CEMETERY RECORDS OF MARSHALL COUNTY TENNESSEE

BY

TIMOTHY R. & HELEN C. MARSH
AND
RALPH D. WHITESELL

MARSH HISTORICAL PUBLICATIONS

Timothy R. and Helen C. Marsh

Southern Historical Press, Inc.
Greenville, South Carolina

Copyright 1981
By: Marsh Historical Publications

Copyright Transferred 1996
To: Southern Historical Press, Inc.

All rights reserved. No part of this publication may be reproduced, stored in a retrieval system, transmitted in any form, posted on to the web in any form or by any means without the prior written permission of the publisher.

Please direct all correspondence and orders to:

www.southernhistoricalpress.com
or
**SOUTHERN HISTORICAL PRESS, Inc.
PO BOX 1267
375 West Broad Street
Greenville, SC 29601
southernhistoricalpress@gmail.com**

ISBN #0-89308-238-4

Printed in the United States of America

FOREWORD

This publication "CEMETERY RECORDS OF MARSHALL COUNTY, TENNESSEE" is a final combination of an earlier partial copy of the county, published in 1968, by Ralph D. Whitesell, now out of print, and the later completed copy of the county by Timothy R. and Helen C. Marsh. This brings together under one cover a copy of all marked gravestones known to be located in Marshall County, Tennessee. We have rechecked, corrected where necessary and added to the 1968 edition. We have attempted to keep the number of persons actively involved in copying the gravestones to a minimum in order to minimize copy error. The final copy lists more than 300 individual, separate graveyards located in the county. The County has been divided into U.S.G.S. Sections or Quadrangles to facilitate in the location of each cemetery. The book contains a complete Cemetery name index as well as a general last name index. The user of this book should keep in mind, the historical fact that Marshall County was formed in 1836. The Eastern portion formed out of Bedford County, the western portion out of Maury and the southern portion south of Elk Ridge was formed out of Lincoln, and in 1870, a small area also containing Cornersville, was removed from Giles County. Most of the early settlers of Marshall County, Tennessee arrived after 1806.

The trials and tribulations experienced by those of us who choose to copy graveyards on a county scale, we leave to the vivid imagination of the reader, with the assurance from the compilers that the rewards are many and the personal satisfaction great. Our fervent hope is that this publication will prove helpful to many in locating the final resting place of their ancestors, and may help in calling attention to the much needed care of some of the old family cemeteries. Some have been neglected to the point of despair while others still receive tender loving care.

The Tennessee Department of Vital Statistics maintains vital records (death certificates) from 1914 to date. In the 1968 publication which is now a part of this complete edition, Mr. Whitesell expressed gratitude to Mrs. Lounora B. Pickens, Miss Myrtle Lee Walker, Mr. and Mrs. Frank R. Boyd, Mr Tom Chunn, Mr. and Mrs. Joe Harris and Miss Dean Poarch. We would like to add special thanks to Mr. Haskell Roden for his help in the south west portion of the county, Mrs. Carolyn McAdams for her help in the Liberty Valley area and Mr. Franklin Blanton for his help in the north east portion of the county.

                                          Timothy R. Marsh
                                          Helen Crawford Marsh
                                          Ralph D. Whitesell

                                                      1981

TIMOTHY R. MARSH HELEN C. MARSH RALPH D. WHITESELL

TABLE OF CONTENTS

CONTENTS	PAGE,NO.
INDEX TO CEMETERIES	v-viii
COUNTY MAP WITH U.S.G.S. QUADRANGLE OVERLAY	ix
RALLY HILL QUADRANGLE	1 - 10
CHAPEL HILL QUADRANGLE	11 - 29
VERONA QUADRANGLE	30 - 57
FARMINGTON QUADRANGLE	58 - 94
CAMPBELLS STATION QUADRANGLE	95 -109
LEWISBURG QUADRANGLE	110- 149
BELFAST QUADRANGLE	150 - 180
BRICK CHURCH QUADRANGLE	181 - 188
CORNERSVILLE QUADRANGLE	189 - 232
PETERSBURG QUADRANGLE	233 - 263
MAP OF LONE OAK CEMETERY	264
GENERAL NAME INDEX	320 - 329
EVOLUTION MAP OF MARSHALL COUNTY,TN	329

****

INDEX OF CEMETERIES

ADAMS	29
ADAMS - STILWELL	189
ALLEN	34
ALLEN	29
ANDERSON	111
ANDREWS - LIGGETT	31
ARTHUR	193
ATKINSON	28
BACHMAN	190
BARNES	191
BAXTER	113
BEAR CREEK (OLD)	97
BEAR CREEK (NEW)	99
BEASLEY	246
BEASLEY	18
BEATTY	114
BEECHWOOD	195
BELL	13
BELL - HEMPHILL	248
BEREA	48
BETHBIREI	84
BETHEL	158
BETHLEHAM	53
BIGGERS - EZELL	27
BILLINGTON	31
BILLS	159
BILLS	252
BISHOP	191
BALCKWELL - JOYCE	16
BOWDEN	114
BOYD	22
BOYET	115
BOYET - HILL	115
BOYET	48
BOYETT	112
BRADEN	191
BRADFORD	246
BRECHEEN - COGGINS	120
BRENTS	234
BRINTLE	189
BRITTAIN	11
BRITTAIN - EZELL	12
BROOKS	252
BROOKS	252
BROWN	116
BROWN	39
BRYANT	99
BRYANT	188
BURROW	73
BUTLER	6
CALTON	148
CAMPBELL - HOWZE	251
CAMPGROUND	160
CANNON	157
CARLTON	76
CARLTON - CLAXTON	58
CARR	30
CARUTHERS - DUCKWORTH	244
CATHEY	2
CATHEY	90
CATHEY	244
CAVNAR	104
CHAPMAN	83
CHEEK	40
CHEEK	110
CHEATHAM - RONE	111
CHILTON	180
CHILTON	93
CHRISTMON	29
CLAXTON - CARLTON	58
COBLE	193
COCHRAN	121
COCHRAN	116
COCRILL - McCORKLE	120
COGGINS - BRECHEEN	120
COLE - WILSON	19
COLLINS	16
COLLINS	120
COLLINS	121
COLVETT	96
CONFEDERATE	155
COOK	243
COX	210
CRUNK - RIVES	251
CRUTCHER	19
CUMMINS - THOMAS	30
CUNNINGHAM	40
DABNEY	181
DABNEY	181
DANIEL	74
DAVIS	194
DAVIS	110
DAVIS - MARSH	134
DAVIS - MOORE	121
DERRYBERRY	8
DEVEN - MYERS - MADISON	135

INDEX OF CEMETERIES

DOWNING...................190	HAMPTON......................150
DRIVER....................246	HARDIN.......................126
DUCKWORTH.................246	HARDIN.......................127
DUCKWORTH - CARUTHERS.....244	HARGROVE..................... 9
DUNCAN....................121	HARPER - TAYLOR.............. 3
DYSART....................160	HARRIS....................... 13
DYSART....................180	HARRIS....................... 60
	HARRIS.......................148
EADY...................... 11	HARRIS.......................191
EDMONDSON................. 95	HASKINS...................... 77
EDWARDS...................122	HASTINGS.....................249
ELLIOTT................... 60	HAYNES - PATTERSON........... 21
ELLISON...................160	HAYWOOD - MARSH..............210
ERWIN.....................155	HAYWOOD......................127
EWING.....................123	HEAD SPRINGS.................161
EZELL..................... 22	HEMPHILL - BELL..............248
EZELL - BIGGERS........... 27	HENDRICK.....................110
EZELL - BRITTAIN.......... 12	HIGGS - ROBERTS.............. 41
EVANS.....................319	HIGHTOWER....................111
	HILL......................... 41
FAGAN..................... 19	HILL.........................128
FALLWELL.................. 15	HILL - BOYET.................115
FALLWELL.................. 16	HOBBY........................189
FINLEY....................245	HOBBY - PRUITT...............189
FINLEY....................245	HOPPER....................... 73
FISHER.................... 90	HOPPER....................... 78
FORREST................... 23	HOPWOOD......................129
FOWLER....................123	HOPWOOD - WILLIS.............129
FOWLER....................124	HORTON (HAUGHTON)............191
FOX - WHEATLEY............125	HOUSTON......................129
FREELAND..................109	HOWZE - CAMPBELL.............251
	HUGHES....................... 14
GABBERT...................252	
GARRETT................... 14	ISLEY........................147
GARRETT................... 96	
GARRETT...................113	JOBE.........................193
GENTRY.................... 21	JOHNSON...................... 15
GENTRY.................... 40	JOHNSON......................132
GIBSON - MORTON...........108	JONES........................ 91
GIBSON....................250	JOYCE........................ 28
GILLS CHAPEL..............122	JOYCE - BLACKWELL............ 16
GIPSON....................126	
GOLD......................180	KING......................... 72
GRAY...................... 3	
GREEN..................... 77	LANIER....................... 10
GREER.....................252	LARWOOD......................242
	LARWOOD......................243
HAISLIP...................211	LAWS HILL.................... 91
HAISLIP - MURDOCK.........243	LEE..........................18
HALL......................240	LEONARD......................241

INDEX OF CEMETERIES

LIGGETT - ANDREWS	31
LITTLE	16
LONDON	132
LONDON	133
LONE OAK	265
LONG	76
LONG	83
LUKER	242
LUNA	240
LUNA	254
LUNN	9
LYONS	254
MACEDONIA	5
MADISON - DEVIN - MYERS	135
MANIER	23
MARLIN	59
MARRS HILL	182
MARRS HILL (OLD)	95
MARSH - DAVIS	134
MARSH - HAYWOOD	210
MARTIN	27
McADAMS	179
McATEER	135
McCLAREY	136
McCONNELL	104
McCORD	15
McCORD	26
McCORD	181
McCORKLE - COCRILL	120
McCURDY	41
McKNIGHT	108
McKNIGHT	254
McLAIN	170
McLEAN	43
McLEAN	43
McQUIDDY	73
MEADOWS	242
MEDEARIS	170
MOORE	253
MOORE - DAVIS	121
MORRIS	78
MORTON	29
MORTON - GIBSON	108
MOSES	4
MOSES	4
MOSES	20
Mt. CARMEL	130
Mt. LEBANON	82
Mt. ZION	233
MURDOCK	26
MURDOCK - HAISLIP	243
MYERS - DEVIN - MADISON	135
NEIL - RAINEY	4
NEW HOPE (CHERRY CORNER)	227
NEW HOPE (FISHING FORD)	234
NICKENS	77
NIX - TAYLOR	190
OAKLEY	72
OGILVIE	28
OLD BEAR CREEK	97
OLD LEBANON	43
OLD MARRS MEETINGHOUSE	95
OLD SHILO	137
OLD - TINDELL	44
OLIVER	189
O'NEAL	180
ORR - VINCENT	108
OWENBY	30
OWENBY	44
PALMETTO	153
PARK	190
PATTERSON	16
PATTERSON - HAYNES	21
PATTON	156
PERRYMAN	77
PICKENS	104
PIGG	253
PLEASANT HILL	137
PORTER	250
POWELL	84
POWELL	139
PRATT	10
PROMISE M. E. CHURCH	11
PRUITT - HOBBY	189
PURDOM	146
RAINEY - NEIL	4
RAINEY	58
RAMBO	112
RECORD	149
REED	6
REED	139
REED - WALKER	171
RIGGS	14
RING	1
RIVES - CRUNK	251

INDEX OF CEMETERIES

ROBERTS - HIGGS	41
ROBERTSON FORK	105
ROBINSON	74
RONE - CHEATHAM	111
ROUND HILL	171
SANDERS	241
SANDIFER	250
SHARP	141
SHEARIN	73
SHEFFIELD	23
SHILO (OLD)	137
SHIRES	31
SHORT	211
SHORT	254
SMITHSON	45
SMYRNA	93
SORRELL	253
SOWELL	246
STEAGALL	15
STILWELL - ADAMS	189
SWAIM - WHITEHEAD	5
SWANSON	62
SMYRNA CHURCH	93
TALLEY	141
TALLEY	255
TAYLOR- HARPER	3
TAYLOR - NIX	190
TANKERSLEY	45
TANKERSLEY	45
TEMPLE	150
THOMAS	84
THOMAS	92
THOMAS -CUMMINS	30
THOMPSON	112
THOMPSON - WELCH	112
TILLMAN	142
TINDELL - OLD	44
TOPPING HILL	10
TOWNSEND	59
TROOP	248
UNNAMED	193
UNKNOWN	109
VEST	29
VINCENT - ORR	108
WALL	59
WALLACE	45
WARNER	74
WARNER	75
WARNER	75
WELCH	143
WELCH - THOMPSON	112
WELLS	234
WHEATLEY - FOX	125
WHITE	58
WHITE	58
WHITEHEAD - SWAIM	5
WHITESELL	46
WHITWORTH	25
WHORLEY	147
WILHOITE	93
WILKES	105
WILKES	108
WILKERSON	243
WILLIAMS	158
WILLIAMSON	251
WILSON	2
WILSON	20
WILSON	20
WILSON - COLE	19
WILSON	59
WILSON (GREEN)	126
WILSON	142
WILSON HILL	144
WILLIS - HOPWOOD	129
WRIGHT	19
WOODS	47
WOODWARD	157
WOODWARD	179
YOWELL	249

****

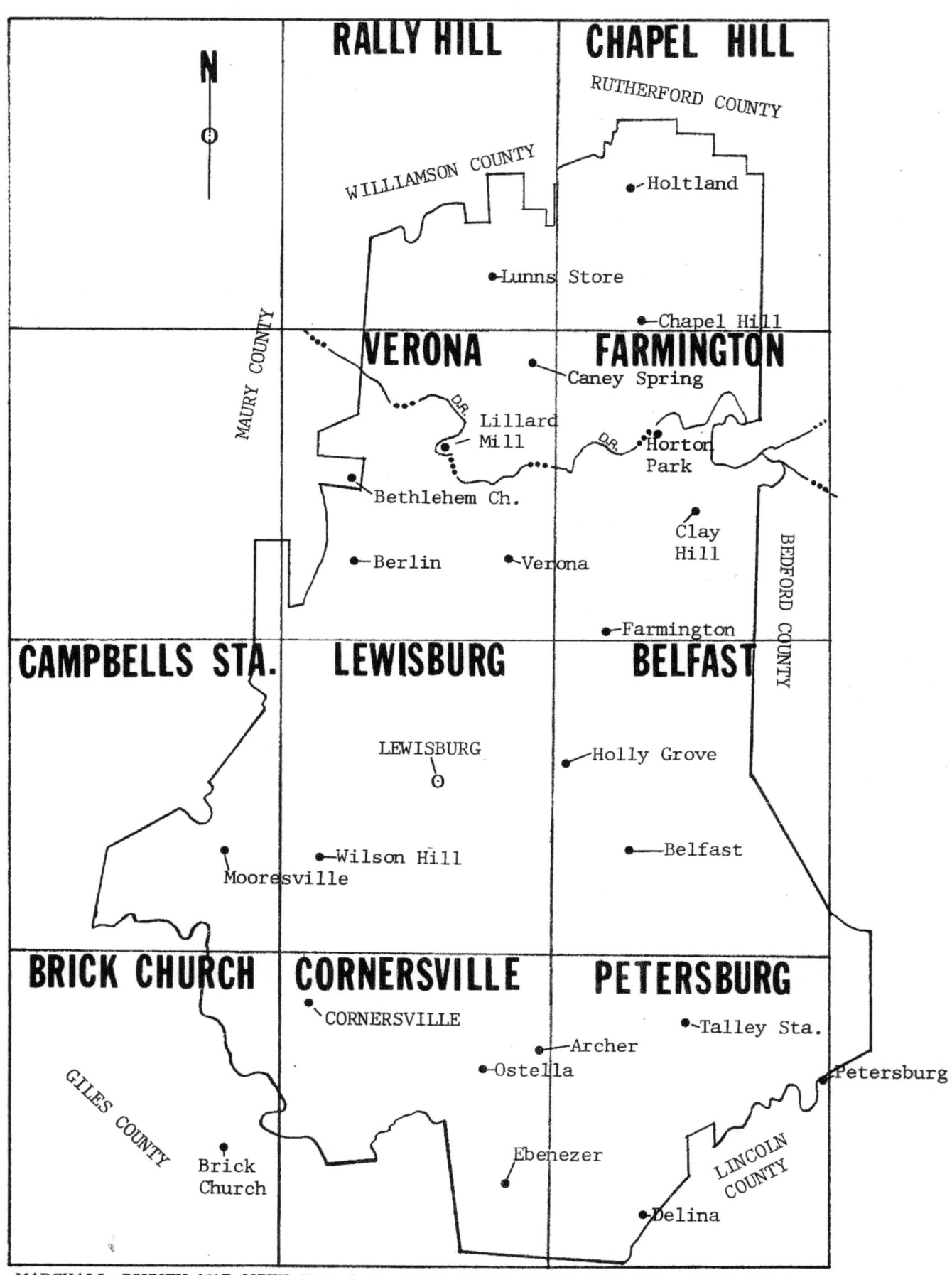

MARSHALL COUNTY MAP WITH U.S.G.S. MAPS QUADRANGLE OVERLAY- 1981 TRM

RALLY HILL
Q U A D R A N G L E

RING CEMETERY
Located on Murrey Lane, 3½ miles northwest of Caney Spring.
Copied in 1968, rechecked September 2, 1978.

Annie Lether Ring
Sept 9, 1911
Jan 13, 1921

"Mother"
Louise Dean
1917-1943

Owen S. Potts
1864-1935
&
Lucia B. Potts
1871-1937

Thomas F. Hargrove
1928-1965
&
Edith P. Hargrove
1931-

Terry R. Hargrove
1958-1958

J. W. Hargrove
1888-1943
&
F. A. Hargrove
1895-1970

Willie B. Hargrove
1910-1964
&
Susie L. Hargrove
1909-1974

J. P. Ring (Jacob Pinkney)
Jan 16, 1835
May 30, 1910

Sarah M. A.(Matilda Anna Walker)
wife of
J. P. Ring
Jul 13, 1844
Feb 10, 1906

Anna E. Ring
Jul 19, 1876
Oct 12, 1910

Father
John M. Ring
May 14, 1841
Aug 20, 1899

Wife
M. M. H. Ring
Jan 11, 1851
Feb 18, 1910

Brother
Alonzo F. Ring
Dec 28, 1868
Jan 16, 1887

Ellie M. Ring
Jun 26, 1877
Jul 18, 1878

Walter Mays
1886-1959
&
Jimmie Mays
1886-1948

John H. Adair
Feb 26, 1895
Sep 17, 1961
&
Hazel S. Adair
Dec 30, 1921

Harry Adair
1887-1975
(Lawrence FH)

Jimmie Joe Horton
Sept 13, 1952

Auleain Horton
Apr 10, 1918
Sep 19, 1919

Thomas Morgan Harper
Jun 1, 1907

&
Mary Jane Harper
Mar 4, 1899
Feb 15, 1959

Joe L. Ring
1881-1941
&
Bessie M. Ring
1885-1948

Maggie Lucile Ring
Dec 13, 1904
Aug 20, 1921

Mother
Ettie M. Derryberry
1870-1947

Infant of
H. F. & Nannie Harris
(no dates)

Isola Harris
Feb 28, 1890
Apr 3, 1891

Infant of
H. F. & Nannie Harris
(no dates)

Infant of
H. F. & Nannie Harris
(no dates)

Sarah Harris
May 15, 1904
Mar 4, 1905

J. T. "Bud" Ring
1868-1944
&
Mollie Ring
1870-1951

John Walker Ring
Nov 17, 1893
Jun 30, 1920
"Served with A. E. F.,
Co. A, 117th Inf., 30th Div"

Ether Ring
1897-1948

G. R. Neathery
Feb 18, 1850
Feb 9, 1903

beside above grave, there
are two fieldstones and is
said to be:
Father
William Neathery
born 1815, died ?.

Mother
Nancy C, Neathery
born 1822, died ?.

Uncle George Harmon
Jun 26, 1845
Dec 24, 1926

George M. Collins
Sep 8, 1868
Jul 31, 1930

B. Ring, wife of
G. M. Collins
Jan 6, 1867
Jan 11, 1919

James M. Neathery
Feb 18, 1844
Mar 14, 1876
&
Malisse W. Neathery
Aug 19, 1844
Oct 31, 1929

W. L. Neathery
Apr 8, 1867
Oct 22, 1897

Ella J. Sharp, wife of
W. L. Neathery
Mar 29, 1868
Oct 4, 1899

Infant son of
A. J. & M. E. King
May 9, 1900

Gennie Ring
1904-1922
&
Hattie Ring
1899-1923

Maggie T., dau of
Mr. and Mrs. J. F. Adair
Dec 23, 1889
Jul 27, 1921

Woodson King
Jun 18, 1887
Jul 28, 1966
&
Lee King
Apr 20, 1890
Sep 15, 1969

John W. Thomas
1861-1912
&
M. Alice Thomas
1870-1946

Mother
Hattie Cherry Hayes
Feb 8, 1913
May 14, 1934

Father
John W. Cherry
Jan 3, 1884
Dec 14, 1929

Mother
Mattie T. Cherry
1894-1944

Carl F. Patterson
Tennessee
Pvt 1cl 7 Engrs 5 Div
Mar 9, 1934

Leslie, wife of C. F.
Patterson
Aug 6, 1900
Jul 24, 1925

Newton C. Neathery
Nov 16, 1846
Mar 14, 1887

Walter Lee Neathery
Jan 13, 1882
Jun 27, 1888

Father: Frank Harris
Jan 5, 1868
Jul 20, 1925
&
Mother: Nannie Harris
Nov 4, 1871
Feb 25, 1946

1

RALLY HILL

Father: J. B. Ring
Sep 25, 1851
Mar 2, 1930
&
Mother: Sallie Green
wife of J. B. Ring
Aug 10, 1844
Oct 25, 1922

Leroy, son of
W. O. & N. E. Ring
Sep 24, 1895
Apr 18, 1914

W. O. Ring
Aug 17, 1870
Aug 11, 1921

Nannie E. Ring
Apr 5, 1873
Aug 6, 1918

Samuel Brooks Aldridge
May 11, 1839
Dec 5, 1914

S. E. Aldridge
Sep 20, 1842
Aug 10, 1911

Bertha W., dau of
S. B. & S. E. Aldridge
Jan 20, 1883
Dec 11, 1901

Mary M., dau of
S. B. & S. E. Aldridge
Aug 30, 1867
Jan 6, 1893

Many unmarked graves.

Edgar Whitehead
Aug 26, 1903
Jul 7, 1909

Lolie Whitehead
Aug 25, 1897
Sep 27, 1897

J. N. Chestnut
1864-1897
&
M. M. Chestnut
1866-1898

Father: Walter Ring
1872-1941

Mrs. Bettie Ring
Aug 11, 1876
Nov 4, 1909

Joseph W. Ring
Pvt Co F 23 Regt Tenn Inf
Confederate States Army
1826-1900

Sarah Ann Ring
1831-1904

James L. Ring
Feb 14, 1861
Aug 15, 1932

Buford Ring
Dec 22, 1898
Jan 17, 1899

Mary Ring, mother of Lewis
is buried under the tree.
The grave is unmarked.
She was living in 1850
census of Marshall Co., TN.

* *

CATHEY CEMETERY

Located on Caney Spring Road, about one and one-half miles north
of Caney Spring. Copied April 29, 1962, rechecked 1980.

Katherine P. Smith
Jun 12, 1820
Dec 5, 1899

(4 or 5 Smith graves, not
marked. RDW.)

Loucinda, wife of
James Patterson
1844-May 16, 1905

Sarah Chadwell, Consort of
Johnson Chadwell
Apr 8, 1821
Oct 9, 1845

Sarah Elizabeth Aldridge
May 10, 1842
Sep 6, 1845

Stephen H. Vaden
Sep   1799
Jun 22, 1868

Aaron H. Dark
Mar 8, 1825
May 31, 1898

Wm. H. Dark, son of
A. H. & L. Dark
Jan 24, 1862
Jan 9, 1892

W. T. Hardison
(TM) (no dates)

Nannie M., wife of
W. T. Hardison
May 20, 1856
Apr 29, 1902

Laura Bedora Hardison
wife of J. Chesley Cundiff
Sep 30, 1870
Jul 11, 1906

Annie Louise Cundiff
Nov 12, 1897
Dec 29, 1917

James Chesley Cundiff, Jr.
Sep 29, 1871
Mar 25, 1942

John Cathey
1776/9 - 1875/6
(no marker) under large
oak tree.

Elizabeth (Calhoun) Cathey
1770/8 - 1840/50
mrd - 1800 Mecklenburg Co.
N.C.
(no dates) under large
oak tree, no marker.

COLORED SECTION:

Father: Morgan Duncan
1873-1928

Mother: Etta McClain
1871-1927

Robert L. Adams
Died Apr 18, 1952
(Scales & Son)

Mother:
Pearl Duncan
1885-1922

* *

WILSON CEMETERY

Located 1 mile east of Pottsville, TN, on Kennie Nelson Road.
Copied by Ralph D. Whitesell, April 28, 1968, rechecked 1979.

J. A. Wilson (Jonathan)
Aug 20, 1819
Apr 16, 1891

Charity S(Sugar). wife of
J. A. Wilson
May 11, 1824
Nov 23, 1890
(she was a McLemore)

Maggie M., wife of A. T.Wilson
Jan 27, 1862
Aug 8, 1892

Nicholas A. Wilson
1861-1943
&
Elizabeth J. Wilson
1868-1911

William Eli Nelson
1858-1919
&
Margaret Ann (Wilson) Nelson
1869-1932

James F. Nelson
Oct 26, 1832
Apr 27, 1901

M. E.(Mary McLemore) wife
of George (D.) Neil
Jul 17, 1822
Apr 8, 1905

Kennie R. Nelson
1904-

RALLY HILL

Mr. Loucis Wilson
(no marker)

Otto Nelson
(no marker)

Mary Ann Elizabeth Jackson Sellars,
wife of James F. Nelson
(no marker)

Information by Mr. Kennie R. Nelson, 1979.

* *

TAYLOR-HARPER CEMETERY
Located about 3 miles north of Caney Spring, Tennessee. Copied September 2, 1978.

John Harper
1875-1955
2nd marker says:
John Harper
1874-1955
(Lawrence FH)

Father
L. T. Harper
Aug 26, 1848
Sep 9, 1918

Brother
Doss J. Harper
Jan 1, 1888
Aug 23, 1914

William M. Taylor
1847-1931
&
Martha L. Taylor
1865-1939

Thomas H. Taylor
Utah
Pvt U. S. Marine Corps
Nov 11, 1927
Aug 13, 1966

Fronia H. Hyde
Oct 4, 1882
Sep 12, 1969

Loranza Cromer Harper
Oct 7, 1914
Aug 13, 1916

Gracie Louvenie, dau of
Hyde and Demie Harper
Mar 14, 1913

Ora E. Harper, dau of
James & Minnie Harper
Jan 15, 1908
Jun 16, 1909

William Ivy Taylor
Tennessee
Cpl 32 RCT Co Gen Svc Inf
W W I
Sep 27, 1895
Jan 25, 1959
&
Mattie D. Taylor
Nov 19, 1894
May 8, 1975

John Taylor
aged: 79 yrs & 9 mos.
& wife:
Julia A. Taylor
age: 74 yrs & 9 mos.

J. H. Taylor
May 1, 1846
Nov 11, 1922
&
Bettie Taylor
Mar 27, 1855
Dec 23, 1947

Grady A. Taylor (Father)
Tennessee
Pvt Quarter Master Corps
W W I
Jul 20, 1901
May 24, 1955
&
Mother
Addie L. Taylor
1904-1937

Very few unmarked graves.

W. H. Riley
Dec 8, 1844
Oct 14, 1922
&
Pennie E. Riley
Jul 28, 1850
Jul 11, 1927

William Taylor Riley, son
of W. H. & P. E. Riley
Aug 5, 1883
Apr 15, 1900
&
Dela O., dau of
W. H. & P. E. Riley
Jan 19, 1881
Dec 20, 1915

J. A. Riley
Jul 3, 1811
Aug 7, 1895
&
S. E. Riley
Sep 8, 1812
Oct 8, 1883

* *

GRAY CEMETERY
Located North end of County, on north side of Collins Lane, 2 miles north of Caney Spring. Copied April 27, 1969 and rechecked Sept 2, 1978.

Tom L. Collins
1885-1963
(Lawrence FH)

Mrs. Lula Ledbetter Collins
died Dec 22, 1945
age: 61 yrs, 7 mos, 12 days
(Lawrence FH)

Louise Collins
Jan 6, 1912
Aug 20, 1932

Mamie Lee, wife of
Kellie Collins
Aug 18, 1898
Nov 29, 1915

Will A. Collins
Aug 28, 1870
Apr 24, 1937

Nannie Ann Collins
Dec 31, 1870
Sep 2, 1917

Cordellar Powell
Jun 24, 1877
Oct 2, 1877

V. P. Ledbetter
Nov 10, 1810
Oct 1, 1885

Marshall McLain Ledbetter
Oct 26, 1887
Oct 21, 1913

Infant of
J. W. & V. T. Joyce
Stillborn
Dec 23, 1874

Sampson Gray
Apr 15, 1815
Sep 22, 1873

Funander G. Gray
May 18, 1855
Sep 18, 1870

Mother
Nancy Gray
Dec 1, 1831
Feb 26, 1908

Several graves marked with fieldstones.

* * * * * * * * * * * * * * * * * * *

RALLY HILL

NEIL-RAINEY CEMETERY

Located on the Stephen W. Rainey homeplace, which was at one time owned by the father of Nathan Bedford Forrest, William Forrest. It is located about 4 miles north of Caney Spring, near what is now (1968) the Will Ogilvie farm.

Major Stephen W. Rainey was born in Williamson Co., Tenn., 14 miles of Nashville, 9 miles of Franklin, & 4 miles of Nolensville March 29, 1806 & died May 13, 1884.

In Memory of Zacheus B. Neil son of William & Sarah Neil, who was born 5th January 1822 & died 12th April 1847 Aged 25 yrs, 3 mos, 7 days. "Who left an affectionate father and mother, 5 brothers and 3 sisters to mourn his loss".

In Memory of Charles R. Neil, son of William & Sarah Neil, who was born Feb 5, 1809 and died May 1st 1840 Aged 31 yrs, 2 mos, 27 days "He left an affectionate wife & 5 children to mourn his loss".

In Memory of William C. Lanier, son of B. B. & Mary Lanier, who was born Nov 23, 1840 & departed this life September 15, 1853 Aged 12 yrs, 9 mos, 22 days.

In Memory of James Reid, who was born Sept 17, 1769 & died May 25, 1814.

Another Reid tombstone nearby was broken.

In Memory of James B. Lanier, son of B. B. & Mary Lanier, who was born July 15, 1844 & departed this life October 12, 1852 Aged 8 yrs, 2 mos, 25 days.

In Memory of Sarah A. M., daughter of B. B. & Mary Lanier Born 30th of December 1847 Died June 11, 1849 Aged 17 mos, 11 days.

In Memory of Benj. B. Lanier Born the 23rd of March 1797 & Died September 14, 1849 Aged 52 yrs, 5 mos, 21 days

There are about eight very old "house-top" graves, with no inscriptions in the same cemetery, and at least 12 other unmarked graves with head and foot stones of sandstone rock.

* *

MOSES CEMETERY

Located on the Lunn's Store-Caney Spring Road. Copied Jan 11, 1976 by Ralph D. Whitesell and Mrs. Foster Nicholas.

John F. Moses
Aug 3, 1866
Jan 26, 1949

Jewel Lee, dau of
J. F. & Sallie Moses
Aug 25, 1906
Aug 25, 1906

Enis and Ernest, Infant sons
of J. F. & Sallie Moses
Apr 1, 1905
Apr 1, 1905

Sallie M. Moses
Nov 22, 1874
Jan 29, 1927

Mrs. Geneva Ragsdale
Died July 20, 1939
age: 68 yrs, 5 mos, 3 days.
(TM)

William R. Davis
May 14, 1879
Sep 4, 1912

Samuel J. Moses
Jun 5, 1834
Jan 5, 1918

Sarah E., wife of
S. J. Moses
May 17, 1838
Apr 14, 1910

Sallie B., dau of
S. J. & S. E. Moses
Sep 28, 1868
Apr 3, 1894

Mary E. Covington
Sep 25, 1864
Apr 11, 1928

Jessie L., dau of
J. H. & M. E. Covington
Apr 27, 1901
Jul 12, 1901

Effie M., dau of
J. H. & M. E. Covington
Aug 2, 1894
Aug 3, 1894

This Cemetery is located near the home of Mr. Albert Moses. It is well kept.

* *

MOSES CEMETERY

Located on the Charles Moses farm, north of Caney Spring. Copied April 12, 1967.

William H. Moses, son of
W. S. & E. A. Moses
Nov 14, 1865
Apr 26, 1892

W. S. Moses
1846-1924

Bettie Moses
1846-1923

* *

RALLY HILL

MACEDONIA CHURCH CEMETERY
Located in the northwest corner of Marshall County.

Sam T. Logan
1846-1917

John A. Logan
1909-
&
Mary E. Tisdale Logan
1912-

Maude Logan Green
Jun 5, 1877
Dec 18, 1934

Osteen
Infant son
Feb 9, 1923
Feb 9, 1923

Thomas Logan Osteen
Jun 26, 1921
Feb 4, 1922

Infant Son of
Mr. and Mrs. J. T. Osteen, Sr.
1907

Joe T. Osteen
Oct 29, 1866
Nov 22, 1915
(picture)

Lollie Mai Osteen
Aug 2, 1875
Dec 4, 1946

W. P. Smith
Apr 12, 1819
mrd- Louisa A. Dean
Nov 1, 1843
died Dec 5, 1904

Louisa A. Smith
Aug 1, 1819
mrd W. P. Smith
Nov 1, 1843
died Sep 27, 1898

French and Blanch Moore
1902-1902

Mrs. M. C. Moore
Nov 20, 1838
Apr 15, 1900

W. E. Osteen
Nov 26, 1859
May 24, 1899

Nannie Sisco Osteen
Feb 2, 1867
May 6, 1957

James C. Skinner
Aug 30, 1890
Mar 9, 1969
&
Sally Ann Skinner
Apr 13, 1895
Feb 10, 1961
&
Thomas Skinner
1912-1961

Father
W. E. Jordan
1852-Mar 14, 1890
& wife:
Mother
Mattie G. Jordan
Sep 6, 1867
Jul 5, 1919

Elisha H. Scott
Sep 16, 1827
Jun 3, 1889

Elizabeth G. J., wife of
Elisha H. Scott
Dec 4, 1832
Aug 8, 1895

Nancy Ella Curtis, dau of
R. C. & M. E. Curtis
Nov 14, 1858
Mar 9, 1860

Father
M. R. Fisher
1863-1925

Davie, son of
Mr. & Mrs. M. R. Fisher
Nov 21, 1889
Apr 30, 1893

William C. Moore
1833-1896
&
Catherine T. Moore
1838-1880

John C. Moore
1862-1879

James H. Moore
1809-1877

William Andrew, son of
E. N. & J. W. Moore
Feb 1, 1881
Jul 5, 1883

Andrew J. Moore
Jan 10, 1832
Nov 9, 1881
(broken)

James B. Scott
Mar 1, 1796
Jun 23, 1876

Mary, wife of
James B. Scott
Jun(Jan) 27, 1797
(no date)

M. F., son of
S. F. & H. A. Cox
Sep 23, 1854
Oct 26, 1855

R. S. Whitehead
Nov 5, 1829
Dec 24, 1895

Infant dau of
T. M. & N. L. Whitehead
B&D Jan 23, 1900

Lee Scott, son of
G. E. & L. J. Scott
Nov 15, 1880
Sep 19, 1881

David Fogleman
Jun 8, 1809
Oct 5, 1872

Nancy T. Fogleman, dau of
D. & M. E. Fogleman
Died Oct 15, 1853
Age 12 years.

Mary E., dau of
Rev. A. & E. Bostick,
wife of D. Fogleman
Nov 8, 1817
May 29, 1857

John Collins
1816-Aug 21, 1872
Age 56 years

Milly, wife of
John Collins
Aug 11, 1824
Apr 14, 1903

Robert McLean
Died Jan 16, 1908
Age 41 years.

James A. Collins
Sep 23, 1858
Nov 3, 1924

* *

SWAIM-WHITEHEAD CEMETERY
Located near Lively and New Bethel Church, northwest part of
Marshall County. Copied April 1967 by Ralph D. Whitesell.
Addition, Jan 1976.

Labon H. Hargrove
1890-1955

Lizzie Hargrove
1897-

Joe H. Hargrove
1895-1945

Annie V. Hargrove
1941-1941

Maggie A. Hargrove
1902-

Willie H. Hargrove
1929-1946

There are about 20 graves marked with concrete slabs, no dates
or names. They are the graves of the Swaim and Whitehead families. One child's grave is marked with a beautiful little
wooden house.

* *

RALLY HILL

BUTLER CEMETERY
Located one mile south of Lunn's Store, no markers.

* *

REED CEMETERY
Located one-half mile east of Lunn's Store, on Chapel Hill Road. Copied Sept 1, 1979.

Wilma Christine Howard
1960-1960

Mother
(footstone)

Olive M. Estes
Dec 3, 1898
May 27, 1963

Baby Perryman
Feb 11, 1972
(Lawrence FH)

Kitt Giles
Jan 22, 1907

&
Eddie Lou M. Giles
Nov 13, 1909
Sep 29, 1970
mrd- Nov 2, 1927

Bobby Gene Giles
Sgt U. S. Army
Jul 22, 1934
Aug 8, 1977

Brother
J. N. Elliott
Mar 13, 1838
Mar 23, 1910
&
Sister
Eliza M. Elliott
Aug 12, 1828
Jun 18, 1916

Roy Whitney Thomas
Mar 13, 1878
Aug 23, 1965
&
Mary Frances Thomas
Nov 2, 1877
Jan 24, 1958
(footmarker: Mrs. Mamie)

Judith Ann Simpson
Sep 19, 1947
Dec 7, 1948

Pa
C. M. "Lum" Walker
Apr 2, 1853
Feb 3, 1926
&
Ma
Mary Sue Walker
Jun 12, 1856
Jun 4, 1928

John M. Collins
May 17, 1901
May 24, 1971
&
Janie M. Collins
Aug 14, 1907
Aug 26, 1969
mrd- Dec 1, 1937

Andrew B. McElhaney
Oct 7, 1902
Feb 28, 1969
&
Josephine McElhaney
Jul 27, 1904

Thomas B. McElhaney
1873-1944
&
Ethel McElhaney
1882-19

Hastings S. McElhaney
Feb 11, 1907
Sep 29, 1962
&
Floey M. McElhaney
Sep 26, 1907

Edwin F. Fagan
1869-1959
&
Mary E. Fagan
1874-1947

Marvin Floyd, son of
E. F. & M. E. Fagan
Aug 14, 1906
Feb 29, 1907

Paul W. Fagan
Jan 26, 1894
Oct 12, 1918

Paul White Fagan, Jr.
Apr 12, 1919
May 18, 1941

Mattie Kimmons Fagan
Jul 7, 1903
Oct 25, 1918

T. W. Moses
1873-1943
&
Nannie E. Moses
1873-1962

Mary & Maggie Moses
1906

James Edmondson

&
Nancy Edmondson

Odar W. Howard
1876-1951
&
Florence L. Howard
1883-1917

Father
L. Forest Walker
1863-1935
&
Mother
Anna L. Walker
1875-1931

Mr. Reed Walker
1906-1936

Father
John F. Walker
Aug 30, 1872
Sep 3, 1921
&
Mother
Sarah T. Walker
Dec 8, 1876
Jan 11, 1968

Ennes Walker
Apr 8, 1904
Dec 4, 1917

James Ealem Walker
Sep 1, 1917
Sep 10, 1921

William C. Walker
1907-1965
&
Willie P. Walker
1930-1969

Father
J. M. Walker
1879-1962
&
Mother
Lucy E. Walker
1888-1951

Ruby E. Whitehead
1908-1977
(Lawrence FH)

Patra W. Harper
1873-1958

Father
Henry Young Kincaid
Dec 15, 1863
Nov 25, 1929

Mother
Roxie Anna Mills Kincaid
Feb 7, 1871
Jul 3, 1928

Arthur L. Kincaid
1892-1960
&
Ora F. Kincaid
1895-1976

Jessie L. Kincaid
1917

Elgin E. Kincaid
Jun 5, 1920
Nov 18, 1924

Mary E. Kincaid
Aug 4, 1939

George Harmon Walker
Jul 10, 1876
Jul 30, 1946
&
S. G. Smithson Walker
Jan 28, 1886
Jan 30, 1971
mrd- Aug 14, 1913

W. C. Walker
1847-1905
&
Sue Walker
1848-1948

Mrs. Willie K., wife of
V. M. Wilson
Sep 25, 1882
mrd- Apr 11, 1909
died Apr 29, 1916

Linda Dell Wilson
Dec 21, 1940
Aug 12, 1941

Columbus Walker
Mar 15, 1912
Jul 10, 1912
&
Irene Walker
Dec 12, 1904
Aug 31, 1906

RALLY HILL

Father
M. C. Pruitt
1851-1927

Wife and Mother
Tibatha A. Pruitt
Mar 28, 1856
Sep 24, 1912

Tommie Joe Pruitt
Nov 16, 1887
Sep 27, 1968

Florence E. Kincaid Pruitt
1890-1923

Williard E. Pruitt
1922-1923

Marion A. Pruitt
1925-1926
&
Walter H. Pruitt
(Infant-no dates)

Charley W., son of
R. L. & Mary A. Eley
May 28, 1896
Apr 1, 1900

Joshua C. Walker
1857-1926

Ella B. Walker
1864-1949

Mrs. Mattie Helton Collins
Died May 27, 1919
(no age given)

Albert Lester
Jan 9, 1957
Jan 11, 1957

W. A. White
Died Sep 28, 1935
Age 55 years
(Bills-McGaugh FH)

Mother
Pauline M. Irvin
Mar 5, 1819
Nov 7, 1899

Mickie Howard
May 2, 1896
Apr 7, 1970
&
Thelma Howard
Feb 9, 1898
Nov 29, 1915

Lucy Aldonia Howard
Jun 9, 1862
Aug 19, 1919

Lewis C. Howard
1848-1924

Jesse A. Leverette
Mar 14, 1878
Feb 13, 1960
(Woodfin FH,
Murfreesboro)

Robert S. McElhaney
1870-1959
&
Luella F. McElhaney
1872-1956

Mrs. S. J. McElhaney
Dec 9, 1840
Aug 25, 1906

George B. McElhaney
Jul 9, 1858
Aug 13, 1918
&
Elizabeth Mills McElhaney
Apr 10, 1876
Apr 28, 1953

Mother
Alene Hargrove McElhaney
Mar 10, 1910
Aug 6, 1939

Father
William H. Blackwell
Oct 16, 1880
Nov 2, 1931
&
Mother
Cleve Walker Blackwell
Sep 16, 1884

Aubrey A. Blackwell
1907-1918

Albert O. McElhaney
Tennessee
Pvt U. S. Army, W W I
Sep 17, 1896
Mar 4, 1971
&
Hattie Lee McElhaney
1902-1971

Roy H. McElhaney
TEC 4 U. S. Army, W W II
Aug 20, 1920
Nov 22, 1976

Father
Aaron E. McElhaney
GM 3 U. S. Navy, W W II
Oct 4, 1927
Jun 18, 1957

Father
William James Russell
Jul 30, 1875
Apr 9, 1950
&
Mother
Catherine Vaughn Russell
Feb 15, 1886
Jan 18, 1960

Irene Russell
1911-1962

Manervie T. Russell
1856-1934

James H. Russell
1844-1929

Sam Russell
1888-1975

Mary E. Whitehead
1877-1955

Brenda J. Russell
June 1, 1944

Joyce V. Russell
March 23, 1943

Julious R. Flodeen
Jan 12, 1928
May 1, 1942

D. W. Howard
Sep 28, 1880
Mar 20, 1943
&
Mary Jane Howard
Aug 6, 1886
Jun 5, 1974

Margaret Howard
1905-1977
(Lawrence FH)

John L. Howard
1885-1951
(TM)

John Baxter Howard
Tennessee
PFC 8 Air VEH REP Sq AAF
W W II
Aug 27, 1920
Nov 1, 1959

Josiah Walker
Jun 19, 1824
Mar 24, 1879

E. C., wife of
Josiah Walker
Jan 20, 1829
Dec 5, 1893

James A. Walker
1849-1918
&
Susan S. Walker
1855-1921

Father
S. S. Allen
Feb 1, 1814
Jul 12, 1895
&
Mother
Eliza Allen
Feb 14, 1833
Jan 28, 1890

B. F. Dodson
Dec 25, 1826
Jan 22, 1897

Many graves with fieldstones, no inscriptions.

END OF REED

* *

RALLY HILL

DERRYBERRY CEMETERY
Located in the extreme northwest corner of Marshall County on Flat Creek. Copied October 20, 1968 by Ralph D. Whitesell.

Mollie Sheppard
Sep 17, 1881
Dec 22, 1959

S. D. Sheppard
Apr 13, 1878
Jan 16, 1931

Lela Sheppard
Jul 12, 1902
Dec 29, 1919

Willie Fred, nephew of
S. D. & M. M. Sheppard
Jun 3, 1914
Jul 10, 1923

Loin A. Hargrove
Oct 16, 1910
Aug 1, 1932

Tommey Cathey
Sep 17, 1866
Feb 15, 1939

Melissa E., wife of
Jas. D. Derryberry
Oct 24, 1837
Oct 27, 1894

Joseph H., son of
A. J. & E. P. Derryberry
Dec 17, 1827
Aug 14, 1909

Sallie J., wife of
J. H. Derryberry
Aug 31, 1844
Oct 15, 1915

Mattie J. Morris
Jul 5, 1879
Oct 10, 1910

John R. Cathey
1861-1942
&
Etta D. Cathey
1866-1925

Elgan Cathey
1884-1885

George K. Hazelwood
1907-
&
Willie L. Hazelwood
1912-

Will L. Reynolds
1909-19
&
Maggie C. Reynolds
1911-1961

James Murray Reynolds
Jul 6, 1904
Dec 23, 1944

Father
Luna Derryberry
1896-1956
&
Mother
Luna B. Derryberry
1898-

Mrs. E. Derryberry
1922-1963 (TM)

Thomas J. Derryberry
Jul 1, 1861
Mar 5, 1905

Sussie Elizabeth Derryberry
Aug 4, 1862
Mar 13, 1926

Noble E., son of
T. J. & Sussie Derryberry
Jun 28, 1904
Nov 10, 1908

Steve, son of
M. A. Derryberry
Nov 14, 1936
Jun 24, 1958

Baby Shadden, son of
Homer & Elizabeth Derryberry
B&D July 21, 1914

Homer Derryberry
May 27, 1888

&
Elizabeth M. Derryberry
Mar 2, 1888
----
mrd- Sep 30, 1909

A. Dennis Derryberry
Sep 12, 1877
Jul 11, 1953

Mora Farris, son of
A. D. & M. M. Derryberry
Mar 20, 1900
Mar 27, 1900

Arthur A. Derryberry
May 4, 1883
Oct 10, 1909

William L., son of
B. M. & S. C. Derryberry
Aug 14, 1872
Oct 8, 1873

Elmer Thomas
Sep 7, 1896
Sep 6, 1912

Infant of L. O. &
M. M. Thomas
(no dates)

Nettie S. Collins
Aug 17, 1876
Apr 16, 1937

Annie Henderson, dau of
Mr. & Mrs. H. W. Collins
Aug 21, 1902
Jun 28, 1927

Marvin W., son of
H. W. & N. C. Collins
Jan 13, 1900
Apr 19, 1920

Grady, son of
H. W. & N. C. Collins
Jun 13, 1905
Oct 5, 1914

J. B. Collins
Nov 14, 1847
Feb 18, 1924

E. Calestine, wife of
J. B. Collins
Dec 3, 1845
Sep 22, 1911

Little Babe, son of
J. B. & E. C. Collins
Apr 25, 1887
Apr 1, 1892

John Marshall Collins
1874-1950 (TM)

Mattie Collins
1866-1945

Ilue Collins, dau of
J. M. & M. A. Collins
Oct 15, 1903
Aug 6, 1904

Ennis L. Collins
1926-1968 (TM)

Mother
Martha S. Creswell
Sep 17, 1849
Mar 30, 1930

B. M. Derryberry
Feb 24, 1842
Oct 10, 1923

Calestine, wife of
B. M. Derryberry
May 31, 1847
Nov 20, 1925

Lemon, son of
W. H. & M. C. Thomas
Oct 5, 1876
Oct 3, 1908

David L. Derryberry
Aug 13, 1855
Dec 4, 1913

Ophelia V. Derryberry
Mar 12, 1858
Dec 5, 1940

A. J. Derryberry
May 21, 1813
Nov 14, 1893

Elizabeth P., wife of
A. J. Derryberry
Jul 10, 1816
Oct 6, 1889

Patrick H. Aldridge
1878-1947
&
Ethel Aldridge
1879-1963

Infant of
P. H. & J. E. Aldridge
Dec 17, 1902
Jan 4, 1903

Gretchen Aldridge
Dec 21, 1912
Nov 24, 1914

S. Thomas Mangrum
1883-1954
&
Lantie O. Mangrum
1888-19

Harold W. Derryberry
1921

William Gordon, son of
D. I. & M. B. Derryberry
Feb 15, 1919
Jun 5, 1919

J. W. Jarrett
Mar 30, 1873
Jan 21, 1927
&
Bettie Jarrett
Aug 27, 1881

Myrtle M., wife of
L. O. Thomas, dau of
J. F. & M. J. Adair
Apr 17, 1879
Mar 18, 1910

Lena, dau of
J. B. & S. A. Lamb
Sep 20, 1888
Nov 26, 1900

RALLY HILL

Johnie M., dau of
W. F. & M. C. Derryberry
Jul 29, 1873
Nov 18, 1875

Lorene, dau of
C. H. & M. W. Moore
Oct 27, 1908
Dec 12, 1911

Willie, wife of
C. H. Moore
1886-1913(8)

Walter Dean
1880-1955
&
Bettie J. Dean
1879-1950

J. A. Derryberry

Minnie M., wife of
J. A. Derryberry
Sep 16, 1873
May 17, 1893

John W. Moore
Dec 2, 1889
Mar 12, 1962
&
Evie Reynolds Moore
May 9, 1891

J. A. Thomas
Aug 3, 1867
Jul 23, 1913

Edward, son of
J. A. & B. G. Thomas
Nov 14, 1902
Jul 18, 1904

Ella F., wife of
Robert Cathey, dau of
W. H. & M. C. Thomas
Jul 24, 1871
Mar 16, 1901

William Jeff, son of
W. H. & Nannie Thomas
Aug 17, 1882
Mar 26, 1899

W. H. Thomas
May 5, 1845
Dec 21, 1915

Nannie J. Thomas
Oct 2, 1847
Jan 20, 1935

Mary C., wife of
W. H. Thomas
Feb 16, 1844
Oct 28, 1876

Lillie A. Reynolds
Feb 19, 1871
Dec 3, 1938

Susan Ann, wife of
James B. Lamb
Dec 22, 1868
Jan 12, 1893

Alma A. Lamb
1924-1924

Jewel W. Lamb
1916-1943
&
Mary L. Lamb
1923-1946

Robert Holt Lamb
Sep 25, 1893
Apr 22, 1938
&
Lucille Broadway Lamb
Jan 14, 1897

Martha S. Lamb
1921-1923

Lany, son of
Mary & Robert Lamb
Apr 2, 1954
Feb 21, 1959

Will K. Reynolds
Jan 1, 1863
Aug 6, 1935

Ida G., wife of
W. K. Reynolds
Oct 22, 1868
Feb 22, 1900

J. W. Broadway
Dec 15, 1875
Jun 20, 1915

Paul Broadway
Dec 29, 1904

Grady Smith, son of
J. W. & I. S. Broadway
Sep 11, 1900
May 2, 1901

W. I. Smith
Jan 11, 1850
Oct 8, 1918

S. F., wife of
W. I. Smith
Dec 27, 1850
Nov 3, 1886

Thomas K. Broadway
Oct 12, 1854
Aug 16, 1934
&
Lucinda Broadway
Jan 12, 1863
Dec 5, 1946

Suzanne Roberson
1961-1968

Jennie Anna Reynolds
Jul 10, 1911
Jul 15, 1953

END OF DERRYBERRY

* *

HARGROVE CEMETERY

Located on the farm now owned by Lewis J. Anderson, 1967, just off the Macedonia Road, north of Caney Spring. Copied April 12, 1967.

Annie V. Hargrove
1941-1941

Labron H. Hargrove
1890-1955
&
Lizzie Hargrove
1897-

Joe H. Hargrove
1895-1945
&
Maggie A. Hargrove
1902-

Willie H. Hargrove
1929-1946

A house has been built over a grave. There are approximately 20 graves marked with fieldstones, no inscriptions.

* *

LUNN CEMETERY

Located at Lunn's Store. This Cemetery is located on land once owned by Mathew Wallis. Copied April 12, 1967 and re-checked 1980 by Ralph D. Whitesell, Tim & Helen Marsh.

Sarah Martin
Feb 19, 1842
May 17, 1863

Wm. D. Martin
Jul 21, 1816
May 10, 1851

Mahu McCall
Dec 24, 1857
Aug 15, 1862

William E. Wallace
Jun 30, 1830
Nov 12, 1884

Sophia Wallace
July 1804
Apr 19, 1878

(broken away), wife of
Wm. H. Toppin
May 15, 1847 - Oct 23, 1877

Jennie V. McElhaney,
wife of J. O. Lunn
Jul 7, 1876
Jul 7, 1911

John Oscar Lunn
Nov 3, 1873 - Mar 27, 1944

RALLY HILL

Felix G. Lunn
Apr 2, 1814
Aug 8, 1895

Ruth, wife of
F. G. Lunn
Jan 1, 1814
Aug 14, 1888
"She was a member of the Baptist Church for more than 50 years."

Felix Oslin Lunn
Jun 25, 1879
Jul 31, 1944

Mrs. Sally B. Lunn
Aug 17, 1880
Jan 12, 1957

Mary L. Lunn
May 10, 1913
Aug 27, 1923

In Memory of Thomas A. Jones, Native of Buckingham Co., VA. Born December 25, 1783, Died in Marshall Co., Tenn. March 10, 1848 (This grave is enclosed in a rock wall with 4 or 5 other graves marked only by stacks of stones)

There are probably two Revolutionary Soldiers and wives buried in this Cemetery, Nathaniel Laird and Mathew Wallis. For information on these Soldiers, see REVOLUTIONARY WAR PATRIOTS OF MARSHALL COUNTY, TENNESSEE by Jane Wallace Alford.

* *

TOPPING HILL CEMETERY

Located one mile south of Lunn Store on hill. Many unmarked graves, no inscriptions.

* *

PRATT CEMETERY

Located in the northwest corner of Marshall County, on the north side of Flat Creek. Copied Jan 29, 1971 by Ralph D. Whitesell.

Arthur Pratt
1875-1947

K. Otis Pratt
1811-1920

Paul Pratt
1905-1945

Clara Pratt
1921

There are 8 unmarked graves.

* *

LANIER CEMETERY

Located in the northwest part of Marshall County, on Don Smith's farm, near New Bethel Church. Copied Jan 15, 1976.

Father
B. J. Lanier
Sep 30, 1842
Sep 6, 1916

and

Mother
C. A. Lanier
Jun 29, 1848
Mar 7, 1921

* *

END OF RALLY HILL QUADRANGLE

CHAPEL HILL
QUADRANGLE

EADY CEMETERY
Located at Holtland. At Promise Methodist Episcopal Church.

J. T. Daniel
Dec 4, 1886
Dec 13, 1965
&
Emma E. Daniel
Aug 8, 1879
Dec 31, 1969

John William Ghee
Aug 25, 1880
Aug 26, 1965
&
Mattie Belle Ghee
Jan 13, 1886

W. T. Eady
Sep 17, 1878
Jan 7, 1964
&
Emma F. Eady
Jan 23, 1881
Aug 24, 1956

Fannie Eady Dies
1890-1955

Eugene Eady
1891-1940
&
Avie Eady
1899-19

Father
W. P. Eady
Jun 24, 1855
Mar 14, 1947
&
Mother
Narcissus Eady
Sep 4, 1855
Apr 5, 1930

Ella Hayes Eady
1877-1955

Clarence E. Eady
1883-1946
&
Mattie V. Eady
1886-19

J. L. Lamb
Mar 9, 1875
Aug 27, 1956
&
Ella Lamb
Sep 23, 1874
Mar 23, 1955

Scott Lamb
Nov 2, 1898
Feb 26, 1970
&
Alice Lamb
Mar 8, 1890
Feb 10, 1944

Leon Dean Eady
1893-1967
&
Myrtle Lynch Eady
1894-

Audrey K., dau of
Mr. & Mrs. J. E. Isom
Jul 4, 1926
Jul 7, 1938

Jas. Ellis Isom
Dec 27, 1900
Nov 13, 1961

John W. Ghee
3 months
1935

W. Durgan Eady
1905-1958
&
Bernice H. Eady
1907-1951

James Oliver Slaughter
1930-
&
Bobbie Jean Slaughter
1935-1970
mrd- Dec 20, 1952

* *

BRITTAIN CEMETERY
Located behind Promise Methodist Church at Holtland, Tenn.
Copied November 8, 1970.

Sarah Harris Wilson
Dec 12, 1856
Feb 10, 1931

Baby Tanner
Jan 22, 1904
Jan 22, 1904

Cecil P. Tanner
Apr 21, 1908
Jun 19, 1909

George W. Tanner
Jan 14, 1882
Apr 3, 1935

Beulah P. Tanner
Dec 10, 1879
Feb 24, 1921

Joseph F. Brittain
1860-1927

Robert G. Brittain
1896-1915

R. H. Brittain
Oct 8, 1837
May 26, 1895

Josie H. Brittain
1863-1954

John H. Brittain
1886-1931

Nathan R. Hyde
Nov 7, 1905
Apr 23, 1935

Samuel R., son of
Dr. R. H. & O. M. Hyde
Mar 10, 1896
Dec 7, 1897

Daughter of
M. F. Moena Harris
Jul 18, 1888
Sep 20, 1894

William Edwin, Infant son of
Hale & Eunice Harris
Aug 25, 1920
Aug 27, 1920

Joseph Fulton Brittain
Dec 9, 1831
Jun 23, 1917
&
Elizabeth C. Brittain
Jun 25, 1836
Feb 5, 1916

Edwin Hale Harris
May 27, 1899
Nov 14, 1928
&
Eunice Holder Harris
Nov 30, 1900
----

* *

PROMISE METHODIST CHURCH CEMETERY
Located behind the Church at Holtland, Tenn. Copied in 1979
by Franklin Blanton.

M. R. D. Bryan
Oct 15, 1817
Oct 23, 1877
&
Sarah O. Bryan
Sep 14, 1831
Sep 17, 1907

Mildred Eugene, son of
S. L. & Ruby Craig
May 14, 1918
Jun 16, 1920

Claudie Ferrell Kelly, dau of
Mr. & Mrs. Lonnie Ferrell
Jul   1920
Mar 3, 1966

Martha C. Thomas
1881-1916

* *

CHAPEL HILL

BRITTAIN-EZELL CEMETERY

Located one mile south of the Williamson County line, about one and one-half miles west of Holtland, Tenn. Copied January 23, 1973 by Ralph D. Whitesell.

John Thomas Alford
Oct 1, 1853
Aug 26, 1931

Bettie Elizabeth Alford
Aug 1, 1859
Dec 17, 1933

Mollie Loftin Alford
Nov 5, 1866
Oct 18, 1906

Mary Riggs Alford
Sep 28, 1824
Jan 4, 1889

Large stone on ground, could not be turned over to read.

John F. Bruin
Dec 23, 1853
Jul 16, 1884

John Fleming Ferguson
Dec 9, 1797
Nov 7, 1870
&
Amelia Brittain Ferguson
Feb 26, 1803
Aug 9, 1854

James M. Ferguson
Feb 28, 1831
May 15, 1921

Infant Son of
M. H. & Susan Scales
(no dates)

James H., son of
Dr. M. H. & Susan Scales
Who was born 1850
(no death date)

H. F., son of
S. L. & Annie Tucker
Jul 16, 1902
Jul 18, 1902

John F. Ferguson
Dec 21, 1839
Nov 18, 1916
&
Sallie S. Ferguson
Jan 9, 1845
(no date)

Mary J. Brittain
Mar 3, 1811
Jun 25, 1863

J. W. Brittain
Jul 7, 1830
Aug 18, 1856

Joseph H. Brittain
Nov 30, 1810
Jun 20, 1848

Constantine LaFayette
            Brittain
Jun 1, 1840
Jun 9, 1844

William Fletcher Brittain
Mar 12, 1842
Jun 29, 1844

J. H. Adams
Jan 27, 1843
Nov 28, 1918
&
Jemima, wife of
A. J. Ring, & 2nd wife of
Jas. H. Adams
May 27, 1837
May 24, 1904

John M. Adams
1868-1942
&
Josa E. Adams
1870-1941

N. O. Redmond
1872-1937
&
Mother
Letha Ann Johnson Redmond
1873-1962
&
Father
J. M. Johnson
1867-1933

Aaron Boyd
Dec 29, 1794
Jun 5, 1858

Mary, wife of
Aaron Boyd
May 27, 1801
Sep 30, 1845
Age 44 yrs, 4 mos, 3 days

Mary, wife of
Aaron Wells
Born 1770
Died 1861

Sacred to the Memory of
Joseph Brittain, Esq.
who departed this life
August 11th, 1823
Age 67 years.

Dorothy Brittain
Departed this life
July 9, 1844
Age about 75 years.

Joe M. Swaim
Oct 30, 1854
Nov 20, 1915

Robert M. Swaim
Born 23 June
Died Jan 12, 1888

Nancy G. Swaim
Dec 1, 1833
Mar 6, 1873

Sarah J. Smiley
Sep 11, 1835
Mar 20, 1876

Sarah Ann McMurry,
wife of
S. E. Johnson
Died Jul 6, 1887
(no age given)

Mary Frances McMurry,
wife of
H. F. Ezell
Died May 24, 1877
(no age given)

Mary Franklin, baby of
M. F. & H. F. Ezell
B&D Dec 8, 1876

Elizabeth Fulton
Dec 25, 1790
Aug 9, 1852

James C. Fulton
Dec 28, 1777
Mar 5, 1831
Age 53 yrs, 2 mos.

James C. Fulton
Apr 29, 1815
Oct 6, 1843

Dorothy H. Fulton
Apr 15, 1813
Jul 15, 1837

Nicholas P. H. Fulton
Born June 2, 1822
Died 1831

Elizabeth B. Holt
Nov 10, 1826
Oct 2, 1836

Joseph B. Fulton
Nov 12, 1824
Aug 30, 1865

Isabella P. Holt
Aug 15, 1832
Jun 26, 1848
Age 15 yrs, 10 mos, 11 days

Martha F. Fulton
Apr 26, 1821
Jun 30, 1847

William Ezell Haynes
Aug 6, 1914
Feb 16, 1915

Father
H. F. Ezell
Jan 31, 1844
May 19, 1918
&
Mother
Lizzie D. Ezell
May 19, 1862
Dec 9, 1922

Jepp. J. Ezell
Jun 20, 1887
Jun 6, 1916
&
Jepp. J. Ezell, Jr.
Nov 28, 1914
Dec 8, 1914

Sarah, dau of
H. F. & Lizzie Ezell
Feb 23, 1907

About 15 graves with fieldstones, no inscriptions.

* *

CHAPEL HILL

HARRIS CEMETERY

Located north of the Holtland-Lunn's Store Road and west of Harris Cemetery Road. Copied August 30, 1979.

Sam D. Harris
1904-1964

L. Ernest Harris
1875-1939
&
Minnie V. Harris
1882-1949

Sherwood D. Harris
Jun 19, 1839
Nov 25, 1897

Catherine, wife of
S. D. Harris
Feb 14, 1846
Jun 24, 1920

Ola Harris
1919-1927

Alice Faye Harris
Dec 5, 1936

Mrs. Mamie Lovings
Died June 10, 1946
age 51 yrs, 6 mos, 4 days
(TM)

Philip E. Smith
1970-1970 (TM)

J. L. Loving
died Aug 28, 1936
age 69 yrs, 10 mos, 13 days
(TM)

Mrs. J. L. Loving
died Nov 7, 1939
age 76 yrs, 5 mos, 29 days
(TM)

Mary Ann Lovings
died May 1, 1951
age 0 yrs, 11 mos, 25 days
(TM)

Mrs. Ida Harris
1885-1967 (TM)

John W. Ferguson
Nov 8, 1978
Oct 26, 1979

J. H. Cristwell
Sep 5, 1847
(no date)
&
M. L. Cristwell
May 15, 1862
(no date)

E. E. Cole
1835-1898

A. L. Cole
1835-1919

T. W. Cole
1864-1922

Mary Emily Cole
May 26, 1865
Apr 12, 1896

Anna Cole
1857-1881

John Patterson Cole
Jan 19, 1871
Sep 14, 1882

Elzer Franklin Cole
Apr 11, 1878
May 14, 1879

Sarah M. T. Cole
Oct 17, 1855
Feb 28, 1879

Infant Twins of
A. L. & E. E. Cole
July 1856

Allen Dalton
1881-1957
&
Mattie Dalton
1883-1912

Thelma (Irene) Dalton
Dec 14, 1946
Dec 18, 1946

Clarence Dalton
Dec 25, 1901
Jan 28, 1969

John W. Ferguson
1879-1970 (TM)

Jimmy Lee Williams
1959-1976
(TM - Cornersville FH)

Eddie B. Love
Jul 15, 1955
Jul 11, 1960
&
Edith Love
Jul 15, 1955
Jul 15, 1955

Alex Victory
1869-1944
&
Tlithey D. Victory
1870-1945

Tom M. Victory
1897-1967 (TM)

Martha James
1963-1963

Dars Johnur James
Jan 17, 1938

Doak James
1914-
&
Mary V. James
1926-1972

Douglas N. James
1871-1943
&
Belle James
1891-1965

Shelia Ann Williams
died Dec 24, 1961
age 11 months (TM)

Patrick J. Brown
Jul 29, 1972
Jul 30, 1972

Cynthia Millicent Jennette
Dec 25, 1972

Willie Joe Lovins
1946-1969 (TM)

Alfred T. Lovins
1896-1958

William R. Anderson
Dec 27, 1930
Jul 10, 1949

James B. Anderson
1935-1935

Milton Aldridge
Dec 3, 1931
10 days
(Lawrence FH)

Eva Aldred
Aug 3, 1890
May 6, 1914

H. Aldrid
Dec 27, 1915
Dec 9, 1927

Henry Alredge
Nov 10, 1843
Feb 2, 1916
&
Sue Alredge
Dec 9, 1851
(no date)

Doss B. Aldredge
1881-1972 (TM)

James O. Aldridge
1876-1959 (TM)

William Bryant Harris
Oct 22, 1976
Jun 1, 1977

Rebecca B. Harris
Sep 26, 1932
Jun 8, 1979

Herschel Edward Harris
Dec 8, 1941
Dec 26, 1973

* *

BELL CEMETERY

Located 3 miles north of Caney Spring, north of old Hwy 99.
Copied by Ralph D. Whitesell, Dennis and Alice Coble.

Jane G. Bell
Died Feb 18, 1821
Age 21 yrs, 1 mo, 10 days

12 to 15 unmarked graves.

* *

CHAPEL HILL

RIGGS CEMETERY
Located on Billie Warner's place, east side of Highway 31-A, North of Chapel Hill, Tennessee. Located at <u>Old Gideonville</u>. Copied Jan 20, 1973.

Sacred to the Memory of James E. Street, son of John T. and Lucin, was born November 8, 1844 and departed this life October 11, 1846.

In Memory of Edward Riggs Born April 16, 1786 and Died 30th Jan. 1824. Age: 58 years.

Elizabeth B. Riggs, Consort of Edward Riggs, born 10th November 1793 and departed this life 5th day September 1855.

In Memory of Mary B., Consort of Jas. T. Bryles, Born Oct 5th, 1814, died Jan 11, 1843. Age: 29 years.

There are 5 or 6 graves that have markers so badly broken, that they could not be read.

* *

GARRETT CEMETERY (COLORED)
Located west of Chapel Hill, Tennessee. Copied June 26, 1978.

Mother
Frances Garrett
1862-1949
&
Daughter
Ardie Garrett
1885-1901
(Mrs. Frances, died May 18, 1949, age 87.
Morton & Sons FH)

Jasper F. Johnson
Mar 18, 1901
Apr 1, 1970 (Anderson FH)

Lillie Garrett Johnson
1879-1973

Mary G. Hudson
Jan 19, 1884
Nov 14, 1977

Leonard M. Braden
May 19, 1924
Apr 20, 1975

1 grave with fieldstone.

* *

HUGHES CEMETERY
Located about 3 miles south of Eagleville near the Marshall County Line. This cemetery was in bounds of Marshall County at one time, now in Rutherford County.

Madison R. Hughes
Mar 9, 1789
Oct 21, 1877

M. R., son of
M. R. & S. S. Hughes
Dec 17, 1846
Oct 17, 1847

Samuel, son of
M. R. & S. S. Hughes
Jan __, 1836
Oct __, 1836

Almira, dau of
M. R. & S. S. Hughes
Apr 11, 1845
Oct 31, 1845

George W., son of
Charles & M. J. Royster
Aug 31, 1853
Jan 18, 1861

Mary, wife of
Rubin Hughes
Apr 2, 1775
Feb 6, 1839

Wm. R. Hughes
Dec 25, 1802
Sep 11, 1840

William T. Hughes
Feb 25, 1825
Jan 29, 1891
&
Mary J. Hughes
Jul 12, 1829
Jan 30, 1891

Arch Hughes
May 20, 1833
Aug 27, 1891

William P. Murrey
Nov 14, 1875, drowned
Aug 16, 1886
&
Willie T. Hughes
Oct 6, 1875, drowned
Aug 16, 1886

Matilda D. Work
Oct 12, 1833
Jan 20, 1869

Mary J., wife of
R. G. Ogilvie, dau of
W. T. & M. J. Hughes
Jun 21, 1850
Oct 16, 1870

Madison R. Hughes
1847-1937
&
Susie F. Hughes
1853-1937

Sallie J., wife of
Wm. H. Roane
Died July 10, 1854
Age 19 yrs, 7 mos, 2 days

Walter A. Hughes
Dec 19, 1902
Jul 20, 1921

Dovie D. Hughes
1875-1955

Robert B. Hughes
Feb __, 1806
Sep 11, 1840

Pattie Hill, wife of
W. Y. Wilhoite
died Oct 17, 1892
age 51 yrs, 8 mos.

W. Y. Wilhoite
__ __, 1841
Oct 17, 1892
(marker now gone, 1979)

Lou L. Hughes
May 9, 1850
Jun 11, 1862

Hollie Jones, wife of
D. H. Hughes
Mar 13, 1868
Nov 12, 1905

* *

CHAPEL HILL

McCORD CEMETERY

Located 1 mile north of Chapel Hill on 31-A, at Old Civil Order. Copied October 21, 1979.

Lucy Porch, deceased
January 11, 1850
Age 60 years.

Daniel Williams
Warm harted friend, for
to none, died in peace
with God and the world
on the 11 day of May 1846
aged: 68 years.

Father
H. G. McCord
Aug 12, 1847
Dec 12, 1910
&
Mother
Lillie V. McCord
May 13, 1856
Oct 15, 1935

Fletcher Williams
(child, no dates)

Nancy Williams
(child, no dates)

James Elgin McCord
9 of Dec 1844
25 of March 1850

Maude Ogilvie
1859-1924

In Memory of
Elizabeth Sophronia Murdock
by her parents
16 July 1842
Died 22 March 1845

A Memorial of
Sarah Williams,
kind hearted and affectionate
mother and friend to her
family and being the affectionate consort of James
Williams, who was born the
13 day of January 1789 and
deceased the 6 day of October
1843 in peace with God.

Sacred to the Memory of
Rev'd James Williams
who was born 26th Decr. 1785
Departed this life 22nd Oct.
1850 in peace with God.

Ann Williams, wife of
Rev. James Williams
Died 1882 (no age given)

Cowden McCord
Jan 14, 1809
Departed this life
Aug 4, 1879

Sarah A., wife of
Cowden McCord
Mar 14, 1826
Jun 8, 1863

Sallie E., dau of
Cowden & Sarah A. McCord,
and wife of
Albert N. Miller
Sep 20, 1849
Sep 1, 1874

Nancy McCord
1896-1974 (TM)

There are 2 or 3 unmarked graves.

* *

JOHNSON CEMETERY

Located about one-fourth mile of Holtland. Copied Oct 21, 1979.

Mittie, daughter of
J. M. & C. M. Johnson
Oct 8, 1870
Apr 7, 1882

This is the only grave. The
cemetery is about 40' X 40'
hewn rock post enclosure.

* *

STEAGAL CEMETERY

Located one-half mile southwest of Beasley. Copied Oct 27, 1979 by Franklin Blanton.

Infant child of
R. H. & M. L. Temple
Age 11 days
Departed this life
Oct 6, 1853

Other graves, no inscriptions.

In Memory of
Amanda Adams, dau of
Jasper Dazy & Mary his wife,
Born 16 of Sept 1808
Dec'd this life
21 of Aug 1840

Mr. Ralph Steagal (Steagall)
Apr 16, 1793
Aug 22, 1871

Nancy Green, wife of
Ralph Steagal
Dec 1, 1806
Mar 17, 1877

In Memory of
Samuel J. Steagal
Born March __, 1829
and departed this life
Aug the __, 1852
(stone broken)

Randolph Steagal (no Insc.)
born ca 1767-Died after 1850

* *

FALLWELL CEMETERY

Located two miles northeast of Chapel Hill, near Bedford County Line. Copied by Franklin Blanton in 1978.

Sacred to the Memory of
Elisha Fallwell
Nov 23, 1776
Jan 25, 1857

In Memory of
Elizabeth Fallwell, Consort
of Elisha Fallwell, was born
Feb 14, ____, died Sept 3,
18__. "She being the mother
of six children."
(stone broken)

1 child grave, unmarked.

* *

CHAPEL HILL

FALLWELL CEMETERY
Located two miles northeast of Chapel Hill, near Bedford County line. Copied by Franklin Blanton, 1978.

Moses Fallwell
May 31, 1803
May 18, 1868

J. F. Fallwell
Jun 26, 1867
Apr 27, 1868

* *

LITTLE CEMETERY
Located on the Old Samuel Vest land. 1 mile northeast of Chapel Hill, Tennessee. Copied by Franklin Blanton, 1978

S. M. Little
Feb 7, 1831
Mar 24, 1851

Nancy Little
Born 1832
Died ____

Infant daughter of
S. M. & N. Little
(no dates)

Infant daughter of
S. M. & N. Little
(no dates)

* *

COLLINS CEMETERY
Located about two miles east of Chapel Hill, Tennessee. Copied by Franklin Blanton, 1978.

Almon A. Collins
    Co F
1 Ala & Tenn.
Vidette Cav

* *

PATTERSON CEMETERY
Located two miles northeast of Chapel Hill, Tennessee, near Bedford County line. Copied by Franklin Blanton, 1978

John Stanley, Sr.
Feb 15, 1797
May 18, 1869

Nancy L., wife of
J. Stanley
Mar 9, 1802
May 17, 1868

Anna, wife of
James Patterson
May 10, 1788
Mar 20, 1870

Nancy Dillie Patterson
Feb 27, 1839
Sep 23, 1870

Martha J., wife of
D. D. Stanley
Died Jan 8, 1880
Aged: 37 yrs, 1 mo, 2 days

There are other unmarked graves.

* *

BLACKWELL-JOYCE CEMETERY
Located north of Chapel Hill, Tennessee, on Blackwell-Lunn Store road. Named SMITH on U.S.G.S.Map. Copied by Franklin Blanton and re-checked June 26, 1978.

Lem A. Vaughn
Aug 29, 1911
Jun 5, 1949

Johnnie Baxter Vaughn
Aug 30, 1928
Dec 20, 1967

Johnnie Neal Vaughn
1876-1941
(Thompson Service)

Lou Vaughn
1874-19(no date)

Infant dau of
Myrel & Hazel Holland
Aug 22, 1938

Wife
Lena Roberson
Apr 3, 1902
Jun 17, 1928

William Oscar Davis
Mar 28, 1890
Aug 2, 1954
&
Esther Lamb Davis
Feb 9, 1895
Jun 5, 1976

Kenneth Howard Davis
Apr 5, 1921
Sep 9, 1942

Billie Ray Ghee
1940-1945

B. F. Walker
1854-1939
&
Bettie O. Walker
1858-1940

Bernice Orr Walker
May 31, 1887
Apr 2, 1957
&
Ruby Trout Walker
Aug 3, 1898
Jan 12, 1973

W. Norman Davis
Jun 19, 1914
Jul 20, 1971
&
Mildred B. Davis
Apr 29, 1916

mrd- Dec 25, 1936

Mack M. Brown
1872-1936
&
Martha L. Brown
1882-1959

CHAPEL HILL

John Lee Watkins
1886-1943

Eliza J. Watkins
1854-1936

Edd S. Ferguson
1869-1932
&
Lillie H. Ferguson
1869-1946

W. T. Robinson
Oct 24, 1866
Mar 31, 1936
&
Lula Dillard Robinson
Jan 7, 1869
Jan 1, 1930

S. L. Dies
Oct 26, 1875
Mar 12, 1952
&
Alice Cromer Dies
May 25, 1881
Feb 1, 1958

Joseph Powell Clyde
SMSGT U.S.Air Force
W.W.II, Korea, Vietnam
1926-1976

Frank M. Sweeney
1903-1960
&
Fannie M. Sweeney
1902-1978

Paul M. Sweeney
Sept 2, 1941

E. S. Stammer
Jan 21, 1872
May 16, 1921

Maggie, wife of
E. S. Stammer
Apr 29, 1883
Dec 20, 1919

Margaret Letitia, dau of
James A. & Mary J. Joyce
Nov 16, 1876
Jan 27, 1877

Annie May, dau of
J. A. & M. J. Joyce
Jun 19, 1879- Apr 9, 1897

Thomas Dewey, son of
W. T. & S. J. Joyce
May 10, 1898
May 20, 1898

Sallie C. Orr
Died Mar 13, 1918
Age about 75 years

Joe G. Cromer
Dec 29, 1861
Nov 3, 1932
&
Martha E. Cromer
Nov 20, 1861
Jun 8, 1940

Ottie Cromer Tanner
Oct 25, 1906
Oct 3, 1947

Jennie Cromer Tanner
Feb 26, 1888
Feb 11, 1944

John Wallace Cromer
Jul 4, 1890
Jul 12, 1969
&
Allene Brown Cromer
Apr 26, 1899

John Wallace Cromer
Tennessee
Pvt 5 Co 157 Depot Brig WWI
(same as above)

Martha Lillian, dau of
J. W. & Alleen Cromer
May 29, 1924
Apr 23, 1925

Mary Ruth, dau of
J. W. & Alleen Cromer
Aug 21, 1922
Feb 6, 1923

William Handerson Smithson
May 7, 1925
May 18, 1941

Marion C. Smithson
Tennessee
Cpl U.S.Army, W.W.II
Jan 29, 1892
Nov 12, 1969

Sacred to the Memory of
Losson Rickman
who was bornd Oct the 8th
1809 and departed this life
Sept. the 15th 1852.

Thomas B. Joyce
1865-1947
&
Mattie Joyce
1874-1928

Edward Cole, son of
T. B. & Mattie Joyce
Dec 14, 1905
Jul 10, 1906

Infant dau of
T. B. & Mattie Joyce
Jul 18, 1909
Sep 12, 1909

Thomas Andrew Blackwell
1909-1962
&
Ella Turner Blackwell
1911-

Infant Son of
Tom & Ella Blackwell
March 23, 1929

Milton Thomas Blackwell
Oct 11, 1877
May 10, 1965
&
Mary Brittain Blackwell
Apr 1, 1892
Mar 18, 1976

D.(Doctor) F. Joyce
Jan 15, 1822
Oct 14, 1870
& wife
Lucinda Joyce
Dec 22, 1828
Mar 3, 1914

Infant of
D. F. & L. Joyce
who was born the 30th of
Oct 1847

Infant of
L. & D. F. Joyce
who was born & died the
22nd of Nov 1851

William A. Joyce
Apr 12, 1871
Jan 17, 1916

Lillie E. Joyce
Jan 27, 1872
Sep 10, 1925

G. W. Joyce
Mar 22, 1830
(no date
&
Mrs. M. E. Joyce
Oct 31, 1841
Jan 30, 1916

J. Fulton, son of
G. W. & Elizabeth Joyce
Mar 13, 1857
Oct 21, 1904

Chas. Harris, infant of
C. A. & Ruby Blackwell
Nov 9, 1918
Nov 26, 1918

Our Son
Johnny Blackwell
1950-1959

Thomas M. Smith
Nov 24, 1835
Apr 8, 1911
(wife on next page)

In Memory of
John Burns
Who was born March the
13th and died Nov the
9th 1841

In Memory of
Robert Burns
Who was born Dec the
25th, 1833 and died
Nov the 26th, 1836

In Memory of
Mary E. Roberson
Who was bornd May the
30th, 1788, Died Aug the
30th, 1866.

John R. Joyce
Oct 27, 1855
Apr 10, 1916

T. C. Joyce
Apr 15, 1823
Oct 14, 1898

Nannie H. Joyce
Apr 15, 1828
Aug 20, 1903

_____ Joyce
1897-1939 (TM)

Carrie S. Joyce
1902-1976 (TM)

Virginia Lucille Joyce
1923-1926 (TM)

J. A. Joyce
Feb 1, 1844
Aug 10, 1932
&
Mary Jane Joyce
Jan 17, 1848
Oct 14, 1917
mrd- Dec 20, 1866

Infant dau of
Louise & Bob Blackwell
July 2, 1958

Thomas Blackwell
Dec 22, 1848
Aug 24, 1925
& wife
Livonia Elizabeth Blackwell
Nov 9, 1848
Mar 3, 1924

Charles Andrew Blackwell
Nov 8, 1881
Aug 31, 1957
&
Ruby Harris Blackwell
Aug 3, 1897

CHAPEL HILL

Ella Morgan, wife of
T. M. Smith
Dec 31, 1856
Nov 7, 1916

Lucinda, wife of
Thomas S. Smith
Jul 8, 1811
Jan 27, 1880
(broken)

E. B. Joyce
Feb 9, 1887
Nov 8, 1913

Eva Joyce Lamb
Feb 6, 1878
Jun 10, 1912

Anna Joice Rainey
Jun 19, 1877
Mar 16, 1915

Sister
Maude Rainey Vaughn
Mar 21, 1907
Aug 31, 1930

Brother
William Thomas Rainey
Jun 8, 1902
May 30, 1937

Claude Esten Joyce
1903-1972
&
Minnie Belle Joyce
1913-

Sacred to the Memory of
Daniel McClaren
Born the 17 of May 1749
and depa.......   P.H.
(never finished,-in the book
Revolutionary Patriots of
Marshall County by Alford,
states he died in Hickman
County, Tenn. in 1844)

Grave (TM)

Sue Ella Joyce
1909-1931

Dock Joyce
1908-1978
(Lawrence FH)
END OF BLACKWELL-JOYCE

James W. Joyce
Sep 18, 1853
Dec 6, 1921

V. T. Joyce
Jul 13, 1855
Feb 20, 1911

Papa
Frank McKinley Rainey
Jun 28, 1863
Feb 3, 1940

Mama
Hattie Sullivan Rainey
Mar 31, 1881
Dec 15, 1934

4 unmarked graves.

* *

BEASLEY CEMETERY
Located one mile northwest of Beasley, near the Rutherford
County line.   Copied 1978 by Richard A., Blanche & Tim Marsh

Rev. J. A. Burton
Jul 14, 1849
Jun 23, 1918

M. A. Burton, wife of
J. A. Burton & dau of
Rev. J. B. Beasley
Mar 26, 1849
May 16, 1910

A. Mason Burton
Nov 26, 1894
Oct 16, 1956

Mrs. W. T. Hall(broken)
Oct 28, 1870
Mar 5, 1889

Florence Evans
1881-1949

Edgar W. Burton
1872-1934
&
Anna Burton
1874-1905

Thomas Elgen Beasley
Jul 26, 1867
Sep 9, 1918

Approximately 6 unmarked
    graves.

Fred St. John
Jun 10, 1878
Jun 31, 1954
&
Kate St. John
Dec 16, 1878
Jan 28, 1948

Hardin Fitzgerald
Apr 2, 1893
Jan 24, 1973

James B. Beasley
Oct 17, 1826
Feb 23, 1890

Sallie, wife of
James B. Beasley
Oct 16, 1828
Nov 18, 1873

Tommie L. Beasley
Jul 3, 1900
Oct 2, 1952

Peggy Ann Beasley
3 days 1934

Dave Henry Clinard
Feb 23, 1862
Sep 18, 1945

Eula Beasley Clinard
Aug 29, 1872
Dec 26, 1949

* *

LEE CEMETERY
Located at Beasley, east of Highway 99. Copied 1979 by Franklin Blanton

John L. Lee
Dec 1, 1821
Jan 4, 1897
&
Tennessee Lee
Jan 9, 1824
Nov 10, 1896

Leila Annie, dau of
W. B. & K. V. Marshall
Jul 18, 1872
Jun 18, 1890

Daisey Ella, dau of
W. B. & K. V. Marshall
Sep 18, 1879
Jul 16, 1880

Walter, son of
J. C. & M. J. Lee
Jan 7, 1878
Jan 18, 1900

Hattie, wife of
P. B. Thomas
Aug 21, 1883
Jul 1, 1909

Francis Marion Harris
Sep 22, 1860
Jun 4, 1913
&
May Josephine Harris
Jan 6, 1866
Apr 10, 1950

* *

CHAPEL HILL

FAGAN CEMETERY
Located at the junction of New Lunn's Store Road and Harris Cemetery Road. Copied April 27, 1969, up-dated Sept 1, 1979.

Cecil M. Newcomb
Apr 23, 1940
Jun 5, 1948

Mary Jane Studivan
Mar 24, 1840
Oct 6, 1893

Malissa Clark
1867-1950

Henrietta Clark
1871-1957 (TM)

Margie Fay Flippin
1946-1957 (TM)

David Edward Flippin
Died Nov 23, 1934
Age 0 yrs, 1 mo, 22 days (TM)

Leonard Hyde Fagan
Jun 19, 1897
Jan 18, 1974

Urban B. Fagan
1867-1949
&
Lena E. Fagan
1879-1943

Several unmarked graves.

Thomas H. Fagan
Dec 14, 1828
Jan 17, 1887

Maggie T., dau of
T. H. & M. E. Fagan
Nov 7, 1875
Dec 2, 1878

Mrs. Mary Owens Fagan
(no dates, Bills-McGaugh FH)

T. H., son of
U. B. & L. E. Fagan
Dec 15, 1902
Jan 16, 1906

John W. Fagan
1877-1960 (TM)

Mrs. Mamie S. Fagan
1878-1959 (TM)

Miss Ella Mai Fagan
1944

Dewey C. Newcomb
1899-1970
&
Charlie F. Newcomb
1894-1971

Elizabeth Ann Newcomb
Jul 5, 1941
(Lawrence FH)

* *

CRUTCHER CEMETERY
Located on the north end of Thick Road. Copied by Charlene Nicholas.

Ulner B. Crutcher
Tennessee
Pvt Co E 307 Engineers
W. W. I
Feb 12, 1894
Oct 9, 1971

Alta Sampson Crutcher
Jul 24, 1880
Apr 15, 1958

Olora Mettie Crutcher
1923-1923

* *

WRIGHT CEMETERY
Located at Thick Community. Re-checked by Ralph D. Whitesell, Helen and Tim Marsh, November 17, 1979.

Andy D. Wright
Mar 5, 1871
Jul 5, 1939
&
Emma C. Wright
Sep 30, 1896
Jan 4, 1943

David Michael Wright
1955-1972 (TM)

John Watson Wright
Tennessee
TEC 4 U.S.Army W. W. II
Aug 14, 1917
Apr 30, 1969

Marie W. Wright
Oct 24, 1922
May 18, 1950

James Thomas Wright
1970-1971
(McDaniel FH)

Several unmarked graves.

Edd F. Adgent
Died June 8, 1942
Age 37 yrs, 11 mos, 4 days.
(Lawrence FH)

* *

WILSON-COLE CEMETERY
Located at Thick Community. Copied November 17, 1979 by Ralph D. Whitesell, Helen and Tim Marsh.

Aaron A. Wilson, son of
Jas. & S. Wilson
Nov 13, 1784
Aug 29, 1832
(marker now gone, 1979)

James D. M., son of
A. J. & H. Wilson
Sep 21, 1825-May 4, 1842

Marilla D. Wilson, dau of
A. J. & H. Wilson
Born 1820
Died Jul 18, 1835

Mary M., dau of
A. J. & H. Wilson
Dec 19, 1818-Sep 12, 1836
(marker now gone, 1979)

Jane Long, dau of
Hugh & Anna Long
Dec'd 3 Dec 1819
Age 1 mo, 3 days

W. L.
(footmarker)

Lethe A. Cole
Jan 27, 1840
Mar 17, 1870

Inda, dau of
A. J. & R. A. Cole
January 25, 1870

CHAPEL HILL

Andrew J. Cole
Apr 3, 1842
Oct 8, 1908

Rebecca Ann Cole
Mar 27, 1847
May 24, 1928

J. A. Cole
1840-1870
&
Alora Cole
185_-187_

John Cole
Feb 14, 1780
Jan 12, 1859

4 Pyramid graves.
Many unmarked graves.

Col. T. C. H. Miller
Died July 15, 1869
Age about 65 years

* *

MOSES CEMETERY
Located at Thick. Copied November 17, 1979 by Ralph D. Whitesell, Helen and Tim Marsh.

Solon Marlin
1888-1939
&
Ola Marlin
1894-1961

J. Homer Marlin
Dec 8, 1911
May 29, 1942

Barbara Darlene, Infant
dau of Billy & Bobbie Gray
January 17, 1955

Marsh C. McCollom
1884-1939

Mother
Willie O. Moses Lofton
  McCullom
1884-1952

Buddie Ragan
1935-1936

James H. Ragan
Mar 24, 1901
Jul 21, 1966

Lela Ruth Ragan
1953-1963 (TM)

Nowles Pinkston
Dec 24, 1890
Jul 1, 1928
&
Johnnie Moses Pinkston
Apr 11, 1892
Apr 17, 1940

Miles Moses
May 13, 1843
Nov 4, 1918
&
Martha A. Moses
Feb 10, 1848
Nov 21, 1918

Peter H. Moses
1850-1932
&
Mary F. Moses
1850-1923

F. Imogene Lofton
May 24, 1914
Oct 24, 1940

Dad
Bob E. Murdock
1883-1951

Mother
Jessie B. Murdock
1889-

Mary Ruth Murdock
1908-1926

George W. Ramsey
Jun 19, 1907
May 2, 1978
&
Alice Murdock Ramsey
Mar 27, 1911

Several graves with fieldstones, no inscriptions.

* *

WILSON CEMETERY
Located at Thick, next to the Moses Cemetery. Copied November 17, 1979 by Ralph D. Whitsell, Helen and Tim Marsh.

Edward E. Wilson
Aug 25, 1894
        1979 (TM)
&
Mamie Powell Wilson
Jan 15, 1899
Jun 18, 1953
&
Lucy Dean Wilson
Apr 22, 1923
        1979 (TM)

Sam Joe Wallace
1879-1916
&
Ora Neely Wallace
1879-1938

Joe W. Wallace
Tennessee
PFC U.S.Army
W. W. II
Sep 7, 1906
Apr 4, 1971

* *

WILSON CEMETERY
Located three miles west of Chapel Hill on the Thick Road, about one-half mile south of Thick. Copied by Ludelle C. Dickey, Covington, TN.

Tarissa Wilson
Jan 13, 1806
Dec 23, 1869

Hiram Wilson
Feb 6, 1802
Mar 16, 1852

Eliza Wilson
Aug 10, 1801
Jul 7, 1854
(wife of Hiram Wilson)

Columbus Wilson
Jul 5, 1831
Dec 15, 1851

CHAPEL HILL

William P.(Pitt) Wilson
Aug 5, 1834
Mar 14, 1902

Edd E. Wilson
Jun 25, 1824
Nov 13, 1891

Emma E. Wilson
Sep 20, 1829
Sep 30, 1906

Cynthia, dau of
E. E. & E. Wilson
May 25, 1858
Jul 3, 1859

John Shires
Aug 2, 1825
Mar 16, 1853

Mary T. Shires
Sep 1, 1827
Apr 16, 1893

Gordie C. Loften
Nov 15, 1867
Aug 22, 1891

Jonathan Bright Wilson
1875-1965
&
Lula Blanton Wilson
1879-1952

Infant Son of
E. E. & E. Wilson
B&D Mar 16, 1853

Hiram Franklin, son of
E. E. & E. Wilson
Dec 24, 1868
Dec 11, 1871

Jennie E., dau of
E. E. & Emma Wilson
Mar 12, 1855
Oct 21, 1885

J. M. T. White
Apr 6, 1846
Oct 1, 1914

Lela, dau of
J. M. T. & B. D. White
May 15, 1875
Feb 26, 1893
Age 17 yrs, 9 mos, 11 days

J. T. Neely
May 4, 1844
Nov 5, 1913

Sarah C. Neely
May 24, 1852
Apr 24, 1930

Bettie D., wife of
Mark T. White
Dec 28, 1849
Jul 23, 1886

Columbus B. Wilson
1861 (Nov 4)
1904 (Sep 13)
&
Jonna Brown Wilson
1863 (Nov 1)
1963 (Jul 5)

Alma Wilson Cathey
1889-1919

W. M. T. White
Feb 14, 1818
Jul 27, 1905
& wife
Alcie R. White
Jan 20, 1820
Feb 27, 1904

Eula, wife of
S. M. Little
Dec 14, 1870
May 6, 1900

Edward Delwyn Wilson
1884-1969
&
F. Gertrude Wilson
1890-1969

Edward T. Wilson
Apr 4, 1866
Jan 5, 1949
&
Minnie Boyd Wilson
Jul 2, 1870
Oct 14, 1935

Hattie Mai Hazlett
Nov 16, 1931
Jun 17, 1975

William M. Neil
Oct 22, 1874
Jul 9, 1897

Emma J. Neil
Sep 12, 1849
Mar 30, 1926

This cemetery is in very bad condition and very hard to get to.

* *

GENTRY CEMETERY

Located at Thick. This is a small cemetery, is fenced and a large metal monument is situated in the cemetery with only name GENTRY inscribed on it. There are 4 or 5 graves in the enclosure. Perhaps the family of Theophillis Gentry.

* *

HAYNES-PATTERSON CEMETERY

Located about one and one-half miles west of Chapel Hill, and about one-half mile north of Highway No. 99. Copied September 16, 1968.

C. P. Patterson
Jun 6, 1851
Jan 25, 1854

Aunt
Mary "Polly" Patterson
Born 1789 or 1790
Died Sep 4, 1864

Edgar, son of
T. J. & L. H. Patterson
Nov 5, 1870
May 20, 1892

Louisa H. Patterson, wife of
Dr. T. J. Patterson
Dec 29, 1832
Jul 22, 1890

John P. Patterson
Jul 25, 1860
May 14, 1932

F. M. Patterson
Jan 1, 1854
Oct 29, 1862

John Patterson
Dec 9, 1802
Dec 8, 1886

Sarah W., wife of
John Patterson
Nov 26, 1822
Mar 29, 1899

Thomas J. B. Patterson
Dec 23, 1861
Oct 22, 1889

Dr. T. J. Patterson "Father"
Jun 13, 1828
Mar 3, 1901

Tabitha Pauline Patterson
Jan 7, 1872
Jun 15, 1947

Charles Ewing Waddington
Honolulu 1927
Louisa Hardin Waddington
Chapel Hill 1931
Infant children of
Mr. & Mrs. C. F. Waddington

William P. Crockett
Aug 11, 1888
Jul 26, 1910

Mary C. P. Crockett
Aug 8, 1890
Nov 13, 1891

Thomas M. Haynes
1852-1930

J. Genora, wife of
T. M. Haynes
Mar 6, 1861
Oct 29, 1899

CHAPEL HILL

Malissa Patterson, dau of
T. M. & J. G. Haynes
May 20, 1892
Sep 24, 1892

Walter B., son of
T. M. & Genora Haynes
Sep 10, 1882
Nov 8, 1899

Clarence H. Haynes
1884-1927

Katie B. Haynes
1885-1957

J. P. Haynes
Dec 16, 1854
Feb 5, 1912

Col. P. C. Haynes
Dec 9, 1826
Dec 12, 1907
"A Veterin of the Mexican & Civil Wars".

Malissa, wife of
P. C. Haynes
Sep 24, 1825
May 26, 1892

John B. Haynes
Oct 29, 1859
Oct 22, 1892

Bessie Haynes
1866-1922

Landon C., son of
J. B. & Bessie Haynes
Feb 13, 1891
Oct 18, 1893

Vera Genora Haynes
Feb 22, 1883
Jun 12, 1903

Miss M. A. Haynes
Jan 23, 1837
Feb 18, 1906

* *

BOYD CEMETERY

Located two and one-hald miles north of Holtland. This cemetery is in Rutherford County, Tennessee.

John Boyd
Jul 1, 1769
May 12, 1831

Rebecca, wife of
John Boyd
Jan 1, 1772
Dec 13, 1835

Joseph Henry, son of
J. H. & M. W. Robinson
Nov 15, 1836
Feb 27, 1838

W.(?) W. Boyd
Nov 1, 1835
Sep 8, 1837

8 or 10 unmarked graves.

Joel Riggs
Apr 22, 1776
Dec 13, 1835

Rebecca B. Lane, dau of
Joel & Elizabeth Riggs
& wife of
Thomas C. Lane
Apr 11, 1821
Sep 22, 1845

* *

EZELL CEMETERY

Located on Unionville Road, near Chapel Hill. Copied Oct 27, 1979 by Ralph D. Whitesell, Helen and Tim Marsh.

Annie M. Ezell
Apr 20, 1823
Dec 4, 1862
&
George W., youngest son of
Eld. Balaam & Keziah Ezell
Apr 10, 1824
Jan 9, 1892
Age 67 yrs, 9 mos, 29 days.

Nancy R. Ezell
Oct 3, 1839
Dec 19, 1923

Georgia A., dau of
G. W. & Annie M. Ezell
Jul 27, 1861
Feb 16, 1862

Willie F., son of
G. W. & N. R. Ezell
Nov 10, 1868
Oct 12, 1881

Infant Daughter of
G. W. & N. R. Ezell
B&D Jul 25, 1864

Infant Son of
J. J. & Omie Henly
B&D Jan 6, 1885

Eugene Price, son of
James & Elizabeth Price
Mar 1898
Apr 1968

James Alex Price
1858-1941
&
Annie Elizabeth Price
1865-1902

George Ezell, son of
James & Elizabeth Price
Dec 14, 1890
Jun 20, 1969

Omie Ezell Henley
Aug 14, 1855
Feb 12, 1935

E. C. Ezell
1872-1949
&
Sonia J. Ezell
1894-

Eula K. Ezell
1880-1913

Kate M. Ezell
1875-1911
(NOTE: Edd C. Ezell was known as "Black Edd" to distinguish him from his first cousin, Ed. A. Ezell, who was a blond. He married three times, Kate M., Eula K. & Sonia J.)
  on another side of stone:
Earl
Jas. Morton
Kathleen (footstone:1900-1930)
  (continued in next column)

Beulah
Frank
Douglas
  another side of stone:
Henry
George
Gaylor
Rebecca
Doris

James M. Ezell
Pvt U. S. Army W. W. II
Apr 8, 1897
Apr 8, 1972(3)

Edward Carl, Infant son of
Henry & Eula Ezell
April 30, 1947

Earl C. Ezell
Jan 28, 1937
Feb 11, 1937

CHAPEL HILL

Father
Thos. M. Ezell
1852-1939
&
Mother
Frances A. Ezell
1855-1901
&
Cassie V. Ezell
1892-1894
&
Willie P. Ezell
1891-1891
&
Emma C. Ezell
1876-1880
&
Infant Sons
1875-1875

John Morgan Stammer
Mar 14, 1863
Jan 9, 1926
& wife
Eugena Ezell Stammer
Feb 18, 1867
Mar 3, 1945

Rev. David B. Smith
Nov 26, 1880
Sep 22, 1948

Annie Stammer Smith
Dec 8, 1888
Mar 29, 1972

Louella, dau of
J. M. & E. Stammer
Feb 24, 1894
May 19, 1896

Lottie, dau of
J. M. & Eugena Stammer
Feb 17, 1887
Apr 7, 1902

Earl W. Ezell
1894-
&
Mabel L. Ezell
1906-1977

Dr. Charles Hazard Gurney
1867-1951
&
Ella Ezell Gurney
1874-1953

Patti Elizabeth Bearden
Apr 13, 1908
Oct 22, 1914

Hugh H. Giles
Sep 11, 1902

&
Beulah A. Giles
Jan 30, 1903
Jul 10, 1971

END OF EZELL

* *

FORREST CEMETERY

Located west of Chapel Hill, on west side of Railroad, and about 3/4 mile from Highway No. 99, on Aubrey Fagan farm. Copied October 30, 1966.

Frederick Siler
Aug 29, 1757
Aug 29, 1826

Mary, wife of
John Sheffield
Who was born July 1799
and Died 1837

Margaret J. Forrest
Who was born Feb the 5th,
1832, & departed this life
October the 1st 1833.

Mary M. Forrest
July 5, 1831
May 17, 1851

Brigli Roberts
Born 1792
Died Dec 10, 1827

James M. R., son of
W. A. & Margaret Fleming
Feb 7, 1811
Sep   1815

* *

MANIER CEMETERY

Located one mile northwest of Chapel Hill. Copied July 30, 1967.

Lemuel Manier
Who was born January the
8th, A.D. 1792 & Departed
this life January 19th
1837.
Age 45 yrs & 11 days.

John Manier
Who was born Sept the 20th
1763 & departed this life
March 4th 1844
Age 80 yrs & 12 days.

Sally Manier
Who was born Aug the 5th
1787 & departed this life
April 15, 1841
Age 53 yrs, 8 mos, 10 days.

Joseph Henry Manier
Aug 16, 1884
Sep 4, 1892

J. W. Manier
Nov 16, 1824
Sep 25, 1903

Several unmarked graves.

Bettie E., wife of
J. W. Slaughter
Apr 5, 1855
Jan 22, 1913

* *

SHEFFIELD CEMETERY

Located northeast of Chapel Hill, on the Eagleville Road. Copied September 7, 1959 by Ralph D. Whitesell and Mrs. Lounora Pickens. Re-checked 1979.

In Memory of
Arthur Shuffield
Born September 12, 1750
Departed this life
December 26, 1824
"Was a Capt. in Rev. War."

In Memory of
Lucretia Sheffield
Born 3rd of November 1756
Departed this life
July 10, 1837

Albert Cass Shuffield
Was born April 16, 1846
Departed this life
July 17, 1855

Ephraim R., son of
J. A. & S. J. Sheffield
Born July 13, 1846
Died November 19, 1872

CHAPEL HILL

Elizabeth, Consort of
James M. Taylor
Apr 8, 1815
Apr 27, 1850
Age 35 yrs & 19 days.

J. M. Taylor
Nov 4, 1814
Jun 18, 1896

Mira W. Taylor, wife of
J. M. Taylor
May 23, 1822
Apr 9, 1882

James K., son of
James M. & Mira W. Taylor
Jan 9, 1855
Died   1856

Daniel, son of
D. W. & Hannah Little
Feb 20, 1843
Jul 14, 1844

Daniel W. Little
Jan 21, 1810
Oct 11, 1846
"Who left an affectionate
wife, 4 sons & 4 daus to
mourn his loss."

Hannah D., wife of
Daniel W. Little
Jun 3, 1813
Jul 29, 1878

Col. Isaac Shook Wilson
Mar 13, 1827
Sep 25, 1851

Elizabeth J., Consort of
Col. Isaac Shook Wilson
Apr 16, 1830
Apr 18, 1861

James A. Hall
(illegible)

Infant son of
Moses & Sarah Falwell
(no dates)

Infant son of
Moses & Sarah Falwell
(no dates)

Sarah Falwell, Consort of
Moses Falwell
Aug 31, 1810
Sep 12, 1848

Georgie G., son of
John G. & Jemima Hall
Nov 10, 1841
Jul 13, 1844

Eli Page Belcher
1827-1909
   &
Mary Ann Belcher
1838-1910

James F. Rickman
Aug 25, 1841
Jun 29, 1880

Cleopatra A., wife of
J. F. Rickman
Mar 12, 1839
Aug 11, 1916

Harriet J., wife of
J. F. Rickman
Apr 12, 1842- Died (no date)

Thomas J. Cooper
Apr 28, 1854
Feb 7, 1924
Age 69 yrs, 9 mos, 9 days

Arthur D. Shuffield
Feb 2, 1811
Sep 13, 1829

Pleasant Rufus Little
Sep 1, 1843
Jun 12, 1844

John R. Little, son of
Wm. & H. B. Little
May 22, 1831
Nov 14, 1836

John L. Little
   &
Lucinda Little
   Twins
May 5, 1842
Jun 5, 1842

William Hogan Little
Jun 28, 1839
Jun 26, 1844

Powell H. Marlin
1889-1975
   &
Irene R. Marlin
1898-1977

Alex Hughes Marlin
1921-1948

Ada Sue Boyd
1886-1969

Thomas A. Boyd
4th Cpl Co C 11 Tenn Cav
Confederate States Army
Jul 25, 1844
Oct 28, 1917
   &
Martha S. Boyd
Dec 2, 1849
Jul 17, 1938

John M., son of
T. A. & M. S. Boyd
Sep 16, 1876
Sep 18, 1882

P. Vaughn
Apr 13, 1826
Oct 13, 1898

Lucindia J., wife of
P. Vaughn
Oct 22, 1837
Jul 6, 1907

Claborn L. Vaughn
Apr 6, 1876
Feb 23, 1879

Robert D. Vaughn
Oct 13, 1873
Jan 6, 1889

Arthur Shuffield
Mar 13, 1787
Jun 8, 1837

Mary, wife of
John Shuffield
Born 1800, Aug 8th.
Died May 26, 1828

Col. John Shuffield
Dec 16, 1799
Mar 30, 1860
Age 60 yrs, 3 mos, 14 days

Lucretia Hogan Sheffield
dau of J. B. & N. Shuffield
Mar 24, 1818
Jun 12, 1844

John Watson, son of
J. W. & E. Sheffield
Dec 7, 1857
Dec 6, 1871

B. K. Sheffield
1851-1929
   & wife
Sarah L. Falwell Sheffield
1856-1884

M. Callie S.
1856-1892

Alice S. S.
1877-1884

Mollie C. S.
1851-1908

Lillie F. S.
1888-1902

Willie W., son of
T. A. & M. S. Boyd
Feb 8, 1868
Feb 15, 1868

Tommie A., son of
T. A. & M. S. Boyd
Nov 16, 1881
Sep 6, 1882

Mitanmelissa Little
May 5, 1869
Nov 15, 1869

Nancy, wife of
John Little
March 1789
Jan 18, 1845

Median Elizabeth Shuffield
Jul 31, 1816
Aug 13, 1841

Nancy Shuffield
Aug 23, 1792
Jul 11, 1824

Dr. Jason B. Sheffield
Mar 5, 1822
Aug 16, 1852

Harriett Brinson Little
Consort of William Little
& Daughter of
J. B. & Nancy Shuffield
Sep 15, 1809
Sep 1, 1843
"Destroyed by Dr. Brock
on child bed 8 O'clock".

Condall H. Shuffield
wife of J. B. Shuffield
Nov 23, 1778
May 6, 1825

William M. Neely
Jul 15, 1843
Feb 15, 1915

Malissa Ann, wife of
W. M. Neely
Oct 31, 1847
Jan 3, 1885

Ewing, son of
W. M. & M. A. Neely
Aug 1, 1877
Oct 19, 1899

J. A. Marlin
1861-1951

Nannie P. Marlin
1859-1944

John Alex, son of
J. A. & Nannie P. Marlin
Apr 5, 1887
Nov 23, 1917

Alice Marlin
1890-1943

Bessie Lee Marlin
Aug 1, 1881
Jun 23, 1969

Lucie M. Marlin
Jul 5, 1885
Nov 5, 1972

CHAPEL HILL

Joe A. Marlin
S2 U. S. Navy
Oct 22, 1922
Nov 15, 1974

William D. Sheffield
1834-1898
&
Susan G. Sheffield
1851-1925

Mrs. Martha M. Sheffield
Aug 24, 1805
Apr 28, 1883

J. B. Sheffield
Aug 2, 1785
Mar 17, 1874

John A. Sheffield
Jan 8, 1814
Feb 2, 1894

Susan Stegall Sheffield
Feb 26, 1819
Jun 2, 1900

Lewis Peach
1836-1927
&
Susie S. Peach
1844-(no date)

J. W. Sheffield
1820-1915
& wife
Evaline Sheffield
1822-1912

Franklin Pierce McGuffee
Apr 29, 1905
Jan 30, 1977
&
Thelma Sheffield McGuffee
May 17, 1911
Apr 26, 1969

E. V. Sheffield
Nov 8, 1840
Dec 14, 1922
&
Mary E. Sheffield
Apr 20, 1854
Mar 17, 1939

Ephraim N. Sheffield
Jul 13, 1879
Jun 11, 1946

Alice L. Sheffield
Oct 9, 1882
Nov 1, 1957

Nannie E. Owen
1872-1961

Gertrude Sheffield
wife of
J. B. Hyde
Mar 13, 1878
Apr   1922

Baby
Charles Sheffield Hyde
Apr 29, 1900
Feb 14, 1901

J. M. Sheffield
1874-1931
&
Lou Sheffield
1868-(no date)

C. Ethridge Sheffield
May 6, 1898
Mar 20, 1927

Elisha Jackson Sheffield
Nov 11, 1909
Apr 10, 1968

Alice Wheeler Sheffield
Dec 7, 1910

Johnny Sheffield
Tennessee
SP4 68 Assault Heli Co
Vietnam, AM & 2 OLC - PH
Oct 16, 1945
Mar 19, 1967
(color picture)

C. J. Sheffield
Jan 27, 1832
Jan 3, 1892
&
Lura A. Dobson Sheffield
Nov 23, 1850
Jan 23, 1935

Samuel J., son of
C. J. & L. A. Sheffield
Oct 20, 1874
Oct 17, 1909

Martha Bell Sheffield
Died May 22, 1942
Age 22 yrs, 9 mos, 8 days
(TM)

Charley M. Sheffield
Dec 18, 1903
Jun 20, 1978

Willie Sue, wife of
J. C. Kimbro
Aug 31, 1880
Jul 15, 1917
&
William Thomas, Infant Son
of J. C. & Willie Kimbro
May 24, 1905
Jun 14, 1905

Henry Baker Sheffield
1877-1958
&
Maude C.(Crutcher)
          Sheffield
1881-1959

Corrine Sheffield
1915-1918

Suzanne S. Giles
Sep 18, 1937

Sam Lee Giles, Jr.
Mar 5, 1901
Dec 21, 1963

Senora S. Giles
Dec 27, 1901
Aug 24, 1961
(DAR Emblem)

Ann Lou Vaughn
1916-1925

John W. Vaughn
Jun 13, 1878
Mar 4, 1934
&
Sallie H. Vaughn
Feb 13, 1878
Aug 26, 1935

END OF SHEFFIELD

Several graves marked with fieldstones, no inscriptions.

* *

WHITWORTH CEMETERY

Located on Old Warner farm between Chapel Hill and Holts Corner, near Old Gideonville, east of Highway No. 31-A.

Sacred to the Memory of
Ann Whitworth, who was
born Nov 15, 1790 &
Departed this life
July 29, 1833

Edward Whitworth
Who was born in the year of
our Lord, 1781, & departed
this life June the 1st 1838
Aged 57 years.

Mary Whitworth, Dec'd
Who was born in the year
of our Lord 1804 & departed
this life on the 14th of
November 1849.
Aged 45 years.

Elizabeth D. Herron
Who was born December the
27, A.D. 1809 & departed
this life Jan. the 13,
1834.

* *

CHAPEL HILL

McCORD CEMETERY

Located in Rutherford County, Tennessee, at the County line, on Highway No. 99. Copied October 21, 1979

Mary B. McCord
Born A.D. 1798
Sep 14th 1849

Mrs. Nancy Parthena, wife of
William A. McCord
Aug 1, 1831
Jun 9, 1893

William A. McCord
Jun 24, 1824
Oct 23, 1886

Mary Ann Haley, dau of
Benjamin & Martha J. Haley
Mar 20, 1843
Aug 25, 1844

William Jason, Infant Son of
J. P. & M. L. Ogilvie
Sep 13, 1861
Dec 19, 1861

B. W. Haley
Feb 2, 1815
Jul 8, 1848
Age: 33 yrs, 5mos, 6 days

Martha Jane, wife of
Benjamin Haley & dau of
Mary B. McCord
Mar 3, 1822
Sep 6, 1846
"Who left an affectionate husband & one dau to mourn her loss."

* *

MURDOCK CEMETERY

Located two miles west of Holtland on Dowdy Road. Copied October 27, 1979 by Ralph D. Whitesell, Helen and Tim Marsh and Mr. Dowdy.

James M. Roberson
borned
Nov 21, 1816
Feb 16, 1879

Caroline J. Thacker
born in Madison County, Ala.
July the 23, 1822, daughter
of the Rev. E. J. &
Elizabeth Dodson,
Who died Dec the 9, 1844.
Aged 22 yrs, 4 mos, 16 days.

Sacred to the Memory of
the Red. Elisha J. Dodson
Who was born in Stokes
Co., N.C., March the 31,
1788 was married to
Elizabeth Blackwell May the
5, 1814 & died July the
29, 1842. Aged 54 yrs,
3 mos, & 29 days.

Mary F. Pearcy
Mar 24, 1824
Feb 6, 1901

Wm. Thomas Vaughn
Nov 25, 1909
Aug 28, 1929

Henry P. Russell
May 1, 1814
Nov 5, 1889
&
Harriet T. Russell
Jan 23, 1813
Sep 4, 1895

This Monument is erected to
the Memory of
Thomas Murdock, husband of
Mary Murdock, by his children,
who died 31 March 1845.
Aged 67 yrs, 18 days.

With hearts of love &
gratitude, this Monument is
erected to the Memory of
Mary Murdock, wife of
Thomas Murdock, by her
children, who died 18th
Aug 1838. Age 59 yrs, 6 mos,
& ___ days.

Sarah A. Murdock
Apr 15, 1856
Apr 10, 1881

Hiram Murdock
Nov 30, 1810
Jan 21, 1879

Jane Murdock
Nov 29, 1812
May 13, 1899

Elgin Murdock
Jan 1, 1852
Apr 26, 1906

Mollie, wife of
E. Murdock (was Martha
Jan 29, 1854   Kimmons)
Feb 17, 1891
(NOTE: Elgin married 2nd to
Margaret Belinda Green.)

Infant Son of
Mr. and Mrs. G. B. Redman
Feb 18, 1900

Millia Ogilvie
Who was born
Oct the 22, 1838 and
died June 17, 1840

Thomas Powell
Born June 19, 1781
Died Oct 11, 1864
"Erected by Grandson,
M. T. Powell".

Sarah, wife of
Thomas Powell
Who was born Dec 18, 1784
and died Dec 18, 1841
Aged 57 yrs & was a member
of the Methodist Church.

W. A. Murdock
Mar 29, 1835
Feb 3, 1912

Elizabeth J. Blackwell,
wife of
W. A. Murdock
Feb 1, 1836
Jul 10, 1920

Walter Murdock
1882-1942

Ada Murdock
1870-1938

Children of
R. E. & Mollie Kimmons
Murdock
Mary O.
Jul 25, 1883
Aug 2, 1884
&
Infant
Mar 9, 1886
Mar 17, 1886

J. W. Blackwell
Mar 30, 1814
Mar 19, 1898
& Mother
Sarah Louiza, wife of
J. W. Blackwell
Jan 25, 1819
Dec 17, 1891

William M., son of
J. W. & S. L. Blackwell
Apr 4, 1857
Nov 11, 1862

S.(Sarah) E., dau of
J. W. & S. L. Blackwell
and wife of F. Rainey
Aug 17, 1843
Dec 4, 1864

Cynthia A. Dowdy
(dau of Hiram Murdock &
wife of Wm. Dowdy, B ca 183
Jul 20, 1837
Sep 27, 1912
(above Wm. Dowdy, son of
Wm. Dowdy b 1795 N.C. &
Elizabeth b 1802 N.C.)

Wm. Leroy Dowdy
Sep 25, 1869
Nov 6, 1931
&
Ivie Wilson Dowdy
Mar 15, 1877
Dec 8, 1975

Holt Cherry
1910-1941

Clara B. Cherry
Apr 19, 1880
Aug 16, 1880

CHAPEL HILL

J. B. Cherry
Aug 13, 1846
Dec 8, 1925

and

Mary Cherry
May 22, 1846
Sep 4, 1915

* *

MARTIN CEMETERY
Located near Beasley, at the Rutherford County line.
Copied October 27, 1979.

In Memory of
Maria Martin, Consort of
Henry Martin who departed
this life 28 July 1842, she
was a tender mother and
affectionate wife. She was
sincere and devout, who left
husband, 8 sons & 6 daus
who deeply lament the loss
of her consolation in this
life. Age 39 years.

Maria S., dau of
Henry & Maria Martin
Who was born June 1830 &
departed this life 5 Dec
1831, Who left Father,
Mother, & 8 brothers & 6
sisters to lament her loss.
Aged 1 year, 5 mos, 6 days.

* *

EZELL-BIGGERS CEMETERY
Located one mile south of Beasley, on Highway No. 99.
Copied October 27, 1979 by Ralph D. Whitesell, Helen and
Tim Marsh.

W. C. Ezell
Oct 14, 1816
Sep 22, 1877

Elizabeth A., wife of
W. C. Ezell
Oct 2, 1825
May 11, 1889
Age 66 yrs, 7 mos, 9 days.

Francis M. Ezell
Apr 11, 1835
Oct 23, 1863
"At Johnson Island, a
Prisoner of War."
Age 28 yrs, 6 mos, 12 days.

Lucinda L. Ezell
May 27, 1846
Aug 3, 1857 at 4 o'clock,
p.m. Age 11 yrs, 2 mos,
16 days.

Balaam H., son of
J. D. & M. C. Ezell
Apr 7, 1836
Jul 7, 1861
Age 25 yrs, & 3 mos.

Mary Brittain Dudley,
wife of
Guilford Dudley
Jul 26, 1861
Aug 18, 1889

Mary A., wife of
J. Britt Fulton
Oct 29, 1823
Aug 28, 1903

Father
John N. Bigger
Jul 2, 1830
Feb 27, 1904
&
Mother
Elizabeth Bigger
Jan 26, 1841
Mar 31, 1920

Joseph D. Ezell
Mar 15, 1810
May 8, 1880
Age 70 yrs, 1 mo, 23 days

Mary C. Ezell
Feb 18, 1817
Mar 28, 1901

Sally Matt, dau of
J. Britt & Sallie J. Ezell
Jul 17, 1876
Aug 23, 1876

Clarence Fulton Ezell
Mar 23, 1864
Sep 25, 1883
Age 19 yrs, 6 mos, 2 days.

J. Britt Ezell
Jul 14, 1838
Dec 16, 1912
&
Sallie J. Ezell
Apr 26, 1843
Aug 31, 1915

E. M. Ezell
Jan 1, 1873
Jul 22, 1899

Joseph F. R. Ezell
Feb 24, 1852
Mar 22, 1882
Age 30 yrs., 28 days.

"Pappy"
John S. Joyce
Aug 7, 1849
Apr 12, 1946

"Mammy"
Fannie Ezell Joyce
Mar 22, 1855
Jul 9, 1918

Tommie Slator Joyce
Age 11 months

Frank W. Ezell
Sep 10, 1880
Feb 18, 1881

Joseph B. Fulton, son of
Joe R. & Mary F. Ezell
Mar 23, 1878
May 5, 1879

Infant Son of
Joe R. & Mary F. Ezell
Oct 13, 1874
Oct 25, 1874

I. A. Stammers
Jan 1, 1868
Jul 16, 1914
&
Jennie Stammers
Oct 18, 1859
Mar 23, 1914

John Francis, son of
I. A. & Jennie Stammers
Nov 21, 1885
Jun 13, 1887

Mary Glenn, dau of
W. B. & Mattie Glenn
Dec 12, 1886
Jul 15, 1887
Age 7 mos & 3 days

Maggie Morton, dau of
W. B. & Mattie Glenn
Dec 22, 1880
May 14, 1882

Cornelia C., wife of
E. W. Poindexter
Jul 21, 1854
Mar 1, 1886

W. B. Glenn
Oct 25, 1846
Mar 26, 1918
&
Mattie Morton Glenn
Sep 2, 1856
Jun 5, 1890

CHAPEL HILL

John A. Glenn
1849-1935
&
Mollie A. Glenn
1851-1940

Tennessee E. Ezell
Sep 4, 1846
Aug 26, 1863
Age 16 yrs, 11 mos, 22 days

Joseph E. Ezell
Jul 7, 1849
Aug 23, 1857
Age 8 yrs, 1 mo, 16 days.

Elizabeth K. Ezell
Dec 28, 1837
Mar 4, 1855
Age 17 yrs, 2 mos, 6 days.

E. E. K., dau of
B. H. & M.A. Ezell
Jan 1, 1846
Aug 8, 1888

Elizabeth H. Ezell
Jul 14, 1819
Aug 29, 1857
Age 28 yrs, 1 mo, 15 days

Jephthah Ezell, Dec'd
Born May 16, 1811
Died Feb 10, 1855
Age 43 yrs, 8 mos, 24 days.

Littleberry R. Ezell
Jul 19, 1807
Jun 1, 1850

Martha Holmes, wife of
L. R. Ezell
Nov 26, 1820
Apr 22, 1910

Nancy E. Ezell
Sep 17, 1843
Jul 1, 1861

Mary Elizabeth Rickman
Jan 22, 1882
Nov 26, 1909

W. B. Rickman
Mar 28, 1880
Feb 14, 1915

W. C. Rickman
1843-1919
&
M. E. Rickman
1841-1927

Fannie D. Ezell, dau of
T. B. Ezell
Dec 28, 1877
died --------
&
Infant
(no dates)

Thomas Balaam Ezell
1850-1893

Martha E., wife of T.B.
Mar 17, 1853   Ezell
Mar 23, 1882
Age 29 yrs & 6 days

Mother
Nannie C. Ezell Hoover
Nov 15, 1868
May 5, 1937

William Marvin Ezell
Nov 28, 1891
Oct 16, 1918

John Balaam Ezell
Nov 11, 1889
Jun 11, 1920

Several graves with fieldstones, no inscriptions.

* *

OGILVIE CEMETERY
Located Two and one-half miles northeast of Chapel Hill, and one mile east of Highway No. 99, near Bedford County line. Copied November 5, 1979 by Helen & Tim Marsh.

Overton S. Ogilvie
1839-1905
&
Mary A. Ogilvie
1849-1922

Willie Ogilvie
1869-1887

All graves marked.

Price O. Ogilvie
1879-1893

Mary Jane Ogilvie
1871-1887

* *

ATKINSON CEMETERY
Located one-half mile south of Holtland and 300 yards east of Highway No. 31-A. Grave is on the edge of the Old Fishingford Road. Copied Nov 17, 1979, by Ralph D. Whitesell, Helen and Tim Marsh.

Amoral for
Esq.
John Atkinson, wos bornd
July the 9th 1773 and
deces this life March the
9, 1829.

(John Atkinson was a first
Justice of Bedford County
in 1807 and represented the
area until his death. Eds)

Only grave.

* *

JOYCE CEMETERY
Located 1 mile southeast of Holtland, west side of Spring Creek, one-half mile east of Highway No 31-A on Harris Farm. Copied by Ralph D. Whitesell, Tommy Joyce, Helen and Tim Marsh, 1980.

Theodocia G. Joyce
Sep 26, 1822
Oct 7, 1847
(Theodocia G. was a Poindexter
 and 1st wife of Doctor F. Joyce.)

Several graves marked with fieldstones.

* *

CHAPEL HILL

ADAMS CEMETERY

Located one and one-half miles west of Holtland, on south side of Thick-Holtland Road. Copied November 17, 1979.

Martha T. Adams
Aug 29, 1866
Jun 30, 1886   6 or 8 graves, unmarked.

* *

ALLEN CEMETERY

Located on west side of Chapel Hill, on Highway No. 99. Copied November 21, 1979.

Elizabeth Minton	Caroline, Consort of	
Born 1795	Thomas A. Allen	
And died Aug 29, 1842	Feb 11, 1816	
(1st wife of Zachariah	Sep 3, 1840	There may have been
Minton)	Age 23 yrs, 5 mos, 8 days.	graves.

* *

VEST CEMETERY

Located one-half mile east of Highway No. 31-A and east side of Spring Creek, one-fourth mile north of Mt. Vernon Church Road and two and one-half miles north of Chapel Hill. Copied 1980 by Ralph D. Whitesell, Helen and Tim Marsh.

Several unmarked graves, no inscriptions. Located on the Old William W. Vest land, formerly Rickman. W. W. Vest and family are buried in Swanson Cemetery at Chapel Hill. May have acquired the name of Vest because W. W. Vest owned land. Samuel Vest, the father of Wm. W., lived two and one-half miles down Spring Creek and ran a Mill and died there in 1838, appears to have been only this one family in Marshall County, Tennessee. Eds.

* *

CHRISTMON CEMETERY

Located north of Chapel Hill City Limits, west of Highway No. 31-A on Clarence Powell Farm, 1980. Investigated by Mr. Tommy Joyce.

3 or 4 graves, no inscriptions, said to be graves of David V. Christmon and members of his family. Said to have been an old Soldier. Eds.

* *

MORTON CEMETERY

Located two miles west of Chapel Hill, west of Thick Road on Caney Spring Creek. Copied by Mr. Tommy Joyce and Jack King, 1980, Ralph D. Whitesell, Helen & Tim Marsh.

                one marker

John Morton	and	Allice, wife of	
1782-Jan 23, 1873		C. P. Morton	
		Jun 11, 1852	
		Dec 3, 1871	

Large marble square stone lying on side, may have had other Names but too large to move. (C. P. Morton, born Feb 10, 1810, died Oct 10, 1884, Eds)   2 or 3 other graves.

* *

END OF CHAPEL HILL QUADRANGLE

VERONA QUADRANGLE

OWNBY CEMETERY

Located between Berlin and Ellington Airport, east of 431.

Chellie, Infant dau of
J. T. & Sally Hardison
Ownby
Oct 5, 1897
Nov 20, 1897

Cora, dau of
J. T. & Sally Hardison
Ownby
Feb 13, 1899
Jun 3, 1901

James Thadeous Ownby
Oct 7, 1851
Oct 26, 1939
&
Sarah L. Hardison Ownby
Nov 18, 1859
Apr 19, 1933

Alice Lee, wife of
W. S. Duggan
1879-1919

Mary E. Johnson
Feb 9, 1926
Aig 1, 1926

Ruby Moses
1915-1924

Frank H. Moses
Mar 8, 1922
Mar 24, 1922

Felix Samuel Ownby
Apr 6, 1905
Jul 24, 1963

Maud Fergus, wife of
J. F. Ownby
Feb 10, 1890
Aug 9, 1911

John H. Moses
1873-1949
&
Maggie Moses
1880-1953

Fannie Louise, wife of
L. B. Johnson
Jan 27, 1907
Jun 17, 1926

Edna Viola (& Baby)
wife of
L. B. Johnson
May 31, 1911
Sep 13, 1938

Infant of
M. S. & Mattie Richardson
1901

Rena Richardson
Jan 27, 1904
May 4, 1923

Milton S. Richardson
1872-1945

Hattie Ownby Richardson
1881-1965

Mrs. J. D. Hardison
(Alice Capley)
1869-1943

W. J. Scott
Jan 21, 1868
Jul 1, 1889

R. A. Scott
Mar 4, 1875
Jan 2, 1896

Mamie May, dau of
C. T. & M. T. Johnson
1915-1919

Tennie Johnson
Jan 20, 1878
Dec 24, 1922

J. D. Hardison
1859-1937

Fredonia, wife of
J. D. Hardison
Jan 8, 1854
Jul 11, 1901

Infant Son of
J. D. & wife,
Hardison
Born July 7, 1892

W. C. Scott
Feb 2, 1845
Dec 22, 1902

Susan M. Scott
Dec 9, 1845
May 21, 1889

Infant of
W. C. Scott
Nov 28, 1887

Infant of
W. C. Scott
(no dates)

M. J. Scott
Mar 1, 1884
May 18, 1885

Susie Scott Johnson
Mar 27, 1873
Aug 10, 1953

In the southeast corner of this cemetery are some of the Faucett family. The graves originally were marked with fieldstones which have been destroyed..per Miss L. K. Ownby.

* *

CUMMINS-THOMAS CEMETERY

Located on the farm formerly owned by Cummins, now owned by B. D. Spence. One mile south west of Verona. 1979.

Mary Alexander
(no marker)

Martha Alexander
(No marker)

Fannie Thomas
(no marker)

Olivia Thomas
(no marker)

M. Will Pickle
(no marker)

Nannie Thomas
(no marker)

Jimmie Zack, child of
Joe & Sally Edwards
(no marker

Mary Jane Thomas
(no marker)

Cummins Thomas
(no marker)

* *

CARR CEMETERY

Located at Bethleham, west side of Highway No. 31. This cemetery is in Maury County, Tennessee, near Marshall County Line. Cemetery has been destroyed. 1980.

John F. Carr
Nov 12, 1764
Died   1836
(He was a Soldier of the
Revolutionary War.)

* *

VERONA

BILLINGTON CEMETERY
Located west of Caney Spring on Highway No. 99.

Jennie M., wife of
E. P. Billington
Jun 15, 1844
Aug 13, 1876
&
Laura, dau of
E. P. & Jennie Billington
Apr 13, 1876
Aug 9, 1876

John Billington
Sep 16, 1816
Feb 2, 1892

Caroline V., wife of
John Billington
Dec 23, 1819
Feb 29, 1888

Rubin Billington
Mar 23, 1823
Died   1899
&
Matilda Billington
Feb 2, 1825
Mar 3, 1904

* *

SHIRES CEMETERY
Located south of Highway No. 99, west of Caney Spring.
Copied by Ralph D. Whitesell, March 3, 1968.

Martha M. Chunn
Aug 13, 1866
Dec 24, 1955

Vonie W. Chunn
Jan 4, 1878
Nov 8, 1934

Joel Shires
   13, 1818
Apr 24, 1891

Sarah C., wife of
Joel Shires
May 11, 1818
Jun 18, 1890

Lena V. Butler, wife of
J. O. Chunn
Sep 23, 1855
Aug 16, 1920

Orville, son of
Mr. & Mrs. J. O. Chunn
Jun 29, 1908
Oct 4, 1908

J. W., son of
Mr. & Mrs. R. M. Gates
Nov 18, 1924
Dec 16, 1924

B. F. Doyle
Oct 27, 1873
Nov 24, 1902

Kate Dark
(stone marker)

Dark
(child, no marker)

Parlee, wife of
F. W. Shires
Jan 27, 1851
Nov 14, 1889

Lottie, dau of
F. W. & M. M. Shires
Apr 5, 1897
Jul 2, 1899

Ephrim P. Butler
Aug 12, 1856
Aug 15, 1943
&
Susan M. Gates
Dec 20, 1862
Mar 27, 1944

H. L. Gates
May 30, 1904
Oct 5, 1904

William Carrol Harris
Dec 20, 1844
May 12, 1918

Sarah C. Shires Harris
Mar 6, 1846
Sep 21, 1916

Tom Harris
Dec 4, 1861
Aug 20, 1937

Kate Sledge Harris
Nov 1, 1868
Feb 6, 1916

Laura Harris, wife of
V. E. Watson
Dec 20, 1844
May 12, 1918

J. M. Gates
Oct 3, 1839
Mar 31, 1927

Hannah Adline, wife of
J. M. Gates
Nov 5, 1842
Nov 16, 1896
"Joined the M. E. Church,
  1877."

J. E. Harris
Mar 27, 1853
Mar 31, 1930

Annie E., wife of
J. E. Harris
Jul 10, 1856
Aug 7, 1918

Grover L. Summers
1902-1942

James F. Gates
1870-19
&
Neatie Gates
1872-1926

Infant son of
J. F. & N. A. Gates
Dec 25, 1907

Nancy Victory Gates
Apr 7, 1859
Dec 21, 1914
"Joined the M. E. Church,
  1876."

No unmarked graves.

* *

ANDREWS-LIGGETT CEMETERY
Located on 431, Old Franklin Road, near Airport, one-fourth
mile west of runway.

Father
Luther T. Liggett
May 26, 1893
Sep 1, 1930

Mary Loftin Liggett
Apr 26, 1899
Jun 10, 1936

Baby Ruby Loftin Liggett
   (no dates)

Sankey Liggett
Nov 29, 1875
Oct 29, 1950

Lula E. Jones
Nov 27, 1866
Oct 6, 1922

J. L. Secrest
Jul 4, 1835
Nov 19, 1910

John T. Pearson
Nov 28, 1849
Sep 22, 1905
   & Mother
Martha E., wife of
John T. Pearson
Feb 3, 1844
Apr 23, 1925

Julia Calahan Webb
1881-1946 (TM)

Jim Webb
1872-1933 (TM)

Harold Knowis
Oct 11, 1897
Apr 27, 1924

VERONA

S. S. Craig
Dec 14, 1833
Aug 22, 1916
&
Mary A. Craig
Jan 13, 1833
Jan 21, 1910

Thomas J. Knowis
Mar 16, 1869
Nov 6, 1954
&
Mary B. Craig
Jan 15, 1872
Nov 11, 1896
&
Luella Craig Knowis
Dec 30, 1869
Mar 14, 1947

Martha Hayes
Nov 5, 1898
Mar 28, 1963

Terry Beatty
May 9, 1885
Feb 1, 1935

Mahaley Jane Fisher Beatty
1858-1931

T. S. Beatty
Jul 23, 1854
May 8, 1927

George Beatty
Jan 25, 1882
Oct 8, 1933

A. H., son of
T. S. & M. Beatty
Mar 20, 1873
Aug 15, 1899

Ervin, son of
T. S. & M. J. Beatty
Born 1891
Died Apr 15, 1919
Pvt in Inf A.E.E.

Rock marker, no
inscription.

D. D. Green
Nov 21, 1802
Apr 14, 1878
Age 75 yrs, 4 mos, 23 days.

Thomas Green
Feb 19, 1809
Dec 26, 1829
Age 20 yrs, 10 mos, 7 days.

In Memory of
Jane Curl & her dau
Tabitha Gray
(no dates)

Thomas J. Barhom
--- --, 1814
--- --, 1880

L. J. Barhom
Dec 13, 1822
May 1, 1904

Garnet, dau of
------ Liggett
(no dates)

J. G. Liggett
May 8, 1844
Jan 12, 1928
&
Louise Hill Liggett
Aug 28, 1843
Apr 24, 1924

Sam Liggett
1868-1936
&
Maggie Liggett
1872-1955

Eugene Fenton Liggett
Capt. U. S. Air Force
Jul 19, 1913
Apr 14, 1958

T. Fenton Liggett
1870-1931
&
Eugenia Ewing Allen Liggett
1872-1941

Father
Dr. T. A. Allen
Oct 19, 1837
Aug 14, 1917
&
Mother
Mary F. Allen
Mar 7, 1846
Dec 21, 1918

Jones B., son of
A. G. & S. L. Andrews
Jan 20, 1886
Aug 24, 1886

Elizabeth T. Cundiff
1880-1922

Victoria L. Cundiff
1840-1900

Capt. J. C. Cundiff
1827-1917

W. M. Cundiff
1869-1888

Clarence Cundiff
1870-1890

Slab, unmarked & overturned.

Drucille Secrest
Born Mar 19, 1810
Died --- --, ----
(illegible)

Father
William H. Secrest
Sep 22, 1841
Sep 28, 1907
&
Mother
Sarah Frances, wife of
William H. Secrest
Dec 15, 1848
Nov 25, 1913

Sam Secrest
1883-1960

William Liggett
was born 1775 & died
Jul 14, 1847
Age 72 yrs.

Jane B. Liggett
Jun 1, 1784
May 30, 1858
Age 74 yrs.

Sampson Liggett
Sep 1, 1814
Apr 28, 1892
&
Sarah E., wife of
Sampson Liggett
Jun 18, 1813
Jul 4, 1849

Amanda P., wife of
James C. Cundiff
Feb 12, 1832
Jun 1, 1852

Sarah A., dau of
J. C. & A. P. Cundiff
Mar 18, 1852
Jan 24, 1859

Sarah J., dau of
Sampson & Sarah Liggett
Dec 2, 1836
Jul 27, 1857

Americus D. Liggett
Jun 25, 1841
Jan 8, 1877

Hampton Liggett
Nov 27, 1807
Nov 24, 1876
& wife
Jane Liggett
Jun 22, 1802
Oct 19, 1888

_____ J., wife of
_____ Gray
1835-Aug 19, 1878

Infant dau of
_____ & Mattie Patterson
(dates illegible)

Infant dau of
F_____ & Mattie Patterson
Mar 12, 1892
Apr 16, 1892

Walter Liggett
May 29, 1868
Jul 20, 1896

Elizabeth A. Baxter
--- --, ----
--- --, ----
(dates illegible)
&
Ida Baxter
Oct 9, 1871
Apr 23, 1909
(rock marker)

E. S. Baxter
Dec 22, 1865
Nov 10, 1955

Jere Baxter
Jun 21, 1907
Jul 23, 1908

Ira H. Baxter
Sep 5, 1896
Oct 6, 1918

Ethel, dau of
H. H. & Bettie Liggett
Sep 12, 1886
Jul 13, 1892

W. H. Drake
Oct 18, 1815
Jul 15, 1881

Infant of
(unable to read names)
Liggett
Aug 24, 1890
Sep 12, 1890

Hampton H. Liggett
1856-1888
&
Bettie H. Liggett
1858-1939

J. C. Liggett
May 22, 1830
Jul 26, 1875
&
Sarah E. Liggett
Oct 3, 1834
Jun 18, 1913

Margaret A., dau of
J. C. & S. E. Liggett
Born Jun 12, 1855
Died (broken away)

VERONA

Lamyra, wife of
B. W. Tindell
Sep 16, 1822
Dec 5, 1869

John A., son of
R. W. & Lamyra Tindell
Nov 26, 1859
Feb --, 1862

S. G. Liggett
Aug 22, 1806
Mar 30, 1862
& wife
Elizabeth Liggett
Apr 26, 1831
Aug 1, 1914

J. K. Hardison
Dec 13, 1846
May 21, 1929

Ann E. J., wife of
J. K. Hardison
Aug 29, 1854
May 4, 1872

Infant Son of
J. N. & M. H. Baxter
Born dead Jul 12, 1892

Leslie, son of
J. N. & M. H. Baxter
Born (illegible)
Died Jul 7, 1894

Orville E., son of
Dr. J. N. & M. H. Baxter
Feb 3, 1883
Oct 15, 1926

Jasper A. Yarbrough
Nov 7, 1839
Aug 13, 1890

Gerry Orlando, Infant Son
of J. A. & L. Yarbrough
Apr 29, 1881
Oct 23, 1882

M. E. Bradley
Oct 7, 1873
Mar 25, 1887

J. B. Bradley
May 15, 1846
Sep 22, 1879

Mary P. Bradley
Sep 14, 1841
Aug 1, 1916

George Yarbrough
1807-1878
&
Nancy Yarbrough
1808-1878

Sallie Tanner
Jun 28, 1843
Mar 7, 1912

Felix Harden Gray
Dec 3, 1865
May 5, 1951
&
Cora Andrews Gray
Mar 1, 1868
Oct 9, 1912

Rufus W. Liggett
Jul 3, 1880
Oct 29, 1895
&
Elizabeth, wife of
W. A. Liggett
Dec 2, 1841
Oct 30, 1880

Thomas J., son of
W. A. & E. R. Liggett
Jul 18, 1863
Feb 19, 1864

Rufus Wiley, son of
J. W. & A. G. Calahan
Dec 21, 1849
Mar 29, 1873

Hattie Adelaid, dau of
J. W. & A. G. Calahan
Aug 21, 1859
Jan 25, 1862

Robert Hampton, son of
J. W. & A. G. Calahan
Feb 3, 1857
Feb 12, 1862

Carlos Johnson
Oct 5, 1910
Nov 23, 1963
&
Lora Johnson
Apr 26, 1928

John D. Beatty
1888-1951
&
Emma Lou Beatty
1903-

Jane Gray Beatty
Feb 8, 1926
Dec 26, 1935

L. S. Finley
Apr 12, 1872
May 30, 1929
&
Nannie Finley
Dec 5, 1879
Jan 15, 1939

Dr. J. N. Baxter
Dec 22, 1857
Apr 14, 1937
&
Mary H. Baxter
Apr 27, 1860
May 25, 1933

Henry Jose Liggett
Feb 12, 1874
Jan 25, 1960
&
Annie Hardison Liggett
May 1, 1872
Sep 13, 1936

Roy Bryant Andrews
Jan 17, 1891
Mar 4, 1949
&
Dora Keel Andrews
Sep 10, 1884
Oct 13, 1953

N. G. Andrews
1854-1934

Lamyra Jane Gray
1918-1946

J. Jack Gray
1889-1961
& wife
Lola Pinkston Gray
1889-1930

W. L. Andrews
1881-1924

Harris Brown
Feb 7, 1901
May 8, 1935

James Brice Cheek
1879-1942
&
Nannie Mai Cheek
1883-1946

David N. Hillard
Jan 4, 1902
Jan 3, 1964
&
Ada L. Hillard
Jun 11, 1906

Bengie M. Hillard
1891-1957

Leslie H. Ramsey
1886-
&
Josie J. Ramsey
1885-1962

Carla J. Church
Sep 21, 1962
Mar 21, 1963

Ernest P. Hillard
Sep 19, 1898
Oct 23, 1952

Billy S. Cole
Jun 17, 1907
Jan 10, 1924

Luther L. Thornhill
1876-1924
&
Fannie L. Thornhill
1880-1918

R. L. Cole
1885-19
&
Gladys Cole
1888-1951

Frederick Fisher
Virginia
Pvt Col Campbell's Regt
Rev. War
1762-1846

Mary Fisher, wife of
Frederick Fisher
1767-1848

J. Brown Fisher
Sep 7, 1891
Apr 1, 1940

George R. Fisher
Apr 30, 1856
Apr 21, 1926

J. R. Hillard
Dec 11, 1883
Jul 25, 1944

Sarah J. Matney
1856-1927

Cornelia M. Thornhill
Sep 30, 1899
Apr 7, 1923

Rickie Levan Wright
Jul 22, 1964
Sep 16, 1964

John T. Weaver
1860-1926
&
Mattie C. Weaver
1864-1928

W. A. Harris
1872-1920
&
Myrtle Harris
1878-1952

Fronie Jenkins Rains
Jul 24, 1899
Aug 27, 1943

Ella Patterson Jenkins
Feb 24, 1871
Jul 14, 1953

Wade H. Brown
Jun 27, 1886
Oct 24, 1966

VERONA

Mary Emma, dau of
J. W. & A. G. Calahan
Nov 21, 1854
Jun 22, 1874

Adelaide Grutrude, wife of
J. W. Calahan
Sep 9, 1825
Jun 30, 1880

James W. Calahan
Feb 1, 1818
Nov 11, 1895

Alex. E. Calahan
Jan 3, 1852
Mar 1, 1912

Vera E. M., wife of
W. A. Davis
Jan 12, 1886
Dec 8, 1912

Infant Son of
W. A. & Mrs. Davis
Aug 3, 1911

Infant Son of
W. A. & Mrs. Davis
June 22, 1910

Infant Son of
W. A. & Mrs. Davis
Mar 1, 1909

Reavis Allen Stacey
July 19, 1889

Josie Ethel Stacey
Mar 31, 1884
Sep 3, 1962

Hettie C., dau of
T. M. & M. J. Bryant
Dec 14, 1876
Mar 17, 1909

Johnnie P., dau of
T. M. & M. J. Bryant
Jul 2, 1886
Mar 29, 1905

Thomas Monroe Bryant
1848-1901
&
Maggie M. Bryant
1853-1933

James Finley
May 15, 1814
Jul 20, 1904
& wife
Malinda P. Finley
Mar 12, 1817
Aug 19, 1882

Paul Finley
Nov 25, 1897

&
Nannie Finley
Dec 5, 1879
Jan 15, 1939

David A. Harris
Mar 26, 1907

&
Evelyn Hill Harris
May 28, 1911
Apr 28, 1965

END OF ANDREWS-LIGGETT

* *

ALLEN CEMETERY
Located at Caney Spring, just off the Verona road. Copied 1959. Re-checked and updated Apr. 20, 1980 by Helen & Tim Marsh.

William G. Allen
May 3, 1832
May 10, 1880
&
Eugenia E. Allen
Jul 30, 1838
Jun 14, 1921

Hattie H. Allen
Aug 31, 1877
Jul 18, 1879

Mary Ida Allen
Jul 1, 1859
Aug 28, 1885
&
Fannie Lou Allen, wife of
J. J. Collins
Dec 31, 1865
Mar 3, 1933

George H. Allen
1874-1940

Callie Mae Allen
1873-1950

George H. Allen, Jr.
1903-1914

Dorann Clymore
Sep 23, 1935
Sep 11, 1940

Deac Clymore
1933-1973

Ruby Dean Brown
1909-1966

Calvin Clymore
Jun 4, 1900
Jul 5, 1936

J. Shannon Dean
1883-1946
&
Willie Mai Dean
1888-1974

George S. Allen
Oct 11, 1868
May 19, 1873
&
Nancy T. Allen
Sep 6, 1870
May 13, 1873
Children of T. A. &
M. F. Allen

Stone (no name)
died Nov 17, 1877

F. W., son of H. & D. Martin
Nov 9, 1847
May 22, 1848

Pauline Dean
Jul 7, 1907
Jun 30, 1909

Cynthia, dau of
J. J. & J. T. Whitehead
Jan 1, 1895
Aug 7, 1896

John J. Whitehead
1857-1926
&
Tennie Harris Whitehead
1858-1926

Walter Whitehead
Dec 7, 1878
Dec 27, 1954

Mrs. Jane Knight
Departed this life
Jul 20, 1859
Age about 78 years

Capt. James Knight
Sep 13, 1791
Jun 29, 1858

James W. Knight
Dec 28, 1853
Jul 1, 1858

Thomas D. Knight
Feb 12, 1860
Jan 27, 1862

Alice T. Knight
Aug 15, 1856
Jun 22, 1863

Mary Elizabeth Cundiff
Jun 15, 1857
Nov 19, 1859

Sacred to the Memory of
Nancy C. Martin
Consort of James M. Martin
Who was born February 1,
1826 & departed this life
the 30th of August, 1856,
Aged 30 yrs, 6 mos, 9 days.
She embraced religion A.D.
1842 in Williamson County,
Tenn. & joined the Methodist Episcopal Church at
Garrett's Meeting House
A.D. 1843, & lived a faithful member the balance of
her days on this earth
with hope of wearing the
immortal crown of everlasting joy with her
Blessed Savior.

Infant daughter of
P. C. & M. H. Haynes
Born & Died Nov 19, 1861

Father
W. U. Cundiff
Jun 11, 1822
Jan 10, 1866
& Mother & wife
Emily J. Clifft
May 30, 1826
Sep 12, 1890

Richard A., son of
J. W. E. & F. A. Floyd
Dec 26, 1891
Oct 1, 1895

VERONA

Ike Gordon Floyd Abernathy
Oct 24, 1896
Dec 19, 1898
& brother
Ike N. Abernathy
Jun 2, 1860
Jul 4, 1903

J. W. E. Floyd
Jul 25, 1842
Jun 13, 1914
&
Fannie E. Floyd
Jul 30, 1857
Dec 17, 1932

Frank L. Freeman
SEA 2 U.S. Navy
Jul 15, 1898
Mar 1, 1975
&
Mona D. Freeman
1904-

Hartwell B. Powell
Jul 29, 1894
Sep 26, 1961

Josephine Baker Powell
Sep 8, 1854
Jan 14, 1928

William L. Powell
May 13, 1834
Dec 22, 1897

William Columbus Baker
May 12, 1852
Apr 3, 1929

Mary Belle Baker
Jun 19, 1856
Mar 21, 1945

Hartwell Garrett Baker
Sep 25, 1804
Sep 13, 1894
&
Jane Haynes Baker
Oct 9, 1817
Jan 10, 1892

Eugenia Baker Fowlkes
Mar 25, 1860
Jun 23, 1890

Elia Baker Hunter
Sep 10, 1838
Nov 17, 1877

Hartie, son of
T. H. M. & Elia B. Hunter
Died Nov 21, 1872
(no age given)

James Rufus Baker
Died May 26, 1860
Age 19 years

W. C. Green
Jan 14, 1830
Feb 12, 1872

Samuel Thomas Allen, Jr.
Apr 18, 1889
Aug 28, 1949
&
Elizabeth Green Allen
Jul 2, 1893
Jan 10, 1978
mrd- Feb 27, 1919

Father
David Green
Jan 9, 1785
Jan 15, 1853
& Mother
Temperance Green
Sep 14, 1792
May 5, 1870

John H. Martin
May 5, 1825
Aug 13, 1855
"Who left a companion, Sarah
A. Martin & 2 children with
a hope of going to rest."

Thomas N., son of
John H. & Sarah A. Martin
Age 7 months. (no dates)

Franklin A. Dillard
Dec 31, 1831
Aug 10, 1861

Dr. J. N. Oslin
Sep 6, 1824
Mar 15, 1882

Margaret M., wife of
Dr. J. N. Oslin
Sep 15, 1829
Jan 26, 1902

Oslin Miller, son of
W. S. & E. O. Morton
Feb 15, 1883
May 25, 1883

Charlie D. Floyd
1900-1901

Maggie Oslin Floyd
1868-1904

Maggie D. Floyd
1904-1905

Sallie B. Floyd
1896-1905

Jesse Boyd Floyd
Tennessee
SGT Co K 117 Inf, W.W.I
Jun 2, 1894
Aug 1, 1968
&
Gretchen Lanier Floyd
Nov 14, 1901

Emma, wife of
John C. Woodall
Mar 26, 1818
Feb 27, 1895

Mary A., wife of
W. R. Winn
Dec 25, 1840
Jul 28, 1881

John Clark Woodall
Born in Compton, Md.
Dec 9, 1804
Died Apr 3, 1887

John T. Woodall
Dec 26, 1847
Aug 15, 1863

James H., son of
John H. Martin & Sarah A.
Martin, Who was born
Aug 28, 1847
Age 14 mos.

Mary P. Falwell, dau of
Henry & Maria Martin, who
was born Feb 1, 1821, who
was a consort of John
Falwell. She an affectionate
companion and a tender mother
departed this life Sep 15,
1850, who left a campanion &
six children to lament the
loss of her consolation.
Age 29 yrs, 7 mos, 14 days.
"Remember, friends, as you
pass by, As you are now so
once was I; As I am now
so you must be, prepare for
death and follow me."

William E., son of
John H. & Sarah A. Martin
Who was born Nov 22, 1848.

James C. Martin
Nancy C. Martin
&
Amanda L. Martin
Dec 19, 1845
Jan 24, 1846

Martha J., dau of
William & Elizabeth
Montgomery
Jul 25, 1838
Sep 16, 1845

Wm. Lee Cherry, Jr.
Infant son of
Mary Allen Lanier &
Wm. Lee Cherry
August 11, 1964

James Allen
Oct 5, 1844
Dec 4, 1845

John O. Lanier
Jan 22, 1873
Mar 13, 1913

Minnie M. Lanier
May 1, 1879
Oct 26, 1966

George H. Allen
Nov 15, 1780
May 8, 1874

Mary Allen
Jun 21, 1782
Aug 11, 1855
"Having been a member of
the M. E. Church 52 yrs."

William Allen
Apr 25, 1818
Aug 20, 1845
Age 27 yrs, 3 mos, 20 days
"He died happy"

Infant dau of
Kendal & Frances M. Dazey
Born Jul 30, 1846

Infant son of
Kendal & Frances M. Dazey
Born Nov 4, 1841

Mary E. & Agness S. Dazey
daus of Kendal & Frances
Dazey.
Mary E. was born
Sep 19, 1836 & died
Feb 8, 1846
Age 9 yrs, 4 mos, 19 days
"She professed religion
at the age of 9 years and
died right"
Agnes was born
Oct 14, 1839 & died
Feb 8, 1846
Age 6 yrs, 3 mos, 24 days

Jasper, son of
Kendal & Frances M. Dazey
Aug 20, 1843
Aug 29, 1843

Amanda M. Dazey, dau of
K. & F. M. Dazey
Died Feb 21, 1858
Age 13 yrs, 2 mos, 25 days

VERONA

Elliott M. Derryberry
1870-1944
&
Iva L. Derryberry
1885-1964

Bettye Jo Derryberry
1930-1934

Harold Derryberry
1907-1956

John Thomas Peay
Jan 9, 1884
Dec 12, 1946
&
Ida Bell Peay
Jan 13, 1892

Ottis Lawton Derryberry
Sep 24, 1905
Apr 1, 1970

Alice Osteen
Oct 26, 1864
Jan 11, 1944

Charlie Keltner
1886-1943

Susie E. Haney
1880-1954
&
Lacy E. Haney
1882-1957

Mother
Icy W. Yowell
Apr 10, 1873
Mar 29, 1964

Bedford (H.) Gulley
Apr 10, 1882
Nov 8, 1954
&
Bertha W. Gulley
Nov 3, 1881
Jan 25, 1954

Alfred Monroe Love
Feb 5, 1905
Jul 25, 1976

Mike Robinson
1947

Willie Love
Jan 27, 1885
Dec 3, 1941

Richard Rice Neil, Sr.
Nov 22, 1875
(no date)

Louis L. Daniel
1910-1971

Lillie Love
Jan 16, 1890
Jul 14, 1946

Robert Love
Jul 18, 1926

Alma Love
March 29, 1930

Adam Stinnett
Sep 28, 1966
Sep 29, 1966

Thomas L. Harper
Jun 10, 1873
Dec 21, 1952
&
Eugene E. Harper
May 29, 1877
Jan 4, 1949

Clara O. Harper
Jul 31, 1896
Feb 6, 1965

Herman M. Stinnett
1900-1974
&
Maudie L. Stinnett
1920-1969

Logan Stinnett
Oct 20, 1938
May 28, 1977

J. Gordon Moore
Jun 23, 1922
May 10, 1940

Andrew R. Moore
Tennessee
S/Sgt 758 Bomb SQ AAF W.W.II
Aug 20, 1916
Apr 7, 1963

John A. Moore
1886-1964
&
Ivie Lee Moore
1892-1972
mrd- Sep 22, 1912

Father
J. B. Richardson
Mar 16, 1916
Apr 15, 1974
&
Mother
Ernestine L. Richardson
Apr 18, 1921

Charles J. Bush
May 8, 1884
in Ford, Ky.
Jan 12, 1971
&
Emma H. Bush
Jul 29, 1900
in Wyatt, W. Va.
----
mrd- Feb 6, 1924

Emmett Brown
Sep 30, 1886
Apr 4, 1971
&
Wilma K. Brown
Feb 14, 1894
Jan 31, 1976

William G. Allen
Jan 19, 1887
Mar 24, 1966
&
Lennie J. Allen
Aug 26, 1890

William G. Allen, II
Aug 26, 1913
Mar 8, 1957
interred in Brookville, Md.

Thomas W. Jones
1870-1942
&
Pearl M. Jones
1877-1959

Kelley P. Simmons
Feb 16, 1902
Aug 29, 1974
&
Louise Jones Simmons
Jan 20, 1906

Steve Jones Simmons
Jan 30, 1945
Jan 30, 1945

Lemuel Franklin Osteen
1862-1944
&
Beadie Jane Osteen
1873-1966

Lottie Mae Beckham
Jun 5, 1920
Nov 15, 1923

James B. Beckham, Sr.
Mar 15, 1892

&
Mary Osteen Beckham
Oct 30, 1896
Mar 11, 1979

Kelly H. Collins
Tennessee
Pvt Co A 319 MG BN 82 Div
W. W. I
Sep 6, 1892
Feb 16, 1967
&
Annie H. Collins
Nov 16, 1899
Nov 11, 1975

Wm. Allen Chadwell
1878-1958
&
Loulene Walker Chadwell
1896-

Delma Lewis Neil Morehouse
1907-1950

Joseph T. Osteen
Jun 3, 1901
Jul 8, 1972
&
Emma Ann Osteen
Dec 10, 1909

George R. Neil
1900-1934

Bertha K. Chopin
Dec 10, 1923

Richard Rice Neil, Sr.
Nov 22, 1875
Mar 15, 1953
&
Flora Stewart Neil
May 31, 1881
Mar 9, 1946

Elizabeth Neil Hudspeth
Aug 16, 1913
May 12, 1972

Aaron K. Stem
Jun 2, 1902
May 21, 1952

Carrie Stanton Scott
wife of Willis H. Scott
Sep 18, 1884
Oct 19, 1973

Willis H. Scott
Feb 1, 1885
Jun 18, 1963

Mary S. Wallace
1887-1971

Harris Newton Scott
Aug 20, 1882
Oct 3, 1935
&
Ossie Bell Scott
Apr 3, 1893
Nov 17, 1966

VERONA

Zora Lee Wallace
Apr 1, 1908
Jun 23, 1929
(picture)

John H. Dark
1870-1957
&
Josephine J. Dark
1862-1951

Price M. Patterson
Jan 25, 1885
Nov 6, 1969
&
Willie W. Patterson
Nov 1, 1884
May 28, 1978

Rachel Oslin, dau of
Morton & Mary Clair Allen
Mar 22, 1924
Feb 9, 1934

Infant son of
Allen & Shirley Jordan
Oct 5, 1963

Bettie Maupin
1850-1951

Ann Love Mattox
1927-1969
(Gowen-Smith FH)

J. Ollie Love
Jan 27, 1889
Jan 21, 1945

Jessie A. Love
Jun 27, 1869
Jul 17, 1967
&
Sallie Love
Jun 4, 1872
Jul 9, 1949

Fred Ernest Smith
Tennessee
Pvt U.S. Army
W. W. II
Dec 4, 1914
Jan 25, 1962

Ollie B. Adgent
1877-1942
&
Leota Adgent
1880-1963

John D. Smith
Dec 24, 1868
Mar 27, 1939
&
Ivie L. Smith
Apr 3, 1875
Sep 19, 1962

Charlie J. Moses
1883-1963
Annie M. Moses
1886-1945

Rev. Nick Oslin Allen
Jun 16, 1898
Dec 10, 1967
&
Laila H. Allen
Sep 24, 1899
Apr 19, 1974

Bernard Mack, son of
Nick & Laila Allen
Oct 20, 1934
Dec 22, 1934

Eugene M. Allen
Oct 8, 1893
Jan 29, 1918

Sam T. Allen
May 2, 1861
Sep 19, 1943
&
M. B. Oslin Allen
Jan 27, 1865
Aug 18, 1942

John Clark Woodall
Sep 16, 1889
Jul 8, 1953

Father
William Preston Woodall
1843-1918

Mother
Sarah Lemuel Woodall
1860-1938

Edward Taylor Woodall
Sep 15, 1886
Oct 8, 1918

Robert D. Woodall
1892-1976
&
Mary F. Woodall
1883-1965

Charles Milton Scott
Sep 20, 1909
Feb 2, 1970

Lillian K. Adams
1891-1921

David R., son of
U. G. & Mary E. Mincy
Jul 28, 1906
Jun 29, 1907

Laura J. Scott
1860-1924

Rev. David E. Scott
1858-1937

J. Louie Neill
1867-1945

B. M. Neill
1833-1914

Adelaide Harris
Feb 20, 1917
Aug 27, 1976

Frederick H. Harris
Dec 8, 1882
Oct 8, 1967
&
Sarah A. Harris
Apr 21, 1893

Ben T. Neill
1912-1976

Susie A. Neill
1841-1920

J. A. Neill
1862-1938

O. A. Neill
1876-1942

Bivins O. Neill
1905-1955

Edgar B. Neill
1878-1932

Salella Neill
1882-1959

John Calvin Montgomery
Jun 4, 1829
May 6, 1916
&
Minerva White Montgomery
Dec 23, 1837
Feb 19, 1914

Jesse H. Baxter
Jul 12, 1897
Oct 4, 1978
&
Irene L. Baxter
Mar 20, 1903

&
John M. Baxter
Mar 23, 1936
Jun 26, 1977

Father
John Fletcher Baxter
Dec 1, 1894
Apr 26, 1972
&
Mother
Bessie Jones Baxter
Apr 24, 1894

Dr. Robert G. Baxter
1860-1931

Minnie M. Baxter
1867-1950

Myrtle C. Pewitt
1879-1964

Lundy V. Chunn
1875-1917

Martha Louise Baxter
Oct 2, 1891
Jun 10, 1979

Thomas R. Martin
Oct 30, 1868
Oct 22, 1950
&
Sarah M. Martin
Mar 24, 1868
May 22, 1934

Horace J. Martin
1898-1945

Robert Thomas Martin
Feb 14, 1897
Jul 10, 1919

Carrie W. Pollard
1908-Mar 23, 1940
(Mrs. James E.,
Lawrence FH)

Ronald Wayne Whaley
May 10, 1942
May 11, 1942

Father
William Aaron Chisam
Feb 16, 1869
Feb 26, 1937
&
Mother
Nolia H. Chisam
Dec 29, 1874
Oct 13, 1959

Rena Chisam
Oct 14, 1903
Oct 30, 1919

Leota T. Evans
Mar 1, 1891
Nov 6, 1972

Rose E. Evans
Dec 25, 1889
Aug 24, 1978

Bob T. Evans
1904-1977
&
Kathleen A. Evans
1906-

Marthie T. Chadwell
Dec 25, 1843
Aug 22, 1921

VERONA

John E. Evans
1931-1972
(Lawrence FH)

Willie F. Evans
Feb 13, 1901
Feb 12, 1973
&
Christine Evans
Jan 19, 1917

J. Evans
(Block, initialed)

John W. Evans
Jan 5, 1857
Feb 2, 1943
&
Julia E. Evans
Aug 2, 1868
Apr 1, 1925

M. J.
(Footstone)

Ida B. Dark
wife of
William Chunn
Aug 3, 1870
Jan 3, 1910

Wm. Chunn
(block, initialed)

Romulus Ogilvie
1846-1928
&
Elizabeth M. Ogilvie
1851-1928

William Harris Ogilvie, Sr.
1885-1964
Sheriff 1940-44
&
Jimmie Floyd Ogilvie
1895-1974
Mrd- Feb 17, 1917

James Rom Ogilvie
Oct 5, 1889
Jan 21, 1969
&
Annie Powell Ogilvie
Oct 7, 1895

Richard T. Dark
Jan 30, 1872
Feb 7, 1872

Robert J. Dark
Jan 20, 1833
Jan 13, 1923
&
Elizabeth Mallard Dark
May 11, 1834
Feb 12, 1872

Maebeth, dau of
J. H. & Pearl Wilson
Apr 19, 1916
Apr 22, 1917

John H. Wilson
1879-1964
&
Pearl O. Wilson
1879-1968
Mrd- Dec 31, 1908

Myrtle P. Allison
1881-1959

Richard B. Allison
1868-1935

Jennie B. Allison
1880-1916

James K. Allison
1853-1938
&
Ann Lou Allison
1880-1916

Bennie C. Neill
1881-1887
&
Lydia M. Junkin Neill
1822-1910

James L. Whitehead
Nov 17, 1910

Lewis Hatton Whitehead
1871-1961
&
Mattie Green Whitehead
1878-1968

Joe Boyd Ogilvie, Sr.
Nov 12, 1921
Jun 11, 1971
&
Ruby Jean Jordan Ogilvie
Jun 2, 1923

James H. West
Born in Iredell Co., N.C.
Feb 1, 1825, Died in
Tishamingo Co., Miss.
Oct 31, 1880
He was an elder in the
Bethlehem Congregation of
the C. P. Church. An Honest
Man, the Noblest work of
God.

W. A. Green
Aug 18, 1871
Dec 2, 1959

Heath Green
Oct 16, 1873
Jun 6, 1952

Ida Green Miller
Apr 16, 1861
Nov 14, 1932

Margaret M., wife of
L. H. Green
Oct 1, 1841
Nov 5, 1921

Elizabeth Green
Jul 22, 1865
Jul 21, 1896

Joe H., son of
J. W. & Julia Evans
Apr 13, 1894
Apr 27, 1897

Joseph Evans
Jul 18, 1860
Feb 9, 1892
&
Mary Evans
Aug 8, 1863
Jul 15, 1895
&
Maggie Evans
Apr 7, 1866
Oct 4, 1905
&
Emma B. Evans
Jun 7, 1869
Apr 6, 1899
&
James Evans
Born 1823
Died Jan 13, 1892
&
Elizabeth Evans
Jul 27, 1828
Apr 11, 1906

Caroline Evans
Died Nov 24, 1899

E. B.
(footstone)

Charlie J. West
Oct 20, 1857
Apr 10, 1860
&
Dovie Jane West
Mar 20, 1855
Mar 17, 1862
"Children of J. H. &
S. A. West"

Fern L. Floyd
1909-1937

Alice M. Floyd
Nov 24, 1868
Jul 13, 1951

William J. Floyd
Jan 4, 1867
Jan 15, 1936

Minta O. Floyd
Dec 2, 1862
Apr 19, 1905

Florence L. Jones
Jan 23, 1885
Oct 6, 1964

Asberry Jones
1848-1917
&
Kansas Jones
1857-1908

T. Mitchell Reynolds
Dec 26, 1902
Sep 29, 1967
&
Lizzie M. Floyd Reynolds
Mar 28, 1898
Apr 22, 1972

a large plot with only
one marker:
   "Garrett Family"

Lidia C., wife of
I. V. Dark
May 11, 1816
Dec 4, 1876

2 unmarked graves,
probably the graves of
Robert Ransom and his wife
Mary (Harris) Ransom.

Joseph W. Mallard
Mar 21, 1809
Jun 2, 1887
was married to
Sarah Ransom, Sep 28, 1831

Sarah Ransom Mallard
August 1804
Mar 10, 1887

Richard T. Mallard
1832-1871

Lemuel A. Mallard
1835-1857

Tabitha, dau of
W. L. & J. H. Mallard
Jul 21, 1875
Feb 9, 1876

VERONA

John G. Dean
Jun 9, 1854
Jul 21, 1924
&
Lillie M. Dean
May 14, 1860
Aug 1, 1925

Jane C., wife of
William M. McLean
Jan 1, 1814
Dec 17, 1856

Infant Son of
William M. & Jane C. McLean
B&D 1856

Wife & Mother
Frances M., wife of
John Laws
Her first husband was
Kendal Dazey
Nov 5, 1815
Sep 4, 1890

Jaspor Dazey
Who was born 12th of May,
1780 & departed this life
30th day of June, 1849.
He died in his 70th year.
He professed religion when
about 20 and joined the M. E.
Church and died an acceptable member.

In Memory of
Mary Dazey, Consort of
Jasper Dazey, Esq.,
Who was born June 19, 1792
Died December 6, 1847

Virginia C., dau of
I. V. & L. C. Dark
Jun 8, 1848
Dec 10, 1872

Joseph E. Mallard
Dec 31, 1839
Nov 28, 1911

Martha A., wife of
J. E. Mallard
Feb 24, 1833
Mar 27, 1904

Nannie Laws, wife of
J. K. Allison
May 9, 1857
Oct 4, 1901
&
Infant dau of
J. K. & Nannie Allison
(no dates)

Lizzie Jane Jones
1852-1879

John Griffith, son of
Nathan H. & Eliza Dazey
Feb 22, 1845
Died 13th, 1847

Nathan I., son of
Kendall & F. M. Dazey
Jul 24, 1852
Jan 26, 1853

Roy A. Thomason
Tennessee
TEC 3 U.S.Army, W.W.II
Mar 13, 1914
Oct 13, 1972
&
Willie R. Thomason
Sep 22, 1916

Father
Gus C. Whaley
Jun 22, 1887
May 1, 1965
& Mother
Annie S. Whaley
Jun 13, 1880
Jun 31, 1960

Graves across the drive:

Clarence Whaley
1905-1979
&
Fannie Mae Whaley
1917-
mrd- May 13, 1935

James R. Hill
Apr 30, 1945

&
Martha S. Hill
Jul 5, 1952
Mar 11, 1979

Terry L. Gulley
1955-1980
(Gowen-Smith FH)

Marshall Butler
Dec 27, 1886
Jan 2, 1977
&
Annie Butler
Jan 29, 1898

Kermit Lee Osteen
Nov 6, 1908
Nov 8, 1977
&
Elizabeth Osteen
Jul 20, 1910

Debra Ann Osteen
1973-1973
(Lawrence FH)

END OF ALLEN

Many unmarked graves, with fieldstones, no inscriptions.

* *

BROWN CEMETERY
Located about one mile east of Franklin Road, in the Bethlehem Community. Copied April 17, 1966.

Mary L., wife of
John Cheatham
Dec 14, 1813
Jun 9, 1874

Brevard Huggins
Sep 13, 1787
Feb 28, 1874

Mrs. Margaret , Consort of
Brevard Huggins, who departed
this life November 11, 1845
in the 58th year of her
life.

Sarah Huggins
Jun 28, 1815
Jun 29, 1850

Ada Brown
Nov 2, 1879
Sep 30, 1919

Imogene N. Huggins
Died Feb 11, 1849
Age 18 years.

John Steele
Sep 14, 1786
Jun 8, 1847

James R. Steele
May 20, 1819
Apr 7, 1847

Mrs. M. A., wife of
Dr. J. M. Rainey & dau of
B. & M. Huggins
Died Nov 27, 1852
Age 28 years.

William B. Morgan
Feb 27, 1824
Apr 29, 1863

Johnie Brown
Apr 4, 1883
Jul 30, 1885

Lucinda E., wife of
Oct 3, 1825
Mar 2, 1887

Richard A. Brown
Jul 16, 1856
May 5, 1890

James Wiles
Feb 15, 1889
Oct 19, 1901

Martha L. Morgan, wife of
W. B. Morgan
Dec 18, 1826
Sep 8, 1877

W. B. Wiles
May 18, 1848
Jul 21, 1915

M. J. Wiles
Apr 15, 1848
Feb 27, 1889

John W. Brown
Jul 8, 1845
Sep 16, 1934

Emaline, wife of
J. W. Brown
May 9, 1853
Jun 8, 1895

Annie Brown
Apr 12, 1885
Dec 13, 1900

* *

VERONA

CHEEK CEMETERY
Located about ten miles north of Lewisburg, and one and one-half miles east of Franklin Road, and west of Lillard's Mill. Copied 1960

Jesse Cheek
Dec 12, 1832
Jun 24, 1921

Cordelia C. Watson Cheek
Jan 30, 1844
Nov 25, 1911

Mary A. Hardison Cheek
Jul 7, 1834
Jun 14, 1874

Della I., wife of
C. L. Cheek
Oct 29, 1869
May 14, 1899

Rebecca E. Manire Cheek
Oct 1, 1834
Feb 18, 1880

Charles Leslie Montgomery
Apr 23, 1887
Aug 23, 1889

Mary Wilson Cheek
Oct 12, 1844
Oct 16, 1882

* *

CUNNINGHAM CEMETERY
Located two miles west of Verona, on the Verona-Berlin Road. Copied 1959.

Amie Lou Hardison
Sep 5, 1897
Aug 13, 1902

Lillie Ann, dau of
J. N. & S. H. Waters
Jan 18, 1865
Sep 17, 1868

Lou A., wife of
J. N. Waters
Apr 10, 1844
Apr 6, 1879

Lizzie E., wife of
W. J. Andrews
Sep 28, 1850
Dec 11, 1880

Ivia J. Hardison
Jul 28, 1866
Aug 6, 1902

Willie Marshall, son of
J. N. & S. H. Waters
Mar 18, 1877
Jul 22, 1877

J. N. Waters
Mar 25, 1838
May 14, 1906

Carey W. Cunningham
May 29, 1817
Oct 12, 1895

George Andrews, son of
W. V. & Tennie Andrews
Jan 24, 1859
Nov 4, 1864

Infant dau of
J. N. & Lou A. Waters
B&D Apr 4, 1879

Sue H., wife of
J. N. Waters
Mar 21, 1839
Apr 13, 1877

Eliza Cunningham
Aug 18, 1825
May 5, 1905

Ada P., dau of
W. V. & Tennie Andrews
Mar 1, 1868
Jul 15, 1868

Susan F., wife of
J. N. Waters
Jan 12, 1837
Jan 26, 1899

C. J. Cunningham
1846-1909
&
Mollie W. Cunningham
1853-1903

Jeffie Cunningham
Jun 22, 1861
Aug 19, 1905

W. V. Andrews
Nov 1, 1824
Feb 22, 1901

Clifford C. Crutcher
Aug 5, 1883
Nov 7, 1907

Alice Cunningham
Feb 19, 1855
Sep 30, 1897

Tennessee, wife of
W. V. Andrews
Jul 16, 1827
Feb 27, 1909

Lula Holly Ownby
(no dates)

Several unmarked graves.

* *

GENTRY CEMETERY
Located one mile north of Caney Spring, North of Chapel Hill Road, Old Highway No. 99.

Watson Gentry
Apr 16, 1828
Feb 8, 1916

William W. Gentry
Sep 17, 1796
Aug 13, 1858

Elizabeth J., dau of
W. W. & Va. B. Gentry
Apr 16, 1835
Mar 28, 1851

W. H. Ogilvie
Dec 17, 1818
Feb 26, 1894

Mrs. Camilla G. Sims
Sep 20, 1832
Feb 15, 1917

Virginia B., wife of
William W. Gentry
Oct 11, 1804
Sep 28, 1889

Dr. Joseph S., son of
Thos. & Elizabeth Gentry,
Nephew of W. W. & Va. B.
Gentry.
Born 1822
Died 1854

Mary R., wife of
W. H. Ogilvie
Dec 16, 1825
Dec 29, 1889

Samuel G. Gentry
Mar 10, 1830
Jun 28, 1908

Richard H., son of
W. H. & E. N. Ogilvie
Jun 11, 1843
Sep 18, 1861
He was a Confederate Soldier
Age 18 yrs, 3 mos, 7 days.

Sister
Susie E., dau of
W. H. & Mary R. Ogilvie
Apr 13, 1861
Aug 28, 1902

* *

VERONA

HIGGS-ROBERTS CEMETERY

Located west of Anes Station. Copied October 18, 1959 by Ralph D. Whitesell and Mrs. Lounora Pickens.

Fanning M. Jones
Who departed this life
Sep 8, 1842
(no age given)

John W. C. Higgs
Jan 15, 1865
Sep 30, 1894

Virginia L. Higgs
Aug 17, 1869
Apr 20, 1921

Lee Higgs
Apr 15, 1820
Oct 4, 1899

Dezzie, dau of
T. F. & A. E. Higgs
Nov 23, 1899
Jun 25, 1900

Thomas Franklin Higgs
Apr 1, 1868
Jun 5, 1930

Agnes Edith Cheatham
Oct 31, 1872
Aug 14, 1936

William H. Cheek
1855-1937

Martha E. Cheek
1863-1934

H. Edward Jones
1905-
&
E. Kathrine Jones
1906-1936

William S. Bryant
1902-
&
Elvie Mai Bryant
1892-1950

Robert M. Higgs
Apr 27, 1862
Oct 31, 1900

Josie Rutledge, wife of
Robert M. Higgs
Jun 30, 1870
Mar 11, 1900

John Higgs
Died April 25, 1902
Age 70 years

Susie E. Thompson, wife of
John Higgs
Nov 22, 1840
Jun 15, 1869

Tommie Louise Bingham
1918-1919

David A. Higgs
Nov 9, 1874
Sep 12, 1877

Susie A. Hart, wife of
John Higgs
Born 1854
Died Sep 15, 1895

Mary E. Higgs
Born 1800
Died March 13, 1898

James M. Higgs
1837-1899

Sallie B. Higgs
1886-1905

Sydney Hunter
May 21, 1903
May 29, 1908

James Isaac Hunter
Jan 19, 1910
Jul 17, 1911

Herman R. Hunter
Jan 5, 1890
Jul 16, 1913

Annie Roberts Hunter
Jun 17, 1891
Nov 9, 1917

Infant of
Herman & Annie Hunter
Oct 1, 1912

Will, son of
S. J. & Maggie Roberts
Mar 10, 1901
Jul 12, 1901

S. J. Roberts
Dec 11, 1865
Apr 21, 1922

Maggie Roberts
Apr 6, 1867
Man 1, 1937

Samuel Richard Crowder
Oct 2, 1851
Jan 26, 1924

Sophronia A., wife of
Sam R. Crowder
Feb 28, 1856
May 1, 1903

Clyde, son of
G. N. & M. E. Hill
Jul 21, 1906
Oct 25, 1906

Giles Newton Hill
1875-1954 (TM)

Edyne Douglas, son of
G. N. & M. E. Hill
Jan 3, 1914
Apr 6, 1918

Richard Hill
1910-1936 (TM)

* *

HILL CEMETERY

Located on Jim Cheek Farm, west of Anes Station. Copied October 18, 1959 by Ralph D. Whitesell and Mrs. Lounora Pickens.

E. M. Hill
Jul 1, 1844
Apr 23, 1900
"A loving wife and Mother dear, lies buried here."

Francis Hill
Feb 13, 1820
Dec 28, 1873

G. L. Hill
May 18, 1820
Oct 22, 1895

2 unmarked graves.

This cemetery is enclosed in concrete wall, dated Oct 19, 1920.

* *

McCURDY CEMETERY

Located at Verona. Copied July 12, 1959.

Lovalla McCurdy
Born 1900
Died Jul 25, 1934

Rosa Anna McCurdy
Born 1874
Died Jul 24, 1928

Cora Drake
Oct 17, 1888
Jul 23, 1900

Mattie, dau of
H. T. & L. H. Drake
Oct 8, 1865
Oct 14, 1884

Henry T. Drake
Sep 8, 1827
Jan 7, 1897

Lemoniza, wife of
Henry T. Drake
May 27, 1826
Mar 16, 1903

Charles Henry Ernest Drake
Feb 21, 1896
Jul 3, 1901

Edward Martin
Jun 8, 1910
Oct 16, 1926

VERONA

F. C. Martin
Jan 27, 1874
Apr 4, 1936

Dora Martin
Feb 3, 1877
Apr 18, 1925

Katie J. Childs, wife of
B. S. McCurdy
Aug 20, 1860
Sep 9, 1886

R. D. Lane
1865-1954

Anna Hay Lane
1872-1900

Elizabeth A., wife of
W. A. McCurdy
Jul 16, 1838
Oct 11, 1881

Martha A., wife of
H. S. Crichlow
Feb 6, 1812
Apr 8, 1869

Dorlene, dau of
W. G. & Eunice Liggett
Jan 4, 1905
Nov 18, 1908

Joel M., son of
J. A. & Mae Regen
Aug 27, 1866
Apr 13, 1871

Maggie Esther, dau of
M. A. & J. A. Regen
Oct 23, 1861
Nov 20, 1885

Mary L., wife of
Lee Woodward
Mar 5, 1890
Mar 18, 1916

Charlie L. Cathey
1889-1947
&
Octa H. Cathey
1893-1930

Thelma Cathey
Apr 13, 1915
Apr 21, 1915

John W. Cathey
Jan 5, 1843
Jan 9, 1897

M. V. Cathey
Nov 11, 1836
Oct 5, 1928

Mary T. Marshall, wife of
M. V. Cathey
1842-1922

Mary E., wife of
M. V. Cathey
1840-1875

Elbert E., son of
N. S. & S. E. Fisher
Jan 3, 1883
Oct 16, 1889

Sallie M. Cathey, wife of
Earnest Taylor
1868-1922

W. B. Long
Aug 15, 1868
Dec 30, 1918

Ella C. Long
Mar 6, 1873
Dec 11, 1956

James Edward, son of
Thos. & Mattie Lamb
Jan 19, 1928
Aug 12, 1928

Mrs. Sam Stutts
Died Feb 12, 1944
Age 29 yrs, 10 mos, 3 days.

Eric Wiles
Jul 21, 1884
Dec 24, 1956

W. T. McCurdy
Sep 22, 1869
Aug 19, 1928

Mary F., wife of
J. P. McCurdy
Jul 26, 1851
Apr 23, 1903

G. L. Hunter
Jul 15, 1860
Mar 15, 1926

Sallie Hunter
1870-1944

John N., son of
J. L. & Susan McCurdy
Dec 8, 1843
Jan 20, 1862

L. M. Fowler
Aug 22, 1857
Jan 9, 1942

Gilbert M. Hunter
1905-1929

Will A. Hunter
1905-1939

Susan, wife of
H. M. McCurdy
Feb 22, 1819
Nov 16, 1898

J. M. McCurdy
Mar 12, 1822
Aug 7, 1891

Allice Adair, wife of
W. H. Reynolds
Aug 10, 1865
Oct 25, 1927

Frank Adair
1855-1906

Bernie Adair
Sep 16, 1902
Jul 1, 1906

Mary E., dau of
J. W. & Leona Cochran
Jan 2, 1903
Jun 17, 1804

Infant Son of
J. W. & Leona Cochran
Died Aug 1, 1907

Mary A. Cathey
Jun 30, 1869
May 24, 1903

W. J. Cathey
Dec 14, 1869
Dec 6, 1921

Mrs. Carrie McCurdy
1886-1951

Infant of
W. K. & Birdie Harris
(no dates)

W. E. Cochran
Jun 14, 1840
Sep 2, 1914

M. A. Cochran
Feb 18, 1845
Jan 12, 1928

James Ralph Cochran
Mar 1, 1925
Nov 8, 1946

Sallie L. Fowler
Apr 22, 1871
Jun 26, 1926

Robert Lee Long
1869-1947
&
Mary Temie Long
1872-1949

Infant Son of
Mr. & Mrs. C. C. Long
(no dates)

Tom Lee Hardison
May 11, 1919
Feb 12, 1927

Tom W. Hardison
1884-1952

Sallie E. Hardison
1868-1947

Billie Hardison
1929-1933

Charles Clayton Long
1894-1955
&
Edna Brown Long
1893-

Dr. Z. W. Neil
Oct 10, 1849
Aug 4, 1916

Allie Neil
Jun 23, 1861
Jan 23, 1927

Jacob Harber
1884-1932
&
Ela May Harber
1887-

Martha Pearl Cathey
1886-1937

James Worth Thomas
Dec 5, 1905
Apr 15, 1914

Stanley Paul Thomas
1880-1954
&
Virgie A. Neil Thomas
1886-19

Camille Hunter
Jan 6, 1909
Nov 10, 1911

Rozelle Hunter
Jul 27, 1910
Jun 13, 1911

* *

VERONA

McLEAN CEMETERY
Located on the old Harvey McLean Farm, about 1 mile west of Lillards Mill, in the mouth of McLean Bend of Duck River. Copied March 19, 1961.

E. H. McLean, Sr. Jan 19, 1808 Mar 29, 1865	Mary Frances, wife of E. H. McLean, Sr. Aug 6, 1826 Apr 14, 1909	E. H. McLean, Jr. Nov 6, 1862 Aug 20, 1941	W. McLean Nov 20, 1872 Jul 29, 1873
Elizabeth S., wife of E. H. McLean, Sr. Feb 17, 1814 Aug 29, 1850	A. McLean Mar 24, 1847 August 1866	S. R. McLean Apr 7, 1864 Feb 26, 1937	

The following three graves are also on land now owned by the Lambert Family. The graves are near the bank of Duck River, McLean Bend. Copied 1957.

Andrew M. McClean
Apr 22, 1803
Aug 12, 1885

Elizabeth, Second wife of
A. M. McClean
Sep 28, 1810
Oct 6, 1867

Elizabeth, wife of
A. M. McClean
Jan 31, 1804
Oct 23, 1839

* *

OLD LEBANON CEMETERY
Located one mile south of Lillards Mill, between the Verona and Franklin Roads. Copied 1958. Re-checked 1979 by Ralph D. Whitesell, Helen and Tim Marsh.

John H. Davis 1811-1859	H. M. Dark* Mar 18, 1851 Jul 12, 1917	William F. Lavander May 11, 1829 Jan 4, 1881 & wife	Sgt Harvey C. Nickens Co A 8 Tenn Cav C.S.A. Mar 29, 1825 Sep 2, 1908
Elizabeth Marks Davis 1816-1849 & Inf Sarah Jane Davis.	Mary Elizabeth Davis, wife of H. M. Dark Born 1845 Died 1909	Fountain Lavander Jan 17, 1837 Jul 31, 1879	Eveline M. Nickens 1833-1907
Lena May, dau of G. H. & E. Edwards Jun 1, 1881 Nov 18, 1886	Bessie House Dark, wife of H. M. Dark (no dates)	Albert J. Gates Aug 1, 1841 Aug 24, 1849 Age 7 yrs & 3 days	Arra Nickens 1857-1908
Eugenia Barnes Edwards Dec 15, 1846 Mar 17, 1933	Pascal W. Ellington Jan 24, 1811 Apr 18, 1846 Age 36 yrs, 3 mos, 24 days "Leaving a wife & one son to mourn his loss."	R. C. Miller Co F 2 US V I Sp. American War	Zilman Spencer 1783-1865 & Mrs. Zilman Spencer 1788-1868
Elbert Dark Barnes* Born 1813 Died 1846 (Concrete block)		A. B., son of A. B. & M. C. Davis May 17, 1868 Sep 11, 1868	Maggie Miller 1889-1901
Betsy Davis Barnes* Born 1814 Died 1903 (Concrete block)	Emma Braden 1863-1886	Susan Davis Died 1899 (no age given)	Nancy L. Miller Sep 11, 1846 Jun 8, 1913
Aunt Mary "Polly" Davis Born 1810 Died 1881	Stonewall Jackson, son of L. J. & S. V. Rice Sep 25, 1865 Aug 1, 1868	Mary E., dau of M. S. & J. F. Green Dec 7, 1868 Nov 8, 1890	Herman "Ham" Stewart Jun 9, 1908 Oct 16, 1970
Rebecca Davis, wife of H. M. Dark Feb 2, 1849 Aug 29, 1884	James F. Green 1849-1928 Info from Bible of Jimmy Dark.	Martha S., wife of J. F. Green Jul 31, 1847 Sep 2, 1893	Mrs. Alice C. Stewart 1878-1961 (London FH) Samuel "Bud" Knowis Died July 29, 1917 (no age given)

VERONA

Infant Sons of
Mr. & Mrs. Howard Wilson
(no dates)

Willis W. Wilson
1893-1935
&
H. Gertrude Wilson
1893-1937

Charlie D. Reed
Dec 31, 1868
Apr 13, 1944
&
Berta A. Reed
Aug 27, 1875
Aug 23, 1966

Kenneth L. Morton
Tennessee
ATN 2 U.S.Navy
Jul 5, 1939
Sep 18, 1973

Many unmarked graves.

Jerry M. Morton, Jr.
1911-1973
(London FH)

* *

OLD-TINDELL CEMETERY
Located one mile south of Hardison Mills Bridge, on highway between Franklin, Tennessee and Lewisburg, Tennessee.

James Old
Oct 1, 1794
Feb 13, 1861

Martha, wife of
James Old
Nov 7, 1798
Nov 24, 1881

Austin G. Stanley
Apr 12, 1820
Apr 11, 1862

D. S., wife of
A. G. Stanley
Mar 8, 1828
Jan 29, 1886

Mary, wife of
J. E. Neil
Sep 1, 1871
Mar 20, 1919

M. T. O'Neal
Sep 6, 1828
Feb 1, 1909

Sarah M., wife of
M. T. O'Neal
Apr 1, 1830
Feb 12, 1885

Mattie T. Davis
1863-1943

Herman T. Davis
Nov 30, 1889
Jul 16, 1912

Robert M. Stewart
Dec 11, 1838
Mar 4, 1911

Rebecca, wife of
R. M. Stewart
Jan 15, 1844
May 8, 1904

Sibba Dianna Fain
Nov 3, 1852
Apr 1, 1909

John Fain
Oct 13, 1813
Feb 17, 1886

Mother
Emily Ann Crowder, wife of
John Fain
Oct 20, 1820
Apr 8, 1895

Mary Jane Fain
May 1, 1855
Oct 15, 1859
&
Sarah Ann Allison Fain
Apr 28, 1857
Oct 30, 1859

Robert Washington Tindell
Feb 13, 1834
Aug 7, 1921

Eliza, wife of
R. W. Tindell
Jul 14, 1833
Jul 20, 1896

Thomas B. Hardison
Feb 14, 1861
Jul 22, 1887

Nancy J., wife of
Jesse Boyett
Sep 22, 1825
Apr 30, 1887

Mildred A., wife of
A. J. Hardison
Dec 20, 1874
Sep 19, 1910

* *

OWNBY CEMETERY
Located in Berlin, Tennessee, on the east side of Lewisburg-Franklin Highway. Copied June 12, 1959.

Joel Thomas Lavender
Dec 8, 1860
Dec 24, 1936

Ida, wife of
J. T. Lavander
Jan 1, 1875
Aug 29, 1898

Matilda, wife of
Joe Davidson
Dec 1, 1805
Jul 17, 1873

Robert L. Weaver
1855-(no date)

M. Elizabeth Weaver
1864-1919

Luchiouse Duggan
1870-1949

Una May Duggan
1878-

Cromer A. Duggan
1923-1924

John M. Green
Jul 22, 1871
Jul 14, 1920

Arra May Green
Jan 22, 1873
Aug 30, 1915

Miss Roxie Mary Ownby
1888-1954

Lemuel Duggan
Sep 24, 1827
Nov 30, 1913

Clarissa T., wife of
Lemuel Duggan
Apr 15, 1832
Dec 23, 1878

Marcus Franklin Ownby
1855-1936

Nora Jackson
1867-1959

Margaret Ownby
Aug 2, 1848
May 31, 1933

Victory Ann Ownby
Dec 6, 1860-Sep 1, 1937

Jeremiah J. Ownby
Aug 3, 1825
Oct 24, 1910

Prissilla, wife of
J. J. Ownby
Apr 4, 1826
Aug 1, 1908

Sallie, dau of
J. J. & Prissilla Ownby
Apr 27, 1866
Jan 30, 1900

Josiah Edward Ownby
Nov 16, 1853-Sep 11, 1941

Sallie O., wife of
J. E. Ownby
Oct 3, 1853-Apr 29, 1915

* *

VERONA

SMITHSON CEMETERY

Located on the Aldridge Farm, north of Highway No. 99, between Caney Spring and the Franklin Highway. This cemetery is not used for burial any more, the last person buried there being Mary Byrns (Rone) Ring. There are only 5 marked graves, but many fieldstones, no inscriptions. The listing here are from my Family Records, and are NOT the EXACT inscriptions on the tombstones. This info. was furnished by Mrs. Webb C. Rizor, Route 2, Goodlettsville, Tennessee. 1968.

Caroline Virginia Smithson Rone	Leman W. Ring 1876-1926	Dempsey Marion Weaver	Harriet E. Smithson Weaver
Jul 14, 1849	&	Aug 13, 1833	Oct 10, 1842
Jul 10, 1918	Mary B. Rone	Aug 24, 1863	Oct 16, 1909
	1876-1927		
Henry Albert Rone			
Apr 18, 1847			
Nov 7, 1923			

* *

TANKERSLEY CEMETERY

Located north of Verona, on farm owned by Mrs. Avis Hunter. Copied October 18, 1958 by Ralph D. Whitesell and Mrs. Lounora Pickens.

W. T. Hardison	Mary F., wife of	John Tankersley	Lota N. Spencer
Sep 21, 1849	W. T. Hardison	Sep 18, 1821	1883-1906
Mar 11, 1903	Oct 26, 1865	Aug 13, 1871	
	Aug 17, 1883		
Emma N., wife of		Nancy Green, wife of	
W. T. Hardison	E. J. Tankersley	John Tankersley	
May 3, 1867	Sep 28, 1850	Feb 15, 1825	
May 17, 1903	Sep 3, 1883	Jul 1, 1901	
	R. D. Green	George W. Spencer	
	May 9, 1835	1845-1924	
	Apr 3, 1906		
		Marthay J. Spencer	
		1846-1903	

* *

TANKERSLEY CEMETERY

Located two and one-half miles north of Verona, on Big Rock Creek. This cemetery has been destroyed. NO MARKERS.

John Tankersley	Frances Muse, wife of
born 1757/8	John Tankersley
died Mar 14, 1840	(no dates)
(A Revolutionary Soldier)	

* *

WALLACE CEMETERY

Located on Highway No. 99, on road from Pottsville, Maury County to Caney Spring, in Marshall County.

Twins of	William Hollis Farris	Nanie Farris	Lula, dau of W. K. &
Leroy & Lucy Farris	Nov 9, 1869	Feb 10, 1850	M. S. Billington
Died Feb 11, 1904	Feb 4, 1901	May 25, 1924	Jul 12, 1884
			May 3, 1885
Leroy Farris	Una Mae, dau of	Kelsie, son of W. K. &	
Sep 4, 1878	G. J. & A. M. Farris	M. S. Billington	Jas. C. Wallace
Apr 23, 1908	Mar 27, 1880	Apr 9, 1877	Sep 24, 1857
	Nov 7, 1881	Jul 24, 1879	Sep 14, 1877

VERONA

Reuben Billington
Mar 23, 1823
Apr 20, 1899

Matilda Billington
Feb 2, 1825
Nov 3, 1904

C. J. Farris
Aug 24, 1843
Apr 27, 1911

J. P. Logan
Aug 4, 1844
Mar 29, 1904

Permilia Emaline Billington,
wife of D. L. Johnson
Apr 7, 1849
Nov 19, 1901

James Wallace
Aug 25, 1827
Jun 6, 1910

Lavina J. Hodge Wallace
Oct 29, 1829
Dec 7, 1877
Mrd- Mar 18, 1850

Sam J. Wallace
Jan 19, 1844
Jan 21, 1897

Jennie M., wife of
E. P. Billington
Jun 15, 1844
Aug 13, 1876

Laura, dau of
E. P. & Jennie Billington
Apr 13, 1876
Aug 9, 1876

Zach W. Wallace
Mar 15, 1820
May 27, 1882
&
Mary P. Wallace
Oct 26, 1820
May 14, 1899
&
Joseph B. Wallace
1795-1849
&
Malissa Wilson Wallace
1801-1854
"Put there by descendants
in 1956 to mark their
graves."

Dallie, wife of
E. A. Hurt
Jun 16, 1847
Jun 25, 1900

David Lowry Johnson
Jan 11, 1847
Nov 15, 1923
Age 76 years

Sarah C. Johnson
Sep 30, 1869
Dec 4, 1876

John Billington
Sep 16, 1816
Feb 2, 1892

Caroline V., wife of
Jno. Billington
--- 23, 1819
Feb 29, 1888

J. P. Doyle
1859-1909
&
Mary M. Doyle
1857-1927

* *

WHITESELL CEMETERY

Located seven miles north of Lewisburg, between the Franklin
and Verona roads, on original Whitesell property. Copied
September 29, 1958, up-dated 1979 by Ralph D. Whitesell,
Helen and Tim Marsh.

Baby grave
(no marker)

3 graves, Bell Family
(no markers)

Eli Rone
1815-1907

Damaris B., wife of
Eli Rone
Jun 1, 1819
Nov 4, 1886

Henry Rone
Jul 29, 1792
Jul 11, 1841
&   wife
Mary Rone
May 23, 1791
May 11, 1883

Robert D., son of
Eli & D. B. Rone
Sep 18, 1843
Sep 19, 1844

Needham Bryan Wiggs
1812-1876

Baby grave

4 Cheek graves,
(unmarked)

Isaac Blakemore Neil
Feb 6, 1905
Jun 1, 1954
&
Mary Rambo Neil
Nov 9, 1905
May 3, 1974

Cordie Neil Reed
Jun 18, 1895
Sep 1, 1975

J. D. Neil
1872-1943

Della Neil
Jun 12, 1875
Feb 10, 1905

Thelma Neil
Apr 5, 1901
Jul 27, 1905

Wilson, son of
J. D. & Della Neil
Jul 18, 1893
Sep 10, 1893

Nannie Neil
1868-1949

James Clyde Whitsell
Aug 23, 1909
Apr 2, 1971

Isaac Justus Whitsell
1886-1952
&
Jamie Mai Cheek Whitsell
1888-1945

John Harvey, son of
I. J. & J. M. Whitsell
May 13, 1907
Jul 6, 1910

Mother
Margaret, wife of
W. W. Whitsell
Dec 25, 1831
Sep 6, 1897

Erected to the Memory of
William W. Whitsell, son of
John Whitesell & Milly
Wilhoite Whitesell, Born
1825, killed April 6, 1862
during the Battle of Shiloh,
Miss., buried there, also a
veteran of the War with
Mexico. Married Margaret A.
Russell, Dec 20, 1847,-by his
descendants, 1959.

Georgia Ann Whitsell
Dec 1, 1890
May 15, 1891

George A. Whitsell
Oct 18, 1860
Aug 1, 1890
&   wife
Margaret L. Whitsell
Sep 3, 1868
Mar 18, 1891

Benjamin H. Cheek
1812-1865

Nannie E. Cheek
1814-1874

Maggie Cheek
1888-1890

Father
Jas. A. Cheek
Feb 28, 1839
Nov 3, 1883
&
Mother
Amy J. Cheek
Apr 30, 1849
Jul 19, 1919

Felix Bledsoe Woodward
Sep 26, 1898
Oct 3, 1958
&
Louise Thomas Woodward

VERONA

Howard Douglas Whitesell
Jul 11, 1899
Oct 30, 1899

Letsey, dau of
W. G. & Lizzie Thomas
Oct 18, 1895
Dec 16, 1895

Willie M., son of
I. B. & R. J. Whitesell
Aug 28, 1883
Sep 27, 1884

Rebecca J., wife of
I. B. Whitesell
Feb 20, 1848
Feb 8, 1884

Sallie D., dau of
I. B. & R. J. Whitesell
Apr 5, 1879
Dec 10, 1879

Infant Son of
J. M. S. & M. A. Whitesell
Mar 9, 1878
Died at Birth
(First Whitesell buried in this cemetery)

J. Otway Whitesell
Sep 22, 1882
Apr 8, 1958
&
Belle A. Whitesell
Apr 17, 1890
May 6, 1976

Jacob B. Austin
1859-1938

Van, son of
J. M. S. & M. A. Whitesell
Jan 27, 1882
Oct 11, 1884

Infant dau of
J. M. S. & M. A. Whitesell
June 6, 1891

Alice, wife of
J. M. S. Whitesell
May 1, 1854
Sep 29, 1892

John F., son of
J. M. S. & M. A. Whitesell
Jan 1, 1877
Feb 25, 1898

Oscar Lee, son of
Johnnie & Cora Whitsell
Nov 22, 1896
Oct 9, 1915

J. M. S. Whitsell
Feb 16, 1853
Sep 11, 1918
&
Tennie Bills Whitsell
Nov 7, 1867
Oct 24, 1920

F. F. Liggett
Jan 3, 1804
Jul 5, 1888

Father
Odell Whitesell
Mar 19, 1901
May 17, 1971
&
Mother
Evelyn C. Whitesell
Dec 6, 1916

Mrd- Mar 9, 1942

Edmond Bradley
1803-1901
Age 98 yrs.

Erected to the Memory of
Rebecca Willis Bradley
1816-1857
dau of Martha Hughes & Davis
Willis & 1st wife of
Edmond Bradley, by
descendants, 1969.

Daniel W. Seay
1902-1977
&
Rebecca W. Seay
1913-

William C. Glasscock
Sep 6, 1876
May 9, 1913

Thomas S. Glasscock
1854-1953
&
Martha J. Glasscock
1851-1926

Mattie Macel, dau of
J. E. & Arie Thomas
Nov 11, 1907
Aug 14, 1913

George Nail, Faithful,
colored servant of the
Whitesell family. The
only colored grave.

Joe Ervin Thomas
Sep 11, 1875-Sep 22, 1958
&
Arie A. Thomas
Jan 14, 1882-Mar 16, 1972

Ruby Whitesell Kerr
1893-1977

James B. Whitesell
1916-1937

Allen W. Whitesell
1893-1935

Artie Missie Whitesell
1857-1932

I. B. Whitesell
1849-1936

Samuel H. Whitesell
Sept 24, 1871
Feb 19, 1938
&
Lula F. Whitesell
Nov 9, 1876
Jan 4, 1950

Dr. Gordon R. Fisher
Sep 15, 1914
Oct 24, 1969
&
Mary E. Fisher
Aug 25, 1918

END OF WHITESELL

* *

WOODS CEMETERY

Located on the Old Sam Whitesell Farm, on Berlin Road.
Copied March 1958.

Charles E. Woods
Born in Madison County, Ga.
Dec 8, 1799, Died
Mar 1, 1868

4 unmarked graves.

* *

VERONA

BOYET CEMETERY
Located near Ellington Airport. Copied October 28, 1979.

J. Frank Boyet
1861-1947
&
Ella O. Boyet
1878-1915

Verginia, dau of
J. F. & Ella Boyet
Jan 20, 1903
Oct 18, 1903

Jimmie, son of
J. F. & Ella Boyet
Oct 16, 1900
Jul 28, 1905

Elizabeth, dau of
J. F. & Ella Boyet
Jan 15, 1906
Jun 10, 1906

Frank Allen Karnes
Feb 3, 1930
Feb 20, 1931

Andrew W. Thompson
Apr 8, 1878
May 6, 1938
&
Mattie O. Thompson
May 30, 1878
Jul 21, 1971

Allen Curtis Thompson
Mar 4, 1899
Mar 4, 1916

N. Gideon Cheatham
Jul 13, 1876
Apr 18, 1955
&
Cofie Mc. Cheatham
Jan 31, 1886
Jul 3, 1974

All graves are marked, well kept cemetery.

* *

BEREA CEMETERY
Located at Berea Church of Christ, one-half mile north of Verona. Copied by Helen and Tim Marsh, Nov 6, 1979.

Joyce Jennette Hazel
died 1953
Age 7 months
(Lawrence FH)

George L. Hussey
Tennessee
Pfc Co D 109 Medical BN
W. W. II   BSM
Oct 8, 1914
Apr 15, 1959

Mrs. Lucille Stewman
1914-1975
(London FH)

Thelma Hussey
1911-1970
(London FH)

Adrain B. Wooten
Jul 29, 1917

&
Gladys S. Wooten
Apr 27, 1922

M. Kenny Phifer
Nov 17, 1902
Nov 13, 1958
&
Laurene A. Phifer
Jan 31, 1917

Algie Phifer
Jan 27, 1909
Nov 25, 1966

Patsy Ann Simmons
Apr 28, 1948
Jun 13, 1955
(picture)

Barbara Jean Dowell
1941-1964
(picture)

Emory N. Poteet
Apr 9, 1919
Jul 8, 1979
&
Virginia J. Poteet
Dec 27, 1922

Joe F. Lee, Sr.
Tennessee
Pvt U.S.Army, W. W. I
Mar 25, 1891
Mar 22, 1974
&
Clara M. Lee
Mar 29, 1909

&
Joe F. Lee, Jr.
Oct 9, 1935

Leonard R. Collins
Jun 21, 1905
Apr 3, 1965
&
Susie S. Collins
Jan 22, 1904

Sarah F. Grammer
Aug 15, 1901
Jul 9, 1970

Leslie S. Collins
Tennessee
Pvt HQ 4 Service Comd.
W. W. II
Nov 21, 1900
Sep 18, 1967

Willie J. McKnight
1883-1952
&
Mattie Joe McKnight
1900-1974

Jim Morton
1886-1968
&
Minnie Morton
1897-1956

M. Douglas Morton
1940-1951

J. B. Morton
Aug 7, 1916
Aug 19, 1957
&
F. Murrel Morton
Dec 1, 1921

Willie Lee Morton
Jun 23, 1919
Dec 15, 1967

Margaret D. Morton
May 25, 1925

Scottie Dewayne Morton
Nov 10, 1968
Jul 17, 1970
(color picture)

Don
Alvin L. Morton
SP 4 U.S.Army
Aug 20, 1944
May 28/30, 1974
&
Susie Morton
Mar 21, 1950

Newt Crowell
Aug 21, 1905

&
Annie M. Crowell
Jul 19, 1919
Mar 19, 1968

Father
Frank B. Luna
Jul 20, 1903
Jul 16, 1972
&
Mother
Sara A. Luna
Feb 2, 1917

Mrd- Dec 23, 1931

Floyd O. Bivins
1888-1964
&
Hattie C. Bivins
1886-1969

Mrs. Mary Ruth Holt
1916-1979
(London FH)

Mrs. Fannie M. Morton
1911-1979
(London FH)

VERONA

Robert Lee Morton
Tennessee
Pfc Btry A 43 Coast Arty BN
W. W. II
Oct 30, 1914
Mar 7, 1964

Tony E. Morton
June 16, 1962

Robert L. Morton, Sr.
1881-1958
&
Ruth E. Morton
1885-1957

Adron P. Phifer
Dec 24, 1869
Nov 13, 1942

Mother
Mattie P. Roberts
1894-1957

Joe C. Phifer
Oct 29, 1893
Aug 11, 1951
&
Sadie E. Phifer
Dec 28, 1899

Nancy Lee Phifer
Aug 10, 1946
Oct 14, 1946

Infant Son, Pruitt
June 1968 (TM)

Timothy W. Davis
May 2, 1965
May 4, 1965

Walter L. Davis
Nov 15, 1893

&
Virgie L. Davis
Oct 14, 1893
Jan 16, 1971
Mrd- Jan 1, 1922

Roy Davis
1900-1977
&
Jessie Davis
1903-

Andrew Richard Crick
Mar 21, 1973
Mar 23, 1973

Father
Otis E. Troop
1895-1960
&
Mother
Jessie Lee Troop
1897-19

Father
Charles A. "Jack" Elrod
Apr 23, 1916
Sep 28, 1977
&
Mother
Cecil Mai T. Elrod
Aug 25, 1915

Charles "Bud" Elrod
Jun 27, 1939
Jan 9, 1972
&
Linda Ervin Elrod
Jul 8, 1944

Thomas E. Jones
Mar 1, 1876
Mar 10, 1958
&
Nancy Ann Jones
Nov 10, 1883
Jun 13, 1971

Cecil Gordon Gilliam
Feb 24, 1893

&
Lula Pearl Gilliam
Apr 22, 1892
May 23, 1969

Kathy Lynn Gilliam
Aug 30, 1958

Harold E. Reynolds
Nov 18, 1903
Aug 31, 1978
&
Lillian W. Reynolds
Dec 10, 1908

Alvin Ross Woodward
Tennessee
Pfc HQ Det 2 Engineers
W. W. I   PH
Sep 27, 1887
Aug 10, 1963

Tiny M. Woodward
Jul 15, 1895
Nov 3, 1969

W. Lee Woodward
1890-1966

John "Ned" Walker
Jan 8, 1912
May 10, 1965
&
Lenis D. Walker
Oct 19, 1913

John Newton Jordan
Jan 17, 1882
Mar 4, 1956
&
Fannie Wilson Jordan
Sep 15, 1882
Aug 26, 1959

Thomas W. Derryberry
Dec 11, 1902
Oct 2, 1975
&
Mary Margaret Derryberry
Aug 12, 1909

Mrd- Mar 14, 1936

James E. Hardison
1893-1953

Blanche E. Hardison
1896-1944

Buford Walker
1910-1941
&
Maycle Walker
1910-19

Wayne Buford Walker
Jun 25, 1936
May 28, 1955

Joe Frank Walker
1874-1952
&
Bettie S. Walker
1879-1974

Infant Son of
Mr. & Mrs. J. P. Walker
Dec 17, 1965

W. Frank Stewart
Apr 5, 1884
Sep 28, 1941
&
Josie Stewart Wood
Oct 3, 1890
Dec 29, 1969
&
Henry B. Wood
Mar 18, 1877
May 10, 1957

Herman C. Reynolds
Tennessee
Pfc U. S. Marine Corps
W. W. I
Jul 12, 1897
Sep 29, 1959

J. Frank Reynolds
1869-1946
&
S. Ethel Reynolds
1878-1948

David A. Lamb
Jan 7, 1868
Feb 22, 1944
&
Kittie R. Lamb
May 12, 1876
Apr 14, 1955

Edd Walker
1880-1946
&
Johnnie Walker
1880-1946

Murrey Walker
1916-1944
(Military Stone)
Columbus M. Walker
Tennessee
Pvt 398 Inf 100 Inf Div
W. W. II
Sep 16, 1916
Nov 23, 1944
&
Willette Walker

Naaman Hill
Sep 23, 1884
Jan 21, 1963
&
Donie D. Hill
Aug 7, 1887
Mar 14, 1974

Fred Hill
May 10, 1893
Dec 18, 1965
&
Margaret B. Hill
Apr 17, 1900
Oct 13, 1961

Father
Earl "Kennie" Hill
Feb 9, 1889
Jan 11, 1969
&
Mother
Elaine Thomason Hill
Dec 26, 1896

Paul E. Ray
Jan 21, 1913

&
Maysel L. Ray
Jan 5, 1916

Alvin L. Cooper
Aug 17, 1912

&
Mai L. Cooper
Apr 12, 1914

VERONA

Stewart Miller
1871-1957
&
Ada Miller
1878-1966

Howard M. Miller
Nov 17, 1905
Sep 3, 1974
&
Helen B. Miller
Mar 16, 1913

Everette W. McConnel
Mar 27, 1962
May 4, 1962

Robert L. Hardison
1900-1955
&
Mattilee B. Hardison
1905-19

Father
Charlie L. Reynolds
Feb 8, 1889
Apr 13, 1962
&
Mother
Argin B. Reynolds
Jun 9, 1890

Robert F. Gaalaas
Minnesota
Pvt Stu Army TNG Corps
W. W. I
Dec 31, 1899
Jun 18, 1970

Clarence Jones Hill
1886-1954
&
Kate Fisher Hill
1890-

Alford Collins
1899-1931
(London FH)

Tom Collins
Born (date gone)
Died 1932
(London FH)

Lizzie Collins Chunn
1878-1958
(London FH)

Tom Chunn
1885-1948

Ben Chunn
1870-1948

Susie Barnett Chunn
1878-1953

Jack Chunn
1894-1948

Maggie Ketchum Quarterman
1915-1977
(Lawrence FH)

Omie Hardison
1885-1966
&
Ellie Hardison
1896-1946

David A. Hardison
May 13, 1854
Feb 26, 1933
&
Flora T. Hardison
Dec 16, 1843
Mar 31, 1930

Robert J. Hardison
Sep 14, 1852
Nov 3, 1930

Nancy C. Garrett Hardison
Apr 19, 1852
Apr 21, 1928

Eddie Long Tankersley
Jan 6, 1900

&
Margaret Louise Tankersley
Dec 22, 1905
Feb 13, 1965

Melvin P. Yarbrough
1882-1947
&
Annie L. Yarbrough
1889-1964

Husband
James H. Ray
May 10, 1916
Feb 18, 1967

Clarence J. Ray
1898-1965

Howard Ray, Jr.
1942-1956

Ollie Howard "Rat" Ray
1910-1951
(London FH)

Lorene Ray
1939-1939

Clemeon C. Ray
Apr 29, 1870
May 4, 1926
&
Sarah J. Ray
Oct 14, 1873
May 8, 1950

W. Claude Ray
1894-1956

Bessie Ketchum, wife of
W. C. Ray
Jun 2, 1899
Sep 22, 1921

W. N. Green
1841-1917

Frances E. Green
1843-1917

Sam M. Braden
1858-1943

Mary R. Braden
1863-1907

W. Oscar Braden
1888-1969

Robert A. Hicks
1879-1961
&
Anna E. Hicks
1882-1949

J. W. Sharp
1861-1898

Glen Sharp
1896-1898

Ernest Sharp
1887-1900

Elmer Sharp
1888-1904

Cora Maud Thompson, wife of
W. B. Caughran
Sep 7, 1883
Aug 6, 1909

Alvin Caughran
1915-1917

Maynita Caughran
1923-1924

Sam J. McCord
May 11, 1901
Oct 24, 1975
&
Sallie M. McCord
Aug 3, 1901

Mrd- Dec 25, 1918

Roy B. Green
1885-1924
&
Ina E. Hill Green
1888-1970

E. Eugene Hardison
May 1, 1910
May 14, 1966
&
Annie Ruth Hardison
Oct 20, 1911

John C. Stewart
Born 1863
Died Jul 25, 1884

Theophilus D., son of
F. P. & M. E. Tankersley
Jul 1, 1882
Nov 28, 1896

F. P. Tankersley
Feb 9, 1853
Jul 11, 1938

Mollie E. Tankersley
Nov 10, 1861
Aug 16, 1903

David E. Tankersley
1897-1964
&
Ruth M. Tankersley
1896-

Demie Tankersley
Feb 2, 1889
Sep 20, 1903

Virgil Tankersley
Sep 23, 1884
Sep 18, 1952

Mother
Dossie Collins, wife of
Virgin Tankersley
Jul 14, 1887
Dec 7, 1927

Infant Son, Tankersley
1911-1911

Raymond O. Kincaid
Sep 11, 1912
May 20, 1966
&
Mary Alma Kincaid
Dec 31, 1912
(new grave, 1979)

Infant dau of
Mr. & Mrs. James Kincaid
1958

John A. Stewart
Sep 2, 1885
Oct 21, 1967
&
Maggie H. Stewart
Dec 24, 1888
Jun 5, 1969

VERONA

Giles Clayborn Hill
Mar 27, 1857
Aug 24, 1937
&
Donna Jane Hill
Dec 8, 1863
Aug 17, 1905

Infant of
G. C. & D. J. Hill
(no dates)

Giles David, son of
G. C. & D. J. Hill
Feb 19, 1903
Oct 22, 1903

Infant Son of
G. C. & D. J. Hill
B&D- May 21, 1901

Roy, son of
G. C. & D. J. Hill
Feb 17, 1899
May 8, 1900

Infant Son of
G. C. & D. J. Hill
B&D- Dec 11, 1897

Fannie D., dau of
G. C. & D. J. Hill
Nov 10, 1890
Jan 17, 1894

Infant Son of
G. C. & D. J. Hill
B&D- Jan 10, 1893

Infant Dau of
G. C. & D. J. Hill
B&D- Oct 8, 1887

Pearl, dau of
G. C. & D. J. Hill
Nov 15, 1893
Sep 17, 1909

Carroll M. Stewart
1856-1934
&
Eliza A. Stewart
1855-1944

Mary A., dau of
David & Eliza Tankersley
Feb 20, 1841
Jul 23, 1887

David Tankersley
Mar 29, 1815
Feb 16, 1882
&
Eliza D. Tankersley
Oct 14, 1818
Sep 10, 1892

Father
James M. Tankersley
Mar 19, 1858
Oct 9, 1900
&
Mother
Lucy Bell Tankersley
Aug 20, 1862
Mar 10, 1958

Billie B. Henson
1910-1964
&
Leota M. Henson
1915-

Odell Henson
Oct 29, 1903
Feb 20, 1973
&
Minerva B. Henson
Mar 14, 1918
Nov 25, 1972

Hoyte Hardison
1927

Edward F. Bigger, Jr.
Jan 6, 1924
Feb 5, 1924

Mary Williams
Jul 3, 1847
Jul 2, 1927

May Bigger
May 15, 1865
Jul 22, 1933

John T. Henson
1908-1963

Jim Allen Henson
1881-1968
&
Lillie Pearl Henson
1882-1952

Elisha Boone Hill
Sep 21, 1884
Dec 5, 1957

Herschel Elam Hill
Tennessee
Cpl U.S.Army W. W. I
Oct 5, 1887
Apr 9, 1955

Mittie E. Hill
Jan 9, 1890
Jun 4, 1895

Ellis O. Hill
Oct 23, 1882
Dec 10, 1883

Tolbert B. Hill
Mar 23, 1880
Feb 23, 1886

Emma A., wife of
T. A. Hill
Feb 5, 1850
Mar 1, 1895

Sam J. Stewmon
May 13, 1886
Nov 25, 1964
&
Myrtle H. Stewmon
Feb 9, 1892
Sep 30, 1961

Clarence Reynolds
Jan 24, 1885
Mar 24, 1921
& daughter
Mary Lou Reynolds
Jun 20, 1916
Mar 24, 1921

W. Henry Reynolds
1861-1935
&
Sara Lou Reynolds
1865-1914

William Carl Reynolds
Pfc U.S.Army W. W. II
1904-1977
&
Annie Mae Reynolds
1911-

M. W. Reynolds
Jan 27, 1863
Aug 26, 1905
& wife
Etta Reynolds
Aug 17, 1866
Aug 29, 1905

Infant Son of
M. W. & M. E. Reynolds
Aug 20, 1905

Allen D. Reynolds
Jul 15, 1889
Apr 13, 1905

Infant Son of
M. W. & M. E. Reynolds
B&D- Nov 5, 1897

M. E. Reynolds
Jun 20, 1837
Mar 26, 1914

Nancy M. Reynolds
Jun 16, 1842
Jul 27, 1915

Infant Son of
J. J. & J. L. Spain
B&D- Jun 16, 1897

Tom Neil Lamb
Jul 11, 1902
Jul 24, 1904

Will Tom Patton
Jul 6, 1897
Jun 14, 1977
&
Mamie E. Patton
Jun 24, 1899

James A. Endsley
Mar 11, 1868
Jun 9, 1917
&
Nora B. Endsley
Aug 9, 1871
Aug 8, 1942

Infant Son & Infant Dau
B&D-   Born Apr 6,
July 1895   1896
(All other info in the
ground, deep)

Willie M. Osborn
Oct 16, 1880
Nov 19, 1912

Liddie R. Braden
1884-1952

Mary D. Walker
Jan 29, 1913

Sherman D. Derryberry
Nov 21, 1889
Aug 14, 1967

Iva Hill Derryberry
Apr 21, 1895
Mar 18, 1935

Mitlon Ross Phifer
Aug 11, 1909
Mar 28, 1936

Sara Elizabeth Phifer
Mar 1899
May 1899

J. C. Phifer
Nov 28, 1844
Oct 12, 1926

Sarah Rebecca Phifer
Aug 29, 1845
Feb 13, 1923

Martha Susan, wife of
J. C. Phifer
Oct 7, 1845
Sep 16, 1886

Ellen M. Phifer
Nov 9, 1869
Jan 26, 1937

VERONA

Infant Son & Infant Dau of
J. R. & G. E. Hardison
B&D- July 7, 1897

John Harvey, son of
J. R. & G. E. Hardison
Oct 27, 1912
Nov 9, 1912

Father
J. R. L. Hardison
1876-1936
&
Mother
Gatha D. Hardison
1878-1962

Clarence Davis
1890-1955
&
Dixie B. Davis
1895-1971

William Auslin Hardison
1895-
&
Minnie M. Hardison
1898-1950

Samuel A. Davis
1863-1931
&
Matilda Davis
1867-1962

Sam Crigger
1882-1972
&
Lola Crigger
1886-1929

J. A. Stewart
Sep 9, 1854
Feb 6, 1920
&
M. F. Stewart
Jan 29, 1857
(no date)

E. B. Stewart
1884-1922
&
N. H. Stewart
1847-1919
C.S.A. 1864-5

Maggie Osburn, wife of
R. L. Madison
Jul 27, 1864
Jan 20, 1898

John Thomas Woodward
Sep 25, 1885
Jul 12, 1905

Hattie May Woodward
Mar 27, 1884
Nov 9, 1908

John Alexander Woodward
Jun 6, 1852
May 8, 1928
&
Martha Margaret Woodward
Apr 7, 1858
May 11, 1924

Will Hume Marshal
1903-1907

Jamie Aldine Marshal
1910-1912

Laura R. Sowell
1883-1971

John Lee Reynolds
Jul 2, 1903
Apr 21, 1936

J. M. Reynolds
Oct 23, 1863
Mar 5, 1927

Laura L. Reynolds
1865-1945

Ezekiel E. Reynolds
Born 1834
Died Aug 2, 1894
&
Thomas J. Reynolds
Aug 18, 1879
Oct 22, 1902

Fannie Bigger
1867-1935

R. Franklin Liggett
Jul 26, 1902
Aug 22, 1920

Fannie P. Liggett
Mar 30, 1881
Feb 11, 1963

Sidney N. Liggett
Aug 23, 1868
Nov 10, 1957

Mary Derryberry Ray
Dec 26, 1860
Feb 25, 1955

John A. Doud
Died Apr 12, 1907
(no age given)

Mary B. Woods
Aug 9, 1813
Aug 6, 1900

Davis K. Hays
Nov 12, 1882
Dec 12, 1892

Sallie R. Hays
Jul 4, 1893
Dec 10, 1899

Andrew J. Hays
1855-1926
&
Nannie J. Hays
1854-1939

Jim H. Hays
1891-1954
&
Vadie T. Hays
1900-

Sam Lee Hays
1889-1961

W. S. Weaver

&
Virginia F. Weaver
Oct 10, 1840
Dec 17, 1904
"In Memory, by 3 gr sons &
1 gr dau."

Girtie N., dau of
W. S. & V. F. Weaver
Dec 24, 1881
Nov 29, 1901

William P. Madison
Jul 8, 1865
Jun 13, 1905
&
M. Frances Madison
Dec 13, 1871
Sep 9, 1911

William Leonard Madison
Oct 8, 1895
Aug 15, 1922

Vashie E. Garrett
Oct 20, 1900
Sep 19, 1929

Hattie Lillard
Apr 8, 1878
Jun 24, 1936

Mother
Nellie M. McCord
1899-1925

George Crigger
1867-1936
&
Cora Crigger
1877-1945

Margaret Pauline, wife of
W. L. Martin
Sep 10, 1900
Jun 15, 1922

Magie Maree Hill
Jan 14, 1916
Mar 29, 1918

Cpl Charlie Webb Hill
Tennessee
Cpl Co A, 512 Armd Inf BN
Korea, PH
Jul 10, 1929
Dec 1, 1954
(picture)

William Lenzie Hill
Aug 12, 1891
Dec 19, 1962
&
Mary Rebecca Hill
Jun 3, 1898
Sep 18, 1964

Father
H. G. Andrews
Aug 25, 1862
Oct 27, 1917
&
Mother
A. M. Andrews
Sep 17, 1864
Jan 10, 1937

George E. Andrews
May 26, 1890
Oct 10, 1917

Mary E., dau of
G. T. & S. E. Yoes
May 16, 1871
Dec 17, 1893

Sister
Mattie May Reed
1897-1899

G. H. O. Weaver "Bud"
1869-1950
&
Cora E. Weaver
1879-1929
"Mother"

Cora I. Weaver
"In loving Memory
 Brother Ben"

Virginia W. Weaver
"In loving Memory
 Sister Sadie"

Ida, dau of
G. H. O. & C. E. Weaver
Mar 8, 1900
Sep 3, 1900

Robert Herschel Adair
Aug 17, 1898
May 25, 1968

Mother
Mollie R. Adair
1865-1942

Louise, dau of
Mr. & Mrs. E. F. Adair
Apr 15, 1914
Jul 6, 1914

VERONA

R. B. Adair
Jul 27, 1860
Nov 13, 1968

Elizabeth Adair
Sep 22, 1832
Aug 13, 1911

J. R. Adair
May 22, 1850
Mar 20, 1917

H. C. McQuiddy
Oct 15, 1846
Oct 11, 1935

Harden W. McQuiddy
Jan 31, 1858
Jul 13, 1944

Richard Everett McQuiddy
Jun 25, 1887
Nov 19, 1890

Robert L. Cathey
1875-1949
&
Emma Lou Cathey
1886-1934

Father
Thomas J. Cathey
Sep 6, 1841
Oct 21, 1919
&
Mother
Roe Elliott Cathey
Aug 20, 1849
Dec 26, 1934

Callie Hill
1885-1926
&
Will Hill
1881-
(TM- Will R. Hill
died 1952)
&
Effie Hill
1886-1922

W. F. P. Derryberry
Jan 9, 1853
Aug 8, 1930

Ella Derryberry
1860-1937

Martha C. Hooten
Sep 15, 1853
Mrd- W. F. P. Derryberry
Oct 3, 1872 & died
Oct 16, 1899

Infant dau of
W. F. P. & M. S. Derryberry
Jun 25, 1893
Jun 26, 1893

John W. Derryberry
Apr 15, 1901
Oct 10, 1902

Myrtle C. Derryberry
Dec 27, 1899
Sep 26, 1901

Chesley W. Derryberry
1875-1939
&
Z. Cordelia Derryberry
1880-1969

Sisters
Nora Hill
Nov 26, 1881
Jun 4, 1957
&
Dora Hooten
Nov 26, 1881
Nov 15, 1960

William Neely Derryberry
Died Aug 9, 1939
Age 64 yrs, 0 mos, 7 days
(Lawrence FH)

Mollie, wife of
W. N. Derryberry
Aug 22, 1872
Jul 19, 1917

Father
James F. Hill
May 9, 1914
Feb 15, 1977
&
Mother
Reba Wolfe Hill
Jul 18, 1920

Rucker B. Hill
1882-1956
&
Pearl G. Hill
1885-1966

Father
John F. Hill
Apr 15, 1852
Aug 3, 1910
&
Mother
Sallie D. Hill
Jul 22, 1862
Jun 11, 1941

W. D. Hill
Sep 20, 1850
May 3, 1919
& wife
Sarah C. Williams Hill
Jul 2, 1857
Jul 4, 1919

END OF BEREA

Several unmarked graves.

* *

BETHLEHEM CEMETERY
Located about 10 miles north of Lewisburg on Highway No 431, one-half mile south of Bethlehem Church. Copied November 24, 1979 by Ralph D. Whitesell, Helen and Tim Marsh.

Nobel F. Brown
Oct 17, 1904
(no date)
&
Mary E. Green Brown
Sep 5, 1902

John H. Crigger
Sep 14, 1845
Dec 27, 1923
& wife
Mary J. Crigger
Mar 6, 1859
Aug 9, 1950

Mary R., wife of
John H. Crigger
Jan 11, 1858
Mar 31, 1886

Tom J. Crigger
Sep 25, 1903

&
Anna M. "Polly" Crigger
Aug 22, 1914

Willie A. Crigger
Jun 5, 1875
May 1, 1894

M. L. Hardison
Aug 27, 1849
Jul 18, 1901

Maggie V. Hardison
Aug 24, 1851
Nov 2, 1928

Infant Son of
M. L. & M. V. Hardison
Aug 12, 1863
Aug 13, 1863

Guy Hardison
1888-1930
&
Lura Hardison
1897-1979

Dennis B. Aldridge
1890-1964

Maxie M. Aldridge
1891-1933

Jim Aldridge
18-- - 1898

Mattie M. Aldridge
1868-1898

Marvin Olen Aldridge
Sep 15, 1888
Nov 10, 1888

Aaron A. Aldridge
Feb 15, 1837
Feb 29, 1898

Lizzie Wiles
Oct 10, 1861
Mar 28, 1897

George P. Blalock
1872-1953

Lillie D. Blalock
1875-1907

Martha P. Blalock
1870-1938

VERONA

W. T. Vaughan
Nov 27, 1863
Sep 2, 1899

Mary Ann Vaughan
1863-1956
(no marker)

John J. Williamson
Feb 11, 1809
May 2, 1882

David Williamson
Born (blank)
Died Feb 25, 1870

J. H. Baird
Nov 30, 1848
Aug 9, 1919

Robert P. Baird
Jan 30, 1854
Mar 10, 1914

Cynthia M. Baird
May 6, 1856
Sep 2, 1882

Charles A. Baird
Mar 30, 1840
Aug 30, 1873

Richard E. Baird
Jan 9, 1859
Jun 19, 1870

James W. Baird
Apr 17, 1812
Aug 26, 1885
&
Sarah J. Baird
Oct 31, 1818
Mar 7, 1868

Dr. J. R. Mallard
Oct 28, 1842
Feb 23, 1925
&
S. A. Mallard
Feb 24, 1846
Nov 25, 1921

Henry J. Davis
1844-1937
"A Confederate Soldier"
&
Nattie J. Davis
1853-1943

Chesley, son of
H. J. Davis
Jul 27, 1888
Aug 8, 1889

Sam McLean Davis
Jun 23, 1890
Feb 22, 1911

A. F. Lillard
1807-1894

Mahala Lillard
1805-1895

John, son of
G. O. Whitesell
Nov 15, 1908
Jun 24, 1910

George O. Whitesell
Co K 4 Tenn Inf
Spanish American War
Jan 9, 1880
Mar 15, 1932

Etta Davis Whitesell
1877-1946

Leota, wife of
J. O. Green
Aug 21, 1878
Oct 13, 1909

J. O. Green
Dec 7, 1869
May 9, 1948

Mary Cora, wife of
J. O. Green
Mar 26, 1875
Jan 18, 1954

J. Ross Green
Mar 25, 1900
Jan 23, 1966

Marvin B. Crigger
Jul 29, 1889
Aug 15, 1976
&
Mattienna M. Crigger
Apr 15, 1898
Dec 6, 1978

Leonard Fain Crigger
Feb 1, 1926
May 8, 1926

J. Crockett Crigger
1856-1934
&
Ellan Fain Crigger
1859-1921

William Herbert "Buddy" Wiles
Oct 9, 1881
Apr 6, 1953
&
Daisy Whitehead Wiles
Apr 1, 1893
Apr 22, 1971

Infant Dau of
Mr. & Mrs. W. H. Wiles
1914

James Herbert "Honey" Wiles
Feb 7, 1919
Aug 20, 1978
&
Mattie Lee Powell Wiles
Jan 7, 1921

Charles Richard Galloway
Sep 22, 1870
Jun 25, 1952

Priscilla J. Baird, wife of
J. A. Galloway
May 27, 1837
Apr 19, 1907

Father
James A. Galloway
Sep 1, 1832
Jul 2, 1900

Sarah Cornelia, dau of
James A. & Priscilla J.
Galloway
Dec 21, 1857
Sep 19, 1894

William Rawley Galloway
Oct 2, 1866
Mar 8, 1929

Elizabeth McLean Porter
1853-1937

Father
Samuel McLean
Aug 1, 1813
Sep 21, 1901

Sarah E., wife of
Samuel McLean
May 26, 1821
Jan 15, 1910

Nannie C., dau of
Samuel & Sarah E. McLean
Nov 7, 1848
Apr 22, 1871

Infant Son of
A. J. & Ella Powell
(no dates)

John L. McLean
Oct 24, 1846
Aug 13, 1924
&
Dolly McLean
Dec 19, 1870
Aug 15, 1962

Brother
Harvey Allen McLean
May 24, 1892-Sep 21, 1952
&
Sister
Pauline Jane McLean
Apr 10, 1894

E. Harvey Mayberry
Mar 21, 1866
Feb 12, 1938

H. Mayberry
Jul 14, 1826
Oct 10, 1910
&
A. P. Mayberry
Aug 11, 1830
Aug 31, 1919

W. P. Gillespie
1851-1921

J. H. Gillespie
Nov 9, 1848
Oct 5, 1910
&
Mary M. Gillespie
Jul 7, 1849
May 24, 1895

Bessie, dau of
J. H. & Mary Gillespie
Jun 26, 1884
May 11, 1896

Fannie May Whitehead
Apr 20, 1881
Sep 5, 1910

James Akin Gillespie
Jan 29, 1887
Jan 1, 1962

H. N. "Jack" Gillespie
Jul 7, 1878
Oct 14, 1968

William H. Gillespie
Mar 3, 1889
Sep 26, 1964

James R. Thompson
1851-1937
&
Nannie E. Thompson
1852-1924

Mag Gilliam
1869-1901

John Gilliam
1866-1936

Catherine Gilliam
1865-1928

Hardin T. Gillespie
Oct 28, 1914

&
Dorothy W. Gillespie
Mar 14, 1919
May 16, 1975

VERONA

John H. Gillespie
Tennessee
PHM 3 USNR, W. W. II
Sep 12, 1912
Oct 28, 1952

Ida Mai, wife of
J. H. Gillespie, Jr.
May 17, 1891
Apr 10, 1923

J. Henry Gillespie
Mar 27, 1876
May 19, 1950

Nannie Liggett Patton
Sep 17, 1873
Jul 23, 1902

Lula Lee Mayberry, wife of
D. T. Harris
May 5, 1864
Apr 16, 1902

Capt. Max Hardison
Sep 14, 1888
Oct 11, 1976
&
Pallen M. Hardison
Oct 23, 1891
Aug 29, 1967
"DAR Marker"

William H. McLean
1890-1954
&
Eleanor G. McLean
1891-

M. Gentry McLean
Jul 20, 1856
Jun 14, 1942
&
Cora M. McLean
Jun 30, 1868
Apr 14, 1943

Emma Lucile, dau of
M. G. & Cora S. McLean
Mar 21, 1894
Aug 11, 1902

Sam Gentry, son of
M. G. & Cora S. McLean
Dec 23, 1895
Jun 25, 1897

Father
W. M. McLean
Aug 27, 1811
Jun 29, 1890

Mother
S. C. McLean
Jan 25, 1825
Dec 24, 1909

J. B. R.(Rutledge)
May 1858
May 7, 1881
(fieldstone)

James L. Galloway
1861-1929
&
Inez M. Galloway
1867-1965

Charles Earl Galloway
Feb 11, 1903
May 20, 1970

Cornelia Aline Galloway
1893-1942

Susie R. Dark
1862-1936

Mother
Mary J. Dark
Aug 17, 1839
Feb 10, 1912

Harris B. C. Dark
1864-1939
&
Zilphia M. Dark
1868-1960

Mamie Elizabeth Crigger
May 19, 1923
May 22, 1923

J. Thad Crigger
Tennessee
Pvt HQ Co 326 Inf, W. W. I
Sep 8, 1891
May 1, 1960
&
Mother
Bessie C. Crigger
Jun 23, 1901

Luster Cheek
1916-1945

Robert L. Cheek
Jul 19, 1925
Oct 15, 1926

R. L. "Bob" Cheek
1895-1971
&
Johnie S. Cheek
1894-
Mrd- Jul 25, 1950

Ewing Dye
Nov 29, 1902
Jun 11, 1975
&
Ruth Dye
Feb 24, 1906

W. Henry Green
1875-1911
&
Maggie H. Green
1875-1934

1st grave,
A Slave (no dates)

Robert Cawthron
1908-1959

William Please Cawthron
1866-1948

Jesse E. Crawford
1878-1951
&
Susie Crawford
1897-

Eddie Vance Crawford
Jun 21, 1955
Jul 5, 1955

Aner Moser
Jul 26, 1874
Jul 7, 1910

Martha A. Clinton
Aug 29, 1832
Jan 1, 1904

Alex N. Crawford
Feb 2, 1834
Jan 28, 1918
"Confederate Soldier"
&
Martha Ann Crawford
Feb 27, 1854
Dec 29, 1912

J. W. Rutledge
Jul 20, 1868
Nov 14, 1907

Nancy E. Rutledge
Feb 28, 1838
Oct 11, 1915

W. J. Rutledge
Jan 18, 1837
Nov 23, 1911

J. G. Aldridge
Jan 15, 1846
Oct 3, 1891
&
Perlina L. Shires Aldridge
Nov 29, 1847
Feb 26, 1926

Infant Dau of
Mr. & Mrs. Willie Beasley
Feb 15, 1929

Robert T. Tindell
Nov 30, 1869
Aug 20, 1915
&
Marilda A. Tindell
Oct 20, 1871
Jan 11, 1965

Paul Porter
Dec 10, 1887
Jul 19, 1896

Rose, dau of
Milton & Lucy Powell
Jan 29, 1897
Sep 10, 1897

Pearl Lunn Galloway
1887-1963

Thomas, son of
W. F. & Lettie Keltner
Aug 10, 1884
Feb 30, 1901

Minnie Lee Hinkle
Jan 13, 1873
Apr 26, 1955

A. C. Hinkle
Sep 4, 1867
Oct 8, 1943

John Hinkle
Nov 4, 1904
Apr 4, 1974

Lottie Andrews Tindell
Jan 12, 1911
Dec 1, 1955

James D. Andrews
1861-1925
&
Hortie E. Andrews
1875-1947

Lou Vergie, wife of
J. D. Andrews
Dec 5, 1864
Jun 10, 1901

W. A. Jackson
1834-1923

Ruth P. Lunn
Aug 29, 1889
Dec 21, 1967

Ethel Lunn Templeton
1883-1963

Charles L. Aldridge
Mar 24, 1883-Oct 2, 1963
&
Vashti V. Aldridge
Dec 13, 1890-May 9, 1965

VERONA

James L. Aldridge
Mar 10, 1888
Nov 26, 1961
&
Susie Lee Aldridge
Nov 2, 1891
Jan 2, 1961

William Richard Aldridge
1878-1937
&
Lee Ida Harris Aldridge
1873-(no date)

Ralph Dewey, son of
F. P. & M. T. Martin
July 21, 1899
        1900

S. Jack Hardison
1867-1946

Nannie, wife of
J. S. Hardison
Oct 7, 1872
Apr 27, 1899

Mary Jane Aldridge
Dec 22, 1842
Apr 30, 1912

Richard Aldridge
Nov 3, 1842
Sep 28, 1897

Samuel R., son of
R. & M. Aldridge
Oct 15, 1880
May 21, 1898

George O. Aldridge
Feb 27, 1870
Jul 23, 1940

Sallie, wife of
G. O. Aldridge
May 31, 1871
May 4, 1935

J. R. Shires
Feb 9, 1850
Mar 26, 1919

M. E. Shires
Jun 29, 1859
Mar 2, 1934

Solomon Oscar Shires
Mar 15, 1887
Jul 19, 1929

Minnie Mai, wife of
S. O. Shires
Jun 5, 1887
Dec 26, 1909

Daisy Trible, wife of
N. B. Shires
Jun 3, 1883
Mar 7, 1910

Loma Lee Shires
Aug 28, 1896
Jul 22, 1921

Ola B., dau of
W. H. & L. E. Duggan
Sep 4, 1905
Oct 25, 1905

W. H. Duggan
May 1, 1861
Oct 30, 1930
&
Elizabeth Brown Duggan
Feb 7, 1878
Oct 29, 1920

Ernest P. Stewart
1906-1952

Ela N. Beard
1906-1933

Father
H. T. Daniel
Feb 11, 1834
Mar 26, 1903

Mother
M. M. Daniel
Sep 14, 1834
Aug 21, 1914

Flora May Jordan
1910

W. H. A. George
Mar 11, 1871
May 30, 1905

George D. Tatum
1855-1904
&
Mattie E. Tatum
1875-1944

Thomas R. Lawrence
Jun 21, 1878
May 29, 1939
&
Ida M. Lawrence
Jan 14, 1881
Dec 21, 1951

W. J. Hardison
Aug 20, 1842
May 7, 1904

Lou Neil Hardison
May 1, 1843
Sep 19, 1918

James J. Spain
1875-1941

Jennie L. Spain
1874-1925

Joe Dark
Apr 11, 1891
May 19, 1961

Father
James Dark
Feb 19, 1848
Mar 8, 1919
&
Mother
Sallie P. Dark
Jul 31, 1850
Aug 14, 1919

Wilson T. Dark
Feb 22, 1870
Sep 4, 1905

Steve Dark
Sep 28, 1874
Apr 19, 1903

Lee Andrew Maupin
Apr 10, 1888
Jul 5, 1954
&
Mary Emma M. Maupin
Sep 15, 1901
Mar 15, 1979

Sarah Margaret Lunn

Ada T. Lunn
Sep 9, 1885
Jan 22, 1977

Justin Lunn
mrd to Ada McKnight
Sep 30, 1915
Born Sep 2, 1885
Died Oct 12, 1918

Wilburn T. Tindell, Jr.
Jun 6, 1923
Aug 19, 1975
&
Frances M. Tindell
Jun 21, 1930

Wilburn T. Tindell
Apr 17, 1878
Mar 16, 1955
&
Annie Mai Tindell
Oct 23, 1882
Jun 24, 1923

John R. Lunn
Oct 20, 1845
Mar 18, 1918

Sallie E., wife of
J. R. Lunn
Feb 5, 1861
Jul 21, 1906

E. G. Lunn
Dec 1, 1879
Sep 17, 1903

Walter Hardison
Jul 30, 1903
Jan 23, 1941

Benjamin T. Hardison
Alabama
Pvt Gen Hosp 6, W. W. I
March 6, 1894
Dec 15, 1946

Lillie L. Hardison, dau of
T. J. & U. D. Tindell
Nov 16, 1871
Oct 10, 1903

Thomas J. Tindell
May 2, 1845
Apr 16, 1932
&
Vannie Cheek Tindell
Oct 7, 1852
Dec 28, 1935

George W. Tindell
May 4, 1869
Apr 30, 1933
&
Lula Liggett Tindell
Dec 25, 1873
Mar 28, 1948

Thomas Julian Liggett
1905-1971
& wife
Ruth McCarley Liggett
1906-1970

Infant Son of
Mr. & Mrs. T. J. Liggett
1934

Thomas Chesley Liggett
1871-1937
&
Annie Tindell Liggett
1867-1953

Robert H. Liggett
Jun 7, 1899
Jul 25, 1952

R. W. Montgomery
Jan 25, 1851
Jul 24, 1933

Laura J. Montgomery
Mar 3, 1866
Jun 9, 1935

George Wendell Martin
Sep 2, 1924
Feb 9, 1925

Minnie Laura, wife of
Henry Martin
Apr 2, 1899-Aug 6, 1945

VERONA

Father
L. A. "Bob" Gillespie
Jan 17, 1892
Sep 26, 1936
&
Mother
Lillian Gray Gillespie
Jun 20, 1893

Billy, son of
Bub & Clara Gillespie
1937-1938

J. Harvey Patterson
1884-1938
&
Myra Ada Patterson
1887-1950

Baby Holton
 1947

Dave Dark
1881-1932

Ura Dark Martin
1893-1966

H. Grady Harris
Jul 16, 1891
Jul 31, 1965
&
Beula A. Harris
Apr 27, 1893
Apr 2, 1978

Well Kept
───────

Natt B. Shires
Jul 12, 1874
Aug 21, 1952

Carlyle Shires
1925-1926

G. W. Rutledge
186_-1940
&
Bettie Rutledge
1860-(no date)

Wesley Gregg
Jan 19, 1899
Jun 8, 1968
&
Mary Loue Gregg
Jun 1, 1892
Jan 8, 1968

Robert S. Cole, Jr.
May 21, 1941
Sep 21, 1971

James D. Endsley
1927-1975
&
Annie C. Endsley
1929-

Cathy Ann Jett
   Aug 1, 1960

George A. Yarbrough
May 14, 1877
Jul 31, 1950
&
N. Clara Yarbrough
Feb 16, 1885
Dec 30, 1952

Mollie Hardison
1869-1944
&
Veva Hardison
1873-1967

John C. Cheek
Apr 5, 1873
Apr 23, 1956
&
Fannie B. Hendrix Cheek
Mar 22, 1880
Apr 4, 1970

Thomas Bascom Hendrix
Jul 14, 1888
Jan 7, 1957
&
Anna Lou A. Hendrix
Feb 16, 1889
Mar 16, 1970

Thomas Mead Hendrix
1850-1947
&
Catherine Tribble Hendrix
1859-1939

END OF BETHLEHEM

Henry Crawford Hendrix
1878-1959

Lee Liggett
1866-1941
&
Genevra Liggett
1867-1951

Wilburn Oslin Cheek
Dec 13, 1911
May 29, 1963
&
Marjorie Aldridge Cheek
May 28, 1911

Mrd- Sep 23, 1937

Joe Pleasant Lunn
Feb 2, 1894
Sep 13, 1965
&
Lila Harwell Lunn
Jan 27, 1893

Charlie F. Ervin
Nov 11, 1897
May 30, 1971
&
Annie Mae Ervin
Feb 2, 1904

Oslin G. Cheek
W. W. I Soldier
Aug 26, 1895
Nov 10, 1967
&
Vannie Tindell Cheek
Mar 25, 1899
----

* *

END OF VERONA QUADRANGLE

FARMINGTON QUADRANGLE

RAINEY CEMETERY

Located east of Caney Spring, Tennessee, on the old River Road. Copied by Ralph D. Whitesell.

Isaac Rainey 1763-1836 "Revolutionary Soldier" and his wife, Sarah Malone Rainey 1765-1843 "Erected by descendants in 1955"	Thomas Lea Wells, husband of Mary Rainey, (died before 1840) (no marker)	Graves of 2 children of Thomas L. Wells and Mary Rainey Wells. (no marker)	Isaac Nelson Rainey, son of Isaac & Sarah M. Rainey Born 1810 & Died 1841 (no marker) 2 or 3 slave graves of the Rainey family.

This Cemetery was destroyed and plowed over in the early 1900's and restored 1955 by Mrs. W. H. Alford (Jane Wallace) and Ralph D. Whitesell.

* *

CARLTON-CLAXTON CEMETERY

Located one mile north west of Mt. Lebanon Church. Copied by Buck Claxton of Shelbyville, TN, 1979.

Cynthia A., wife of
James J. Claxton
Dec 31, 1839
Aug 22, 1880

Baby Claxton
Aug 18, 1880

Other graves, unmarked.

* *

WHITE CEMETERY

Located two and one-half miles south east of Chapel Hill, at the Bedford County line. Copied by Franklin Blanton, 1979.

B. F. White
Jan 19, 1829
Jan 17, 1894

Mary J. Wife of
B. F. White
Mar 13, 1842
Sep 8, 1913

* *

WHITE CEMETERY

Located south east of Chapel Hill, near the Bedford County line, on Wilson Creek. Copied by Franklin Blanton, 1979.

Joshua White 1785-186_ (6) Mary Holt White 1796-186_ (6) John H. White Jul 10, 1830 Aug 24, 1908 William Perry White Aug 28, 1827 Aug 26, 1848	Kittie, wife of B. F. White Feb 6, 1832 Jun 3, 1865 Fannie E. Brown Dec 1, 1873 Jun 27, 1919 Our Mother Nancie Matilda Covington Dec 10, 1855 Feb 7, 1894	Charles L. Marshall Dec 10, 1862 Jan 24, 1896 America White Marshall Jul 25, 1824 Oct 1, 1894 Elizabeth W., wife of S. B. Arnold Aug 4, 1861 Jan 24, 1912	Mary L. White Oct 4, 1832 Jun 27, 1890 Rev. Joshua White Mar 20, 1858 Mar 30, 1891 James B. Cooper Dec 11, 1858 Jan 8, 1949 & Charlottie W. Cooper Dec 16, 1869 Oct 21, 1948

* *

FARMINGTON

TOWNSEND CEMETERY

Located two miles south east of Chapel Hill, near Wilson Creek. Copied by Franklin Blanton, Shelbyville, TN, 1979.

Father
In Memory of
Thomas Townsend
Born in Lunenburg Co., Va., moved to Marshall Co., Tenn. in 1849, Died Mar 11, 1855.

Mother
In Memory of
Susan J. Townsend
Consort of R. W. Townsend
and dau of J. K. & S. C. Poindexter
Aug 14, 1838
Feb 26, 1857

In Memory of
Infant Daughter of
T. P. & A. E. Townsend
Born & Died Aug 22, 1855.

* *

MARLIN CEMETERY

Located two miles east of Chapel Hill, near Bedford County line. Copied by Franklin Blanton, 1979.

Abner H. Marlin
Jan 1, 1809
Jan 6, 1886
Age 77 yrs & 6 days

Nancy K. Marlin
Jan 6, 1822
Aug 1, 1903

* *

WALL CEMETERY

Located two miles east of Chapel Hill, near Bedford County line. Copied by Franklin Blanton, 1979.

Sacred to the Memory of
Nancy J. Wall, dau of
Hugh & Jane Wall
July 1819
Age 3 mos & 16 days.

* *

WILSON CEMETERY

Located south on Highway 31-A to Chapel Hill, turn east at Chapel Hill Post Office, go until cross over narrow bridge over Spring Creek, turn south and go to first gate, large white house. Cemetery is about 100 yards to left of house. NOTE: This land was formerly owned by Aaron Wilson, the land is NOT a Military Grant to Aaron Wilson.

In Memory of Moses Wilson
Born July 1769
Died July 18, 1850
"A bachelor and 11th son of R. & E. Wilson of N.C."

Infant Daughter of
J. M. & C. M. Wilson
(no dates)

In Memory of
Susannah Neese, who died as she lived in quietude Oct 24, 1852. Age 69 yrs.
"Who clung in faith for consolation to her children".

Jas. M. Wilson
Jun 21, 1821
Apr 11, 1862
Age 41 yrs, 9 mos, 29 days.

Charity Malinda Neese,
wife of James Miller Wilson
Jun 23, 1819
Dec 29, 1903
on reverse side of same stone:
Mother of Mrs. James B. Ezell
Grandmother of
Mrs K. F. Dazey
Mrs. Jas. W. Blackmore
Mrs. G. O. Rone
Mrs. C. Howard Miller
J. Ewing Ezell
Mrs. J. M. Lynn
Sallie Fulton Ezell

Elizabeth P. Neese
Feb 14, 1825
Jun 15, 1908

"Cleo"
Cleopatra Texanna, wife of
Jas. B. Ezell
Dec 13, 1844
Oct 19, 1882

James B. Ezell
Jul 15, 1841
Mar 19, 1888

Alice McCord, wife of
James Balaam Ezell
Jan 18, 1861
Feb 7, 1934

Sallie Fulton, dau of
Jas. B. & C. T. Ezell
Jun 26, 1880
Sep 2, 1895

Frances J. Niece
Nov 19, 1822
Mar 22, 1879
"Member of C. P. Church, 40 years".

Joel B. Low
Jan 28, 1803
Oct 29, 1888

Anna E., dau of
T. M. & S. M. Graves
Died Dec 24, 1882
Aged 23 yrs, 3 mos, 14 days

Sallie Giles, Relict of
Cowden McCord
Jul 6, 1814
Jun 7, 1888

FARMINGTON

Genl. Ewing Anderson Wilson
May 10, 1818
Apr 18, 1883
"He was an Elder in the C.P. Church for 40 years. Twice member of the Legislature of Tenn., and twice of the Senate. A Noble man, a true patriot and a conscientious Christian."

Sallie R., wife of
Rev. T. B. Fisher
Aug 31, 1847
May 20, 1889

Brother
Willie Roberts Allison
Oct 29, 1888
Jul 31, 1903

John D. Roberts
Mar 27, 1824
Jan 6, 1884

Susannah M., wife of
Jno. D. Roberts
Jan 4, 1823
Apr 7, 1899

In Memory of Dear Husband,
William A. Roberts
Feb 15, 1850
Sep 21, 1887
"He leaves a wife and little girl to mourn his loss."

M. Ella, wife of
N(H). S. Allison
Jul 16, 1856
Jul 18, 1884
Aged 28 yrs & 2 days

H. S. Allison
Oct 7, 1860
May 12, 1896

Maggie N., wife of
H. S. Allison
Feb 20, 1863
Aug 19, 1895

Maria Jane, wife of
James A. Wilson
Born July 1830
Died Jun 19, 1876

Samuel Leander, son of
Jas. A. & M. J. Wilson
Aug 21, 1850
Jul 3, 1875

J. L., husband of
Mary A. Conley
Feb 24, 1836
Nov 6, 1876

William A. Fleming
Who was born August the 25th 1798 & departed this life Dec 21, 1850.

Aaron Wilson thought to be buried here.
(no marker)

* *

HARRIS CEMETERY
Located Henry Horton Park and near Clay Hill. Copied 1978 by Franklin Blanton.

Robert A. Copeland
Dec 23, 1879
Feb 22, 1901

Mrs. M. J. Bond
Jun 16, 1840
Sep 6, 1899

Ida Belle, Infant of
J. M. & A. E. Harris
Aug 31, 1875
Sep 12, 1875

Hiram Harris
Oct 20, 1806
Oct 10, 1889

Jane P. Harris
Jul 3, 1807
Apr 29, 1892
Age 84 yrs, 9 mos, 26 days

Sarah M. Harris
Mar 9, 1806
Feb 15, 1856

Catherine B. Harris
1824-1913

Watson R. Harris
1858-1874

Mary J. Harris
1860-1887

Mary Elma Harris
Jul 22, 1883
Dec 2, 1887

Elvira Elizabeth Frank
Jun 24, 1838
Jun 6, 1878

Morris Frank
(no dates)

Sophia Jane Frank
(no dates)

Joe Frank
(no dates)

Willis A. Frank
(no dates)

* *

ELLIOTT CEMETERY
Located one and one-half miles west of Highway No. 31-A, just off new Columbia Road No. 99, at the Railroad. Copied August 1978 by Franklin Blanton.

Charlie J. Dalton
Sep 10, 1909

&
Margaret C. Dalton
May 15, 1915
Jan 30, 1973

Willis Owen Dalton
1900-1972
&
Lottie Hazel Dalton
1908-

Jerry M. Dalton
April 14, 1957

Bobby Joe Dalton
Jan 21, 1936-Feb 10, 1956

Virgal Lee Dalton
Jan 29, 1872
Oct 17, 1948
&
Maggie V. Dalton
Jun 4, 1881
Mar 31, 1957

John W. Dalton
1866-1918
&
Susie E. Dalton
1878-1946

Elmer Dolton
1888-1955 (TM)

Mrs. Pearl Dalton
1890-1964 (TM)

Jessie D. Dalton
1920-1964 (TM)

Jesse N. Dalton
1892-1964 (TM)

Gordie Lee Dolton
1890-1944

Mrs. Annie D. Dolton
1901-1956

Zelma Mae Ball
Sep 28, 1915
Nov 1, 1970

George Calhoun
Born Dec 1774
Died Jul 7, 1848
Age 73 yrs & 7 mos.

Mary A. M. Calhoun
Aug 27, 1879
Mar 21, 1940
Age 60 yrs & 7 mos.

Ada E. Walker
1902-19
&
Sam Lee Walker, Jr.
1923-1940
&
Sam Lee Walker
1892-1944

FARMINGTON

Infant of
R. W. & L. L. Ball
Aug 20, 1892
Jun 18, 1894

R. W. Ball
1868-1950
&
Lillie Lee Ball
1868-1937

Robert Eldridge Ball
Oct 12, 1899
Jun 13, 1920

Sam W. Ball
1894-1958
&
Mary B. Ball
1895-1946

Eva Ball
1927-1937

Allen B. Thomas
1856-1937

Mary S. Thomas
Aug 17, 1848
Jun 21, 1925

J. R. Thomas
Aug 26, 1861
May 31, 1911

Martha J. Thomas
Nov 11, 1862
Jun 28, 1918

H. C. Howell
1892-1967

J. C. Howell
Sep 23, 1892
Dec 26, 1918
(picture)

Cecil Garrett Neathery
Feb 29, 1904
Jul 11, 1905

Thomas J. Neathery
Feb 25, 1863
Jan 2, 1935
&
Fannie B. Neathery
Jul 6, 1881
Dec 1, 1957

Robert L. Neathery
1915-1978
&
Ruth A. Neathery
1909-1970

Elizabeth J., wife of
E. L. Thomas
Dec 15, 1826
Sep 22, 1902

M. E. Thomas
Mar 10, 1863
Mar 4, 1896
Age 32 yrs, 11 mos, 24 days.

Mrs. M. A., wife of
J. N. Dalton
Aug 26, 1851
May 2, 1901

Dora Howell Finley
Jan 19, 1882
Jun 21, 1963

E. L. Thomas
Sep 10, 1821
Mar 27, 1890

Mary J., wife of
J. P. Thomas
Nov 24, 1854
Feb 15, 1885

Infant Son of
J. P. & M. J. Thomas
Feb 1, 1885

R. F. "Bob" Thomas
Jan 15, 1869
Mar 23, 1952
&
Annie Lou Thomas
Jan 5, 1882
Dec 19, 1952

William Pierce Thomas
1826-1916

W. R. Taylor
Jul 7, 1838
Jan 31, 1918
&
Ava E. Taylor
Mar 25, 1840
Jul 2, 1925

John T. Taylor
1870-1937
&
Mary E. Taylor
1879-1966

W. P. Ball
1904-
&
Nora Bell Ball
1904-

John M. Thomas
Mar 25, 1891
Jun 21, 1960
&
Mattie P. Thomas
Sep 27, 1902

John Morgan Thomas
Tennessee
Pvt Co F 165 Inf 42 Div
Mar 25, 1891
Jun 21, 1960

Infant Son of
J. C. & E. C. Greer
July 23, 1934

Effie M. Elliott, wife of
W. B. Garrett
Feb 18, 1885
Jan 15, 1906

William Boyd Garrett
1877-1950
&
Maude E. Garrett
1883-1968

Charles H. Tomlinson
Jul 4, 1903
Feb 23, 1969
&
Vera H. Tomlinson
Aug 27, 1910

Mrs. Lucy Thomas
Dec 23, 1798
Aug 6, 1891
Age 93 yrs, 7 mos, 13 days.
"She was a member of M. E. Church, 71 yrs."

Azartah Adcock
1869-1933
&
Iva Ann Adcock
1876-1958

Little Billie Wade Griffin, Jr.
Jun 17, 1974
Dec 16, 1974

Agnes C. Griffin
1902-1971

Charlie E. Griffin
1882-1967

Lula V. Griffin
1886-19

Grandmother Griffin
1845-1920

John P. Elliott
Mar 8, 1851
Oct 31, 1920

Mecca A., wife of
J. P. Elliott
Dec 7, 1851
Jan 30, 1906

W. G. Leonard
May 28, 1855
Mar 24, 1928

Sallie B., wife of
W. G. Leonard
Feb 20, 1863
May 16, 1910

Earnest M. Wortham
Dec 10, 1892
Nov 7, 1917

Clint Wortham
1907-1971 (TM)

Mattie Smithson
May 18, 1891
Jan 26, 1922

Mary Ann Haynes
Aug 16, 1948
Jan 8, 1950

W. A. Holder
Aug 3, 1856
Jul 24, 1912

Lillis Holder Gentry
Dec 29, 1863
Jan 24, 1947

Fate C. Holder
Nov 30, 1895
Dec 10, 1965
Tennessee
Pvt Co C 149 Inf 39 Div
&
Mattie R. Holder
Jan 20, 1905

Oscar L. Holder
Nov 14, 1884
Jan 12, 1970
&
Jennie P. Holder
Jul 15, 1896
Apr 26, 1956

William M. Holder
Tennessee
Pfc. Co L 15 Inf
W. W. II, Korea
Sep 7, 1926
Mar 19, 1970

END OF ELLIOTT

* *

FARMINGTON

SWANSON CEMETERY

Located a short distance south of Chapel Hill, just east of U.S. Highway No. 31-A. The cemetery was originally used by the Patterson family as a family burial ground. Copied August 10, 1969 by Ralph D. Whitesell and re-checked and up-dated July 9, 1978 by Helen and Tim Marsh.

David Jones
Dec 1967
5 months (TM)

Donnie Lee Jones
(TM, marker now gone, 1978)

Unable to read (TM)
(TM now gone, 1978)

Lucindie Mooningham
1847-1932

Estella Mooningham
1897-1967 (TM)
(TM now gone, 1978)

H. Edward Jones
1905-1949

Nettie Carter, wife of
J. M. Jones
Jul 24, 1881
Jul 31, 1907

Henry E. Jones
1868-1904
&
Sallie P. Jones
1869-1942

Edward Powell Jones
Nov 22, 1894
Aug 6, 1912

Milton T. Powell
Dec 1, 1826
Nov 25, 1918
&
Mary G. Powell
Feb 27, 1839
Feb 2, 1915

James M. Patterson
Apr 8, 1820
Dec 27, 1877

Father
Edward Swanson
Oct 8, 1828
Jun 11, 1881
&
Mother
Sallie J. Swanson
Jun 6, 1843
May 31, 1922

Eliza D. Putmon
Mar 26, 1815
Mar 7, 1905

Susie Carter
Sep 20, 1878
Oct 10, 1879

Charles Lewis Carter
Jun 22, 1844
Dec 20, 1883

G. W. Campbell
Jan 6, 1846
May 21, 1910
&
Manerva Bruce Campbell
Dec   1845
(no date)

Charles A. Rogers
Jun 1, 1846
Mar 4, 1888

Charles H. Lavender
Jun 7, 1810
Mar 8, 1892
&
Nancy J. Lavender
May 7, 1838
Jul 13, 1898

W. L. Daughrity
Jul 4, 1843
Oct 10, 1917
&
Mary J. Daughrity
Jan 1, 1849
(no date)

Cleveland H., son of
W. H. & Bettie Bell
Jul 9, 1891
Sep 30, 1893

Mrs. J. H. Bruce
1852-1939

J. H. Bruce
1841-1933

Thomas H. Bell
Feb 27, 1818
Feb 11, 1891
&
Elizabeth J. Bell
Apr 26, 1834
Aug 19, 1920

Alice G. Bell, wife of
S. D. Pickle
Jul 24, 1864
Dec 3, 1887
Age 23 yrs, 1 mo, 10 days

Cordie Bell, dau of
C. W. & M. P. Campbell
May 8, 1874
Nov 17, 1881

J. H. Gault
1866-1956
& wife
Lula C. Campbell Gault
1871-1929

Susan Jane Mullikin
Aug 29, 1826
Mar 2, 1894

Warren Mullikin
Sep 16, 1821
Jan 16, 1860

John Houston Millikin
Mar 10, 1847
Jan 7, 1907

Andrew Patterson
Mar 25, 1770
May 7, 1849

Jane Patterson
Jul 17, 1782
Aug 23, 1868

Prudence Patterson
Oct 18, 1797-
Aug 28, 1856

Mary P. Patterson
Jan 24, 1812
Aug 14, 1855

Bobby L. Young
Frank Young, Jr.
1931
1 day

John Eron Rucker
Jun 18, 1891
Apr 26, 1931
&
Mary Jane Rucker
May 1, 1896
Jul 6, 1932

Alice C., wife of
J. W. Rucker
Sep 19, 1868
Feb 22, 1920

Robert W., son of
Robert & Betsey Ramsey
Dec 25, 1820
Sep 9, 1845
Age 24 yrs, 8 mos, 15 days
"A Son & Brother"

In Memory of
Betsey Ramsey
Who was born Oct 12, 1795
Died Oct 3, 1844
Age 18 yrs, 11 mos, 21 days
"The Dec'd was a dau of
Zacheus Wilson & wife of
Robert Ramsey, a companion
& Mother kind and affect-
ionate"

R. S. (Robert Ramsey)
(fieldstone, no dates)

Robert Patterson
Died Jan 30, 1854
Age 86 years

Elizabeth Patterson
Died Mar 31, 1816
Age 44

In Memory of
James Bruce
Who was born in the year
of 1768 and departed this
life March 1, 1822

Sacred to the Memory of
Lucy C. Bruce
Who was born in the year
1769, departed this life
Oct the 9, 1834.

In Memory of Mary Bruce
Who was born 29th day of
May, 1830 and departed
this life on the 13th
day of Sept 1832

In Memory of John Bruce
Born June 20, 1805 and
departed this life May 24,
1853.

Sacred to the Memory of
Elizabeth, wife of
John P. Bruce
May 26, 1808
Jun 28, 1873

Livona, dau of
J. P. & Elizabeth Bruce
Nov 3, 1849
Nov 1, 1858

John T., son of
W. W. & Lucy G. Vest
(dates illegible)

FARMINGTON

Tennie, wife of
A. J. Huey, dau of
W. W. & Lucy G. Vest
Sep 30, 1852
Jun 3, 1893

Nancy A., wife of
W. M. Redman, dau of
W. W. & Lucy G. Vest
Nov 24, 1856
Jun 28, 1898

Aron V., son of
F. G. & Ida Gray
Feb 23, 1892
Jul 27, 1893

Mary E., dau of
A. J. & Tennie Huey
Jan 29, 1893
Oct 18, 1893

W. W. Vest
Nov 11, 1829
Apr 26, 1910

Mary G., wife of
W. W. Vest
Nov 13, 1825
May 8, 1900

W. J. S. Huey
Aug 12, 1881
Aug 30, 1905

A. J. Hughey
Mar 18, 1837
Dec 1, 1910

Sam A. Huey
Sep 7, 1884
Mar 28, 1968

Albert E. Reynolds
Dec 22, 1876
Feb 24, 1913
&
Nancy Clatie, dau of
S. A. & Tennie Vest Huey
Nov 15, 1881
Jan 30, 1970

Beatrice Mai Wilson
Dec 4, 1907
Apr 21, 1924

Sacred to the Memory of
Mary Patterson
Born Oct the 11th, 1812
departed this life
Aug the 5, 1832

Samuel J. Blackwell
1864-1921
&
Carrie L. Blackwell
1870-1925

Addie Lee Gambill
1878-1961

Fannie B. Helton
1905-1976

Floyd Gerald Hazel
U. S. Navy, W. W. II
Dec 8, 1913
Feb 12, 1977

Marker:
This marker donated by
M'boro Monument Co.,
Murfreesboro, Tenn.
Unidentified man found on
Highway near Chapel Hill,
Tenn., Aug 26, 1948.

Joe Wilson
Co G 57th Pioneer Infantry
Sep 15, 1896
Oct 12, 1918

Susie E. Wilson
Nov 18, 1866
Dec 13, 1924
"Mother"

Lillian Ketchum
1902-1941

Sallie Sue Jones
1887-1943

Sarah Helen Matney
1925-1926

Lelia Blalock
1882-1960
&
Hattie L. Blalock
1883-1958

Margaret Blalock
Jun 20, 1918
Jul 28, 1918

Annie Blalock
Jan 19, 1909
Oct 17, 1918

Jessie T. Blalock
Jan 20, 1905
Oct 27, 1932

George A. Blalock
1906-1962

T. H. P. Morton
Feb 26, 1821
Aug 11, 1884

Angeline Morton
1828-1906

Thomas H. Morton, Jr.
Aug 10, 1869
Sep 17, 1887

Sarah Virginia, wife of
Rufe L. Neely
Mar 30, 1847-Mar 18, 1902

Lottie C. Laws
Mar 26, 1880
Aug 9, 1888

Martha E. Laws
Aug 23, 1848
Jun 25, 1921

John M. Laws
Apr 22, 1882
Nov 2, 1904

Lena R., wife of
W. F. Dozier
Sep 14, 1865
May 20, 1901

Ollie R. Dozier
Oct 3, 1894
Jan 6, 1895

Lena R. Dozier
Jan 7, 1897
Jan 7, 1897

Virginia Catherine Taylor
1853-1934

Annie Rivers Morton
Jan 11, 1889
Jul 1, 1903

Sam E. Morton
Oct 24, 1867
Jan 30, 1898

Sallie Alice Taylor
1878-1954

Dora Helton
1884-1940

Robert Owen Helton
1910-1942

Guilford C. Laws
Apr 24, 1841
Jun 4, 1898

Charles T., son of
W. P. & A. J. Crutcher
Apr 22, 1894
May 5, 1894

Catherine P. Crutcher
Feb 23, 1822
May 16, 1894

S. A. Crutcher
Oct 14, 1818
Jun 13, 1900

Jennie Grigsby
Aug 24, 1867
Sep 29, 1948

G. H. Turner
Dec 8, 1836
Oct 21, 1923

Annie Elizabeth, wife of
G. H. Turner
May 6, 1846
Jun 3, 1894

In Memory of
Nathan Anderson Forrest
was born May 31st, 1821
and died Feb 28, 1847
"By Dillahunty Lodge
No. 112".

Father
D. L. White
Aug 2, 1857
Jun 9, 1922
&
Mother
Sallie G. White
Feb 19, 1856
Nov 18, 1932

Lawrence "Dot" Tomlin
1909-1956

James W. Clark
Aug 30, 1885
Jul 31, 1956
&
Cora Lee Clark
Apr 5, 1894
Mar 12, 1965

John Wesley Tomlin
1881-1941
&
Emma Jean Tomlin
1883-19

Henry Neese
1879-1919
&
Caldonia Neese
1882-1960

Luther W. Neese
1902-1919

Kathleen Mealer
Mar 25, 1924
Jul 15, 1924

Leslie H. Mealer
Mar 22, 1889
May 29, 1926
&
Jennie Perryman Mealer
Sep 3, 1901

Harriet W., Consort of
J. H. Freeman
Died Nov 13, 1855
Age 23 yrs & 1 mo.

FARMINGTON

W. P. Skinner
Oct 9, 1903
Sep 24, 1927

William Skinner
Dec 18, 1924
Apr 5, 1928

Frank M. Skinner
1901-1945
&
Willie P. Skinner
1903-19

J. Howard Mealer
Dec 10, 1923
Dec 12, 1954

John Less Mealer
Tennessee
F2 USNR W.W.II
Sep 3, 1926
Jan 26, 1963

Sally Hopkins Ball
1877-1953 (TM)

Mother
Martha J. Bowling
1875-1947

James E. Wortham
Aug 24, 1896

&
Maggie K. Wortham
Feb 28, 1896
Jan 19, 1952

William H., son of
J. D. & E. Vaden
Apr 15, 1867
Dec 10, 1869

A. W. Elder
Jan 13, 1840
Apr 28, 1902

Annie Matilda Elder
Oct 9, 1844
Jan 14, 1915

Husband
John L. Ramsey
Jan 30, 1838
Jul 5, 1921
& Wife
N. C. Ramsey
Sep 24, 1848
Feb 7, 1919

John Daughrity
1909-1967 (TM)

Joseph E. Loftin
May 5, 1842
Oct 22, 1897

Sallie, wife of
D. L. Johnson
Mar 1, 1856-Feb 21, 1915

Hartwell F. Miller
Nov 19, 1853
Feb 19, 1901

Ida Miller Clark
Dec 1, 1857
Aug 31, 1914

W. H. B., son of
J. E. & N. E. Crockett
Nov 4, 1845
Jul 3, 1871

J. E. Crockett
May 15, 1823
Jul 8, 1871

Nancy E. Crockett
Sep 24, 1820
Jul 14, 1904

John C. Anderson
Sep 21, 1892
Jan 12, 1953

John B. Anderson
1858-1942
&
Susan R. Anderson
1858-1917

James M. Ramsey
1835-1914

Sara L. Ramsey
1843-1888

William L. Ramsey
1862-1884

James D., son of
William & Lena J. Patterson
Nov 28, 1876
Jan 14, 1877

David F. Patterson
Aug 27, 1841
Aug 30, 1926
&
Martha C. Patterson
Mar 2, 1846
Nov 22, 1895

H. H. Estes
Feb 27, 1842
Oct 2, 1918

Martha Chriesman, wife of
H. H. Estes
Born Feb 27, 1844
Mrd- Jan 7, 1869
Died May 16, 1904

Mrs. Mira W., wife of
Dr. J. H. Robinson
Apr 11, 1813
Feb 28, 1887

Dr. John H. Robinson
Jun --, 1800
Sep 4, 1874

Mrs. Ella, wife of
A. B. Robinson
Nov 22, 1860
Apr 3, 1883

Dr. John R. Rickman
Mar 29, 1876
Oct 18, 1916

Mary Rickman Bailey
Jan 10, 1887
Dec 1, 1976

J. Smiley Jones
1892-1948

E. D. Jones
Sep 21, 1841
Mar 24, 1909

Mary A., wife of
E. D. Jones
Dec 14, 1852
Nov 22, 1901

Jane R. Garrett
Jul 12, 1828
May 16, 1888

Aaron R. Ball
Mar 15, 1881

&
Nora L. Ball
Dec 16, 1877
Feb 26, 1932

J. F. Logue
Apr 24, 1854
Apr 13, 1937
&
Roxie Logue
Mar 5, 1857
May 16, 1938

Robert C. Logue
Jan 8, 1859
Nov 21, 1917

John A. Eakin
1854-1931
&
Sarah Little Eakin
1859-1904

Mary Jane, wife of
J. M. Taylor
Oct 5, 1833
Dec 8, 1905

Henry Nowlin Clay
May 22, 1856
Feb 26, 1918
&
Eugenia Clay
May 4, 1861
Dec 8, 1929

Annie Lizzie Clay
Jan 23, 1901
May 5, 1919

Mollie Clay
1891-1938

Henry P. Clay
Sep 15, 1887
Mar 27, 1966
&
Addie A. Clay
Sep --, 1896

Daughter
Benita Sue Holdman
1960-1960

Jennie M. Simmons
1915-1969 (TM)

Robert F. Black
1898-1965 (TM)

Maggie Clark
1875-1923 (TM)

L. M. Shaw
1872-1922 (TM)

Father
Nicholas J. Shaw
May 14, 1850
Jun 8, 1904
&
Mother
Mary J. Shaw
Apr 14, 1856
Mar 16, 1900

Aubrey D. Shaw
1891-1892 (TM)

Annie P. Shaw
1882-1884 (TM)

John P. Ragsdale
1889-1969 (TM)

William A. Cochran, Jr.
Oct 3, 1961
Oct 3, 1961

Frank B. Young
1893-1960
&
Ada K. Young
1895-1967

Mrs. Addie Potts
1875-1968 (TM)

John R. Potts
1883-1956 (TM)

Genora Haynes Ramsey
1909-1931

Nannie Ellen Ramsey
1905-1924

Margaret Marshall Ramsey
Thomas
1880-1959

FARMINGTON

John McBride Ramsey
1875-1920

Lizzie R. Chapman
1874-1905

Ed S., son of
Frank H. & Jennie Swanson
                    Ezell
Oct 18, 1888
Sep 30, 1964

Sara B., dau of
Alfred Young & Pearl Ezell
                    Bailey
Feb 21, 1896

Joe E. Ezell
Feb 25, 1900

&
Rena H. Ezell
May 9, 1903
Oct 20, 1963

James P. Ezell
Tennessee
BN Sgt, Major U.S. Army
1892-Sep 26, 1932

F. H. Ezell
1862-1935

Jennie Swanson Ezell
1866-1935

Ernest Stephens Alford
May 13, 1888
Mar 23, 1959

Tom V. Sheffield
Oct 11, 1885

&
Myra B. Sheffield
May 15, 1889
Jul 13, 1963

W. E. "Billie" Sheffield
May 19, 1911
Mar 28, 1963
&
Mary Ervin Sheffield
Apr 14, 1909

William H. Bell
1858-1932
&
Bettie Taylor Bell
1859-1937

Allen Bruce Bell
Oct 16, 1901
Jul 27, 1963
&
Lena Adgent Bell
Jan 14, 1904

Edgar F. Patterson, Jr.
May 24, 1921
Feb 3, 1925

Edgar Ezell Patterson
Aug 21, 1897
May 20, 1967
&
Riggs Bell Patterson
Sep 25, 1897

Melvin R. Taylor
Aug 19, 1856
May 24, 1931
&
Tinie B. Taylor
Aug 3, 1866
Aug 24, 1933

Riley Harrison
Jul 17, 1875
Apr 19, 1957
&
Ella F. Harrison
Sep 26, 1876
Aug 12, 1953

R. Cecil Harrison
Jul 19, 1904
Aug 26, 1966
&
Bertie B. Harrison
Dec 30, 1911

Brenda Crafton
1956-1957

Mary E. Haynes
1914-1953 (TM)

Charles A. Haynes
Dec 12, 1956
Dec 14, 1956 (TM)

William B. Payne, Jr.
1953-1953 (TM)

Zada Estes
1871-1938
&
Lottie Estes
1880-1936

C. A. "Pete" Ramsey
1898-1968 (TM)

George W. Ramsey
1871-1947
  & Wife
Eliza Ramsey
1876-1928

P. Clyde Haynes
Jan 20, 1885
Jan 18, 1968
&
Zelma P. Haynes
Jul 3, 1904

Elizabeth, wife of
Rev. N. D. Crawford
Mar 1, 1846
Sep 10, 1904

Sister
Louise Oakley, dau of
George E. & Fannie W. Forbes
Sep 6, 1901
Sep 6, 1921

Father
George E. Forbes
May 31, 1869
Sep 17, 1922
&
Mother
Fannie W. Forbes
Nov 17, 1869
Jan 30, 1926

M. D., wife of
S. M. Giles
Jul 22, 1839
May 28, 1915
Age 75 yrs, 10 mos, 6 days

S. M. Giles
Mar 7, 1833
Dec 19, 1910
Age 77 yrs, 9 mos, 12 days

Myrtle Swain Giles
May 22, 1881
Mar 22, 1912

Aubrey Swain
1887-1956

Father
James M. Swain
Sep 7, 1856
Feb 12, 1928
&
Mother
Mary Lee Swain
Mar 16, 1864
Mar 30, 1940

James Cecil Swain
Feb 10, 1884
Dec 22, 1926

W. F. Dozier
1855-1929

G. E. Reeves
1861-1922
&
Vonie Reeves
1859-(no date)

Maud Edwards
Feb 26, 1890
Sep 17, 1923

Walter L. Edwards
1876-1928
&
Nannie J. Edwards
1885-1942

Robert H. Edwards
May 8, 1878
Apr 19, 1953

John B. Edwards
Jan 26, 1902
Oct 9, 1962
&
Charlie F. Edwards
Jan 29, 1904
May 13, 1966

Ted Griffy
Mar 2, 1956 (TM)

Lenard M. Leverette
Mar 11, 1931

&
Betty L. Leverette
Jan 20, 1939
Nov 16, 1958
&
Thomas R. Leverette
Feb 10, 1958
Nov 16, 1958

Marvin F. Watts
1901-1962 (TM)

Lundy M. Skinner
Apr 18, 1893
Nov 10, 1952
&
Vianna H. Skinner
Jul 31, 1893
Mar 2, 1963

William H. Burks
Oct 9, 1871
(no date)
&
Sadie P. Burks
Aug 12, 1878
Nov 6, 1926

Ruby, dau of
W. H. & Sadie Burks
Sep 9, 1899
Dec 29, 1918

Infant Son of
Mr. & Mrs. Ernest Ferguson
(no dates)

Annie Parks Ferguson
Jul 18, 1893
May 30, 1926

FARMINGTON

Ernest Ferguson
Mar 28, 1885
Jul 8, 1957

Sam L. Parks
Jul 21, 1891
Jul 15, 1915

J. R. Parks
Oct 16, 1854
Nov 11, 1932
&
Minnie Parks
Jun 27, 1865
Sep 26, 1939

Virginia McCord Giles
Jan 31, 1922
Jan 2, 1938

Clarence N. Giles
1882-1963
&
Cammie M. Giles
1885-

James W. Morton
Aug 1, 1888
Jun 15, 1965
"Son of Dr. J. W. Morton"

Lowranzy Dow Pugh
1874-1951

William T. Hurt
Mar 26, 1865
Sep 9, 1962

Mother
Etta Swanson Hurt
wife of W. T. Hurt
Feb 5, 1871
Mar 5, 1916

Thomas F. Hurt
Oct 11, 1895
May 28, 1942

Alfred Young Bailey, Sr.
Son of William & Ida Prewett
Bailey
Nov 7, 1871
Feb 18, 1943

Pearl Ezell Bailey, dau of
J. Britt & Sally Reynolds
Ezell
Feb 9, 1872
Sep 13, 1919

Will Ezell, son of
A. Y. & Pearl Ezell Bailey
Feb 28, 1907
Nov 7, 1916

Alfred Young, Jr., son of
A. Y. & Pearl Ezell Bailey
Jul 28, 1901
Mar 2, 1934

Edward Swanson Ezell, III
great grandson of
A. Y. & Pearl Ezell Bailey
Aug 16, 1939
Nov 11, 1940

Sam Prewett, son of
A. Y. & Pearl Ezell Bailey
Jan 13, 1894
Jan 8, 1947

Virginia C. Parks
1830-1918

Lelia Parks Green
1859-1931

Charles A. Hill
1884-1966
&
Addie L. Hill
1885-1955

Dr. John T. Ferguson
1875-1956
&
Martha C. Ferguson
1876-1963

Clifton J. Shaw
Tennessee
Pvt 3 Co Receiving Camp
W. W. I
Mar 30, 1889
Feb 21, 1961
&
Mary Ellen Shaw
Oct 3, 1899

Lawrence Lee Brown
1912-1959
&
Katherine Brown
1914-

Babe Ball
1871-1955
&
Climmie Ball
1877-1953

Henry Griggs
1904-1962
&
Annie Griggs
1904-

William T. Farlow
1891-1953
&
Ella Mai Farlow
1894-1959

William Ewing Eatherly
1892-1919 (TM)

Joseph Henry Thompson
Dec 21, 1877
Nov 28, 1922

William J. Thompson
Tennessee
Pvt Co H 17 Regt Tenn Inf
Confederate States Army
Oct 4, 1836
Sep 9, 1915

James Liggett
1920

Charlie Weaver
1894-1946
&
Ivie Weaver
1892-19

J. M. Jones
1873-1960
& wife
Mary Sue Dozier Jones
1883-1929

Infant Son of
Mr. & Mrs. B. L. Redmond
1933

J. Frank Rickman
Aug 17, 1878
Sep 22, 1954

Beth Rickman
Dec 1, 1914
Feb 8, 1918

Maggie B. Rickman
Nov 26, 1882
May 7, 1927

John W. McCrory
1873-1943

Wilson P. Fisher
1874-1950
&
Elsie Bigger Fisher
1878-1939

Joseph R. Bigger
1869-1921
&
Hettie H. Bigger
1874-1949

Clarence Edgar Logue
Tennessee
Cpl 323 Inf 81 Div
March 14, 1943

Billy Winn Marlin
Emma Jean Marlin
Jun 12, 1927
Aug 20-27, 1927

W. D. Cary
Indiana Noble Co
Apr 1, 1877
Jan 5, 1943

Catherine Cary
1887-1945

L. E. Winn
Oct 21, 1872
May 9, 1936

J. Orville Ezell
1883-1954

Kate H. Ezell
1884-

Otis L. Spencer
Sep 7, 1886
Apr 23, 1968
&
Lora T. Spencer
Jan 15, 1890

Charlie H. Logue
Apr 15, 1907
May 30, 1956

Thomas C. Slaughter
Nov 4, 1906
Jul 26, 1963
&
Mary L. Slaughter
Apr 12, 1897

Grady Lee Clark
Jul 7, 1908

&
Bridgett Clark
Jul 14, 1914
Jul 29, 1967

J. Ralston Scott
Jun 27, 1894
Aug 30, 1958
&
Myrtle R. Scott
Apr 18, 1894

Charles N. Watkins
May 19, 1923
Nov 4, 1968

Ayune W. Watkins
April 21, 1969

Joe Penn Watkins
Apr 16, 1891

Abner C. Marlin
Feb 14, 1882
Sep 18, 1958
&
Avo Winn Marlin
Dec 30, 1900

Walter Stammer
1889-1967
&
Reba Stammer
1891-1946

FARMINGTON

Walter C. Rogers
1884-1967
&
Maude W. Rogers
1887-1961

Grace Rogers Beisinger
1918-1941

Bethe Ezell Van Cleave
Nov 23, 1890
Dec 19, 1965

O. E. Van Cleave
Sep 13, 1886
Sep 27, 1956

John L. Garrett
1881-1959
&
Zula Walker Garrett
1884-1948

Dewey Gene Hargrove
Jan 16, 1934
Nov 29, 1951

Herbert R. Walls
Tennessee
Pfc 24 Medical BN, W.W.II
May 21, 1927
Dec 3, 1957

Tom Walls
1903-1951
&
Mattie Walls
1903-

Father
John C. Walls
Jul 10, 1881
Jan 24, 1951
&
Mother
Margaret R. Walls
Apr 8, 1876
Apr 14, 1962

J. T. Walls
Jul 5, 1905

&
Eula Mae Walls
Nov 12, 1904
Aug 6, 1967

Leon Teal
Oct 17, 1920

&
Zelma Lee Teal
Apr 16, 1923
Aug 6, 1966

James T. Calvert
Tennessee
Pfc Infantry, W. W. II
Mar 8, 1914
Apr 7, 1957

Edgar B. Calvert
Aug 27, 1885
Feb 10, 1967
&
Clarice Mae Calvert
Oct 7, 1907

Timothy E. Burrow
Aug 31, 1953

Kenneth Dwight Walls
1948-1948
&
John Thomas Walls
1949-1949
&
Freda Edwina Walls
1950-1951

Fred W. Walls
1924-1951
&
Marie P. Walls
1929-

Charlie A. Kincaid
Jul 17, 1890
May 25, 1966
&
Ora Haynes Kincaid
Apr 3, 1900

Alton A. Kincaid
Sep 24, 1924
May 4, 1949

Alfred F. Lane
Jun 24, 1898
Nov 6, 1956

Milton Thomas Powell
Nov 30, 1879
Mar 30, 1958
&
Aurora Ralston Powell
Feb 15, 1889

Sam R. Laws
1885-19
&
Berta E. Laws
1886-1956

W. Taft Reed
Aug 19, 1908

&
Lurlie P. Reed
Nov 16, 1911
May 20, 1968

William Reed
Dec 30, 1928
Feb 5, 1949

Father
Thomas Robert King
1890-1954
&
Mother
Daisy Hopper King
1894-1961

Samuel H. Brisby
1866-1958
&
Annie Lee Brisby
1878-1954

Samuel R. Brisby
1904-1955

U. P. Pruitt
Oct 24, 1926
Jun 23, 1927

Leonard B. Harris
1889-1961

Bun Jordan
1884-1965
&
Bessie Jordan
1888-1949

Robert Hammet Hurt
1877-1952
&
Sarah Ruth Hurt
1905-1965

Lillie Smith Hurt
1879-1953

Comer Wilson Dean
1871-1954
&
Viola Pratt Dean
1878-1965

William D. Ferguson
May 23, 1866
Oct 23, 1950

Dewitt Garrett
1882-1961 (TM)

William P. Hurt
1905-1961
&
Ethel F. Hurt
1903-19

W. M. Porter
Jan 11, 1900
Apr 2, 1967

Clarence A. Dean
Sep 29, 1903

&
Alexine T. Dean
May 27, 1914
Apr 11, 1960

Albert D. Vincion
May 3, 1902
Apr 27, 1950

Samuel C. Vincion
Tennessee
S/Sgt 117 Inf W. W. II
Dec 18, 1900
Dec 1, 1951

Joe Frank Dies
Jul 7, 1900
May   1941

Billie Cooper Dies
Sep 25, 1925
May 18, 1946

Oliver S. Cooper
1894-1944
&
Lucy Ray Cooper
1897-1952

William Leonard Shearin
1882-1951
&
Pearl Iris Shearin
1894-1955

W. Thomas Holton
Jan 14, 1897
Oct 28, 1953
&
A. Macil Holton
Jul 18, 1900

Adolphus L. Collins
1880-1947
&
Josie Emma Collins
1885-19

Clifford P. Collins
1916-1946

Sudie Collins
1918-1952

Father
John Thomas Beech
1904-1947
&
Mother
Mary Daughrity Beech
1908-19

Ernest Ring
May 11, 1904
Nov 8, 1962

Andrew J. Ring
Feb 12, 1873
Sep 4, 1941
&
Margaret E. Ring
Aug 20, 1880
Jan 2, 1944

FARMINGTON

Pauline Meeks Joyce
1902-1947

Sam M. Logue
Dec 9, 1881
Feb 24, 1953

Betty W. Logue
Apr 4, 1884
Oct 24, 1965

William Edgar Logue
Mar 21, 1914
Jan 3, 1924

Jack Gwedon
1946-1946

Novella Stacy
1898-1947

John M. Stacy
Tennessee
Pvt Armored Force R.T.C.
W. W. II
Jan 19, 1917
Jun 24, 1959

John William Neathery
Apr 1, 1922
Sep 19, 1956

Sarah Neathery
1914-1966

Buford Mealer
1902-1967

Buddy J. Mealer
1944

Gilbert L. Marshall
1878-1943
&
Ethel E. Marshall
1883-1955

Marilyn, Infant dau of
Mr. & Mrs. J. C. Palmore
1940

Jasper G. Palmore
Jul 8, 1897

&
Jennie M. Palmore
Sep 1, 1908
Aug 14, 1965

Gordon L. Smiley
1936-1942

Andrew Jennings Hardison
Jul 19, 1910-Feb 11, 1966

Lillie Smiley Hardison
Feb 5, 1904-Jun 9, 1967

Erik Jennings Hardison
1872-1951

Alice Idella Hardison
1871-1956

William Andrew Purdom
1884-1957

Mother
Martha G. Vincent
1876-1951

Tip T. Hargrove
1909-1947
&
Annie Laura Hargrove
1910-

John R. Sheppard
Tennessee
S 2C U.S.Navy
Aug 10, 1921
Jul 16, 1943

Louise Sheppard
1919-1936

Stanley M. Cathey
May 1, 1911
Sep 19, 1960
&
Christine B. Cathey
Feb 23, 1917

Ernest Cathey
Jun 6, 1875
Dec 12, 1941
&
Anna Cathey
Feb 20, 1875
Jun 25, 1945

Daniel Q. Walls
1950
Age 11 months

Edwin E. Fagan
Mar 20, 1881
Apr 5, 1962
&
Lula D. Fagan
Mar 22, 1881
Mar 19, 1954

Eugene F. Fagan
1922-1941

Hubert Basil Paul
Mar 25, 1914
Feb 1, 1945

Geraldine Giles
Nov 19, 1951
Nov 20, 1951

Charles Phillip Holton
1941-1944

Robert E. Holton
Sep 26, 1867
Oct 29, 1941
&
Jennie E. Holton
May 28, 1876
Nov 21, 1954

Fred B. Sheppard
Sep 14, 1890
Sep 13, 1964

John W. Cook
Tennessee
S1 U.S.N.R., W. W. II
Sep 28, 1913
Dec 4, 1962
&
Henrietta G. Cook
Mar 4, 1916

John L. Cook
Feb 18, 1877
Jun 29, 1968
&
Melissa A. Cook
Jul 28, 1881
Jan 21, 1967

Guy Warner
1883-1954

William B. Warner
1880-1949
&
Jennie R. Warner
1876-1955

Stella E. Thorne
Apr 10, 1893
Sep 17, 1953

Otto B. Woosley
1891-1946

Norman Wayne Meador
Oct 28, 1947
Jan 19, 1948

Miss Nannie Redmond
1870-1958
&
George B. Redmond
1869-1947
&
Mary T. Redmond
1878-1966

E. Timothy Holder
1870-1949
&
Evelyn Powell Holder
1881-19

William S. Holder
Tennessee
Pvt 26 Marines 5 Marine Div
W. W. II
Mar 27, 1918-Mar 3, 1945

Bill Glenn Crutcher
Sep 21, 1883

&
Powell D. Crutcher
Mar 26, 1886
Oct 28, 1966

John William Ferguson
May 4, 1907
Sep 12, 1949
&
Mattie Ferguson Harris
Oct 12, 1887
Nov 16, 1963

Mary Louise Vincion
Jul 4, 1942
Jan 31, 1943

Robert E. Lee, Sr.
Jun 5, 1893
Jan 3, 1966

Paul P. Tanner
1896-1969 (TM)

Hubert Scott
Mar 6, 1907
Sep 1, 1959

Hannah Scott
Jun 27, 1906

Elgin W. Logue
Tennessee
Horseshoer Co F, 306 Ammo
TN W. W. I
Sep 13, 1894
Nov 22, 1966
&
Annie B. Logue
Mar 9, 1898

Oliver F. Brown, Sr.
Feb 1911

&
A. T. Brown
Feb 8, 1913
Dec 5, 1963

Debra Lynn Gentry
1967-1967 (TM)

Virginia Martin
1920-1966

Joseph Charles Gabard, Sr.
Dec 22, 1912
Feb 3, 1968

Joe Clyde Hamilton
Aug 4, 1914-Oct 2, 1968
&
Marian T. Hamilton
May 8, 1921

FARMINGTON

Infant Son of
Johnny & Fay Cook
Aug 19, 1963

Infant Son of
R. N. & L. M. Galbreath
April 22, 1919

Frances I. Paul
Jun 3, 1928
Jul 11, 1929

B. H. Hayes
Jul 27, 1849
Mar 15, 1910
&
Carolyn Hayes
Oct 2, 1861
Feb 24, 1940

Lish Hayes
1892-1962

Clarence C., son of
D. E. & P. J. Barnes
Aug 15, 1917
Oct 20, 1918

John T., son of
J. T. & V. T. Barnes
Aug 9, 1905
Oct 13, 1918

Grace Melton
1829-1911

Rufus Wood Beech
1871-1943
&
Mary Daughrity Beech
1878-1904

Catherine, dau of
Mr. & Mrs. J. T. Beech
Jun 4, 1927
Jun 6, 1929

Morris E. Beech
1933-1935

James Franklin Daughrity
Jun 12, 1928
Sep 18, 1940

Lou Daughrity
1892-1954

John T. Daughrity
1880-1961

M. B. Rogers Lavander
Mar 22, 1880
Aug 9, 1951

Mary A. Lavender
Oct 10, 1878
May 1, 1958

Cleopatra A. Lavender
Apr 2, 1858
Jan 30, 1938

George W. Lavender
Jun 27, 1866
Jan 20, 1935

Thomas M. Lavender
May 5, 1850
Nov 24, 1930

William L. Lavender
Aug 12, 1863
Jul 9, 1906

Minnie C. Lavender
Apr 6, 1875
Aug 20, 1946

Charley A. Lavender
Feb 1, 1873
Jun 10, 1955

Thomas H. Lawrence
1883-1942

Thomas M. Lawrence
Oct 10, 1850
May 5, 1915

Cleopatra Lawrence
May 1, 1855
Apr 29, 1932

Garrett White, M.D.
May 25, 1865
Nov 29, 1939
&
Lillie M. White
Dec 14, 1869
Dec 18, 1909

Viola M. White
Oct 27, 1876
Jan 1, 1957

"Aunt Lou"
Lou Finley
1859-1950

James J. Shaw
1866-1957
&
Virginia E. Shaw
1875-1940

Warren Carter, son of
Mr. & Mrs. E. P. Crutcher
(no dates)

Edward P. Crutcher
Corp. in Btry F 1st U.S.Art.
Spanish-American War - 1898
Apr 27, 1872
May 29, 1935
&
Nevada T. Crutcher
Mar 22, 1877
Aug 25, 1960

Frank Turner, son of
Mr. & Mrs. E. P. Crutcher
Mar 28, 1903
Aug 29, 1909

Edward W. Crutcher
Tennessee
A2C U.S.Air Force
Oct 21, 1939
Jul 14, 1963

Dr. W. M. Crutcher
Nov 16, 1833
Oct 19, 1917

Mollie L., wife of
W. M. Crutcher
Jul 9, 1846
Dec 26, 1897

Mary Crutcher, wife of
S. L. Giles
Oct 15, 1876
Dec 30, 1918

Harry O'Neal Morton
Oct 8, 1898
Apr 27, 1919

M. B. O'Neal, wife of
Dr. J. W. Morton
Aug 26, 1861
Jan 21, 1912

Dr. James W. Morton
Oct 11, 1850
Aug 30, 1916

Joe D. Stammer
1917-1937

Z. A. Dozier
Feb 13, 1858
Sep 15, 1917
&
Allie P. Dozier
Aug 11, 1864
Feb 6, 1957

Herman W. Dozier
Sep 2, 1895
Mar 17, 1915

Garey Stammer
Aug 3, 1914
Jan 30, 1916

Caelera D. Stammer
1891-1967

Herman Stammer
1915-1968 (TM)

Mary Alice Dozier
Oct 20, 1911
Dec 2, 1911

John P. Dozier
Dec 13, 1887
Jun 25, 1967
&
Mary E. Dozier
Oct 26, 1888
Dec 7, 1966

J. W. Rowland
1900-1958
&
Dollie Holton Rowland
1904-

Lurline Aldridge
Oct 16, 1898
Oct 9, 1917

Moses W. McCrory
1828-1908

Margaret V. McCrory
1837-1914

Annie M. McCrory
1871-1935

Sarah Jane McCrory
1875-1928

Richard W. Brooks
1876-1950

Emily M. Brooks
1877-1961

Elizabeth P. Manier
1915-1967

S. B. Manier
Jul 23, 1880
Apr 29, 1959
&
Elizabeth Modrall Manier
Jan 5, 1883
Sep 21, 1951

George, son of
R. R. & Mary Ogilvie
Dec 9, 1880
Mar 28, 1907

Father
R. R. Ogilvie
Dec 19, 1847
Apr 1, 1919
&
Mother
Mary V., wife of
R. R. Ogilvie
Jun 14, 1849
Dec 8, 1916

James A. Ralston
1851-1937
&
Mary C. Ralston
1856-1923

Frances J. Powell
Mar 28, 1927
Jul 8, 1947

Herman E. McBride
Tennessee
1 Sgt 21 Engr AVN Regt
W. W. II
Dec 16, 1905
Jul 17, 1949

FARMINGTON

Father
Clarence A. McBride
1883-1948
&
Mother
Emma Eady McBride
1887-1967

Bessie Clark Davis
Feb 24, 1897
Nov 29, 1961

Robert L. Clark
1895-19
&
Ellen A. Clark
1889-1938

Mrs. M. P. Manire
Jul 4, 1843
Jul 28, 1933

Katherine R. Manier
1886-1965

Camilla Manier
1882-1965

Albert Manier
1885-1956
&
Katie Lee Manier
1897-1945

Joseph B. Manier
Feb 1925 - Sep 1925

Sara Manier
1938

Porter W. Garrett
1884-1937
&
Martha J. Garrett
1899-1945

Annie Ruth Garrett
1926-1951

Mary Elizabeth Garrett
May 23, 1922
Mar 11, 1926

R. C. B., son of
E. L. & A. L. Brown
Dec 10, 1930
Dec 17, 1930

James Edward, son of
E. L. & A. L. Brown
Jun 9, 1920
Jul 7, 1927

Edard L. Brown
1886-1948

Mrs. W. C. Brown
1854-1939

Lottie McNeese
Feb 19, 1888
Jan 5, 1952

Genie Powell Culbertson
1888-
&
Newton Hunter Culbertson, M.D.
1883-1961
&
Bessie Mai Culbertson
1894-1941

Don, Adopted Son of
Dr. N. H. & Susan
            Culbertson
Dec 17, 1914
Feb 13, 1918

James "Ollie" Paul
1875-1942
&
Lula "Crica" Paul
1878-1945

Father
James Henry Sheppard
Dec 26, 1892
Sep 24, 1927
&
Mother
Lillie Mai Sheppard
Mar 26, 1906

J. T. Smiley
Dec 8, 1851
Mar 19, 1926

John B. Beech
1877-1938
&
Sallie Moore Beech
1871-1950

John Hannah Patterson
1848-1936
&
Susan Haze Patterson
1868-1955
&
Sarah Myrtis Patterson
1904-1958

Robert Wilson Ramsey
1866-1938

Shannon A. Ramsey
Sep 14, 1938
Aug 27, 1939

James L. Ramsey
1907-1941

Cynthia Ring Harper
Jun 28, 1915
Mar 29, 1957

John M. Harshaw
Jan 9, 1897
Feb 1, 1940

Ellis Carlton Mealer (Daddy)
1895-1958
&
Dora Estelle Mealer (Mama)
1900-

Clara, dau of
Mr. & Mrs. E. C. Mealer
Aug 28, 1918
Feb 23, 1931

Dora Ruth, dau of
Mr. & Mrs. Ellis Mealer
Oct 16, 1932
Jul 23, 1934

Herbert Holder
Tennessee
Pvt 1 CL U.S. Army
March 14, 1935

Father
William A. Perryman
1881-1930
&
Mother
Lula J. Perryman
1891-1959

James H. Perryman
1910-1970
&
Blanche S. Perryman
1911-

Ida S. Broadaway
Dec 5, 1877
Dec 15, 1953

Zollie H. Griggs
1936-1938

J. Harmon Griggs
1906-1950
&
Lou Emma Griggs
1906-

Thomas Neathery
Sep 1, 1920
Apr 9, 1936

Ernest P. Neathery
Jul 25, 1889
Apr 27, 1962
&
Fannie Pearl Neathery
Jan 31, 1889
Feb 22, 1959

Ruth Thompson Cooper
1909-1941

Charlie C. Thompson
1886-1934
&
Rebecca L. Thompson
1882-1928

James E., son of
Mr. & Mrs. John Atkins
Jun 15, 1927
Oct 17, 1928

John A. Adkins
Apr 27, 1885
Sep 18, 1953
&
Maggie Lee Adkins
Nov 22, 1892
Aug 13, 1957

In Memory of
Vernon Eugene Adkins
Mar 20, 1931
Dec 31, 1953
"Killed in Korea"

Willie C. Shaw
1886-1966
&
Annie Lee Shaw
1888-1932

Mother
Frances McMurry
1882-1963

Robert Henry Gault
Nov 12, 1885
Jun 24, 1959

Daddy
Charles F. Powell
1900-1952

Charles Griffin
1912-1937

Wm. Montgomery Gabard
1889-1931
&
Nell Haynes Gabard
1888-

Larry H. Chatman
1869-1950

H. Massey Crutcher
1857-1929
&
S. Virginia Crutcher
1863-1929

John E. Logue
Sep 30, 1850
Jan 23, 1934
&
Ada A. Logue
Jan 1, 1863
Mar 14, 1942

FARMINGTON

Eli H. Logue
1875-1955
&
Idi Mangrum Logue
1880-1928

Virginia G., dau of
C. E. & M. V. Paul
Feb 3, 1920
Feb 27, 1929

James H., son of
C. E. & M. V. Paul
Dec 19, 1921
May 7, 1922

Henry H. Rowland
1857-1944

Rebecca C. Rowland
1872-1946

Sallie Rucker Stevens
1866-1936

Roy Wallace Patterson
Aug 23, 1875
Feb 7, 1937
&
Mary Ezell Patterson
Sep 24, 1876
May 11, 1949

Joseph A. Rozell
1890-1944
&
Mary E. Rozell
1895-19

Raymond Nelson Rozell
1921-1925

Virginia L. Rozell
1859-1939

Houlton D. Jones
March 21, 1923

William Marcus Evans
Dec 18, 1927
Mar 12, 1967

William H. Dickson
Dec 16, 1900
Jan 11, 1966
&
Lelia L. Dickson
Jul 14, 1904

Newton Ozro Perryman
Jul 21, 1866
(no date)
&
Bessie Jones Perryman
Jan 23, 1888
Jul 15, 1965

William D. Evans
1904-1964

Jennie B. Swain
1902-1930

Alden Lee Marshall
Jan 12, 1903
May 9, 1967
&
Mayme C. Marshall
May 29, 1903

Betty June White
Jun 9, 1933
Jun 15, 1933

Bobbie Gene Griffin
Nov 24, 1932
Jul 20, 1936

Howard M. Paul
April 1926
Dec 26, 1932

Bob Paul
1903-1970 (TM)

Paul
1906-1953 (TM)

Thomas J. Lee
1849-1934
&
Sarah E. Lee
1855-(no date)

James W. Thompson
Aug 16, 1869
Sep 10, 1938
&
Louella R. Thompson
May 5, 1879
Jan 19, 1958

Jack Wilson
1902-1965

Jimmie L. Neese
Sep 29, 1911
Dec 1, 1967
&
Johnnie B. Neese
Feb 10, 1919

Gilbert Lee Griffin

&
Mary Eva Lynn Griffin
Mar 14, 1928
Sep 20, 1968

Robert V. Morgan, Sr.
Mar 4, 1904
Oct 31, 1970
&
Della Mai Morgan
Jul 2, 1909

James Robert Holder
Aug 2, 1905

&
Clara Mai Holder
Dec 23, 1902
Apr 7, 1968

Mattie, wife of
William J. Rodgers
1861-1939
&
J. A. Rodgers
1879-1943
&
William Oscar Rodgers
1892-1948
&
Elsie Rodgers, wife of
William A. Dyer
1885-1959

Margaret Galbreath Holton
1908-1936

Rollie Holton
1904-1935

Rollie Holton, Jr.
1935-1935

Joe Bob Holton
1923-1942

Sarah Davis
Oct 6,

Susanna Collins
Mar 12, 1853
Jun 30, 1939

Hugh G. Molder
Sep 6, 1893
Nov 23, 1962
&
Ruth Lillian Molder
May 8, 1900

D. L. Clark
Nov 16, 1909
Sep 1, 1970
&
Mildred H. Clark
Oct 3, 1910
Dec 11, 1967

James Edward Cooper
1894-1968
&
Florence C. Cooper
1888-1967

Iva Lee Little
1909-1968 (TM)

Joel M. Collins
1871-1958

Charlie W. Collins, Sr.
Feb 18, 1890
Dec 21, 1964
&
Gracie M. Collins
Jul 23, 1892

J. D. Mealer
1874-1942
&
Sadie Mealer
1878-1960

Ernest B. Shaw
Feb 29, 1884
Oct 18, 1940

J. R. Marshall
1861-1939

Hardy W. Hester
Tennessee
Pvt Co D 117 AMMO TRAIN
W. W. I
Aug 13, 1895
Oct 21, 1965
&
Dorothy E. Hester
Aug 24, 1903

Charlie W. Hester
May 2, 1945
Feb 19, 1964

Herman Jones
Sep 29, 1898

&
Mattie Mai Jones
Jul 12, 1898
Nov 9, 1962

Jimmie D. Hickman
Mar 1, 1915
Apr 2, 1966
&
Edna M. Jones Hickman
May 27, 1918

Erskin Hargrove
Apr 12, 1895
Mar 10, 1969
&
Estella Hargrove
Sep 27, 1890

John D. Crafton
Mar 31, 1897-Aug 12, 1968
&
Sallie C. Crafton
Nov 8, 1907

FARMINGTON

Samuel Thomas Lee
Tennessee
Pvt U. S. Army, W. W. II
Aug 1, 1913
Nov 8, 1969
    &
Louise M. Lee
Sep 3, 1917

Gladys Watkins
Jul 27, 1950
Feb 11, 1970

Myrtle Cooper
1891-1968

Leeroy Crafton
Jun 24, 1900
Oct 22, 1969
    &
Nellie J. Crafton
Feb 6, 1903

Horace Noah
1909-1970
    &
Aline Noah
1921-

H. N. "Bud" Rowlin
1885-1971 (TM)

Myra R. Meathery
1912-1970 (TM)

Hubert Scott
Mar 6, 1907
Sep 1, 1959

Hannah Scott
Jun 27, 1906

Joseph Charles Gabard, Sr.
Dec 22, 1912
Feb 3, 1968

Several unmarked graves.

Virginia J. Martin
Mar 14, 1920
Feb 25, 1969

Amie B. Louge
Mar 9, 1898

Paul Powel Tanner
Tennessee
Pvt U. S. Army, W. W. I
Jan 22, 1896
Jun 4, 1969
    &
Grace L. Tanner
1903-

Elgin W. Louge
Tennessee
Horseshoer
Co F 306 AMMO TN, W. W. I
Sep 13, 1894
Nov 22, 1966

Robert E. Lee, Sr.
Jun 5, 1893
Jan 3, 1966

Infant Son of
Johnny & Faye Cook
April 19, 1963

Debra Lynn Gentry
1967-1967 (TM)

Joe Clyde Hamilton
Aug 4, 1914
Oct 2, 1968
    &
Marian T. Hamilton
May 8, 1921

Oliver F. Brown, Sr.
Feb 19, 1911

A. T. Brown
Feb 8, 1913
Dec 5, 1963

END OF SWANSON
* *

KING CEMETERY
Located on Old Columbia Road, north of New Highway No. 99,
north of Duck River, near L & N Railroad. Copied Mar 1972.

Boling W. King
Apr 4, 1845
Nov 6, 1910

Alice Mosley King
Feb 24, 1854
Aug 20, 1929

J. Fountain King
Mar 17, 1884
Sep 17, 1909

J. D., son of
S. R. & S. A. Crowder
Jan 22, 1878
Feb 23, 1878

Mary M. King
May 10, 1825
Apr 25, 1880
    &
Eudora King
B&D- 1882

Julia M., wife of
Josh King
Born 1818
Died Jun 23, 1856

Josephine King
Age 4 months
(no dates)

4 or 5 unmarked graves.

* *

OAKLEY CEMETERY
Located one-half mile east of Laws Hill. Copied by Ralph D.
Whitesell, Ronnie E. Wilson and Bobby Robinson on July 22,
1974.

Richard Oakley
North Carolina
  N. C. Troops
    Rev. War
     1856   15 or 16 unmarked graves.

* *

FARMINGTON

SHEARIN CEMETERY

Located on the I. N. Green Farm near Rich Creek now owned by Jas. Shaw. Copied by Ralph D. Whitesell, 1970.

Elizabeth, wife of
Fletcher Shearin
May 5, 1826
Aug 15, 1868

James Shearin
Nov 24, 1849
Jun 15, 1868

William Fox
Oct 11, 1829
Feb 2, 1880

C. Ophelia, wife of
M. A. Whitaker
Jan 25, 1858
(no date)

5 or 6 unmarked graves.

* *

McQUIDDY CEMETERY

Located one-half mile west of Highway No. 31-A, on banks of Rock Creek, 2 miles north west of Farmington. Copied by Ralph D. Whitesell.

Father
Newton McQuiddy
Sep 26, 1819
Feb 5, 1894

Mother
Nancy Allen McQuiddy
Jun 6, 1823
Aug 2, 1918

V. W. McQuiddy
Oct 13, 1860
Sep 24, 1863

Infant Dau of
H. G. & M. K. McQuiddy
Mar 4, 1874
Mar 5, 1874

All graves marked.

* *

BURROW CEMETERY

Located north east of Farmington, Mt. Lebanon vicinity. Copied March 27, 1975.

Mr. J. B. Brown
1884-1959 (TM)

Will E. Hill
May 13, 1878
Apr 28, 1951

Aunt
Etta Hill
May 13, 1878
Oct 27, 1958

Bennie H. Hill
1881-1915

Cynthia Hart
1970-1970 (TM)

Eddie B. Thompson
Jun 22, 1923
Sep 18, 1965

Many unmarked graves.

Roy F. Thompson
May 10, 1892
Feb 17, 1965
&
Mary B. Thompson
Jul 13, 1899
(no date)

William J. Thompson
Tennessee
Pfc 16 Armd Inf BN 13 Armd Div
W. W. II
Mar 19, 1926
Aug 23, 1945

Burt B. Burrow
1915-1918

Ephraim Bud Hill
1874-1951 (TM)

Anner E. Nickens
Oct 5, 1855
Jan 18, 1933

* *

HOPPER CEMETERY

Located about one mile east of Laws Hill, on farm owned by Johnny H. Robinson. Copied July 22, 1974 by Ralph D. Whitesell, Bobby Robinson and Ronnie W. Wilson.

Uriah Hopper
Mar 1810
Oct 20, 1896

Susan M. Hopper (2nd wife)
May 4, 1834-May 13, 1907

Thomas Hopper
Died Mar 18, 1874
Age about 81 years

(Mary) Hopper
May 7, 1790-Sep 4, 1875

E. C. Wilson
Aug 29, 1862
Nov 26, 1927

Nancy E. Wilson
Mar 14, 1858-Apr 18, 1897

J. B. Hopper
Co G
5th Tenn Cav

* *

FARMINGTON

DANIEL CEMETERY

Located a short distance north of Mt. Lebanon Church. Copied April 1971, re-checked Dec 30, 1976 by Helen & Tim Marsh.

Joseph F. Cherry, Jr.
Tennessee
Sgt U.S.Army, W. W. II
May 8, 1921
Sep 7, 1971

Ray Thomas Farler
Feb 6, 1938
Mar 22, 1971

John Frank Perry
Oct 28, 1909
Feb 27, 1970

E. G. Perry
Sep 2, 1890
Apr 18, 1957

Margrett C., wife of
Wash Wynn
Died Apr 15, 1907
Age 78 years

Oliver Howard Perry
May 10, 1863
Jun 5, 1916

Nancy Perry
1869-1942

Della, dau of
O. H. & N. A. Perry
Dec 17, 1892
Nov 10, 1905

Matilda C. Gates
Feb 22, 1847
Feb 9, 1915

E. G. Hargrove
Aug 31, 1925
Sep 17, 1926

M. F. Calahan
Nov 3, 1874
Dec 9, 1900
Age 26 years.

T. J. Hargrove
Jun 2, 1888
Apr 2, 1973
&
Annie P. Hargrove
Aug 1, 1896
Apr 17, 1975

Mike Dettman
Feb 1, 1883
Jul 3, 1923

Nancy J., wife of
Simp Daniel
Died Mar 28, 1890
Age 52 years

Edward N. Stephenson
Nov 2, 1835
Feb 22, 1905

Nancy A., wife of
E. N. Stephenson
Jul 11, 1831
Apr 9, 1906

J. Hardin Luna
Jun 11, 1914
Feb 23, 1975
Mrd- May 18, 1944

Vera H. Luna
May 25, 1923

Henry D. Glasscock
Dec 3, 1817
Feb 7, 1899

Manervey Glasscock
Mar 25, 1817
Jul 18, 1891

Lucinda Glasscock
Oct 29, 1848
Feb 28, 1862

* *

ROBINSON CEMETERY

Located south and near Henry Horton State Park, north of Lewisburg.

David Robinson, son of
Joseph Robinson
(no marker)

Nancy Robinson Boyd
Apr 10, 1835
    29, 1915

James Robinson
Nov   1805
Sep 9, 1846
Who left an affectionate
wife, 2 sons & 2 daus to
mourn his loss.

Margaret Robinson, dau of
Joseph Robinson
(no marker)

Joseph Robinson
Born Jan 4, 1776
Mrd- Apr 6, 1797
Died Jan 3, 1850

Sarah Ray, wife of
Joseph Robinson
Mar 2, 1778
Jun 20, 1852

Thomas Wilson Robinson
Born Mar 4, 1823
Died Jun 4, 1857
Mrd- Sep 19, 1844
(no marker)

Martha Victoria, child of
Thomas Wilson Robinson &
wife Martha Adeline Oakley
Robinson.
(no marker)

Batten is said to be buried here. many unmarked graves.

* *

WARNER CEMETERY

Located about one-half mile north east of the Old Warner home, and about 300 yards south of Duck River, behind Henry Horton State Park, on a farm owned by the Curtis family (1974). Copied July 7, 1974.

Sacred to the Memory of
Richard Warner
Born Aug 26, 1794
Died Mar 5, 1876
NOTE:
A first commissioner of
Marshall County,Tn.also
member of General Assembly

Lucy, wife of
Col. Richard Warner
Born Mar 18, 1806 &
departed this life
Apr 2, 1860

John H., son of
R. & L. Warner
Mar 26, 1826
Apr 13, 1862

R. Warner, Jr.
1833-1915

There are 4 or 5 unmarked graves. The cemetery is enclosed in a large rock wall.

* *

FARMINGTON

WARNER CEMETERY
Located at Clay Hill. Facing Church, on the right side. Copied Dec 30, 1976 by David M. Pickens and Ralph D. Whitesell. Re-checked Sept 2, 1978 by Helen & Tim Marsh.

John Morgan Landers
Oct 2, 1877
May 24, 1953

Maggie L. Landers, dau of
B. S. & Bettie Landers
Born in Marshall Co., TN
1883-1885
(2nd stone: Maggie L., dau
of B. S. & M. E. Landers
Jan 8, 1883
May 25, 1885)

Bettie M. Landers
Born in Marshall Co., dau of
Allen and Margaret Morris
1850-1935

Ben S. Landers
Born in Bedford Co., son of
S. A. & Sarah Landers
1846-1939

Scott A. Landers
Mar 9, 1886
May 2, 1969

Etta A. Uselton
Aug 17, 1868
Mar 10, 1969

William Thomas Warner
1863-1920
&
Mary Etta Parks Warner
1858-1936

Infant of W. T. & Etta Warner
(no dates)

William A. Harris
1869-1945
&
Blanch Harris
1874-1947

Father
James Calvin Culbertson
1822-1901
&
Mother
Sarah Strong Culbertson
1830-1895

William J. Nicholas
Mar 4, 1863
Jun 29, 1956

Nannie Claxton, wife of
W. J. Nicholas
Aug 21, 1865
Jul 28, 1939

Flossie Nicholas Eagle
Jul 22, 1900
Mar 15, 1949

Infant of
J. E. & Florence Robinson
Sept 18, 1910

Ann E., wife of
J. W. Whitman
Aug 14, 1841
Sep 8, 1882

James Franklin Ferguson
Mar 19, 1885
Feb 18, 1969
&
Mary Langley Allen Ferguson
Oct 28, 1886
Jun 20, 1966

Sarah J. Robinson, wife of
Dr. F. F. Ferguson
Aug 21, 1854
Mar 29, 1932

Dr. J. F. F. Ferguson
Feb 18, 1848
Sep 17, 1897

Stanley S. Galbraith
1889-1945
&
Argent Park Galbraith
1909-19

Margret E., wife of
T. C. Hutton
Jul 10, 1845
Jul 31, 1884

Martha J. Warner
Oct 8, 1837
Mar 24, 1879

Mrs. Fannie L. Plummer
Jul 31, 1856
Jul 5, 1881

Mattie B., wife of
R. Warner
May 25, 1855
Jan 9, 1899

Mrs. Margaret Warner
1865-1951 (TM)

J. W. Hutton
Aug 6, 1809
Dec 23, 1895
& wife
Francis Moore Hutton
Oct 13, 1810
Aug 5, 1899

Samuel Paul, son of
Mr. & Mrs. S. B. Warner
May 26, 1917
Dec 8, 1921

Sam B. Warner
1896-1955
&
Annette L. Warner
1896-

S. B. Warner, Jr.
1923-1962
&
Laurene K. Warner
1922-1957

Samuel J. Warner
Sep 11, 1831
May 5, 1910
& wife
Sarah E. Warner
Feb 27, 1855
Jan 7, 1916

* *

WARNER CEMETERY
Located at Clay Hill. Cemetery is directly behind the previous Warner Cemetery, enclosed in rock wall. Re-checked Sep 2, 1978 by Helen & Tim Marsh.

J. Britt Bigger
1875-1941
&
Lucy Warner Bigger
1874-1957

J. P. Warner
1842-1928
& wife
Ella Parks Warner
1849-1920

Mattie Polk Warner
1877-1895

Erma Lee Warner
1887

William Charles Hunter
1864-1939
& wife
Annie Warner Hunter
1875-1950

Sallie A. Allen, dau of
Harry & Amanda O'Neal
Jan   1859
Sep 4, 1899

Wm. W. O'Neal
Oct 24, 1850
Nov 17, 1894

William W. Brown
1855-1941
&
Dolly Parks Brown
1860-1902

Infant Dau of
William & Dolly Brown
(no dates)

Jane R. Parks
Apr 2, 1821
May 28, 1882
"Farewell dear Mother"

John R. Warner
1859-1935
&
Lucy J. Warner
1851-1922

3 unmarked graves.

* *

FARMINGTON

LONG CEMETERY
Located at Clay Hill. Directly behind the Church.
Re-checked Sep 2, 1978.

Wallace R. Harris
May 26, 1893
Jul 20, 1963
&
Leola C. Harris
Jul 15, 1897

Mrd- May 12, 1913

Mark Carlton
1878-1955
&
Maggie Campbell Carlton
1863-1950

L. M. Carlton
Dec 21, 1870
Jan 26, 1914

Ella M. Carlton
1868-1914

A. W. Hill
Mar 13, 1853
Aug 28, 1905

M. Kate Wilson, wife of
A. W. Hill
Mar 15, 1859
Sep 6, 1891

Eula R. Hill
1881-1964

Mary E. Jones, wife of
A. W. Hill
Apr 3, 1863
Feb 22, 1915

Mary Aldean Cooper
Jul 3, 1916
Jan 6, 1919

W. Cleveland Cooper
Feb 2, 1886
Jun 25, 1943
&
Nettie S. Cooper
Oct 31, 1887

Infant Son of
D. A. & Ethel Crowell
Born Nov 16, 1895

Jessie Whorley
Aug 23, 1915
Jun 8, 1917

Jesse Whorley
Jan 22, 1864
Apr 7, 1951
& wife
Mattie Carlton Whorley
Oct 23, 1858
Feb 1, 1910

Nora Harbor, wife of
Jessie Whorley
Apr 10, 1880
Feb 4, 1941

* *

CARLTON CEMETERY
Located at Clay Hill. Behind the Church. Re-checked Sep 2, 1978.

W. R. Carlton
Sep 11, 1828
Jun 2, 1901
&
Amanda Carlton
May 17, 1839
Jun 16, 1921

Eli James Hopkins
Feb 21, 1849
Apr 21, 1912
& wife
Sarah A. Hopkins
Jan 27, 1857
Dec 13, 1907

Fred Carlton
Aug 5, 1901
Jan 1, 1923

Filey Carlton
Apr 29, 1899
Dec 19, 1918

Philey C. Crowell
Sep 25, 1927
Feb 27, 1959

Truman Hopkins
1882-1946

Gifford Hopkins
Sep 4, 1886

&
Nancy L. Hopkins
Mar 8, 1895

Mrd- Nov 27, 1913

Lelon T. Hopkins
Sept 8, 1914

Albert Murat Carlton
1872-1948

Clara, wife of
A. M. Carlton
Feb 17, 1881
Mar 28, 1911

David A. Crowell
1875-1952
&
Ethel C. Crowell
1875-1955

Tom W. Hill
1886-1938
&
Bess T. Hill
1902-19

Bertha Erie, dau of
A. W. & M. E. Hill
Aug 14, 1899
Jul 19, 1900

R. L. Powell
Nov 28, 1878
Aug 17, 1918
&
Esther Powell
Apr 2, 1880
Nov 5, 1932

Infant of R. L. &
E. B. Powell
June 10, 1914

A. Odell Powell
Nov 14, 1901
Sep 7, 1926

Albert Jordan
1882-1958
&
Maud Jordan
1883-1923

William B. Cooper
1909-
&
Annie Pearl Cooper
1909-1977

Infant Dau of
W. B. & Annie Pearl Coc
1930

Ernest W. Carlton
1881-1953
&
Willa D. Wright Carltor
1889-1926

Father
Bob C. Crowell
Nov 20, 1901
Dec 11, 1977
&
Mother
Mae W. Crowell
May 31, 1913
----

* *

FARMINGTON

NICKENS CEMETERY
Located at Clay Hill. Facing the Church, small cemetery to the extreme left. Rechecked Sep 2, 1978.

L. J. Nickens
Feb 24, 1860
Jun 1, 1934

Cora B. Nickens
Jan 18, 1867
Jun 12, 1904

* *

GREEN CEMETERY
Located at Clay Hill. To the right of the Nickens Cemetery. Rechecked Sep 2, 1978.

J. C. Green
Mar 13, 1830
May 23, 1919

Infant of
J. A. & M. S. Green
Died Dec 3, 1910

Mrs. M. C. Elliott
Jun 22, 1825
Feb 4, 1903

Georgia Elizabeth Johnson
Sep 8, 1920
Mar 9, 1941

M. A. Green
Feb 24, 1832
Aug 15, 1898

Joseph Long Nicholas
Nov 14, 1852
Jun 19, 1916

J. M. Robinson
Feb 7, 1850
Apr 21, 1908

Joe Elgin Johnson
1880-1959
&
Maggie Robinson Johnson
1890-1959

Elatia Green Powell
Oct 14, 1869
Sep 21, 1944

Sarah Green, wife of
F. M. Dillard
Died Aug 14, 1912
Age 56 years.

Telitha Ann Robinson
Feb 12, 1862
Aug 2, 1939

* *

PERRYMAN CEMETERY
Located at Clay Hill. Directly behind the Green Cemetery. Rechecked Sep 2, 1978.

John T. Perryman
Jul 16, 1872
Nov 6, 1945

James W. Perryman
Indiana
Pfc. Co. C 9 Armored Engr. BN
W. W. II
Mar 2, 1908
Jan 22, 1962

Sarah Izerbel, wife of
John Perryman
Aug 14, 1871
Aug 7, 1916

(name gone)
Aug 27, 1918
Feb 10, 1926

* *

HASKINS CEMETERY
Located at Clay Hill. Across the road from the Church. Rechecked Sep 2, 1978.

Henry C. Johnsey
Dec 13, 1891
Jun 10, 1960
&
Etta H. Johnsey
Mar 31, 1900

W. A. Haskins
1867-1944
&
Nannie R. Haskins
1872-1936

Mattie H. Crowell
Jul 8, 1894
Nov 4, 1922
"Mother"

Mary Beatrice Crowell
1918-1918
6 mo.

Oliver H. Perry
Jan 13, 1904
Aug 7, 1974
&
Mary H. Perry
Sep 1, 1905

Mrd- Mar 23, 1924

Alvin D. Haskins
May 15, 1940
Nov 25, 1940

Clyde A. Haskins
Dec 8, 1898
Nov 25, 1962
&
Jamie D. Haskins
Aug 9, 1906

(moved to another Cemetery)

Charles F. Haskins "Father"
Mar 3, 1875
Aug 15, 1945
&
Sallie F. Haskins "Mother"
Dec 17, 1877
Jul 31, 1958
(moved to another Cemetery)

Vance E. Haskins
Jul 23, 1926
Apr 6, 1936
&
Kate E. Haskins "Mother"
Sep 18, 1900

(moved to another Cemetery)

William A. Perry
Mar 12, 1924
Nov 20, 1927

Mollie H. Agee
Oct 23, 1879
Feb 19, 1959

J. R. Haskins   "Father"
May 5, 1845
Jan 10, 1925
&
Martha V. Haskins "Mother"
Oct 17, 1846
Sep 8, 1909

James Haskins
Sep 29, 1920-Sep 23, 1921

Mary M. Haskins
Mar 6, 1935-Apr 18, 1935

James A. Haskins
Nov 22, 1876-Jan 21, 1956
&
Mary P. Haskins
Dec 1, 1892-Nov 6, 1951

* *

FARMINGTON

MORRIS CEMETERY
Located at Clay Hill. This cemetery is north of the Haskins Cemetery. Rechecked Sep 2, 1978.

Elisha Green Morris
Feb 14, 1843
Jul 22, 1921
&
Chloe Ann Hopkins Morris
Aug 3, 1851
Nov 5, 1927

Thomas Bates Morris
1878-1937

J. Lee Morris
1871-1946

Pearl R. Morris
Aug 18, 1886
May 14, 1949

James S. Morris
1873-1950

* *

HOPPER CEMETERY
Located three miles south east of Henry Horton State Park. Copied April 1971. Rechecked July 9, 1978.

Nellie Collins
1906-1966 (TM)

M. C. Mangrum
Nov 14, 1887

&
Alice Mangrum
May 9, 1877
Aug 22, 1945

Father
Charles Hopper
Jan 14, 1816
Feb 13, 1901
&
Mother
Mary E. Hopper
Oct 7, 1835
Dec 28, 1926

Brother
J. V. Hopper
1873-1934

R. L. Slaughter
Jul 12, 1951
Jul 12, 1951

Mrs. Mamie Slaughter
1914-1937

Dad
Everett H. Slaughter
1902-1936
&
Mom
Ruby H. Slaughter
1910-

Mary L. Slaughter
1926-1927

Everett Slaughter, Jr.
1929-1931

William D. Slaughter
1867-1927 (TM)

Omey E. Slaughter
1881-1954 (TM)

Milisa Horton Slaughter
1876-1947

Father
J. F. Slaughter
Mar 1, 1872
Sep 6, 1934

E. Rice Phifer
Apr 12, 1898
Oct 25, 1966
&
Mildred D. Phifer
May 19, 1907

John G. Green
Sep 8, 1841
Apr 23, 1897

Eluira Caro Perry
Jun 21, 1860
Aug 28, 1925

Elenor Caroline Perry
Aug 24, 1824
Jan 19, 1900

J. H. Hopper
Nov 4, 1831
Dec 29, 1906
& wife
Minerva C. Hopper
Jul 23, 1846
Jul 14, 1921

Martha M., wife of
Merritt Laurence
Oct 15, 1827
Nov 14, 1911

Merritt Laurence
Feb 8, 1808
Jul 27, 1893

William A., son of
J. C. & Lenora Davis
Nov 3, 1910
Jan 8, 1911

James J. Davis
Tennessee
Pvt 1753 SVC Comd Unit, WW II
(dates in ground)

John T. Davis
Nov 16, 1885

&
Lanora Davis
Jul 20, 1887
Dec 30, 1955

Sallie Davis Bills
Sep 9, 1861
Jan 22, 1911

Corp'l W. C. Dickens
Co A 4th Tenn Mtd Inf

Garfield Dickens
Jan 22, 1881
Dec 16, 1900

Murry Claxton
Feb 15, 1884
Aug 9, 1969
&
Minnie Claxton
Feb 26, 1888
Jun 17, 1962

Grace Claxton
1912-

Benjamin H. Davis
Georgia
TEC 4, Co H 409 Inf, WW II
Nov 10, 1916
Aug 12, 1967

Joe J. Davis
1895-1971 (TM) (Soldier)

Paul J. Peterson
Jan 22, 1873
Aug 17, 1963

Gottlieb Peterson
Jul 18, 1871
Jan 12, 1957

Seth Peterson
Aug 19, 1877
May 29, 1956
&
Emma Peterson
Jul 25, 1879
Aug 11, 1969

Lewis Hopper
Mar 13, 1895
Mar 24, 1921

W. "Bill" Plummer
Feb 8, 1882
Apr 17, 1956
&
Mary G. Plummer
May 12, 1884
Jan 27, 1965

Father
W. R. Harbor
Mar 14, 1849
Aug 22, 1930
&
Mother
Sarah E. Harbor
Nov 7, 1843
Aug 17, 1917

Elizabeth J. Harbor
Jun 22, 1871
Apr 23, 1896

George E. Harbor
Mar 22, 1873
Sep 15, 1894

Sallie Hopper
Died Mar 5, 1901
(no age given)

Father
Frank Haynes
Nov 20, 1921

&
Mother
Mary A. Haynes
Aug 8, 1920
Feb 13, 1967

FARMINGTON

Jimmie Hopper
Nov 20, 1891
Sep 20, 1901

T. G. Hopper
Sep 23, 1868
Nov 8, 1892

Clary Hopper
Feb 8, 1879
Oct 23, 1880

Presley J. Hopper
Jan 2, 1882
Nov 11, 1883

A. E. Hopper
Mar 25, 1870
Sep 1, 1890

Everett Martin
Nov 21, 1900

&
Carry B. Martin
Jan 27, 1904
Nov 15, 1958

Tom Martin
1860-1930

Elmer Martin
Oct 5, 1907
Jul 18, 1967
&
Geneva Martin
Jul 3, 1910

Robert H. Young, Sr. "Son"
1864-1911
&
America A. Young "Mother"
1839-1910

W. J. Young
Apr 17, 1836
Apr 10, 1906

J. Lee, son of
W. J. & A. A. Young
Mar 18, 1873
Feb 13, 1890

Sallie Thomas, dau of
W. J. & A. A. Young
Dec 15, 1862
Sep 22, 1875

Euna May Jones
Apr 23, 1873
Aug 6, 1912

Tina Alice Helton
Oct 28, 1898
Feb 17, 1916

Martha Martin
1921

Dovie Martin
1864-1915

Jane Martin
1838-1907

Carrie Martin
1905-1906

Clara Martin
1905-1905

Eugene Martin
1890-1892

Lewis Martin
1894-1896

Ada Martin
1876-1901

Obe Martin
1834-1901

J. W. Batten
Apr 18, 1824
Apr 18, 1904

Alice Young
1859-1929

Coreen Martin
1915-1917

Baby Martin
1930

Infant Son of
Mr. & Mrs. Sam Claxton
Aug 4, 1914

Louise Martin
1911-1912

Ernest B. Blackwell
Jun 17, 1894
Aug 30, 1969
&
Della G. Blackwell
Mar 24, 1895

Hugh G. Molder, Jr.
Tennessee
EM1 US Navy, WW II
Mar 6, 1920
Aug 11, 1969

Pamela Kay Smith
1964-1964

Wanda Joy Hill
Aug 25, 1947
Mar 15, 1959

Burnice W. Claiborne
May 18, 1920
Mar 3, 1933

Claude Lee Martin
Tennessee
Pvt Co I 2 Inf Regt WW I
Apr 21, 1898
Oct 18, 1958

Bessie Thomas Martin "Mother"
Nov 10, 1893
Dec 29, 1953

Annie Ruth Martin
1912-1932

William J. Martin
May 7, 1886
Mar 5, 1952
&
Estella Potts Martin
Jan 7, 1890
Feb 28, 1965

Jennie Osborne
1871-1952

James Martin Osborne
May 22, 1861
Oct 22, 1909

Elmer Anderson
1938-1938

Baby Anderson
1957-1957

Charlie E. Darnell
1877-1966
&
Leeotie Darnell
1884-1949

Carl A. Darnell
1916-1953
&
Nina B. Darnell
1923-

Mr. Ellis L. Baxter
1897-1971 (TM)

Loyd D. Darnell
1904-1971 (TM)

Ellen Neese
1869-1947

Leslie Darnell
May 13, 1910
Jan 29, 1933

Clarie D. Perry
Oct 17, 1902
Mar 20, 1933

Joe M. Claiborne
Tennessee
Pvt 1 Cl 317 Field Arty
8th Div WW I
Oct 12, 1927

Jimmie H. Perry
Sep 4, 1886
Oct 1, 1963
&
Margaret S. Perry
Dec 13, 1909
Jan 24, 1971

George W. Burns
May 24, 1884
Sep 4, 1917

Laurie G. Hardison
May 28, 1883
Aug 6, 1964
&
Mary Leoda Hardison
Feb 2, 1887
Jul 4, 1968
&
Annie Ellen Hardison
Jul 6, 1919

&
Everette Hardison
Sep 30, 1906
Dec 19, 1964

Smithson Baby Girl
1952 (TM)

Paul D. Yell
Apr 8, 1952
Apr 28, 1970
&
Addie P. Yell
1911-1955

James H. Pugh
Dec 18, 1943
Dec 19, 1943

Huston M. Pugh
Jan 12, 1903

&
Sadie B. Pugh
Jan 24, 1910
Jun 29, 1970
Mrd- Jul 14, 1929

Paul E. Pugh
Feb 25, 1937
Dec 26, 1962
&
Teresa F. Pugh
Nov 29, 1943

David Keith Brock
Oct 17, 1957
Feb 15, 1958

Charlie F. Haynes
1895-1967 (TM)

FARMINGTON

Henry Ethridge
Apr 29, 1882
Jun 3, 1968
&
Kate Ethridge
Nov 20, 1897

Cristy Kay Burrow
1968-1968 (TM)

Baby Haynes, of
Mr. & Mrs. Ray Haynes
1968   1 day (TM)

Charles A. Sheppard
Jan 13, 1937
Sep 1, 1958
Tennessee
Pfc US Army

Dorothy Marie Stephenson
1936-1937
8 months

Rebecca Ann, Infant dau of
Jessie & Vera Batten
Feb 14, 1954

Clyde Jones, Jr.
Mar 25, 1944
Oct 7, 1944

James Street Shires
1910-1960

Doyle E. Keel
1930-1969

Betty Ann Baxter
Jun 16, 1949

Claud Lee Cheeves
Oct 18, 1884
Apr 29, 1959
&
Julia Ethel Cheeves
Oct 27, 1889

R. M. Batten
Jan 1, 1867
Dec 13, 1902

Hoyle M. Batten
Tennessee
Tec 5 831 Engr Avn Bn
Apr 25, 1917
Dec 19, 1948

Amanda E. Batten
1912-1913

Emma L. Batten
1905-1906

Thomas A. Batten
Jun 15, 1877
Mar 21, 1961

Hattie A. Batten
1888-1942

Stephen Batten
Nov 8, 1821
Aug 6, 1904

Lucy R. Batten
Jun 21, 1899
Apr 9, 1908

Taylor F. Allen
Jul 10, 1855
Apr 26, 1905

Amanda Batten Allen
Nov 11, 1863
Mar 6, 1938

William S. Daniel
Jan 19, 1864
Sep 29, 1940

Valrie B. Daniel
Jan 8, 1872
Aug 6, 1957

Howard Russel White
Oct 2, 1929
Dec 1, 1940

Sallie R. White
Jul 18, 1903
May 13, 1961

Sallie Bell
Feb 10, 1885
Jul 19, 1945

Martin J. White
1859-1942
&
Nancy A. White
1859-1933

Edward Franklin Batten
Feb 25, 1937
Jun 21, 1938

Infant Son of
Mr. & Mrs. J. N. Batten
(no dates)

Infant Son of
Mr. & Mrs. J. N. Batten
(no dates)

James M. Batten
1874-1952
&
Martha A. Batten
1875-1964

Harvey Bolin
1880-1968 (TM)

Elizabeth Bolin
1885-1965 (TM)

Clarence Bolin
Mar 19, 1925-Feb 4, 1941

T. J. Harber
Dec 1, 1864
Apr 29, 1937

Kattie Lee, dau of
J. E. & Leila Harber
Nov 13, 1909
Jul 13, 1922

J. Edward Harber
Dec 16, 1872
Sep 7, 1943

Leila L. Harber
Aug 22, 1882

Tina A. Harber
Feb 28, 1876
May 12, 1904

J. D. Harber
Feb 21, 1833
Feb 2, 1903

Sarah Elizabeth Harber
Jul 22, 1839
Nov 16, 1916

C. W. Harber
Feb 24, 1859
Mar 11, 1928

Mrs. E. J. Harber
Dec 25, 1860
Oct 22, 1933

Laura Virginia Harber
May 5, 1872
Apr 28, 1920 -

Father
Kenny A. White
Apr 8, 1890
Jan 29, 1957
&
Mother
Rose Etta White
Mar 18, 1895
Sep 18, 1954

Frank R. Haskins
Sep 19, 1903
Aug 1, 1970
&
Louise B. Haskins
Aug 29, 1908

Joseph A. Pugh
1881-1954

C. E. "Dee" Burrow
1885-1960

Lurling Hopper Allen
Aug 18, 1901
Apr 11, 1958

Sarah Elizabeth Hopper
Jun 18, 1869
Jun 29, 1942

Jessee Paul Burrow
Sep 28, 1877
Mar 24, 1961
&
Elizabeth Cook Burrow
May 22, 1880

Clifford S. Keele
Feb 20, 1903
Jun 28, 1960
&
Laura Acree Keele
Sep 1, 1900

Robert V. Haston
1923-
&
Rosa Mae Haston
1921-1970

James Thomas Hopper
May 29, 1871
Apr 7, 1949

Virginia M. Cleek
1921-1943

Father
John L. Baxter
Apr 14, 1860
Oct 21, 1930
&
Mother
Sarah Ann Baxter
Apr 11, 1867
Mar 16, 1921

Lucile Stephenson
1913-1928

Ruben Boyd Baxter
1897-1966

John H. Miller
1881-(no date)
&
Maggie D. Miller
1874-1949

Emmet Harber
1882-1968
&
Mollie Harber
1885-1928

Myrt R. Stephenson
Sep 10, 1876
Sep 5, 1951
&
Betty C. Stephenson
Jun 11, 1888
Jan 19, 1955

FARMINGTON

William Hoyle Stephenson
1916-1918

L. Watt Davis
1862-1945
&
Emma E. Davis
1872-1947

Rita Gale Davis
Mar 4, 1947

Ethel D. Price
Jun 21, 1892
Dec 2, 1961

Thomas Jeff Davis
Aug 10, 1873
Dec 28, 1952
&
Emma Alice Davis
Oct 17, 1884

Thomas M. Gillespie
1868-1937
&
Lillie D. Gillespie
Mar 20, 1878
Feb 10, 1968

Janies, dau of
Mr. & Mrs. Richard Davis
Oct 10, 1935

Maggie A. Davis
Apr 9, 1848
Apr 17, 1937

William G. Davis
Dec 15, 1842
Apr 21, 1928

Samuel W. Sutton
1872-1958 (TM)

Walter G. Sutton
1880-1912
&
Ida L. Sutton
1882-1967
&
Lela Alice Griffin
1888-1963

Samuel Jesse Batten
Dec 11, 1869
Mar 9, 1955
&
Minnie Alma Batten
Aug 10, 1883
Sep 22, 1966

Maymie L. Batten
Jul 25, 1905
Sep 30, 1915

Sarah Ann Miller
Feb 7, 1943
Feb 7, 1943

W. B. Wortham
Oct 19, 1862
Jun 11, 1917

James L. Davis
1880-1960

Samuel J. Sutton "Father"
Nov 15, 1831
Jul 7, 1914
&
Susan G. Sutton "Mother"
Nov 1, 1847
(no date)

Charles Hopper
Feb 20, 1794
Jan 25, 1877
&
Clarkey Hopper
Nov 15, 1808
Oct 26, 1876
(On placque: This work was
put here and paid for by
H. H. Hopper, the youngest
son.)

H. H. Hopper
Sep 12, 1837
Dec 7, 1915
&
Mary A. Hopper
Apr 2, 1835
Dec --, 1919

Carleen Neese McClanahan
Sep 22, 1912
Jul 28, 1959

John, son of
Mr. & Mrs. E. W. Capps
Aug 19, 1938
Aug 19, 1938

D. J. Hargrove
Feb 1, 1875
May 9, 1939

Mrs. D. J. Hargrove
Feb 15, 1877
Jun 19, 1950

Vera L. Capps
Feb 6, 1920
Feb 7, 1941

Allen Otis, son of
C. T. & N. M. Harbor
Oct 13, 1901
Jul 11, 1902

Infant of
C. T. & N. M. Harbor
Nov 3, 1913

Charlie T. Harbor
Jan 18, 1878=Sep 4, 1920
&
Nora M. Harbor
May 10, 1877
(no date)

Lee Roy Keel
1900-1970
&
Ellie Mae Keel
1903-

Lee Less Keel
1929-1969

Pamela Gantley
1970-1970 (TM)

Hobert Perryman
Jun 2, 1906
Mar 18, 1968
&
Bessie Perryman
Jan 10, 1907

William F. Perryman
Dec 27, 1907
Feb 27, 1968
&
Clarice H. Perryman
Dec 6, 1916

Timothy A. Perryman
1961-1961 (TM)

George W. Perryman
1884-1957
&
Maymie L. Perryman
1906-1959

John D. Perryman
1947-1947

Claude Perryman
1945-1945

Riley M. Perryman
1937-1937

J. B. Epperson
1924-1937

S. David Glasscock
Dec 4, 1869
Feb 15, 1962
&
Maggie E. Glasscock
Aug 12, 1879
Nov 26, 1959

Mary E. Burrow
1904-1928

Margaret Burrow
1924-1946

William R. White
Tennessee, Cpl 381 Bakery Co
QMC WW I
May 6, 1896-Jan 31, 1970
&
Edna H. White
Sep 7, 1907
Oct 22, 1970

Eunice Glasscock
1897-1960 (TM)

Rayfield Hoyle Trollinger
1881-1953 (TM)

Rena Trollinger
1888-1955 (TM)

Gloria S. Williams
Nov 7, 1921
Feb 5, 1961

Tillman Williams
1881-1942
&
Lydia Williams
1898-19

Peggy Nell Brannon
Sep 4, 1945
Oct 22, 1952

James Richard Neese
Feb 23, 1907
Aug 12, 1929

Joel Lowe Neese
Jun 23, 1883
May 27, 1932

Mattie E. Neese
Feb 20, 1890
Sep 17, 1957

Sarah E. Pierson
1855-1941

Bob M. Dean
Nov 22, 1921
Aug 15, 1970
&
Mildred S. Dean
Oct 28, 1922

Charles A. Batten
Aug 18, 1910
Dec 1, 1970
&
Maude C. Batten
Dec 18, 1915

R. "Bob" Pierson
Apr 19, 1884
Dec 17, 1957
&
M. Ellen Pierson
Apr 8, 1898
May 25, 1929

Odell Pierson
Tennessee
Pfc Engineers WW II
Apr 25, 1919
Apr 28, 1957

William Thomas Pearson
May 27, 1913
Dec 1, 1970

FARMINGTON

Keifer Ezell
Mar 11, 1907
Jan 17, 1970
&
Addie S. Ezell
Nov 25, 1908

William Edgar White
Nov 3, 1915
Sep 30, 1946

Jennie B. Cooper
Oct 17, 1887
Sep 6, 1959

J. F. Brittain
Nov 14, 1847
Apr 24, 1915
&
A. R. Brittain
Mar 8, 1850
Jun 28, 1917

Frances Louise Caldwell
Dec 22, 1921
Jan 1, 1922

Ozro Caldwell
Co L 151 Inf A.E.F.
Jan 27, 1894
Feb 18, 1922
&
Maggie A. Caldwell
Jun 30, 1897
Aug 2, 1923

Nellie Susan Buckingham
Jul 3, 1843
Aug 19, 1926

Joe W. Buckingham
1871-1950
&
Ada L. Buckingham
1879-1954

Allen W. Buckingham
Jun 12, 1901
Mar 8, 1968
&
Catherine S. Buckingham
Nov 9, 1913

Frances J. A. Broomley
Oct 3, 1860
Aug 14, 1939

Elizabeth Houser
Jun 12, 1860
Mar 21, 1929

Harriet Houser
Mar 11, 1835
Oct 25, 1925

END OF HOPPER
* *

MT. LEBANON CEMETERY
Located at the Bedford County line, on Rich Creek. Copied in 1971. Rechecked July 9, 1978 by Helen & Tim Marsh.

Ellis Clyde Batten
Jul 10, 1892
Jul 17, 1892

Richard W. Hay
Died July 19, 1967
Age 74 years
(Cosmopolitian FH)

Miles T. Pardee
1866-1954
&
Nannie F. Pardee
1867-1947

Sallie P. Glasscock
Feb 4, 1873
Apr   1906

James N. Powell
Feb 23, 1826
May 25, 1904
&
Sallie A. Powell
Nov 30, 1843
Aug 1, 1921

Lina Alice, dau of
J. N. & Sallie A. Powell
Aug 20, 1876
Feb 24, 1895

Andrew Trollinger
Jan 31, 1829
Apr 11, 1905

Sarah A., wife of
A. T. Trollinger
Sep 21, 1840
Apr 1, 1901

Infant of
M. S. & N. F. Bills
May 23, 1905

Mary Gladys, dau of
M. S. & N. F. Bills
Aug 25, 1909
Nov 11, 1913

Jerry Richard Hay
1849-1936
&
Mary Alice Hay
1859-1932

Effie Linley Hay
1885-1966

Gladys, Infant dau of
R. H. & R. E. Trolinger
April 20, 1920

Spencer C. Cates
Tennessee
Pvt Co F 17th Regt Tenn Inf
Confederate States Army
1823-1903

Ernest M. O'Neal
1883-1952

Laura Etta Trollinger
1871-1952
(Lawrence FH)

Elizabeth B. Reavis, wife of
J. H. Bledsoe
Aug 31, 1854
Feb 10, 1923

William R. Stephenson
Jan 20, 1877
Feb 25, 1955
&
Novella O. Stephenson
Apr 1, 1882
Jul 3, 1921

Father
Will C. O'Neal
Jun 1, 1879
Sep 9, 1911
&
Mother
Bertie O'Neal
Dec 10, 1882
Sep 7, 1911

W. B. O.
(footstone)

Infant of
J. H. & M. L. Glasscock
(no dates)

Jimmie D. Glasscock
Oct 19, 1897
Jun 28, 1899

J. H. Glasscock
Jul 17, 1853
Mar 9, 1903
&
M. L. Glasscock
Apr 13, 1864
(no date)

Cummie Glasscock
Jul 18, 1890
Aug 28, 1906

Father
George Reavis
Apr 28, 1841
Oct 3, 1903
&
Mother
Eva Hayes Reavis
Feb 14, 1858
Jul 5, 1913
"Erected by D. Hayes Reavi_

Jimmie Judson, son of
George & Eva Reavis
Mar 12, 1882
Nov 16, 1882

Johnie Wamack, Son of
George & Eva Reavis
Dec 4, 1876
Nov 3, 1882

W. F. Dickens
Feb 21, 1868
Dec 7, 1894

Rosa Dickens
1871-1899

Father
Rev. R. B. Freeman
Sep 18, 1829
Feb 2, 1892
&
Mother
Louise S. Freeman
Mar 6, 1840
Mar 11, 1920

Fannie E. Freeman
May 2, 1870
May 18, 1889

FARMINGTON

James M. Pyland
Dec 2, 1855
Nov 7, 1939

Hardee L. Pyland
May 7, 1812
Jul 15, 1891

Nancy H., wife of
H. L. Pyland
Apr 7, 1820
Aug 7, 1901

S. W. Pyland
Aug 27, 1849
Dec 10, 1919

Lela D. Pyland
Apr 12, 1880
Apr 30, 1956

Jane Glasscock
Dec 17, 1823
Oct 21, 1903

Manervia J. Glasscock
1838-1904

Many unmarked graves.

J. T. Glasscock
Co C 4th Tenn Mt'd Inf
(no dates)

Polly Glasscock
1815- Feb 1862

Charnell Glasscock
Jan 15, 1812
Oct 7, 1894

Richard Reavis
1852-1854

I. N. Reavis
Oct 31, 1816
Jan 25, 1912

Rosanah D., wife of
I. N. Reavis
Jan 7, 1820
Aug 28, 1905

Nancy Glasscock
Jul 10, 1846
Feb 7, 1899

James V. Pyland
Jul 27, 1888
Sep 27, 1936

Charlotte Pyland
Jun 1, 1861
Dec 28, 1940

Hardy C. Robertson
Feb 9, 1871
Oct 18, 1959
&
Jennie Lee Robertson
Sep 2, 1882
(TM: Sep 27, 1969
Age 84 yrs, 11mos, 25 da)
(TM now gone, 1978)

Louisa Glasscock
Jan 20, 1844
Died 1866

Charley Johnson
Jan 26, 1876
Mar 1895

Mary Ann Marrow
1842-1866

Father
Jake O'Neal
1845-1890
&
Mother
Alice O'Neal
1856-1928

Our Baby
Emma E. O'Neal
Nov 24, 1901
Dec 6, 1901

Emma Ethel O'Neal
1888-1899

J.A.J. Pickle
Jul 16, 1868
Age 10 years

M. F. Pickle
Nov 11, 1879
Mar 11, 1882

Francis, wife of
P. M. Pickle
Apr 23, 1837
Jun 3, 1904

* *

CHAPMAN CEMETERY
Located on the Palmetto Cemetery Road, east of Farmington.
Copied January 27, 1974 by Ralph D. Whitesell.

Bennett E. Chapman
Feb 2, 1830
Jun 18, 1906

Nancy Ann Chapman
Apr 3, 1840
Jun 22, 1926

Two graves, enclosed by
Rock wall, large marker,
no inscription, believed
to be the grave of
Robert Chapman & his wife.

Ana Mary Chapman
Jan 15, 1874
Jan 15, 1891

NOTE: Ana Mary and Nora Bell
Chapman were the daus of
Bennett E. & Nancy Ann Chapman.
They died from Typhoid fever.
RDW.

Nora Bell Chapman
Apr 25, 1871
Mar 1, 1891

* *

LONG CEMETERY
Located on the back side of the Memorial Gardens, south of
Horton State Park, on the east side of Highway No. 31-A.

Benton W. Long
Co D 4th Tenn Cav
  C.S.A.
1840-1911

Mary F. Long
1846-1918

Richard Long
Sep 22, 1758
May 30, 1848
(no marker, Rev. Soldier)

Nancy (Stevenson) Long,
2nd wife of Richard Long
Born ------------
Died Sep 23, 1846
(no marker)

Thomas Long
Dec 20, 1793
Apr 11, 1874

Sallie G., wife of
Thomas Long
Mar 11, 1809
Apr 3, 1884

B. B. L. (footstone)
---------, Son of
Thomas & Sallie Long
Dec 1, 1834
Jan 9, 1856
(stone broken)

Claudie, son of
J. L. & S. A. Baxter
Jul 30, 1890
Sep 14, 1892

"My Husband"
David E. M. Woods
Jul 22, 1826
May 26, 1863
&
"My Daughter"
Sallie E. Woods
Feb 9, 1862
Dec 14, 1862

* *

FARMINGTON

THOMAS CEMETERY

Located one-fourth mile south of Anes, on Rock Creek. Copied November 17, 1979 by Ralph D. Whitesell and Helen and Tim Marsh.

Sam D. R. Fowler
Nov 13, 1890
Aug 30, 1921

Walter B. Bills
Feb 26, 1879
(no date)
&
Florence Ann Bills
Jun 3, 1867
Mar 1, 1918

Daisy D. Sellers
1903-1951

J. W. Thomas
Sep 15, 1846
Feb 12, 1936
&
Estelle Thomas
Sep 15, 1845
Aug 12, 1916

John William Clark
404 Co Motor Trans Corps
U.S.A.

Effie T. Houston
1884-1971

James L. Garrett
1852-1933
&
Mary L. Garrett
1862-19(no date)

Myrtle Garrett
Jul 13, 1886
May 25, 1965

R. Howard Leonard
Jul 18, 1898
Feb 9, 1947
&
Sadie M. Leonard
Oct 27, 1904

Loyd Leonard
1931-1974

Members of the Leonard Family, unmarked.

* *

POWELL CEMETERY

Located on Old Columbia Highway No. 99, north east of Caney Spring and three miles south west of Chapel Hill. Copied December 8, 1979 by Ralph D. Whitesell, Helen and Tim Marsh.

E. R.
B- A   3, 1823
D- J 30, 1825
(fieldstone)

E. D. R.
D-Ju + D + 23 + 1825
B + 2 + 10
(Fieldstone)

Son
July 7, 1835
(fieldstone)

J. R.
Sept 9, 1809
(fieldstone)

M. R.
(fieldstone

M. A. R.
Nov 1793
July 3, 1835
(fieldstone)

M. J.
(fieldstone)

"Mother"
Mary Anne Rone
Mar 27, 1855
Dec 10, 1919

Alvin P., son of
H. H. & M. L. Thomson
Dec 31, 1892
Sep 17, 1893

Austin Powell
Nov 15, 1829
Jan 24, 1898

Emily Jimmey, dau of
Hugh & Mary Thomson & wife of
Austin Powell
Dec 17, 1840
Jan 3, 1860

William L. Neely
Nov 7, 1804
Jul 30, 1878

Mrs. Elizabeth, wife of
William L. Neely
Feb 13, 1813
Jan 24, 1875

Rufus L., son of
Wm. L. & Elizabeth Neely
Feb 6, 1851
Aug 21, 1873

William T. Price
Nov 17, 1820
Jan 27, 1894
Age 73 yrs, 2 mos, 10 days.

Rachel J.(Jane) Price
Jun 31, 1821
Jul 24, 1909

Hugh Thomson
Sep 6, 1806
Aug 10, 1892

Henry, son of
H. H. & M. L. Thomson
Apr 28, 1886
Apr 23, 1898

Mary H., dau of
Thomas & Elizabeth
Blackwell & wife of
Hugh Thomson
Sep 20, 1806
Jun 16, 1874

Mary E. Crutcher
Sep 1, 1831
Oct 15, 1908

* *

BETHBIREI CEMETERY

Located five miles north of Lewisburg, about half way between the Verona Road and the old Farmington Road. There are many unmarked graves. Across the road, is the oldest section of the cemetery. Bethbirei Presbyterian Church is the oldest church in Marshall County, its organization dates back to 1810. Copied October 19, 1958 by Ralph D. Whitesell and Mrs. Lounora Pickens.

Martha C. Ewing
1838-1913

John A. Ewing
1818-1893

Thomas S. Ewing
Feb 28, 1872
Oct 4, 1913

Mary Haynes, wife of
T. S. Ewing
Jul 12, 1877-Apr 23, 1909

FARMINGTON

Martha I., dau of
J. W. & V. M. Walker
Died July 13, 1847
Age 16 yrs, 10 mos, 16 days

Grizzella, Second wife of
Alexander Dysart
Jan 18, 1806
Mar 31, 1873

Alexander Dysart
May 27, 1808
Jan 7, 1880

James F., son of
A. & G. Dysart
Mar 31, 1847
Jul 1, 1867

Newton F., son of
A. & G. Dysart
May 8, 1842
Sep 9, 1843

Mary I. S., wife of
Alexander Dysart
Jan 5, 1812
Dec 26, 1835

Sofrona C., dau of
A. & M. Dysart
Apr 14, 1832
Sep 14, 1833

John C., son of
Samuel W. & E. C. Colvert
Died March 1829
Age 22 months.

Kitty, dau of
S. A. & Emma J. Duling
Feb 12, 1866
Sep 12, 1867

Samuel Whitfield, son of
John & Sarah Ramsey
Par 26, 1835
Oct 4, 1836
Age 1 yr, 5 mos, 8 days

Mary Amanda, dau of
John & Sarah Ramsey
May 20, 1838
Aug 13, 1839
Age 1 yr, 2 mos, 23 days

John Ramsey
Apr 23, 1797
Sep 14, 1891

Sarah B., wife of
John Ramsey
Jan 18, 1814
Jan 19, 1898

Rachel, wife of
John LaRue
Mar 8, 1793
Jan 18, 1863

Robert Hunter
Apr 13, 1745
May 3, 1835
Age 86 yrs, 20 days

Rebecca Hunter, Consort of
Robert Hunter
Died Dec 1, 1832
Age 72 years.

Edwin Hunter
Born Oct 1788
Died Jun 10, 1839

Milton B. Hunter
Sep 15, 1817
Jul 10, 1840
Age 22 yrs, 4 mos, 5 days

Elizabeth R. Wiggs
1815-1856

John Richard, son of
P. C. & S. M. King
Died Jun 29, 1857
Age 4 yrs, 7 mos, 13 days

"Our John"
W. S. & R. Y. Anderson
(no dates)

"Our Mary"
(no dates)

"Our Baby"
(no dates)

James B. Laws
Dec 6, 1839
Nov 6, 1854
Age 14 yrs, 11 mos.

John Laws
Feb 13, 1802
May 23, 1874

Mary N., wife of
John Laws
Sep 12, 1813
Jun 22, 1855
Age 41 yrs, 10 mos, 9 days

Willie F. Jett
Tennessee
Cpl 352 Fighter SQ AAF WW II
Nov 5, 1917
Jan 24, 1953

Robert L. Isley
1862-1945

Lizzie Isley
1879-1957

Nancy E., wife of
I. A. Thomas
Mar 18, 1832
Sep 11, 1865

Miles Pardee
Apr 30, 1790
May 26, 1872

Tennessee C., wife of
Miles Pardee
Nov 15, 1832
Jul 24, 1912

Mrs. Collie M., wife of
L. Fuller, dau of
James D. & Elizabeth Ewing
Sep 3, 1837
Apr 6, 1862

Littleton Fuller
Nov 7, 1827
Jan 7, 1896

Mary J., wife of
J. B. Wilkes, Dau of
J. D. & E. Ewing
Apr 1, 1835
Aug 16, 1856
Age 21 yrs, 4 mos, 15 days

Mary Virginia, dau of
I. B. & M. J. Wilkes
Jun 3, 1856
Jul 24, 1856
Age 1 mo, 21 days

Robert H. Hunter
Jul 10, 1819
Jan 3, 1849
Age 29 yrs, 5 mos, 25 days

Sylvester Hunter
Jan 11, 1824
Mar 11, 1847
Age 23 yrs, 2 mos.

Tibza Hunter
Mar 2, 1801
Oct 11, 1851

Priscilla Russell
Apr 1, 1794
Apr 24, 1870
&
William Paley Russell
Age 2 years
(no dates)

Nat Rives
Died Oct 8, 1827
Age 22 yrs, 5 days

Rachel Virginia, dau of
Felix & Rachel Ewing
Jan 9, 1827
Sep 11, 1842

Samuel B. Appleby
1808-1887

In Memory of
Rev. Thomas J. Hall
Who was born in Iredell
Co., N.C. Feb 28, 1774,
Was married Jan 7, 1803
& Died Feb 27, 1859.
Age 84 yrs, 7 mos, 29 days
"Was pastor of Bethbirei
Church 34 years, 7 months
& 16 days, & preached for
the glory of God & not to
please his fellowmen. He
being dead yet speaketh
our flesh shall rest in
hope. This corruptible
shall put on incorrupt-
ion and this mortal shall
put on immortality. Death
is swallowed up in Victory.
1st Cor. 15: 53-54
Debtors continue in Grace."

In Memory of
Emma W. Hall, wife of
Rev. Thomas J. Hall
Who was born in Iredell Co.,
N.C. June 22, 1780. Died
April 25, 1849. Age 68
yrs, 10 mos, 3 days.

Thomas A. Hall, Consort of
Catherine C. Hall & son of
Thomas J. & Emma W. Hall
Mar 10, 1810
Apr 9, 1841
Age 31 yrs, 1 mo.

Catherine C. Hall, Widow
of Thomas A. Hall & dau of
Thompson & Elizabeth Cannon
Sep 25, 1816
Sep 17, 1841
Age 25 yrs.

Elizabeth T. Hall, Consort
of Thomas A. Hall & dau of
John & Mary L. Nowlin
Died Aug 10, 1838
Age 20 yrs, 3 mos, 9 days

Felicia Ann, dau of
Thomas & Elizabeth T. Hall
Died Aug 9, 1838
Age 24 days

James Ewing
Born in Cumberland Co., Pa.
Sep 21, 1782
Oct 18, 1860

Mary, wife of
James Ewing, Born in Burk
Co., N.C. Feb 4, 1798
Died Jul 11, 1828

FARMINGTON

In Memory of
John McClarey
Who was born in the state
of Pennsylvania April 24,
1765, Departed this life
Oct 24, 1810.
Age 75 yrs, 8 mos.

Elizabeth McClarey
Wife of John McClarey
Died Jan 4, 1850
Age 81 years.

Nancy I., Consort of
John Baxter & dau of
Edwin H. & Mary McNail
Died Sep 22, 1853
Age 22 yrs, 7 mos, 14 days

Joseph P. Ewing
Died Aug 10, 1833
Age 44 yrs, 7 mos.

Jane E. Appleby, Consort
of S. B. Appleby & dau of
George & Jane E. Ewing
Jul 31, 1811
Jun 2, 1846
Age 35 yrs, 10 mos.

John Simeon, son of
S. B. & J. E. Appleby
Feb 1, 1844
Jul 24, 1844
Age 6 mos, 24 days

John E. Miller
Aug 10, 1843
Died   1845
Age about 2 years

Mary E. Miller
Oct 23, 1810
May 5, 1844
Age 33 yrs, 7 mos, 12 days

Margaret H., Consort of
Milton H. Dysart & dau of
Wm. D. & Rebecca Ewing
Died May 29, 1836
Age 18 yrs, 11 mos, 1 day

B. T. McRee
May 7, 1807
Nov 8, 1834
Age 21 yrs, 6 mos.

Here lies the body of
Thomas C. Block
Who died AD Nov 20th 1823
Age 30 years

Here lies the body of
Rebecca A. Block
Died AD June 18, 1820
Age 18 mos.

George Ewing
Mar 30, 1775
May 9, 1842
Age 67 yrs, 1 mo, 10 days

John Agnew Duling
Jan 9, 1842
Aug 22, 1870

Eudora James
Apr 23, 1852
Dec 16, 1876

Jane Ewing
Jan 30, 1781
Sep 7, 1855
Age 74 yrs, 7 mos, 7 days

John L., son of
Wm. D. & R. Ewing
Died Aug 31, 1833
Age 4 mos.

David A. Ewing
Died Apr 14, 1833
Age 20 years

In Memory of Mary Ewing
Who was born October, 1750
& Departed this life
10th of August, 1834
Age 83 years, 10 months

Andrew T. Ewing
Aug 9, 1810
Aug 18, 1834
Age 24 yrs, 9 days

Nancy C., dau of
Ephraim & Mary Hunter
Nov 21, 1817
Oct 21, 1831
Age 13 yrs, 8 mos, 4 days

Rob. M., son of
Robert & Mary Hunter
Nov 13, 1820
Aug 1, 1821

Infant Son of
Mary & Ephraim Hunter
Born 11th of May, 1830

W. D. Ewing
Oct 12, 1786
May 1, 1872
Age 85 yrs, 20 days

Rebeckah, Consort of
W. D. Ewing
Jan 17, 1791
Jun 4, 1847

Ann E., Consort of
W. D. Ewing
Died 13 ---, 1867
Age 67 years.

Louisa Miller
May 28, 1811
Aug 7, 1836
Age 25 yrs, 3 mos, 10 days

Frances Dysart
Nov 31, 1788-___ 22, 1824

Mary Ann Dysart
Nov 22, 1818
August 1824

Francis R. Dysart
Dec 1, 1820
Died   1824

T. W. A. Ewing
Died Oct 1, 1860
Age 5 months

R. R. Ewing
Died June 13, 1860
Age 23 yrs, 3 mos, 2 days

Harriet Rebeccah, dau of
T. B. & R. R. Ewing
Nov. 6, 1858
Dec. 3, 1858

W. N., son of
S. D. & J. E. Ewing
Jun 25, 1848
May 18, 1852

L. G., son of
S. D. & J. E. Ewing
Jul 26, 1845
Nov 8, 1852

T. J. H. Ewing
Jan 31, 1827
Mar 7, 1855

Floyd B. Ewing
Sep 7, 1833
Jul 21, 1903
&
Mary J. Ewing
Sep 5, 1841
Apr 4, 1913

Knox Ewing
1871-1941

Mamie Ewing
1880-1945

Mittie E., dau of
T. S. & S. J. Ewing
May 15, 1855
Oct 1, 1868

Jas. S. Ewing
Jul 5, 1824
Mrd- Jan 16, 1845
Oct 9, 1906

Eliza J., wife of
Jas. E. Ewing
Dec 19, 1829
Nov 15, 1904

Ittie Ewing
1875-19(no date)
&
Mittie Ewing
1875-1954

S. D. Ewing
Dec 8, 1819
Apr 3, 1883

Jane E., wife of
Dr. S. D. Ewing
Jul 12, 1825
Aug 8, 1886

Addie M., wife of
B. H. Fisher
Jun 2, 1856
Nov 20, 1889

Samuel J. Ewing
Oct 26, 1877
Mar 26, 1945

Hattie Liggett Ewing
Jul 13, 1880
Sep 3, 1957

Mary E., dau of
M. H. & H. C. Dysart
Dec 26, 1851
Jul 17, 1853

(Iron fence enclosure,
with "Samuel Ewing".
2 graves.)

Alberta Ewing
Sep 7, 1843
Nov 21, 1926

Argyle A. Ewing
Jun 4, 1840
Jul 30, 1892

Wilber T. Ewing
Apr 6, 1885
Nov 2, 1911

Sallie Rebecca Nowlin
Dec 19, 1873
Dec 26, 1890

James Ozro Nowlin
Dec 8, 1843
Oct 30, 1879

Dr. Bryan W. Nowlin
1820-1861
&
Rebecca Neill Nowlin
1821-1880

Matilda, wife of
L. A. Thomas
Mar 30, 1836
Nov 9, 1902

Dora L. Barron
Dec 29, 1872
Dec 4, 1903

Robert E. Ewing, son of
J. C. & Hattie Collins
Jan 19, 1896
Dec 24, 1915

FARMINGTON

Infants of
J. C. & Hattie Collins
Sep 24, 1899
Feb 17, 1900
&
Dec 3, 1903
Dec 7, 1903

Father
John C. Collins
Sep 15, 1858
May 4, 1929
&
Mother
Hattie P. Collins
Aug 28, 1860
Mar 7, 1930

Dorothy Ann Jett
Died Mar 9, 1958
Age 20 days.

Mrs. Nannie Jett Shirley
1883-1953

Rev. L. M. Hunter
May 1, 1826
Mar 3, 1908
& wife
Phoebia Ann Hunter
Oct 18, 1833
Mar 13, 1908

William O. Rutledge
Feb 16, 1867
Oct 20, 1943
&
Annie May Rutledge
Sep 22, 1871
(no date)

William O. Rutledge
Nov 5, 1810
Sep 10, 1880
&
Amanda E. Rutledge
Nov 18, 1833
Jul 1, 1912

Grady, son of
H. M. & Z. M. Roberts
May 26, 1890
Sep 1, 1894

A. M. Roberts
Jul 20, 1861
Jan 30, 1904

Myrtle Rutledge Roberts
Nov 13, 1872
May 6, 1946

Justin O. Rutledge
Feb 20, 1869
Dec 10, 1956

Rena Rutledge Anderson
May 25, 1863
Dec 30, 1932

William T. Jett
1863-1950
&
Catherine Jett
1867-1946

Ittie, wife of
T. D. Ramsey
Mar 18, 1856
Feb 16, 1891
& husband
(no marker)

Fannie T. Ewing
Nov 14, 1869
May 6, 1873

William W. Bond
1829-1891

Margaret Appleby Bond
1837-1887

Emma Bond
1860-1890

Lena Bond
1866-1872

Infant Son of
S. A. & A. R. Appleby
Jun 10, 1873
Jun 28, 1873

Flora Bell, dau of
S. A. & A. R. Appleby
Jan 28, 1867
Oct 1, 1875

Samuel Argyle Appleby
Jun 1, 1845
Jan 7, 1923
& wife
Ann Rebekah Ewing Appleby
Mar 2, 1846
Jul 9, 1928

Alvan B. Ewing
Jan 9, 1819
Dec 20, 1900
Age 81 yrs, 11 mos, 11 days

Louisai, wife of
A. B. Ewing
Dec 25, 1824
Feb 20, 1879
Age 54 yrs, 1 mo, 26 days

Scott Dryden Davis
Jun 14, 1844
Mar 6, 1929

Kitty Ewing Davis
Mar 23, 1846
May 28, 1926

Olivia "Lolly" Davis
Oct 30, 1875
Sep 25, 1947

Sheryl I. George
1952-1957

John M. Hayes
1877-1945
&
Myrtle Hayes
1879-1953

M. J. Beatty
Oct 1860
Dec 13, 1914
&
Mattie Beatty
Aug 16, 1868
Dec 20, 1914

Tom M. Little
Aug 8, 1854
Sep 18, 1914
&
Bettie Little
Mar 23, 1860
May 18, 1914

Effie Beatty
Nov 12, 1886
Died (no date) &
Infant, born 1888

Callie, wife of
Spencer Snell
Jun 28, 1831
Dec 30, 1876

Adelaide Snell
Sep 17, 1851
Jan 10, 1921

Spencer M. Snell
Oct 21, 1840
May 8, 1918

Walter L. Burgess
Dec 27, 1874
May 13, 1890

William T. Burgess
Oct 5, 1884
Oct 16, 1903

Martha C. Burgess
Oct 27, 1848
Aug 19, 1918

Brice H. Burgess
Apr 3, 1849
Dec 13, 1900

Florence L. George
Nov 13, 1925

Infant Son of
J. & E. Carpenter
Aug 7, 1874
Sep 29, 1874

Mattie K., wife of
H. C. McQuiddy
Born Sep 25, 1845
Died (broken)
(New Stone: Kate McQuiddy
Sep 25, 1845
Jul 12, 1880)

Sallie A., wife of
Dr. J. C. Hill
Feb 22, 1859
Mar 10, 1888

Sallie H., wife of
B. H. Fisher
Apr 28, 1856
Mar 30, 1882

Luther R. Hill
Dec 3, 1859
Sep 27, 1885
Age 25 yrs, 9 mos, 24 days

Mary K. McClarey
1858-1932
&
Jas. O. McClarey
1845-1908
&
Mary W. Woods
1816-1882
&
Elizabeth Leeper McClarey
1807-1890

William Leeper McClarey
1884-1916

William Carlton
1819-1905

Martha Carlton
1827-1894

Mattie J. Stewart
Mar 5, 1865
Dec 26, 1943

Jas. A. Stewart
Dec 12, 1860
Oct 22, 1917

Ozro Nowlin Hardison
1875-1939

Ida Thomas Hardison
1876-1936

William Howard, son of
O. N. & Ida Hardison
Jan 19, 1896
Jun 16, 1905

Monroe Bills
1831-1886

Susan Osborn Bills
1842-1883

FARMINGTON

Enoch M. Osborne
Jan 29, 1862
Feb 8, 1894
& wife
Sarah E. Osborne
Jun 22, 1858
(no date)
&
Infant
Jul 15, 1882
Jul 17, 1882
&
Robert Cecil Osborne
Dec 22, 1886
Sep 25, 1913

Floyd A. Bills
1835-1891

Infant of
J. W. & J. B. Turner
Feb 6, 1889

Jennie C., wife of
John Lane
Jul 7, 1844
Aug 23, 1887

Elizabeth D., wife of
W. L. Thomas
Nov 25, 1846
May 26, 1889

W. L. Thomas
Apr 8, 1846
Mar 17, 1913

Claude Bills
1878=1932

Daisy E., wife of
Claud Bills
Sep 22, 1876
Aug 10, 1901

Helen, dau of
Claude & Daisy Bills
May 13, 1900
May 18, 1907

Lura Bills
1875-1946

Mary Neill Walker
Feb 19, 1843
Aug 2, 1923

Loyd Walker
Apr 29, 1886
Aug 6, 1902

Loila Walker
Nov 11, 1882
Nov 21, 1902

John H. Walker
Sep 16, 1867
Jul 10, 1934

Samuel Knox Walker
Mar 22, 1869
Jul 7, 1935

Henry Marshall Adams
1889-1948

William Hoyle Adams
Dec 9, 1925
Feb 3, 1929

Infant Son of
A. W. & Kate Cochran
Sept 18, 1909

Leander N. Ewing
1817-1911

Jane W. Ewing
1818-1908

George A. Endsley
1865-1935

Lessie W. Endsley
1866-1940

Clarence Endsley
1904-1927

Will Knox Endsley
Apr 2, 1899
Feb 2, 1910

Charles T. Stewart
1929-1929

Thomas Fagan
1900-1902

Martha Fagan
1903-1903

Charles Fagan
1905-1905

George B. Walker
Dec 13, 1875
Apr 30, 1902
&
Carrie B. Walker
Feb 4, 1875
Oct 15, 1904
&
Frank Lyle Walker
Feb 3, 1889
Mar 21, 1913
&
Robert Scott Walker
Jan 10, 1839
Feb 28, 1922

Mrs. Jane Woods, wife of
John Lawrence
Dec 1, 1874
Sep 3, 1927

Cecil Stewart
Tennessee
Pvt 318 Field Artillery
81st Div
Mar 22, 1939

Mary J. Purdom
Oct 18, 1861
May 11, 1940

George D. Purdom
May 31, 1862
Nov 23, 1936

Robert D. Glenn
Jan 7, 1873
Aug 5, 1949
&
Anna Bell Glenn
Jul 8, 1875
1960

Alice Cathey Fagan, dau of
Lyndal & Nell Fagan
1948

Robert S. Fagan
1889-1963
&
Alice S. Fagan
1886-1945

Claude C. Fagan "Son"
Feb 3, 1913

William H. McKee Orr
Jul 11, 1873
Dec 12, 1937

Sallie C. Orr
Oct 16, 1875
Feb 2, 1932

Mary J. Orr
Sep 14, 1837
Dec 25, 1915

William L. Orr
Mar 30, 1825
Oct 6, 1902

Mrs. Julia Ketchum
1897-1958

Lyle W. Ewing
Sep 4, 1879
Mar 25, 1951

Billy Ewing
May 17, 1913
Aug 15, 1913

Clair W. Ewing
Jul 17, 1915
Sep 24, 1936

W. B. Hill
Feb 13, 1813
Sep 6, 1897

Martha A. Hill
Mar 4, 1818
Oct 22, 1902

James Osborne
Oct 7, 1872
Oct 8, 1905

Sallie Miller, wife of
James Osborne
Apr 5, 1875
Feb 23, 1898

James O. Miller
1868-1940

Mary Lou Miller
1876-1951

John Orr
May 14, 1792
Aug 22, 1879

Johnnie
(no other information)

William Mayfield, son of
William & M. C. Robinson
Dec 4, 1876
Oct 4, 1900

William Mayfield Robinson
Aug 30, 1831
Apr 17, 1914
&
Marilyn Robinson
Aug 24, 1841
Mar 23, 1923

Nancy Robinson, wife of
R. R. Whitaker
Jan 23, 1861
Aug 17, 1926

Virginia Robinson Landy
Jun 10, 1863
Aug 2, 1953

R. M. Landy
Feb 14, 1857
Jun 24, 1896

Richard Robinson Landy
Jul 2, 1890
Aug 20, 1910

Mamie Claire Miller
Apr 12, 1893
Jul 3, 1894

J. L. Miller
1845-1923

Aramintta Miller
1845-1896

Nancy L., wife of
W. T. Osborne
Aug 21, 1866
Jan 7, 1894

FARMINGTON

Charley A. Hays
Tennessee
Pvt Co I 323 Inf WW I
Aug 31, 1886
Sep 6, 1953

Samuel D. Russell
Died Aug 23, 1909
(no age given)
&
Arrivella C. Russell
Died Mar 2, 1895
(no age given)
&
Martha E. N. Russell
Died Jan 14, 1910
(no age given)
&
Jemima T. Russell
(no dates)

Infant Son of
G. C. & N. T. Houston
Born & Died 1888

Burke Akin Houston
Dec 5, 1889
Sep 24, 1894

Euphra May Houston
Dec 5, 1891
Oct 10, 1894

Andrew J. Hicks
Feb 22, 1853
Jan 22, 1918

Bessie L. Hicks
Jun 1, 1884
May 22, 1904

Florella J. Ewing
Born May 3, 1835
Mrd- May 3, 1853
Died Jun 29, 1895

Newton B. Ewing
Nov 2, 1826
Feb 6, 1899

James A. Ewing
Feb 26, 1843
Jan 22, 1930
&
Mary Dysart Ewing
Jun 12, 1836
Jul 2, 1921

Bethenia E. Hightower
Apr 6, 1838
Feb 15, 1923

James H. Hightower
Feb 10, 1838
Nov 5, 1893

Otway Hightower
(unmarked)

Iire Little Leeper
Dec 7, 1881
Jul 7, 1941

Mary J. Wiggs
1852-1876

Florella Wiggs
1854-1878

John Calvin Wiggs
1849-1873

Hannah W. Stewart
1844-1919

Elizabeth, wife of
W. J. Snell
May 15, 1869
Mar 22, 1909

William J. Snell
1871-1955

Sara E. Snell
1883-19(no date)

R. N. Glenn
Oct 8, 1845
Sep 20, 1909
&
S. H. Glenn
May 9, 1844
Mar 28, 1935

Marguerite Elizabeth, dau
of William L. & Dixie Bond
Jul 17, 1900
Dec 6, 1901

Annie Ewing, dau of
W. L. & Dixie Bond
Nov 5, 1890
Oct 29, 1905

Milton Waddey
(Grave not marked)

J. B. Jett
1872-1957

R. R. Rainey
Feb 24, 1807
Dec 11, 1886
"He was a Soldier in the
Mexican War."

Mother Jett
(no dates)
&
Our Baby Jett
(no dates)

Fannie Drucilar Shirley
Jun 14, 1878
Jul 18, 1921

Bert F. George
1901-
&
Maple George
1909-1964

Virginia B., dau of
William D. & Mary E. Fisher
1841-1842

Calvin Church
1862-1937 (TM)

H. Lee Hicks
Jan 28, 1893

&
Mable P. Hicks
Feb 6, 1896
Mar 18, 1965

Willie R. Jett
1886-1964
&
Beulah M. Jett
1896-

John R. McClarey
Tennessee
Pfc 1716 SVC Comd Unit WW II
Dec 29, 1897
Mar 14, 1962

Ollie Purdom
Dec 29, 1869
Mar 11, 1944
&
Lula Purdom
Dec 27, 1870
Jun 14, 1960

Walter R. Jett
Mar 7, 1892
Feb 21, 1965
&
Gatha L. Jett
Mar 8, 1900

Bessie S., dau of
W. S. & Fannie Gambill
May 18, 1878
Nov 8, 1907

Una E. Gambill
Jul 10, 1876
Feb 22, 1893

Alpheas L., son of
William D. & Mary E. Fisher
Died Jun 20, 1837
Age 3 mos, 9 days

A marble slab bolted to a
hugh native stone in the
northwest corner of the
churchyard bears the
inscription:
June 1, 1810
On this spot was preached
by Rev. Samuel Finley the
first and organization
sermon of Bethbirei Church,
from "Upon this rock I will
build my church".

BETHBIREI CEMETERY
(Across road from Church)

Lutisha Melton, wife of
J. A. Christopher
1861-1906

John Appleby
Who was born Dec 21, 1778
& Died April 6, 1863
Age 84 yrs, 5 mos, 15 days

Sarah Appleby
Was born Jan 8, 1772
Departed this life
Dec 8, 1852
Age 80 yrs, 11 mos.

Calvin B. Ewing
Died Dec 8, 1857
Age 27 years

Rebecca A., Consort of
Lile A. Ewing
Aug 14, 1809
Apr 11, 1877

Lile A., Consort of
Rebecca A. Ewing
Died Mar 26, 1853
Age 43 yrs, 5 mos, 29 days

Infant Son of
L. A. & R. A. Ewing
Born & Died
Mar 7, 1849

In Memory of
Rebekah Leeper, wife of
Allen Leeper, Who departed
this life Feb 4, 1856
Age 83 years

Sacred to the Memory of
Allen Leeper
Consort of Rebekah Leeper
Who departed this life
Feb 21, 1839
Age 65 yrs, 6 mos, 3 days

In Memory of Mary Ewing,
Consort of Jas. L. Ewing &
dau of Allen & Rebekah
Leeper, Born 31st of Oct AD
1797. Departed this life
28th of Oct AD 1824 in the
27th year of her age.

FARMINGTON

Jane Neill, Consort of
Samuel Neill, dau of
Allen & Rebekah Leeper
Jun 14, 1801
Jul 29, 1824
Age 25 years.

James, son of
Allen & Rebekah Leeper
Mar 13, 1804
Sep 30, 1823
Age 20 years

Samuel J., son of
B. W. & R. E. Nowlin
Mar 1, 1842
Oct 30, 1843

Infant Son of
Allen & Rebekah Leeper
(no dates)

Slave of Ewing Family
"Died Happy"

Elizabeth, dau of
J. L. & M. Ewing
Died Jul 30, 1828
Age 8 yrs, 6 mos.

Gideon H. Ewing, Consort of
H. C. Ewing & son of
J. L. & Mary Ewing
Died Apr 8, 1838
Age 23 years.

N. B. Ewing, Son of
James L. & Mary Ewing
Sep 10, 1817
Jul 29, 1834

E. E. Vernor
Died Apr 19, 1881
Age 75 years.

Jane Vernor
(no dates)

Many unmarked graves.

David C. Creswell
Jan 29, 1805
Sep 1, 1842

3 other pyramid type graves
(probably Henry Creswell &
wife)

In Memory of
H. V. Turner
Who departed this life
Apr 23, 1830
Age 45 years

Nancy Orr
Jun 27, 1799
Jan 22, 1866

In Memory of
John Herron
Who died December 1814
(no age given)

In Memory of
E. W. Hunter
Mar 18, 1798
Oct 22, 1876

In Memory of
Jane Herron, who died
October 1818
(no age given)

William Whitfield Hunter
May 1, 1850
Jul 30, 1884
Age 34 yrs, 1 mo, 29 days

Mary E. Baxter
Jul 25, 1837
Feb 18, 1880

A. Baxter
Nov 10, 1832
Jul 1, 1873

Delia, wife of
Hamp Drake
1824-1883

Susan W. Hunter, Consort
of E. W. Hunter
Who died Aug 1, 1848
(no age given)

END BETHBIREI

* ***

CATHEY CEMETERY

Located one-half mile north east of Bethbirei Church and
five miles north of Lewisburg. Property now owned by Mrs.
Frank B. Houston, Sr. Copied April 30, 1958 by Ralph D.
Whitesell and Myrtle Lee Walker.

Peggie Cathey
Wife of
George Cathey
Age 64 years
(no dates)

George Cathey
Oct 16, 1784
Dec 3, 1866

Sarah A. Cathey
Sep 19, 1818
Nov 20, 1901

George, son of
George & Peggie Cathey
Feb 10, 1822
Oct 5, 1844

* *

FISHER CEMETERY

Located East of Verona & one mile north of Bethbirei Church.
Cemetery is in good shape. Copied in 1959.

Sally Mary, dau of
R. M. & M. C. Haggard
Jan 25, 1866
Dec 15, 1866

John Lee Bradley
1875-1955

Fay Fisher Bradley
1878-1957

Jose Burr Fisher
Oct 22, 1878
Nov 8, 1951

Frank M. Haggard
1863-1900

E. B. Green
Sep 18, 1868
Dec 23, 1885

D. B. Green
Aug 4, 1879
Nov 10, 1891

E. J. Green
Sep 22, 1875
Mar 24, 1894

M. A. Green
Jun 13, 1850
Nov 25, 1902

T. P. Green
Dec 27, 1842
Jul 25, 1905

E. M. Fisher
Jul 29, 1836
Jun 18, 1896

John Fisher
Sep 17, 1806
Apr 13, 1882

Mildred Stratton, wife of
John Fisher
November 1810
Jul 20, 1882

Bascom Hurt Fisher
Oct 25, 1852
Feb 28, 1917

William Thomas Bradley
May 25, 1877
Aug 29, 1941

W. F. Smith
1860-1911

James Dean, son of
Jacob & Mattie Bell Fisher
Jan 28, 1879
Sep 15, 1899

A. B. Green
Mar 19, 1872
Aug 25, 1918

Ella Green
Jun 14, 1877
Jun 26, 1918

Manie B. Green
Sep 11, 1887
Jul 22, 1909

George Adrin
Dec 18, 1873
Dec 5, 1945

FARMINGTON

Annie May
Sep 8, 1885

Sadie, dau of
Mr. & Mrs. Bacone Haggard
(no dates)

Sadie Haggard Schuessler
Jul 29, 1876
Feb 5, 1951

Bettie Cathey Haggard
1856-1946

Rev. Berry S. Haggard
Feb 2, 1857
Jul 13, 1892

Betty L., dau of
Rev. Robert M. & Mary C.
Haggard
Dec 29, 1858
Jun 25, 1882

B. A. Mannan
1886

Many unmarked graves.

Over fence are several
colored graves, unmarked.

Mary C., wife of
Rev. R. M. Haggard
Apr 1, 1833
Oct 16, 1896

Rev. R. M. Haggard
Oct 15, 1819
Jun 11, 1902

William S. Fisher
Dec 7, 1842
May 17, 1884

Mary Arnold
Born 1858
Died Aug 31, 1898

Millie, wife of
G. W. Fisher
Died Sep 18, 1899
Age 69 years

G. W. Fisher
Jul 17, 1812
Oct 16, 1897

Ella L. Fisher
Jul 29, 1871
Jan 7, 1892

N. M. Hicks, dau of
T. P. & M. A. Green
Feb 14, 1881
Jan 14, 1895

J. E. Fisher
Aug 29, 1831
Nov 23, 1895

J. W. Fisher
Feb 1, 1838
Oct 13, 1873

Mary E. Fisher
Feb 18, 1847
Apr 9, 1926

Robert Lee Fisher
1869-1959

Sallie J. Fisher
Sep 25, 1878
Dec 13, 1879

John F. Fisher
Oct 24, 1873
Jan 10, 1892

Infant
Feb 8, 1881

W. D. Tate
Aug 15, 1845
Feb 5, 1888

Mary Haggard Tate
1842-1926

J. William Graham
1857-1943

Martha B. Graham
1867-1939

D. M. Wright
Jun 3, 1853
Jan 28, 1919
&
M. F. Wright
Jan 13, 1866
Feb 28, 1945
(picture)

Cora B. O'Neal
1883-1954

Arthur W. O'Neal
1881-1950

Edna O'Neal
Mar 28, 1920
Feb 15, 1947

* *

JONES CEMETERY
Located about one-half mile south of Powell Road and one-
fourth mile east of Railroad.

Redding Jones
Feb 1, 1825
Jul 13, 1901

Martha, wife of
J. R. Jones
Died Nov 29, 1884
Age 82 yrs, 8 mos, 12 days

J. R. Jones
Nov 2, 1866
Age 71 yrs, 1 mo, 24 days

Slave. (no marker)

Rufus, son of
J. R. & Martha Jones
Sep 27, 1837
Age 10 years & 10 months

Tommie, son of
Thos. G. & M. E. Jones
Aug 7, 1864
Sep 3, 1867

* *

LAWS HILL CEMETERY
Located west of Nashville Highway No. 31-A, on farm of
Charlie Webb Fowler. Copied 1962.

James Boren
Aug 27, 1791
Feb 12, 1866

James Boren
Aug 3, 1861
Dec 1, 1881

Nicholas F. Boren
Oct 3, 1861
Oct 19, 1892

Maggie, wife of
J. C. Fisher
1827-1892

Mary Cyntha Shaw
Feb 8, 1854
Feb 11, 1913

James Jackson Shaw
Apr 10, 1825
Jun 22, 1919

James Hayes Shaw
Jan 31, 1829
Nov 30, 1911

Nancy Ann, dau of
J. J. & Jane Shaw
Jan   1860
Jun 3, 1862

Philetus M. Hayes
Mar 14, 1835, was lost
Feb 3, 1843 & found dead
on the 5th of the same
month. Age 7 years, 10 months
& 25 days. Son of Anderson
& Cyntha Hayes.

Cyntha, wife of
Anderson Hayes
Feb 25, 1795
Sep 23, 1846

Nancy Irene Hayes
Mar 31, 1815
Jul 28, 1893

John R. Hill
Nov 30, 1858
Jan 12, 1931

Lena H. Hill
Mar 11, 1881
Sep 26, 1894

W. L. Hill
Feb 14, 1822
May 3, 1894

W. J. Boren
Jul 30, 1824
Oct 7, 1873

FARMINGTON

Sarah H. Boren
Sep 1, 1828
Jul 23, 1880

Margaret M. Hunter
Mar 30, 1834
Aug 6, 1884

William L. Neil
May 1, 1814
Mar 27, 1884

Mary L., wife of
William L. Neil
Mar 2, 1815
Nov 16, 1887

James D., son of
William L. & Mary Neil
Nov 25, 1844
Jun 25, 1867

James M. Boren
Feb 24, 1823
Dec 27, 1881

Bessie Lee Green, dau of
J. N. & Addie Green
Aug 17, 1902
Jun 6, 1904

Sarah, wife of
David Robinson
Aug 5, 1822
Dec 26, 1896

Enola, wife of
L. S. Thomas
Jan 7, 1889
Feb 14, 1905

Stella Mai, dau of
C. R. & K. L. Thomas
Jan 27, 1911
Apr 19, 1912

Charles M. Neil
Sep 24, 1846
Dec 27, 1887

Susanah E. Hill
Feb 8, 1855
Nov 19, 1861

Polly A. R., wife of
John F. Hill
Dec 5, 1860
Jul 22, 1885

Infant Son of
J. F. & P. A. R. Hill
Feb 21, 1885
Jul 26, 1887

Temperance H. Bills
Nov 8, 1828
Sep 28, 1866

Manning S. Bills
Nov 7, 1824
Jun 11, 1907

Infant of
J. & M. T. Bills
Jun 1, 1891
Jun 6, 1891

Uncle
Elbert G. Warren
Apr 4, 1856
Oct 30, 1913

Mattie Bell Bradley
Mar 17, 1897
Sep 8, 1898

George H. Cathey
Oct 30, 1875
Mar 26, 1898

G. A. Cathey
Feb 5, 1839
Feb 6, 1916

Mary J. Cathey
Jun 9, 1841
Oct 6, 1920

Eli Coble
Aug 5, 1833
Feb 2, 1916

John T., son of
L. M. & S. L. Fowler
Jun 30, 1889
Jun 25, 1895

Dora Hunter Slate, dau of
J. N. & C. A. Hunter &
wife of
T. G. Slate
Born Feb 5, 1854
Mrd- Jan 15, 1880
Died Sep 23, 1894

James N. Hunter
Born Nov 15, 1815
mrd- C. A. Hayes May 2, 1849
Died Jul 19, 1885
"Left a wife & 6 children"

Cyntha Ann Hunter
Born Nov 6, 1825
Died Jun 17, 1914
Buried in Larissa, Texas

Rush, son of
J. N. & C. A. Hunter
Feb 19, 1872
Nov 8, 1876

Mary J. Hunter
Jan 23, 1860
Feb 2, 1889

W. A. Hunter
Feb 8, 1831
Apr 2, 1909

James D. Cathey
May 5, 1874
Jul 27, 1915

Lou Ella, wife of
J. D. Cathey
Sep 7, 1870
Sep 22, 1912

C. P. Powell
Feb 21, 1824
Mar 29, 1902

Margaret Powell
Jan 16, 1832
Jun 22, 1916

Uncle
Johnnie Fowler
Jun 24, 1827
Oct 11, 1899

W. L. Cathey
Dec 15, 1834
Jul 25, 1902

Sarah A. Cathey
Sep 23, 1844
Jul 29, 1927

Mollie Cathey, wife of
Jerry Loftin
Nov 9, 1872
Jan 17, 1908

W. Loftin, dau of
Jerry Loftin
Feb 28, 1906
Mar 6, 1906

Leila Fowler, wife of
K. D. Cathey
Dec 19, 1887
Feb 19, 1909

Nannie M., dau of
J. K. & E. K. Kephart
Nov 12, 1861
Oct 18, 1885

Maggie M. Cathey, wife of
W. J. Loftin
Feb 22, 1868
May 11, 1924

* *

THOMAS CEMETERY

Located East of Verona and about one mile north of Bethbirei
Church, across the road from the Fisher Cemetery.

Only three graves.

Jonathan Thomas
Aug 31, 1798
Jun 9, 1884
Age 86 yrs, 9 mos.

Susan T., wife of
Jonathan Thomas
Nov 18, 1807
May 31, 1858

Nancy Jane, dau of
Jonathan Thomas
Sep 28, 1834
Jan 23, 1858

* *

FARMINGTON

WILHOITE CEMETERY

Located near Chapel Hill, in the Henry Horton State Park, Highway No. 31-A. In 1962, the bodies of Governor and Mrs. Henry H. Horton were moved from Lone Oak Cemetery in Lewisburg to this location.

*Gov. Henry Hollis Horton
1866-1934
&
Anna Adaline Wilhoite Horton
Mar 28, 1878
Apr 26, 1960

Ann Adaline Robinson
Jan 6, 1814
Mar 16, 1876

John Wilhoite Horton
Tennessee
2nd Lieutenant F. A. Res.
World War I
Oct 6, 1897
Feb 9, 1962

Lizzie Bullock Wilhoite
Aug 25, 1840
Nov 11, 1908

Jacob Richard Wilhoite
Jan 2, 1870
Sep 3, 1927

John B. Wilhoite
Dec 23, 1830
Mar 15, 1911

Jacob R. Wilhoite
Jun 23, 1836
Oct 24, 1863
"He leaves a Kind & affectionate Mother & Brother to Mourn his Untimely Loss"

* Governor of Tennessee

* *

CHILTON CEMETERY

Located on the south side of Duck River, one and one-half mile north of Anes, TN. The entire cemetery is covered with concrete slab.

J. M. Chilton
Sep 8, 1815
Mar 19, 1893
Age 77 yrs, 6 mos, 11 days

Rebecca J. Bramblett, wife of J. M. Chilton
Jan 30, 1833
Feb 18, 1918

In Memory of
Elmore D. Chilton
who was instantly killed
Dec 13, 1885
Age 27 yrs, 3 mos, 18 days

J. Newton Chilton
Aug 29, 1869
Jan 7, 1897
Age 27 yrs, 4 mos, 8 days

* *

SMYRNA CHURCH CEMETERY

Located on the south boundary of Henry Horton State Park, on east side of Highway No. 31-A. Copied Aug 30, 1979 by Helen and Tim Marsh.

Robert G. Whitman
Aug 14, 1884
Oct 7, 1911

Roy T. Mayhew
1879-1953
&
Hazel A. Mayhew
1884-1963

Tommie Lee McCormack
May 17, 1899
Jan 31, 1961
&
Elise A. McCormack
Jan 30, 1897

Joe Lee Lofton
1895-1961 (TM)

Harvey Lee Hopper
Jul 27, 1887
Sep 10, 1930

Edward E. Hopper
1865-1946
&
Josie B. Hopper
1871-1959

Rev. Robert L. Bell
1872-1926

W. J. Lane
1877-1921

Grace L. McCown
1881-1944

J. F. Lane
1873-1953
&
Sallie O. Lane
1874-1972

A. J. Lane
1848-1921
&
Alice O. Lane
1853-1930

J. B. Hastings
1872-1945

Mary L. Hastings
1876-1954

Lucinda Hopper Stewart
1897-1947

Emmett E. Hopper
1860-1951
&
Madora Hopper
1860-1940

C. R. McCullough
Feb 25, 1841
Apr 4, 1918
&
M. R. McCullough
Oct 21, 1843
Jul 10, 1913

Father
D. S. McCullough
May 11, 1838
Mar 28, 1907

Mother
Julia A. Saunders
Dec 7, 1850
Mar 19, 1931

Rubin J., son of
D. S. & Martha McCullough
Jul 11, 1866
Nov 6, 1917

Nannie Whitehead
1874-1961 (TM)

Paulie S. Bell
1877-1926

Julia E. Bell
1907-1929

Charles M. Bell
May 27, 1875
May 29, 1915

Carl Milton Cook
Age 6 hours, 1953
(Lawrence FH)

---- Cook
(Baby, no dates)

Tom Cook
(Adult, no dates)

Viola Cook
(Adult, no dates)

Nanie Lee Cook
1916-1916

Baby Cook
(no dates)

Laura Ann Cook
1818-1818 (this date is on stone but may be 1918)

FARMINGTON

Nancy Ann Cook
1889-1930

Walter P. Cook
1929-1930

Rufus Cook
(no dates)

Rosie Cook
(no dates)

Flossie May Haynes
1930-1939

James H. Horton
1883-1953
&
Clara B. Horton
1890-1978

Joe Horton
Feb 25, 1847
Apr 26, 1917
&
Mandy Horton
May 20, 1849
Mar 29, 1936

Annie Ruth Horton
Jul 6, 1907
Dec 23, 1918

Joe L. Horton
Jul 6, 1904
Feb 23, 1937

Wiley S. Hastings
1857-1937
&
Mary F. Hastings
1864-1936

Will J. Horton
Dec 7, 1873
Feb 8, 1947
&
Bettie E. Horton
Sep 17, 1873
Oct 23, 1954

Fount Iva Cook
Jun 8, 1917
Sep 18, 1965

Ruby P. Cook
Sep 19, 1926

Flora Ella Cook
Dec 24, 1921

Ann Cook Timmons
1882-1957
(Lawrence FH)

George W. Timmons
Died Nov 14, 1946
Age 77 yrs, 4 mos, 7 days
(Lawrence FH)

Mother
Louise Collins
May 14, 1914
Jun 30, 1945

Jodie Farlow
1901-1937
&
Belle Farlow
1906-

Jesse H. Adgent
Oct 1, 1897
Jan 14, 1968

Ira L. Adgent
1864-1938
&
Ella W. Adgent
1874-1953

William H. Martin
Mar 13, 1865
Sep 15, 1936
&
Lee Martin
Oct 20, 1870
(no date)

Lee Martin
Nov 20, 1866
Mar 22, 1962

John R. Farlow
1864-1946
&
Victoria Farlow
1871-1942

Charlie J. Farlow
Tennessee
Pvt 318 Field Arty 81 Div
Oct 19, 1918

James Luther Hastings
1926-1926

John Robert Wilson
1902-1979
&
Jessie Hastings Wilson
1902-

Bob W. Cook
1884-1951
&
Martha J. Cook
1893-19

Wallace E. Walker
Jan 17, 1913
Nov 20, 1972

Eloise A. Walker
Nov 25, 1912
Oct 4, 1960

Several unmarked graves.

Herbert L. Overton
1880-1959
&
Rubye D. Overton
1895-

Achsah Tankersley
1849-1927

Alice E. Parsons
Mar 8, 1929
Mar 24, 1929

Minnie Dryden
1873-1926

James A. Dryden
1870-1961

Lula E. Dryden
1873-1962

H. H. Hopper
1867-1950 (Lawrence FH)

William Charlie Hopper
1890-1954 (Lawrence FH)

Mattie Hopper
1895-1971 (Lawrence FH)

Carl Noblett
Tennessee
Pfc Co M 322 Inf WW II
Oct 31, 1916
Oct 16, 1968

Oliver J. Singleton
South Carolina
Mech US Army WW I
Sep 5, 1895
Apr 30, 1972

* *

END OF FARMINGTON QUADRANGLE

CAMPBELL STATION
Q U A D R A N G L E

EDMONDSON CEMETERY

Located one-half mile west of Interstate 65 and one-half mile north of State Road No. 129. Copied Oct 9, 1979 by Helen and Tim Marsh.

Jane E., Consort of
J. G. Edmondson
Mar 10, 1809
Jan 8, 1864   3 unmarked graves.

* *

OLD MARRS MEETING HOUSE CEMETERY

Located about four-tenths mile north of Marrs Hill Church Cemetery on Lynnville-Cornersville Road. Recopied Oct 7, 1979 by Helen and Tim Marsh.

In Memory of
John Andrews
born Sep 15, 1783
died Aug 3, 1835
Age 51 yrs, 10 mos, 19 days

Richard Brown
Born May 31, 1756
Died Oct 28, 1839

Sarah Brown
Born Apr 4, 1774
Died Dec 24, 1852

Zenes M. Brown
Apr 7, 1804
Jul 20, 1839

Richard Harvey Brown
Jun 26, 1808
May 6, 1835

J. M. M. Brown
Aug 26, 1836
Oct 8, 1858
Age 22 yrs, 2 mos, 7 days
"Worthy member Master Mason of Petersburg Lodge # 123 F.A.M."

J. M., son of
J. T. & U. J. Dixon
died day of birth, 1887

Sarah A., wife of
G. W. Doggett
Nov 15, 1812
Mar 8, 1885

Marge Goodrum
died Sep 26, 1827
Aged 31 yrs.

Colena McCray
Mar 23, 1799
Feb 12, 1848

F. M. McCollumn
Aug 30, 1830
Feb 19, 1850

Sacred to the Memory of
James Massey, Sen.
Who departed this life
Nov the 4th in the year
1839. Aged 94 years.

Ephraim M. Massey, Esq.
deceased Feb 27 AD, 1836
Aged 47 yrs, 9 mos, 0 days.

Andrew Miller Massey
died Feb 16, 1828
Aged 5 yrs, 8 mos, 11 days

James Esselman
A Native of Scotland
(no dates)

Our Father
Alexander Esselman
died Oct 22, 1854
Aged about 60 years

Elizabeth M. Esselman
Oct 13, 1791
Sep 23, 1842

M. Kerr
Age 77
D'd 1826
(fieldstone)

W. Black
(no dates)

Mary E. Black
died Aug 21, 1844
Aged 67 yrs.

William Black
Mar 27, 1808
Sep --, 1827

Mary S. M. Black
Aug 6, 1810
Sep --, 1826

William Johnson, dec'd
who departed this life
Apr 28, 1840
Aged 55 years.

James C. Esselman
Jun 15, 1806
Apr 21, 1848

Ma---- A. Esselman
Dec 5, 1814
Nov 28, 1845
(broken)

Samuel Alexander Esselman
May 14, 1839
Mar 21, 1840

Elizabeth Jane Esselman
May 14, 1839
Dec 11, 1839

Martha Frances Esselman
Oct 14, 1844
Apr 14, 1845

Nancy, Consort of
E. R. Davis
Mar 8, 1805
Feb 16, 1856

I. E. Davis
Jun 15, 1823
May 27, 1825

(David Hill)
(fieldstone, no dates)

Rebecca, wife of
David Hill
May 19, 1779
Jun 2, 1850

S. H.
(footmarker)

Samuel I. Kincaid
Oct 9, 1825
Mar 5, 1857

Martha J. Johnson
Dec 14, 1828
Aug 30, 1834
Aged 5 yrs, 9 mos, 16 days

Annie Ball
Dec 30, 1800
Jan --, 1881

Mary, dau of
G. W. & R. A. Davis
May 16, 1870
(date in ground, deep)

George, son of
G. W. & R. A. Davis
Jan 1, 1883
Feb 6, 1884

Emily J., dau of
Hugh & Jane Carothers
Feb 28, 1840
Sep 6, 1858
Age 18 yrs, 6 mos, 8 days

R. J., son of
Hugh & Jane Carothers
Apr 25, 1852
Aug 19, 1857
Age 5 yrs, 5 mos, 21 days

J. P. (John Patrick)
B - 1739
D - 1827 (fieldstone)

Ephraim Patrick
(marker broken)
(Born 1778-Died 1850-60)

Isabella, wife of
Ephraim Partick
Dec 31, 1779
Mar 11, 1866

Andrew J. F. Patrick
died 1815
Age 9 months

Marget Isabella Addeline
                    Patrick
Who died Feb 10, 1834
Age 6 yrs, 4 mos, 1 day

CAMPBELL STATION

F. W. King
Feb 13, 1807
Sep 13, 1872
Age 65 yrs, 7 mos, 0 days

Harriet L. King
wife of F. W. King
May 22, 1816
Jun 28, 1881

Joseph Nance
Feb 3, 1793
Mar 13, 1847
NOTE: another Box-type
      tomb next to above.

In Memory of
____ _. ____sery
Born --- --, 1798
Died --- 18, 1855

(Name broken away)
Born Nov --, ----
Died Feb 13, A.D. 1852
"Mother & Sister"

Ella Campbell, dau of
J. B. & L. J. Warden
Jan 16, 1882
Jul 22, 1882

H. Nance
Dec 1815
-ried to W.

Beuna Francis Alfedine
                Winston
Apr 6, 1850
Aug 12, 1850
Dau of T. F. & M. E.
Winston.

William London
died Feb 9, 1859
Age 77 years

Tennessee, wife of
William London
died Feb 5, 1859
Age 61 years

Ann C. London
Dec 15, 1812
Nov 25, 1881
"Wife & Mother"

Florence Ella Wilkes
Nov 2, 1864
Nov 28, 1867

Elisha D., son of
Thomas & Mary Wells
died Oct 28, 1855
Aged 25 yrs, 6 mos, 9 days

Many unmarked graves.

Allen Williams
Apr 1, 1803
Jul 12, 1886

P. M. Williams
Sep 27, 1837
Oct 3, 1859

Mary J. M. D. Newland
Feb 5, 1845
Aug 4, 1865

Rev. J. C. Mitchell
died Aug 25, 1841
Age 27 yrs, 5 mos, 25 days

Hannah Patterson
Born   1774
Died Nov 28, 1847
"Mother of Thomas Ross"

Elizabeth, wife of
T. Ross
Aug 7, 1807
Mar 15, 1837

Henrietta A. Ross
Jun 8, 1846
Aug 1, 1847
&
Infant not named
"Two Infants of T. & E. A.
  Ross"

Jacob Shanks
died Oct 13, 1855
Aged about 23 years

Loutisha H., wife of
H. M. McClure
Nov 12, 1849
Dec 28, 1875

Evert M., son of
H. M. & P. W. McClure
Jun 13, 1889
Jan 4, 1892

Frank M. Steele
Feb 25, 1859
Nov 7, 1885

John Bell Wadley
Feb 9, 1853
Feb 1, 1856
Aged 3 yrs, less 8 days
&
Will Burr Wadley
Jul 29, 1855
Feb 1, 1856
Age 6 mos, 3 days
"Lived together-died
 together" children of
S. J. & T. J. Wadley.

* *

GARRETT CEMETERY
Located three miles north of Mooresville, at county line.

J. J. Arney
Feb 15, 1840
Jul 31, 1914

E. F. Arney
Nov 24, 1842
Jul   1929

Willie W. Arney
Jan 22, 1878
Mar 27, 1878
(no marker)

James Garrett
Born   1775
Died Aug 2, 1854

Mary, Consort of
James Garrett
Born   1784
Died May 19, 1849

Johnson Garrett
Jul 13, 1822
Sep 7, 1892

Elizabeth Garrett
Born   1798
Died Oct 9, 1848

J. M. Burris
1836-(no date)

M. J. Burris
1835-(no date)

Some unmarked graves.

* *

COLVETT CEMETERY
Located in the Pickens Hollow, about two and one-half miles
south of Mooresville. Copied Mar 23, 1976 by David Pickens
and Ralph D. Whitesell.

Frederick Colvett
Apr 3, 1805
Oct 15, 1868

Jane, wife of
Frederick Colvett
Mar 9, 1821
Jun 5, 1881

L. E. C.
died Mar 15, 1880

8 to 10 unmarked graves.

* *

CAMPBELL STATION

OLD BEAR CREEK CEMETERY

Located on hill in front of Bear Creek Church on Bear Creek Road, south of the Lewisburg-Columbia Highway and just beyond the community of Mooresville.

Susie, wife of
J. T. Van Cleave
Dec 9, 1876
Nov 1, 1909

Jno. Orvis, son of
J. T. & Susie Caneer
(Van Cleave)
Aug 11, 1908
Jan 20, 1909

Emiline B. Calvert
Feb 3, 1819
May 22, 1887

William Calvert
Nov 14, 1806
Oct 5, 1877

Bettie C., wife of
G. A. Brown
Aug 6, 1833
Apr 14, 1873

Josie C., wife of
G. A. Brown
Feb 8, 1836
Jan 12, 1897
Age 61 years

Oscar L., son of
G. A. & Bettie C. Brown
Jul 10, 1863
Oct 22, 1864

Dr. G. A. Brown
Died Feb 2, 1913
Age 81 years

W. L. Orr
Jan 30, 1838
Oct 8, 1861

Capt. James Wade Nowlin
Jan 15, 1830
Feb 15, 1862

Bentley Jabus Nowlin
Jan 31, 1855
Feb 27, 1864

Emma G. Swanson
Oct 14, 1840
Feb 15, 1875

C. T. Swanson
Dec 8, 1832
May 26, 1896

Anna B. Swanson
Apr 3, 1871
(no age given)

Infant Son of
J. E. B. & I. I. Park
Apr 14, 1899

Ida I., wife of
J. E. B. Parke
Feb 19, 1866
Jul 18, 1902

James T. Thomas, son of
S. S. & N. K. Cross
Nov 29, 1862
Apr 14, 1886

Evia Blanche Cross
Oct 20, 1884
Feb 27, 1885

J. W. Wilson
Feb 8, 1845
May 6, 1870
Age 23 years

Andrew Wilson
Oct 19, 1806
Feb 2, 1864
Age 58 years

Dewitt C. Orr
Aug 24, 1827
Nov 7, 1891

Sarah V. Orr
Jan 19, 1837
Sep 20, 1905

Berthunia P. Orr
Sep 6, 1857
Oct 5, 1861

Willie T. Orr
Sep 6, 1869
Sep 13, 1869

Agnes A., dau of
D. C. & S. V. Orr
Feb 4, 1855
Apr 24, 1900

Isaiah Morton
Apr 5, 1763
Jun 22, 1844

Phebe, Consort of
Isaiah Morton
Died Dec 13, 1852
Age 90 years

E. B(or R). Fry
Jan 8, 1844
May 13, 1844

Ashley Moore
May 19, 1798
Mar 5, 1881

Martha, Consort of
Ashley Moore
Died Aug 28, 1840
Age 38 years

Frances H. Moore
Mar 3, 1807
Nov 15, 1863

James C. Moore
Died Oct 13, 1835
Age 3 years

L. P. Walker
Oct 7, 1834
Apr 26, 1851

Sacred to the Memory of
Mary Calvert, Consort of
Joseph Calvert
Who departed this life
Jan the 11, A.D. 1842
Aged 72 years

Sacred to the Memory of
Joseph Calvert
Who departed this life
July the 22, A.D. 1827
Aged 56 yrs, 6 mos, 16 days

Infant Child of
William & Margaret Calvert
Who died Apr 17, 1837
(no age given)

Margaret, Consort of
William Calvert
May 13, 1816
Feb 17, 1839

William Anderson
Feb 1, 1825
Aug 10, 1848

Robert Orr
May 21, 1803
Oct 17, 1848

Mary A. Orr
May 4, 1805
Dec 30, 1877

Virgil B. Moore
Jul 18, 1876
Sep 11, 1879

Allie L. McConnell
Dec 25, 1875
Sep 17, 1879

Allena H., dau of
N. W. & E. G. Orr
Jan 14, 1882
Jun 1882

Annie Kirkland, wife of
Rev. J. W. Simmons
Nov 14, 1869
died at Newman, Calif.,
May 24, 1902

Annie Narcis, dau of
M. A. & M. L. Hardison
Mar 22, 1887
Nov 21, 1888

W. B. Hariss
Mar 23, 1822
Mar 25, 1877

John Kirkland
Died Jan 5, 1862
Age about 25 years

Josephine D. Fry
Jul 26, 1854
Aug 12, 1854

Joseph Fry
Sep 19, 1800
Oct 31, 1858

Mary, wife of
Joseph Fry
Oct 18, 1811
Jun 21, 1894

A. E. T. Fry
May 6, 1853
Aug 30, 1861

Wilmoth M. Stone
Aug 27, 1867
Jul 17, 1876
&
Katie C. Stone
Apr 18, 1870
Dec 27, 1880
"Children of J. W. &
N. A. Stone"

James C. Moore
Departed this life
Oct 13, 1838
Age 3 yrs, 8 mos, 21 days

Elizabeth Moore
Departed this life
--- --, 1838
(broken)

Sacred to the Memory of
Samuel B. Moore
(broken)

In Memory of
Samuel Moore
May 11, 1763
Nov 3, 1852

Thomas M. Moore
Oct 13, 1820
Jan 1, 1843
Age 22 years

CAMPBELL STATION

Lavina, Consort of
John Moore
Aug 1, 1805
Aug 18, 1848
Aged 44 years

Andrew Jackson Moore
Apr 11, 1842
Dec 16, 1859
Age 17 years

Bettie J. Lyon, dau of
S. K. & M. E. Orr
Born Feb 27, 1848
(broken)

Joseph W. Calvert
Nov 15, 1800
Sep 17, 1845

Catherine N., Consort of
Joseph W. Calvert
Aug 18, 1802
Aug 16, 1825

Samuel K. Orr
Apr 4, 1817
Oct 11, 1900
Aged 83 years

Rev. Robert J. Orr
Dec 25, 1847
Jan 15, 1894

Harvy P. Orr
Mar 14, 1841
Jan 31, 1842

Florence, dau of
J. & M. E. Goldman
Aug 31, 1877
Jul 1, 1879

Mary Ann, wife of
T. W. Orr
Sep 9, 1825
May 16, 1902
Age 76 years

W. J. Hodge
May 18, 1814
Jan 13, 1894
&
L. D. Hodge
Feb 21, 1817
Aug 9, 1893

Sallie L., wife of
W. J. Williamson
Nov 6, 1839
Feb 22, 1879

Sarah Emma A. Z., wife of
John J. McConnell & dau of
J. T. & S. E. Cavanar
Apr 21, 1875
May 7, 1898

Sarah Elizabeth, wife of
George Cavnar
Apr 22, 1825
Feb 11, 1866

George Cavnar
May 25, 1804
Jul 12, 1883

Fannie K., wife of
John Wilson
Sep 4, 1820
Jan 22, 1897

Alice Cynthelie Arillah
       Wilson
Aug 13, 1871
Feb 9, 1883

William Boyd Wilson
Mar 24, 1846
Aug 24, 1878

Annah Malissie Magnolia
       Wilson
Born 1874
Died 1875

George Henry Perry
Aug 23, 1859
Aug 7, 1896

James Edward Mathis
Jun 21, 1887
Aug 12, 1916

J. F. Peartewheimer
Born 1834
Died 1891

John M. Clark
Born 1820
Died 1901

Harriet P., wife of
W. A. Clark
Born 1823
Died May 22, 1859

Mary D., wife of
T. Terry
Born 1840
Died 1876

Joe Casteel
Born 1878
Died 1923

Joe T. Cavnar
1850-1935

Sarah E. Cavnar
1852-1921

Catherine C., wife of
Joe E. Gupton
Feb 28, 1853
Nov 1899

Joe E. Gupton
1841-1929

John H. Lowrance
1826-1828

Julia C., wife of
J. W. Lowrance
1849-1885

J. W. Lowrance
1840-1897

Evie A., wife of
James Lowrance
1844-1874

Lucy, wife of
J. W. Lowrance
1844-1921

James P. Orr
1817-1895

Jane, wife of
J. N. Lowrance
1800-1876

Doctor Josiah Lowrance
1799-1890

Jane E., wife of
Josiah Lowrance
1809-1875

Sarah, Consort of
J. W. Lowrance
1803-1848
Age 45 years

William Dickson
Mar 22, 1786
Jun 18, 1849
Aged 63 years

Ebenezer Orr
Born 1797
Died Aged 55 years (1852)

Clarissa Rushing
1816-1818

William McGee Orr
Oct 21, 1800
Aug 7, 1844

Linfred Rushing
Mar 13, 1825
Nov 1846

Mary King, wife of
W. M. Orr
May 29, 1805
Dec 7, 1870

Thomas Orr
Born 1797
Died Oct 19, 1855

Mattie C., dau of
W. A. & S. J. Pickens
Sep 18, 1860
Died 1886

Emily J. Orr
Sep 1838
Sep 1839

David A., son of
J. B. & Elizabeth Lowry
Jul 1856
Nov 1864

James B. Lowry
Born 1793
Died 1864
Aged 70 years

Elizabeth Lowry
Born 1806
Died 1869

Jacob Lowrance
"Revolutionary Soldier"
Born 1759
Died 1855

Rebecca, wife of
Jacob Lowrance
Born 1766
Died 1852

James Orr, Esq.
Born Nov 1787
Died 1876
Age 89 years

Elizabeth, wife of
James Orr
Born 1787
Died 1863

Ann Orr
May 21, 1796
Died 1876
Aged 80 years

Thomas J. Jeter*
Aug 18, 1861-Oct 26, 1889

Bessie May,*dau of
T. J. & L. A. Jeter
Sep 14, 1882-Oct 14, 1883

Lavada,* dau of
J. R. & E. A. Jeter
Dec 13, 1873-Jun 28, 1888

Monrow,*son of
J. R. & E. A. Jeter
May 3, 1879-Jul 17, 1886

* Submitted by Don Jeter

END OLD BEAR CREEK

CAMPBELL STATION

NEW BEAR CREEK CEMETERY
Located north of Bear creek church

Minitis Dodson
1896-1958

Velma, wife of
Minitis Dodson
1894-

M. A. Hardison
Jan 11, 1854
Oct 9, 1928
& wife
Mollie E. Hardison
1884-1966
&
Mary Harris Hardison
Apr 11, 1880
Feb 4, 1928

Rev. James Kirkland
Jun 27, 1818
Dec 27, 1886
& wife
Malinda Kirkland
Jul 28, 1834
May 19, 1910

William J. Lowrance
May 8, 1831
Feb 20, 1917
& wife
Martha A. Lowrance
Apr 16, 1842
Jul 2, 1921

Josiah P. Lowrance
Apr 21, 1865
(no date)
& wife
Josie Lowrance
Nov 22, 1863
Aug 2, 1923

Walter Orr
May 17, 1912
Jul 26, 1912

Charles L. Orr
1860-1913

Jackson W. McConnell
1838-1924
& wife
Mary Jane Orr McConnell
1844-1929

James Wear Orr
Dec 10, 1853
Jul 16, 1899
& wife
Nannie Orr
Dec 9, 1854
Mar 9, 1934
& Dau
Annie B. Orr
1886-1918
& Dau
Gracie Orr
Feb 23, 1880
Oct 1, 1886
& Son
Franklin Orr
Jan 25, 1892
Jan 29, 1892

Henry W. Orr
May 24, 1850
1902
& wife
Bettie P. Orr
1857-1944

Newton W. Orr
Dec 16, 1854
Mar 14, 1936
& wife
Eula Orr
May 4, 1866
Feb 21, 1949

Nelson M. Orr
Feb 7, 1850
Mar 14, 1934
& wife
Martha A. Orr
Nov 10, 1859
May 15, 1947

Lockard Meredith Pickens
Sep 8, 1870
Dec 21, 1944
& wife
Delta Orr Pickens
Mar 28, 1881
Feb 1, 1958
&
Infant Son
1915-1915

James H. Orr
Nov 19, 1852
Jan 3, 1914
& wife
Addie B. Orr
Jun 21, 1868
Feb 26, 1934

Robert M. Orr
Jun 9, 1819
Feb 25, 1910
& wife
Mary A. Orr
Sep 15, 1827
Sep 18, 1918

C. Lafayette Orr
Dec 12, 1846
May 29, 1937
& wife
Sallie J. Orr
Oct 6, 1856
Jul 3, 1929

J. Woodson Orr
Mar 9, 1858
Apr 19, 1939
& wife
Mattie M. Orr
Aug 19, 1868
Jan 5, 1925

Harvey R. Orr
1851-1951
& wife
Emmer C. Orr
1858-1944

Zella Mae Orr
Oct 31, 1915
Apr 29, 1961

Shook Orr
Mar 26, 1863
Dec 15, 1938
& wife
Lula A. Orr
Dec 20, 1870
Oct 27, 1943

Robert Riggs Orr
Dec 23, 1854
Jun 8, 1937

Samuel D. Pickens
Jun 9, 1929
Sep 25, 1906

Theresa, dau of
R. A. & Hettie Pickens
Jul 11, 1902
May 7, 1904

Sarah J. Pickens
Feb 12, 1839
Sep 12, 1903

* *

BRYANT CEMETERY
Located at Mooresville on Highway 50-A East. Copied April 12, 1966.

Beulah Orr
Jul 17, 1884
Jul 6, 1962

Jamie Walker Orr
Dec 11, 1892
Dec 9, 1965

DeWitt Clinton Smith
Tennessee Colonel US Army
WW I & WW II
Mar 26. 1894-Jan 5. 1963

DeWitt C. Smith
1894-1963
&
Leila M. Smith
1892-

Eliot Coyle
Nov 11, 1915
Sep 24, 1964
&
Robbie Coyle
Mar 2, 1917 - -------------

Stewart Angus
Tennessee
Pvt Co D 88 Chemical BN
WW II
Aug 24, 1918
Dec 2, 1964

Emory F. Gupton
Aug 30, 1913
May 26, 1933

Sid J. Gupton
Jan 12, 1878
Mar 24, 1951
&
Virgie B. Gupton
Mar 21, 1884

Fannie B. Ewing
1882-1944

CAMPBELL STATION

William P. Holder
Tennessee
Pvt Co A 25 QM TNG BN WW II
Jul 23, 1908
May 26, 1963

Margaret A. Fleming
1851-1930

Elizabeth Grove
1841-1934

William A. Bryant
Sep 24, 1839
Sep 24, 1889
&
Eliza B. Bryant
Oct 11, 1851
Mar 29, 1936

David Xenophon, son of
W. A. & Eliza Bryant
Born Jun 12, 1874
Died Nov 30, 1879
of Diptheria

Sarah, dau of
Whit & Lizzie Bryant
1908

Virginia, dau of
Reavis & Grace Bryant
1913

Dora, dau of
Jas. & Rebecka Bryant
Died Apr 15, 1900
age 56 years

Twin Sons of
S. J. & Ida Reavis
Born & Died Aug 28, 1901

Son of
S. J. & Ida Reavis
1905-1905

Samuel J. Reavis
1859-1934
&
Ida R. Reavis
1861-1935

Bivian Lynn Reavis(V)
Feb 20, 1957
Oct 5, 1960

Joe W. Reavis
1857-1942
&
Cornelia B. Reavis
1869-1953

Twin Infants
Sons of J. A. & S. C.
Bryant
Born & Died May 10, 1874

Willie, son of
J. A. & S. C. Bryant
Aug 9, 1869-Sep 19, 1869

Lura, dau of
J. A. & S. C. Bryant
Born Mar 1, 1866(?)
Died --- 3, ----

Wallace, son of
J. A. & S. C. Bryant
Sep 1, 1863
Jan 3, 1864

John A. Bryant
Born in Granville Co., N.C.
Jun 21, 1829
Died Nov 21, 1899
& wife
Sallie C. Bryant
May 9, 1835
Sep 26, 1904

Martha E., wife of
A. D. Bryant, Sr.
Nov 5, 1843
Jan 3, 1922
&
James R. Bryant
Jan 1, 1854
Oct 30, 1915
&
Dr. Patrick Henry, son of
A. D. & S. W. Bryant
Born Mar 21, 1866
Died in Newport, R.I.
Dec 28, 1896
Past Assistant Surgeon
USN 1891-1896
&
Sarah Williams Bryant
wife of A. D. Bryant, Sr.
Aug 30, 1827
Sep 22, 1889
&
Andrew D. Bryant
Mar 14, 1825
May 21, 1910
&
Andrew D. Bryant, Jr.
Dec 14, 1863
Dec 8, 1888
&
W. T., son of
A. D. & S. W. Bryant
Dec 1, 1859
Apr 29, 1901

Dr. William R. Orr
1861-1939
&
Elizabeth B. Orr
1868-1932

William B. Orr
1910-1957
&
Frances G. Orr
1911-

Robert S. Crawley
1889-1963

David P. Orr
Nov 7, 1880
Aug 4, 1909
&
John B. Orr
Sep 15, 1883
Mar 8, 1901
&
Dr. R. A. Orr
Dec 11, 1852
Mar 25, 1901
&
Johnnie Orr
Jul 5, 1857
Mar 4, 1940

James W. Holder
1873-1953
&
Mary A. Holder
1883-1957

Mary Ratcliffe Cromartie
Mar 11, 1897
Mar 2, 1938

Father
R. G. Ratcliffe
Nov 7, 1863
Jul 4, 1926
&
Mother
Lettie W. Ratcliffe
Jul 20, 1868
Feb 2, 1959

Mary Orr Gracey
Mar 29, 1879
Dec 15, 1944

Clarence B. Gracey
Dec 13, 1875
Apr 6, 1944

Willie T. Jones
1886-
&
Sallie O. Jones
1891-1959

S. W. Bryant
Apr 1, 1794
Apr 14, 1870

John F. Bryant
May 14, 1790
Dec 6, 1857

Joe Frank Coyle
1880-1952

Hugh Thomas Bryant
Tennessee
Pfc Co G 117 Infantry
Jul 3, 1887
Jul 3, 1965

Rowland F. Bryant
Born Jan 26, 1831
Died in the Confederate
Army Oct 10, 1861(4)
&
Henrietta Bryant Taylor
Dec 8, 1820
Oct 31, 1915

Henry Edwards
Dec 4, 1909
Sep 10, 1960
&
Mary L. Edwards
Feb 4, 1912

J. F. Mullins
1836-1918

Sara Jane Robbins Mullins
1858-1937

G. H. Mullins
1851-1934

T. F. Mullins
1844-1914

Susie M. Allen
Aug 27, 1883
Mar 29, 1958

Will T. Allen
Apr 9, 1887
May 6, 1954

Infant Son of
Lewis and Chas Bain
May 1916

W. J. Mullins
1875-1944

William J. Mullins
Nov 23, 1836
Feb 19, 1906

Leila R. Mullins
1873-1924

J. S. McGibbon
Sep 22, 1867
Dec 19, 1936

Ozro Earl Frye
1890-1955

J. Van Frye
1884-1950

Amos Frye
1895-1937

Ozro N. Frye
Mar 11, 1850
Jul 21, 1919
&
Ophelia E. Frye
Oct 7, 1856
Mar 4, 1931

CAMPBELL STATION

Ina Frye
1892-1953
&
Irma Frye
1892-1942

Rev. John McKelvy
Jul 26, 1809
Mar 18, 1907

Jane McKelvy, nee
Jane McKibbon
Nov 23, 1812
Jan 23, 1897

J. V. McKibbon
Jan 30, 1827
Jun 29, 1902

Elizabeth, wife of
J. V. McKibbon
Aug 8, 1831
Jul 9, 1897

Mollie E., dau of
J. V. & E. P. McKibbon
Oct 31, 1860
Jan 12, 1864

Buford Jones
1864-1950
&
Blanche Vincent Jones
1869-1947

Emma Belle Vincent
1871-1954

Lena M. Davis, dau of
H. B. & D. M. Tate
Jun 13, 1890
Aug 20, 1911

Henry B. Tate
Nov 5, 1858
Jun 23, 1930
&
Dena Tate
Dec 12, 1867
Sep 17, 1944

Odell Tate
Dec 1, 1897
Aug 21, 1937

Johnie Clyde Tate
Tennessee
Pvt 22 RCT Co GEN SVC Inf
WW I
Apr 24, 1897
Jan 26, 1918

W. Robert Tate
May 19, 1886
Oct 28, 1946
&
Cora Lee Tate
Oct 13, 1890
Oct 31, 1955

Anna Bowden Wilkes
Nov 26, 1880
(new grave in 1966)

Father
Richard G. Bowden
Mar 31, 1859
Feb 11, 1893
&
Mother
Emma J. Bowden
Apr 1, 1851
Jul 29, 1941

Robert R. Bowden
1889-
&
Etta M. Bowden
1889-1950

Walter O. Freeland
1872-1951
&
Myrtle K. Freeland
1876-(no date)

Amanda E., wife of
W. F. McKibbon
Jan 4, 1863
Nov 14, 1889

W. F. McKibbon
Oct 9, 1855
Feb 21, 1919

Lula King McKibbon
1870-1942

J. Willie Barron
1880-1940
&
Anna King Barron
1878-(no date)

Richard W. Collier
1899-1930

Nannie Lou Collier
1894-1951

Infant Dau of
Raymond & Carrie Lee Phillips
October 4, 1846

A. L. Ledford, Jr.
Oct 10, 1914
Apr 30, 1962
&
Mary A. Ledford
Jan 13, 1917

Mrd- Dec 24, 1937

Judy Von Coyle
1946

Robert T. Redding
1874-1949
&
Elizabeth I. Redding
1882-

Myrtle C. Bryant
1886-1941

Marion R. Bryant
1856-1923
&
Laura V. Bryant
1859-1943

Nannie May, dau of
M. R. & L. V. Bryant
Jun 27, 1887
Oct 15, 1888

William Scott Bryant
1882-1916

Nancy C., dau of
Isaac H. & M. Hill
Oct 9, 1825
Jul 11, 1862

Walter S. Clark
Oct 17, 1876
Apr 10, 1953

Roy M. Clark
1880-1947

Tansel D. Clark
Died Oct 29, 1902
Age 63 years

J. B. Clark
1871-1897

Sallie Alberts Phillips
Aug 18, 1868
Nov 20, 1958

William B., son of
R. T. & I. F. Phillips
Nov 17, 1863
Oct 27, 1922

R. T. Phillips
May 15, 1831
Sep 14, 1904

Iowa F., wife of
R. T. Phillips
Jun 18, 1843
Jan 19, 1913

T. J. Frye
1848-1922

J. M. Frye
May 1, 1841
Jan 25, 1925
&
Cornelia Pickens Frye
Dec 30, 1845
Dec 4, 1913

J. V. McKibbon
Dec 5, 1897
Mar 8, 1934

Herbert McKibbon
Aug 25, 1899
Mar 17, 1934

W. H. McKibbon
May 20, 1902
Apr 29, 1964

Ida J. McKibbon
1867-1926

I. H. McKibbon
1859-1920

John H. Phillips
Nov 22, 1877
Nov 27, 1942
&
Ruth W. Phillips
Oct 10, 1875
May 18, 1963

E. J. King
Dec 15, 1841
Dec 25, 1910

Elizabeth P., wife of
E. J. King
May 16, 1838
Aug 24, 1907

Nan Belle King
Jan 1, 1872
Feb 28, 1957

Joe Frye
Tennessee
Pvt 1 Cl 13 Regt US MC
Aug 16, 1941

Annie Sue H. Frye
Mar 18, 1897
Jul 23, 1961

Cecil King
1882-1930

Willis Perry
Feb 24, 1818
Jan 4, 1908

Jim Tate
1858-1912
&
Lucindy Tate
1858-1932

W. S. Scallorn
Co F 8th Texas Cav
C.S.A.
Age 34 Years
(no dates)

Father
James Loyd Tate
1897-1953

Mother
Irene E. Tate
1902-1938

CAMPBELL STATION

John R. Tate
1888-1941

Katie R. Johnson
Sep 11, 1880

Thomas L. Raney
Nov 14, 1880
Feb 12, 1955

Everette E. Madison
1888-1950

Lyndell Massey
1914-1940

Callie Pickens
1843-1920

John Roy Tate
Tennessee
Pfc 310 Aux RMT Depot QMC
WW I
Dec 9, 1888
Jul 13, 1963

Mary R(P)., wife of
Wiley F. Stone
Nov --, 1823
Apr 17, 1901

Wiley F. Stone
Feb 26, 1822
Sep 4, 1880
Age 58 yrs, 6 mos, 8 days

Emmette W. Orr
1871-1919
&
Estelle K. Orr
1878-1958

Infant Son of
E. W. & Estelle Orr
Born & Died Feb 25, 1901

W. R. "Dick" Stone
1875-1952

William Henry Stone
1845-1917
&
Eugenia J. Stone
1850-1924

Nannie C. Stone
1877-1946

James S. Hill
1863-1939

Ella P. Hill
1867-1938

Jas. W. King
1851-1921
&
Kate W. King
1853-1919

Annis Fox Raden
1898-1956

John E. Raden
Florida
Cook 138 AERO SQ
Aug 13, 1892
Mar 5, 1946

Everette T. Orr
1864-1939

John V. Orr
1857-1940

Della Jones Orr
1870-1963

Robert Orr Wilkes
Aug 4, 1899
Jul 23, 1952

John Samuel Thomas
Oct 20, 1861
Nov 21, 1961
&
Hannah E. Wilkes Thomas
Aug 22, 1877
Apr 22, 1948

Ethel C. Eubank
1881-1943
&
Flournoy Eubank
1893-

Rebecca Orr Langley
1903-1953

William Joe Langley
1901-1942

Louie Lawrence Raden
1925-1938

Orless Cheek
1909-1931

Charles L. Cheek
1864-1962
&
Sallie C. Cheek
1877-1937

B. F. Fox
Jan 15, 1855
Mar 11, 1919
&
Nanie Fox
Sep 3, 1866
Jan 24, 1922

Annie Watts, dau of
Oscar & Zada McConnell
Dec 22, 1914
May 4, 1916

Martha Bryant McConnell
1928-1934

Father
Oscar J. McConnell
1878-1924

Bruce K. Orr
1869-1939
&
Edna King Orr
1871-1958

Grace Bryant
1885-1955

Reavis Bryant
1878-1935

Burgess O. Bryant
1907-1935

Bettie O. Pickens
1881-1941

Macie Kirkland
1899-1919

Pearl P. Kirkland
1879-1957

James A. Kirkland
1876-1937

Elizabeth M. Bryant
Apr 4, 1888
Jan 20, 1962

J. G. Coffey
1871-1933

C. B. Bryant
Jan 20, 1888
Mar 7, 1920

Clarence Paul Bryant
1916-1934

Robert L. Colvett
1851-1926

Janie Colvett
1869-1932

Mark L. Funderburke
1878-1963 (TM)

Margaret Funderburke
1881-1960 (TM)

Thomas D. Erven
1888-1958

Cynthia Erven
1842-1926

James Erven
1845-1933

Nina Lula, dau of
W. E. & Addie McConnell
Dec 12, 1878
Apr 22, 1894

Father
W. E. McConnell
May 22, 1844
Aug 30, 1920
&
Mother
Mary Adelaid McConnell
Aug 4, 1848
Jan 4, 1938

Ashley Pickens
1858-1920
&
Maggie Pickens
1866-1952
&
Ina Pickens
1894-

Guy Orr
1888-1949
&
Mary Orr
1888-

Jimmie L. Gupton
Dec 16, 1882
Jan 1, 1961
&
Ellen N. Gupton
Dec 26, 1887

James L. Gupton, Jr.
Jul 18, 1916
Dec 16, 1916

James R., Jr., son of
Robert P. & Edna McKibbon
Feb 5, 1915
May 10, 1921

John R. McKibbon
1857-1928
&
Ada P. McKibbon
1865-1943

George F. Kennedy
Tennessee
Corp 316 Field Arty 81 Div
Mar 19, 1937

John Newton Ayers
Sep 16, 1871
May 24, 1925
&
Dora Ayers
Mar 3, 1872

Odell W. McConnell
1870-1948
&
Mary A. McConnell
1873-1954

Henry, son of
Odell & Mary McConnell
Sep 11, 1911
May 2, 1925

CAMPBELL STATION

William H. Secrest
1880-1932
&
Elizabeth Secrest
1883-1937

Mary Ann Lusby
Nov 29, 1926
Nov 30, 1926

Jennie Boyd
Jul 13, 1887
Nov 14, 1955

Eliza A. Wilkes
Jul 7, 1882
(no date)

Joseph B. Wilkes
Tennessee
Sgt 307 Engrs
Dec 20, 1887
Jul 18, 1944

Rosevelt Wilkes
Oct 26, 1900
Sep 12, 1922

John R. Orr
Mar 27, 1921
Oct 29, 1961

John Reznor Orr
Oct 28, 1889
Nov 4, 1926

Ward D. Orr
1860-1944
&
Belle B. Orr
1866-1953

Ward Davis Orr, Jr.
Sep 20, 1898
Sep 18, 1921

Robert M. Orr
Jan 18, 1902
Jul 11, 1952

Kenneth Fowler
1877-1947

Hugh O. Boring
1906-1956
Grace W. Boring
1907-

Etta Orr
1873-1941

Richard C. Bowden
1909-1946

John, son of
Mr. & Mrs. E. C. Grubbs
Nov 11, 1936

Louis Ingrum
Jun 28, 1918
Sep 21, 1921

Dan M. Ingrum
Sep 1, 1864
Aug 6, 1956

Arch S. Bryant
Apr 6, 1862
Jun 1, 1933
&
Lura G. Bryant
Dec 21, 1863
Jul 1, 1945

Weldon Brent Wilkes
Jul 14, 1959
Dec 19, 1964

E. L. Grissom
1862-1931
&
Margaret E. Grissom
1868-1953

M. B. Grissom Morris
Jul 9, 1896
Jan 13, 1923

Sallie Batey, wife of
S. T. Sewell
1864-1938

Elizabeth Beckham
Jul 20, 1927
Nov 12, 1939

Charles W. Beckham
Aug 1, 1879
Aug 7, 1951

Blanche Beckham
Jan 1, 1889
Apr 3, 1965

James H. Orr
Tennessee
Sgt 10 Prov Regt QMC
Jul 20, 1891
Nov 24, 1964

J. Frederick McKibbon
1905-1955
&
Claudia D. McKibbon
1906-

Marshall A. McConnell
1876-1958
&
Mattie E. McConnell
1886-1958

Fred Secrest
1904-1961
&
Lillian Secrest
1906-

Luther R. Edwards
Sep 2, 1908
Mar 10, 1963
&
Ladye C. Edwards
Apr 30, 1926

Amos Lewis Bowden
Died Mar 20, 1965
Age 72 years & 1 day

"Son"
Bobby Joe Bowden
Jan 2, 1947
Feb 14, 1964

John Michael Ayers
Aug 3, 1955

William Loyd Fowler
Tennessee
Pfc US Air Force
WW II, Korea
Nov 1, 1927
Feb 14, 1955

Bryan Herman Ledford
Tennessee
Cpl Co K 117 Inf Regt
WW I PH
Mar 27, 1896
Apr 29, 1955

Walter Wilson Brisby
1875-1953

Mrs. W. W. Brisby
1877-1951

Preston J. McConnell
Oct 19, 1904

&
Mary Alice McConnell
Dec 20, 1911
Sep 30, 1955

Bobby Wayne Miller
Jan 19, 1953
May 7, 1961

J. Morgan Gupton
1875-1950
&
Ola H. Gupton
1872-1962

William John Pickens
Nov 7, 1862
Dec 31, 1954

Mattie Maude P. Pickens
Dec 13, 1871
Feb 12, 1948

George W. Wilkes
Tennessee
Pvt 157 Depot Brigade
WW I
Nov 19, 1891
May 12, 1962

Walter McKnight
Sep 25, 1875

&
Anna G. McKnight
Sep 23, 1880
Nov 3, 1952

Zeb Vance Gupton
Ohio
Pvt US Marine Corps
Aug 28, 1936

Margaret C. Gupton
Oct 8, 1872
Sep 6, 1962

Lennie Wilson
1877-1962
&
Mark Wilson
1876-1930

John Royall
1756-1823
&
Catherine Dudgen Royall
Died 1830
(No Marker, a Revolutionary
Soldier & wife)

END BRYANT

* *

CAMPBELL STATION

CAVNAR CEMETERY

Located on top of the hill behind the old George Cavnar home, two and one-half miles from Mooresville in Wilkes Hollow and about 6 miles from Lynnville, TN.

George Washington Cavnar
Nov 15, 1845
Jan   1916

Martha Malinda (Wilson)
            Cavnar
1842-1912

Sally Wilkes Cavnar
Born 1808
Died May 1846
(no marker)

Ida Day Cavnar
Jan 25, 1876
Mar 17, 1889

Callie Mae Boyd
Jan 21, 1902
Jun 21, 1903

Mattie Cavnar Boyd
Nov 28, 1906
Mar 11, 1908

* *

McCONNELL CEMETERY

Located one mile west of Mooresville on the Campbell Station Road. Copied August, 1958.

Manuel McConnell *
"A Revolutionary Soldier"
Born 1757
Died Sep 9, 1842
(no marker)

* Dates from McConnell Bible.

Three pyramid type graves, no inscriptions. Two are Revolutionary Soldiers, Armstrong brothers and the other is a sister. Information from McConnell Bible.

Martha Armstrong,*wife of
Manuel McConnell
Died Aug 12, 1824
(no marker)

Jeremiah McConnell
Oct 14, 1797
Feb 11, 1871

Annabel Martin McConnell
Nov 26, 1803
Oct 13, 1886

Elizabeth McConnell
(no marker)

Tabitha McConnell
(no marker)

Nancy McConnell
(no marker)

James McConnell
(no marker)

Infant Son of
W. E. McConnell
(no marker)

* *

PICKENS CEMETERY

Located in Pickens Hollow, south of Mooresville, Tennessee. Copied 1959.

Hamilton Pickens
1862-1944

Zula M., wife of
H. Pickens
Nov 15, 1870
Dec 17, 1914

Maggie, wife of
H. Pickens
May 19, 1864
Jul 17, 1899

David B. Pickens
Aug 9, 1816
Mar 12, 1902

Mary A. Pickens
Aug 14, 1824
Oct 28, 1900

William H. Pickens
Jun 13, 1792
Jun 22, 1872

Hannah, wife of
W. H. Pickens
Sep 19, 1795
Sep 15, 1882

Martha J. Hill
Oct 8, 1820
Feb 28, 1876
"Erected by her Brother,
  David Pickens"

Solomon H. Hudson
Jun 20, 1813
Departed this life
Apr 4, 1844
Age 30 yrs, 9 mos, 14 days

Robert S. Hudson
Nov 3, 1844
Jan 29, 1865

Margaret Procilla Berry
Jun 22, 1837
Mar 17, 1870
"Erected by W. H. &
  J. M. Berry sons"

Dr. James M. Hudson
Jul 9, 1839
Jan 3, 1883

Mamie A. E., wife of
Dr. James Hudson
Apr 10, 1851
Sep 12, 1890

Johnnie B., son of
J. M. & M. E. Hudson
Jul 17, 1871
Apr 12, 1886

Lucinda Jane Pickens
Jun 29, 1843
Jul 2, 1874
Age 29 yrs & 23 days

Hattie P., dau of
J. K. & I. A. Wilkes
Oct 9, 1877
Oct 15, 1877

William D. Hudson
Nov 14, 1838
Aug 2, 1844

James N., son of
F. G. & A. C. Furgeson
Mar 25, 1872
Jan 5, 1874

G. E. Yates
Apr 15, 1843
Jun 7, 1903

Mary Ann, wife of
G. E. Yates
Jan 3, 1845
Feb 12, 1922

Infant Dau of
M. A. & G. E. Yates
Jun 15, 1873
Jun 17, 1873

Bettie T., dau of
M. A. & G. E. Yates
Sep 12, 1880
Mar 20, 1882

Nannie T., dau of
G. E. & M. A. Yates
Sep 12, 1880
May 7, 1900

Penina D., wife of
W. D. L. Pickens
Dec 5, 1853
Jan 9, 1892

CAMPBELL STATION

W. D. L. Pickens
Jun 4, 1864
Nov 18, 1916

William Pickens
DAR marked, 1976
Oct 5, 1748
May 6, 1835
(Revolutionary Soldier)

Jane Hamilton Pickens
wife of William Pickens
1758-1839
(no marker)

Several unmarked graves.

* *

WILKES CEMETERY
Located two and one-half miles south of Mooresville, in Pickens Hollow. Copied September 25, 1958.

Mary Elizabeth, wife of
James E. Collins
Jul 15, 1865
Aug 9, 1893

Alfred McConnell
1829-1919

Margaret H. McConnell
1850-1937

William A. McConnell
1871-1939

Nancy S. Moore
Oct 17, 1814
Jun 27, 1905

John A. Evans
Dec 20, 1837
Mar 26, 1892

Tabitha C. Evans
Dec 27, 1834
Mar 18, 1915

Approximately 11 unmarked graves.

N. H. Grove
Mar 31, 1821
Oct 25, 1915

Jane A., wife of
N. H. Grove
Mar 9, 1829
May 6, 1889

Maria V. Bryant
Sep 24, 1848
Nov 12, 1868

Martha L. J. Bryant
Dec 26, 1846
Aug 31, 1856

Cyrena T. Dugger
Jan 20, 1818
Aug 14, 1883

S. L., wife of
Elisha Hurt
Oct 7, 1811
May 31, 1875

Emily V. Turner, dau of
John & Martha P. Wilkes &
Consort of R. E. Turner
Mar 11, 1831
Apr 30, 1852

John Wilkes
Oct 25, 1790
Nov 20, 1857
Age 61 yrs & 25 days

Martha P., wife of
John Wilkes
May   1792
Nov 19, 18-8
(still living in 1850 census)

Margaret E. Wilkes
Feb 16, 1833
Jul 21, 1861
Age 28 yrs, 5 mos, 5 days

Walter M. Wilkes
Oct 7, 1859
Nov 17, 1862

Sally Pickens, wife of
H. M. Wilkes
Mar 29, 1837
Apr 6, 1892

H. Marshall Wilkes
Jun 2, 1827
Oct 18, 1906

M. Floyd Wilkes
1864-1934

Almanza J., wife of
W. N. Wilkes
Nov 23, 1829
Jun 19, 1909

William Nelson Wilkes
Apr 9, 1816
Feb 16, 1899
Age 82 yrs, 9 mos, 27 days

E. Wilkes, wife of
John S. McKnight
Jul 3, 1853
Feb 12, 1929

Mary C. Wilkes
Oct 10, 1850
Sep 20, 1866

Benjamin F. Wilkes
Dec 19, 1854
Aug 17, 1865

* *

ROBERTSON FORK CEMETERY
Located two miles west of I-65 and one-fourth mile north of Highway 129. The site of the old Robertson Fork Baptist Church. Copied Oct 7, 1979 by Helen and Tim Marsh.

J. D. Boatright
1856-1913
&
Clemmie Boatright
1861-1916

Floyd Boatright
Sep 11, 1881
Oct 15, 1904

Thomas Brown, son of
J. D. & Clemmie Boatright
1888

Sallie Mary, dau of
J. D. & Clemmie Boatright
1892

S. J. Bills
Dec 6, 1857
Aug 26, 1896
Age 38 yrs, 6 mos, 26 days

Tobitha Ionis Griffis
Born Aug 17, 1851
mrd- T. J. Holly
Aug   1873
Died Nov 7, 1887
Age 36 yrs, 2 mos, 20 days

James Monroe Griffis
1849-(no date)
& wife
Francis Farmer Griffis
1854-1908

Ethel Griffis Boatright
Apr 14, 1881
Aug 14, 1905
(NOTE: large stone face down
beside above stone)

Thomas Martin Griffis
1826-1915
&
Nancy E. Griffis
1829-1879

Julia Fox
1842-1935

Andrew Jackson Griffis
1847-1914
&
Martha Elizabeth Griffis
1852-1888
&
Nannie H. Griffis
1847-1928

Vesta Valeria Griffis
1878-1899

Pearl Griffis Wilkes
1880-1907

CAMPBELL STATION

Andy M., son of
J. M. & F. A. Griffis
Jul 30, 1878
Sep 24, 1882

R. A., son of
R. N. Nix
Sep 6, 1866
Apr 14, 1889

Leotia M., dau of
J. M. & F. A. Griffis
Aug 28, 1876
Aug 28, 1877

James Griffis
Apr 12, 1799
Dec 20, 1873
Age 72 yrs, 8 mos, 8 days
&
Rebecca Griffis
Aug 20, 1801
May 26, 1881
Age 79 yrs, 9 mos, 6 days

H. J. Griffis
Dec 11, 1861
May 26, 1884

Sarah A. Griffis
Feb 2, 1825
Oct 20, 1880

W. J. Griffis
Jan 3, 1823
Nov 10, 1873

Sadie Bell, dau of
J. H. & Z. M. Harris
Aug 13, 1899
Jun 21, 1903

Napoleon B. Gregg
1855-1917
&
Sarah C. Gregg
1861-1945

J. B. L.
(fieldstone, at large
 cedar tree)

John Perry
Oct 11, 1828
Oct 26, 1886

E. Holly
born ----
Died ----
(fieldstone, illegible)

Millar Doggett
Mar 30, 1789
Sep 7, 1841
Age 52 yrs, 5 mos, 8 days

Mary N. Doggett
Oct 17, 1811
Jul 25, 1835

Sallie A. C. Colvett
Bornd Jan 7, 1864
Died Feb 23, 1886

Rebecca J. Colvett
Jan 14, 1829
Aug 3, 1885

Father
S. G. Calvert
Feb 16, 1812
Apr 11, 1896
Age 84 yrs, 1 mo, 25 days

Sarah B., Consort of
S. G. Calvert
Feb 5, 1818
Jul 2, 1881

Joseph M., son of
S. G. & S. B. Calvert
Nov 27, 1852
May 15, 1872
Age 19 yrs, 5 mos, 19 days

Otis E., son of
A. J. & Anna Calvert
Died Apr 3, 1883
Age 15 mos & 27 days

Children of
A. J. & Annie Calvert
(no names or dayes)

Samuel D. Colvett
Nov 26, 1820
Aug 25, 1892

H. W. Walker
Jun 25, 1833
May 6, 1887

Mattie Walker
Mar 22, 1856
Nov 22, 1878

Louis, dau of
J. M. & D. A. Walker
Feb 18, 1904
Mar 25, 1904

Infant Child of
J. M. & D. A. Walker
(no dates)

Here lies ....
(Hugh fieldstone, never
 finished)

Sacred to the Memory of
Collen Campbell, Native of
Scotland who was born 1 of
August 1754 and died 27 of
May, 1832.

Babby Kristalane Hardison
Died Sep 23, 1906
Aged 1 week

Floy May Kiser
Jul 15, 1911
Oct 17, 1911

J. L. Kiser
Oct 26, 1902
Aug 20, 1911

S. M. Kiser
Jan 10, 1910
Jan 17, 1910

T. O. Kiser
Aug 28, 1904
Nov 17, 1908

Delilah A. Fraser
May 18, 1838
Sep 15, 1906

Brother
C. C. Keiser
Mar 17, 1868
Oct 1, 1891

J. S. Kiser
Jul 11, 1901
Nov 20, 1901

W. C. Kiser
Nov 25, 1897
Sep 3, 1898

Father
John M. Keiser
Oct 10, 1830
Dec 28, 1891

Mother
Sarah M. Keiser
Sep 25, 1831
Nov 16, 1894

Eliza M. Boyd
Dec 6, 1846
Apr 18, 1904

Infant Son of
W. F. Martin
Sep 17, 1907

Sacred to the Memory of
Peter Ussery
Who was born May 8th 1762
and departed this life
Dec 28, 1834

P. C., Consort of
J. J. Fleming & dau of
D. G. & Mary Ussery
Jul 15, 1838
Feb 19, 1862

W. B. McMillon
Born 1823 & Died 1878
Age 55 years

W. J. Hickman
1863-1935
 & wife
Minervia E. Hickman
1859-1925

Robert S. Doggett
Nov 22, 1848
Jul 3, 1936
&
Alcie H. Doggett
May 17, 1849
May 15, 1907

Mary A. Doggett
May 31, 1870
Jul 7, 1873

Jesse B. Doggett
Jan 20, 1882
Jan 13, 1883

Mag. Lusel Doggett
(fieldstone, no dates)

Father
William F. Doggett
Nov 17, 1811
Mar 11, 1883
&
Mother
Elizabeth C. Doggett
May 29, 1831
Jan 18, 1904

Tennessee Doggett
(fieldstone, no dates)

Martn. Doggett
(fieldstone, no dates)

Father
G. W. Doggett
Jun 12, 1818
Mar 2, 1890
&
Mother
Sarah A. Doggett
Jan 26, 1821
Dec 28, 1854

Maggie Hudson
Jan 19, 1876
May 23, 1901

Pyramid marker
(no names or dates)

Harriet T., dau of
James & Evaline Colvett
Apr 9, 1845
Jan 8, 1846

Thomas G. Martin
Apr 20, 1861
Feb 20, 1900

M. C., son of
W. C. West
May 6, 1888
Jun 19, 1888

Brownie H. Hickman
1902-1940

CAMPBELL STATION

J. Y. Stem
Apr 8, 1848
(no date)
& wife
Mehulda Stem
Mar 1, 1842
Dec 25, 1924

J. H., son of
J. Y. & M. A. Stem
Dec 18, 1874
Sep 22, 1906

Lem D. Beasley
Jun 2, 1877
Jul 20, 1930

Annie Lee, dau of
Mr. & Mrs. Lem Beasley
Oct 14, 1905
Jul 7, 1907

John B. Caskey
1870-1951
&
Virgie V. Caskey
1877-1944

Many unmarked graves.

Joe Franklin, son of
Roy & Dezzie Beasley
July 8, 1930
Jul 13, 1930

David T. Roberts
Feb 11, 1848
Apr 7, 1913

T. J. Calvert
Nov 30, 1844
(no date)
&
Fannie Calvert
Dec 11, 1844
Dec 29, 1914

Orah, dau of
T. L. & M. F. Calvert
May 25, 1880
Jul 6, 1900

Father
Robert A. Lee
Sep 5, 1899
Feb 27, 1977
&
Mother
Lorean Lee
Feb 22, 1905
Apr 3, 1967
Mrd- Jun 11, 1925

Mother
Anna G. Caskey, wife of
A. J. Calvert
Apr 23, 1860
Oct 1, 1913

Husband
John T. Stone
Apr 15, 1883
Jun 4, 1925
& Wife
Gertrude Stone
Apr 11, 1883
Mar 30, 1957

John R. Terry
1881-1947
&
Florence Nix Terry
1881-1916

Claud Hurt
Nov 11, 1934
Nov 11, 1934

Matla S. Lee
Born 1862 & Died 1935
(McDaniel-McClintock FH)

R. K. Wells
Dec 21, 1870
Aug 1, 1926
&
M. E. Wells
Jun 15, 1876
Feb 28, 1956

Mattie Sue Wells
Nov 30, 1905
Oct 11, 1919

H. J. Doggett
Jan 31, 1845
Oct 26, 1927
&
Pairlee Doggett
Nov 22, 1846
Nov 11, 1940

M. V. Doggett
Oct 5, 1860
Nov 7, 1939

Thomas A. Doggett
Mar 20, 1867
May 6, 1931
&
Eva E. Doggett
Dec 10, 1871
Nov 9, 1935

Colored Section:

Mother
Jane Brown
1862-1956

Lizzie Gant
1883-1973
(Queen Ann FH)

Julia, wife of
Lee Brown
Died Jul 1, 1908
Aged about 43 years

Lewis Brown
Mar 10, 1870
Apr 8, 1906

Bony Brown
Died Dec 5, 1910
Aged about 70 years
No. Lodge 55-77

Andrew Jackson Marchbanks
1882-1933

Isabel W. Reynolds
Feb 17, 1863
Dec 24, 1944

Lavoy Henderson
May 25, 1916
Dec 25, 1942

Ritchmond Ursy
1880-1930

Fronie
(in ground, deep)

Louella Boyd
Dec 18, 1892
Oct 14, 1946

Willie Marchbanks
(no dates)

Thomas Marchbanks
Aug 15, 1848
Mar 18, 1913
&
Violet Marchbanks
Aug 11, 1849
Apr 22, 1917

Pearlie Marchbanks
1884-1931

H. Newman Marchbanks
1921-1930

Tom Mitchell
Oct 30, 1881
Oct 20, 1940
&
Isabel Mitchell
Aug 22, 1876
Oct 21, 1951

Thedore Ursy
1902-1963

Andrew Jackson
Apr 12, 1869
(no date)
&
Mary J. Jackson
Nov 16, 1874
Jan 16, 1944

Julia Duff, dau of
Andrew & Mary Jackson
Dec 6, 1900
Feb 6, 1934

Cassins Jones
(no dates)

Flournoy Walker
Tennessee
Pvt Pioneer Inf
Aug 24, 1893
Oct 23, 1944

Robert Walker
Tennessee
Pvt Co I 812 Pioneer Inf
WW I
Oct 24, 1895
Nov 11, 1965

Hannah Ursy
1885-1963

_____ Marchbanks
Apr 8, 1900 (fieldstone)

Flournoy Jackson
Aug 26, 1886
Apr 29, 1954
&
Pearl Jackson
Nov 2, 1887
Feb 4, 1944

Isado Mitchell
Jan 31, 1908
Mar 19, 1908

J. H. Mitchell
1903-1978
(Queen Ann FH)

Lizzie Gant
Born ----
Died Jan 3, 1974

Merit Simmons
Jan 25, 1864
Apr 19, 1926

Supreme Royal Circle of
Friends
Henry Mitchell
Greys Circle No. 1878
Died Nov 26, 1926
(no age given)

John Henry
Dec 21, 1881
Jun 15, 1910

CAMPBELL STATION

Mother
Eliza Jane, wife of
Jas. Henry
Jul 5, 1853
Dec 22, 1912

Robert K. Jackson
Tennessee
S/Sgt US Air Force WW II
Mar 11, 1924
Jun 17, 1959

John A. McClure
Died Aug 31, 1925
Age 66 years

Many unmarked graves.

Thomas D. Henry
Tennessee
Corp 847 Co Trans Corps
July 5, 1935

Hansel Holt
Tennessee
Pvt 159 Depot Brig
Mar 25, 1942

Lessie Holt
Mar 29, 1893
Mar 24, 1919

Leroy Jackson
Indiana
Pvt 1 Cl 809 Pioneer Inf
Feb 22, 1926

Edd L. Henry
1888-1942
&
Cora L. Henry
1899-1934
Mrd- Aug 2, 1915

Mollie Holt
Dec 16, 1867
May 30, 1907

John A. Holt, Sr.
Mar 16, 1895
Jun 18, 1963

George D. Boyd
1914-1962

END ROBERTSON FORK

Callie Kennedy
Mar 29, 1864
Oct 8, 1922

Henry Kennedy
Died Jan --, ---6
Age 73 years
(Queen Ann FH)

Robert L. Anthony
Aug 30, 1922
Jan 11, 1937
Age 14 yrs, 4 mos, 11 days

Jackson Eldridge
Nov 11, 1889
Nov 3, 1971
(Queen Ann FH)

* *

WILKES CEMETERY

Located one-half mile north of Robertson Fork in Wilkes Hollow. Copied Dec 8, 1979 by Ralph D. Whitesell, Helen and Tim Marsh.

Father
R. A. Wilkes
Feb 15, 1830
Sep 23, 1907

Frances A., wife of
R. A. Wilkes
Aug 18, 1824
Oct 18, 1895

C. E. B. Woods
Mar 8, 1831
Sep 18, 1898

Few unmarked graves.

* *

MORTON-GIBSON CEMETERY

Located west of I-65, one and one-fourth mile north of the Lewisburg-Mooresville Exits. Copied Dec 11, 1979, by Ralph D. Whitesell, Helen and Tim Marsh.

Andrew Gibson
1850-1935

William E. Gibson
1848-1921

Franklin Gibson
1818-1894

Nancy Gibson
1816-1897

J. C. Harris
Nov 12, 1848
Nov 3, 1913

15 or more unmarked graves.

H. L. Morton
1839

* *

McKNIGHT CEMETERY

Located two miles north of Mooresville-Lewisburg Exit of I-65, on west side of Interstate, on Kipp Gupton's farm. Copied Dec 11, 1979 by Ralph D. Whitesell, Helen and Tim Marsh.

John S. McKnight
Feb 12, 1839
Jul 12, 1889

Eliza B., wife of
M. A. McKnight
Feb 3, 1814
Mar 6, 1897

M. A. McKnight (Marlin)
Mar 4, 1805
Dec 17, 1875

abt 8 unmarked graves.

* *

VINCENT-ORR CEMETERY

Located two miles north of Mooresville-Lewisburg Exit of I-65, on west side of Interstate, on Kipp Gupton's farm. Copied Dec 11, 1979 by Ralph D. Whitesell, Helen and Tim Marsh.

Bettie Orr
Nov 10, 1855-Aug 1, 1880

Infant of Thos. A. &
Minerva Orr (no dates)

Martha C. Vincent
Mar 14, 1846-Jun 7, 1882

Wesly Vincent (fieldstone)
died Jun 20, 1918 (no age)

CAMPBELL STATION

J. A. Vincent (on same stone
Oct 17, 1840   as wife)
Jul 31, 1933
3rd Tenn Reg C.S.A.
  CHILDREN
Nannie, Bet, Maude, Thomas G.

Pearl M., dau of
Thomas & Minerva Orr
Apr 3, 1876
May 17, 1886

Father
Hezekiah J. Garrett
Oct 20, 1845
Feb 6, 1924
     &
Mother
Emma V. Garrett
Oct 17, 1853
Mar 23, 1931
  CHILDREN
Claud, John, Lewis

Thomas A. Orr
Feb 9, 1827
Sep 15, 1899

Minerva E., wife of
Thomas A. Orr
Jul 12, 1830
Aug 9, 1886

Many unmarked graves.

Cara Lee, dau of
Thomas A. & Minerva Orr
May 11, 1866
Nov 5, 1866

Mattie G., dau of
Thomas A. & Minerva Orr
Born --- --- ----
Died Dec 5, 1862
(broken)

* *

NAME UNKNOWN CEMETERY
Located on top of Elk Ridge on west side of the Robertson Fork-Mooresville Road. This was part of the old Wilkes Estate, this portion owned in 1816 by David Copeland.

Two graves, marked with fieldstones, no inscription.

* *

FREELAND CEMETERY
Located south west of Mooresville, Tennessee. Information submitted by Donald C. Jeter, Lewisburg. This cemetery is on the farm owned by Mr. & Mrs. Brenard Richardson, 1980.

James Freeland
Died 1819
(no age given)
    &
Wife

Peter Garron

Rebecca Freeland Garron,
dau of James Freeland

William Freeland
Born 1800 N.C.
Died Feb 1858
(son of James Freeland)

Martha (Patsy) Wright
                Freeland
Born 1805 VA
Died 1870-1880
mrd - Mar 28, 1840 Maury Co.

Henderson D. Pigg
Born 1837
Died before 1900

Sarah A. Freeland Pigg
Born Jul 1844
Died after 1900
(dau of William Freeland)

Mostly unmarked stones with one sandstone with hand carving. Probably several others in this cemetery but unknown.

* *

END OF CAMPBELL STATION QUADRANGLE

LEWISBURG QUADRANGLE

CHEEK CEMETERY

This Cemetery has been completely destroyed. It is inside the City of Lewisburg. Mr. John T. Ownby stated that in the garden of the late Algie Phifer's homeplace, on the west side of the Cornersville Road, south of the public square of the Town of Lewisburg, were these graves. They are completed destroyed now, July 1st 1966.

Jeremiah Cheek
Born --------
Died 16 May 1823

Tabitha Doyle, wife of
Jeremiah Cheek
Born ----------
Died --------1834

* *

DAVIS CEMETERY

Located between the Snake Creek and Spring Place Roads. Copied by Mr. & Mrs. J. Davis Calahan, Mrs. Thomas A. McAdams and David M. Pickens.

J. D. Davis
Nov 12, 1823
Nov 12, 1884
&
Polly Ann Davis
Sep 4, 1826
Nov 16, 1905
&
Dave Davis
Aug 24, 1876
Apr 30, 1898

One stone, no inscription.

* *

HENDRICKS CEMETERY

Located on the east side of Old Columbia Road. Three miles north west of Lewisburg, on the Davis Farm. Copied Oct 1, 1976 by Miss Martha Fox and Ralph D. Whitesell.

John Martin McKnight
1887-1966
&
Clarence H. McKnight
1894-1955

Thomas J. McKnight
Feb 14, 1854
Sep 22, 1921

Manervy Hendrix McKnight
Sep 19, 1859
Apr 12, 1948

W. B. Hendricks
Nov 3, 1894
Sep 8, 1919

Charlie L. Stenbeck
Mar 31, 1875
Dec 5, 1965
&
Izora D(Davis) Stenbeck
Oct 18, 1871
Sep 6, 1961

Joseph J., son of
John & Caroline Hendricks
Oct 15, 1848
Jul 20, 1931

Father
I. A. Hendricks
Nov 27, 1852
Jun 8, 1927
&
Mother
Aug 18, 1866
Apr 25, 1904

Infant Son of
Andrew Hendricks
Born & Died 1835

Sara Shaw
Sep 6, 1850
Jan 8, 1929

H. B. Hendricks
Aug 10, 1854
May 18, 1917

Bettie, wife of
B. W. Renfro
Mar   1846
Apr 15, 1891

Infant Dau of
J. & Caroline Hendricks
Born & Died 1836

John Hendricks
Jun 18, 1794
Sep 23, 1890

Caroline (Shaw), wife of
John Hendricks
Nov 17, 1819
Feb 16, 1886

S. B. Davis
Dec 23, 1869
Jan 25, 1962
&
Gus Davis
Dec 22, 1877
Aug 12, 1958

Ada Davis
Dec 15, 1874
Dec 20, 1958

Mann Davis
Sep 15, 1879
Jan 30, 1962

Cecil Owen, son of
R. L. & J. M. Davis
Jan 21, 1901
Dec 28, 1906

A. M. Davis
Apr 1, 1840
Mar 1, 1902
&
Martha (Hendricks) Davis
Apr 1, 1844
Aug 24, 1921

Garland Davis Fox
Tennessee
Sgt Co B 640 TD BN WW II
Apr 14, 1914
Jun 25, 1972

Allen Monroe Fox
Jan 6, 1906
Mar 22, 1972

Walter W. Fox
Apr 11, 1880
Jun 15, 1930
&
Suella D(Davis) Fox
Sep 1, 1882

LEWISBURG

Wiley C. Davis
Jul 14, 1878
Sep 14, 1949
&
Clatie L. Davis
Jan 2, 1900

This Cemetery is well kept.
All graves are marked.

* *

RONE-CHEATHAM CEMETERY
Located one mile west of Ellington Airport. Copied Oct 3, 1976.

Earl Vestil, son of
Mr. & Mrs. J. L. Cheatham
Nov 28, 1898
Oct 14, 1904

Jessie, dau of
W. E. & M. R. Osborn
Apr 25, 1900
Jul 2, 1902
"Erected by her mother".

Mother
Jennie Mai Cheatham
Aug 9, 1894
Apr 3, 1968

M(Martha). J., wife of
J. N. Cheatham
Jul 12, 1854
Jun 1, 1914

J. Dailey Cheatham
Jan 10, 1878
Jan 1, 1963

Bettie, wife of
J. D. Cheatham
Dec 1, 1872
Nov 30, 1919

About 15 unmarked graves.

Henry Rone
Mar 18, 1819
Dec 12, 1856

M. J. Rone
Apr 26/28, 1850
Aug 21, 1868

* *

ANDERSON CEMETERY
Located one and one-half mile west of South Berlin, east of Old Highway 50, Silver Creek. Copied Oct 3, 1976 by Susan and Frances Tindell, Ralph D. Whitesell and Charlene Nicholas.

On one large stone

Dr. William Inslee Anderson & Ann Eliza Anderson
&   &
Martha E. Wallis Anderson   Joseph Anderson
&   &
Dr. Stephen D. Anderson   Children of
&   Dr. William Inslee & Martha E.
Robert Hamlin Anderson   Wallis Anderson
&
William Inslee Anderson

(Stone on ground)

Rev. R. A. Erwin
Minister of the C. P. Church,
Departed this life
Aug 6, 1845
Aged: 29 years.

* *

HIGHTOWER CEMETERY
Located one and one-half miles north east of Lewisburg, on Rock Creek.

Two graves, no signs of graves, today. 1980. Ralph D. Whitesell and Helen & Tim Marsh.

* *

LEWISBURG

THOMPSON CEMETERY

Located one mile north east of Yell. Copied April 25, 1976 by Mr. Pruitt and Ralph D. Whitesell.

Levona Jobe, dau of Dulin & America Cochran (no dates)	Dulin Cochran Born Nov 1812 Died Dec 1906	America Cochran Aug 31, 1831 Dec 2, 1905	Lucrety Thompson, wife of C. Cochran Oct 1839 Jun 30, 1868
Pelias H., dau of Dulin & America Cochran Mar 23, 1857 Oct 9, 1862	There are two graves with headstones, Mr Pruitt told us that one was the grave of Bedford Thompson, the other is a small child whose name is unknown.		

* *

BOYETT CEMETERY

Located three-fourths mile south west of Lewisburg, near the Railroad.

Sam Boyette
(no marker)

About 45 unmarked graves.

* *

RAMBO CEMETERY

Located 5 miles south of Lewisburg, on Spring Place Road.

F. K. Rambo Nov 26, 1805 Oct 8, 1875	Mary B., wife of F. K. Rambo Jan 16, 1809 Mar 1899	J. K., son of F. K. & Mary B. Rambo Born Jul 28, 1845	Brant W., son of F. K. & Mary B. Rambo Feb 12, 1847 Sep 12, 1860

* *

THOMPSON-WELCH CEMETERY

Located nr. the Industrial Park, Lewisburg, TN. Re-checked 1979.

Lee R. Thompson 1855-1947 & Bright R. Thompson 1864-1940	Father C. S. Welch Dec 8, 1838 Oct 12, 1894 & Mother Margaret C. Welch Jul 23, 1846 (no date)	L. L. Thompson Jun 25, 1841 Jan 16, 1923 & wife Mary R. Brown Thompson 1843-1870	Sarah Gilmore Mar 23, 1815 May 26, 1903
Robert Hubert Thompson Jul 4, 1903 Nov 6, 1928			A. D. Calahan Jul 12, 1848 Feb 21, 1920
Nannie B. Thompson 1905-1906	Sarah J. Welch Mar 28, 1879 Jan 13, 1897	John West, son of J. H. & M. E. Welch Died Jul 15, 1895 Age 13 yrs, 2 mos, 14 days	
Mattie V. Thompson 1860-1928	S. J., wife of A. D. Calahan Mar 3, 1845 Sep 23, 1908		
Hanna G. Thompson Died Aug 6, 1896 Age 77 years		Mary Elizabeth, wife of J. H. Thompson Sep 18, 1850 Jun 15, 1899	
Father John R. Thompson 1853-1929 & Mother Sarah E. Thompson 1862-1934	Infant Children of N. E. & M. E. Wiley Son, died Apr 28, 1882 Dau, died Oct 8, 1880		
Robert W. Thompson 1857-1933			

LEWISBURG

GARRETT CEMETERY
Located about two miles from Lewisburg on Highway 431.

Ed Sanders
1871-19(no date)
&
Nannie Sanders
1879-1948

J. L. Elmore, son of
J. M. & H. H. Garrett
Feb 5, 1894
Jul 30, 1908

James E. Garrett
1918-1921

E. G. Garrett
Born Feb 17, 1832
Mrd- Oct 26, 1851
Died Oct 20, 1909
 & wife
Elizabeth A. Caudle Garrett
Nov 19, 1832
Mar 27, 1922

Elizabeth, wife of
John Helton
Jun 22, 1830
Mar 30, 1900

Elisha Garrett
Oct 23, 1791
Sep 15, 1882

Nancy, 1st wife of
E. Garrett
Jul 6, 1790
Apr 7, 1853

Alcy, 2nd wife of
E. Garrett
Jun 1, 1804
Mar 16, 1873

Several unmarked graves.

Son of
J. M. & H. H. Garrett
Born May 20, 1884
&
Dau & Son of
J. M. & H. H. Garrett
Born Sep 22, 1897
&
Son of
J. M. & H. H. Garrett
Born Aug 15, 1881
&
Son of
J. M. & H. H. Garrett
Born Sep 1, 1879

W. W. Hall
Sep 20, 1830
Oct 23, 1901

Sarah, wife of
W. W. Hall
Jan 28, 1822
Mar 21, 1890

L. A., wife of
A. J. Thompson
Feb --, 1846
Feb 18, 1882

Infant of
L. A. & A. J. Thompson
Born 1882

Infant of
L. A. & A. J. Thompson
Born 1883

S. E., wife of
A. J. Thompson
Feb 14, 1849
(illegible)

Cora C. Garrett
Nov 10, 1885
Jun 24, 1887

Eula Lottie McDaniel
Aug 22, 1895
May 25, 1909

Loyd, son of
J. M. & Nannie Falkenberry
Mar 29, 1890
Dec 10, 1902

J. M. Falkenberry
Aug 24, 1862
Mar 22, 1910

Ivy Trammel
1882-1920

Infant of
J. M. & N. A. Falkenberry
(no dates)

Bubbie Isley
1898-1919 (TM)

John Isley
1854-1939 (TM)

Mrs. Clemmie Isley
1872-1959 (TM)

E. B. Jewel
Nov 12, 1813
Mar 7, 1889
 & wife
Annie Jewel
Apr 16, 1823
Jun 17, 1904

Judy Thomas
Aug 13, 1798
Jun 21, 1894

Girtie, dau of
E. B. & A. E. Jewel
Jun --, 1890
Dec --, 1894

Alcy Emmeline Jewel
Jul 22, 1862
Jan 6, 1914
"Mother"

James J. McCabe
Born & Died Oct 20, 1924

Maurice L. McCabe
Jan 12, 1926
Jan 19, 1935

Mary Vivian McCabe
Sep 21, 1932
Feb 12, 1935

James Morgan Hobby
1866-1956
&
Nancy Ella Hobby
1876-1937

Noless Novella Hobby
Sep 3, 1898
May 14, 1918

Ethel, dau of
J. M. & Ella Hobby
Sep 9, 1902
Nov 22, 1908

William Rambo
Oct 23, 1845
Oct 13, 1923

M. J. Rambo
Jul 30, 1858
Nov 2, 1902

Archie Odell Ramsey
Apr 4, 1895
Feb 10, 1920

James Floyd Garrett
Oct 16, 1921
Oct 18, 1921

Jim Shade Garrett
Aug 24, 1861
Apr 20, 1931
&
Mary H. Garrett
Dec 12, 1857
Jul 5, 1910

* *

BAXTER CEMETERY
Located at Jeremiah Baxter Home Site, now owned by Earl
Harris, on Old Columbia Road, at Silver Creek. Copied
Jul 11, 1966.

Jeremiah Baxter
Who was born the 4th of
November 1777 & Died the
20th of August 1833

Catharine Baxter
Who was born the 20th of
March 1778 & Died the 21st
of September 1844

Jer. F. Baxter
Was born 25th of December
1823. Embraced the religion
of Christ Sept 1840. Departed
this life Sept 9th, 1844.

* *

LEWISBURG

BEATTY CEMETERY

Located two and one-half miles north of Cornersville, on the old road. On property now owned by A. G. Van Horn. Copied 1959.

Rev. Samuel Henry Polk
Oct 13, 1863
Jul 26, 1946

Virginia Pearl Beatty Polk
Dec 17, 1869
Feb 10, 1945

Samuel Beatty
Dec 26, 1837
Jan 11, 1877

X Antippa C., wife of
S. Beatty
Nov 10, 1840
Sep 30, 1911

John Beatty
1812-1892

10-12 unmarked graves.

One grave on Mr. Van Horn's farm, across the valley from Beatty Cemetery:

In Memory of
Mrs. Martha London
Aged 67 years
(no dates)

* *

BOWDEN CEMETERY

Located one mile north east of Lewisburg on property of the Bowden heirs. Copied June 10, 1858 by Ralph D. Whitesell and Myrtle Lee Walker.

William J. Bowden
Jul 21, 1837
Dec 11, 1893
&
Elizabeth N. Bowden
Sep 17, 1843
Apr 27, 1904

James M. Bowden
Mar 10, 1810
Jul 18, 1849
& wife
Ann H. Bowden
Jan 3, 1818
Apr 27, 1900

"A Confederate Soldier"
John G. Bowden
Feb 22, 1833
Dec 18, 1910

R. Lucius Bowden
1838-1922
&
Margaret E. Bowden
1841-1924

Birdie Bowden
1868-1948

Thomas A. Cathey
Nov 22, 1862
May 27, 1924
& wife
Addie Cathey
Sep 26, 1865
(no date)

Mattie J. Ewing
May 24, 1851
Mar 29, 1918

Elaine, dau of
T. A. & Addie Cathey
Jan 22, 1890
Dec 7, 1898

Scott Ewing, son of
R. L. & M. E. Bowden
Died Oct 14, 1898
In the 24th yr of his age.

Jimmie, son of
R. L. & Maggie Bowden
Died Apr 7, 1873
Age 2 yrs, 3 mos.

Boddie, son of
R. L. & Maggie Bowden
Died Apr 7, 1873
Age 2 yrs, 3 mos.

Sallie, dau of
R. L. & Maggie Bowden
Died Aug 16, 1866
Age 3 yrs, 5 mos.

Mildred Ann Ophelia Bowden
Jun 24, 1845
Jul 20, 1859

Carless, son of
W. J. & N. E. Bowden
May 21, 1871
May 1, 1877

Trim K. Bowden
Mar 2, 1881
Sep 11, 1911

H. E. Bowden
(Wooden marker, no dates)

James Knox Reed
Feb 22, 1860
May 24, 1919

Blanch Bowden Reed
Jul 17, 1862
Dec 26, 1918

J. M. Fraley
Oct 3, 1858
Mar 30, 1877

M. Hattie Fraley, wife of
H. C. Willson
Feb 29, 1856
Apr 18, 1878
Age 22 years

Cecil S. Bowden
1904-1911

Wilbur W. Cathey
1890-1933

R. Cecil Bowden
1881-19
&
Lillie L. Bowden
1885-1922

* *

LEWISBURG

BOYET CEMETERY

Located one mile south west of Lewisburg on the Boyet property.

Edmon Elliott
Died Mar 24, 1891
Age 76 years

Patsy, wife of
G. W. Elliott
Oct 25, 1877
May 28, 1897

George W. Elliott
Sep 18, 1875
Aug 24, 1906

Fannie, wife of
James C. Snell
Dec 28, 1832
Aug 19, 1877

Nancye ----, wife of
O. P. Sheppard
Last married to
Henry Collins
Apr 6, 1821
Oct 16, 1861

M. H. Gilbert
wife of R. Gilbert
Born 1821
Died Sep 26, 1875

Catharine, wife of
L. P. Bills
Oct 27, 1830
Mar 12, 1862

Joseph E. Lee
Mar 8, 1831
Jul 22, 1863

Sue F., wife of
James D. Elliott
Aug 11, 1852
Jul 30, 1875

Sammie R., dau of
Jas. D. & Sue F. Elliott
Jan 12, 1872
Feb 15, 1876

John W., son of
B. W. & L. P. White
Aug 3, 1857
Oct 30, 1876

S. T. Calton
Jan 7, 1850
Oct 12, 1931

W. N. Calton
Feb 18, 1826
Jul 27, 1891

Catherine Chunn
Oct 6, 1846
Jan 27, 1911

Jesse Boyet
Mar 28, 1821
Oct 24, 1901

Henrietta, wife of
Jesse Boyet
Aug 25, 1825
Jan 17, 1854

Zilpha H. & Elizabeth, daus
of J. & H. Boyet
Dec 15, 1853
Jun 26, 1854

Mary A., dau of
J. E. & M. F. J. Boyet
Mar 29, 1879
Oct 9, 1879

Mamie J., dau of
J. E. & M. F. J. Boyet
Mar 29, 1879
Jun 18, 1879

William A., son of
J. E. & M. F. J. Boyet
Sep 16, 1858
May 21, 1859

Husband
James E. Boyett
1831-1882
& wife
Mary F. J. Boyett
1839-1916

W. Thomas Boyet
May 14, 1839
Feb 27, 1913

Brother
John T. Boyett
1876-1940
&
Sister
Kate M. Boyett
1884-1917

Josiah Boyet
Jan 26, 1819
Jan 11, 1888

Zilpha, wife of
A. C. Tucker
Jan 2, 1816
May 30, 1884

Elizabeth Boyett
Jul 6, 1797
Sep 6, 1883

James Boyet
Aug 3, 1790
Mar 25, 1868

B. F. Boyet
Sep 24, 1836
Oct 31, 1859

Nancy Boyet
Mar 12, 1833
May 5, 1834

Edith Boyet
Sep 18, 1823
Apr 22, 1894

Gilelley J. Boyet
Jan 31, 1829
May 24, 1898

Husband
Willis Menifee
1841-1902
& wife
Mattie M. Menifee
1867-1946

T. H. London
Oct 10, 1824
Feb 16, 1862

Priscilla A., wife of
Thomas H. London
Sep 3, 1820
Dec 18, 1905

Martha V. London
May 4, 1858
Sep   1864

Darthula Octavia, dau of
Martha & H. Chunn
Dec 13, 1873
Sep 8, 1880

* *

BOYET-HILL CEMETERY

Located two miles from Lewisburg, on Highway 50-A, turn
left just past Pleasant Hill Cemetery. Cemetery is behind
Odie Poteet's residence. 1968.

James M. Boyett
May 11, 1849
Jun 13, 1929

Mary E., wife of
J. M. Boyett
Jan 25, 1851
Apr 27, 1912

J. Clifford Boyett
1885-1949 (TM)

Leila, dau of
J. M. & M. E. Boyett
Jan 23, 1890
Sep 4, 1905

2 unmarked graves, (one is a child).

John R. Hill
Mar 12, 1818
Jan 16, 1900

Louisa T. Hill
Jan 6, 1832
Apr 19, 1865

Jno. W. Barron
Oct 29, 1848
Jul 13, 1880

Roena Thomas, wife of
John William Barron
Feb 18, 1850
Jan 17, 1919

* *

LEWISBURG

BROWN CEMETERY

Located one and one-half mile north of Lewisburg, on property of Miss Tiny Clay. There are only a few graves, Brown, Doud, and perhaps Turner. Last buried was Miss Malinda Liggett in early 1900. Now completely abandoned. This information obtained from Mr. Cecil Bowden and Miss Della Walker, both having lived in this community and attended Miss Liggett's burial. June 12, 1958. Myrtle Lee Walker.

* *

COCHRAN CEMETERY

Located on Cochran Road, between Lewisburg and Cornersville. Copied Apr 10, 1966 by Deane Porch. Rechecked 1979.

G. C. Franklin
1883-1941

W. C. Jourdan
Oct 20, 1843
Oct 29, 1912
"Confederate Soldier"

N. E. Jordan
Jan 11, 1879
Dec 29, 1910

Octa Jordan
1904-1924
&
Fannie Jordan
1873-1929

"Baby Son"
James Patrick Little
Sep 18, 1953
Dec 8, 1953

Lula Kate Emerson
Dec 29, 1892
Feb 16, 1905

William Everett Emerson
Jun 2, 1889
Apr 7, 1926

Joseph A. Emerson
1859-1938
&
Lona Emerson
1868-1960

Betty Joe Freeman
1933-1934

W. D. Pyles
Jul 16, 1871
Apr 27, 1922
& wife
Bonnie Smith Pyles
Nov 8, 1880
Feb 3, 1962

W. G. Pyles
Sep 29, 1847
Oct 3, 1910

Mother
Neoma S., wife of
W. G. Pyles
Mar 10, 1849
Aug 27, 1916

R. J. Lee
1860-1946

Howard Lee
Jun 2, 1899
Dec 21, 1966
Tennessee
Pfc 37 Pioneer Inf WW I
&
Vera Pearl Lee
1902-1957

Ernest D. Gillum
May 30, 1884
Aug 23, 1965

Robert Lee Turner
Mar 22, 1883
May 1, 1935

Cpl. Kenneth W. Turner
Age 32
Co B 704 T D BN
Gave his life in the Service
of his Country in France
May 15, 1945

L. D. "Bud" Turner
1856-1936
&
Callie Turner
1856-1932

Eliza, wife of
Ward Fowler
Aug 11, 1886
Dec 2, 1920

Mrs. Maude Fowler
1884-1960 (TM)

Sherman Endsley
Apr 16, 1893
Mar 3, 1920

Basil Manley Cooke
Aug 24, 1867
Feb 13, 1905
&
Octa Willis Cooke
Jan 1, 1869
May 8, 1957

Mary E., wife of
L. M. Cook
Jul 18, 1843
Jan 14, 1915

Mrs. Fannie Williams
1865-1920

Alice Williams
Jun 28, 1889
Mar 4, 1904

William Thomas Hazlett
January 12, 1948

Robert S. Williams
1886-1955 (TM)

Ebbie E. Luna
Apr 15, 1891

&
Charlie Luna
May 11, 1893
Mar 12, 1958

Marcena E., wife of
T. F. Moffitt
Mar 13, 1861
Nov 2, 1896

Airrow Moffitt
Feb 1, 1903
Feb 9, 1903

O. L., son of
L. O. & Olie Hawkins
Jun 29, 1878
Feb 19, 1901

C. C. Cochran
Aug 7, 1831
Feb 29, 1918

Sgt Thomas O. Jobe
May 13, 1883
Sep 4, 1938

Albert Church
1887-
&
Ada Ann J. Church
1886-1951

Tommy Church
Mar 24, 1912
Apr 3, 1965
&
Selma Church
Sep 9, 1920

George F. Cheek
Nov 20, 1896
Dec 16, 1962
&
Janie A. Cheek
Jul 9, 1898

Creola Childress
1871-1956

Ida Cheek
Nov 27, 1888
Oct 25, 1941

R. O.(or R. D.)
Feb 20, 1881
(fieldstone)

Murdock M. Malone
Oct 24, 1840
Jun 14, 1903
&
Sarah J. Malone
Jul 27, 1846
Apr 21, 1923

Steven Clay Gillum
Dec 28/30, 1960

Alice McLean Kelly
1933-1934

LEWISBURG

Otis Tell Pruitt
Aug 16, 1897
Jul 9, 1916

Bob Pruitt
Mar 10, 1866
May 26, 1952
&
Alice Pruitt
Dec 16, 1877
Dec 26, 1960

O. B. Paxton
Jan 24, 1869
May 6, 1900

Lula Cochran
1879-1940

Brother
William B. Turner
Jun 15, 1872
Aug 17, 1895

Sister
Sallie E. Turner
May 28, 1870
Aug 6, 1888

J. Newt Henry
1883-1947
&
Gertie Henry
1890-1964

Lushion E. Smith
1892-1945

Henry M. Pruitt
1879-1961
&
Erma P. Pruitt
1891-

Francis F. Pruitt
1882-1948
&
Minnie B. Pruitt
1891-

Eugene Cochran
1883-1941
&
Audie Cochran
1885-1948

H. Loyd Burgett
1890-1917
&
Irene S. Burgett
1894-

J. Willoughby Ownby
1886-
&
Lillie Shaw Ownby
1892-1941

Charlie Brown, son of
Mr. & Mrs. E. D. Gillum
Dec 20, 1916-Jan 6, 1917

Myrta S. Gillum
Aug 25, 1884
Aug 14, 1952

William Anderson Shaw
1829-1893

Kenneth W. Shaw
1898-1898
&
Eula H. Shaw
1887-1894
&
Johnnie W. Shaw
1889-1894

Polk Cochran
1848-1933

Pearlee, wife of
W. J. Cochran
Mar 12, 1838
Jun 12, 1892

W. J. Cochran
May 17, 1837
Dec 14, 1905

E. A. Cochran
Sep 25, 1819
Dec 11, 1890

David Cochran
1810-Aug 17, 1899
&
Lizzie Cochran
1810-Mar 1, 1900

Francis J. Pruitt
1862-1914
&
Lillian I. Pruitt
1867-1938

Evline Shaw
Jan 1, 1849
Jan 27, 1885

J. C. Shaw
Jan 2, 1832
Jun 17, 1896

Mary Elizabeth Shaw
Nov 9, 1853
Feb 18, 1935

Olcie Davis
Aug 13, 1892

&
Pernie Davis
May 27, 1882
Jan 10, 1960

Bertha A. Davis
May 26, 1878
Aug 10, 1905

Mildred, dau of
F. P. & Bettie Davis
Aug 9, 1895-Oct 17, 1910

F. P. Davis
1849-1926
&
Bettie Davis
1858-(no date)

James C. Cochran
Jan 7, 1813
Apr 6, 1883

Margaret C., wife of
James C. Cochran
Nov 4, 1833
Aug 17, 1905

Annie Frances Gamel
Nov 3, 1923
Aug 23, 1946

Robert L. Shaw
1841-1925
&
Polly V. Shaw
1855-1914

Thomas Loyd Hobby
Sep 6, 1925
May 11, 1944

Emmett Loyd Hobby
Mar 11, 1900
Nov 2, 1934

Ophelia Agent Hobby
Jan 16, 1899
Jun 30, 1952

Shirlie Cochran
Mar 6, 1884
Sep 19, 1937
&
Georgie Cochran
Dec 17, 1890

Father
L. V. "Sine" Cochran
1852-1947

Clem Raney
(no dates)

Infant Son of
Mr. & Mrs. T. C. Holly
(no dates)

Mother
Nancy P., wife of
L. V. Cochran
Jun 26, 1858
Nov 25, 1926

Thomas D. Cochran
Oct 19, 1895
Feb 5, 1917

Elisha Cochran
Mar 7, 1827
Aug 8, 1901

Myrtle E., wife of
E. D. McCollum
Nov 25, 1879
Mar 31, 1906

George W. Turner
1851-1939
&
M. J. Turner
1855-1900

J. T. Turner
Oct 4, 1878
Dec 20, 1891

John Franklin Turner
Nov 1, 1853
May 2, 1878

William T. Turner
Jul 24, 1882
May 13, 1883

Tempy, wife of
William Turner
1812-1890

Martha S. Simpson
1863-1939

Ambros B. Simpson
1857-1933

E. N., wife of
J. H. Simpson
Died Apr 27, 1899
(no age given)

C. B. Simpson
Oct 27, 1848
Sep 24, 1882

Carrah Hopwood
Aug 7, 1889
Apr 8, 1890

L. O. Simpson
Jan 25, 1880
Mar 14, 1924

Granny
L. C. "Doll" Simpson
Apr 16, 1858
May 22, 1938

Earnestine F., dau of
S. D. & N. M. Shaw
Mar 22, 1912
Feb 16, 1914

Robin Howard Tankersley
1954-1960

Sam Shaw
Aug 27, 1887
Jan 6, 1959
&
Nannie D. Shaw
Jun 10, 1888
Sep 11, 1973

LEWISBURG

John "Pid" Shaw
1893-1963

John L. Divin
1857-1928
&
Eva Divin
1876-1948

Dee Shaw
1878-1938

J. W. Shaw
Jan 26, 1837
Aug 10, 1902

Mrs. A. F. Shaw
Jan 18, 1851
Jun 19, 1916

William J., son of
J. W. & A. F. Shaw
Apr 7, 1873
Oct 11, 1873

Infant Son of
J. W. & A. F. Shaw
Born & Died Jun 22, 1874

Ola Ethel, dau of
J. W. & A. F. Shaw
Oct 22, 1883
Jul 6, 1885

J. T., son of
J. W. & A. F. Shaw
Nov 5, 1891
Feb 28, 1892

Clyde Shaw
1871-1945
&
Emma Shaw
1874-1950

Newell Shaw
1896-1965

W. H. Rambo
1868-1934

Artie Missie Rambo
1872-1944

W. A. Barnett
1853-1922

Thomas F. Barnett
1895-1924

M. E. Purdom
Jan 5, 1859
Mar 9, 1910

William C. Hedgcoth
1869-1955
&
Ellen Hedgcoth
1869-1943

Earnest T. Hedgcoth
1888-1945
&
Ana P. Hedgcoth
1888-1967

George T. Hedgcoth
1912-1957
&
Ruby Hedgcoth
1920-

Wiley Neil Moffitt
Sep 1, 1872
Jan 19, 1873

C. W. Thompson
Dec 16, 1874
Feb 24, 1935
& wife
Florence Thompson
Sep 24, 1881
Aug 9, 1951

George Washington Wood
Pvt US Army WW I
Jan 13, 1888
Dec 1, 1977
&
Frances B. Wood
Feb 7, 1888

Married 68 years

Infant Dau of
Mr. & Mrs. G. W. Wood
(no dates)

Calvin F. Woods
Tennessee
Pvt 149 Inf 38 Div
Jan 19, 1927

Sarah E. Wood
1920-1924
&
Ela L. Wood
1923-1931

Thomas F. Wood
Nov 25, 1860
Sep 12, 1952
&
Senora E. Wood
May 20, 1861
Aug 22, 1946

Louisa Crigger
Jan 13, 1837
May 15, 1917

Dolly, dau of
Z. T. & B. J. Hedgcoth
Sep 13, 1882
Oct 17, 1882

James Walker
Born 1801
Died 1873

David Rambo
Dec 28, 1839
Mar 3, 1900
&
Elizabeth Rambo
Jun 10, 1844
(no dates)
& Son
J. T. Rambo
Jan 20, 1877
May 13, 1896

Infant Son of
Z. T. & B. J. Hedgcoth
Apr 7, 1880
Apr 15, 1880

Bettie J., wife of
Z. T. Hedgcoth
Jun 17, 1847
Sep 26, 1884

Simmie, dau of
Z. T. & Bettie Hedgcoth
Apr 17, 1880
Oct 10, 1899

Bodie E., son of
Z. T. & L. C. Hedgcoth
May 31, 1896
Feb 6, 1897

James H. Bigham
Nov 5, 1881
Oct 4, 1963
&
Bertha P. Bigham
Oct 15, 1888
Mar 26, 1977

Drucilla Moffitt
1839-1926 (TM)

B. F. Moffitt
Feb 17, 1837
Jan 11, 1898

Charles D. Moffitt, M.D.
1883-1910

Alice Hobby, wife of
Van Moffitt
Oct 30, 1874
Mar 31, 1917

Bula Glenn, wife of
Van Moffitt
1882-1938

Marthie, wife of
J. P. Pruitt
Bornd 1829
Died Mar 11, 1868

Father
Sign C. Pruitt
Feb 5, 1849
Nov 17, 1929
& Mother
Dorcas Pruitt
Sep 3, 1858-May 30, 1937

Marvilene Moffitt
Sep 11, 1903
Nov 23, 1911
&
Turney Moffitt
Mar 4, 1893
Sep 26, 1894
"Children of
W. N. & Zular Moffitt"

Olie L. Moffitt
Tennessee
F 1 US Navy WW I
May 26, 1896
Jan 10, 1960

Kenneth Lee
1888-1924
&
Nettie Frances Lee
1880-1950

Humphrey C. Moffitt, Jr.
1909-1910

Humphrey C. Moffitt
1880-1910

Cora Mae Moffitt
1883-1915

N. D., wife of
W. F. Finley
Feb 13, 1841
Jan 22, 1912

W. H. Lee
Sep 12, 1856
Apr 19, 1936
&
Judie Lee
Aug 7, 1871
Apr 25, 1936

Ruth Martin Gillum
Aug 12, 1923
Nov 20, 1943

William Roy Freeman
Jan 9, 1902
Aug 26, 1921

William N. Freeman
1871-1910
&
Inez Freeman
1876-1947

John W. McDowra
Feb 2, 1876
May 12, 1961
&
Alice M. McDowra
Jun 25, 1871
Feb 24, 1933

Alice E. McCay
Oct 9, 1933
Feb 22, 1934

LEWISBURG

Thomas E., son of
J. D. & J. E. Thomason
Dec 23, 1882
Feb 18, 1884

Carlene Bigham
Jul 18, 1918
Sep 17, 1918
&
Infant
Feb 4, 1916
Feb 6, 1916

Bettie Jane Cochran
(child, TM)

Luther L. Pruitt
(no dates)
&
Delia B. Pruitt
(no dates)
&
Mazie C. Pruitt
(No dates)
&
Leonard L. Pruitt
(no dates)

Luther Lee Jack Pruitt
1875-1954 (TM)

Mabel Pruitt
Aug 6, 1908
Jul 6, 1909

John W. Bigham
May 4, 1885
Dec 20, 1956

A. C. Bigham
1857-1905
&
Caroline Bigham
1854-1944

N. C., wife of
J. H. Cochran
Mar 12, 1864
Feb 7, 1902

John Henry Cochran
1869-1951

Martha J., wife of
Wilson Cochran
Jan 1, 1847
Sep 1, 1898

Wilson Cochran
Jan 27, 1834
Aug 15, 1904

T. Alphus Cochran
1885-1960
&
Lillie Lee Cochran
1886-1969

Minnie Lee
1875-1958

Mahaly A. Cochran
Sep 18, 1852
Apr 9, 1854

Azor Cochran
Nov 29, 1803
Apr 7, 1851

Hannah Cochran
Jun 12, 1797
Jul 4, 1858
"Wife of Azra Cochran
A smart & industrious
woman."

Dovey Cochran
Dec 4, 1831
Jun 25, 1853
"A Smart & industrious
Woman."

Infant Son of
Dolphus & Laura Whitsett
Jun 30, 1905
Jul 7, 1905

Sadie B. Whitsett
Oct 14, 1902
Dec 3, 1910

Adolphus Whitsett
1870-1949
&
Laura Ann Whitsett
1868-1948

Bee Lee, son of
C. W. & L. E. Lee
Jan 1, 1882
Jul 24, 1893

Wash Lee
1856-1932
&
Lydia Lee
1854-1932

William Roy, son of
J. W. & Maggie Pruitt
Nov 21, 1898
Dec 13, 1910

Mrs. Maggie Ann Pruitt
1878-1955 (TM)

Edd C. Cochran
1878-1931
&
Annie Maxie Cochran
1884-1918

Sarah F. Morris
Jun 9, 1853
Jun 12, 1884

W. M. Morris
Mar 15, 1851
Nov 29, 1883

M. J. Morris
Jul 29, 1859
Jul 30, 1880

Lucinda, wife of
W. H. Morris
Mar 27, 1812
Oct 7, 1879

Mrs. Oma Smith Green
1890-1963 (TM)

Infant Son of
Mr. & Mrs. W. B. Barrett
Feb 21, 1910
Feb 22, 1910

Infant Son of
David & Violet Bigham
(broken, dates gone)

Mamie Kate Barrett
Dec 12, 1917
Dec 13, 1936

W. B. Barrett
1886-1965
&
Nannie Barrett
1883-(no date)

Dovey Ann Narcis Bigham
Sep 21, 1852
Nov 8, 1852

Nancy Tennessee Crunk
Sep 27, 1860
Jul 7, 1861
"Daughter of David &
Violet Bigham

J. C. Hedgcoth
Mar 6, 1842
Apr 11, 1908

Eliza, wife of
J. C. Hedgcoth
Died Feb 18, 1884
Aged 46 years

T. S. Cochran
Died Mar 18, 1880
Age 94 years

Catharine, wife of
Thomas S. Cochran
Feb 25, 1791
Jun 1, 1873

Julius Clinton Cochran
Aug 8, 1872
Aug 29, 1950
&
Emma Pruitt Cochran
Feb 29, 1876
Aug 10, 1957

A. G. Fisher
Apr 22, 1894
Sep 16, 1958
&
Sallie B. Fisher
Aug 20, 1894
Apr 3, 1951

Several unmarked graves.

END OF COCHRAN

* *

LEWISBURG

COCRILL-McCORKLE CEMETERY

Located at Cocrill Gap at Cornersville, and named for the family, on the farm of Mrs. Will Murrey, south of Lewisburg on the Cornersville Road. Copied Dec 16, 1960 by Ralph Stephens and Ralph D. Whitesell.

In Memory of Unity McCorkle
Died Oct 6, 1845
Age 48 yrs, 3 mos, 24 days.

1 child grave, unmarked

Two crude stones mark the grave of twin Cocrill boys killed when felling trees. The stones, unmarked, may have been moved from the actual grave site.

* *

COGGINS-BRECHEEN CEMETERY

Located one-fourth mile north of the Mooresville Road and two miles west of Lewisburg, on the C. Barron place. Copied 1959.

Effie L. Coggins, wife of
L. H. Twitty
Jan 16, 1893
Apr 17, 1920

John T. Gibson
Oct 29, 1856
(no date)

Octa Gibson
Nov 20, 1868
Nov 23, 1926

J. A. Coggins
Jul 15, 1848
Jul 27, 19-5

Sarah J. Coggins
May 16, 1849
Feb 29, 1920

G. W. Beckham
May 1, 1840
Nov 19, 1909

Mary A. Beckham
Feb 24, 1853
Jan 5, 1913

Susan H., dau of
Levi & Susan Brecheen
May 2, 1859
Jun 18, 1859

Sgt L. R. Brecheen
1st Tennessee & Alabama Cav.
Oct 10, 1823
Oct 31, 1899

Susan J. Brecheen
Sep 12, 1822
Jun 29, 1911

Jas. W. Welch
Nov 25, 1816
Dec 28, 1893

Dr. Fletcher M. Beckham, V.S.
Oct 13, 1895
Oct 5, 1919

Robert L. Beckham
Nov 28, 1874
Jul 21, 1921

Susan L., wife of
J. W. Darnall
Aug 9, 1874
Sep 29, 1904

Infants of
Reavis & Grace Coggins
Son,
Apr 26, 1917
Dec 15, 1919
&
Infant
Dec 17, 1910

Will Baxter
1858-1930

E--- A. Baxter
Feb 22, 1862
Feb 21, 1916

* *

COLLINS CEMETERY

Located south of Lewisburg, on the Spring Place Pike, near the Twitty Farm. Copied 1958.

Phebe Ann, dau of
Thomas & Sally Davis
Jul 20, 1842
Feb 13, 1879

Thomas Collins
Jul 27, 1818
Oct 16, 1838

A. L. Smith
Dec 25, 1846
Jul 9, 1912

Bula, wife of
R. O. Davis
Aug 24, 1876
Aug 18, 1907

C. W. Smith
Jan 20, 1822
Dec 9, 1844

H. T. Pruitt
Sep 11, 1860
Dec 25, ----
Married Nora P. Collins
Born Sep 19, ----
Died --- --- ----

S. H. McDoura
Mar 2, 1856
Nov 20, 1923

W. W. Wade
Co F St. Tenn & Ala
VIO Cavalry
(no dates)

Mary Smith
1835-1933

Henry L. Collins
Sep 28, 1845
Aug 27, 1917

G. W. Smith
Oct 26, 1872
Aug 1, 1903

Minnie Davis
Aug 9, 1872
Sep 20, ----

Sally, wife of
Thomas Collins
Apr 8, 1816
Apr 23, 1884

Sarah, wife of
A. L. Smith
Aug 27, 1852
Mar 8, 1885

R. O. Davis
Sep 3, 1868
Jun 9, 1920

Thomas Henry Neil
Apr 29, 1902
May 17, 1918

Adah, wife of
Granville Cockrell, &
Dau of H. L. & F. L.
Collins
Mar 16, 1870
May 14, 1907

Fanny L. Collins
Oct 28, 1849
Jan 24, 1932

LEWISBURG

COLLINS CEMETERY
Located on the Spring Place Road, on Old Wheatley Farm.
Copied May 9, 1958.

Willis Collins Feb 1785 Nov 24, 1854 Phebe, wife of Willis Collins May 20, 1787 Dec 10, 1867	James Collins, son of Henry & Frances Collins Dec 27, 1825 Jul 23, 1844 in Memphis, Pichett(Pickens) Co., Ala. & Willis, son of Henry & Frances Collins Jan 26, 1828 Jan 9, 1847 in Brazos St. Iago, Texas. On his return from Monteray, Mexico	William H., Grandson of Phebe Collins Born Jan 26, 1844 & Died A prisoner in Indiana- polis, Indiana, Mar 16, 1862 Frances, Consort of Henry Collins May 3, 1797 Dec 26, 1841	Sidney D. Collins Feb 7, 1847 Aug 22, 1851 Henry Harvey, son of C. C. Richardson Dec 29, 1838 Feb 12, 1862 Sidney R. Short, dau of C. C. Richardson Feb 14, 1861 Apr 21, 1885

* *

COCHRAN CEMETERY
Located on the Cornersville Road, south of Lewisburg.
Copied Dec 16, 1960 by Ralph Stephens and Ralph D. Whitesell.

J. B. Cochran Aug 21, 1823 Jan 2, 1883	Jane M., wife of J. B. Cochran Aug 16, 1820 Died in Paris, Tennessee May 11, 1893	Nannie, dau of J. I. & S. C. Rollings Born June 29, 1883	Sallie Cochran, wife of J. I. Rollings Jul 23, 1859 Jun 9, 1894 Mrd- Dec 19, 1878

* *

DAVIS-MOORE CEMETERY
Located about three miles south of Lewisburg on Cornersville Highway.

Samuel Davis Aug 8, 1814 Sep 1, 1909 Sarah A., wife of Samuel Davis Jan 9, 1826 Aug 2, 1901	James B. F. Moore Jun 27, 1840 Feb 12, 1884 Emma Moore Mar 16, 1847 Feb 6, 1909	Willie L. C., son of J. B. & E. Moore Aug 15, 1879 Jun 26, 1886 Tom Moore 1876-1950 & Mai Moore 1877-1953	Josie Davis Jun 10, 1854 Aug 16, 1899 Unmarked graves: Mr. Rhiner & Infant of Jack & Elsie Moore

* *

DUNCAN CEMETERY
Located one mile north west of White Acres, Lewisburg, west of Lewisburg, on farm now owned by Walter T. King. Copied June 11, 1966.

Horatio M. Phillips Dec 11, 1801 Oct 19, 1871 Nancy, Consort of H. M. Phillips Jun 4, 1804 Aug 30, 1856 Isaac R., son of R. T. & I. F. Phillips Nov 7, 1860	Mary F. Phillips Dec 17, 1835 Oct 27, 1870 Nancy H. Phillips Nov 30, 1829 Sep 23, 1866 B. Pigg (slave section) Jan 8, 1855	W. H. Phillips Aug 11, 1803 Apr 23, 1882 Mary R., Consort of William H. Phillips Apr 8, 1808 Sep 7, 1855	Two graves walled with square stones, probably the graves of Micajah (Cager) Duncan and his wife. Joseph Duncan Feb 14, 1790 Oct 16, 1844 Next to the above, is a grave, probably his wife Wynefred Phillips Duncan.

LEWISBURG

Josiah Duncan
May 19, 1787
Jul 2, 1856

Several unmarked graves.

Nancy (Bigham), wife of
Josiah Duncan
Nov 7, 1789
May 11, 1833

Martha J. Duncan
Wife of (First wife)
A. S. Duncan
Apr 26, 1834
Sep 25, 1855

Leota F., dau of
A. S. & Martha Duncan
Born March 13, 1855

* *

GILLS CHAPEL CEMETERY
Located on Elk Ridge at the Fire Tower, former location of Gills Chapel Methodist Episcopal Church. Copied May 30, 1971 by Mrs. Foster Nicholas, undated 1979 by Helen and Tim Marsh.

Joe Loyd Chapman
1920-1973
&
Melba Park Chapman
1922-

Jacob McCoy
Mar 16, 1833
Dec 15, 1902

Margareta Greggs McCoy
Jan 25, 1840
May 30, 1913

S. T. Holly "Father"
Jun 1, 1830
Jan 17, 1880
& "Mother"
Annie C. Holly
Aug 12, 1826
Jul 6, 1917

E. H.
(footstone, no dates)

M. H.
(footstone, no dates)

Clifford Dale Holly
Oct 12, 1913
Oct 24, 1914

Dorothy Phylis Holly
Jul 21, 1912
Aug 9, 1912

Eugenia S. Phifer, wife of
W. K. Holly
Oct 14, 1856
Oct 5, 1882

Martha J. Doggett, wife of
W. K. Holly
Nov 29, 1862
Jul 18, 1887

Thomas A. Holly
Oct 25, 1878
Nov 18, 1906

W. K. Holly
Dec 5, 1852
Nov 1, 1919
& wife
Mary J. Green Holly
Oct 29, 1853
Apr 3, 1920

A. L. Holly
Feb 9, 1877
Dec 8, 1908

Loyd, son of
A. L. & R. C. Holly
Oct 22, 1904
Mar 8, 1906

Clifford, son of
A. L. & R. C. Holly
Jul 9, 1908
Nov 4, 1908

Father
T. J. Holly
May 28, 1850
Jul 9, 1918
&
Mother
Tinnia A. Holly
Jan 30, 1864
Nov 7, 1934

Anne C. Holly
Aug 12, 1826
Jul 6, 1917

Kittie Holly
1885-1907
&
William Owen Holly
1876-1949
&
Cora Holly
1883-1944

Wilma Holly
1895-1923

Annie Ruth Holly
Aug 31, 1919
Feb 17, 1920

J. B.
(fieldstone, no dates)

J. _.
(fieldstone, no dates)

Neil F. Bigham
Jun 12, 1855
Jul 22, 1933
&
Mary E. Bigham
Feb 14, 1855
Feb 24, 1905

Buford White Holly
1921-1923

John N. Holly
1890-1938

Mary White Holly
1927-1942

Grady G., son of
J. K. & M. E. Jobe
Oct 20, 1892
Apr 30, 1907

Urah Alma, dau of
W. K. & M. J. Holly
Feb 2, 1887
Jul 28, 1887

Ruth Holly Collins
1883-1958

7 graves with fieldstones, no dates.

* *

EDWARDS CEMETERY
Located south west of Lewisburg by the New Lake. Copied 1957 by Frank Boyd and Ralph D. Whitesell.

James Edwards
Nov 28, 1800
Jul 28, 1882

Several unmarked graves.

Mary, wife of
James Edwards
Oct 16, 1823
Jun 26, 1885

G. H. Edwards
Apr 19, 1830
Jul 20, 1908

Lucinda, wife of
G. H. Edwards
Feb 3, 1834
Jul 12, 1879
Mrd- Oct 17, 1852

* *

LEWISBURG

EWING CEMETERY

Located two and one-half miles north of Lewisburg, south of the Airport, on the Franklin Road. Copied June 15, 1957.

Joseph A. McRady
Jan 18, 1827
Aug 7, 1895

Margaret Elanor, wife of
Joseph A. McRady
Feb 9, 1833
Aug 31, 1898

Marion H., son of
J. M. & L. A. Hawkins
Born & Died Sep 22, 1868

Mary E. Ewing
Died Aug 9, 1874
(no age given)

Mrs. Hettie E., wife of
W. J. Leonard
Died Mar 9, 1882
Age 84 years

Carl, son of
W. J. & H. E. Leonard
Died Oct 27, 1876
(no age given)

Mary Virginia, wife of
Ewell M. Bryant
Age 23 years
(no dates)

Robert K. Kercheval
Died Apr 27, 1867
Age 50 years

Mrs. Sue C., wife of
R. K. Kercheval
Aug 1, 1823
Apr 11, 1885

Elisha Hurt
Oct 31, 1780
Nov 10, 1853
Age 73 yrs, 9 days

Ellen J. Kercheval
Died Apr 15, 1860
Age 4 yrs, 4 mos.

Patrick Ewing
Dec 2, 1802
Apr 4, 1860

Elizabeth E., wife of
James V. Ewing
Feb 12, 1813
Nov 19, 1886

James V. Ewing
Feb 14, 1805
Jun 13, 1878

James Ewing
Died Jan 4, 1826
Age 52 yrs, 12 days

Nelly Ewing
Died Oct 1831
Age 62 yrs, 10 mos, 15 days

Elizabeth Hurt
Died Aug 8, 1842
Age 49 yrs, 9 mos, 14 days

Mary F. J. Ewing
Oct 14, 1842
Sep 21, 1845

Ophelia J. Ewing
Jul 21, 1842
Sep 22, 1845

James O. Ewing
Jan 3, 1855
Oct 26, 1868

Dr. J. C. C. Ewing
Nov 12, 1839
Oct 30, 1917

R. C. Williams
Mar 4, 1828
Oct 2, 1863
Age 35 yrs, 6 mos, 28 days

S. K. Ewing
1841-1923

Georgia W. Ewing
Jul 21, 1842
Sep 17, 1845

Calvin L. Ewing
Oct 12, 1844
Mar 10, 1861

Lizzie D. Ewing
Sep 20, 1845
Jul 25, 1905

Orville S., son of
S. B. & Hattie Ewing
Feb 19, 1860
Aug 5, 1891

A. J. Ewing
1834-1917

* *

FOWLER CEMETERY

Located one mile south west of the new Lewisburg Reservoir just off the Lynnville-New Lake Road. Copied Aug 31, 1958.

E. L. Fowler
Aug 2, 1887
Oct 30, 1891

Joseph L. Fowler
Jul 17, 1850
Sep 15, 1895

J. L. Fowler
May 6, 1812
Feb 17, 1888

Lucinda Perkins, wife of
J. L. Fowler
Jan 29, 1816
Dec 27, 1900

V. B. Hall, wife of
Emmet Allen
Apr 11, 1867
Oct 19, 1910

P. C. Hall
Born 1834
Died Mar 10, 1912

Mary A. Hall
May 2, 1844-Oct 8, 1913

James L. Emmerson
May 3, 1837
Sep 5, 1907

Nancy J., wife of
J. L. Emerson
Oct 2, 1839
(no date)

Leonidas Emmerson
May 17, 1866
Jun 16, 1887

W. L. Colvett
Died Jan 21, 1901
Age 15 yrs, 2 mos, 7 days

Marcus, son of
J. L. & M. J. Emerson
May 21, 1867
Sep 26, 1868

James William, son of
J. L. & M. J. Emerson
Nov 7, 1862
Feb 9, 1863

Nezzie May Fowler
May 12, 1883
Nov 2, 1883

R. L. Fowler
Jul 5, 1867
Jun 26, 1873

Tennie Fowler
Sep 10, 1873
Jun 23, 1890

C. Fowler
Jan 22, 1870
Mar 24, 1871

B. Fowler
Nov 29, 1877
Jan 8, 1895

Mary J., wife of
J. M. Fowler
Sep 22, 1843
Jul 24, 1897

Josie, dau of
J. M. & M. J. Fowler
Dec 30, 1873-Jun 20, 1901

Aurcilla A. Hall
Jan 29, 1879
Sep 28, 1882

Dona, wife of
H. M. Lindell
Feb 27, 1862
Jun 28, 1894
Age 32 yrs, 4 mos, 1 day

Bruce Duncan
Nov 29, 1877
Jul 28, 1878

Several unmarked graves.

* *

LEWISBURG

FOWLER CEMETERY

Located on the west side of the Cornersville Road, about four miles south of Lewisburg. Copied Sep 6, 1958 by Ralph D. Whitesell and Lounora Pickens.

Jamie H. Higdon
Jun 10, 1901
Dec 27, 1918

William "Bill" H. Higdon
1876-1950

James David Carroll
1855-1922

Nancy Emma Carroll
1861-1932

Virgil Lee Fowler
Nov 10, 1915
Jan 7, 1954

Nado London
Nov 9, 1860
May 20, 1943

Vinnie London
Aug 1, 1870

Julius M. Fowler
1875-1932

W. H. "Babe" Cochran
1871-1955

Mrs. Lula Jordan
1882-1955

James Albert Fowler
1883-1944

Bertha Fowler Pettes
Jan 18, 1885

James Gus Pettes
Jan 28, 1880
Mar 9, 1924

L. B. Fowler
Jul 17, 1852
Apr 27, 1931

L. P., son of
L. B. & W. A. Fowler
Jan 21, 1885
Sep 10, 1926

Winnie A., wife of
L. B. Fowler
Jul 20, 1856
Dec 2, 1935

Mai, dau of
L. B. & W. A. Fowler
Dec 26, 1894
Oct 15, 1908

Leola, dau of
L. B. & W. A. Fowler
Jul 4, 1901
Jul 17, 1901

Amy, wife of
E. B. Fowler
Feb 24, 1828
Feb 19, 1893

E. B. Fowler
Feb 21, 1821
Oct 28, 1887

J. H. Fowler
Dec 24, 1857
May 2, 1919

E. E., wife of
J. H. Fowler
Aug 3, 1857
(no date)

Margaret E., wife of
J. P. Thompson
May 2, 1826
Feb 24, 1918

Joseph P. Thompson
Jan 16, 1812
Dec 30, 1899

Robert C. Thompson
Jun 30, 1836
Oct 1, 1912

Fannie P., wife of
R. C. Thompson
Dec 19, 1839
Jun 16, 1918

Infant Son of
Paul C. & Mamie Davis
Oct 3, 1906

Mamie Thompson Davis
May 26, 1870
Mar 24, 1908

Flora, dau of
R. C. & F. P. Thompson
Sep 5, 1859
Oct 25, 1872

Amie C. Fowler
1856-1945

Vergie Fowler
Jul 17, 1898

May F. Hilliard
May 22, 1882

Maude F. Childress
Sep 9, 1880
Jul 14, 1947

Arthur O. Fowler
Sep 9, 1887

Monroe Daugherty
May 7, 1879
Mar 6, 1948

Myrta W. Fowler
Nov 20, 1865
Aug 22, 1945

J. Edwin Fowler
Aug 25, 1855
Dec 21, 1932

Thomas J. Fowler
Sep 8, 1849
Nov 4, 1872

Alanthus L. Fowler
Oct 26, 1822
May 21, 1901

Tennessee Ann Fowler
Aug 14, 1831
Mar 2, 1860

Amhers F. Fowler
Jun 3, 1850
(no date)

Sarah H., wife of
William Fowler
Jun 2, 1816
Jun 17, 1887

William N. Fowler
Apr 12, 1816
May 18, 1894

O. B., son of
W. N. & S. H. Fowler
Mar 28, 1841
May 12, 1858

William P. Fowler
Died Mar 7, 1853
Age 1 year.

Martha A., dau of
G. W. & M. S. Smith
Jun 11, 1853
May 31, 1855

Armantha S., wife of
B. F. Rambo
Sep 20, 1834
Aug 30, 1855

Mary Wilson, wife of
Van Gardner
Jan 14, 1836
Jul 27, 1855

Mark W., son of
Van & Mary Gardner
Nov 31, 1854
Jan 21, 1855

Lee Fowler
1857-1937

Martha S., wife of
G. W. Smith
Sep 25, 1818
Oct 3, 1871

Thomas H. Wilson
Feb 10, 1842
Jan 19, 1862
"Killed in the Battle of Fishing Creek."

Infant Son of
W. P. & M. F. Collins
Died Dec 7, 1874

Margaret F., wife of
W. P. Collins
Jan 10, 1849
Dec 12, 1874

Margaret E., wife of
H. L. Smith
Born 1856
Died Sep 10, 1891

Kenneth Paul, son of
H. L. & S. F. Smith
Jun 9, 1874
Sep 14, 1875

Nancy B. Fowler
Sep 24, 1825
Oct 3, 1905

Osborn Fowler
Jan 11, 1824
Aug 5, 1857

Demeatry L., dau of
Jacob & Sara S. Sowell
Aug 24, 1834
Sep 24, 1835

John B. Fowler
Sep 8, 1785
Oct 17, 1865

Elizabeth Fowler
Oct 2, 1785
Aug 15, 1867

LEWISBURG

M. T. Knudson
Jul 7, 1845
Dec 19, 1926

Oleo Knudson
Aug 14, 1838
Oct 13, 1901

Syddie Knudson
Apr 18, 1871
Dec 20, 1952

Sidney J. Fowler
Jul 28, 1862
Dec 1, 1883

Alice F. Sanders
May 5, 1863
Mar 23, 1937

A. H. Sanders
Jan 20, 1859
Mar 12, 1930

James N. Garrett
May 11, 1848
Feb 20, 1917

Mary E. Garrett
Apr 22, 1856
Sep 30, 1918

Maxie Fowler
Nov 24, 1874
Apr 16, 1955

Sarah Ada Fowler
May 27, 1865
Jan 31, 1951

Margaret E. Fowler
Sep 17, 1858
Aug 23, 1948

J. Lucien Fowler
Jun 30, 1867
Aug 3, 1947

Several unmarked graves.

Sallie H. Fowler
Mar 27, 1835
Dec 15, 1899

Lucien B. Fowler
Aug 15, 1830
May 27, 1905

Maggie Fowler
& 8 months old baby
1874-1900

Robert L. Fowler, Sr.
1866-(no date)

Andrew Fowler
Oct 22, 1878
Apr 29, 1946

Annie Ruth
1913-1914

Ollie J. Fowler
1880-1929
Wagoner's 1st Tenn Inf N.G.

Roena Fowler
1855-1929

Mary Jane Fowler
1887-1957

R. H. H. Hall
(no dates)

J. D. Henry
Jun 9, 1861
Sep 20, 1882

Andy Henry
Oct 5, 1883
Dec 27, 1883

Marion Simmons
Mar 10, 1862
Dec 24, 1944

* *

FOX-WHEATLEY CEMETERY
Located two miles south of Lewisburg, on the Cornersville Road. Copied by Mrs. Felix B. Fox.

Pervines Fox, Sr.
Born Mar 26, 1810 & Died
Aug 16, 1887

Frances Fox
(no dates)

NOTE:(From Mrs. Fox:
Pervines married
1st Narcissus Bennett on
  Jul 21, 1828, who was
  born Dec 29, 1809
  died Mar 23, 1848
2nd Frances Clymore on
  Feb 13, 1849, who was
  born Oct 4, 1831
  died Nov 1, 1857
3rd Frances Bercheen on
  Oct 12, 1858, who was
  born Nov 22, 1811
  died (no record).)

Frances M. Wheatley
Aug 7, 1825
Jul 4, 1885

William Harris Wheatley
Dec 29, 1861
Feb 29, 1942

Felix B. Hays
Jan 25, 1888
Apr 8, 1963

Harold D. Hays
Mar 27, 1917
Killed in WW II, A.F.
May 10, 1942

Articile Hays Roberts
May 27, 1911
Nov 7, 1965

W. Claud Fox
1870-1952

Wilba Fox Trigg
1899-1944

Infant of
Sam P. & Rowena Fox
Jun 13, 1898
Jun 14, 1898

Twins, Infants of
W. C. & Donnie Fox
1892

Mary Ann (Fox) Wheatley
Nov 6, 1832
May 14, 1881

Olive V. Wheatley
May 4, 1867
Nov 19, 1945

Volenia Wheatley Hays
Mar 2, 1891

Joel McConnel
Nov 4, 1937
Nov 28, 1937

Infant of
J. A. & Bettie Wheatley
Feb 12, 1865-Aug 12, 18--

Infant Son of
Mr. & Mrs. Guy Hatley
Mar 10, 1930

Infant Son of
Mr. & Mrs. Guy Hatley
Dec 13, 1938

Eugene J.(Burr) Willis
Aug 7, 1862
Feb 7, 1945

Moss Pyles Willis
Feb 11, 1868
Dec 24, 1936

Sarah Hughs Willis
Dec 26, 1835
Apr 16, 1916

John C. Fox
Jun 3, 1864
Apr --, 1944

Tommy W. Fox
Sep 21, 1870
Jun 16, 1943

Lillian Fox Baxter
Feb 5, 1880
Feb 3, 1901

William D. Fox
Feb 23, 1862
Jan 19, ----

Eva Calton Fox
Jan 22, 1871

J. R. Logue Taylor
1852-1933

Martha Ann Taylor
1856-1931

John A. Wheatley
Aug 9, 1859
Mar 7, 1928

Bettie Bercheen Wheatley
Feb 17, 1886
May 4, 1938

Samuel Wheatley
1857-(no date)

Winnie Sparkman, wife of
W. V. Willis
Died Apr 18, 1913
(no age given)

Sam P. Fox
Oct 11, 1877
Nov 15, 1949

Kathrine C. Fox
Oct 31, 1885
Mar 27, 1957

Clabe Pigg
1881-1938

LEWISBURG

Effie, wife of
Clabe Pigg
1884-

Pervines Fox
Dec 10, 1882
Feb 9, 1938

Georgia Fox Bartlett
Jul 1, 1878
Dec 31, 1957

Joshua Fox
1853-1892

Frances M. Fox
1856-1925

John H. London
May 28, 1855
Feb 10, 1908

Octie Fox London
Oct 21, 1865
Aug 2, 1899

Hays London
1890-1952

Ava Stinson London
1891-1956

Olie Fox
Oct 5, 1884
Apr 7, 1967

Lucille Brown Fox
Feb 13, 1888

Pervines Fox, Jr.
Feb 6, 1835
Apr 10, 1905

C. A. Fox
Oct 25, 1832
Jan 23, 1912

J. L., son of
Mr. & Mrs. Carl Fox
Nov 24, 1904
Jan 5, 1937

Ethel W. Fox
1884-1961

Opal Fox
1913-1967

Ed Taylor
1876-1952

Alphonso Taylor
Dec 2, 1881
Dec 3, 1899

This cemetery has two graves marked only by sandstones. These were the first two graves. The privilege was granted by Pervines Fox, Sen. to a Mr. Jones to bury his wife and infant. They were traveling by wagon, and no further information has been found. - Mrs. Felix Hays

* *

GIPSON CEMETERY
Located on the Rambo Hollow Road, about five miles south west of Lewisburg. Copied January, 1961.

Marcelous Gipson
Sep 28, 1852
Sep 29, 1876

Aron Gipson
Jan 10, 1859
Aug 26, 1866

Three unmarked graves.

* *

GREEN WILSON CEMETERY -
Located on hill across Globe Creek on Wilson Hill Road, in edge of woods. Copied Dec 5, 1979 by Ralph D. Whitesell, Helen & Tim Marsh.

Daughter of
Mark & Lennie Wilson
1900-1900

M. L. F. Wilson
Mar 22, 1852
Nov 11, 1856

J. C. Wilson
Jun 17, 1845
Mar 12, 1889

Telitha Cochran Wilson
1841-1916

5-6 unmarked graves.

Green Wilson
Mar 10, 1815
Nov 15, 1853

L. T. Phillips, nee wife of
Green Wilson
May 1, 1821
Aug 31, 1887

Oscar, son of
W. C. & R. M. Gates
Oct 5, 1872
Aug 11, 1887

D. Bills (Daniel Bills
Died 1848 (1789-1848)
(fieldstone, no age given)

* *

HARDIN CEMETERY
Located on the Spring Place Road, near Linton Pencil Company. Copied 1959.

T. Jeff Chapman
1862-1948

Dora E. Chapman
1862-1897

Lola Chapman
1888-1890

Thomas M. Chapman
Died May 9, 1865
Age 50 years

M. S. Woodward
(no dates)

J. D. Woodward
(no dates)

Margaret W., dau of
J. D. & Martha S. Woodward
Aug 10, 1857
Sep 26, 1863
Age 6 yrs, 1 mo, 16 days

John F. Glenn
May 25, 1816
Dec 7, 1854

Thomas H., son of
M. J. & E. P. Hardin
Sep 20, 1846
Aug 29, 1852

Mattie R. Nowlin, wife of
J. M. Ledbetter
Jan 22, 1851
Jul 14, 1874

LEWISBURG

Mattie Lou, dau of
J. M. & H. M. Ledbetter
Nov 20, 1884
Aug 15, 1897

G. M. D. Twitty
Mar 9, 1845
Jul 13, 1874

Infant Dau of
D. B. & M. L. Elliott
Jun 24, 1874
Jul 9, 1874

Patrick H. Twitty
Born Oct 9, 1836
Was wounded at the Battle
of Murfreesboro, Tenn.
Dec 31, 1862, in the C.S.A.
Died Feb 19, 1863
Age 26 yrs, 4 mos, 10 days

Several unmarked graves.

Judith, wife of
L. H. Twitty
Aug 31, 1814
Feb 11, 1905

Leonard Twitty
Born 1806
Died Jun 30, 185-

Martin H., son of
L. H. & J. L. Twitty
Jan 8, 1847
Sep 14, 1854

William W., son of
L. H. & J. L. Twitty
Sep 17, 1853
Sep 17, 1857

Bathiah J. Hardin
Born Jun 5, 1822
Mrd- J. N. Nowlin
Died Jun 14, 1849

A. Blakemore
Feb 9, 1858
May 23, 1901

J. B. W. Nowlin
Died Jul 14, 1854
(no age given)

Martha, Consort of
L. H. Twitty
Jan 27, 1812
May 31, 1836

Bryant Nowlin
Oct 18, 1768
Jun 13, 1835

Lucy, Consort of
Thomas H. Hardin, Sr.
Feb 28, 1791
Nov 15, 1858

Dalas P., son of
M. J. & E. P. Hardin
Jun 13, 1850
Jul 25, 1851

Elizabeth P., wife of
J. M. Hardin
Dec 11, 1823
Sep 16, 1853

James P. Hardin
Sep 17, 1844
Died 1865

John F., son of
M. J. & E. P. Hardin
Sep 3, 1853
Jul 14, 1855

Mary Glenn
Dec 1, 1787
Aug 5, 1866
Age 78 yrs, 9 mos, 4 days

James Glenn
Sep 1787
Mar 28, 1868
Age 80 yrs, 6 mos.

* *

HARDIN CEMETERY
Located on Tilden Collins Farm, owned by W. B. Coughran, 1968.

R. A. Endsley
Apr 18, 1860
Jun 23, 1925

L. T., son of
Laura Collins
Nov 8, 1914
Jan 18, 1916

Tilden Collins
Nov 26, 1879
May 14, 1920

Mary, Consort of
John L. Hardin
Dec 13, 1794
Mar 15, 1820

Sandstone
(Presumably the grave of
John L. Hardin)

Norma Davis, wife of
R. A. Endsley
Jan 3, 1859
Jul 7, 1937

Laura N. Endsley, wife of
T. L. Collins
Nov 31, 1879
Nov 17, 1914

F. K. Rambo
Nov 26, 1805
Oct 8, 1875

Mary B., wife of
F. K. Rambo
Jan 16, 1809
Mar 1899

Mary Ann, Consort of
Richard Daugharety
Dec 22, 1818
Dec 10, 1844
(Her grave is below the
house, other graves, un-
marked)

J. K., son of
F. K. & Mary B. Rambo
Born Jul 28, 1845

Brant W., son of
F. K. & Mary B. Rambo
Feb 12, 18--
Sep 12, 1860

* *

HAYWOOD CEMETERY
Located three and one-half miles south of Lewisburg, on the
J. T. McKnight property, south of the Rambo Spring. Copied
May 27, 1966.

Dr. J. D. S. Haywood
May 6, 1829
Jul 3, 1856
Age 27 yrs, 1 mo, 27 days

Dr. George W. Haywood
Oct 7, 1798
Sep 22, 1846

George W. L. Haywood
Jan 8, 1844
Sep 21, 1844

5-6 unmarked graves.

* *

LEWISBURG

HILL CEMETERY

Located off State Highway 50-A, between Mooresville and Lewisburg, near the turn off to Wilson Hill, but on the Silver Creek cut off, about one-half mile from highway. Webb-Globe Road. A Hill family cemetery with others buried there, about half with no identity. Likely to become inactive, as the last burial was in 1959 and now badly grown up in bushes and trees, some large, when copied by Joe Harris and wife, March 1964.

James Kennedy
Born 1777
Died Oct 20, 1837
in the 60th year of his age.

Mary Kennedy, wife of
James Kennedy
Feb 2, 1773
Jan 25, 1864

Col. John R. Hill
Born 1802
Died Jun 13, 1880

Elizabeth (Kennedy), wife of
John R. Hill
Born 1806
Died Jun 6, 1879

Mary Ann, dau of
J. R. & E. Hill
Jul 16, 1830
Jun 10, 1837

Elizabeth P., dau of
J. R. & E. Hill
Nov 26, 1831
Apr 1, 1852

James K., son of
J. R. & E. Hill
Nov 22, 1836
Sep 24, 1849

Nancy M., dau of
J. R. & E. Hill
Jan 14, 1840
Mar 14, 1841

John T., son of
J. R. & E. Hill
Sep 6, 1846
Jul 17, 1922

Missie McClean Hill (wife)
Jun 3, 1848
Sep 15, 1941

Grandison McClean Hill
Jun 29, 1887
Sep 8, 1892

Capt. Isaac H. Hill
1833-1923

Cornelia Stone Hill (wife)
1844-1924

Mollie E., dau of
I. H. & C. A. Hill
Apr 13, 1865
Jan 1, 1866

Isaac H. Hill, Jr.
1874-1927

William F. Hill
Mar 7, 1867
Oct 13, 1896

Sue E. Hill
1869-1934

John Davis Hill
1877-1937

Laura Rose Hill
1880-1959

Noble C. Hill
1882-1947

Maymie S. Hill (wife)
1885-1943

Sallie H., Consort of
G. J. Harris
May 27, 1841
Apr 4, 1873

Sallie Hill, dau of
G. J. & S. H. Harris
Aug 16, 1872
Mar 27, 1878

Mattie Hill Towner
May 17, 1842
Dec 1, 1870

Infant Child of
W. W. & H. L. Gordon
Feb 18, 1859
Feb 18, 1859

Calvin D. Ritchie
1836-1921

Frances C. (Harris) Ritchie
(wife)
1843-1919

Thomas W. Bryant
moved to Tenn. 1827,
married Eliz. Bell
Sep 15, 1814
(broken)
(first marriage issued in
Marshall County)(stone down)
(wife may be on other side)

Vannie J., dau of
T. W. & Eliz. Bryant
Sep 21, 1853
Feb 11, 1884

Bettie Bryant
May 18, 1864
Oct 7, 1867

Hattie Bryant
(no dates)

Brother
Thomas H. Malone
May 10, 1867
Oct 22, 1898

Mother
Eliza Lamyra Malone
Mar 30, 1845
Jan 27, 1912

Sister
Clara Bell Malone
Oct 22, 1877
Sep 7, 1915

William H. Osburn
Dec 16, 1805
Oct 20, 1880

Margaret Osburn (wife)
Jul 14, 1810
Jul 8, 1881

William Osburn
Jun 21, 1835
Sep 14, 1881

W. T. Osburn
May 13, 1831
Dec 24, 1886

Monroe Osburn
May 5, 1851
Sep 30, 1889

G. M. London
Nov 29, 1861
Mar 27, 1924

Artie M. Frances London (wife)
Dec 8, 1853
Jun 23, 1901

Annie London
(no dates)

Green B. London
(no dates)

Marcus London
(no dates)

E. R. Tilman
Nov 18, 1849
Aug 27, 1882

Mary P., wife of
Richard Tilman
Mar 29, 1843
Aug 1, 1903

James R., son of
E. R. & Mary Tilman
Feb 20, 1881
May 7, 1900

Jane, wife of
S. G. Huggins
Dec 3, 1825
Dec --, ----

Mary Eliz. M. Frances
                Huggins
Nov 13, 1865
Mar 2, 1885

J. N. Bailey
(no dates)

Minerva V., wife of
J. D. Thompson
Mar 7, 1876
Sep 1, 1897

Emily T., wife of
D. M. Barro (Barron)
Oct 28, 1839
Jun 7, 1903

NOTE: The above Frances C., wife of Calvin D. Ritchie, was an aunt of the copier, being a half-sister of his father, John Lindsey Harris

The negro cemetery is on the next page. Eds.

LEWISBURG

NEGRO SECTION OF HILL CEMETERY

Florence Hardy
Dec 20, 1870
Oct 27, 1920

Martha, wife of
John Williams
Jun 4, 1874
Dec 23, 1919

Melissa Hill
May 1, 1894
Jun 5, 1948

Elsie C. Rhodes
1897-1957

James Rhodes
Oct 8, 1927
Apr 31, 1929

Cornelia, dau of
Willie & Susie Wilkes
Oct 22, 1925
Jul 1, 1927

Henry F., son of
Charles & Connie
Fitzpatrick
Apr 28, 1904
Jun 15, 1918

Infant Son of
Craig & Ida Moore
Aug 8, 1920
Aug 8, 1920

* *

HOPWOOD CEMETERY
Located four miles south of Lewisburg, between the Yell and
Spring Place Roads, on the farm of Charlie Lasater. Copied
1957.

Calvin Hoopwood
Born 1816
(hand carved stone)

Mary Hoopwood
Died 1830
(hand carved stone)

Nancy Jones
Died 1848 at age of 41 yrs.
(hand carved stone)

Probably Eld. Willis Hopwood
Oct 29, 1777 - Oct 6, 1850
& wife: Penelope P. Hopwood,
no marker.

John Hoopwood
Age 43   1823
(hand carved stone)

NOTE: Willis Hopwood & wife
were natives of Pittsylvania
Co.Va. Early settlers of MCT

Betsy Nowlin
Was born Oct 15, 1830
(no date)
(hand carved stone)

Several unmarked graves.

* * * * * *

HOPWOOD-WILLIS CEMETERY
Located on Yell Road, near the site of Old New Providence
Church.

A. C. Hopwood
Born Dec 23, ----
Jan 5, 1888

NOTE: This inscription may not be authentic since the stones
were so deteriorated, they could not be read. An oak tree
about five feet in diameter encases one stone. The size of
the tree gives an idea of it's age and the time of these
graves. Several stones were only markers. I well believe
Davis and Martha Willis found this their last resting place.
1979, Ralph D. Whitesell.

* *

HOUSTON CEMETERY
Located west of Lewisburg, on Globe Road. Near Interstate
65. Copied 1964.

In Memory of
Christopher Houston
Born 19th February 1744
Died 17th May, 1837
&
Sarah Houston
Who died July 18th, A.D.
1821 in the 79th year of her
age. "Now the God of peace be
with you all - Amen."

Martha E., dau of
William & S. M. Holley
Aug 14, 1860
Oct 9, 1862

In Memory of
Jane Bills
Born Mar 28, 1798 & departed
this life July 13, A.D. 1825

Alfred M. Houston
Aug 21, 1833
Sep   1861

Elenor Cummings
Apr 10, 1772
Dec 14, 1832

Archibald McConnell
Jan 29, 1795
Mar 15, 1847
"He was in the War of 1812 &
in the Battle of New Orleans
Jan 8, 1815.

Eliza M., wife of
Archibald McConnell
Aug 31, 1799
Jan 14, 1884

Rachel, wife of James Jackson
Jan 27, 1778
(no date, died after 1850)

Sacred to the Memory of
Daniel & Deborah Bills
He was born Sep 28, A.D.
1740, Died Mar 18, A.D.
1829.
She was born Dec 28, A.D.
1745. Died Jun 26, A. D.
1819. "They lived in union
56 years". "He that feareth
God & worketh righteousness
is accepted with Him."

James Jackson
Apr 3, 1767
Sep 3, 1851
Age 84 years

LEWISBURG

B. F. Houston
Oct 7, 1805
Feb 16, 1862

Niccie B. Houston
Feb 14, 1813
Nov 10, 1878

Dawson B. Elliott
Sep 11, 1820
Aug 16, 1883

Archibald, son of
W. J. & P. J. McConnell
Jul 26, 1880
Aug 24, 1880

William B., son of
W. J. & P. J. McConnell
Jul 26, 1880
Apr 28, 1881

Infant Son of
W. J. & P. J. McConnell
Jun 19, 1887
Apr 16, 1888

Clyde E., son of
W. J. & P. J. McConnell
Jan 3, 1890
Jun 6, 1895

W. J. McConnell
Oct 17, 1846
Sep 10, 1904

Sanford W. Elliot
Jan 21, 1858
May 28, 1888

Our Father
A. C. Beasley
May 1, 1836
Dec 5, 1899

Mary E., wife of
A. C. Beasley
Dec 14, 1847
Sep 2, 1893

A. C., son of
A. C. & M. E. Beasley
May 8, 1893
Aug 20, 1893

Oscar, son of
A. C. & M. E. Beasley
Jan 22, 1877
Dec 30, 1890

Sue B., dau of
E. B. & P. O. Perkins
Sep 21, 1864
Dec 12, 1880

S. L. Meadows
Aug 4, 1878
Sep 30, 1899

Patience O., wife of
J. K. P. Meadows
May 25, 1841
Sep 14, 1900

Robert Loyd, son of
J. M. & B. J. Davis
Dec 29, 1894
Dec 29, 1894

Infant Son of
J. L. & Bessie Davis
July 10, 1917

I. P. Jackson
Born Jun 20, 1801 Surry Co.,
N. Carolina, Died Mar 22,
1881

M. A. Jackson
Born Mar 22, 1807 in South
Carolina, Pendleton Co.,
Died Oct 6, 1895

Claudius, son of
J. K. P. & Jesie Meadows
Oct 2, 1870
Oct 11, 1870

Infant Son of
P. D. & M. A. Houston
Buried Dec 16, 1869

Mrs. Ada _____-(illegible)
Died 1928

Josephene, wife of
J. K. P. Meadows
Feb 6, 1848
Jul 30, 1871

* *

MT. CARMEL CEMETERY

Located in Lewisburg. This cemetery was established as a Church and Community Cemetery many years before Lewisburg existed. Rechecked May, 1980 by Helen & Tim Marsh.

James McMorris
Mar 28, 1784
Aug 2, 1815

Lydia McMorris
Mar 20, 1777
Jul 20, 1818

Mary Nelson
Died May 6, 1822
(no age given)

Peggy Nelson
Died Nov 6, 1822
(no age given)

Robert Ewing
Feb 4, 1767
Apr 9, 1852

Jonah Phifer
Died Mar 18, 1860
Age 82 yrs, 3 mos.

Jincy, wife of
Jona Phifer
Aug 27, 1814
Jul 12, 1891

W. W. Phifer
Jun 26, 1840
Jun 20, 1861

Levi Phifer
Age 33 years (no dates)

Cyrus Houston
Mar 6, 1822
May 29, 1846

John M., son of
Abner & Phoeby Houston &
Husband of Jane D. Houston
Oct 6, 1813
Jul 17, 1838

H. T. B.
(footmarker)

James R., son of
Jane D. & John M. Houston
Dec 22, 1834
May 3, 1836
Age 16 mos & 10 days

Peggy, dau of
W. A. & M. A. Houston
Jun 22, 1858
Sep 19, 1868
&
W. A. Houston
Nov 27, 1815
Mar 3, 1868
& wife
Matilda A. Houston
Jun 23, 1820
Oct 22, 1873

Ann C., Consort of
W. A. Houston
May 29, 1817-Aug 9, 1843

Elizabeth Jane, Consort of
Wm. A. Houston
Jun 24, 1825
Jan 28, 1847

Margaret Ann, dau of
Wm. A. & E. J. Houston
Feb 15, 1846
Jul 20, 1854

Rufus C. Jackson
Jan 29, 1860
Aug 24, 1867

Wm. A., son of
W. A. & M. F. Jackson
Oct 30, 1857
1857

Thomas J., son of
W. A. & M. F. Jackson
May 29, 1876
Oct 22, 1877

Willie A., son of
W. A. & M. F. Jackson
Jun 25, 1872
Nov 10, 1892

Wm. McGregor
1779-Sep 9, 1853

Francis McGregor
(no dates)

George McGregor
(no dates)

Cynthia McGregor
(no dates)

James Patterson
Aug 8, 1794
May 30, 1875

Polly Patterson
Jun 11, 1791
Aug 18, 1874

Wm. M. Patterson
Feb 28, 1833
Nov 30, 1864
"Franklin, Tenn. Killed
in Battle."

Manervy Patterson
Sep 17, 1831
Jun 7, 1860

James Washington Kelly
                    Goodrich
Nov 27, 1849
Sep 27, 1850

Drucilla, wife of
J. W. Calahan
Nov 24, 1816
Aug 13, 1848
Age 31 yrs, 8 mos, 17 days

LEWISBURG

R. J., son of
L. & E. Cochran
Apr 13, 1828
Sep 7, 1840

H. L., dau of
L. & E. Cochran
Mar 2, 1836
Oct 27, 1852

Levi Cochran
Oct 3, 1799
Jan 29, 1885

Elizabeth, wife of
Levi Cochran
May 24, 1803
Jan 7, 1873

E. J. McCorkle, dau of
L. & E. Cochran
Nov 26, 1833
Dec 3, 1852

R. F., son of
P. W. & E. J. McCorkle
Nov 6, 1852
Jan 22, 1853

John Hatchett
Jan 26, 1784
Jan 8, 1848

Clitus F. Hatchett
Jun 28, 1824
Jul 8, 1854

Robert L., son of
Samuel & S. A. Davis
Jan 30, 1844
Sep 16, 1858

John A., son of
Sam & Sarah A. Davis
Mar 24, 1849
Jun 20, 1853

Infant of
J. B. & C. J. Moore
Born & Died Jan 5, 1871

F.
(footstone)

William Coleman
Jun 15, 1805
Jun 15, 1896
&
Nancy Coleman
Apr 12, 1811
Oct 17, 1891

Collins Nichols
Nov 23, 1908
Nov 6, 1911

Wilson P. Davis
Dec 8, 1808
Feb 20, 1862

Sally, wife of
Wilson P. Davis
Jan 13, 1811
Jan 25, 1889

Alford Davis
Oct 15, 1817
Oct 30, 1896

John Davis
Died Aug 14, 1842
Age 24 years

Jonathan G. Ewing
Apr 7, 1804
Jun 15, 1828

Elisha Collins
Sep 18, 1845
Dec 11, 1862

David Collins
Mar 16, 1827
Aug 8, 1906
&
Margarett A. Collins
Oct 21, 1823
May 25, 1909
mrd- Jul 12, 1853

William B., son of
David & M. A. Collins
May 12, 1861
Oct 1, 1862

R. Becket
D- 1841
(hand hewn stone)

John Columbus, son of
Ebenezer & Dorcus Stillwell
Apr 28, 1820
Feb 13, 1831

W. M. McKnight
Jan 17, 1846
May 23, 1882, 36y, 4m, 6 da.

Cynthia C. McKnight
Dec 8, 1842
Sep 27, 1861
&
Sara McKnight
Aug 17, 1849
Sep 19, 1869

PLAQUE:
Eliza Cochran Coleman
Wm. Jasper Coleman
Sam Coleman
Sallie Coleman Glenn
Peggie Coleman
William Cochran
(no dates)

Russell Bryant
Died Feb 4, 1888
Age 90 years

Sidney, wife of
R. Bryant
Jun 15, 1793
Sep 2, 1866

Col. W. B. Holden
1814-1873
&
Ellen B. Holden
1859-1872
&
Emily Holden
1821-1886

Gaston Braly
Aug 30, 1825
Oct 10, 1861
&
Willie Gertrude, dau of
W. A. & M. I. Braly
Feb 16, 1874
May 6, 1874
&
Rachel L. Braly
Sep 1, 1825
Jun 19, 1858
&
Louise E. Braly
Jun 12, 1858
Jul 15, 1858

Robert Harvey McCrory
Feb 18, 1823
Mar 25, 1893

Frances M., wife of
R. H. McCrory
Nov 2, 1825
Dec 22, 1902

Emma McCrory
Apr 25, 1855
Sep 8, 1925

Joseph McKnight
Sep 18, 1820
Sep 22, 1839
Age 19 yrs & 4 days

James McKnight
Jul 24, 1814
Feb 27, 1886
&
Margaret McKnight
Jun 15, 1820
Jun 16, 1902

Naomi, dau of
J. & M. McKnight
Oct 16, 1851
Oct 24, 1855

Eula LaDelle, dau of
S. E. & Sally McCrory
Sep 9, 1897
Jan 9, 1902

William Davis
Dec 9, 1774
Nov 7, 1854

Naomi, wife of
William Davis
Mar 17, 1791
May 5, 1876

Cynthia J. A. Davis
Feb 8, 1828
Aug 23, 1883

Rachel M., wife of
S. L. Davis
May 17, 1845
Feb 6, 1879

Joseph I., son of
S. L. & R. M. Davis
Aug 29, 1877
Sep 26, 1878

Nancy, dau of
F. & M. McKnight
Died Mar 14, 1845
Age 3 months

Margaret McKnight, wife of
Robert Davis
Jul 21, 1824
May 2, 1848

Robert Davis
Jul 27, 1808
Jun 12, 1897
& wife
Elizabeth Davis
Feb 21, 1830
Oct 26, 1899

Robert J. Davis
Oct 10, 1847 (died)
Age about 5 years
&
Sarah C. McKnight, wife of
Robert Davis
Oct 24, 1812
Jun 5, 1844

Jane McKnight
Oct 17, 1816
May 20, 1844
Age 27 yrs, 7 mos, 3 days

John M. Christopher
Aug 16, 1837
Aug 6, 1838

S. Ann Christopher
Aug 18, 1839
Sep 5, 1840

LEWISBURG

James W. Christopher
Son of John & Susannah
Christopher
Mar 10, 1830
--- --- 1836

George F., son of
J. E. & M. T. McAteer
Apr 17, 1889
May 31, 1889

R. L., son of
W. E. & S. J. McAteer
May 23, 1866
Nov 25, 1866

George W. Birmingham
Dec 17, 1806
Oct 8, 1878

Rosanna C. Birmingham
May 1, 1812
Mar 6, 1885

Leroy Neese
1914-1943
&
Pauline Neese
1915-1938

Bobby Lee Neese
1936-1937

Jona A. Snell
Sep 25, 1809
Jun 11, 1869

W. S. Calahan
Mar 10, 1799
Apr 3, 1862

Rachel, wife of
W. S. Calahan
Feb 27, 1802
May 14, 1889

Dorcus E. Rone, dau of
F. & D. Stilwell
Sep 21, 1836
Sep 26, 1863
mrd Dec 28, 1853

John S. Cheek
May 11, 1831
May 13, 1834

E. Bruce Hamlin
Oct 1, 1886
Dec 19, 193-
&
Mary L. Hamlin
Jul 28, 1876
Jul 26, 1943

On one stone:
E. B. & C. H. B.
(no dates)

Elisha Collins
May 2, 1807
Nov 16, 1872
& wife
Elizabeth Collins
Dec 19, 1807
Mar 19, 1893

L. C. Gupton
Aug 27, 1842
Nov 25, 1875

S. Thompson
Died May 13, 1821
Age 54 years
(hand hewn stone)

Mother
Mary A. Rambo
Oct 21, 1852
Oct 16, 1906

George Phifer
Oct 20, 1850
Dec 30, 1888

Williams
(footmarker)

Infant Son of
J. & H. Williams
Born dead Feb 22, 1847

Many unmarked graves.
END MT. CARMEL

Frederick W. Foster
Died Jul 12, 1932
Pvt Q M Corps
(no age given)

Fannie Foster
1872-1950

Tennie, dau of
B. F. & Mary Foster
Jan 4, 1887
Mar 29, 1902

John A. Smith
May 11, 1891
Oct 16, 1935

Sallie E. Smith
Mar 21, 1891
Oct 30, 1936

W. L. Church
(no dates)

Mollie B., wife of
W. L. Church
Apr 20, 1861
Oct 10, 1899

Sara H. Clendening
Jul 28, 1914
Apr 24, 1934

* *

JOHNSON CEMETERY
Located about three miles south of Lewisburg on the Cornersville Highway.

William E. Johnson
Jan 30, 1830
Jul 6, 1861

James B., son of
Wm. & J. D. Johnson
Jul 11, 1838
May 31, 1863

Virgil Johnson, son of
W. J. & M. B. Hunter
Mar 8, 1902
Oct 2, 1902

Jimmie Lee, son of
W. J. & M. B. Hunter
Mar 31, 1901
Apr 2, 1901

Joseph T. Johnson
Apr 4, 1836
Dec 3, 1896

Bennie V. Johnson
May 17, 1872
Feb 26, 1901

M. E. Johnson
Sep 30, 1838
Mar 6, 1876

Sacred to the Memory of
My wife Mary E. Herndon
Born Aug 30, 1833. Departed
this life Oct 2, 1852
Age 19 yrs, 1 mo, 3 days

Nannie J., dau of
J. G. & M. A. Johnson
Jun 23, 1859
Mar 8, 1864

Bennie G., son of
J. G. & Mary A. Johnson
May 1, 1854
Jun 23, 1857

John G. Johnson
May 22, 1826
Jul 23, 1860

* *

LONDON CEMETERY
Located on the Bill Duncan Farm. Copied Dec 9, 1958 by
Ralph D. Whitesell.

Neil E. Gipson
1882-1900

Sallie D. Gipson
1874-1949

Ann Gipson
Apr 7, 1825-Oct 24, 1889

Enoch London
Aug 15, 1885 (died)
Age about 43 years

Sarah London
Died Mar 28, 1875
Age 75 years

John London
Died Dec 9, 1868
Age 71 years

Two graves with headstones,
no inscriptions. Said to be
one of the London girls and
her husband, an Edwards.

7 graves with initials:
R. L.; M.A.; H. L.;
S. C. L.; M. J. L.;
W. L.; and N. L.
(no dates)

* *

LEWISBURG

LONDON CEMETERY
Located southwest of Wilson Hill on New Lake Road, on a hill
near the Lewisburg reservoir. Copied Oct 31, 1960 by
Ralph Stephens and Ralph D. Whitesell.

I. G. Osburn
Mar 28, 1837
Jul 6, 1899

Rachel J., wife of
I. G. Osburn
Aug 12, 1838
Sep 11, 1893

William Thomas G., son of
G. & B. J. Osburn
Jan 8, 1870
Feb 26, 1893

Mary, wife of
John Cochran
Oct 22, 1811
Jul 20, 1884

J. H. Cochran
Jul 11, 1850
Jan 24, 1882

S.
(fieldstone)

W. C. M.
(footstone)

In Memory of
Washington Day
(no dates)

W. H. & W. E. McConnel
Born Apr 10, 1851
Was taken sick on the 9th
& Died on the 10th of
April, 1856, of scarlet
fever.

Joseph S. McConnel
Dec 7, 1886
Aug 5, 1887

A. Ras. McConnel
Mar 2, 1883
Feb 10, 1891

P. C. McConnel
Aug 22, 1868
Apr 30, 1898

Josie Lou, dau of
A. S. & M. V. McConnel
Oct 25, 1880
Jul 25, 1901

A. S. McConnel
Feb 11, 1842
Oct 13, 1909

His wife
Mary V. McConnel
Dec 2, 1846
May 30, 1926

N. Berry London
Sep 15, 1828
Sep 8, 1868

E. M. C. (no dates)

Amos London
(no dates)

S. L.
(no dates)

W. L.
(no dates)

M. L.
(no dates)

Amos M. London
1836-(no date)

J. A. L.
(footstone)

George W., son of
Alex Baron
Jun 1, 1863
Aug 30, 1884

S. C. McDaniel
Sep 16, 1849
Jan 21, 1921

A. L. McDaniel
Jul 22, 1862
Feb 12, 1920

James H. Thompson
Nov 25, 1853
Jan 31, 1908

Wilson London
Mar 10, 1820
Jan 12, 1891
Age 70 yrs, 10 mos, 2 days

Nola F. W., dau of
A. L. & S. G. McDaniel
Aug 22, 1885
Sep 14, 1890

John P., son of
Wilson & J. London
Dec 29, 1841
Dec 24, 1887

Alfred B., son of
W. & J. London
May 26, 1861
Sep 29, 1862

Jemima, wife of
Wilson London & dau of
P. W. & M. McCorkle
Nov 18, 1819
Feb 20, 1862

W. & J. London's Infant
(no dates)

Ann London
Died Jul 20, 1856
(no age given)

F.
1844

Catherin Thomas, dau of
William & Mary C. Barron
May 15, 1859
May 2, 1888

William Barron
Oct 11, 1837
Feb 27, 1909
& wife
Mary C. Barron
Oct 22, 1834
Mar 18, 1883

Malinda Barron
May 10, 1801
May 27, 1880
(E. J. Scholz, Evansville, Ind.
Monument Mfgr.)

Mary Matilda, dau of
William & Mary C. Barron
Jun 22, 1868
Jul 18, 1884

Marcus L. Caneer
Mar 24, 1856
Oct 28, 1862
Age 6 yrs, 7 mos, 4 days

E. A., dau of
William & Nancy London
Jun 8, 1838
Aug 22, 1849

H. H.----
(illegible)

A. C., dau of
W. M. & Nancy London
Apr 28, 1836
May 25, 1844

J. A., son of
W. M. & Nancy London
Sep 10, 18--
Jun 5, 1840

N. J., dau of
W. M. & Nancy London
Mar 31, 1841
--- 8, 1882
(broken)

Nancy, wife of
William London
Jan 9, 1801-Mar 2, 1890

Nellie M., wife of
J. T. Lawrence
Sep 23, 1843
Jan 25, 1892

Mary V. London
Jan 26, 1824
Dec 4, 1895

William Shehane
Jun 10, 1785
Aug 18, 1867

M.S.O.G.
1858

J. F. Shehane
Was murdered January 1855

R. Jones
Apr 14, 1844
(no date)

John London
1760-1832
& 2nd wife
Permelia Cheek London
(assumed to be buried here
in unmarked graves)

Miss B. S. Shehane
Aug 4, 1811
Jul 4, 1867
Age 56 years

Mr. D. D. Shehane
Aug 22, 1808
Jul 22, 1867

B. L. Richardson
(no dates)

W. C. R.
(died) May 25, 1845

R. Richardson
(no dates)

Infant of
C. F. R. & --- Shehane
------- (name illegible)
Oct 13, 1835
Jan 18, 1836

William Barron
Jun 11, 1801
Sep 30, 1868

Francis C., wife of
Daniel Barron
Apr 27, 1829
Oct 24, 1860

T. J. P.
(no dates)

LEWISBURG

W. D. M.
(no dates)

-. D. M.
(no dates)

J. B. Mc.
(no dates)

S. B. Jones
Died Aug 7, 1847
(no age given)

S. E. Wilson
Aug 28, 1827
Jul 24, 1887

Isaac Newton Wilson
Sep 3, 1837
Nov 12, 1876
Age 39 yrs, 2 mos, 9 days

George J. Wilson
Jan 19, 1840
Killed at Murfreesboro
Jan 1, 1863

H. T. Barron
Mar 14, 1844
(no date)

William T. W., son of
H. T. & M. S. Barron
Jul 22, 1863
Apr 17, 1864

Mary A. Wilson
Aug 11, 1835
Jul 25, 1856

Nancy M. Wilson
May 22, 1833
Nov 13, 1853

Tempy, wife of
John Wilson
Dec 19, 1813
Jun 3, 1852
"The mother of Enoch, Nancy,
Mary & George Wilson."

Enoch Wilson
Dec 25, 1830
Jul 25, 1851

H. W.
D. 28, 1848

John Wilson
Jun 7, 1808
Aug 25, 1879

Matilda Wilson
Jan 12, 1803
Feb 8, 1879

Mary F., dau of
J. P. & M. Osburn
Aug 13, 1867
Mar 20, 1869

Infant Son of
J. P. & M. Osburn
Born & Died Oct 26, 1860

Rachel Wilson
Oct 26, 1812
Aug 17, 1872

M. S. Barron
Oct 15, 1846
Oct 8, 1913

Father
James P. Osburn
Mar 22, 1833
Sep 25, 1905
&
Mother
Matilda Osburn
Oct 10, 1833
Feb 17, 1901

Bonnie Mae, dau of
J. F. & Ella Boyet
Jun 25, 1899
Oct 22, 1899

Mattie B., dau of
J. F. & Ella Boyet
Apr 30, 1898
Aug 16, 1898

Anne S., dau of
J. F. & Ella Boyet
May 3, 1897
Jun 29, 1897

Several unmarked graves.

Maggie M. Whitesell
May 6, 1865
Mar 19, 1886

Infant of
D. J. & M. L. Stafford
Born Jan 24, 1867

S. L. Osburn
Jun 22, 1869
Jun 8, 1888

Alonzo Osburn
Died Jan 1863
(no age given)

Winney F. Osburn
Died Jan 1863
(no age given)

Henry F. Caneer
Died Apr 22, 1902
Age 48 yrs, 5 mos, 2 days

J. D. Caneer
Oct 23, 1829
May 11, 1914

Susan A. L. London,
wife of J. D. Caneer
May 28, 1830
Sep 5, 1892
Age 62 yrs, 3 mos, 8 days

C.
(on both head & foot stone)

* *

MARSH-DAVIS CEMETERY
Located on Globe Road, one mile south of the Columbia Highway, west of Lewisburg. On east side of road, on property belonging to Mrs. Walter Hill. Copied July 14, 1960 by Mrs. Ray Farley.

Albert Mathis
1861-1944
&
Jennie Mathis
1882-1943

Mrs. Laura Woods
1864-1957 (TM)
(same as below)

W. J. Woods
Jan 10, 1861
Apr 24, 1922
&
Laura A. Woods
Aug 1, 1864
(TM: 1957)

Mattie Mundy Davis
Apr 6, 1831
May 7, 1904
"My Grandma
Margaret Davis"

Thomas P. Marsh
Nov 17, 1817
Sep 21, 1878

Thomas Edwards
1856-1936
&
Eliza B. Edwards
1856-1903

Infant of
R. _. & M. M. Phillips
Aug 7, 1872
Sep 14, 1872

Mrs. E. L. Marsh
Jan 20, 1828
Jan 13, 1907

Ole, son of
J. P. & P. V. Turner
Nov 25, 1872
Mar 30, 1899

Robert Marsh
Jan 1795
Oct 25, 1869
&
Elizabeth Marsh *
Aug 23, 1859 (died)
Age 105 years
(Mother & Son, Eds.)

James Davis
Died Jan 20, 1840
Age 55 years
&
Christian Davis
Died Aug 30, 1854
Age 65 years

J. W. Davis
Oct 7, 1817
May 28, 1893

*Widow of Thomas Marsh
native of Anson Co. N.C.

Father
Jerome P. Turner
Mar 3, 1849
Jun 1, 1930
&
Mother
Permelia V. Turner
Mar 24, 1851
Jun 29, 1930

M. B. Dyer
Jan 22, 1842
Jun 22, 1862

Mary J. Dyer, wife of
J. B. Breecheen
Nov 18, 1837
Nov 24, 1862

Nancy Davis, wife of
F. F. Dyer
Dec 13, 1818
Aug 27, 1904

LEWISBURG

Edgar Howell, son of
J. M. & Selma Burrow
Sep 29, 1898
Nov 20, 1898

Mrs. Robert Flanakin
Born 1800
Died Apr 30, 1844

Clide Edwards
Mar 13, 1881
Aug 5, 1881
&
Infant
Nov 22, 1888
Apr 23, ----
"Children of
W. F. & M. E. Edwards"

Annie May, dau of
W. H. & Mrs. Edwards
Feb 26, 1906
Feb 8, 1908

Cora, dau of
W. A. & M. Matney
Sep 1873
Died 19--

W. A. Matney
Born --- 19, 1844
Died Jan --, 1897

Mrs. Mary H. Slimp,
wife of W. A. Matney
Born 1844
Died Feb 3, 1---(?)

Several unmarked graves. A few colored, marked graves on the outside, many unmarked ones.

* *

MYRES-DEVIN-MADISON CEMETERY
Located east of Nashville Highway # 31-A, north of Lewisburg, on farm owned by Edd M. Crigger, about two miles north of Lewisburg. Copied Jun 10, 1958 by Ralph D. Whitesell and Myrtle Lee Walker.

W. D. Madison
1858-(no date)
& wife
E. E. Madison
1858-1926
& Sister
Jennie Mai Myres
Feb 22, 1874
Jun 24, 1900
& Mother
Mary Charlotte Temple Myres
Jan 16, 1840
Jun 20, 1889

C. H. Myres
Mar 3, 1860
Oct 17, 1901

Rachel B. Myres
(Died) Oct 10, 1901
Age 63 years

Mary Etta, wife of
J. D. Whitt
1877-1917

Elmo, Jr., son of
Elmo & Mary Madison
1924
Age 3 weeks

Davie William Devin
Mar 12, 1830
Jul 12, 1911
& wife
Lucy Nowlin Devin
Jun 15, 1834
Jan 19, 1908

Lucy G., dau of
D. W. & L. N. Devin
Mar 28, 1859
Apr 4, 1860

William, son of
D. W. & L. N. Devin
Mar 26, 1871
Nov 7, 1872

Many unmarked graves.

Sherrod J. Orsborn
Aug 1846
Nov 1914

Nancy, wife of
S. J. Orsborn
May 28, 1849
Jan 19, 1885

Muel Gilmore
Feb 11, 1811
Sep 23, 1822
Age 11 yrs, 7 mos, 13 days

Sebe Ren Gilmore
Jul 31, 1825
Feb 1, 1835
Age 10 yrs, 8 mos, 1 day

John McDanell
1823 (all)

On one marker:
Elizabeth Devin
Annie B. Devin
Mary E. Devin
(no dates)

Herman Barron
Sep 10, 1895
Jan 10, 1899

Harriet E. Hamilton
Mar 16, 1838
Jun 28, 1906

Mary Jane Caughran
Sep 2, 1887
Aug 26, 1927

E. H. Hamilton
Apr 27, 1834
Nov 4, 1896

Mother
Rebecca Beckett, wife of
John Devin
Born April, 1812
(broken)

John Devin
Sep 12, 1792
Jun 12, 1877

* *

McATEER CEMETERY
Located about one mile west of highway 31-A, south of Lewisburg and two miles from Cornersville, between New Lewisburg Reservoir and 31-A. Perhaps not more than 20 unidentified graves with fieldstones, complete to date, as copied May 26, 1963 by Joe C. Harris and wife.

Robert McAteer
Aug 8, 1814
Apr 14, 1903

Hanna, wife of
Robert McAteer
Sep 10, 1822
Sep 8, 1891

H. D. McAteer
Mar 26, 1836-Aug 12, 1912

Elizabeth, wife of
H. D. McAteer
Aug 2, 1842
Apr 22, 1910

James P. McAteer
Feb 1, 1846
Feb 19, 1900

N. A., wife of J. P. McAteer
Nov 7, 1848-Sep 26, 1890

Florence, dau of
J. P. & N. A. McAteer
Mar 8, 1876
Oct 23, 1879

M. M., wife of
J. P. McAteer
Nov 13, 1860
May 26, 1947

R. E. McAteer
Dec 17, 1848
Jun 22, 1871

W. W. McAteer
Jun 9, 1857
Jan 11, 1927

Nanie R., wife of
W. W. McAteer
Sep 6, 1866-Nov 30, 1925

LEWISBURG

J. H. McAteer
Nov 15, 1858
Mar 25, 1902

Mary E., wife of
J. H. McAteer
1866-1948

Robert McAteer
1892-1948

Newt McConnell
Dec 8, 1873
Jun 15, 1943

Fanny, wife of
Newt McConnell
Nov 4, 1866
(no date)

J. G. Fox
Sep 22, 1855
Mar 27, 1903

Allis D., wife of
J. G. Fox
Feb 17, 1855
Sep 16, 1890

Robert Pervines Fox
Apr 27, 1878
Sep 23, 1895
Son of J. G. &
A. D. Fox

Harris W. Fox
Sep 5, 1884
Dec 18, 1937

C. C. L. Glenn
May 1, 1883
May 31, 1909

Martha E., wife of
C. C. L. Glenn
Sep 23, 1843
Jun 25, 1923

Fannie, wife of
W. H. Glenn
Jun 21, 1863
Jul 30, 1903

Gess King
1871-

Angie, wife of
Gess King
1880-1929

Amanda Bearden
Apr 8, 1843
Feb 20, 1912

Robert J. Bearden
Dec 6, 1869
Jun 16, 1900

James F. Bearden
May 21, 1877
Nov 30, 1902

Thomas B. Bearden
Sep 9, 1879
Jul 16, 1919

Cowden Bearden
Sep 21, 1883
Jul 18, 1916

Sarah London
(no dates)

William Thomas Parks
Jun 13, 1859
Feb 28, 1939

Mary Morphis, wife of
Wm. T. Parks
May 9, 1861
Feb 12, 1931

Robert W. Hill
Apr 13, 1798
Aug 27, 1866

Elizabeth C., wife of
Robert W. Hill
May 18, 1802
May 19, 1835

Mary LaRue
1854-1934

Several unmarked graves.

M. G. Shehane
Born 1814
Died Jun 25, 1879
Age 65 years

W. Shehane
Jul 2, 1825
Jun 27, 1839

Martha W., wife of
A. J. Cole
Mar 7, 1829
Feb 18, 1849

Alvin A., son of
A. J. & M. W. Cole
Oct 15, 1846
Feb 18, 1849

J. C. Emerson
Aug 6, 1813
Feb 3, 1886

Martha, wife of
J. C. Emerson
Mar 10, 1820
Mar 17, 1890

John W. Emerson
Nov 30, 1851
Apr 30, 1918

Nancy Emerson
Aug 3, 1856
May 18, 1917

J. T. Emerson
May 4, 1858
May 29, 1936

Winnie Emerson
Feb 22, 1853
Oct 21, 1925

William S. Turner
Jun 12, 1847
Dec 8, 1909

J. T.
(headstone)

W. B. "Billy" Clift
1862-1933

Bettie Emerson, wife of
W. B. Clift
1855-1943

Margaret Richardson
Feb 5, 1801
May 1, 1886

Margaret C. Richardson
Sep 8, 1837
Feb 28, 1880
"Dau of H. C. &
M. R. Richardson"

James C. Richardson
May 18, 1824
Sep 15, 1897

Frances A., wife of
James C. Richardson
May 25, 1833
Jan 6, 1909

Infant Son of
A. H. & Ruth Richardson
Nov 1, 1900
Nov 3, 1900

James Rhea Richardson
Jul 7, 1906
Jul 9, 1906
"Son of A. H. &
Ruth R. Richardson"

Jon Richardson
Jan 17, 1826
Apr 10, 1883

James Turner
Feb 14, 1812
Jul 24, 1875

Amanda J., wife of
James Turner
Oct 3, 1825
Oct 17, 1901

Joseph M., son of
James & A. J. Turner
Oct 2, 1854
Jun 6, 1856

* *

McCLAREY CEMETERY
Located two miles north east of Lewisburg, on Holly Grove Road. Copied Sept 7, 1958.

W. D. McClarey
Died Nov 2, 1863
Age 59 yrs, 9 mos, 22 days

Mrs. Annie M. G. Liggett,
wife of
Wm. D. McClarey
Feb 4, 1854
Dec 4, 1872

Rebecca E., Consort of
Wm. Stegall & dau of
Wm. D. McClarey
Dec 9, 1828
Professed hope in Christ
1843. Married Feb 19, 1847
Died May 1, 1848

Infant Son of
W. D. & Elizabeth McClarey
(no dates)

Infant Son of
W. D. & Elizabeth McClarey
(no dates)

According to Land Deeds,
Members of the James
Hightower family are
buried here. Eds.

* *

LEWISBURG

OLD SHILO CEMETERY

Located four miles west of Lewisburg, on left of Old Columbia Road. Site of Old Shilo Baptist Church. Copied Sep 5, 1958.

Andrew Jackson Davis
Apr 10, 1844
Sep 28, 1920

Lucy Weaver
Mar 4, 1774
Oct 15, 1825

John Duncan
Apr 1, 1773
Aug 3, 1853

Margaret Duncan
Aug 4, 1773
Jul 2, 1859

Infant Son of
J. R. Duncan
Born Nov 15, 1849

James, son of
J. & M. Duncan
Nov 20, 1811
May 10, 1860

John W., son of
James & Rebecca Duncan
Dec 4, 1841
Aug 9, 1856

Martha P., dau of
James & Rebecca Duncan
Jan 3, 1838
Mar 7, 1864

Winnie Elizabeth Thompson
1852-1903

Sallie Bettie, dau of
James S. & L. M. Duncan
Feb 8, 1891
Dec 7, 1894

Ula Wilkie, dau of
W. & E. Thompson
May 1, 1825
Mar 14, 1876

James Story Duncan
1847-1914

Nimrod S. Caudle
Jul 12, 1832
Mar 31, 1834

Margaret Duncan
1849-1922

Rebecca Duncan
Mar 9, 1818
Feb 22, 1890

Irenia Duncan
Mar 21, 1821
Mar 3, 1887

James E. Emerson
Aug 12, 1845
Mar 5, 1906

Margaret W. Emerson
Sep 11, 1843
Feb 28, 1905

"Revolutionary Soldier"
Shadrack Weaver
1766-1849
said to be buried here in
an unmarked grave. Eds.

* *

PLEASANT HILL CEMETERY

Located at Duncanville, on Mooresville Road, west of Lewisburg. Copied by Joe C. Harris and wife, Jan 1963.

Janice Mai Andrews
Feb 24, 1953 (died)
Age 1 day

William Baxter Andrews
Jan 11, 1958 (died)
Age 6 years

Allen T. South
Aug 29, 1883
Feb 2, 1961
&
Pearl G. South
Mar 5, 1908

William W. Rambo
1849-1934
& wife
Leota (Collins) Rambo
1856-1938

Edgar Bruce Malone
Jun 15, 1874
Sep 7, 1944

Ella Fount (Rambo), wife of
Edgar B. Malone
Mar 31, 1876

Feliz K. Hill
1861-1939

Mary E. (Stacy), wife of
Felix K. Hill 1866-1942

Jessie M. Hill
1888-1943

Annie Mai (Rambo), wife of
Jessie M. Hill
Nov 4, 1891
Jun --, 1962

J. Thomas Hill
1883-1948

Ollie (Fowler), wife of
J. T. Hill
1883-1962

Essie Louise, dau of
Tom & Ollie Hill
Aug 23, 1909
Jan 7, 1911

J. P. Stacy
Mar 5, 1845
Nov 5, 1893

Nancy J.(London), wife of
J. P. Stacy
Sep 16, 1849
Nov 7, 1920

Eva Roena (Stacy) Fox Bryant
Aug 16, 1881
May 14, 1914

Lyndhal Polk, dau of
K. E. & Roena Bryant
Dec 12, 1904
Jan 11, 1907

William Clearance Stacy
1890-1957

Harry D. McGee
May 2, 1874
Dec 9, 1932

John Howard Hughes
Mar 24, 1902
Oct 20, 1918

Atlas J. Bills
1850-1920

Nancy A. Bills
1847-1931

A. D. Bills
Sep 5, 1871
May 3, 1947

Fannie (Walker), wife of
A. D. Bills
Jun 23, 1873
Mar 7, 1942

L. E. Boyett
Aug 3, 1879
Jul 4, 1916

Adolphus -----(illegible)
May 1947 (TM)

A. W. Talley
Aug 8, 1860
Mar 15, 1905

Bula M. (Young), wife of
J. W. Thompson
Sep 24, 1877
Jul 5, 1901

William M., son of
J. W. & B. M. Thompson
Jul 29, 1900
May 30, 1903

Arch A. Webb
Sep 18, 1872
Apr 7, 1933

Knoxie (Young), wife of
Arch A. Webb
Nov 18, 1879
May 7, 1942

John A. Webb
1869-1940

Elma Lena (Killingsworth)
wife of John A. Webb
1871-1953

LEWISBURG

John Thomas Killingsworth
1845-1923

Nancy Emeline (Tillman)
       Killingsworth
1845-1930
"wife of
John T. Killingsworth"

Joe Atlas Killingsworth
Nov 3, 1876

James N. Killingsworth
WW I Vet.
Jun 4, 1886
Jan 21, 1956

James A. Wright
Nov 15, 1845
Aug 25, 1901

Susan C. Wright
Dec 11, 1847
Sep 30, 1930

John M. Wright
Apr 23, 1873
Sep 20, 1927

Daughter
Mary E. Wright
Mar 5, 1875
Aug 5, 1893

5th Son
James Lafayette Wright
Oct 17, 1878
Dec 24, 1937

Brother
Lee Ernie Wright
Nov 15, 1881
Jan 20, 1962

Sister
Minnie V. Wright
May 13, 1883
Apr 1, 1951

"Motorcycle"
Willie M. Wright
Aug 29, 1892
May 23, 1929

Ezra O. Phillips
Aug 18, 1888
Apr 18, 1961
   & wife
Ellen (Barron) Phillips
May 11, 1896

Waymon Harmon
Jun 19, 1899
Apr 17, 1962
&
Sadie W. Harmon
Feb 12, 1901
Sep 2, 1930
&
Carrie S. Harmon
Oct 15, 1914

Charles McGregor
Apr 5, 1870
Feb 4, 1935

Maud D. McGregor
Jun 4, 1872
Jul 13, 1909

Preston A. McKnight
Jun 30, 1857
Jan 3, 1941

Maggie (Young),
wife of
Preston A. McKnight
Sep 30, 1858
Mar 21, 1923

Jonas A. McKnight
Oct 7, 1880
Nov 15, 1956

Ella (Vaughn), wife of
Jonas A. McKnight
Jan 19, 1892
Aug 16, 1914

Douglas, son of
J. A. & Ella McKnight
died Aug 15, 1914
(no age given)

Eula J. (Jewell) McKnight
Jul 1, 1889
Mar 9, 1956

Eulas H. Barron
Apr 18, 1879
Jul 1, 1928

Selma K., dau of
E. & F. Barron
Apr 25, 1918
Jul 1, 1920

Several unmarked graves.

Ida M. Thompson
Aug 2, 1869
Aug 15, 1901

J. C. Duncan
May 15, 1820
Sep 28, 1914

Peggie Duncan
Dec 20, 1818
Dec 26, 1908

James C. Duncan
1848-1926

Simmie (Gipson), wife of
James C. Duncan
1850-1901

Ollie F., son of
J. C. & E. S. Duncan
Sep 29, 1879
May 29, 1902

Ellen, dau of
J. C. & E. S. Duncan
Apr 23, 1884
Jan 24, 1889

Allison M. Duncan
Nov 15, 1870
Nov 14, 1951

Mattie (Bills), wife of
A. M. Duncan
Oct 3, 1874
Feb 19, 1960

George, son of
A. M. & M. B. Duncan
Feb 22, 1911
Aug 31, 1912

Clarence E. Duncan
1892-
   & wife
Edith (Lavander) Duncan
1899-1955

Mother
Sarah Duncan Gipson
1845-1935

Charles Alex Crane
1909-1964
   & wife
Pearl Crane
1913-

N. P. Gipson
Nov 16, 1862
Jun 13, 1917
   & wife
Annie R. (Doggett) Gipson
Jun 1, 1869
Nov 6, 1928

John R. Gipson
Dec 28, 1880
May 7, 1937
   & wife
Elizabeth (Casteel) Gipson
Jul 7, 1888
Dec 18, 1950

Morgan M. Gipson
Oct 13, 1904
Dec 19, 1945

Elisha D. Gipson
1914-
   & wife
Maudie L. (Fly) Gipson
1908-1946

Lacye (Gipson), wife of
Orrin Barron
May 24, 1898
Feb 25, 1917

Otis N. Osburn
1881-1941
   & wife
Laura (Barron) Osburn
1884-

Andrew W. Barron
Mar 10, 1851
Oct 2, 1899
   & wife
Callie D. (Hill) Barron
Feb 29, 1856
May 16, 1920

T. J. Barron
Aug 18, 1852
Dec 28, 1925
   & wife
Alice (Gipson) Barron
Feb 29, 1864
Nov 17, 1935

Mary Emma Rambo
Sep 29, 1873
Apr 29, 1965

* *

LEWISBURG

POWELL CEMETERY

Located one mile from Wilson Hill Church, south of Highway 50-A, on Globe Road. Copied April, 1962 by Joe C. Harris and wife. Rechecked by Ralph D. Whitesell and Helen and Tim Marsh, 1979.

Robert A. Adams
1828-1903
&
Malinda P. Adams
1832-1902

Will M. Bobo
Jun 13, 1881
May 1, 1967

Jas. C. Powell
Jan 10, 1798
Sep 20, 1854

Sallie L., wife of
J. C. Powell
Nov 6, 1807
Apr 4, 1896

Green Wilson, Junr.
Aug 16, 1827
Nov   1856
&
J. A. Wilson
Jan 4, 1852
Nov 29, 1856

Annie L. (Powell), wife of
Green Wilson
Dec 8, 1830
Jul 2, 1876

Mother
Martha L. Bobo
1850-1917

5 unmarked graves.

P(eter). L. Houston
Aug 19, 1836
Jan 26, 1930
&
Mary E.(Powell) Houston
Jan 11, 1839
Jun 26, 1930

Johnnie B. (Houston, wife of
J. W(alter). Beasley
Jan 24, 1875
Jul 2, 1898

Brother
James E(lisha) Bobo
1870-1950

G(eorge). W. Gupton
1850-1900
(wife, Donie Houston
Gupton is buried at
Wilson Hill Cem.)

Era Clara Gupton, dau of
Geo. W. Gupton
Feb 27, 1893
Jan 5, 1908

Ella Mai (Bobo), wife of
T. K. Phillips
Sep 29, 1873
Sep 12, 1899
(T. K. Phillips is buried
at Wilson Hill Cem.)

* *

REED CEMETERY

Located one mile north of Lewisburg, on Verona Road. Copied Jun 26, 1958 by Ralph D. Whitesell and Myrtle Lee Walker.

Mattie J., wife of
W. J. Little
Mar 11, 1865
Dec 30, 1920

Susie W., dau of
M. J. & W. J. Little
Jan 8, 1883
Dec 22, 1902

Martha W. Bills
Dec 21, 1835
Aug 21, 1918

J. J. Bills
Sep 14, 1826
May 1, 1893

A. B. Stilwell
Oct 31, 1842
Aug 24, 1901
&
Kate Stilwell
Died Apr 27, 1923
(no age given)

James H., son of
William H. & M. H. Hooten
Aug 9, 1865
Jul 2, 1882

Deborah L., wife of
J. J. Elliott &
Formerly the widow of
O. S. Stilwell
Jul 31, 1816
Apr 28, 1882

J. J. Elliott
Feb 27, 1820
Aug 15, 1905

Mattie W. Collins
Mar 3, 1848
Oct 2, 1898

P. W. McCord
Died Oct 1843
Age 17 years
&
Mary McCord
Died Sep 2, 1873
Age 75 years
&
Joseph McCord
Died May 1855
Age 63 years

Gabe L. Long
May 19, 1808
Jul 1, 1854

Wayne Elliott, Jr.
Died Apr 4, 1852
Age 10 yrs, 10 mos, 5 days

Marcus King
Died Oct 3, 1946
Age 33 years
&
Homer Carl King
July 1945
(no age given)

Herman M. Thomason
Tennessee
Tec 5 945 Field Arty BN
Jan 4, 1912
Jun 13, 1946

Ada Thomas
1880-1926

Robert Roy Montgomery
Jul 14, 1902
Nov 17, 1915
&
Pauline Troop Montgomery
1876-1918

Martha Ann McConnell
Apr 12, 1909
Mar 26, 1929

Sadie L. Murray
Aug 3, 1906
Jan 7, 1910

Elder
John Hooten
Oct 6, 1811
May 28, 1886
& 1st wife
Susan T. Hooten
Nov 24, 1814
Oct 20, 1862
& 2nd wife
Partheney Hooten
Died Mar 8, 1892
Aged about 78 years

Harvy McCord
Mar 21, 1818
May 28, 1890

Jodie, son of
D. H. & E. A. McCord
Mar 12, 1858
Oct 26, 1861

George R. Braley
Apr 20, 1851
Feb 26, 1921

Mary M., wife of
George Braly
Nov 28, 1855
May 30, 1896

John Wilson Hooten
Nov 17, 1856
Oct 2, 1924
&
Mary Celestia Hooten
Dec 8, 1855
May 26, 1935

Mary Neill Cathey
1894-1926
&
Brown Cathey
1904-1928

S. J. Neill, wife of
J. B. Cathey
Mar 12, 1832
Aug 18, 1893

LEWISBURG

J. W. Barron
Sep 8, 1878
Died   1944

Lola Lee, wife of
J. W. Barron
Sep 4, 1882
Oct 2, 1915

W. M. Turner
Aug 31, 1865
Sep 14, 1896

Talitha Barron
Oct 2, 1862
Nov 20, 1946

Esley F. Reedy
Apr 10, 1883
Sep 19, 1899

Ada E. Reedy
Nov 20, 1886
May 11, 1892

Julious J. Hooten
son of W. J. &
T. C. Hooten
Aug 30, 1898
Sep 8, 1900

Infant Dau of
W. J. & T. C. Hooten
Died Oct 27, 1898

William A. Johnson
Oct 7, 1888
Jul 3, 1903
  & wife
Eliza J. Johnson
Mar 18, 1887
Feb 5, 1927

Infant Son of
R. L. & Sallie Davis
1907

Charlie Toy Johnson
1873-1954

Grover Bills
1892-1934

Andrew J. Bills
Sep 20, 1875
Jan 23, 1926
  & wife
Mattie T. Bills
Jul 14, 1862
Jun 10, 1927

J. W. Hooten
May 15, 1859
Mar 3, 1900

Tempie Hooten
Jul 11, 1866
Apr 20, 1926

Archie C. Jordan
Feb 19, 1895
Oct 23, 1918

B. S. Jordan
Died 1896
(no age given)

Mary E., wife of
B. S. Jordan
Jul 26, 1842
Jan 29, 1895

David Hashaw
Oct 6, 1849
(no date)
  & wife
Sue Williams Hashaw
Jan 1, 1856
Jan 14, 1918

Arthur L. Nix
Apr 5, 1880
Sep 28, 1920
  &
Mattie Wells Nix
(no dates)

Elder P. H. Hooten
Nov 22, 1870
Jul 19, 1905

W. H. Hooten
Oct 3, 1837
Jul 30, 1912
  & wife
M. H. Hooten
Dec 25, 1831
Mar 18, 1913

Bettie Louise Hooten
1935-1940

Andrew R. Crutcher
Infant
(no dates)

Patricia Ann Smith
Feb 23, 1948
  Infant

Patricia Gail Cooper
1957 Infant

William D. Nix
1876-1895
  &
Martha Fox Nix
1855-1895
  &
George W. Nix
1851-1931
  &
Martha Pickle Nix
1867-1930

Marion Nix
1851-1945

Eldridge Fraser
Mar 30, 1826
Aug 10, 1895

L. L. Farmer
Oct 1, 1829
Oct 18, 1895

Mary J. Farmer
Aug 22, 1844
Apr 3, 1900

William Vivie, son of
W. T. & Lizzie Fox
May 2, 1887
Dec 5, 1899
Age 12 yrs, 7 mos, 3 days

Vivian Lee, dau of
W. T. & Lizzie Fox
May 2, 1887
Aug 10, 1904
Age 17 yrs, 3 mos, 8 days

John Alvin Warner
(no dates) Infant

William Powell Hale
Jul 3, 1870
Sep 5, 1932

William M. Gipson
1887-1956
  &
C. B. Gipson
Jan 29, 1907
Jul 22, 1932

John N. Price
Mar 18, 1881
Apr 27, 1925

William Thomas Fox
1869-1928
  &
Fannie Elizabeth Fox
1869-1939

J. D. Hooten
Jan 23, 1859
(no other date)

Wilson L. Hooten
Dec 24, 1890
Oct 5, 1918

Addie Hooten
Nov 9, 1860
Jul 4, 1925

Janie P. Williams
1870-1945

R. W. Pickle
1847-1912
  &
S. J. Pickle
1841-1918

George W. Reed
1857-1933
  & wife
Addieline V. Reed
May 1, 1858
Sep 22, 1905
  &
Lena Reed Davis
Sep 10, 1886
Oct 6, 1910

Nancy Ann Savage
Aug 12, 1860
Jul 22, 1900

Marshall Savage
Apr 14, 1830
Jan 16, 1914

Sarah E. Savage
Apr 22, 1841
Dec 8, 1917

Miss Alice Savage
1870-1956

Several unmarked graves.

This cemetery is named for the man who gave the land for burying ground, Mr. James L. Reed, father of George Reed who is buried here. This information given by elderly citizens, Mr. Cecil Bowden and Miss Della C. Walker.

* *

LEWISBURG

SHARP CEMETERY

Located two miles north east of Lewisburg, on the Holly Grove Road. Copied Sep 7, 1958

Charles Henry George
1883-1956

Mace C. Sharp
1873-1939
&
Mary L. Sharp
1880-

Infant
Ronnie Reynolds
Jul 2, 1953

Mrs. Maggie Toseland
1897-1936

Willie Lavin Toseland
1917-1936

T. J. Sharp
Nov 26, 1836
Oct 20, 1908
"Death loves a Shining mark"

John A. Ramsey
1856-1918
&
Cynthia J. Ramsey
1859-1929

Cynthia B., dau of
M. G. & M. L. Sharp
Jun 16, 1890
Sep 28, 1900

J. N. Vanhooser
May 11, 1863
Apr 29, 1906

Carrie Hall Tate
Died May 2, 1939
Age 49 yrs, 11 mos, 19 days
(TM)

Cynthia, wife of
W. A. Sharp
Feb 15, 1852
Jun 11, 1905

W. A. "Jack" Sharp
1851-1934
&
Cynthia Parlee Sharp
1852-1934

Lula Sharp Fox
1878-194-

Maggie Bell Sharp
1911-1912

Susie Lake Sharp
1907

Olie Woodward Davis
Dec 5, 1918
Sep 6, 1921

H. Moses Sharp
Feb 26, 1841
Apr 20, 1893
&
Susan E. Sharp
Aug 24, 1843
Dec 24, 1918

John N. Bowden
1869-1940
&
Alice Bowden
1873-1948

Rex Bowden
Sep 16, 1896
Feb 15, 1921

Ora E., dau of
John N. & Alice Bowden
Sep 28, 1899
Jan 26, 1903

Several unmarked graves.

* *

TALLEY CEMETERY

Located on Barnes Hill, west of White Acres Subdivision, and west of Lewisburg, on Highway 50-A. Copied Sep 4, 1958 by Ralph D. Whitesell and Lounora Pickens. Rechecked Apr 16, 1980 by Helen and Tim Marsh.

Mahulda, wife of
------- Record & dau of

(broken & illegible)

J. H. Killingsworth
Aug 28, 1831
Jan 26, 183-

Elizabeth, wife of
G. W. Record & dau of
William & Alsey Hughs
Age 21 yrs, 11 mos 21 days
Died Mar 11, 1835

William H., son of
George W. & Amanda Record
Aug 16, 1842
Feb 20, 1844

Mary E. J., dau of
E. & M. A. P. Stilwell
Apr 29, 1850
Dec 17, 1850

Margaret M. T., dau of
G. W. & A. A. Record
Mar 25, 1844
May 13, 1850

Infant Son of
G. W. & A. A. Record
Born & Dead
Nov 4, 1849

Infant Son of
G. W. & A. A. Record
(broken, dates gone)

Eliza, wife of
William H. Record
Dec 25, 1811
Jan 25, 1835

Child's grave
(marker illegible)

Sion S. Record
Sep 27, 1793
Sep 26, 1821

Mary M., wife of
John Record
Apr 24, 1769
Jul 12, 1850

Rev. John Record
Feb 3, 1765
Jul 26, 1814

John J., son of
James C. & N. R. Record
Jan 9, 1831
May 23, 1831

T. S. Tarry
(fieldstone)

G. W. Killingsworth
Jan 30, 1828
Dec 24, 1835

E. C. Killingsworth
Oct 1, 1824
Oct 4, 1838

William T., son of
James C. & N. R. Record
Nov 27, 1825, was
killed accidentally
Aug 10, 1837

A. M. F. G. Squires
wife of Uriah E. Squires
Died Jan 11, 1855
Age 28 years

W. H. Collins
Died Jan 20, 1893
(fieldstone, no age given)

(NEW SECTION)
Lucinda Bills
Apr 10, 1818
Apr 6, 1899
&
Sandy K. Bills
Jan 5, 1816
Jun 4, 1855

Oscar J. Rutledge
Jun 9, 1865
Aug 7, 1868

Monroe Young
1850-1895
&
Nancy J. Young
Dec 12, 1856
Aug 7, 1886
&
Clide Young
Mar 18, 1874
Sep 7, 1876

Rufus G. Whitsell
1871-1937

Mary Martha Whitsell
1868-1938

LEWISBURG

William Whitsell
May 22, 1837
Jan 15, 1914
&
Rachel Whitsell
Jun 7, 1840
Jul 31, 1909

Willis Collins
Died Nov 2, 1879
"Wife, children, friends,
Dry up your tears."
(no age given)

Neal McDaniel
Sep 1, 1875
Oct 26, 1948

Salena McDaniel
Nov 26, 1880
Dec 28, 1951

Thomas Helmick, Jr.
Born & Died Jun 7, 1932
(TM)

Imogene Helmick
Jun 7, 1924
Jun 4, 1926

Jesse Harison
Oct 1863
Confederate Soldier
C.S.A.

McClure Gipson
1856-1937
&
Leota Gipson
1857-1938

Joe Gipson
Mar 29, 1886
Aug 22, 1929

Father
J. P. "Bunk" Gipson
1882-1956
&
Mother
Ethel Mai Gipson
1884-1961

Roland, son of
J. P. & E. M. Gipson
Jan 14, 1906
Oct 6, 1908

Matt M. Neese
Dec 9, 1873
Sep 1916
Age 42 years
&
Eula L. Neese
1879-1963

Many unmarked graves.

W. D.
-1914
(fieldstone)

Henry Lee Gipson
Feb 18, 1874
Nov 1, 1949
&
Susie Terry Gipson
May 26, 1882
Nov 6, 1947

Soldier
Edd H. Gipson
Tennessee
Pvt 1Cl 306 Mil Police
81 Div
Sep 27, 1934

P. S. Gipson
Sep 20, 1854
Mar 6, 1932
&
Elizabeth Gipson
Jan 15, 1855
Apr 29, 1936

Grover Gipson
Aug 15, 1885
Sep 1, 1924

James Gipson
Jun 6, 1892
Dec 11, 1913

William G. Bone
1882-1946
&
Wilsie M. Bone
1890-1968

H. E. "Gee" Woosley
Feb 8, 1887
Nov 6, 1962

E. J. Woosley
1848-1923
&
Nancy Woosley
1858-1934

Grace W. Coggins
1885-1954

S. E. Duncan
Feb 14, 1847
Sep 2, 1879
(fieldstone)

Martha L., wife of
H. D. McAteer
Jul 17, 1842
Jun 3, 1871

* *

WILSON CEMETERY
Located about one-fourth mile north of Wilson Hill Church
Cemetery. Thomas Wilson, who gave the land for the Wilson
Hill Church, is reportedly buried here but no marker was
found when copied in April 1963 by Joe C. Harris and wife.

Many unmarked graves.

James T. Beech
1861-1899
& wife
Arrelia E.(Wilson) Beech
1869-1898
"Erected by son
W. C. Beech"

In Memory of Mary A. K. Holt
(no dates)

In Memory of Martha C. Holt
(no dates)

P x W
Decd x Dec -- A.D.
1827

* *

TILLMON CEMETERY
Located on the Old Tillmon Homestead. One-fourth mile
southwest of Rambo Hollow Road and one mile southwest
of Duncanville. Copied Mar 15, 1961.

William, son of
John Tillmon
Nov 6, 1813
Apr 9, 1831

Joseph W. W. Carroll
Born Jan 9, 1843
(no date)

John, son of
Joshua Tillmon
Dec 29, 1780
Aug 25, 1839
Age 59 years.

Susan Tillmon
Feb 14, 1786
Jun 11, 1864

Sarah, wife of
William Tillmon
Born 1833
Died Jan 14, 1893

Martha N. Henry
1857-1928

Nancy, wife of
Joe Wilson
Born 1810
Died Jan 8, 1892

Joseph Wilson
Jul 7, 1810
Feb 12, 1872

LEWISBURG

Walter Royal Hill
1868-1956
&
Paralee T. Hill
1883-

Sarah, wife of
John Wilson
Died Feb 8, 1867
(no age given)

Hannah Eliza Jane Tillmon
Nov 5, 1852
Mar 25, 1863

Manerva N., dau of
B. G. & H. R. Tillman
Apr 8, 1856
Mar 6, 1857

Thomas W., son of
B. G. & H. R. Tillman
Jan 26, 1853
Sep 26, 1862

Hazy P., wife of
B. G. Tillmon
Apr 14, 1825
Jul 13, 1878

M. Jerome, son of
Brantley & Paralee Tillmon
Dec 12, 1849
Jun 9, 1928

Several unmarked graves.

Naomi, dau of
Robin & Betsy Davis
wife of
M. J. Tillmon
May 12, 1856
Sep 18, 1896

* *

WELCH CEMETERY
Located one mile south of South Berlin, off the Old Columbia Road, on Webb Road. Copied September 1959.

Charles H. Welch
1884-1937

Batty Mae Welch
1930-1931

Bettie Welch
May 7, 1861
Jan 30, 1950

G. W. Welch
Apr 10, 1855
Aug 7, 1914

J. R. Barron
Oct 10, 1865
Sep 28, 1927

Eva Thomas Barron
1865-(no date)

Daniel M. Barron, Jr.
Nov 2, 1863
Jun 16, 1931

Mattie M. Barron
Dec 3, 1863
Jul 16, 1948

Mrs. Anna Lou Ervin
1890-1947

George W. Ervin
1888-1942

Mary L. Griffin
Age 64 years
(no dates)

J. H. Finley
1867-1940

G. G. Finley
1876-1936

J. F. Fisher
Born (no date)
Died 1926

Martha Ann Finley
Apr 14, 1846
Nov 5, 1910

W. F. Finley
Feb 19, 1841
Feb 14, 1918

A. T. Wallace
Sep 26, 1845
Jun 12, 1931

Margaret A. Wallace
May 7, 1832
Apr 26, 1912

H. P. Rone
Sep 4, 1881
Jul 5, 1910

T. B. Ridner
1884-1951

Parlee Purdom
Sep 20, 1844
Apr 6, 1916

M. F. Purdom
Sep 6, 1844
Apr 18, 1906

Gothie, wife of
J. L. Brown
Aug 7, 1879
Mar 17, 1915

Infant of
J. L. & G. W. Brown
Born & Died Sep 1, 1901

W. C. Brown
Aug 5, 1854
Feb 16, 1929

Mary T., dau of
James G. Harris, Esq. &
wife of J. H. Brown
Jan 24, 1834
Nov 15, 1897

Jefferson Brown
Nov 21, 1809
Apr 7, 1891

James Brown
Aug 28, 1781
May 21, 1868

Mary L., wife of
S. J. Welch
Apr 21, 1850
Jun 4, 1872

Infant Dau of
S. J. & M. L. Welch
Born & Died Jun 3, 1872

Margaret, dau of
J. W. & Ida Jackson
Born Mar 18, 1889

Julius, son of
C. W. & C. M. Ewing
May 19, 1897
May 27, 1898

Infant Son of
C. J. & E. W. Crutcher
Jan 1, 1878

Charles J., son of
C. J. & E. W. Crutcher
Aug 20, 1859
Feb 23, 1862

Infant Dau of
C. J. & E. W. Crutcher
B & D Feb 15, 1875

Mary E., dau of
C. J. & E. W. Crutcher
Feb 2, 1862
Mar 2, 1876

Elizabeth W., wife of
C. J. Crutcher
Apr 3, 1841
Feb 16, 1925

C. J. Crutcher
Jan 16, 1834
Jan 19, 1908

John B., son of
H. B. & E. H. Welch
Mar 2, 1839
May 2, 1853

Ada Stewart Rambo
1875-(no date)

Elias S., son of
H. B. & E. H. Welch
Mar 21, 1833
Apr 3, 1854

Harvey B. Welch
Jul 2, 1805
Jul 4, 1860

Eliza H., wife of
H. B. Welch
Sep 17, 1811
Jul 28, 1891

George W. Rambo
Jul 3, 1851
May 4, 1932

Eliza J. Rambo
Apr 12, 1852
Nov 15, 1938

Frances Harvey Rambo
Mar 24, 1873
Mar 9, 1947

Lemirah Ellen, wife of
W. H. Welch
Jun 28, 1838
Oct 15, 1863

J. L. Ewing
Died Sep 9, 1897
Age 26 years.

John W. Purdom
Jan 4, 1871-Sep 4, 1905

LEWISBURG

Thomas J. Tillman
Feb 18, 1859
Sep 13, 1927

Mary J. Ewing, wife of
T. J. Tillman
Mar 3, 1862
Apr 25, 1909

Ida Gracie, dau of
T. J. & M. J. Tillman
Apr 20, 1895
May 16, 1896

Florah Othella, dau of
G. W. & S. L. Rone
Sep 13, 1871
Feb 1, 1873

Henry Birch, son of
G. W. & S. L. Rone
May 22, 1867
Nov 9, 1867

George W. Rone
Nov 6, 1846
Jun 9, 1905

Sarah H., wife of
I. F. Murphey
May 18, 1841
May 25, 1914

I. F. Murphey
Nov 25, 1834
Nov 12, 1899

B. T., son of
I. F. & S. H. Murphey
Apr 1, 1880
Feb 12, 1903

George A. Welch
1874-1952

W. H. Welch
Feb 17, 1837
Jul 30, 1905

E. H., wife of
W. H. Welch
Feb 18, 1842
Mar 29, 1893

Ethel M. Welch
Jan 16, 1882
Mar 18, 1885

Jocie A., dau of
J. J. L. & M. H. Bryant
Sep 4, 1863
Jun 26, 1870

John W., son of
J. J. L. & M. H. Bryant
Nov 19, 1875
Dec 13, 1875

Eliza T., dau of
J. J. L. & M. H. Bryant
Feb 23, 1868
Jun 13, 1877

Mary H. Bryant
Oct 20, 1843
Dec 23, 1908

J. J. L. Bryant
Aug 24, 1837
Feb 23, 1898

Martha Barron Hendrix
Dec 5, 1846
Sep 17, 1928

Elizah H. Hendrix
May 12, 1838
Apr 5, 1893

Ethel P. Bills
May 3, 1871
Jan 26, 1894

Flora B. Jones
Jan 10, 1869
Oct 21, 1930

Othella, dau of
J. N. & P. J. Green
Nov 14, 1894
Sep 24, 1911

J. N. Green
Mar 4, 1869
Dec 2, 1928

Pinina Green
Jul 15, 1865
Mar 27, 1951

James W. Hendrix
Mar 4, 1840
Jun 1, 1946
(as copied)

Nancy H., wife of
James W. Hendrix
Mar 23, 1858
Sep 1919

D. M. Barron
Apr 1, 1821
Sep 5, 1895

Luther Hilliard
Nov 21, 1880
Aug 12, 1904

Walter T. Hendrix
1873-1931

Andrew Barron
Sep 26, 1885
Jul 29, 1904

Virgie Barron
1895-1896

G. Arthur Barron
1899-1899

Annie Mae G. Rone
Dec 7, 1887
Feb 11, 1923

Mary L. Roberts
Jul 11, 1917
Sep 4, 1918

Rebecca Inez Thomason
Nov 12, 1876
Nov 15, 1917

W. W. Thomason
Mar 6, 1835
Jan 13, 1917

S. A. Thomason
Mar 1, 1858
(no date)

J. Fount Harris
Feb 9, 1883
Jan 1, 1949

Zillah Whitesell Harris
Dec 22, 1891

J. P. Harris
May 17, 1848
Apr 13, 1922

Sallie R., wife of
J. P. Harris
Sep 28, 1851
Jun 22, 1906

Several unmarked graves.

* *

WILSON HILL CEMETERY
Located at Wilson Hill Church, on left of Globe Road, four miles from Highway 50-A. Copied April 6, 1966.

J. E. H.
(Foorstone)

Samuel Gentry Richardson
Dec 12, 1897
May 26, 1918
&
Martha Eliza Richardson
Mar 17, 1893
Feb 1, 1911

William Henry Richardson
1882-1958

Otis M. Marshall
1883-1940
&
Eva R. Marshall
1880-

R. Claude Richardson
1896-1963 (TM)

W. L. Richardson
Jan 6, 1856
Jun 29, 1931

Sallie C. Richardson
Jan 3, 1863
Feb 13, 1894

M. Addie Richardson
May 10, 1857
Dec 19, 1938

Joe Head
1860-1903
&
Dora Head
1862-1942

Henry J. London
Oct 21, 1852
Sep 6, 1923

Donie London
Jan 29, 1861
Sep 6, 1917

Angie Richardson
Jan 17, 1890
Jan 20, 1931

Clarence London
Mar 18, 1884
Apr 16, 1902

Clyde London
Jun 9, 1882
Jun 3, 1906

LEWISBURG

Lively Ann Richardson
Mar 25, 1839
Oct 24, 1908

J. J. Richardson
Jan 1, 1828
Nov 5, 1912

Josie Richardson Barron
1872-1910

John C. Richardson
May 5, 1870
Oct 26, 1951

Neil E. Gipson
1882-19
&
Sallie D. Gipson
1874-1949

Lucille Higgs
1910-1940

Donie Houston Gupton
Sep 11, 1859
Sep 18, 1946

W. L. Gupton
Jan 3, 1876
Oct 21, 1948

Homer L. Haislip
Jun 15, 1908
Jun 19, 1942
&
Nannie L. Haislip
Jun 1, 1912

Earl Davis Ketchum, Jr.
Tennessee
Cox US Navy WW II
Dec 28, 1924
Dec 6, 1957

Bryan K. Lines
Oct 16, 1960
Nov 28, 1960

Diana Lynn Lines
Jan 7, 1958
Aug 26, 1959

James B. Reaves
Died Mar 8, ----
(TM)

C-- D-- -----rt
1927 (illegible)
(London FH)

W. Fount Emerson
Feb 16, 1850
Jun 30, 1921
&
Lula E. Emerson
Oct 24, 1873
May 19, 1931

Athol, son of
W. F. & L. E. Emerson
B&D Sep 21, 1894

J. W. Duncan
1845-1902
&
Mary A. Duncan
1847-1927

Florence Duncan
1883-1960
&
Mallica Wallace
1876-1946

W. L. Richardson
Oct 25, 1867
Feb 23, 1954

Wilma May Higdon
Sep 28, 1916
May 19, 1918

Johnnie Powell Dobyns
Oct 30, 1868
May 5, 1941

J. C. Powell
1836-1912
& wife
Ann McKnight Powell
1837-1912

S. Bright Orr
1874-1951
&
E. Lettie Orr
1878-1962

Wendall, son of
S. B. & E. L. Orr
Apr 21, 1909
Oct 29, 1910

Jesse Cowden, son of
C. C. & S. S. Stacy
Oct 8, 1898
Oct 13, 1898

Lewis London
Nov 9, 1899
Dec 11, 1954
&
Selma London
Feb 28, 1905

Alonzo C. Edwards
1857-1901
&
Cordelia Edwards
1865-1901

Emma C., wife of
William Forehand
Jan 22, 1860
Jan 4, 1906

Henry McCord
Oct 18, 1860
Feb 14, 1938
&
Mattie McCord
Nov 20, 1867
May 9, 1944

Franklin H. Bills
Jan 28, 1823
Nov 14, 1904

Elizabeth Bills
Sep 4, 1823
Nov 4, 1905

Davis Bills
Dec 3, 1862
Aug 19, 1900

Leo Davis
Sep 8, 1868
--- --, 1898

John B. Edwards
Dec 30, 1858
Jul 3, 1934
&
Emma C. Edwards
Feb 20, 1869
May 29, 1934

Earnest B. Miller
1906-1949
&
Vonie E. Miller
1894-

Elisha L. Duncan
1876-
&
Ada Bone Duncan
Oct 8, 1873

Virginia, wife of
C. C. Duncan
May 19, 1859
Oct 22, 1905

Christopher Columbus Duncan
Feb 27, 1853
Oct 20, 1925

Thomas Wilson Doggett
Jul 21, 1873
Dec 24, 1957
&
Della Barron Doggett
Jun 29, 1882

Sarah U., wife of
J. P. Doggett
Mar 17, 1846
Mar 6, 1899

James Polk Doggett
Mar 18, 1846
Jul 15, 1910

T. H. Walker
Oct 30, 1857
Nov 13, 1897

John Lindsey Harris
Feb 16, 1859
Dec 16, 1934
&
Elnora R. Phillips Harris
Nov 12, 1867
Jan 30, 1941

J. Clifford Harris
Feb 24, 1892
Dec 31, 1926

Clella May, dau of
J. L. & E. R. Harris
Apr 28, 1895
May 12, 1895

Frank Harris Richardson
Apr 23, 1859
Feb 25, 1931
&
Annie Stacy Richardson
Jul 21, 1871

Nannie M., dau of
F. H. & A. J. Richardson
Jan 27, 1891
Sep 12, 1895

Mable Wilson London
Feb 1, 1901
Dec 8, 1935
&
Elwanda, dau of
Fred & Mable London
June 4, 1925

J. Charley London
Jul 27, 1870
Mar 11, 1920
&
Effie Maud London
Nov 22, 1872
Jan 20, 1915

B. F. Phillips
Jan 1, 1834
Jun 1, 1916
&
Hannah Phillips
Nov 11, 1845
Oct 9, 1914

Elisha L. Phillips
Sep 14, 1878
Jan 6, 1913
&
Lula M. Phillips
Jul 9, 1878
Mar 10, 1964

Joe M. Phillips
Dec 14, 1871
Apr 18, 1961

LEWISBURG

Thomas K. Phillips
Mar 16, 1869
May 7, 1944
&
Maxie O. Phillips
Jul 18, 1883

J. D. "Polk" Phillips
1845-1918
&
Mary Melissa Phillips
1854-1932

Kittie, dau of
W. C. & E. C. McGregor
Jul 14, 1871
Apr 20, 1888

Mary Alice, dau of
W. C. & E. C. McGregor
Dec 27, 1866
Jan 15, 1894

William C. McGregor
Mar 15, 1837
Jan 25, 1910

Elizabeth, wife of
W. C. McGregor
Dec 30, 1833
Aug 21, 1900

Arrena London
Oct 15, 1840
(no dates)
&
Johnie Caneer
Oct 15, 1861
Jun 29, 1901
"Weep not, she is not dead
 but sleepeth."

Mark J. Wilson
1857-1907
&
Jonnie C. Wilson
1858-1939

Laura B. McGregor, wife of
T. A. K. London
Mar 22, 1868
Jul 13, 1920

T. A. K. London
Feb 10, 1869
Sep 30, 1941

N. Worth Fowler
Mar 7, 1851
Jun 13, 1923
& wife
Mattie A. Fowler
Aug 15, 1851
Jul 17, 1906

Nola T. Fowler
Jun 23, 1886
Dec 11, 1945
&
Mary Eula Beech Fowler
May 29, 1888
Dec 31, 1961

Adron T. Beckham
1884-1949
&
Essie M. Beckham
1894-1959

William H. Matney
1877-1935
&
Cornelia F. Matney
1871-1951

Everette Wilson
Sep 13, 1887
Aug 27, 1959

James A. Fowler
Nov 17, 1855
Jul 1, 1934

Leila F. Gupton
Jan 23, 1882
Mar 3, 1961

Herschell, son of
J. T. & Lura McConnell
1900-1901

J. T. "Tom" McConnell
1869-1905
&
Lura V. McConnell
1875-1935

Ira Mai McConnell
Mar 21, 1896
Nov 8, 1956

J. T. Wilson
1851-1938

Katie M. Denton, wife of
V. C. Summerford
1889-1926

Soldier
M. K. Lowrance
Sep 17, 1894
Aug 22, 1927

Mother
Josie Lowrance
Dec 31, 1865
Jan 25, 1942

T. J. Lowrance
Sep 26, 1850
Oct 18, 1918

Husband
O. B. Lowrance
Aug 11, 1881
Jul 3, 1929

Martha, wife of
J. B. Loftin
Apr 1, 1829
Mar 24, 1914

Era Edith, dau of
J. T. & A. E. Wilson
Jun 21, 1889
Apr 22, 1899

Clare Wilson
Jul 30, 1885
Dec 12, 1920

Mother
Ann Elizabeth Wilson
1859-1930

Blanche Beasley
Sep 3, 1883
May 26, 1904

Atlas L. Wilson
Jun 24, 1854
Jan 26, 1938
&
Elma Beasley Wilson
Feb 23, 1879

H. Knox McConnell
1871-1937
&
Mary L. McConnell
1879-1958

Mary E. Wilson
1909

James Claud Wilson
1876-1965
&
Josie Houston Wilson
1877-1959

Several unmarked graves.
END OF WILSON HILL
* *

PURDOM CEMETERY
Located on New Lake Road at Lewisburg Reservoir. Copied
Dec 4, 1979 by Ralph D. Whitesell, Helen and Tim Marsh.

Infant of
W. H. & Paralee Purdom
(no dates)
NOTE: only marked
grave with inscription.

* Information from a Bible
  of E. A. Holly of
  Lewisburg, TN.

*Washington Haywood Purdom
Jan 26, 1826
May 28, 1900
& wife
Paralee (Collins) Purdom
Apr 10, 1831
Mar 2, 1894
Mrd- Feb 6, 1850

*Elizabeth Collins
Mar 16, 1827
Sep 5, 1898

* Also buried in this
  Cemetery are members
  of the Bearden family.

* Other members of the
  Purdom and Collins
  family.

* *

LEWISBURG

ISLEY CEMETERY

Located one and one-half mile east of Lewisburg at the City limits. Copied Dec 4, 1979 by Ralph D. Whitesell, Helen and Tim Marsh.

Mrs. Betty Wright
1875-1964
(Bills-McGaugh FH)

George W. Cozart
1894-1972
(Bills-McGaugh FH)

Baby Whitehead
1967-1967
(London FH)

Infant of
A. J. & F. E. Thompson
Mar 6, 1885
Age 3 days

Sarah, wife of
A. J. Isley
Died Jan 22, 1916
Age 75 years

Morgan Isley
1868-1947

Ada Isley
1874-1953

Miss Mattie Pearl Isley
1866-1955
(Bills-McGaugh FH)

Mrs. Stella Rogers
1940-1979
(London FH)

Mrs. Mary Kate Wright
1910-1972
(London FH)

Linda Paulette Wright
Died J-- -, 1949
(no age given)

Samuel Isley
A Confederate Soldier
Dec 24, 1824
Jun 15, 1919

Elizabeth, wife of
Sam Isley
Sep 22, 1829
Mar 6, 1913

Lillie, wife of
B. M. Isley
Aug 5, 1876
Nov 2, 1911

"Gave his life for his Country"
Samuel Isley
Apr 4, 1897
Oct 4, 1918

George D. Whitsell
Mar 28, 1866
May 2, 1928

Several unmarked graves.

* *

WHORLEY CEMETERY

Located on Old Belfast Road, between Needmore and Hickory Heights. Copied Dec 4, 1979 by Ralph D. Whitesell, Helen and Tim Marsh.

Linton Blackwell
1943-1952
(London FH)

Grady Finley
Jan 7, 1936
Nov 24, 1937

Juanita Finley
Jul 19, 1942
Jul 19, 1942

Elizabeth Whorley
Apr 17, 1791
Dec 10, 1843
Age 52 yrs, 7 mos, 23 days

Virginia Roberts
1907-1940

Mother
Eliza Hallock
1881-1958
   & Daughter
Louise Keel
1916-1948

Reba Juanita Davis
Died Mar 3, 1952
Age 1 day

Mrs. Annie Lou Davis
1925-1972
(London FH)

Riley Scott Davis
1904-1968
(Bills-McGaugh FH)

Emmet Chilton
Tennessee
Pvt Btry D 318 Field Arty
WW I
Jul 24, 1893
Dec 29, 1946

Mamie (Brewer) Chilton
Nov 11, 1893
Oct 20, 1949

Kenneth Lee Chilton
Died Apr 16, 1944
Age 0, 0, 0.
(London)

Henry Lee Chilton
1925-1977
(London FH)

Mrs. Margaret Chilton
1921-1979
(London FH)

"Son"
William J. Isley
1946-1946

Clyde Cozart
1913-1974
(London FH)

James Odell Cozart
1907-1967
(London FH)

Mrs. Brownie Mealer
1936-1968

Mrs. Eunice Dean
1909-1977
(London FH)

Joe Rogers
Feb 28, 1922
Jul 2, 1974

George Rogers
(Blank)-1951
(London FH)

John Rogers
1868-1942
  &
Mollie Rogers
1875-1962

Father
Narve Rogers
Dec 15, 1903
Apr 15, 1971

James E. Hargrove
1957-1957
(London FH)

William L. Chilton
1932-1932

Roy D. Chilton
Dec 20, 1935
Jun 9, 1951

Cecil L. Chilton
1933-1961

Joe P. Chilton
1902-1975
  &
Bessie L. Chilton
1907-1971

Robert D. Chilton
Nov 3, 1969
Nov 21, 1969

Joe Chilton, Jr.
Nov 10, 1939
Aug 9, 1973

Johnie F. Chilton
Jan 8, 1895
Jun 1, 1939
  &
Georgia B. Chilton
May 13, 1902

Mrs. Callie Brewer
1872-1954
(London FH)

Robert Lee Shirley
Tennessee
Pvt 417 Inf   WW II
Nov 8, 1913
Oct 31, 1966

Kareen (Chilton) Shirley
Dec 24, 1918
Apr 21, 1952

LEWISBURG

Frank Rodgers
Jan 11, 1905
Apr 12, 1970
&
Mildred Ruth Rodgers
Mar 31, 1917

Daughter
Pauline Rodgers
July 10, 1953

Jess Rodgers
Feb 16, 1902
Aug 19, 1972

Ed Rodgers
1868-(no date)
TM: Ed Rodgers
1864-1951
(London)
&
Lizzie Rodgers
1864-1943

Brother
Ollie O. Rodgers
1896-1956

Daddy
Jim Russell
1874-1958
(London FH)

Mrs. Annie R. Russell
1884-1962
(London FH)

Herman Russell
1907-1963
(London FH)

Darrell Farrell Rodgers
Died Mar 30, 1945
Age 0, 0, 0. (TM)

_____ Rodgers
Died (date gone)
(TM)

Many unmarked graves.

Clifford E. Jones
1901-(TM: Elmer, d 1959)
&
Laura K. Jones
1895-1958

Robert Russell
1916-1969
(London FH)

Judy Lynn Shirley
1969-1969

* *

CALTON CEMETERY
Located one and one-half mile north of Lewisburg on Verona Road. Information by Ralph D. Whitesell.

Mary D. (Russell) Calton
Jul 27, 1816
Apr 23, 1864
"She was 1st wife of
George Whitesell of
Bedford County, TN. &
2nd wife of William Calton
of Marshall Co., TN."
(no marker)

Her grave is in the southwest
corner of an Old garden on west
side of Lewisburg-Verona Road.

Only one grave.

* *

HARRIS CEMETERY
Located north of the Lewisburg-Columbia Highway 50, on South Berlin Road. Copied April 1962 by Joe C. Harris and wife. This is the old Gideon Harris farm, later owned by a nephew David Harris and now owned by his grandson David Harris.

Gideon Harris
Jul 30, 1772
Oct 26, 1860

Martha T. (Gilliam),
wife of
Gideon Harris
Feb 3, 1786
May 14, 1860

David Harris
Dec 31, 1781
Jun 22, 1864
(Born blind, a brother
of Gideon)

Mary C., wife of
Jesse Harris
Dec 14, 1793
Jul 2, 1864

Lindsey Arnold
Dec 28, 1798
Aug 11, 1868
(nephew of Gideon Harris)

James G. Harris
Dec 13, 1811
Apr 22, 1882
(son of Gideon Harris)

Susan A. (Hill), wife of
James G. Harris
Feb 7, 1818
May 22, 1900

W. F. Baxter
May 5, 1820
Oct 28, 1898

Martha J. (Harris), wife of
W. F. Baxter
Apr 11, 1826
Dec 9, 1918

W. L. Harris
May 18, 1821
Jan 15, 1897
(Blind, son of David
Harris)

Mary A. (Patterson),
wife of W. L. Harris
Jun 29, 1823
Jul 15, 1905

Lewis T. Harris
Aug 10, 1825
          1853 br 1858)
(son of David Harris,
stone down & broken)

R. G. Ramsey
Nov 26, 1826
Feb 14, 1909

Mariah (Hill), wife of
R. G. Ramsey
Dec 27, 1829
Jul 28, 1893
(sister of Susan A. Hill)

David L., son of
W. L. & M. A. Harris
Jan 21, 1845
Feb 13, 1916

Mildred (Tidwell), wife of
David L. Harris
Jan 14, 1852
Oct 18, 1934

LEWISBURG

Gertrude, dau of
G. L. & M. T. Harris
Jan 31, 1874
Sep 20, 1949

William Thomas, son of
Jas. G. & S. A. Harris
Aug 2, 1853
Aug 29, 1913

Martha Elizabeth, wife of
Garrett Harris
Apr 20, 1854
Dec 21, 1893

Clarissa B., wife of
Hunter Harris
Nov 15, 1861
Jul 27, 1938

John Bryce, son of
W. T. & M. E. Harris
Feb 16, 1880
Apr 7, 1895

Charles R., son of
W. T. & C. B. Harris
1900-1929

Many unmarked graves.

* *

RECORD CEMETERY

Located about four miles west of Lewisburg, on the New Columbia Highway. The farm now owned by Miss Laura Hill, and formerly by her father, Isaac H. Hill. Copied Oct 23, 1958 by Ralph D. Whitesell and Mrs. Ray Farley.

In Memory of
Elizabeth M. Cowden
Who departed this life
Sep 5, 1854
Age 64 years.

Josephas N. Cowden
Was born A.D. 1817
And died 1840
Age 22 years

Rev. Sion Record
Was born A.D. 1812
& professed religion in
1838 & joined the
Tennessee Conferance in
1839 & Died in 1859
Age 47 years.

* *

END OF LEWISBURG QUADRANGLE

BELFAST
QUADRANGLE

HAMPTON CEMETERY

Located on Endsley Road, one mile east of the Fishing Ford Road. Copied by David Harris.

In Memory of
Mary Hampton
Who died Aug 3, 1822
Age 75 years.　　　　　Many unmarked graves.

* *

TEMPLE CEMETERY

Located four miles north east of Lewisburg, and one and one-half mile west of Farmington. Copied 1968. And 1979.

Ransom F. Chapman
Jul 14, 1881
Nov 22, 1960
&
Lennie D. Chapman
Oct 17, 1890

James H. Dillard
Sep 17, 1883
May 24, 1966

Thomas G. Dillard
1888-1977
&
Pearl P. Dillard
1894-1952

John Howell Kennedy
New York
Sgt 13 Air Force WW II
Sep 26, 1907
May 19, 1947

John Herschel Culbertson
1888-1971

Ann E. Hurt Culbertson
1893-1957

Turner Madison
1915-1960

Lottie Mae Madison
Jul 2, 1893
Jan 30, 1967

Walter Oscar Junge
Jan 16, 1891
Feb 19, 1968
&
Marietta T. Junge
Jan 1, 1907

Chesney C. Gold
Sep 23, 1891
Dec 20, 1939
&
Annie Mae Gold
Mar 28, 1892

Ruby Elizabeth Gold
Sep 25, 1925
Dec 18, 1925
"Our Baby"

J. W. Gold
Mar 22, 1924
May 26, 1924
"Our Baby"

Sam E. Gold
Nov 21, 1887
Jun 20, 1920

Bonnie Fox Gold
Jan 27, 1892
Dec 22, 1974

Elmore Oscar McCullough
Dec 23, 1888
Aug 19, 1959

Billy G. McCullough
Tennessee
Pfc 346 Inf 87 Div WW II
Dec 18, 1925
Mar 4, 1945

Pvt Fred H. Dysart
Feb 19, 1917
Killed in Action
in France
Aug 10, 1944
&
Harrison R. Dysart
1880-1954
&
Flora Preslar Dysart
1876-1942

Willie Joe Wilson
Apr 8, 1902
May 12, 1961
&
Annie Mae Wilson
Dec 2, 1906
Aug 11, 1956

Sam A. Wilson
1862-1939
&
Della J. Wilson
1870-1953

Joseph Holston Wilson
Jul 4, 1878
Mar 29, 1959
&
Lena R. Gold Wilson
Mar 25, 1882
Dec 24, 1969

Infant Son of
Mr. & Mrs. J. H. Wilson
June 23, 1917

William J. Cathey
1866-1954

Luther Cathey
Mar 11, 1882
Dec 25, 1956
&
Jannie H. Cathey
Oct 12, 1886
Feb 22, 1973

James W. Jackson
May 8, 1897

&
Nora D. Jackson
Feb 7, 1897
Jan 4, 1976
&
J. G. Jackson
Aug 2, 1894
Oct 15, 1934
NOTE: The above stone had
JACKSON-DOUGLAS

J. Len Miller
1872-1943
&
Lula M. Miller
1870-(no date)

E. W. Woodward
Jul 31, 1837
Mar 15, 1925
&
Mary A. Woodward
Mar 18, 1847
Jun 26, 1930

Olie B. Miller
1904-1946
&
Mary D. Miller
1906-

James Melvin Chapman
1874-1946
&
Sallie Davis Chapman
1877-1954

Father
James M. Davis
1840-1914
&
Mother
N. M. Davis
1843-1928

Hiram Tennison, Jr.
Oct 29, 1894
May 31, 1966

Mattie V. Tennison
Nov 4, 1861
Dec 15, 1931

Nancy C., wife of
Hiram Tennison
Dec 12, 1848
Oct 6, 1880
Age 31 yrs, 9 mos, 24 days

Hiram Tennison
Confederate Soldier
Aug 23, 1842
Jul 13, 1910
"Our Father"

Edith Hobby Woodward
1913-1953

Robert Edward Woodward
1901-1945
&
Annie Ruth Woodward
1903-1972

Dick Mosley
1848-1934
&
Lute Mosley
1851-1927

BELFAST

Olie L. Mosley
Dec 19, 1878
Mar 31, 1944

Hubert A. Woodward
Jun 25, 1884
Dec 22, 1920

Ida L. Woodward
Jul 2, 1871
Nov 18, 1957

George D. Bradley
Dec 18, 1869
Feb 3, 1941
&
Mary Anne Bradley
Aug 31, 1873
Jun 6, 1945

"Duck"
Leslie James Lasater
1900-1951
&
Nannie Bradley Lasater
1899-

Wade Bills
Feb 1873
Mar 1924

Lily Bills
Sep 13, 1876
Dec 16, 1953

Father
William H. Orr
May 26, 1834
Jun 6, 1923

Mother
Martha A. Orr
Nov 7, 1844
Sep 10, 1918

Retta Orr
1866-1957

Alfred Orr
1858-1935

William Newton Orr
Apr 2, 1894
Sep 25, 1961

Rhessa Cross Orr
Nov 24, 1894
Feb 3, 1952

Douglas, son of
W. N. & Rhessa Orr
Nov 16, 1924
Feb 22, 1934

Ted Orr
1937

Mary Lou dau of
G. R. & Rebecca Woodward
May 21, 1912
Nov 20, 1913

George Robert Woodward
1874-1964

Rebecca Ellen Woodward
1880-1940

Margaret N. Woodward
Jan 22, 1905
Oct 6, 1930

William Kenneth Woodward
Cpl USMC
Dec 1, 1926
Feb 4, 1951
Killed in action in Korea

Henry J. Liggett
1875-1933

Willie F. Liggett
1876-19(no date)

R. D. Palmer
Mar 29, 1841
Dec 26, 1913
& wife
Lucinda P. Palmer
Nov 27, 1844
Dec 15, 1912

Janie D. Palmer
1883-19

James R. Palmer
1877-1942

Allen Coleman McCullough
Dec 5, 1858
Apr 16, 1942

Tina Goldman McCullough
Oct 2, 1872
Mar 21, 1942

William Virgil, son of
A. C. & Tina McCullough
Nov 22, 1895
Feb 12, 1910

Swanson McCullough
Apr 15, 1864
Apr 2, 1946

Fannie McCullough
Jan 6, 1871
Feb 29, 1940

Carl Swanson McCullough
Mar 21, 1898
May 28, 1962

Minta Lambert McCullough
June 4, 1900

Vera Wilson Musgrave
1893-19

Frank C. Musgrave, Sr.
1893-1954

Evelyn "Lyn" Musgrave
Jul 30, 1946
Sep 12, 1955

Ollie Bartlett, wife of
W. S. Yarbrough
Aug 5, 1881
Nov 2, 1912

W. Scott Yarbrough
(no marker)

Clifford Brown Taylor
Feb 22, 1922
Mar 22, 1922

Mrs. Maggie Anderson
1897-1927

William P. Anderson
Tennessee
Pfc Co A 861 Engr Avn Bn
WW II
Sep 16, 1920
Sep 1, 1963

Clabe P. Palmer
Jun 20, 1882
Nov 29, 1954

Carrie Long Palmer
Apr 13, 1881
Jun 6, 1948

Carolyn Lee Braswell
1934

Son of
C. P. & Carrie Palmer
Mar 15, 1911
Dec 1, 1911

John Calvin McGuire
Oct 31, 1886

Jennie Long McGuire
Apr 21, 1886
Aug 23, 1962

L. A. Temple
Mar 3, 1819
Jun 13, 1870

W. A. Temple
May 21, 1857
Aug 12, 1880

W. L. Hurt
(no dates)

Father
Newton K. Long
Feb 7, 1849
Jun 8, 1908

Mother
Sallie H. Long
Nov 24, 1851
Feb 17, 1934

M. J., dau of
J. C. & S. J. Burlen
Feb 20, 1866
Jul 30, 1879

Abe Smith
(no dates)

Sara Smith
(no dates)

Kate Brown Walker
Dec 19, 1873
Sep 27, 1911

Mattie Belle, wife of
J. J. Word
Dec 15, 1868
Nov 25, 1894

W. B. Brown
Mar 10, 1829
Jul 4, 1891
& wife
L. E. Brown
Jan 24, 1831
Nov 15, 1903

Little Daisy
(in Adams Plot, no dates)

Father
W. C. Adams
1848-1925

Mary Virginia, wife of
W. C. Adams
Dec 12, 1849
Aug 7, 1885
"Mother of four children,
one of whom preceded her
to heaven."

Riceoslin Adams
1869-1919
"Mother"

Evie Adams
May 1, 1877
Jun 6, 1899

Sarah, dau of
W. C. & Rice Adams
Oct 19, 1898
Jan 18, 1901

Father
Joseph Adams
May 28, 1809
Feb 6, 1894

Mother
Evaline Garrett, wife of
Joseph Adams
Jan 26, 1813
Jul 20, 1885

W. A. Gold
May 16, 1850
Aug 12, 1924

BELFAST

Lou C. Gold
Oct 23, 1856
Nov 19, 1936

Willie Harris, son of
W. A. & L. C. Gold
Nov 29, 1898
(date in ground)

Kittie G. Bills
1896-1951
&
Jesse S. Bills
1890-(buried in
Lone Oak Cemetery)

Nancy Culbertson
Feb 29, 1920
Jul 4, 1921

Annie Mai Culbertson,
wife of S. L. Giles
Aug 5, 1886
Mar 28, 1925

John Houston Culbertson
1855-1928

Alice Hunter Culbertson
1856-1949

Sallie Boren, dau of
J. H. & Alice Culbertson
Jan 10, 1885
Oct 15, 1886

R. M. Gold
1866-1925
& wife
M. D. Gold Stallings
1871-1948

Annie Adams Anderson
May 2, 1875
Nov 8, 1957

James Baird Anderson
1872-1919

Mary, dau of
J. B. & Annie Anderson
Apr 26, 1896
Sep --, 1900

J. M. Gold
Jun 14, 1825
Aug 1, 1897

Harriett E., wife of
J. M. Gold
Nov 12, 1829
Apr 8, 1903

Isaac Posey McCullough
1861-1939
&
Ada Chilton McCullough
1867-1947

Elbert, son of
J. W. & Estelle Thomas
Jun 30, 1869
Oct 28, 1885

J. H. Fowler
Jun 30, 1862
Jan 14, 1892

William Wallace Mount
Apr 24, 1838
Nov 20, 1901
&
Parmelee Coffey Mount
Jul 16, 1842
Aug 8, 1897

William Henry Mount
Apr 8, 1875
Sep 15, 1900

William Thomas, son of
Dr. T. C. & Mary A. Mount
Aug 9, 1887
Dec 17, 1888

Thomas C. Mount, D.D.S.
Aug 6, 1861
Dec 2, 1901
"Father"

Annie B. Bell
Dec 14, 1897
Nov 15, 1959

Luther M. Bell
Aug 29, 1871
May 21, 1923

Lula D. Hunter, wife of
L. M. Bell
Jul 11, 1868
Jan 4, 1912

Thomas Bruce, son of
L. M. & Lula Bell
Jul 28, 1899
Oct 15, 1900

Eliza Gold
1847-1927

Bettie Bartlette
1853-1904

Mary Brechen
1843-1905

Hollie Pickle
1856-1950

Nancy McCullough
Mar 31, 1820
Jun 14, 1895

Isaac McCullough
Apr 30, 1816
Mar 28, 1908

Paul DeWitt, son of
F. M. & A. C. McLean
May 10, 1893
Oct 2, 1894

Joe Doug., son of
F. M. & A. C. McLean
Sep 17, 1891
Sep 24, 1891

Etta H. R. Boren
Sep 18, 1864
Oct 31, 1909

Mira Dora, dau of
Bright C. & Ida Hunter
Jun 9, 1887
Aug 14, 1888

Ida T. Hunter
1861-1927

B. C. Hunter
1861-1954

Burt Hunter
1893-1962

Edwin Penn Long
Nov 15, 1870
Sep 2, 1892

G. C. Houston, Sr.
Nov 17, 1853
Aug 20, 1938
&
Nannie T. Houston
Feb 8, 1861
Apr 3, 1937

Tennessee C. Adams,
wife of J. C. Hayes
Feb 17, 1837
Jun 5, 1904

Mattie, dau of
Riggs & Hattie Hayes
Dec 21, 1894
Mar 12, 1898

T. M. Noblin
May 3, 1849
Dec 19, 1937
&
Florence Warren Noblin
Jul 30, 1849
Jun 18, 1926

Esther Ada Brown
Apr 1, 1895
Nov 4, 1901

Samuel V. Johnson
Oct 5, 1812
Jul 31, 1886

Ollie W.
(no dates, infant)
(prob. Johnson)

Dulcenia Johnson
Apr 8, 1819
Apr 13, 1889

James A. Noblin
Feb 12, 1851
Apr 4, 1892
& wife
Martha F. Noblin
May 18, 1850
Jun 21, 1892

Pearl Bartlett Brechen
Mar 3, 1870
May 28, 1935

Paul Q. McDill
Dec 22, 1902
Jan 3, 1940

Bettie W. Parks
1862-1935

Lily Mai Parks
1879-1926

John Lem, son of
W. M. & Virgie Parks
Oct 27, 1900
Sep 22, 1910

Kitty C. Parks
1836-1896

Sammie Harris
1876-1964

J. Lewis Harris
1873-1967

Birdie E. Harris
1919-

Edna Pauline, dau of
J. P. & Lillie Cunningham
May 6, 1910
May 11, 1910

Ida Bell, wife of
S. K. Dillard
Feb 2, 1859
Aug 3, 1900

S. K. Dillard
Nov 30, 1854
Aug 23, 1939

Nannie Mai Dillard
Feb 8, 1882
Jun 8, 1919

L. Dow Reed
1864-1938
&
Gertie Reed
1883-

Mother
Mary Ann Reed
Sep 3, 1841
Feb 7, 1907

BELFAST

Mary C., wife of
J. E. Musgrave
Nov 12, 1879
Mar 24, 1899

Joel Ozro Musgrave
1881-1941

Carlyle Hayes Musgrave
1889-1916

Infant Son of
T. R. & Bennette Musgrave
Born Aug 10, 1899

W. E. Musgrave
Aug 22, 1842
Dec 10, 1900
&
Susan G. Musgrave
Apr 25, 1850
Sep 14, 1918

Charley, son of
W. E. & Susan Musgrave
Mar 3, 1883
Nov 14, 1887

Babe Sweeney
1865-1943

V. C., wife of
A. N. Sweeney
May 9, 1840
Jan 27, 1902

Adolphus N. Sweeney
Jun 8, 1839
May 23, 1885

Amanda Bartlett
Feb 16, 1842
Feb 15, 1906

George Logan Bartlett
Jun 18, 1897
Nov 7, 1915

Annie Z., dau of
P. H. & Josie Bartlett
Jul 12, 1895
Jul 29, 1896

P. H. Bartlett
Jan 21, 1846
Jul 9, 1923
& wife
Josie Bartlett
Sep 26, 1856
Mar 5, 1899

Several unmarked graves.
END OF TEMPLE
* *

PALMETTO CEMETERY
Located near Farmington. Take 31-A north from Lewisburg
6.2 miles to 64, East for 2.7 miles and turn left, a short
distance. Copied Sep 21, 1969 by Charlene Nicholas.

Robert Elgin Phillips
Aug 3, 1899
Dec 9, 1958

William Claude Phillips
Mar 28, 1905
Oct 27, 1966

Infant Dau of
Mr. & Mrs. Claude Phillips
Mar 3, 1935

Edgar Wesley Phillips
Oct 23, 1866
Dec 12, 1932
&
Daisy Montgomery Phillips
Jan 6, 1877

Claude Montgomery
Aug 8, 1870
Sep 25, 1954

William R. Montgomery
Jun 12, 1884
Mar 26, 1926

Peter H., son of
W. A. & Sarah Montgomery
Jan 12, 1878
Aug 5, 1904

W. A. Montgomery
Apr 4, 1846
Feb 12, 1903

Sarah E., wife of
W. A. Montgomery
Jan 27, 1847
Jan 15, 1938

Peter Hoyle
Sep 27, 1818
Nov 18, 1890
Age 78 yrs, 1 mo, 21 days
&
Esther Orr, wife of
Peter Hoyle
Apr 18, 1809
Dec 28, 1891
Age 82 yrs, 8 mos, 10 days

Susan L., wife of B.M. Logan
Sep 2, 1849
Oct 1, 1879
"She hath done what she
 could."

Infant Son of
B. N. & Susan L. Logan
Mar 17, 1879
Mar 26, 1879

Martha Cleveland
Dec 6, 1899
Apr 3, 1901

Sudie Montgomery, wife of
George W. Chapman & dau of
William A. & Sarah A.
Montgomery
May 29, 1880
Jul 2, 1968

Jess S. Woodward
Aug 15, 1877

&
Leila L. Woodward
Sep 3, 1882
Feb 8, 1867

Lee H. Woodward
Nov 24, 1910
May 24, 1913
&
Liggett E. Woodward
Jul 20, 1909
Jul 23, 1910
"Sons of J. S. &
Lela Woodward."

Lora Dell, wife of
B. T. Tiller
Aug 22, 1871
Jul 18, 1920

William Phillips
1835-1922
& wife
Mary J. Phillips
1851-1941

Charley W. Bills
1879-1950
&
Lillie L. Bills
1880-19

M. W. Bills
Mar 4, 1856
Feb 6, 1937
&
Ella J. Bills
Jan 25, 1868
Jul 25, 1897

Arthur E. Bills
1883-1948
&
Bettie Bills
1881-1935

Robert Mount
1877-1938
&
Vashti Mount
1883-1967

Maggie Zearl Hayes
Jun 9, 1881
Nov 8, 1902

Thomas R. Logan
May 28, 1864
Aug 28, 1931
&
Flora Montgomery Logan
Oct 12, 1869
Apr 16, 1939

Frank Edwin Funk
1881-1951
&
Susie Montgomery Funk
1880-

Thomas S. Montgomery
Mar 30, 1843
Jan 4, 1914
&
Margaret L. Montgomery
Feb 13, 1844
Jun 25, 1926

Story of
Mary Ethel, wife of
Jno. Royal Harris
May 2, 1875
mrd- Mar 16, 1898
Died Sep 18, 1898

Infant Dau of
T. S. & M. L. Montgomery
B&D Jul 6, 1867

BELFAST

Infant Son of
F. W. & Sallie Baber
Still born
Jan 21, 1893

W. E. Collins
Feb 19, 1825
Aug 6, 1866

Mary J., dau of
Thomas & Mary Montgomery
May 23, 1835
Jan 29, 1912

Mary Flemming, wife of
Thomas Montgomery and
Mother of R.S., Sarah E.,
Mary J., J. F., J. B.,
T. S., W. A., Margaret E.
and H. C. Montgomery
Born Nov 15, 1805,
married Nov 20, 1828
Taken to heaven
Dec 11, 1898

Henry Clay, youngest son of
Thomas & Mary Montgomery
Jul 4, 1852
Dec 19, 1878

Henry C., son of
J. B. & M. E. Ramsey
Jun 17, 1879
Sep 8, 1879

J. B. Ramsey
Dec 1, 1841
Mar 9, 1899
& wife
Margarete Ramsey
Jan 1, 1849
Oct 27, 1886

John T. Ramsey
Dec 29, 1871
Feb 5, 1919
&
Lillie R. Bondurant Ramsey
Apr 14, 1881
Oct 25, 1931

Fred M., son of
J. B. & Margaret E. Ramsey
Dec 10, 1873
Jul 22, 1932

William Robert Montgomery
Dec 26, 1887
Nov 8, 1952

Rossea L. Montgomery
1865-1922

John O. Montgomery
1860-1914

Robert Montgomery, Sr.
Sep 10, 1810
Feb 3, 1903

Margaret P., wife of
Robert Montgomery
Feb 6, 1824
Mar 12, 1867

Jane Montgomery
Feb 19, 1816
Mar 20, 1876

Mary A. Montgomery
Feb 22, 1813
Sep 6, 1886

Logan Wesley Hayes
Jul 20, 1835
Nov 26, 1922
& wife
Adeline D. Montgomery Hayes
May 22, 1837
Jan 2, 1918

Joe A. Hayes
Jul 7, 1869
Jun 16, 1922

Elizabeth, wife of
A. J. Montgomery
Oct 28, 1818
Jul 23, 1890

J. Robert Mount
Aug 30, 1847
Aug 25, 1912

Ettie E. Mount
Jul 20, 1857
Nov 29, 1931

Maggie L. Mount
Oct 15, 1882
Aug 29, 1916

John M. Mount
Feb 16, 1879
Nov 19, 1940

I. T. Wiggs
1846-1916

Jennie Larkin Montgomery
Wiggs
1863-1968
(At the time of her death,
Mrs Wiggs was the oldest
resident of Marshall County)

Robert G. Wiggs
Tennessee
Pvt 115 Field Arty 30 Div
Feb 29, 1896
Jul 14, 1944

Thomas Johnson
1884-1952

Fern Wiggs Johnson
1885-1919

Marion Thomas Wiggs
1907-1933

Miss Etta London
1881-1952 (TM)

(name gone)
1877-(date gone) (TM)

Cell Levi London
1871-1952 (TM)

J. B. London
1875-1947

P. D. London
1888-1937

Ella, dau of
Dr. E. C. London
Dec 6, 1881
Jul 5, 1897

Hill, son of
Mrs. Gerty Adams
Jan 20, 1920
Jan 28, 1921

Jose C., son of
A. S. & Garnette Gaines
Nov 13, 1922
Nov 14, 1922

Gertrude H. Adams
1875-1942

Anna E., wife of
W. C. Hill
Jul 29, 1854
Jul 12, 1886

Frank Montgomery "Pete" Woods
1907-1960

Dorothy Woods Bragg
Jan 11, 1904
Dec 25, 1936

Martha Susan Woods
1902-1923

William Leonard "Billie" Woods
1916-1921

Ross A. Woods
Jul 4, 1876
Sep 16, 1937

Gertrude M. Woods
Oct 9, 1873

Jimmy, son of
R. S. & S. D. Montgomery
Oct 3, 1860
Mar 26, 1862
Age 17 mos & 23 days
(oldest marked grave)

Mary, dau of
R. S. & S. D. Montgomery
(stone repaired and dates
are illegible)

Susan D., wife of
R. S. Montgomery
Born Aug 29, 1831
passed away Apr 19, 1881
married Mar 13, 1855
"The sweetest wife and
kindest Mother"

Thomas Alfred, son of
R. S. & S. D. Montgomery
Jul 31, 1863
Dec 24, 1890

Robert Strong Montgomery
Nov 30, 1829
Apr 27, 1905
"The most loving husband
and the most indulgent
parent."

J. Fount Tillman
1853-1899
&
R. S. Tillman
1884-1899
&
Alice Montgomery Tillman
1856-1945
&
J. Fount Tillman
1894-1946

Sadie Wilson Tillman
1896-19

Susan Ransom, wife of
Dr. N. H. Culbertson
Mar 18, 1884
Jul 18, 1918

Sara Anne, dau of
W. C. & L. M. Ransom
1889-1942

W. C. Ransom, M.D.
Aug 28, 1851
Jul 31, 1914
&
Lily Montgomery Ransom
Feb 15, 1866
Jun 30, 1957

Lillian, dau of
W. C. & L. M. Ransom
Jan 5, 1896
Sep 30, 1896

Elvira Herron
Jun 21, 1815
Dec 3, 1877

Clinton, dau of
James P. & Leah Dysart
Jul 18, 1836
--- --, 1878
(stone broken)

BELFAST

James P. Dysart
Nob 19, 1804
Aug 26, 1879
   & wife
Leah Dysart
Jan 6, 1806
Oct 14, 1881

Lucy Dysart
"Our Black Mammy, The
faithful nurse of three
generations."
Died Jany 4, 1893
Age 75 years
"Erected by her white
children."

Odus Barnett
Sep 8, 1893

&
Mattie B. Barnett
Sep 17, 1903
----
mrd- Jun 6, 1925

Infant
William Barnett
July 4, 1941

Susie Loftin Mount
1899-1918
&
Maggie Adams Mount
1879-1900

Maggie B., dau of
W. E. & S. O. Waddey
Jul 3, 1896
Apr 21, 1899

Father
William E. Waddey
Feb 29, 1843
Jul 31, 1918
&
Mother
Susie O. Waddey
Jul 12, 1861
Feb 27, 1939

Fay Barnett
Sep 4, 1928
Nov 20, 1932

Infant
J. O. Barnett
Feb 8, 1938

About 6 unmarked graves.

Leila Aileen, wife of
Marvin Morris
Nov 1, 1876
Feb 22, 1903

W. J. Biggers
Co F
1st Tenn and Ala
VID CAV
(no dates)

Susie Biggers
Sep 9, 1857
Jun 19, 1863

William T., son of
J. N. & R. V. Dalton
May 4, 1859
Sep 3, 1864

Father
William Thomas
Died Jan 25, 1878
(no age given)
  & wife
Susan Ann Ferguson Thomas
Died Mar 28, 1876
(no age given)

END OF PALMETTO

Father
W. Lewis Thomas
Apr 9, 1842
Jul 1, 1914
&
Mother
Roanne Thomas
Jan 3, 1842
Jun 17, 1921

Infant Dau of
A. H. & Cora Cathey
Jan 29, 1904

A. H. Cathey
1876-1937
&
Cora T. Cathey
1875-1922

Wilson Dallas Cathey
1868-1930
&
Belle Thomas Cathey
1869-1948

Mary Anna Cathey
1907-1935

* *

CONFEDERATE CEMETERY
Located at Farmington, north side of Highway 64-E. Copied Oct 27, 1978.

NAMES OF CONFEDERATE SOLDIERS KILLED ON THIS FIELD, IN BATTLE, ON OCT 7th., 1863. CAVALRY.

_____ Bodie	Thomas Grinstead	Daniel Hoffman	J. W. Lane
_____ Evans	_____ Gilleott	Peter Kesterson	_____ McDonald
Ben Easley	H. T. Hunter	C. W. Love	William Smith

NOTE: Some bodies were moved after the war.

* *

ERWIN CEMETERY
Located two and two-tenth miles south of Farmington-Belfast Road (Fishingford Road). Copied 1979 by Helen and Tim Marsh.

Martha Elizabeth Chilton
May 18, 1928
Jun 16, 1929

Hazel Lee Chilton
Oct 4, 1922
Dec 15, 1922

Tina M. Little
1899-1926

Robert M. Darnal
Jun 19, 1881
Jan 22, 1897

Maggie E., dau of
John F. & Elmira Darnal
Jun 29, 1867
Jun 25, 1890

Elmira G., wife of
John F. Darnal
May 26, 1838
Mar 10, 1880

Mattie C., wife of
R. H. Hunter
Jan 12, 1862
Jan 5, 1883

Milton A. Coffey
Jun 24, 1855
May 21, 1902

Susie E., dau of
M. A. & H. O. Coffey
Dec 19, 1885
Sep 17, 1887

R. D. Erwin
Nov 14, 1860
Jun 14, 1881
Age 20 yrs, 7 mos.

Mittie, wife of
F. L. Woods, Sr.
Jan 11, 1843
Apr 9, 1868

Mittie H. Mays, dau of
F. L. & Mittie Woods
Mar 25, 1868
May 6, 1885

Hannah O., wife of
F. L. Woods, Sr.
Sep 6, 1832
Jun 25, 1866

BELFAST

James P. Erwin
Aug 16, 1836
Feb 8, 1864

Hannah B., Consort of
John R. Erwin
May 18, 1777
Oct 16, 1851

John R. Erwin
Sep 4, 1773
Dec 23, 1859
(broken)

Rev. William F. Erwin
Who died in the
triumphs of faith
Oct 30, 1852
(Pyramid)

Thomas H. Erwin
Sep 22, 1838
Jul 9, 1873

C. C. Lancaster
Mar 12, 1852
Feb 4, 1902

A. C. Lancaster
Dec 22, 1849
Apr 10, 1917

Nettie Lancaster
May 12, 1865
Mar 6, 1895

Pauline, dau of
M. A. & H. O. Stallings
Dec 2, 1905
Mar 26, 1907

Hannah O. Erwin
Born Sep 12, 1859
Mrd M. A. Coffey
Nov 4, 1877
mrd M. A. Stallings
Oct 7, 1903
Died Dec 12, 1915

John D. Logan
May 10, 1826
Apr 30, 1879
Age 52 yrs, 11 mos, 20 days
&
Matilda H. Logan
Jul 21, 1828
Feb 25, 1877
Age 48 yrs, 7 mos, 4 days

J.(or L.) W.
(illegible stone)

J. B. Lancaster
Oct 11, 1889
Feb 1, 1922

Sam B. Lancaster
Feb 1898
Nov 1919

William Candor, son of
John E. & Elizabeth Erwin
Jan 20, 1839
Nov 21, 1845

John Edward Erwin
Jan 18, 1810
Aug 22, 1845

James Porter Erwin
Dec 9, 1811
Sep 11, 1836

L. E. N.
(probably child of
James & Sarah (Erwin)
Newton)

H. B. Erwin
Jan 9, 1808
Mar 18, 1890
Age 82 yrs, 2 mos, 9 days

_amanda M. Anderson
Oct 12, 1869
Dec 15, 1888
(broken)

John A. Keele
1858-1937
(could be another stone
for this man)

Many unmarked graves.

D. L. Carothers, wife of
H. B. Erwin
Mar 12, 1807
Jul 6, 1889
Age 82 yrs, 3 mos, 24 days

James Miller Anderson
Mar 29, 1840
Aug 14, 1905

Amanda M., wife of
James M. Anderson
Aug 31, 1845
Jul 22, 1888
Age 42 yrs, 10 mos, 21 days

William H., son of
Jas. M. & Amanda M.
Anderson
Oct 12, 1869
Dec 16, 1888
(broken)

John A. Keele
1860-1937
&
Jessie E. Keele
1866-1914
&
Infant Dau
1909-1909

Robert Lee Duddy
Jan 2, 1904
Jun 6, 1904

* *

PATTON CEMETERY

Located west of Fishingford Road, south of Head Springs.
Copied Dec 5, 1979 by Ralph D. Whitesell, Helen and
Tim Marsh.

Leona, wife of
James T. Martin
Apr 2, 1887
Sep 22, 1909

Alma F., wife of
J. R. Patton
Aug 21, 1887
Nov 5, 1906

J. R., Jr., son of
J. R. & A. F. Patton
Oct 20, 1906
May 30, 1907

Lucy L., wife of
D. V. Greer
Jun 9, 1866
Sep 19, 1907

A. I. Patton
Mar 28, 1817
Feb 15, 1890
 & wife
Alsie M. Patton
Apr 5, 1838
Oct 24, 1908

2 or 3 unmarked graves.

J. F. Patton
1807-May 30, 1893

Jno. T. Patton
Mar 1, 1871
Oct 31, 1893

Charlie S., son of
T. S. & K. P. Hopwood
Mar 15, 1891
Oct 15, 1894

Thomas S. Hopwood
Jul 31, 1864
Apr 10, 1911

William R. Green
Jul 16, 1857
Jan 11, 1942

G. A. Green
Jan 15, 1863
Feb 2, 1885

Connie Green
May 5, 1883
Jul 2, 1885

* *

BELFAST

CANNON CEMETERY
Located at Belfast, Tennessee. at railroad

Arthur Shaw
Apr 12, 1882
Oct 23, 1954

Mabel Shaw
Dec 13, 1887

Susan K., dau of
Thomas W. & Susan L. Smith
Nov 6, 1811
Sep 2, 1812

Susan L. Smith
Who was born --
(illegible)

Thompson Cannon
Aug 20, 1793
Oct 5, 1834

Elizabeth Cannon
Apr 15, 1795
Mar 23, 1864

Owen Lane
1907-
&
Lottie B. Lane
1907-1955

Roy Woods
Nov 7, 1893

&
Katherine M. Woods
Oct 3, 1903
Apr 11, 1966

Frank Henry Cannon
Oct 2, 1869
Aug 14, 1959

Robert Cannon
Dec 9, 1825
Apr 5, 1894

Sarah Elise, dau of
Mr. & Mrs. A. C. Sweeney
Mar 28, 1923

Grady J. Sweeney
1891-1935
&
Mary Adams Sweeney
1892-1921

Michael Cannon
Dec 7, 1828
Jul 2, 1907

Mary E., wife of
M. Cannon
Nov 3, 1839
Jan 5, 1900

Charlie C. Lancaster
Nov 13, 1883
Jan 14, 1961
&
Lena May Lancaster
Jun 28, 1893

John S. Sweeney
Dec 4, 1866
Nov 3, 1955

Ola Cannon Sweeney
Oct 26, 1870
Nov 5, 1920

John D. Adams
Feb 28, 1859
Apr 11, 1926
& wife
Lizzie Adams
Apr 5, 1861
Jan 2, 1946

Sarah Woods Cannon
Mar 15, 1838
Mar 9, 1917

Henry C. Cannon
Feb 22, 1832
Feb 2, 1889

Charlie E., son of
H. C. & S. E. Cannon
Jun 16, 1823
Nov 11, 1823

David K. Cannon
Nov 14, 1822
Aug 26, 1843

Father
Newton Jasper, son of
Barnett & Sarah Smiley
Aug 9, 1833
Dec 14, 1894

Mother
Catherine Elizabeth Smiley,
dau of Thos. & Catherine Hall
Sep 17, 1841
Feb 22, 1900

Infant Sons of
J. S. & Ola Sweeney
(no dates) (two small
footstones)

Lena May Cannon, wife of
J. P. McAdams
May 6, 1866
Jul 12, 1897

Ralph McAdams
Nov 16, 1859
Mar 1, 1919

Cora McAdams
Feb 25, 1868
Mar 10, 1944

Henry D. McAdams
Tennessee
Pfc PMG School Det WW II
Sep 18, 1899
Oct 29, 1965

Thomas L. McAdams
Oct 16, 1865
Jun 30, 1910
&
Myrtle Mc Gabbert
Apr 14, 1873
Nov 29, 1936

Jasper S."Pete" McAdams
Tennessee
Pvt Student Army TNG Corps
WW I
Jun 16, 1897
Jul 7, 1947

* *

WOODWARD CEMETERY
Located near Liberty Valley, three miles southeast of Belfast.
Copied Jan 27, 1970 by Hoyte Ledford and Mrs. Thomas McAdams.

An Infant of
Josiah & Rebecca Blackwell
Feb 8, 1812
Jun 13, 1812

Rion Seaton
(no dates)

Infant of
F. (Frank) P. &
Cora Margaret (Foster)
Carter
Feb 1, 1907

Mrs. Margaret Cortner
            Johnson
1847-1926

John William Foster
Feb 4, 1849
Mar 27, 1904
&
Sarah Elizabeth
(Woodward) Foster
Jun 6, 1847
Sep 16, 1919

Patrick, son of
J. W. & S. E. Foster
Feb 11, 1874
Oct 1, 1888

Calham Luna
1829-Oct 20, 1877

Frances Victoria(Woodward),
wife of A.(Anthony). S(Smith).
Foster, Jr.
Jan 27, 1852
Feb 25, 1883

Emmie, dau of
Joseph & Mary A. Hastings
Sep 28, 1870
Apr 4, 1890

Infant of
Jas. A. & Louise A.
(Woodward) Mosley
(no dates)

George Woodward
Aug 26, 1796
Dec 12, 1868

Margaret, wife of
George Woodward, dau of
John & Margaret Porter
Apr 11, 1808
Jan 31, 1888
Age 79 yrs, 9 mos, 19 days

William L., son of
J. C. & M. J. McAdams
Nov 21, 1858
Aug 10, 1884
Age 25 yrs, 8 mos, 20 days

BELFAST

Joseph C. McAdams
Apr 12, 1822
Oct 5, 1908
&
Mary Jane (Woodward) McAdams
Sep 2, 1832
Feb 6, 1908

John Woodward
Sep 3, 1801
Jul 7, 1881
Age 79 yrs, 10 mos, 4 days

(Mary) Elizabeth (Mayes) Woodward
Died Mar 18, 1890
Age about 84 years old.

Father
William Richard Woodward
Sep 1, 1848
Jan 19, 1923

Mother
Eliza Jane (Mayes) Woodward
Mar 12, 1850
Mar 24, 1927

Henry Clay, son of
W. R. & E. J. Woodward
Aug 19, 1880
Apr 27, 1904

Several unmarked graves.

* *

WILLIAMS CEMETERY
Located on the west slope of the Round Hill, one and one-half miles east of Belfast, Tennessee. Information from Mrs. Daisy Orr of Belfast on Oct 31, 1972.

William Williams
Feb 13, 1774
Sep 26, 1840

Elizabeth Allison, wife of
William Williams
Born ----
Died Apr 4, 1850

one child grave, unmarked.

The markers have been removed and the graves are still enclosed by large long lime-stone rocks.

* *

BETHEL CEMETERY
Located one mile east of Old Belfast, on Needmore Road. Rechecked 1979 by Helen & Tim Marsh.

John, son of
S. & S. P. Ramsey
Died Mar 22, 185-
(no age given)

David, son of
S. & S. P. Ramsey
Died 1853
age 18 years, 3 months

Florence Adams
Aug 30, 1867
Jul 28, 1920

S. J. Adams
Sep 27, 1840
Apr 22, 1922

Cleopatria, wife of
S. J. Adams
Dec 18, 1844
Sep 11, 1910

Mary E. Adams
Jun 15, 1835
Jul 24, 1959

John S. Glenn
1871-1944
&
Rachel C. Glenn
1873-1913

Sammie Glenn
1875-1878

Jon W. Adams
Dec 26, 1836
Apr 29, 1892
& wife
Mary S. Adams
Jan 1, 1844
(no date)

Infant Son of
J. W. & Mary S. Adams
B&D Sep 28, 1862
&
Moddie, dau of
J. W. & Mary S. Adams
Aug 15, 1873
Aug 21, 1873

Archibald Adams
Born in Bedford County, Tennessee
Sep 30, 1811
Died Feb 3, 1850
Age 38 yrs, 4 mos, 3 days

Jane Adams
Jul 21, 1810
Sep 2, 1854

Father
L. C. Glenn
1841-1903
&
Mother
Lucy Glenn
1853-1909

Malissa A., wife of
M. T. Smith
Oct 29, 1846
Mar 25, 1885

Esther A. Jones
Jun 15, 1844
Jun 25, 1933

Mary Adams
Feb 15, 1879
Dec 16, 1882

William L. Davidson
Dec 21, 1835
Feb 7, 1853
Age 17 yrs, 1 mo, 16 days

Sophia Chapman
Nov 11, 1819
Jul 20, 1885

Kimbro Ogilvie Chapman
Sep 8, 1814
Jan 20, 1849

Eula Glenn
1882-1903

Infant Dau of
J. M. & M. J. E. McKee
Aug 4, 1883
Aug 9, 1883

Mary, dau of
William & Catharine Martin
Jan 11, 1802
Jun 9, 1884

Elizabeth P., Consort of
G. M. Coffey
May 14, 1848 (died)
Age 25 years.
&
Also an Infant Son

Sacred to the Memory of
John C. Garrison
&
His three children
(no names or dates)

S. I. Low
Aug 23, 1870
Nov 19, 1902

Seymor S. Low
1824-1881
&
Mary Bethira Low
1825-1908

Ana S., dau of
J. M. & M. J. E. McKee
Sep 18, 1884
Sep 26, 1884

BELFAST

Dovie E., dau of
J. M. & J. E. McKee
Oct 30, 1884
Nov 28, 1885

H. J. Brown
Jun 5, 1834
Aug 31, 1899
&
J. A. Brown
Nov 15, 1827
Nov 22, 1898

Little B., son of
D. & S. P. Adams
Jan 1, 1883
Oct 24, 1883

Father
W. P. O'Neal
Jan 7, 1826
Apr 8, 1880

Mother
Elizabeth H. O'Neal
Jul 24, 1837
Oct 6, 1866

Robert W., son of
P. K. & A. C. Ewell
Sep 25, 1850
Aug 24, 1872

Robert Williams
May 3, 1806
Jul 19, 1884
&
Julia F. Williams
Apr 19, 1811
Oct 20, 1884

Several unmarked graves.

Mother
Sallie L. Orr
Aug 16, 1843
Aug 14, 1911

Sadie Lee Orr
Jan 21, 1881
Nov 14, 1946

Julie Ann Adams
Died July 17, 1864
(no age given)

* *

BILLS CEMETERY

Located six miles northeast of Lewisburg and about three miles south of Farmington. Copied Apr 30, 1958 by Ralph D. Whitesell and Myrtle Lee Walker. Rechecked 1979 by Helen & Tim Marsh.

John A. Bills
1838-1915
&
Harriet N. Bills
1839-1921

Miss Jennie M. Bills
1867-1955

Infant Son of
J. A. & H. N. Bills
B&D Nov 16, 1880

Robert Lee, son of
J. A. & H. N. Bills
Jul 29, 1869
Nov 26, 1870

Clyde, son of
J. A. & H. N. Bills
Aug 16, 1882
Oct 1, 1882

Mrs. Sallie J. Dysart
Dec 27, 1827
Sep 7, 1906

Leila, wife of
M. A. Stallings
Aug 27, 1891
Jul 26, 1918

Marshall A. Stallings
Jan 25, 1868
Mar 19, 1956

James H. Neil, Sr.
Oct 19, 1809
Sep 7, 1849

Elizabeth P., wife of
J. H. Neil, Sr.
Apr 23, 1811
Jul 15, 1878

John A. Stegall
Aug 1, 1864
Mar 13, 1944

Nancy E. Stegall
Mar 10, 1872
Sep 4, 1959

D. M. Stegall
Jan 27, 1839
Feb 3, 1922

Mollie S., wife of
D. M. Stegall, Is resting
here, after many years of
suffering. She was Born
Sep 2, 1841
Died Dec 13, 1906

Tommie Stegall
Sep 27, 1873
Fell Asleep
Feb 15, 1876

Douglass Bliss Stegall
Born Dec 25, 1877
Suffered patiently & died
Peacefully Jan 16, 1907

Jane, wife of
Andrew Dysart
Feb 18, 1799
Apr 16, 1866
Age 67 yrs, 1 mo, 22 days

Cornelius Dysart
Aug 12, 1831
Dec 2, 1844
&
Arsenath Dysart
Nov 25, 1809
Feb 27, 1857

Infants of
T. M. & F. J. Noblin
(no dates)

Rebecca L., wife of
T. P. Wilson
Oct 31, 1841
Apr 1, 1899

G. B. Dysart
Apr 25, 1813
Mar 18, 1889

Mary B., wife of
Gideon B. Dysart
Feb 22, 1810
Nov 6, 1865

Infants of
J. A. & M. S. Ewing
(no dates)

George M. Coffey
Apr 13, 1825
Jan 14, 1902
&
Mary A. Coffey
Feb 23, 1825
Apr 6, 1908

Lizzie Coffey
Feb 19, 1850
Apr 27, 1926

Celia Noblin
Died Feb 12, 1859
(no age given)

John Dysart, Sr.
Dec 25, 1749
Sep 10, 1842
&
Martha Dysart
Jun 30, 1770
Sep 25, 1848

Charles T. Dysart
Jul 19, 1881
Aug 10, 1903

Celia E. Noblin Pyland
Dec 6, 1853
Apr 3, 1873

Laura A. Noblin
Sep 23, 1868
Jan 28, 1910

William Noblin
Co G 1 Tenn VID Cav
Mar 14, 1829
Nov 21, 1903

Louvenia Noblin
1837-1930

Amos L. Bills
Jul 21, 1807
Jan 4, 1843
Age 36 years

Mary A., wife of
Amos L. Bills
Jan 14, 1806
Nov 1, 1883

Hester A., wife of
Dr. T. A. McNail
Jun 10, 1832
Oct 16, 1852

Mrs. Martha N. Brown
May 23, 1832
Oct 17, 1900

Maggie F. Dysart
Dec 10, 1847
Feb 24, 1874

Father
John Dysart, Jr.
Aug 16, 1804
Dec 14, 1870
&
Mother
Rachel Dysart
May 10, 1805-May 23, 1874

BELFAST

L. W., son of
D. L. & M. E. Barnett
Jul 2, 1875
Jun 19, 1877

Ola Dysart
Jun 26, 1887
Sep 6, 1960

Ozro Dysart
(no marker)

Father
John H. Dysart
Jan 10, 1837
May 15, 1913
&
Mother
Margaret H. Dysart
Apr 6, 1843
Aug 31, 1897

William Dodridge, son of
W. H. H. & Mary C. Dysart
Oct 28, 1877
Nov 10, 1878

M. D. Dysart
Jan 18, 1852
Jul 24, 1924
& wife
Lou Ella Homes Dysart
Aug 27, 1856
Oct 10, 1894

W. H. H. Dysart
Sep 2, 1840
Sep 1, 1914

Several unmarked graves.

Mary C. Holmes, wife of
W. H. H. Dysart
Nov 18, 1844
Dec 29, 1891
Age 47 yrs, 1 mo, 11 days

John Palmer Dysart
May 13, 1875
Feb 2, 1910

Foxie Elizabeth Dysart
Oct 30, 1872
Oct 16, 1911

* *

CAMP GROUND CEMETERY
Located three miles east of Farmington, south of the Shelbyville Highway. Land owned by Robert Mason and Joe Ransom. The site was once a campground near a spring on East Rock Creek. Originally white people, later colored people. Copied Aug 12, 1958.

Calvin H., son of
L. J. & M. F. Sweney
Dec 2, 1853
Oct 5, 1856

Amanda V., dau of
L. J. & Mary F. Sweney
Aug 20, 1858
Feb 29, 1864

75-100 unmarked graves.

Nancy C. McCrory
Dec 12, 1812
Oct 25, 1853
Age 40 yrs, 10 mos, 11 days

Mary, wife of
Jeremiah Claxton
Oct 5, 1805
Oct 6, 1836

* *

DYSART CEMETERY
Located two miles south of Farmington, on the Belfast Road.

Robert L. Dysart
Jan 9, 1775
Jul 11, 1835
Age 60 yrs, 5 mos, 2 days

Susan Dysart
Dec 28, 1775
Oct 25, 1831
Age 55 yrs, 5 mos, 28 days

1 unmarked grave.

* *

ELLISON CEMETERY
Located east of Farmington, on the Jess Woodward farm. Copied in 1965.

Sacred to the Memory of
John Ellison
Oct 20, 1762
Jul 24, 1831

Sacred to the Memory of
Polly Ellison
Who was born
May 6, 1776
Died Oct 30, 1826

Joseph S. Ellison
Oct 13, 1798
Oct 6, 1826

Robert E. Ellison
Sep 16, 1840
Sep 15, 1855

Infant Son of
James & Polly Adams
(no dates)

William Warren, son of
John & Miranda Ellison
May 1, 1834
Oct 31, 1845

William A. D., son of
James L. & Betsy Ewing
Dec 6, 1825
Jul 2, 1827

3 unmarked graves.

Joseph S., son of
Thomas & Nancy Ellison
Died August 1827
age 7 months

Hanah A., dau of
Thomas & Miranda M. Ellison
Nov 10, 1830
Jan 5, 1831

* *

BELFAST

HEAD SPRINGS CEMETERY

Located two miles south of Belfast, on Old Fishingford Road. The Old Head Springs Associate Reformed Presbyterian Church, now inactive, is located beside this Cemetery. Copied Oct 25, 1959 by Ralph D. Whitesell and Lounora Pickens.

Jesse, son of
Joseph & Mary McAdams
Died Jun 3, 1839
Age 1 yr, 2 days

Jesse McAdams
Died Nov 4, 1839
Age 24 yrs, 6 mos, 8 days

Mary, Consort of
William P. O'Neal
Mar 22, 1834
Aug 15, 1851

Sarah, dau of
Peter M. & Elizabeth
Glascock
Oct 1, 1834
Mar 15, 1835

Susie, wife of
H. C. Wherley
Jan 1, 1865
May 27, 1885

Elizabeth, wife of
H. C. Wherley
Mar 8, 1871
Mar 3, 1890

William Tobe Cockran
1875-1952

Robert Hoyle
1824-May 15, 1904

George C. Neill
Aug 15, 1783
Aug 27, 1844
Age 61 yrs, 12 days

James Neill
Jul 13, 1807
Sep 22, 1872

Lively Roberts, wife of
James Neill
Nov 9, 1805
Feb 20, 1895

Sarah McAdams
Died Jan 17, 1874
Age 65 years

James Thomas Shirley
1866-1960

Ida Jane Shirley
1876-1958

William S. King
1863-1949

Mary Moore King
1890-19

Luther Dayton King
1901-1959

Gertrude Adams
1887-1957

Albert Adams
1885-1961

Myra S., dau of
Mr. & Mrs. Jirel Brown
Jul 11, 1952
Aug 31, 1955

Leonard H. Twitty
1882-1947

Vertie Twitty
1887-1946

John Tosland
9th Ohio Batry
1810-Jun 6, 1900

James E., son of
M. J. & M. A. O'Neal
Sep 14, 1901
Dec 27, 1901

Augusta E. Wingfield
Tenn. Wagoner Supply
Co 52FA   WW I
Apr 7, 1891
Aug 27, 1957

Joe Cowden Bills
Mar 4, 1904
Jan 8, 1945

Mattie Sue Bills
Sep 6, 1902

Clemma Bethume
Jul 11, 1871
Jun 13, 1878

Emily L. Bethume
Feb 20, 1870
May 13, 1870

Dempy E. Caughran
Died Apr 24, 1864
Age 18 years

Jane, dau of
John & V. McLain
Sep 20, 1810
Sep 30, 1812

Douglas McLain
Died Sep 16, 1863
Age 80 years

Erwin McLain
Was murdered for his
Money Dec 15, 1863
Burried Jan 21, 1864
Age 24 years.

Henry M. McLain
Jan 31, 1811
Mar 26, 1842

Nancy McLain
Died Oct 9, 1888
Age 75 years

Mary Katharin, dau of
Henry & Nancy McLain
Nov 8, 1839
Dec 13, 1841

Elizabeth Adams
Jul 17, 1819
Apr 1, 1847

Alice B., wife of
J. C. Whitsett
Jan 15, 1857
Sep 1, 1890

Allen Whitsett
Mar 15, 1868
Mar 3, 1904

James M. Bartlett
Died Aug 25, 1871
Age 4 yrs, 7 mos, 15 days

Era, dau of
H. S. & C. C. Bartlett
May 4, 1896
Mar 15, 1897

H. S. Bartlett
Dec 27, 1851
Mar 19, 1900

C. Ernest Bartlett
Nov 20, 1877
Nov 1, 1910

Absalom Whitsett
1812-Aug 22, 1854

James Kidd
1803-Jan 3, 1887

Sarah Ann, Consort of
George Glascock
Died Nov 10, 1845
Age 27 yrs, 10 days

H. B. Cummings
Jan 29, 1811
Sep 9, 1889

Mary P., wife of
H. B. Cummings
Jan 13, 1813
Jun 23, 1897

Hettie, wife of
J. M. Petty
1861-1940

J. M. Die
Feb 24, 1860
Oct 17, 1898

M. J., wife of
N. A. Freeman
Mar 9, 1865
Mar 23, 1899

Frank Allen McDaniel
Jul 6, 1938
Jul 6, 1938

Merlene Dyer
Apr 29, 1937

Arthur Moore
Mar 15, 1882

Etta Moore
Aug 29, 1883
Nov 2, 1957

Luther McAdams
Jan 1, 1887
Mar 25, 1945

Walter McAdams
1873-1946

J. B. McAdams
May 19, 1828
Jul 28, 1911

Maggie, dau of
William & Mary Cummings
Jul 20, 1877
Jan 22, 1903

Minnie, dau of
William & Mary Cummings
Jan 1, 1870
Oct 28, 1871

BELFAST

Cecil Cummings
Jun 14, 1880
Jan 22, 1956

William Cummings
Feb 1, 1844
Nov 13, 1930

Sarah Glascock Sanders
Sep 16, 1846
Aug 18, 1930

G. E. Glascock
Jul 17, 1838
Dec 10, 1884

Catherine Orr
Dec 25, 1804
Aug 14, 1888

J. C. Orr
Feb 4, 1813
Sep 10, 1885

Margaret, wife of
John Orr
Died Sep 7, 1868
Age 85 years

John Orr
Died Apr 11, 1862
Age 92 years

John Riley, son of
Allen & Rachel Orr
McDaniel
Nov 1846
Sep 1857

Rachel Orr, wife of
Allen McDaniel
Dec 7, 1819
(illegible)

Elizabeth Orr
Sep 27, 1811
Died   1837

Robert, son of
R. H. & Susan Orr
Aug 9, 1832
Jul 9, 1847

Fredrick, son of
John & Nancy Jane Orr
Aug 19, 1862
Nov 7, 1862

Beaugard, son of
Samuel & Catherine Orr
Sep 7, 1861
Nov 1, 1862

Marmadore, son of
Samuel & Catherine Orr
Aug 8, 1870
Feb 10, 1871

Infant of J. H. & M. F. Orr
B&D Feb 18, 1878

Samuel Orr
Feb 21, 1803
Oct 23, 1879

Robert A. Orr
Jun 7, 1801
Mar 21, 1878
Age 76 yrs, 9 mos, 14 days

S. F., son of
Samuel & Margaret Orr
Dec 9, 1863
Feb 3, 1887
Age 23 yrs, 1 mo, 25 days

Susannah, wife of
R. A. Orr
Dec 4, 1807
Dec 5, 1895

Margaret Catherine, wife
of Samuel Orr
Mar 14, 1843
Jan 2, 1913

Samuel Orr
Nov 30, 1828
Jul 27, 1901

Maggie P., wife of
W. E. Welch
Jan 29, 1880
Jan 25, 1907

Henry W. McDaniel
Tennessee
Pvt 157 Depot Brigade
Died Jan 5, 1933

Sallie G. Lasater
Sep 1, 1886
Mar 12, 1907

Mary C., dau of
M. T. & S. G. Lasater
Jun 10, 1905
Aug 13, 1905

Andrew J. Blackwell
Dec 19, 1836
Feb 4, 1905

Mary Jane, wife of
A. J. Blackwell
Mar 3, 1847
Jun 28, 1898

William Luther Blackwell
Sep 1, 1870
Nov 8, 1890

Mary E. Blackwell
Jan 20, 1875
Sep 16, 1890

John T. Blackwell
Oct 12, 1868
Aug 20, 1890

John, son of
E. & D. McAdams
Oct 13, 1812
Jul 8, 1842

Erwin Calvin, son of
Erwin & Dorcas McAdams
Jan 29, 1828
Oct 8, 1845
Age 17 yrs, 8 mos, 9 days

Erwin McAdams
Died Oct 21, 1861
Age 76 years

Dorcas McAdams
Died Nov 17, 1865
Age 73 years

Joseph McAdams
Aug 22, 1810
Aug 16, 1842

Maggie, dau of
C. W. & Mary E. Hunter
Died 1861
Age 5 years

Mary E., wife of
C. W. Hunter
Oct 5, 1834
Sep 28, 1871

Philip B. Adams
Aug 18, 1861
Jul 15, 1936

Annie C. Adams
Nov 13, 1871
Dec 26, 1954

Lawrence R. Harris
1874-1933

Ollie J. Luna
1869-1945

Mary M. "Kate" Luna
1873-1950

Alice F., dau of
J. W. & L. J. Crunk
Aug 21, 1891
Sep 15, 1892

Lula Edna, dau of
J. W. & L. J. Crunk
May 3, 1882
Sep 25, 1882

Daniel, son of
Samuel & M. E. McAdams
Died Dec 1878

Mary E., wife of
Samuel McAdams
Mar 10, 1840
Jan 8, 1878
Age 37 yrs, 9 mos, 28 days

S. H. McAdams
Dec 6, 1833
Jan 25, 1900

Luther E., son of
S. H. & M. E. McAdams
Oct 16, 1867
Sep 6, 1887

Elizabeth Jane, dau of
Erwin & Dorcus McAdams
Oct 14, 1840
Age 9 yrs, 2 mos, 4 days

Infant Son of
J. & D. E. Leonard
Jun 30, 1854
Jul 24, 1854

Margaret E., wife of
J. H. Glenn
Sep 8, 1842
Sep 26, 1911

J. H. Glenn
May 28, 1837
Mar 23, 1888

Knox, son of
J. H. & M. E. Glenn
Aug 15, 1877
Jun 20, 1880

Infant Son of
J. H. & M. E. Glenn
Feb 11, 1875
Feb 12, 1875

Mary E. L., dau of
J. H. & M. E. Glenn
Jan 2, 1864
Feb 11, 1868

James D. King
Apr 24, 1843
Dec   1864

Joseph, son of
F. F. & S. F. Crabtree
Oct 13, 1907
Jul 20, 1908

Grace, dau of
F. F. & S. F. Crabtree
Apr 26, 1903
May 25, 1903

Fannie, wife of
F. F. Crabtree
Dec 25, 1868
May 24, 1908

Fred Crabtree
1868-1939

Thomas W. Twitty
Mar 8, 1841
Jan 12, 1912

BELFAST

Mary M. J. Twitty
Oct 15, 1846
Jan 20, 1915

M. O., dau of
I. W. & M. J. Twitty
Aug 25, 1866
Feb 9, 1890

S. L. Twitty
1872-1958

Anna Sue Twitty
1876-

A. D. McAdams
Apr 22, 1818
Aug 12, 1870

Nancy A., wife of
A. D. McAdams
Jan 4, 1824
Apr 12, 1885

Nina Bell & Tomie,
Children of
E. J. & Fannie McAdams
(no dates)

Faney Eler (McAdams)
Jan 18, 1857
Aug 14, 1857

Samanthey Adaline, dau of
J. B. & M. C. McAdams
Dec 20, 1852
Sep 19, 1867

Infant Son of
A. S. & S. E. Ledford
B&D Apr 14, 1884

A. S. Ledford
Nov 22, 1859
Mar 26, 1938

Sallie E. Ledford
Mar 4, 1867
Apr 19, 1884
(1st wife)

Virginia E. Ledford
Feb 8, 1857
Mar 3, 1908
(2nd wife)

John Leonard
Mar 21, 1819
Feb 8, 1892

Dorcas E. Leonard
May 4, 1818
Feb 10, 1900

James Davis
Dec 29, 1813
May 6, 1894

Malinda P. Davis
Apr 8, 1818-Sep 12, 1887
Age 69 yrs, 4 mos

Sarah A. Ellison
(nee Davis)
Sep 30, 1839
Mar 2, 1858
Age 18 yrs, 5 mos

Mary Thompson
Apr 24, 1786
Nov 28, 1860

Elizabeth McAdams Haskins
1887-1949

Infant of
Mr. & Mrs. Lee Marsh
B&D 1939

J. C. McLain
1876-1946

Allie, wife of
J. C. McLain
1875-1930

Thomas H. Twitty
May 8, 1882
Feb 21, 1938

Maggie E., wife of
T. C. Ellis
Jul 1, 1867
Nov 24, 1890
Age 23 yrs, 4 mos, 23 days

Infant of
L. H. & M. M. Twitty
B&D Apr 20, 1880

Samie L., son of
L. H. & M. M. Twitty
Sep 15, 1878
Sep 1, 1879

L. H. Twitty
Jan 1, 1843
Jan 13, 1929

Mary Harper Twitty
Sep 30, 1845
Jun 11, 1911

Infant Son of
R. S. & M. C. Walker
B&D Sep 28, 1889

Infant Son of
R. S. & M. C. Walker
Jul 26, 1884
Aug 20, 1884

Infant Son of
R. S. & M. C. Walker
Jun 11, 1881
Jun 21, 1881

Gertie, dau of
R. S. & M. C. Walker
Sep 30, 1879
Jun 25, 1880

James R. Neill
Sep 5, 1818
Jul 29, 1885

Matilda Neill
Aug 5, 1818
Aug 17, 1886

Esther Montgomery
Died Nov 10, 1859
Age 83 years

Lois M., dau of
J. M. & S. S. Leonard
Sep 12, 1837
Dec 22, 1872

Infant Son of
J. M. & S. S. Leonard
B&D Dec 24, 1874

W. Truman Leonard
Jul 27, 1887
Feb 19, 1920

Nettie M. Leonard
Aug 3, 1853
Mar 19, 1918

W. J. Leonard
1846-1898

Mary B. Beard
Jan 6, 1901
Nov 28, 1901

James S. Beard
Oct 22, 1872
Nov 28, 1879

Willie & Jimmie,
Infant Sons of
G. H. & O. M. Waters
May 13, 1886
Aug 6, 1886

M. W. Beard
Mar 2, 1800
Jan 12, 1888

Mary H., wife of
W. D. Beard
Aug 30, 1840
Nov 2, 1888

W. D. Beard
Mar 29, 1842
Jul 15, 1925

O. W. Rowland
1923-1936

Thomas L. Rowland
1890-1944

Ina M. Rowland
1889-

John T. Ray
1870-1943

Myrtle Ray
1874-1942

J. B. Armstrong
Dec 14, 1840
Nov 10, 1925

E. J. Armstrong
Sep 30, 1851
Oct 22, 1929

R. L. Davis
Dec 9, 1871

M. E. Davis
Oct 6, 1876

Carrie Chalmers, dau of
M. D. & Carrie Bell
Feb 4, 1886
Oct 4, 1886

Infant Son of
C. S. & M. B. Young
Mar 15, 1872
Mar 23, 1872

J. W. Bell
Nov 5, 1813
Oct 12, 1892

Ester Orr, wife of
J. W. Bell
Mar 20, 1815
Nov 23, 1895

Andrew J., son of
J. W. & Hettie Bell
May 15, 1860
Apr 12, 1862

J. W. C., son of
W. N. & M. J. Davis
Aug 26, 1873
Oct 14, 1876

James L. Davis
May 5, 1884
Dec 15, 1904

W. N. Davis
1849-1931

Mary Davis
1853-1921

Robert Orr, II
Jul 8, 1871
Mar 15, 1947

M. Della Orr
Sep 9, 1871
Mar 1, 1947

William B. McAdams
Oct 10, 1852
Sep 9, 1903

BELFAST

Bessie McAdams
Jun 27, 1882
Aug 3, 1897

Johnnie, wife of
W. D. McAdams
Dec 4, 1858
Dec 4, 1885

John T. Caughran
1875-1930

H. T. Burt
1858-1946

Maggie F. Burt
1872-1950

Leila Brown McAdams
1882-1957

Sherman McAdams
1866-1948

Bettye Jane, dau of
R. A. & J. E. Lancaster
Oct 15, 1926
Nov 25, 1926

E. J. McAdams
Apr 6, 1835
Mar 27, 1906

Fannie A. McAdams
Feb 8, 1839
Dec 23, 1906

Mary Ida, wife of
J. W. Adams
Dec 10, 1862
Aug 15, 1895

Julia McAdams
Jul 25, 1871
Jul 20, 1931

Dan W., son of
Sherman & Leila McAdams
Nov 16, 1917
Dec 23, 1936

Leila McAdams Walker
1909-1950

Ada Cummings
1870-1930

Zola Cummings
1884-1938

Deed Cummings
1847-1922

Evie Cummings
18-- - 1904
(illebible)

Undine Armstrong
1884-1946

A. D. Armstrong
Jan 12, 1844
Jun 19, 1906

L. M. Armstrong
Mar 13, 1846
Jan 1, 1912

Bonner D., son of
A. D. & L. M. Armstrong
Jan 10, 1888
Dec 20, 1905

May M., dau of
A. D. & L. M. Armstrong
Feb 21, 1877
Nov 22, 1902

S. D. Cunningham
Feb 24, 1823
Jun 12, 1896

E. A. Cunningham
Apr 5, 1828
Dec 1, 1922

Joe B. Cunningham
Died 1940
(no age given)

Robert L. Cunningham
Dec 9, 1863
Nov 16, 1900

Mary K. Cunningham
Oct 29, 1858
Aug 1, 1880

George A. Cunningham
Jun 25, 1852
Oct 25, 1887

Maggie E. Cunningham
May 28, 1847
Dec 3, 1878

Margaret, wife of
George A. Armstong
Feb 15, 1807
Mar 29, 1894

Joseph McLean
Jan 4, 1831
Feb 2, 1868

Rachel, wife of
Joseph McLean
Mar 3, 1829
Nov 4, 1903

Gus A. McLane
Aug 14, 1836
Jul 31, 1905

Margaret Eliza McLane
Jun 12, 1850
Nov 26, 1920

Alfred, son of
G. A. & M. E. McLane
Died May 15, 1881, 6 mos.

Flora N., dau of
G. A. & M. E. McLane
Oct 7, 1886
Oct 31, 1887

Lura Glenn
Nov 10, 1863
Nov 27, 1922

John Glenn
Jun 4, 1861
(no date)

W. M. Glenn
Nov 11, 1869
Sep 28, 1902

Oliver Caughran
1822-Apr 10, 1882

Sallie J. Caughran
Feb 9, 1855
Jun 22, 1882
Age 27 yrs, 4 mos, 13 days

America, wife of
O. H. Caughran
1819-Oct 4, 1902
Age 83 years

B. D. Caughran
Sep 24, 1853
May 5, 1883

Lou N., wife of
W. J. Caughran
Jul 13, 1858
May 20, 1912
Age 53 yrs, 10 mos, 7 days

W. J. Caughran
Mar 31, 1858
Aug 12, 1926

Mrs. R. L. McDaniel
1856-1931

R. L. McDaniel
Aug 31, 1859
Jul 11, 1912

L. J. Wherley
Jul 6, 1880
Mar 17, 1915

Mary Emma Craig
Dec 25, 1844
Jul 2, 1910

Sallie Davis
1866-1938

Gus T. Craig
Jun 3, 1868
Mar 29, 1889

Jessie Brison McAdams
Apr 5, 1830
Sep 22, 1894

M. M., son of
J. B. & M. C. McAdams
Jul 11, 1858
May 6, 1882

Kate McKamie, wife of
J. B. McAdams
Mar 22, 1828
May 15, 1921

Vernie, son of
J. N. & Dora Petty
(no dates)

Infant of
J. N. & Dora Petty
(no dates)

Dora Petty
1867-1898

Nathan Petty
1861-1943

Wiley Davis
1865-1933

Hattie Davis
1868-1940

Lottie C. Beatty
Nov 21, 1889
Apr 2, 1942

Hettie Lou Cummings
Feb 8, 1881
Nov 8, 1950

Newt Petty
1864-1899

Etta Petty
1867-1945

Mary E., dau of
M. N. & M. E. Petty
Oct 18, 1888
Oct 9, 1894

Zana Petty
Nov 11, 1896
Sep 13, 1900

Mary E., wife of
Dillard Petty
Nov 15, 1859
Oct 2, 1904

Dillard Petty
Aug 26, 1855
Oct 21, 1886

Infants of
J. E. & D. S. McLain
Sep 25, 1886
Oct 24, 1886

Granville P. Montgomery
Mar 27, 1873
Dec 31, 1942

BELFAST

Cordelia E. Montgomery
Apr 8, 1881

Minnie E. Montgomery
Jun 1, 1901
Jul 12, 1957

Infant Son of
J. D. & V. J. Miller
B&D Jan 25, 1883

Charlotte S., wife of
Andrew Miller
Feb 20, 1816
Oct 18, 1903

John D. Miller
Aug 6, 1855
Jun 5, 1920

Josie Neil Miller
May 1, 1855
Jul 5, 1935

D. M. Wilmer Leonard
Jul 29, 1882
Jan 26, 1896

Albert Sydney Leonard
Dec 2, 1867
May 24, 1890

J. C. Leonard
Nov 28, 1840
Jul 21, 1917

M. A., wife of
J. C. Leonard
Apr 14, 1846
Mar 25, 1918

Esmond Willis
1895-

Julia Willis
1894-1948

Tommy K. Woodward
1957-1960

Julia Ann Woodward
1953-1956

Oliver Holt
Tennessee
Cpl HV Mort Co 5th Inf
24 Inf Div Korea
Jun 13, 1927
Apr 19, 1951

Lewis W. Davis
Apr 9, 1872
Apr 9, 1957

William J. Adams
1868-1935

May Etta Adams
1867-1959

Ethel, dau of
W. M. & M. E. Hardy
May 6, 1904
Jul 20, 1904

Ethel, wife of
W. M. Hardy
Aug 5, 1875
May 16, 1904

D. C., wife of
G. W. Foster
Jan 13, 1849
Jun 6, 1889

G. W. Foster
Nov 18, 1842
Sep 22, 1922

Nannie Wilson Foster
Apr 2, 1865
Dec 12, 1951

Joseph C. Orr
Feb 21, 1853
Apr 4, 1928

Dorcas Tennessee Orr
Jul 8, 1848
Sep 4, 1913

Joe Orr
Mar 18, 1889
May 18, 1890

Tommie Orr
1886-1951

Lessie Orr
1879-1959

Sam Orr
1875-1958

Margaret C., wife of
N. A. McLain
Oct 13, 1821
Oct 4, 1893

Other & Niner, children of
D. J. & Addie Lasater
(no dates)

Riley Calahan
Feb 24, 1888
Sep 13, 1904

Luther Calahan
Jun 26, 1883
Dec 2, 1901

Allen McDaniel
Born around the year 1821
Died Feb 8, 1890

Margaret C., wife of
J. K. Calahan
Dec 23, 1853
Jun 3, 1907

Mary Fox
Dec 17, 1826
Dec 5, 1900

Maggie E., wife of
S. O. Crutcher
Jun 16, 1867
Apr 6, 1891

Mary Kate, dau of
S. O. & M. E. Crutcher
Jul 28, 1889
May 27, 1890

Joe Shearin, son of
S. O. & M. E. Crutcher
Mar 5, 1891
Jun 4, 1891

Jocephus Turner
1874-1894

Fannie Turner Brown
1871-1954

John A. Orr
Mar 12, 1855
Jan 5, 1903

John Orr
Oct 17, 1826
Apr 28, 1914
Age 87 yrs, 6 mos, 5 days

Nancy Jane, wife of
John Orr
Feb 2, 1828
May 28, 1908

R. B. Cummimgs
1855-1940

Mary Petty Cummings
1857-1942

Robert C. Cummimgs
Apr 7, 1884
May 30, 1945

Lessie C. Orr
1880-1957

Daisy E. Orr
1878-

Robert Knox Orr
1872-1937

Joseph L. Orr
Tennessee
Corp 427 Motor SUP Inf MTC
Oct 7, 1868
Feb 14, 1937

Joe P. Orr
May 27, 1888
Mar 11, 1941

Clemmie Orr Brown
Dec 18, 1868
Sep 30, 1919

J. N. Brown
Mar 7, 1870
Aug 11, 1950

Estelle, dau of
W. R. & R. T. Stallings
Jun 15, 1894
Jun 21, 1894

J. J. Endsley
Jun 9, 1858
Jul 11, 1894

Herman B., son of
R. E. L. & M. J. Watson
Aug 12, 1890
Feb 3, 1892

A. M. Endsley
Mar 7, 1826
Mar 3, 1908

Nancy L. Endsley
Oct 4, 1834
Jul 15, 1909

Julia E. Endsley, wife of
A. L. Smith
Jul 5, 1868
Jun 2, 1913

W. M. McLain
Oct 22, 1833
Oct 22, 1890

Mary C. McLain
Dec 25, 1821
Aug 10, 1908

William J. Petty
May 29, 1891
Sep 29, 1892

James W. Petty
Feb 28, 1895
Feb 14, 1896

Sidney Catherine Petty
Dec 8, 1857
Jun 28, 1905

Daisy F., dau of
W. T. & M. M. McAdams
Oct 10, 1898
Aug 27, 1913

Margaret Jane Johnson
Sep 2, 1862
Dec 30, 1911

Willie Johnson
Jan 27, 1901
Jul 11, 1911

E. D. Spray
1878-

Leota Spray
1878-1945

BELFAST

Janie, dau of
E. D. & L. Spray
Jan 28, 1905
Feb 7, 1905

J. H. McAdams
Dec 25, 1830
Dec 9, 1900

A. L. Calahan
Dec 7, 1840
Oct 8, 1905

Mrs. A. M. Calahan
Dec 7, 1841
Jan 13, 1926

Frank Adams
1842-1934

Jimme Joe Jordon
1940-1941

John Lyons
Mar 26, 1888

Erby Tate Lyons
Aug 29, 1894

Cecil C. Lyons
Jun 2, 1914
Jul 25, 1936

Hilda W. Pigg
May 31, 1928
Jul 25, 1933

Norah Hawkins
Nov 10, 1886
Oct 10, 1896

Infant of
D. E. & L. Spray
Jan 11, 1906
Jan 14, 1906

James A., son of
D. E. & L. Spray
Jan 14, 1909
Aug 6, 1910

James E. Spray
Nov 2, 1926
Dec 7, 1926

A. A. McAdams
Dec 5, 1858
Jul 17, 1927

J. A. Hawkins
Jan 9, 1843
Oct 19, 1922

M. E. Hawkins
Mar 17, 1850
Feb 15, 1931

T. H., son of
J. A. & M. E. Hawkins
Feb 19, 1891-Oct 2, 1892

W. O., son of
J. A. & M. E. Hawkins
Apr 12, 1870
Aug 4, 1892

Sam Hawkins
1888-1954

Atha Hawkins
1895-1961

Mary F. Ray
Oct 22, 1851
Jul 3, 1911

Joel F. Ray
Oct 5, 1846
Jul 12, 1917

Susan I. Ray
Feb 6, 1840
Aug 3, 1894

Anna F. Ray
Nov 26, 1880
Jul 18, 1893

J. Clarence Tate
Dec 22, 1871
Oct 9, 1939

Julia Orr Tate
Jun 22, 1875
Jun 22, 1960

Robert S. Orr
1850-1938

Alpha Orr
1856-1934

Una Davis Ring
1880-1940

Ozro E. Ring
1882-1953

Mary, dau of
O. E. & Una Ring
B&D May 7, 1903

R. C., son of
O. E. & Una Ring
Jun 15, 1905
Jul 27, 1905

Luteshie Davis
Jun 18, 1841
Mar 26, 1929

J. W. Davis
Mar 8, 1838
Oct 23, 1902

Knox D. Bethune
Jul 20, 1877
Feb 17, 1899

George L. Bethune
Feb 11, 1880
Feb 4, 1899

D. A. Bethune
Dec 15, 1837
Nov 30, 1895

Euel G., son of
C. D. & N. T. Sanders
Jul 30, 1888
Jul 22, 1894

George D. Sanders
Mar 20, 1859
Feb 22, 1925

N. Tennie Sanders
Apr 25, 1860
Aug 8, 1927

W. J. Williams
1850-1928

Eliza McAdams Williams
1846-1930

Joe Ted Petty
1871-1942

Maggie B. Petty
1877-1898

James Earl, son of
S. A. & M. C. Whitsett
Sep 19, 1901
Dec 10, 1901

Alice Pearl, dau of
S. A. & M. C. Whitsett
Sep 1901
Jan 28, 1902

Samuel A. Whitsett
1856-1957

George Allman Harris
Sgt 538 Motor Truck Co
MTC WW I
Nov 4, 1895
Sep 19, 1957

Mary Lucille Calahan
Dec 17, 1901
Jan 5, 1906

Murphee T. Calahan
Nov 7, 1896
Oct 18, 1897

Lee Calahan
Aug 24, 1862
Jun 6, 1928

Ida L. Calahan
May 28, 1868
Jul 5, 1957

Gabbert Ray Davis
1926-1932

Roy C. Lasater
1894-1960

Sabra G. Lasater
1898-

Jennie M. Thompson
1905-

Sam Thompson
1887-1959

Leonard W. Martin
1956-1959

Orr McLain
Tennessee
WW I
Jul 8, 1894
Dec 6, 1951

Jackie Guthrie
Aug 5, 1951
Oct 26, 1951

George W. Crabtree
1874-1945

Ella M. Crabtree
1875-

Ewell Hawkins
1863-1936

Mary McAdams Hawkins
1869-

J. H. Orr
1837-1918

Martha F., wife of
J. H. Orr
May 27, 1845
Aug 4, 1910

R. D. Orr
Jan 20, 1872
Mar 3, 1901

Sallie D., wife of
A. L. Sanders
Jan 1, 1823
Dec 1, 1898

S. E. Davis
Oct 13, 1872
Feb 17, 1903

Mary E. Blackwell
1867-

John A. Blackwell
1867-1929

R. Ollie Williams
1872-

Nora E. Williams
1873-1940

John Whitsett
Oct 24, 1839
Jun 3, 1914

S. E., wife of
John Whitsett
Sep 28, 1846
(no date)

BELFAST

Wilburn W. Wells
1917-1939

Jimmie Dale Adcock
B&D 1943

Marshall Allison Gragg
Oct 16, 1890
Jan 13, 1905

Donie Bradshaw
Jul 21, 1843
Nov 3, 1911

J. M. Bradshaw
Mar 28, 1844
Mar 1, 1903

Everette Wade
1889-1929

Claudia Wade
1896-

Infant of
Marvin & Claudia Jones
(no dates)

Kenneth Calahan
Oct 18, 1881
Feb 23, 1903

Ross Calahan
Jul 28, 1897
Oct 22, 1898

E. M., Jr., son of
E. M. & Vera Harris
Sep 1, 1910

Alice A. Calahan
Nov 30, 1863
Aug 2, 1919

Bertha McAdams Petty
Mar 28, 1881
Apr 21, 1899

E. W. Petty
Feb 23, 1875
Feb 22, 1899

C. F. Petty
Jun 28, 1835
Oct 4, 1922

W. M. Petty
Oct 1, 1825
Feb 1, 1899

L. E. Petty, wife of
W. S. Cummings
Feb 9, 1878
Nov 4, 1898

H. Clyde Gabbert
1877-1938

Charles E. Gabbert
Apr 22, 1873
Jul 8, 1935

Lelar A. Ray
Dec 3, 1878
Mar 16, 1925

Lottie E. Miller Wilson
Mar 2, 1885
May 19, 1915

Ben T. Wilson
1883-1960

Mary Orr, wife of
W. B. McAdams
Oct 11, 1881
Jun 28, 1914

Mary C. Hazelwood
1864-1949

William D. Hazelwood
1863-1934

John Bryson McAdams
1871-1931

Mary Blackwell McAdams
1873-1952

J. P. Adams
Jan 28, 1853
Aug 12, 1935

Mrs. N. L. Adams
Mar 14, 1855
May 14, 1913

Amie Margaret
wife of J. T. &
L. B. Thrasher
Jan 28, 1906
Oct 21, 1909

L. M. Roberts
1856-1938

Emma Roberts
1845-1913

Hettie Lou Roberts
1883-

W. R. McAdams
Nov 12, 1847
Mar 11, 1925

M. A., wife of
W. R. McAdams
Oct 28, 1853
Jan 27, 1902

Rebecca, wife of
John Cavender
Jun 25, 1829
Jan 27, 1902

M. E. McKinney
1862-1914

R. L. McKinney
1886-1891

Charlie Tucker
Sep 18, 1885
Jan 18, 1902

Johnnie Tucker
Aug 28, 1892
May 9, 1900

Harris E. Adams
Aug 7, 1836
May 10, 1915

Sara A. Adams
Nov 4, 1836
Sep 26, 1915

George Sewell
1865-1938

Mayme Sewell
1894-1950

Tola Sewell
1869-1941

M. T. Sewell
Nov 3, 1831
Jun 29, 1905

Mary Sewell
1826-1923

Robert A. McCool
1880-1937

John Thomas McKinney
1891-1953

Alene McKinney
1901-

Will R. McKinney
1877-1941

Lois V. McKinney
1884-1946

Rolla Cummings
1874-1945

Eddie B. Leonard
Apr 11, 1870
Jul 7, 1927

Iola Twitty
Apr 15, 1870
Apr 15, 1945

Cora McCool
Dec 15, 1882
Jun 1, 1952

A. L. McCool
May 15, 1877
Oct 14, 1917

Martha Jane McCool
Jun 17, 1842
Dec 10, 1917

A. E. McCool
Jun 18, 1835
Oct 31, 1907

Wilma E. Laurine, dau of
E. B. & E. I. Leonard
Jun 18, 1899
Oct 24, 1911

Fannie E., wife of
Ewell L. Leonard
Sep 28, 1870
Mar 16, 1900

Infant of
T. S. & M. E. Leonard
Dec 3, 1908
Dec 6, 1908

Tolbert S. Leonard
1880-1959

Eunice H. Leonard
1887-

William Robert, son of
J. A. & S. W. McAdams
Jan 14, 1909
Dec 22, 1920

Mary Belle, dau of
J. A. & S. W. McAdams
Jan 17, 1900
Oct 11, 1907

J. A. McAdams
1875-1957

Sallie McAdams
1877-1943

Herman B. McAdams
1896-1960

Willie C. McAdams
1896-

Robert A. Pearson
(no dates)

Frank B. Robinson
Dec 26, 1887
Oct 15, 1918

Emma Adams Robinson
Apr 11, 1886

Lyndal, dau of
J. R. & F. L. Waters
Dec 12, 1913
Aug 21, 1916

Mary Waters
Oct 12, 1890
Feb 1, 1908

Henry Waters
1861-1907

BELFAST

Ophelia Waters
1860-1932

Myrtle Louise McDaniel
1914-

Lawson Landis
1904-1948

Luther McDaniel
1874-1950

Carrie W. McDaniel
1882-1944

J. W. McDaniel
1925-1931

James Whitsett
1859-1927

Nanie J. Whitsett
1859-(no date)

Sallie G., wife of
R. J. Crawford
Aug 26, 1886
Jul 31, 1909

A. D. Marsh
May 2, 1870
Feb 11, 1918

Susie F. Orr
1872-1940

F. March Orr
1880-1937

Rev. William Orr
Oct 8, 1842
Mar 21, 1929

Emily E. Orr
Jul 23, 1843
Feb 1, 1913

J. R. McDaniel
1877-1959

Susie P. McDaniel
1879-1953

N. F. Davis
Mar 14, 1847
Jul 19, 1933

Margaret Elizabeth Davis
1846-Mar 1, 1917

J. K. P. Davis
Mar 20, 1841
Jul 6, 1913

Maggie, dau of
Mr. & Mrs. Bob Pearson
Mar 28, 1886
Feb 27, 1913

Bessie, dau of
Mr. & Mrs. Bob Pearson
Jan 9, 1890
May 21, 1917

Robert C. Pearson
1853-1928

Nannie J. Pearson
1853-1933

Joe L. Beard
1880-1953

Lillian Elsa Beard
Sep 25, 1912
Feb 20, 1918

Wendell Wayne McDaniel
May 29, 1923
Jul 23, 1924

Russell McDaniel
Dec 22, 1920
Jul 2, 1922

William T. McAdams
1867-1935

Minnie Pearson McAdams
1880-

John E., son of
W. A. & M. C. Prosser
Mar 11, 1877
Dec 27, 1907

W. A. Prosser
Nov 7, 1849
Nov 5, 1926

M. C. Prosser
May 28, 1859
Aug 23, 1946

Will Welch
1873-1960

Mollie Welch
1872-1950

R. S. Welch
Dec 27, 1904
Mar 4, 1961

Jewell C. Whitsett
1907-

V. Roy Whitsett
1903-1959

Buddie Whitsette
1885-1951

Clara Mai Whitsette
1903-

T. A. McKinney
1850-1933

Willie H. Whitsett
Tennessee
Pvt Co A 138 Engineers
WW I
Sep 27, 1896
Feb 6, 1953

John Whitsett
1861-1936

Lina Whitsett
1861-1931

J. P. Calahan
Feb 18, 1833
Mar 10, 1913

Nancy J., wife of
J. P. Calahan
Dec 16, 1836
Apr 4, 1912

W. J. McClain
Mar 11, 1866
Jul 28, 1909

Fannie M., wife of
W. J. McClain
Oct 13, 1864
(no date)

Sallie L., wife of
A. S. Watson
Aug 29, 1874
Jul 13, 1911

R. W. McRee
Mar 25, 1854
Jun 12, 1915

H. Bell, wife of
R. W. McRee
Feb 18, 1863
Apr 10, 1911

Nannie May McRee
Nov 9, 1894
Nov 6, 1915

William B. McRee
(no dates)

Fannie McRee
(no dates)

J. Oscar McRee
(no dates)

George W. Marsh
Nov 11, 1847
Sep 22, 1915

Mable Odessa, dau of
W. W. & G. E. Marsh
Jun 16, 1913
Oct 16, 1918

Julius McKinney
1909-1911

James Ira, son of
W. W. & G. E. Marsh
Mar 25, 1917
Oct 14, 1918

Ruby Tiller
Jan 30, 1894
Nov 22, 1920

G. W. Dockery
Dec 5, 1850
Jul 6, 1921

Elizabeth Dockery
May 30, 1856
(no date)

James J. Gragg
Dec 13, 1865
Jan 15, 1935

Ardella T. Gragg
Jun 9, 1868
Feb 28, 1936

Comer T. Gragg
Aug 21, 1889
Feb 23, 1910

Rollie M. Gragg
Nov 7, 1901
Oct 1, 1909

Emma Lee, dau of
A. O. & M. E. Gragg
Nov 5, 1906
Sep 26, 1908

M. E. "Betty" Gragg
1886-1958

Francis Gragg
Dec 13, 1920
Sep 11, 1924

Joe T. McLain
1879-1943

Mary W. McLain
1881-1958

A. M. Murray
Feb 12, 1841
Dec 22, 1908

Edward Lee Gragg
Oct 16, 1911
Jul 17, 1919

James Helton
Dec 25, 1875
Mar 7, 1920

Janey Helton
Feb 14, 1822
Nov 13, 1849

Julia A., wife of
J. B. Helton
Oct 8, 1858
Feb 6, 1918

BELFAST

Jodie McKinney
1881-1946

Elser McKinney
1888-

Lena Lee, wife of
Albert McKinney
Mar 12, 1882
Nov 27, 1926

Mina McKinney
1890-

Albert McKinney
1880-1948

William B. Twitty
1882-1953

Macie Twitty
1893-1939

William F. Twitty
1913-1959

Christine A. Twitty
1917-

Paul Preston, son of
J. C. & Ola Twitty
1920-1930

Ada Jane, dau of
J. C. & Ola Twitty
Mar 8, 1922
Oct 10, 1923

G. H. Armstrong
Feb 6, 1836
(no date)

Susan, wife of
G. H. Armstrong
Feb 14, 1842
Jun 21, 1911

Blanch Armstrong
1869-1951

Blie Armstrong
1871-1955

Stonewall J. Ketchum
1875-1956

Maggie Sue Ketchum
1876-

Oliver L. Martin
Died Jun 17, 1915
Age 88 years

Dorcas E. Martin
Died Mar 19, 1916
age 65 years

Fountain Allison Martin
Tennessee
Pvt US Army
Died Jun 6, 1922

Clayton, son of
G. C. & Itis Marsh
Dec 24, 1913
Jul 7, 1915

J. C. McDaniel
May 6, 1851
Apr 30, 1932

Margaret Ann McDaniel
Jul 21, 1857
Mar 22, 1918

Will Woodward
May   1888
Dec 7, 1926

Zana Woodward
Nov   1887
Jul 22, 1955

W. M. Vernie Woodward
Nov 4, 1914
May 6, 1917

John Reed Adams
Jul 20, 1879
Jan 24, 1919

Sarah Ruth Adams
May 29, 1869
Aug 12, 1955

Dorothy Sanders Archer
1910-1954

William T. Sanders
1874-1920

Bettie L. Sanders
1888-

William F. McDaniel
Nov 4, 1847
Dec 29, 1936

Mattie P. McDaniel
May 13, 1850
Feb 2, 1921

Losson O. McDaniel
Sep 24, 1870
Mar 16, 1919

Jessie Lasater
1898-1920

Bonnie Lasater
1905-1921

Addie Lasater
1871-1934

Daniel Lasater
1868-1949

G. A. Armstrong
1878-1940

Mary M. Reed
1894-1951

Neal B. Reed
1890-1959

Emma M. Reed
1892-

James L. Wright
1911-1938

Edgar B. Watson
Apr 28, 1878
Nov 23, 1921

Ella McRee "Bim" Watson
Jun 13, 1879
Oct 11, 1950

Sadie Irene Watson
Dec 20, 1903
Nov 19, 1923

Julian Maryland Salisbury
1881-(no date)
Spanish American War
Veterian

James Buford Salisbury
1915-1917

Ellie Nora Salisbury
1879-1955

Bessie Beatty
Oct 20, 1883
Jul 8, 1925

Zora Priscilla Beatty
              Whitesell
Dec 8, 1883
Dec 28, 1959

Dora Ray, wife of
G. W. Beatty
May 29, 1868
Oct 10, 1927

George W. Beatty
Apr 26, 1841
Jan 31, 1917

James A. Leonard
Feb 10, 1932
Jul 8, 1932

Infant Son of
Mr. & Mrs. H. A. Leonard
1937

Hugh A. Leonard
1910-

Winona D. Leonard
1910-1955

Lela J. Daws
1890-1952

Thomas Clifford Caughran
Mar 25, 1906
Aug 11, 1958

James N. Caughran
Apr 13, 1883
May 16, 1961

Sammie L. Caughran
Jun 24, 1884
Oct 14, 1945

Hugh M. Cummings
1872-1941

Kate Cummings
1874-1957

Maggie Mai Cummings
Oct 15, 1905
Jan 11, 1917

Benjamin F. Adams
1868-1925

Earl Hanaway
1883-1937

Greta Hanaway
1888-

Catherine Hanaway
1928-1929

William T. McLain, Jr.
1885-1954

Callie McLain
1884-1945

Knox Bills
1869-

Maude Bills
1874-1945

Birdelle (no last name)
1900-1946

W. T. McLain
Aug 14, 1850
Jun 2, 1934

M. C. Armstrong, wife of
W. T. McLain
Apr 17, 1852
Apr 16, 1915

Emma McLain
Jun 22, 1872
May 10, 1950

D. W. Green
May 30, 1868
Aug 1, 1953

J. Anna Calahan, wife of
D. W. Green
May 21, 1872
May 2, 1926

Ralston F. Foster
Jul 17, 1912
Jun 30, 1959

BELFAST

Elizabeth, wife of
Ralston F. Foster
Jan 27, 1922

Jim Bell Graham
1890-1961

Hazel M. Graham
1890-

Emma K. McAdams
1881-1925

Will Cortner
(no dates)

Mary Cortner
(no dates)

Richard Lasater
1872-1943

Josie Lasater
1877-1939

Loyd Lasater
1915-1915

Willie Hunter Mosley
1916-1917

Reps H. Farler
1890-1955

Annie R. Farler
1895-1956

Dallas Bruce Mosley
1874-1952

Etta Glenn Mosley
1878-1954

Earl Prosser
1891-

Ester Prosser
1895-

Mary Hugh Prosser
1934-1935

Hugh Allen Prosser
1923-1934

Joe D., son of
J. D. & S. M. Madison
Oct 1, 1918
Nov 3, 1920

Doria F. Woodward
1857-1931

Sue E. Woodward
1860-1948

Noble Guy Barron
Tennessee
Seaman US Navy
Mar 8, 1894
Jul 21, 1932

Bennie Wright
Mar 1, 1850
Nov 16, 1923

Joe Frank, son of
Carl & wife, Wright
1934-1935

Roe Beney Gragg
Aug 30, 1893
Jun 26, 1926

Rosa L. Gragg
Nov 11, 1896

James E. Bass
May 20, 1902
May 16, 1954

Walter McCool
1868-1947

Ida McCool
1884-

Clara Eakes
Aug 17, 1898
Jan 5, 1947

Eliza Duckworth Calahan
1876-

Tom Calahan
1887-1955

END OF HEAD SPRINGS

John Chapman
Jun 20, 1894
Jun 7, 1960

G. R. "Buddie" Davis
1873-1947

Elsa J. Davis
1879-1958

George L. Foster
1878-

Nannie A. Foster
1876-1949

Edward H. Prosser
1868-1948

Bertha F. Prosser
1881-

Ever Dell Jernigan
B&D Jul 18, 1950

Joe Edd Spray
1906-1950

Grace M. Spray
1907-

Joe W. Spray
1929-1956

Betty J. Spray
1932-1957

Several unmarked graves

* *

MEDEARIS CEMETERY

Located on the Liberty Valley Road, on farm of Ernest McAdams, on the Old Petersburg Road from Lewisburg to Petersburg.

Capt. John Medearis
1744-1834
"A Revolutionary Soldier"
Erected October 1953 by
his descendants.

George W. Medearis
1823-1860
(This stone was moved to
this graveyard in 1950)
A grandson of John Medearis.

Other family members are believed to be buried here.

* *

McLAIN CEMETERY

Located on Old Fishing Ford Road, south of Belfast. Copied October, 1958.

Nancy Payton McLain
Was born 4th of May A.D.
1784 & departed this life
Jan 26, 1826. Age 42 yrs,
8 mos, 22 days.

8 graves marked with
fieldstones.

Jesse McLain
Died 1844
(no age given)

Flora Patterson McLain
1803-1867

All markers are broken.

* *

BELFAST

REED-WALKER CEMETERY

Located four miles northeast of Lewisburg and one and one-half mile west of Farmington, large rock enclosure adjoining the Temple Cemetery. Copied Apr 24, 1958 by Ralph D. Whitesell and Lounora Pickens. Re-checked 1979 by Helen & Tim Marsh.

Isaac W. Walker
Aug 6, 1800
Jul 11, 1887
& wife
Violet M. Walker
Jan 7, 1802
Jul 6, 1865
& Son
George W. Walker
Nov 13, 1837
Dec 26, 1865

Nancy A., Consort of
George C. Reed
Died May 22, 1861
Age 64 years

George C. Reed
Died Jun 14, 1822
Age 30 yrs, 4 mos

Melissa F., wife of
J. C. Pyland
Mar 2, 1818
Sep 19, 1885

Chapman B. Davis
Jul 13, 1820
Sep 13, 1855
Age 35 yrs, 2 mos

In Memory of
Violette Cathey
Who departed this life
Oct 28, 1848
Age 87 years

J. F. Tenison
Died Oct 6, 1871
Age 32 years

Eliza Tenison, wife of
Rev. T. A. Hardin
1866-1891

John Reed
Jun 15, 1767
Apr 6, 1847
Age 79 yrs, 9 mos, 22 days

Esther Reed
Apr 8, 1767
Sep 28, 1840
Age 73 yrs, 5 mos, 17 days

Violet M. Walker
Jan 2, 1802
Jul 6, 1865
Age 63 yrs, 6 mos
(2nd marker)

George C. Cathey
Son of J. & E. Reed
Died Jun 14, 1822
Age 30 yrs, 4 mos

James L., son of
J. & E. Reed
Died Oct 15, 1820
Age 20 yrs, 4 mos

Mary, dau of
George & Jane Bishop
Feb 20, 1837
Jun 22, 1837
Age 4 mos, 2 days

Joseph Alexander, son of
Alexander B. & Jane Reed
Died Dec 8, 1837
Age 8 yrs, 4 mos, 8 days

J. A. Tenison
Died Jan 12, 1873
Age 41 years

Isabella Dryden
Nov 28, 1805
Aug 18, 1884
Age 78 yrs, 8 mos, 20 days

Nathaniel Dryden
Died Sep 27, 1835
Age 38 years
"He left a beloved wife
and three little daughters
together with a great many
friends and inlaws to lament
his loss."

Infant Son of
A. B. & J. Reed
(dates broken)

Alexander B., son of
J. & E. Reed
Died Oct 31, 1836
Age 38 yrs, 8 days

John P., son of
J. & E. Reed
Died Jul 28, 1831
Age 24 yrs, 9 mos

Infant Son of
B. C. & E. M. Brantley
Jun 10, 1830
Died in a few hours.

James, son of
N. & I. Dryden
Died Aug 8, 1829
(broken)

Benjamin Brantley Tenison
May 20, 1861
May 30, 1924
&
Mattie Preslar Tenison
Jan 15, 1874
(no date)

Judith Esther, Second dau
of Benj. C. & Eliza M.
Brantley
Born Saturday night
Oct 22, 1836
Died Sunday morning
Dec 19, 1841
Age 3 yrs, 1 mo, 26 days

Infant Son of
N. & I. Dryden
Died December, 1831
First day of his life.

John N., son of
N. & I. Dryden
Died Jul 14, 1833
Age 9 months

Robert A., son of
N. & I. Dryden
Died Aug 20, 1835
Age 9 months

William W. Walker
Mar 23, 1842
Jun 16, 1923

Joseph Walker
Jan 14, 1901
Feb 4, 1976

Myrtle Lee Walker
Oct 21, 1902
Nov 25, 1976

Eva Belle Walker
Jul 16, 1900
Nov 17, 1975

J. Herman Walker
Feb 21, 1894
Nov 6, 1960

* *

ROUND HILL CEMETERY

Located one and one-half miles northeast of Belfast. Copied October and November of 1959 by Ralph D. Whitesell and Lounora Pickens.

Mary H. McBride
Born in Mecklenburg
County, Virginia
Dec 30, 1808
Died in Giles County,
Tennessee
Aug 5, 1868

George W. McBride
Born in Guilford County,
North Carolina
Feb 3, 1800
Died in Giles County,
Tennessee
Oct 12, 1862

J. P. Thompson
Jan 5, 1819
Nov 5, 1856

Rebecca B. Kerr
Nov 11, 1856
Sep 10, 1882

"Children of
K. K. & R. B. Kerr"
Infant Son
Jan 10, 1882
Jun 2, 1882
&
Little Mac
Jul 3, 1879
May 5, 1882

BELFAST

Eliza Kerr, dau of
David McGahey
Dec 11, 1820
Aug 8, 1875
Age 55 years

Mary, Infant dau of
Eliza Kerr
(no dates)

James McGahey
Born in North Carolina
Thursday Aug 10, 1797
Died Jul 2, 1876
Age 79 years

David McGahey
Born in North Carolina
Sep 25, 1794
Died in his 81st Year
in 1875

Sally McGahey
Born in North Carolina
Jan 29, 1794
Died Apr 22, 1884
In the 91st year of
her age.

Leah, dau of
David McGahey
Mar 28, 1824
Dec 23, 1896
Age 72 yrs, 9 mos, 17 days

Margarette, Dau of
David McGahey
Oct 19, 1837
Nov 27, 1908

Jean McBride
Died Jun 9, 1841
Age 82 years

Sally McBride
Died Dec 23, 1834
Age 71 years

Elizabeth Shaw
Died Nov 30, 1836
Age 88 years

James McBride
Died Jan 25, 1836
Age 85 years
(A Revolutionary Soldier)

Floyd Curtis
1900-1952

Margaret McGahey
May 28, 1757
Oct 24, 1849
Age 92 yrs, 5 mos

Joseph McBride
Apr 2, 1789
Aug 26, 1850

Robert J. Orr
Feb 11, 1813
Nov 29, 1913

Sarah Laws Orr
May 5, 1833
Mar 30, 1915

Tinie Mayes
1861-1933

Louis Mayes
1860-1944

Infant Son of
B. B. & M. J. Craig
B&D Aug 23, 1873

R. E. Lee, son of
B. B. & M. J. Craig
Mar 28, 1865
Nov 12, 1867

Mahala E. C., dau of
Samuel & Mary J. Coffey
Jan 6, 1860
Aug 9, 1865
Age 5 yrs, 7 mos, 3 days

John M., son of
R. J. & S. E. Orr
Jan 29, 1854
Jul 7, 1857
Age 1 yr, 5 mos 8 days

Robert Orr
Jun 14, 1764
Jan 5, 1855
(Revolutionary Soldier)

Leah, Consort of
Robert Orr
Died Jul 21, 1830
Age 62 yrs.

Alfred M. Orr
Born in North Carolina
Departed this life
Apr 16, 1826
Age 25 yrs, 7 mos, 14 days

Nellie M., dau of
R. J. & S. E. Orr
Oct 18, 1867
Sep 29, 1887
Age 19 yrs, 11 mos, 17 days

Elizabeth H. Dysart
May 2, 1803
Died   1884
Age 81 yrs, 5 mos.

John Dysart
Feb 14, 1802
Mar 15, 1835
Age 33 yrs, 1 mo, 5 days

R. E. Dysart
May 4, 1830-Jul 10, 1854
Age 24 yrs, 2 mos, 15 days

Alfred A. Dysart
Oct 9, 1832
Mar 7, 1863

John McBride
1752-Feb 12, 1826
(Revolutionary Soldier)

Margaret McGahey McBride
1760-Jul 5, 1821

Margaret, Consort of
Peter Carpenter
Who was born in N.C.
Sep 6, 1774 &
Departed this life
Nov 6, 1812
Age 48 yrs, 2 mos

James L. Coffee
Dec 25, 1791
Jun 22, 1837

Samuel Ramsey
Born in N.C.
Jul 29, 1767
Departed this life
Aug 18, 1829
Age 62 years

Mary, Consort of
Samuel Ramsey
Born in N.C.
Feb 6, 1770
Died May 17, 1847
Age 77 yrs, 3 mos, 11 days

Sarah P., Consort of
Samuel Ramsey & dau of
Robert B. & Jane Glenn
Apr 9, 1810
Feb 20, 1844
Age 33 yrs, 10 mos, 11 days

David Ramsey
Oct 9, 1799
Oct 27, 1844
Age 45 yrs, 18 days

John Endsley
Born in N.C.
Aug 13, 1769
Departed this life
Sep 21, 1828

Mary, Consort of
John Endsley
Aug 17, 1775
Oct 13, 1854
Age 79 yrs, 4 mos, 27 days

J. B. E., son of
Rev. W. & C. Burgess
Died Apr 13, 1850
Age 13 years

Martha Bingaman
Died Sep 22, 1840
Age 13 yrs, 2 mos, 2 days

Jane Coffey, dau of
James & Mary Coffey
Born Mar 20, 1797
Died (illegible)
(broken)

Jane, Consort of
Joseph Bigger
Died Nov 10, 1820
Age 43 years

Jefferson H. Brown
Oct 26, 1836
Jul 6, 1905

Malinda, wife of
J. H. Brown
1816-Feb 20, 1906

Joel Darnel
(no dates)
       & wife
Nancy Darnell
(no dates)

Sacred to the Memory of
James Coffey, Who was
born in Pennsylvania
August the 17th, 1761 &
Died the 20th of December
in Tennessee in the year
1836.
(Revolutionary Soldier)
Age 77 yrs, 4 mos, 3 days

Mary, wife of
James Coffee of Revolutionary Fame
Born Jan 28, 1769 A.D.
Died Jul 27, 1861 A.D.

Charles Ewing
(no marker)

Sacred to the Memory of
James Leeper, Son of
Allen & Elizabeth C.
Leeper
Born in Pennsylvania
28th of February A.D. 1745
Died 14th of April A.D.1811
in the 69th year of his
age.
(James Landsdown Scpt. Col.
Tenn - Revolutionary
             Soldier)

Mary, Consort of
James Leeper
Died Mar 29, 1828

Sarah, Consort of
J. L. Lowrey
Feb 7, 1750
Nov 10, 1837
In the 87th year.

Jane, Consort of
J. C. Coldwell
Aug 3, 1797-Apr 22, 1822
Age 43 years(dates wrong,?)

BELFAST

David, son of
J. L. & Sarah Lowrey
Feb 22, 1792
May 24, 1814
Age 22 yrs.

John L. Smiley
Sep 17, 1825
Oct 15, 1859

Our Father
W. C. Cummings
Apr 15, 1820
May 26, 1876

James M. Price
Sep 19, 1826
Jul 6, 1884

W. T. Arnold
1859-1934

Donie Arnold
1871-1936

W. L. Cummings
1852-1934

Louisa Cummings
1856-1920

Maggie Elizabeth Cummings
Nov 7, 1874
Feb 24, 1907

Sarah, wife of
H. B. Smiley
Dec 7, 1786
May 23, 1878

H. B. Smiley
Oct 22, 1795
Sep 17, 1870

Jane, Consort of
James Woods & dau of
Samuel & Ann Long
Jun 22, 1789
Aug 26, 1840
Age 51 yrs, 2 mos, 4 days

Harriet L., dau of
James & Jane Woods
Jan 10, 1825
Aug 24, 1840
Age 15 yrs, 7 mos, 4 days

Mary Bishop
Died Aug 10, 1823
Age 34 years.

David Patrick
Born Aug 10, 1796 in
State of S.C.
Departed this life
Mar 12, 1841

Thomas N. A., son of
Thomas P. & Mary Adms
Aug 12, 1834
Jul 13, 1875

Edward Jefferson, son of
James & Nancy M. Darnall
Nov 24, 1859
Sep 14, 1869

John Westley, son of
James & Nancy M. Darnall
Jul 9, 1861
Dec 19, 1863

Mary Malinda, dau of
James & Nancy M. Darnall
May 14, 1864
Apr 18, 1886

Sarah Amanda, dau of
James & Nancy M. Darnall
Feb 14, 1866
Aug 6, 1885

Mary T., wife of
W. R. Sanders
Jul 13, 1848
Jul 21, 1876

Sallie Davidson
Dec 29, 1798
Feb 12, 1874
Age 75 yrs, 1 mo, 14 days

Thomas Davidson
May 29, 1783
Mar 3, 1864
Age 80 yrs, 9 mos, 4 days

Napoleon B. Davidson
(no dates)

Rachel C., dau of
David & Elizabeth Cook
Mar 17, 1814
Dec 24, 1835

David, son of
Thomas & Nancy Cook
Sep 11, 1781
Sep 2, 1829

Elizabeth Cook
Sep 1, 1786
Nov 7, 1868

Mary B., wife of
Flavis Dysart
Oct 23, 1792
Dec 31, 1875

Harriet Ann, wife of
W. A. Hunter & dau of
E. B. & M. S. Woods
Jun 3, 1851
Aug 22, 1872

Francis H. Woods
1776-1849
&
Martha L. Woods
1775-1851
(NOTE: They gave the ground
for this cemetery)

Martha E., dau of
Martha & Francis H. Woods
Oct 6, 1814
Jan 13, 1817

Isaac Larue
Who departed this life
Oct 3, 1818
Age 65 years

Bethire Larue
Who departed this life
Feb 14, A.D. 1827
Age 60 yrs, 4 days

James H., son of
Isaac B. & Martha C. Larue
May 23, 1820
Jan 14, 1835
Age 14 yrs, 7 mos, 16 days

Sacred to the Memory of
William, son of
William & Elizabeth Anderson
Born in North Carolina in
the year of our Lord 1796,
March 10th. Departed this
life 1857, December 4.
Age 61 yrs, 8 mos, 24 days

Elizabeth, wife of
William Anderson
Oct 6, 1806
Aug 1, 1899

John L. Thomas
Jul 11, 1850
Sep 9, 1924

Susan Thomas
Apr 30, 1851
Jul 15, 1928

Infant of
Mr. & Mrs. J. J. Gragg
B&D Feb 27, 1893

Elizabeth Anderson
May 2, 1792
Dec 20, 1867

Synthia, wife of
Albert Anderson
Born in Georgia
Mar 26, 1797
Died Jul 28, 1861
Age 64 yrs, 4 mos, 20 days

E. H., Consort of
James L. Hazelett
Sep 7, 1816
Jul 1, 1859
Age 43 years
and
An Infant Daughter

Infant Daughter of
Albert & Synthia Anderson
Jul 9, 1835
Aug 4, 1835

Infant Dau of
Albert & Synthia Anderson
Jul 11, 1841
Aug 28, 1841
Age 1 mo & 11 days

Sarah E., dau of
Albert & Synthia Anderson
Dec 14, 1836
Sep 19, 1851
Age 14 yrs, 9 mos, 5 days

Robert Anderson
Bornd in South Carolina
the --(illegible)
Died Aug 14, 1826 in the
55th year of his age.

Robert W. Wood
Oct 14, 1824
Sep 2, 1851
Age 26 yrs, 10 mos, 18 days

Ollie Lee Jones
1909-1928
"From Detroit, Mich."

Audley W. Jones
Apr 17, 1875
Dec 5, 1948

Myrtle E. Jones
Nov 28, 1880
Jan 18, 1949

Son
Willie Lee Stephenson
Jan 23, 1900
Jun 4, 1929

Mother
Etta Stephenson
Jul 22, 1872
Jul 14, 1912

Mary L., wife of
W. L. Jones
Sep 29, 1836
Feb 10, 1908

W. L. Jones
Sep 3, 1833
Sep 14, 1909

Flavia A., wife of
W. L. Jones
Oct 27, 1834
Aug 17, 1883

Martha S. L., dau of
Ollie & Annie Coffey
Nov 15, 1844
Oct 12, 1887

L. J. Coffey
Died Jun 5, 1845
Age 21 yrs, 7 mos, 2 days

E. H. Coffey
Died Jun 28, 1845
(no age given)

BELFAST

Annie, wife of
Allen Coffey
Dec 28, 1804
Jul 2, 1873

Allen Coffey
Sep 26, 1800
Jun 26, 1884
Age 84 yrs, 4 mos

J. M. Coffey
Aug 27, 1830
Sep 10, 1901

M. C. Bradley
May 1, 1815
Aug 26, 1844

Joel Bradley
Died May 29, 1856
Age about 50 years

Thomas P., son of
Joel & Mary C. Bradley
Feb 26, 1837
Feb 2, 1838
Age 1 yr, 11 mos

L. N. Bradley
Dec 11, 1843
Jul 4, 1883

Gideon Dysart
1820-1845

Elizabeth A. Dysart
1816-1888

Mary J., wife of
Francis L. Woods
Oct 28, 1841
May 29, 1866

Infant Son of
J. H. & E. E. McAdams
Aug 4, 1850
Aug 21, 1850

Elizabeth, Consort of
John Miller & dau of
Francis H. & Martha S.
Woods
Apr 20, 1801
Sep 26, 1837
Age 36 yrs, 5 mos, 6 days

Infant of
Samuel & Sarah -------
1829

Andrew M. Woods
Jan 2, 1835
Sep 8, 1884

Thomas G. Woods
1869-1899

J. B. Woods
1845-1910

Addie B. Woods
1845-1919

Father
J. C. Woods
1887-1956

Mother
Annie M. Woods
1890-1949

Francis Bedford Woods
1873-1926

Margaret E. Woods
1875-1950

John Blackburn Woods
Nov 20, 1881
May 7, 1940

Sarah Woods Wilson
1878-1930

Father
S. L. Woods
Nov 10, 1867
Jul 2, 1926

Margaret E. Woods "Mother"
Sep 5, 1869
Nov 4, 1917

Jessie Woods
Nov 29, 1889
Dec 5, 1915

Infant of
S. L. & M. E. Woods
Jul 2, 1906
Jul 8, 1906

Sarah F. Miller
Jul 21, 1909
Nov 30, 1919

H. L. Miller
Apr 5, 1886
Mar 21, 1926

Hattie E. Miller
Sep 30, 1884

Will Cheeves
1883-19

Mary E. Cheeves
1891-1923

James B. West
1897-1924

Robert Arnold
1886-1951 (TM)

W. B. Hinton
Feb 17, 1882
Oct 20, 1957

Bobby
1939
(no last name on stone)

W. E. Woods
1879-1929

Ettie Mosley Ledford
Aug 27, 1871
Feb 3, 1946
mrd Apr 5, 1893

P. A. Ledford
Jan 26, 1870
Dec 30, 1951

Mary E. Woods
1885-

James A. Mosley
Feb 27, 1841
Sep 14, 1929

Lou A. Mosley
Dec 19, 1844
Jan 13, 1952

Gertrude Woods Endsley
1871-1950

Fount Endsley
Sep 2, 1907
Jan 16, 1910

Maggie Woods
1875-1950

Bedford Woods
Feb 14, 1809
Jun 21, 1892

Margaret Woods
Mar 9, 1810
Aug 15, 1895

Our Mother
Jane E., wife of
W. O. C. Smith
Jan 11, 1848
Aug 11, 1893

Vance Smith
Aug 6, 1873
Apr 2, 1902

W. O. C. Smith
Aug 20, 1840
Jan 30, 1909

Ethel J., wife of
J. H. Kinnard
Jun 27, 1871
Nov 14, 1910

Martha Caldonia McGahey
Dec 31, 1832
Sep 25, 1909

Alfred McGahey
Mar 6, 1827
Dec 16, 1914

Otto McGahey
Jan 4, 1858
Mar 20, 1926

Walter Lee Vickery
Sep 5, 1887
Jul 16, 1903

Mary Jane Vickery
Dec 20, 1885
Jun 24, 1921

Thomas A. Vickery
Apr 23, 1863
Nov 12, 1912

Brother
Bennie C. Vickery
Aug 23, 1889
Feb 23, 1923

Esther M., wife of
J. T. Jeanette
Apr 23, 1905
Sep 6, 1929

Dixie L. Cummings
1886-1959

John H. Cummings
1886-1937

Robert L. Cummings
Oct 24, 1891
Oct 20, 1918

Allen N. Woods
Died Jun 15, 1837
Age 25 yrs, 8 mos, 9 days

Amelia Woods
Jun 30, 1805
Apr 11, 1882
Age 76 yrs, 9 mos, 11 days

Mary F. Dysart
Nov 11, 1849
Mar 29, 1934

Jane M. Dysart
Jun 22, 1843
Jul 13, 1905

Thomas B., son of
James & Mary Dysart
Feb 5, 1875
Nov 26, 1908

Robert N. Allison
1869-1936

Jeffie W. Allison
1883-1956

Infant Son of
R. N. & Jeffie Allison
Oct 5, 1909
Dec 12, 1909

BELFAST

Thomas Allison
1871-1942

Maud W. Allison
1875-1955

Infant Son of
Mr. & Mrs. C. L. Bussart
1952

Infant Dau of
Mr. & Mrs. C. L. Bussart
1950

Allie Jones
(no dates)
&
Lula Jones
(no dates)

Sister
Sallie B. Allison
1867-1957

Brother
Julian M. Allison
1877-1948

Magness W. Allison
1874-1890

Mary Allison
1887
Age 18 days

Margaret E., wife of
M. W. Allison
Jul 22, 1844
Aug 8, 1887

Mattie J. Andrews
May 24, 1852
Oct 6, 1896

W. Jones Andrews
Jul 16, 1850
Nov 19, 1894

Sarah H. Allison
Died Jan 30, 1887
(no age given)

T. H. Allison
Died Apr 6, 1880
(no age given)

Mary A. Allison
Dec 25, 1834
Nov 22, 1885

Dr. M. W. Allison
Sep 10, 1832
Sep 10, 1911

Arthur Emanuel Overholser
1884-1953

Mattie Dysart Overholser
1885-

Mary Jane Stockton
Jun 31, 1838
Jul 2, 1838
&
W. M. Stockton
Aug 20, 1839
"Infants of
L. D. & S. W. Stockton"

S. W., Consort of
L. D. Stockton
Dec 25, 1809
Mar 10, 1846

Virginia Josephine, dau of
H. D. & Elizabeth Adams
Feb 5, 1841
Jul 3, 1842

James Dennie Adams
Dec 9, 1842
Jun 8, 1917

James Adams
Born Feb 24, A.D. 1775 &
Departed this life
Oct 11, A.D. 1842
In the 67th year of his age.

Sarah Latricia Caperton
Jan 29, 1844

A. L. Rodgers
1883-195- (TM)

Vaun, son of
J. T. & S. H. Endsley
Dec 28, 1870
Oct 5, 1875

J. D. Rodgers
1914-1931

Lena M. Daniel
1888-1942

Mrs. F. Curtis
1881-1958 (TM)

Walter C. Curtis
1872-1952

Susie C. Curtis
1882-19

Lucinda M. Anderson
wife of James Price
May 28, 1862
Oct 28, 1884

W. C. Hazelette
Mar 26, 1835
Sep 1, 1843

M. E. Hazelette
Sep 29, 1837
Sep 4, 1848

Robert M., son of
Milion & Connie P. Cummings
Apr 7, 1834-Aug 17, 1843

Mary Lee Smith
1891-1954

Shirley Ann, dau of
J. B. & Lucille Smith
1945

J. B., Jr., son of
J. B. & Lucille Smith
1938

Cleveland Smith
Jul 17, 1886
Nov 26, 1953 (TM)

Bryce Smith
1871-1936

Susie Smith
1883-19

Floyd McKay
Feb 2, 1878
Dec 13, 1929

Lake McKay
Jun 26, 1880
Feb 2, 1945

James Hoyte McKay
Aug 1, 1902
Mar 14, 1926

Margaret Emily, dau of
James H. Miller
May 15, 1839
Sep 25, 1880

John W., son of
James H. Miller
Sep 23, 1834
Dec 25, 1880

Harry A. Muse
1888-1930

John T. Muse
Feb 18, 1848
Sep 12, 1925

Jennie E. Muse
Sep 17, 1851
Aug 18, 1880

M. L., dau of
J. H. & Susie Miller
Aug 17, 1844
Mar 2, 1875

Francis L. Woods, wife of
James H. Miller
Jun 28, ----
May 2, 1875

Elizabeth H., wife of
S. A. Armstrong & dau of
J. H. & Sallie Miller
Sep 17, 1829
Dec 6, 1873

James H. Miller
May 18, 1803
Dec 22, 1879

Sallie, wife of
J. H. Miller
Dec 14, 1806
Jul 10, 1872

Andrew, son of
J. H. & Sallie Miller
Mar 11, 1832
Feb 4, 1845

Mattie L., dau of
J. H. & Sallie Miller
(dates illegible)

Nancy Amanda, wife of
John Anderson
Feb 7, 1827
Jun 6, 1851

Nancy D., First wife of
A. Miller
Jun 19, 1812
May 1, 1843

Andrew Miller
Oct 6, 1808
Apr 18, 1882

Robert E. Hopkins
Jul 13, 1871
Dec 20, 1914

N. A. Hopkins
Mar 11, 1849
May 11, 1911

Bettie Hopkins
1869-1955

A. D. Hopkins
Jun 24, 1840
Apr 25, 1897

Robert W. Adams
Mar 14, 1885
Aug 11, 1885

Winfield Scott Adams
1852-1927

Alice Stephenson Adams
1856-1885

Carrie L., wife of
Benjamin Thompson
Jul 6, 1832
Sep 25, 1894

B. Thompson
Mar 7, 1827
Jun 17, 1899

Emaline A., wife of
B. Thompson
Feb 3, 1826
Sep 28, 1868

BELFAST

Madora A. Thompson
Jan 5, 1856
Apr 5, 1858

Harriet L. Thompson
Nov 22, 1849
Apr 4, 1854

Thomas R., son of
J. W. & C. Coffey
Nov 29, 1841
Jul 13, 1853

Robert M., son of
J. W. & C. Coffey
May 28, 1869
Jun 29, 1871

Cyrena Coffey
Jan 25, 1821
Aug 26, 1898

J. W. Coffey
Jan 4, 1814
Oct 23, 1893

Mary Miller, wife of
Thomas Coffey
Feb 23, 1795
Jan 10, 1887

Thomas Coffey
Jan 17, 1788
Nov 14, 1852

A. P. Coffey
Nov 5, 1835
Jun 2, 1905

C. L. Coffey
Jan 23, 1830
Apr 18, 1914

Angie Coffey
Jun 4, 1839
Feb 3, 1934

Daisy Rankin, wife of
T. V. Allen
Feb 6, 1877
Mar 5, 1904

Mary E., wife of
R. S. Rankin
Feb 9, 1851
(no date)

R. S. Rankin
May 1, 1844
Jul 11, 1900

Gailia Furn Rankin
Aug 9, 1887
Oct 19, 1888

Herman Knox Rankin
Apr 7, 1892
Jul 8, 1900

Birdie Casteel
1907-1948

Marvin A. Neil
1878-1951

Maggie L. Neil
1886-

Bonnie Sue Rankin
Jun 27, 1909
Apr 26, 1910

R. S., son of
S. G. & A. H. Rankin
Nov 27, 1861
Feb 15, 1884

J. G. Rankin
Oct 1, 1830
May 19, 1891

Amelia H., wife of
J. G. Rankin
Dec 31, 1839
Aug 16, 1876

J. Howard Leonard
Nov 23, 1879
Apr 16, 1915

Samuel G. Leonard
Nov 9, 1877
Nov 30, 1942

Martha L. Shriver
1882-

Cannon C. Shriver
1877-1954

I. S. Brown
Jul 24, 1853
Aug 6, 1883

A. E. Brown
Mar 19, 1856
Mar 5, 1894

Isaac Carl, son of
W. R. & Cyrena Mosley
Jul 25, 1907
Oct 17, 1907

William R. Mosley
Mar 19, 1874
Nov 3, 1908

Cyrena Mosley
Jan 24, 1879
Oct 25, 1941

D. J. E. Coffey
Mar 7, 1831
Aug 28, 1907

Mary E. Crabtree
Died Oct 24, 1946
(Wayne Crabtree,
Elizabeth Crabtree) 3
children (TM)

Mary McWhirter
Oct 12, 1804
Feb 2, 1894

Mary O. Adams
Mar 1, 1833
Jul 1, 1885

R. A. Adams
Sep 20, 1837
Jun 21, 1913

Charles Hume McAdams
1876-1952

Lillie May McAdams
1879-19

Lucy A. Woods
1873-1874

Della, dau of
C. H. & Bessie McAdams
Jan 12, 1906
Feb 9, 1911

Francis Leroy Woods
May 15, 1829
Nov 9, 1909

Sallie Hall Woods
Jan 7, 1842
Mar 28, 1924

James L. Woods
1875-1948

Bessie, wife of
C. H. McAdams
Sep 22, 1881
Dec 16, 1906

Mary E., dau of
T. B. & Mary Leonard
Jun 13, 1884
May 18, 1902

Mary E., wife of
T. B. Leonard
Apr 23, 1854
Jul 24, 1885

Bedford Endsley
Jan 3, 1815
Jun 3, 1895

M. L., wife of
Bedford Endsley
Dec 3, 1816
Feb 8, 1901

J. F. Endsley
Sep 23, 1847
Sep 28, 1923

Sallie A., wife of
J. F. Endsley
Jul 24, 1846
Oct 21, 1907

B. B. Craig
Nov 21, 1831
Aug 7, 1885

Martha J. Craig
Jul 31, 1835
Feb 18, 1925

Margaret A. Phillips
1857-1952

Stephen F. Phillips
1855-1939

Gary H. H. Woods
Aug 29, 1816
Jul 17, 1885

Matilda A., wife of
Gary H. H. Woods
Dec 27, 1833
Jul 7, 1910

Calvin J. Woods
1878-1941

E. H. Hazlett
Nov 10, 1805
Jan 12, 1888

M. B., wife of
E. H. Hazlett
Aug 24, 1805
Aug 17, 1891

Mary M. Hazlett, wife of
G. W. P. Jones
Jun 22, 1849
Sep 4, 1907

Dewey Glenn
Oct 7, 1883
Jul 21, 1906

Z. T. Adams
Oct 5, 1848
Feb 8, 1929

Della Adams
1869-1956

Mollie Craig Fisher
1859-1947

Thomas E. Bishop
Oct 29, 1816
Jul 9, 1883

John Lee Endsley
Nov 22, 1887
Nov 4, 1956

Jessie Lee
Apr 22, 1890
Feb 21, 1951

Charlie, son of
J. B. & M. A. Endsley
Mar 19, 1878
Jun 2, 1878

BELFAST

George Rufus Endsley
1870-1943

Mary Anna, wife of
J. B. Endsley
1847-1928

James B. Endsley
1836-1917

William McGee Endsley
1868-1940

Levinia Shearin
Jun 12, 1845
Sep 10, 1897

Eva E. Shearin
Aug 3, 1882
Aug 22, 1902

Henrietta E., wife of
Stephen C. Wood
Dec 24, 1832
Feb 22, 1905

Stephen C. Wood
Dec 28, 1830
Mar 9, 1886

Clarence Beech
Nov 10, 1890
Nov 30, 1895

Frank Beech
May 25, 1902
Oct 28, 1903

Herman Beech
Aug 9, 1900
Nov 21, 1903

Lometa Wood Beech
Apr 30, 1865
Nov 3, 1957

William L. Beech
May 28, 1862
Feb 11, 1939

Lee A. Regin
1900-1954

Sallie Beech
1904-

Stephen Wood Beech
1888-1945

Lottie Lee Beech
1888-19

Della Wood
Nov 23, 1858
Dec 18, 1933

W. L. Wood
Nov 10, 1858
May 22, 1917

Roy Wood
Sep 25, 1890
Jan 3, 1892

Sallie H., dau of
W. L. & A. J. Wood
Sep 21, 1883
Jul 22, 1887

Maggie Eller, dau of
W. L. & A. J. Wood
Jun 17, 1886
Age 7 days

J. M. Endsley
Mar 19, 1803
Dec 5, 1884

C. B. Endsley
Oct 16, 1810
Apr 7, 1890

Addie Craig
Nov 17, 1904
Dec 8, 1908

Addie Hunter, wife of
W. T. Craig
Sep 3, 1870
May 2, 1913

William T. Craig
1868-1947

Polly T. Craig
1882-1956

Mattie Endsley
Oct 10, 1859
May 10, 1939

I. M. Endsley
Dec 2, 1808
Jan 30, 1882

S. M. Endsley
Oct 4, 1824
Aug 16, 1890

Vetron London
1904-1905

Enoch London
Co H 17th Tenn Inf
C.S.A.

E. C. London, Jr.
1913-1917

Samuel K. Glen
Jan 5, 1848
Jul 20, 1914

Fannie J. Glen
Oct 1, 1846
Aug 27, 1891

J. W. Anderson
Feb 1, 1857
Jan 12, 1916

L. H. Anderson
May 16, 1858
Mar 12, 1937

Tiny Lucille, dau of
H. M. & Callie Anderson
1919-1921

Mary Ann Dillard
Aug 12, 1866
Apr 15, 1937
(SMOOT on marker)

F. M. Dillard
Apr 16, 1840
Oct 2, 1922

Sallie G. Dillard
May 30, 1840
Jul 25, 1899

H. D. Adams
May 26, 1855
Oct 14, 1920
& wife
Nancy E. Dillard
Oct 23, 1867
Sep 17, 1894

Stephen L. Dillard
Aug 4, 1880
Jun 13, 1919

William A. Dillard
1869-1939

Ethel G. Dillard
1882-19

William James Whitaker
Tennessee
Pvt US Army
Aug 31, 1888
Oct 25, 1937

Jewell London
Jul 3, 1909
Nov 25, 1941

R. F. "Fob" Adams
1857-1948

Adlishia Adams
1866-1945

John Henry Adams
1886-1959

M. E. Bradley
Feb 4, 1842
Sep 2, 1891

J. C. Bradley
Mar 5, 1839
Oct 28, 1894

Virginia C., wife of
Thomas Pickle
Oct 7, 1856
Jan 6, 1942

Thomas Pickens
Mar 5, 1820
Feb 22, 1901

L. J. Swiney
Jan 20, 1832
Aug 18, 1909

M. E. Haislip Swiney
Dec 14, 1828
Aug 14, 1884

Dan Pickle
May 12, 1852
Oct 19, 1933

Josephine Pickle
Jan 26, 1852
Mar 10, 1883

Mother
L. Lois Pickle
1885-1936

Epps Roberts
1847-1931

Caddie B. Roberts
1855-1932

Ewell D. Neill
Sep 16, 1881
Dec 19, 1954

Mary M. Neil
Jun 9, 1858
Jun 11, 1948

James H. Neill
Oct 31, 1844
Oct 10, 1917

Gennettie E. Neil
Apr 23, 1887
Oct 7, 1889

E. C. Pickle
Oct 17, 1858
Jul 4, 1925

Sallie Wood Pickle
Jan 10, 1861
Jan 16, 1934

D. Frank Pickle
1866-1942

Johnnie C. Pickle
1878-19

Billie F. Pickle
Dec 21, 1945
Dec 24, 1945

Lawly P. Craig
Aug 23, 1873
Nov 13, 1954

Algie B. Craig
Jun 7, 1873

BELFAST

Brownie T. Craig
Jun 15, 1899

Ross W. Neely
1889-1954

Flora C. Neely
1892-

John W. Pickle
1861-1931
   & wife
Neely H. Pickle
1875-1942

Infant Son of
Epps & C. B. Roberts
B&D Jun 9, 1891

Lucy J. Neely
1895-1936

Infant of
R. W. & F. M. Neely
Oct 17, 1920

James A. Neely
1849-1926

Cornelia Coffey Neely
1861-1933

Thomas N. Neely
May 5, 1863
Mar 11, 1931

Joe W. Pickle
1890-1950

Sammie M. Pickle
1890-1952

Infant Son of
Joe & Sammie Pickle
(no dates)

Joe Calvin, son of
J. W. & S. M. Pickle
Jun 17, 1911
Jul 1, 1911

James Alex Majors
Apr 11, 1889
Feb 21, 1920
   & wife
Mamie Lee Majors
Jul 12, 1894

J. S. Thorne
1859-1921

Tennie Thorne
1872-1903

Etta D. Turner
1865-1918

John T. Turner
1867-1950

S. E. Drake
Jan 13, 1838
Mar 2, 1895

J. R. Drake
Aug 15, 1823
Dec 22, 1891

Ettie, wife of
T. A. McAdams
Jan 8, 1867
Aug 10, 1896

Mattie J., wife of
T. A. McAdams
Jan 16, 1864
Apr 8, 1905

Infant of
J. W., Jr. & H. A. Coffey
1912

Selene Tally
Jan 15, 1905
Jun 22, 1924

Anderson Tally
1879-1957

Lillian C. Tally
1883-

Wilkes Coffey
May 20, 1891
Jul 25, 1934

Lane
Sherman - Tom - Lela
(no dates)
Coffey
Sherman - Jane
(no dates)

Sam D. Woodward
Oct 25, 1875
Dec 31, 1952
&
Nona A. Woodward
Jul 21, 1884

J. W. Woodward
Oct 19, 1914
Sep 18, 1956
&
Louise Woodward
Apr 25, 1914

Nettie W. Davis
Oct 12, 1917
May 6, 1930

Marsia Emaline Endsley
1860-1949

Robert C. Pickle
1881-1949
&
Vera A. Pickle
1884-19

Willie Wilkes Talley
1906-1949
&
Mary Louise Talley
1914-

Clara P. Adams
1893-1932

Infant Dau of
Mrs. W. L. Endsley
1915

Ethel, wife of
W. L. Endsley
Jul 21, 1879
Aug 10, 1901

Mary E. Wilson
Mar 4, 1852
Mar 6, 1910
&
Lula Wilson
Aug 17, 1875
Aug 2, 1913
&
Myrtle Wilson
Oct 13, 1883
Feb 26, 1913
&
Joseph B. Wilson
Mar 13, 1855
Jan 16, 1926

Henry B. Wilson
Jun 13, 1887
Mar 8, 1917

Frank Falcon
1888-19
   & wife
Daisy Falcon
1889-1930

Wendell C. Blanton
May 23, 1936

Sandra Faye Wood
Nov 12, 1942

William N. Endsley
Dec 19, 1906
Aug 11, 1922

Effie L. Bowden
1888-1925

Mother
Ida May Gregory
May 16, 1871
Dec 5, 1955

Carolyn M. Neill
May 14, 1951

Earnie McCollum
1885-1946

Willie L. McCollum
1892-19

Mildred Lucile, dau of
Mr. & Mrs. E. A. McCollum
May 30, 1917
Apr 23, 1920

E. A. McCollum
Dec 19, 1834
Apr 1, 1917

M. J. McCollum
Oct 30, 1842
Sep 16, 1922

Dolly, wife of
R. A. Adams
Mar 4, 1844
Jun 26, 1927

Winson Chapman
Aug 26, 1881
Mar 12, 1903

J. W. Chapman
1839-1918

Mattie Chapman
1844-1925

Carolyn F. Smith
1945-1956

Lura I. Anderson
Mar 9, 1888
Apr 15, 1950

James W. Neely
World War II
Tenn Pfc 629 TD BN
28 Inf Div
Oct 31, 1920
Sep 30, 1954

William C. Smith
Tennessee
Tec 4 Co 1 194 Glider Inf
WW II
Mar 29, 1915
Mar 9, 1958

R. E. L. Sweeney
May 26, 1868
Nov 10, 1931

Rice Manier Hill
Apr 26, 1925
Apr 29, 1925

Mamie Woodward Pickle
1887-1930

Willie Vaun Woodward
Oct 2, 1890
Mar 23, 1922

BELFAST

Eula C., wife of
T. F. Woodward
Dec 18, 1867
Apr 25, 1917

T. F. Woodward
Aug 13, 1863
May 31, 1931

Mary Francis Woodward
Oct 23, 1916
Jan 10, 1919

Willie Frank McCollum
1909-1957 (TM)

Infant Son of
O. S. & B. D. Adams
1912

W. Horace Anderson
1882-1945

Ethel M. Anderson
1879-1930

Susie McCollum Phifer
1875-1934

James D. Curtis
1891-19

Zula G. Curtis
1833-1935

Betty Jean Sissom
1940-1941

William J. Williams
1875-1940

Mary Beulah Williams
1877-1956

Gordon "Jack" Endsley
1907-1957

Brownie H. Endsley
1907-

Meta A. Chapman
1884-1940

Hardy L. Chapman
1870-1921

Walter Wood
1873-1944

Neeta Wood
1884-19

J. Paul Wood, Jr.
Aug 2, 1942
Dec 12, 1942

N. C. Snell
1855-1934
& wife
Bell Snell
1861-1939

M. Franklin Rankin
1869-1957

Many unmarked graves.

* Revolutionary Soldier

Sallie M. Rankin
1872-1959

Cathey M. Stewart
Jun 6, 1955
Jun 8, 1955

Mother
Georgia K. Stewart
1910-1957

Marylyn Elizabeth, dau of
Mr. & Mrs. Jack L. Martin
Mar 25, 1955

Hugh B. Leonard
1875-1954

Katie B. Leonard
1880-

Alexander Davidson*
Born 1755 in Rowan Co., N.C.
Died 1818 (no marker)

Henrietta Clayton Davidson
wife of Alexander Davidson
Born 1745 in Rowan Co., N.C.
Died ----
mrd 1769 in Rowan Co., N.C.
(no marker)

END OF ROUND HILL

* *

WOODWARD CEMETERY
Located on the south side of Elk Ridge, right on Liberty
Valley Road, five and one half miles east of Belfast.
Copied by Mrs. Thomas McAdams, 1965.

William Woodward
Oct 31, 1769
Sep 30, 1843
Age 74 years

Nancy, wife of
William Woodward
Born --- --, 1766
Died Aug 20, 1865
Age 99 years Old.
(Nancy Mayes)

Marget C. Woodward
Jan 11, 1804
Aug --, 1857
"wife of Jerman
Woodward".

Mary E., wife of
J. Woodward
Oct 29, 1815
Sep 12, 1853
Age 37 yrs, 11 mos, 17 days

Jermon Woodward
Mar 25, 1794
Mar 14, 1860

Vanburen, son of
J. & M. E. Woodward
Aug 1, 1810
Aug 29, 1817
Age 7 years old

Infant of
J. & Mary E. Woodward
Feb 8, 1831
Died the same day.

Several unmarked graves.

* *

McADAMS CEMETERY
Located about six miles south of Belfast, on Old Fishing
Ford Road. Original land belonged to Joseph McAdams.

Joseph McAdams*
Apr 3, 1761
May 18, 1823
(Revolutionary Soldier)

* no markers

Margaret (Whittsett)*
wife of
Joseph McAdams
Born ----
Died Aug 1, 1844
mrd Jan 2, 1782

William S. McAdams
Jul 12, 1804
Mar 17, 1884

This Cemetery was destroyed many years ago. Copied by
Mrs. Thomas McAdams.

Levina (McLain) McAdams
Jan 27, 1810
Aug 22, 1888

* *

BELFAST

GOLD CEMETERY

Located two and one-half miles southeast of Lewisburg on Robinson Road, one-fourth mile north of Highway 431.

David Gold *
Born ca 1819 in TN
Died after 1850

Catherine Caroline (Smith)*
wife of David Gold
Born ca 1828 in TN
Died in Newton Co., MO
after 1892.

1 child's grave *
(David Gold's grand child)

* Info from Deed Records in Marshall Co., TN.

* *

CHILTON CEMETERY

Located south of Belfast, on the Billy Willis' farm, on the Old Fishing Ford Road. One and one-fourth mile southwest of Belfast, west of Fishingford Road. Copied 1980, by Mrs. Billy Willis, March 1980.

Nancy Gossage, wife of
Richard Chilton
Born 1804
Died Feb 18, 1844

Richard Chilton
(no marker, said to be
 buried here)

Also three unmarked graves.

* *

O'NEAL CEMETERY

Located two miles south of Palmetto on Gold Road, at the Bedford County line. Copied Apr 18, 1980 Helen & Tim Marsh.

Elizabeth B., wife of
J. M. O'Neal
Nov 28, 1815
Feb 19, 1864
Age 49 yrs, 2 mos, 23 days   About 3 unmarked graves.   Overgrown.

* *

DYSART CEMETERY

Located two and one half miles south east of Farmington on Phillips farm. Copied January 3, 1981 by Ralph D. Whitesell and Parks Gold. Only three graves.

Sarah E. Dysart
Jan 21, 1830
May 23, 1864

William E. Dysart
Sep 30, 1849
May 24, 1895

Marker with the top and inscription, broken away and unable to locate. This was probably the marker of Robert C. Dysart, husband of Sarah E. Dysart. He died in Spring of 1865.

* *

END OF BELFAST QUADRANGLE

BRICK CHURCH
Q U A D R A N G L E

DABNEY CEMETERY

Located on Buck Allison's farm, at Giles & Marshall County Line, one and one-half miles west of Interstate 65. Copied 1978.

Narcissa R., Consort of
R. C. Dabney
Aug 23, 1824
Mar 8, 1861

John E. Dabney, son of
R. C. & N. R. Dabney
Mar 8, 1845
Oct 17, 1857

Joseph H., son of
R. C. & N. R. Dabney
Nov 27, 1852
Jan 11, 1863

Infant of
R. C. & N. R. Dabney
(no dates)

Infant Son of
R. C. & N. R. Dabney
(no dates)

Win C. Bearden
Dec 5, 1798
Oct 24, 1858

N. F., dau of
J. O. & Eliza Dabney
May 21, 1850
Jan 25, 1853

N. A., dau of
J. O. & Eliza Dabney
Dec 15, 1854
Jul 28, 1855

Bettie E. Dabney
Dec 27, 1852
Feb 1, 1878

Taswell A. Dabney
Died Nov 8, 1847
Age 15 mos, 4 days

Eliza N. D., dau of
G. W. & M. Day
Died Aug 31, 1857
Age 8 yrs, 10 mos, 10 days

Eliza, wife of
John O. Dabney
May 30, 1818
Aug 16, 1890

J. O. Dabney
Nov 22, 1807
Apr 10, 1892
"Our Father"

William M. Dabney
May 12, 1839
Oct 22, 1874

H. C. Dabney
Sep 6, 1847
May 6, 1893

John, son of
J. E. & A. E. Hyde
Nov 15, 1892
Nov 19, 1895

Anna Belle, dau of
J. C. & A. E. Hyde
May 8, 1895
Jun 3, 1895

John H. Dabney
Jun 8, 1840
Jun 1, 1889

John Dabney
Jan 21, 1779
Aug 14, 1857

Gustavia T. Dabney
Dec 25, 1848
Jul 11, 1877

M. E. V., dau of
John O. & Eliza Dabney
Jul 24, 1851
Aug 21, 1855

John C. Young
Nov 1, 1828
Jan 18, 1858

John C., son of
J. C. & Mary E. Young
Feb 17, 1857
Oct 17, 1857

* *

DABNEY CEMETERY

Located on Charlie Thomas farm, at Giles & Marshall County Line, west of Interstate 65. Copied 1978.

Gustavia T. Dabney
Died Dec 31, 1837
Aged 2 yrs, 3 mos, 7 days

F. M., son of
J. O. & Eliza Dabney
Born --- --, 1846

John D. C., son of
S. P. & M. S. Smith
Died Jul 26, 1836
Age 1 yr, 4 days

Emily Dabney
Died Feb 28, 1826
Age 14 yrs, 8 mos, 1 day

Margaret S., dau of
John & Nancy Dabney &
Consort of
S. P. Smith
Died Jan 8, 1838
Age 22 yrs, 8 mos, 30 days

Emily O., dau of
S. P. & M. S. Smith
Died Jan 8, 1838
Age 1 yr, 11 mos, 11 days

* *

McCORD CEMETERY

Located one mile south of Robertson Fork and Highway 129, Ash Gap. Copied 1979 by Helen & Tim Marsh.

John Claiborn McCord
May 24, 1864
Oct 20, 1895
&
Sarah Virginia McCord
Aug 13, 1827
Oct 1899

Vernon Latham
Apr 20, 1883
Sep 14, 1903

Julia A., wife of
Jno. T. Dugger
Apr 13, 1862
Mar 14, 1886
(broken)

R. B. McCord
Feb 7, 1854
Oct 2, 1886

Zipporah (Wilkes) McCord
Oct 31, 1857
Aug 9, 1906
&
Florence McCord
Died Apr 12, 1901
Age 19 years

Infant dau of
R. B. & Zipporah McCord
(no dates)

Father
T. F. McCord
Nov 9, 1847
May 8, 1919
&
Mother
Nannie H. McCord
Apr 24, 1850
Oct 6, 1917

BRICK CHURCH

J. J. Latham
Jul 9, 1846
Sep 13, 1906
&
Mrs. J. J. Latham
Jun 27, 1850
(no date)

Stella McCord
Feb 13, 1878
Nov 18, 1881
&
Horace Linsy McCord
Aug 27, 1882
Mar 14, 1883
&
Robert Linus McCord
Feb 2, 1884
Mar 20, 1891
(children of T. F. &
N. H. McCord)

Father
D. H. Jones
Dec 11, 1823
Mar 11, 1904

and

Mother
Emily F. Jones
Jul 20, 1829
Jun 16, 1897

Several unmarked graves

* *

MARRS HILL CEMETERY
Located 100 yards west of the Lynville-Cornersville Exit of
Interstate 65. Copied Sep 16, 1978 by Helen & Tim Marsh.

Herbert W. Hodge
Feb 21, 1922
Jun 27, 1973
&
Annie D. Hodge
Sep 26, 1927

Steve J. Drapchaty
Sep 11, 1908
Mar 21, 1964
&
Louise Nox Drapchaty
Mar 28, 1919

Father Roy N. Nix
1898-
&
Mother
Cora M. Nix
1901-1975

Janice Wade
Jan 29, 1940
Oct 3, 1975

William Collins Wright
Oct 23, 1910
Mar 3, 1973

James E. Helmick
May 22, 1950

&
Elizabeth B. Helmick
Apr 22, 1919
Dec 18, 1973

Tom Adams
1876-1938
&
Ollie Adams
1880-1957

Henry Adams
Oct 29, 1900
Aug 23, 1922

Dora Zell Adams
Jun 16, 1914
May 10, 1920

Miss Martha G. Adams
1899-1978
(London FH)

George M. Adams
Sep 2, 1872
Sep 6, 1951

Mary S. Adams
Aug 7, 1876
Jan 1, 1928

Mary E. Poarch
1928-1932

Ervin Poarch, Jr.
May 8, 1925
Sep 4, 1967

Loyd Adams
1910-
&
Elnora Adams
1915-1970
&
Brenda Adams
1952-1970

Alvie Adams
Nov 25, 1894
Oct 2, 1933
&
Edith Adams
Feb 17, 1897

Baby
Virginia Adams
B&D Nov 15, 1924

Wiley G. Boatright
Mar 15, 1895
Feb 28, 1977

Father
S. J. Ramsey
Oct 2, 1861
Sep 12, 1923

A. Horace Jett
Jan 20, 1883
Mar 26, 1969
&
Lillie M. Jett
Nov 1, 1892
Jul 1, 1933

Ira Brown Cross
1872-1938
&
Ella Terry Cross
1879-1927

Charles Q. Fralix
1967-1967 (TM)

Tracy Fralix
1969-1969
(Bennett-May, Pulaski FH)

Barbara Jean Fralix
Jun 20, 1949
Feb 17, 1950

Billy Dean Fralix
Jun 20, 1949
Jun 22, 1949

Bert Williams
Jul 10, 1910
May 9, 1957
&
Jewell Williams
Jul 8, 1919
Jan 23, 1955

Rena Cross Jeter
May 9, 1896
Feb 26, 1971

Annie Cross Adams
1907-1927

George W. Wade
Nov 16, 1858
Sep 29, 1919

Izabell Wade
Jan 18, 1858
Jun 1, 1923

Mary Lou Williams
Sep 28, 1913
Feb 24, 1977
&
Thomas J. Williams
Dec 26, 1918

&
Francis E. Williams
Oct 12, 1922
Sep 18, 1973

Jim O. Orr
1876-1950
&
Mattie E. Orr
1884-1973

Mahlon Orr
Dec 18, 1919
Oct 9, 1923

James Harvey Orr
Tennessee
Pfc 2 Marine Air Wing
Jun 20, 1915
Apr 28, 1952
&
Robert Dean Orr
1912-

Eliza, wife of
T. B. Wisdom
1847-1919

William Knox Sharp
1904-1929

BRICK CHURCH

W. D. Sharp
1867-1943
&
Lula B. Sharp
1868-1934

James Edwin Sharp
Nov 8, 1915
Oct 5, 1916

Henry Franklin Wisdom
Dec 11, 1877
Apr 18, 1915
"Farewell, wife & children".

Billie Jean Locke
1928-1965

W. H. Doggett
Oct 24, 1860
Oct 7, 1938
&
Donnie C. Doggett
Feb 21, 1856
Jul 22, 1920

Louginnia Doggett
Feb 9, 1877
Dec 2, 1945

H. H. Coble
Jan 23, 1861
May 2, 1918
&
Myrtle L. Coble
Jun 12, 1874
Sep 23, 1951

Cleophas S. Coble
Tennessee
BM2 US Navy WW I
Sep 17, 1895
Jul 19, 1962

Evalena Taylor Coble
Oct 20, 1904
Sep 24, 1975

Mary Edna Roland
Apr 5, 1951
Jan 22, 1953

Della Estes Hopkins
Dec 10, 1880
Jul 23, 1955

Alice June Hopkins
1938-1944

H. Clifton Hopkins
Apr 6, 1903
Aug 29, 1974
&
Willie B. Hopkins
Aug 26, 1906

Mrs. Frances Hopkins
1923-1976
(London FH)

Tommie Nix Perman
1908-1934

Tommie's Baby
(no dates)

Robert Earl, son of
Paul & Sara Nix
1935-1939

J. H. Pierce
1905-
&
Lula Bell Pierce
1910-1963

Hulda Ann Nickens
Oct 24, 1878
Oct 6, 1956

Boyd Chapman
May 2, 1901
Feb 7, 1948
&
Lamoria J. Chapman
May 18, 1911
May 24, 1948
&
Ronald Chapman
Oct 28, 1946
Aug 16, 1947

Della P. Cortner
1873-1938

Nora Jean Roberts
1941-1965

Earl Tucker
1890-1950

Infant Boy Tucker
(no dates)

Thomas "David" Watkins, Jr.
B&D Nov 24, 1969

Father
H. M. McClure
Dec 25, 1840
Oct 25, 1913
&
Mother
Pallie W. McClure
May 30, 1870
May 1, 1906

Martha Ann Woods
1873-1918

Allen E. Hopkins
1904-1962
&
Thelma B. Hopkins
1910-

Mother
Charity M. Malone
Oct 12, 1825
Jun 2, 1915

Henry K. Malone
1869-1947
&
Sara E. Malone
1872-1961

Father
John H. Harris
Oct 14, 1865
Feb 24, 1921
&
Mother
Zilla M. Harris
Jun 9, 1876
Jan 17, 1949

Mother
Hannah, wife of
Henry Walker
Dec 25, ----
Jan --, ----
(broken, cemented over dates)

Alma Walker Hewitt
Apr 14, 1893
Sep 1, 1973

J. M. Walker
Jan 21, 1866
Jan 31, 1915

Dora A. Walker Turner
Nov 26, 1870
Jul 22, 1924

Father
James Herman Walker
1900-1978
&
Mother
Thelma Inez Walker
1910-

S. P. Lowrance
Sep 18, 1859
Mar 18, 1949

Manda V., wife of
S. P. Lowrance
Mar 5, 1856
Mar 11, 1918

Henry Lowrance
1883-1965
&
Jonnie Lowrance
1887-1943

Infant Clift
1924

Cecil Clift
1926

Rufe Clift
1882-1936
&
Lucile Clift
1890-1957

Benjamin N. Tucker
Tennessee
Pvt US Army WW I
Dec 16, 1892
Jan 9, 1965
&
Dessa W. Tucker
1900-

Sherlie Adams
1898-1953
&
Lillian Adams
1913-

Baby
Bobby Adams
Mar 13, 1943
Jan 13, 1944

James M. Woods
1896-1946

Vera Allen
Feb 13, 1899
Jun 15, 1955

Wiley Allen
Nov 10, 1873
Mar 20, 1951
&
Callie Allen
Oct 3, 1868
Dec 14, 1942

Velma A. Stokes
May 27, 1903

Johnnie T. Jett
1891-1937
&
Jennie Mai Jett
1895-1971

James M. Jett
1864-1947
&
Margaret A. Jett
1869-1948

James Rollie, son of
J. M. & M. A. Jett
Aug 12, 1893
Dec 3, 1924
(picture)

Lonnie H. Follis
1889-1957
&
Ada L. Follis
1881-1969

Van Doggett
Died Nov 27, 1920
(no age given)
&
Jennie Doggett
Died Jul 26, 1959
(no age given)

BRICK CHURCH

James W. Keele
Dec 23, 1853
Jul 23, 1920
&
Sophia C. Keele
Mar 20, 1851
Aug 15, 1902
&
Orminda J. Keele
Jan 1, 1871
Jun 17, 1917

Miller Doggett
Died Feb 25, 1915
(no age given)

Pvt Willie T. Lee
3998824 Medical Dept.
US Army
Jan 2, 1968

Sadie Doggett Lee

John Lapsley McMahon
1848-1933
&
Alice Allen McMahon
1860-1939

Bruce Allen
1858-1943

Edwin Allen
1872-1926

Edwin Allen
Aug 3, 1831
Nov 7, 1916
&
Martha Harper Allen
May 22, 1831
Apr 17, 1920

M. M. Perry
May 10, 1861
Oct 6, 1923

Allice M., wife of
M. M. Perry
Apr 14, 1858
Aug 23, 1913

Mary C., wife of
Woodson Walker
Nov 9, 1833
Mar 11, 1916

Husband
J. B. Smithson
Nov 5, 1844
Sep 3, 1919
&
Wife
S. E. Smithson
Dec 25, 1852
Jul 27, 1943

Father
George Doggett
Jul 15, 1874
Feb 8, 1939
&
Alberta Doggett
Jan 26, 1877
May 25, 1960

N. A. Parks
Feb 19, 1862
Mar 10, 1902

James Houston Alford
Jan 11, 1853
Dec 12, 1924
&
Virginia Austin Alford
Oct 12, 1861
Dec 19, 1935

Dewitt Clinton Alford
1863-1944

H. C. Casteel
May 3, 1866
Dec 12, 1937

John D. Colvett
1855-1933
&
Josie D. Colvett
1859-1948

W. C. Colvett, Jr.
1026-1928

Asbery Allen
1867-1931
&
Jennie Allen
1863-1932

W. Ruth Wright
1922-1940

Mary E. "Lizzie" Doggett
1878-1952

William Clarence Colvett
Tennessee
Pvt Co E 168 Inf WW I
Apr 30, 1894
Jun 12, 1970
&
Zora M. Allen
Aug 12, 1888
(new grave) 1978

James Oscar McClintock
1904-1966

Lula H. McClintock
Oct 14, 1896

Maggie McClintock
1884-1961

J. E. McClintock
1856-1936

Clifford Hurman McClintock
1915-1917

Annie Bell McClintock
1864-1901

Emma Claribel McClintock
1892-1895

T. Eugene Tate
1903-1904

James F. Woods
1870-1917

Sallie Woods
Jul 23, 1842
Jan 3, 1896

Homer C. Tate
Mar 5, 1905
Sep 29, 1958

Arzenia Cowan Tate
1870-1902

Emma Wilkes
May 3, 1863
Jun 8, 1897

Frenchie T. Wilkes
Dec 10, 1895
Jun 2, 1896

Thomas Woodson Wilkes
Aug 9, 1823
Sep 22, 1899

Patsy Wilks
Born 1819-
Died Jun 9, 1893

Maude H. Handly
Jul 29, 1882
Jul 4, 1966

Virgil E. Wilkes
Aug 9, 1885
Nov 28, 1947
&
Bessie Mae Wilkes
Sep 11, 1895

Jay Collins Wilkes
B&D Jul 28, 1962

John Woodfin Gardner
Mar 1, 1891

&
Wilma Stacy Gardner
May 25, 1892
May 29, 1953

Katie, dau of
C. R. & Jennie Wilkes
Feb 2, 1880
Jul 3, 1903

Charles Richard Wilkes
1851-1932
&
Mary Jane Wilkes
1853-1934

Raymond Eugene, son of
Kenneth & Ethel Wilkes
Sep 14, 1906
Jun 27, 1907

Russell Aubrey Wilkes
Nov 28, 1909
Nov 5, 1912

Kenneth S. Wilkes
Nov 5, 1880
Aug 10, 1961
&
Ethel O. Wilkes
Oct 14, 1886

William Percy Charlton
Nov 5, 1869
Feb 12, 1924

Elmer Pearl Charlton
Aug 19, 1877
Dec 6, 1895
&
Sarah A., wife of
M. M. Charlton
Sep 2, 1840
Feb 13, 1901

Mabel Pearl Bryant
May 20, 1900
Jan 1, 1906

Jeff D. Bryant
1861-1929
&
Lillie C. Bryant
1862-1947

Guss H. Farmer
1856-1910
&
Tonie Anette Farmer
1869-1952

Susan Farmer
1858-1906

Nancy E. Farmer
1833-1903

Samuel, son of
J. S. & N. E. Farmer
Sep 19, 1859
Aug 8, 1893
Age 33 yrs, 10 mos, 21 days

Grady Wright
1891-1938

Lois Wright
1894-1972

BRICK CHURCH

Pauline Key, wife of
Orville Wilkes
1918-1943

Shirley Doggett
1892-1959
&
Elsie Doggett
1904-

Homer Cason
Jan 14, 1893
Nov 26, 1971
&
Gladys Cason
Jul 19, 1895
Nov 18, 1952

John A. Smith
1877-1963

A. Cowan
Jun 6, 1848
Feb 6, 1893

William Thomas Cowan
Aug 4, 1868
Jun 12, 1893

Louellen, dau of
J. T. & Eliza Adams
Oct 1, 1917
Nov 21, 1917

Martha J. Smith
May 7, 1838
Jun 14, 1895

J. M. Adams
Dec 3, 1841
Jan 10, 1916
&
E. M. Adams
Sep 28, 1851
(no date)

Richard P. Wilkes
Jun 10, 1848
Apr 13, 1895
&
Mary M. Wilkes
Apr 12, 1852
Mar 29, 1923

Nettie M. Townsend
1961-1964

Minnie May Watkins
Oct 28, 1899
Dec 5, 1942

Robert L. Rohelier
1873-1951
&
Alice Rohelier
1873-1959

Liston C. Van Cleave
New York
QM2 US Navy WW I
Dec 3, 1894
Aug 24, 1947

John Mylus Kaiser
Tennessee
Cpl Co D 307 Eng. WW I
Sep 9, 1889
Apr 23, 1971
&
Mary Mahoney Kaiser
1904-1976
(DAR marker & Ladies
Aux. VFW)

Lenice Alford Kaiser
1889-1941

M. D. Alford, M.D.
Sep 13, 1855
Nov 23, 1908
&
Emma B. Alford
Mar 4, 1864
Jun 9, 1931

T. C. Tucker
1864-1898
&
G. A. Tucker
1863-1938

Waymond Carl Tucker
Mar 11, 1911
Mar 4, 1913

Thomas J. Steete
1858-1942
&
Olivia R. Steete
1868-1951

Aaron X. Steete
Aug 8, 1818
Nov 10, 1910
&
Martha E. Steete
Jul 26, 1833
Jul 21, 1924

Susie S. Clark
1893-1934

Walter Scott Doggett
Jul 1874
Jan 1962
&
Lula Wisdom Doggett
Apr 1879
Aug 1964

Henry Russell, son of
W. S. & Lula Doggett
Dec 25, 1900
Feb 19, 1903

Dovie Williams, wife of
W. E. Bledsoe
Aug 12, 1877
Apr 3, 1900

M. J. W.
(all on stone)

Father
Cleophous Lee Roberts
Feb 15, 1860
Aug 28, 1940
&
Mother
Dazzreen Roberts
Mar 30, 1872
Feb 18, 1936

Mother
Fannie E. Ball, wife of
G. W. Hobby
Apr 2, 1866
Jul 30, 1908

Morgan Hobbs
1889-1931
&
Ruth Hobbs
1892-1966

Sgt John Thomas Hickerson, Jr.
1918-1945
148th Inf. 37 Div

Larry Donaldson
Feb 3, 1946
Feb 3, 1946

William Harvey Madison
Aug 27, 1906

&
Myrtle M. Madison
Mar 21, 1907

Avie L. Stokes
1895-1970
&
Millie D. Stokes
1888-1966

William J. Davis
Jul 8, 1858
Apr 8, 1931
&
Nancy C. Davis
Nov 14, 1860
Dec 13, 1936

C. L. Riner
Sep 28, 1891
Dec 1, 1891

Ada Doggett Ephlin
1869-1926

Moses D. Doggett
Feb 25, 1838
Dec 19, 1905
&
Elizabeth P. Doggett
Nov 24, 1840
Oct 5, 1899

William Colvett
1861-1935
&
Theora Colvett
1858-1900
&
Ella J. Colvett
1858-1942

John H. Freeman
Apr   1843
Nov 21, 1915
&
Harriet H. Freeman
Jan 1, 1833
Feb 22, 1905

Robert A. Nix
1881-1940
&
Jennie B. Nix
1885-1940

Cordell, son of
R. A. & Jennie Nix
May 14, 1902
Dec 13, 1919

Harper Edmondson
Nov 17, 1899
Nov 7, 1966

Norborn Philip Edmondson
Jul 15, 1898
Apr 25, 1976

James Horace Rodgers
Cpl US Army WW I
May 30, 1889
Feb 28, 1978
&
Ada Mae D. Rodgers
Oct 29, 1902

Vol Pruit Rodgers
1858-1943
&
Florence Wilks Rodgers
1864-1923

C. E., wife of
D. H. Colvett
Jun 23, 1865
Jan 3, 1917

Alice A. Doggett, wife of
R. J. Fowler
Mar 20, 1871
Sep 3, 1896

BRICK CHURCH

Father
John L. Gower
Apr 4, 1872
May 26, 1913
&
Mother
Cora B. Gower
Jul 22, 1878
Mar 1, 1924

Florence E., dau of
M. D. & E. P. Doggett
Jan 10, 1880
Nov 3, 1893
&
Maxie H., dau of
M. D. & E. P. Doggett
Aug 23, 1877
Nov 22, 1893

E. L. McMahon
1857-1945
&
Sarah A. McMahon
1856-1939

Flora Lee, dau of
E. L. & R. A. (S.A.) McMahon
Jun 20, 1886
Oct 8, 1891

Joseph A. McMahon
Mar 24, 1884
Mar 4, 1968
&
Annie R. McMahon
Apr 24, 1886
Aug 8, 1972

Raymond C., son of
J. A. & Annie McMahon
Dec 12, 1910
Jan 14, 1918
Age 7 yrs, 1 mo, 1 day

Mother
Clara V. Hickman
Dec 31, 1897
Sep 28, 1967

Ealon B., son of
Arlie & Clara Hickman
1930

Ross Estes
Jul 4, 1898
Mar 16, 1974

Gladice O. Estes
Jan 20, 1909
Oct 29, 1976

James Billy Ramsey
1935-1935

Barbara Jean Ramsey
1937-1937

J & T
(fieldstone)

Thomas Percy Harwell
Tennessee
Pvt US Army WW I
Jul 8, 1892
Jan 21, 1970

Olon B. Thompson
Sep 30, 1901
Dec 19, 1974
&
Maggie B. Thompson
May 20, 1903
Dec 13, 1970

Father
James W. Smith
Jan 29, 1871
Mar 29, 1939
&
Mother
Clemmie Smith
Jun 11, 1874
Jun 21, 1944

William L. Head
1856-1926
&
Mattie M. Head
1871-1949

J. W., son of
J. A. & T. M. Grammer
Nov 7, 1883
Jun 13, 1909

Annie Mae, dau of
J. A. & T. M. Grammer
May 10, 1894
Dec 27, 1912

William Howard, son of
J. A. & F.(T) M. Grammer
Oct 3, 1900
Feb 1, 1917

Adine Thompson
Died Mar 1905
(no age given)

Nettie Doggett
Mar 12, 1866
Sep 17, 1905

U. Grant Doggett
Oct 9, 1865
Oct 14, 1934

McClure
1895

William Clarence McClure
Nov 21, 1860
Jul 27, 1938

Videau Allen, wife of
W. C. McClure
May 25, 1862
Apr 13, 1904

A. B. Edmondson
1872-1951

Adelia Allen, wife of
A. B. Edmondson
1868-1946

Edmondson
1897

Norburn P. Moore
Jul 5, 1871
Apr 12, 1966
&
Dora Allen Moore
Mar 21, 1866
May 3, 1937

Jasper Doggett
May 16, 1831
Jan 28, 1913

Father
Robert C. Gawer (Gower)
Nov 29, 1865
Dec 25, 1921

Sammie Davis Gower
Dec 31, 1901
Mar 1, 1919

John William Van Cleave
1872-1931
&
Ida Bell Van Cleave
1873-1920

Clifford M. Van Cleave
Tennessee
Cpl Co G 139 Inf WW I
Jan 13, 1896
Jun 20, 1971

Joyce Briggs
Oct 24, 1934
Nov 8, 1934

Winfred S. Gabriel
Dec 23, 1897

&
Carrie C. Gabriel
Jul 20, 1902
Jan 31, 1976

Dewey Edmond Bivens
May 28, 1898
Jun 23, 1973
&
Ora Lucille Bivens
Jul 28, 1900

Joseph N. Pinkston
1861-1946
&
Susie D. Pinkston
1861-1958

Joe A. Pickens
1879-1941

Lillie Pickens
1886-1945

Wilbur L. Smith
Aug 28, 1901
Nov 17, 1967

Joseph Shirley Pinkston
Oct 22, 1894
Apr 19, 1926

Bernie D. Pinkston
1892-1949
&
Rubie Walker Pinkston
1894-1950

Wave Loyd Pinkston
1924-1947
Pvt Co D 129 Inf
Training Btn USA Armory

Joe Anderson, son of
B. D. & Ruby M. Pinkston
Sep 23, 1920
May 24, 1925

Herman O. Pinkston
Tennessee
Pvt 3505 AAF Base Unit
WW II
May 11, 1926
Jul 6, 1952

Walter Allen Pinkston
Pvt US Army Korea
1932-1976

C. B. Gower
Jun 16, 1853
Feb 15, 1899

Newton Doggett
Jun 15, 1836
Dec 24, 1901
Age 65 yrs, 11 mos, 9 days

Father
L. W. Wilkes
Jun 14, 1832
Sep 5, 1892

Narsissa B. Wilkes "Mother"
Jan 9, 1840
Aug 5, 1898

Ida E., wife of
R. C. Gower
Mar 7, 1869
Jul 4, 1892

William Collins
1st Tenn 8th Ala
Vid. Cav.
Dec 15, 1840
Jun 30, 1898

BRICK CHURCH

Infant Son of
J. F. Berlin & wife
B&D Jul 18, 1907

Loise Parks
Sep 28, 1894
Aug 31, 1899

Father
Henry Allie Grammer
Apr 3, 1880
Feb 23, 1940

M. G. Grammer
Jan 16, 1853
Aug 25, 1914

Robert E. Head
1868-1931

Ada D. Head
1878-1958

Elijah H. Williams
1900-1978
(Cornersville FH)

B. Frank Grammer
1898-1956
(fieldstone)

William J. Roberts
1876-1951
&
Mamie G. Roberts
1882-

Jim B. Foster
Sep 18, 1875
Jul 28, 1954
&
Oda V. Foster
Apr 15, 1887
Sep 12, 1972

Ervin R. Grammer
1885-1944
&
Hettie May Grammer
1888-1954

James A. Grammer
Feb 13, 1859
Aug 26, 1940
& wife
Teresa Maria Tinnon Grammer
Sep 14, 1859
Dec 12, 1932

John B. Doggett
1866-1941
&
Mollie A. Doggett
1866-1940

Maudie L., dau of
J. B. & M. A. Doggett
Mar 26, 1888
May 19, 1890

Audie L., son of
J. B. & M. A. Doggett
Mar 26, 1888
May 28, 1892

L. O. Lee Doggett
Oct 11, 1892
Mar 27, 1959

Bettie, dau of
J. J. & M. J. Wilkes
Aug 27, 1809
Sep 19, 1890

W. R. Hewitt
Apr 29, 1866
Mar 3, 1923
& wife
Elizabeth Hewitt
Nov 13, 1869
Jan 21, 1935

Mother
Effie Hewitt Carpenter
1899-1950

Mrs. Maggie Beatty
1886-1970
(McDaniel FH)

Ruby Mai Gower
Aug 18, 1915
May 28, 1959

Betty Lynne Allen
May 10, 1954
May 11, 1954

Donna Jean Allen
Oct 17, 1960
Oct 18, 1960

Joe Lynn Allen
Jun 28, 1934
Nov 21, 1971
&
Betty Ann Allen
Dec 22, 1933

Thomas Brown Jeter
Sep 19, 1920

&
Mary Katherine Jeter
Apr 12, 1925
Jun 22, 1970
mrd Sep 16, 1939

Ronnie Brown
Apr 8, 1950
Dec 15, 1976
&
Kathy Brown
Nov 10, 1953
----
mrd Jan 22, 1971

George W. Townsend
Mar 19, 1892
Nov 24, 1971
&
Nettie R. Townsend
Jul 7, 1893
----
mrd Jan 3, 1912

Father
Richard R. Whitsett
1916-1963
&
Mother
Corene Whitsett
1915-

Tony Lee Whitsett
Oct 15, 1960
Mar 4, 1972
(color picture)

J. D. Madison
1889-
&
Sallie M. Madison
1890-1954

Joe D., son of
J. D. & S. M. Madison
Oct 1, 1918
Nov 3, 1920

Marion Stone
Feb 2, 1895

&
Rowena K. Stone
Feb 10, 1901
----
mrd Mar 13, 1919

Orbin F. Haley
Sep 13, 1889
Jan 22, 1973
&
Gertie L. Haley
Jul 2, 1889

Mrd Sep 6, 1908

Melvin C. Haley
Jun 3, 1912
Jul 12, 1975
&
Lillian B. Haley
Jan 21, 1921

Mary Alice Williams
Mar 11, 1908
Oct 15, 1943

Father
Andrew Biega
Nov 28, 1886
Nov 26, 1956

James E. Adams
Oct 12, 1881
Oct 9, 1944
&
Nora E. Adams
May 23, 1883
Aug 21, 1959

Bennie, son of
J. E. & Nora Adams
Dec 8, 1902
May 15, 1919

Father
William Ottis Talley
Nov 21, 1877
Mar 11, 1960
&
Mother
Maude Hewitt Talley
May 18, 1880
Jul 16, 1958
mrd Oct 2, 1899

Willie Whitehead
1899-1936

Gambelle McLin
Sep 9, 1902
Oct 9, 1904
&
Lizzie McLin
Jul 3, 1872
Jul 20, 1909
"Wife & Mother"

R. D. Hewitt
Sep 26, 1832
Nov 8, 1898

Sarah E. Hewitt
Aug 24, 1840
Apr 10, 1902

James D. Griffis
Jul 1, 1831
Aug 13, 1901
&
Lucinda Griffis
Nov 9, 1827
Jan 26, 1900

Josie Griffis Ealy
1866-1956

Ewing Griffis Martin
Feb 12, 1900
Oct 22, 1900

Zennie Olis, son of
J. L. & R. J. Martin
Feb 18, 1892
Apr 20, 1892

Wesley W. Griffis
Sep 21, 1828
Apr 12, 1911

BRICK CHURCH

Sarah A., wife of
W. W. Griffis
Aug 13, 1837
Dec 23, 1889

Mary Emma Griffis
Oct 11, 1861
Oct 24, 1922

W. Almos Hickman
Nov 26, 1887
Mar 14, 1974
&
Emma M. Hickman
Dec 10, 1894
----
mrd Sep 14, 1911

Josie Stem Beasley
Oct 1, 1871
Sep 5, 1940

William D. James
Oct 19, 1935
Oct 23, 1935

J. D. James
Jan 21, 1872
Aug 31, 1946
&
Janie James
Mar 13, 1876
Feb 28, 1945

Johnie M. Grammer
1889-1977

Oscar Hickerson
Feb 9, 1889
Aug 13, 1961
&
Agnes Hickerson
Sep 11, 1894
Apr 3, 1978

John Thomas Hickerson
Sep 16, 1876
Mar 14, 1960

Anna Belle Hickerson
Oct 19, 1882
Jun 3, 1938

Harvey C. Hatfield
Jun 28, 1907
Dec 21, 1974
&
Mary L. Hatfield
Aug 8, 1908

Leonard Wayne, son of
Jim & Helen Hatfield
Oct 5, 1967
Oct 20, 1967

Annie Ruth Pettus
1873-1962

Robert W. London
1854-1939
&
Vera J. London
1877-1963

Wesley Wilson, son of
R. W. & Ida London
Jun 12, 1884
Nov 21, 1891

Orvous Porter, son of
R. W. & Ida London
Jun 18, 1887
Sep 4, 1894

Ida, wife of
R. W. London
Jun 26, 1857
Oct 3, 1901

Father
J. W. Wallace
Feb 27, 1862
Jan 27, 1932
&
Mother
Sallie Wallace
Nov 26, 1866
Mar 20, 1944

Thomas Ernie Wallace
Nov 7, 1889
Nov 11, 1911

Several unmarked graves.
END OF MARRS HILL

Anna Lou Doggett
Jan 1, 1923
Nov 7, 1923
&
Sallie N. Doggett
Jan 22, 1917
Jul 6, 1917

William Thomas Edmondson
1869-1940

Annie Follis Edmondson
1871-1901

Grace Elise Edmondson
1896-1896

Infant Son of
W. T. & Annie Edmondson
1901

Annie Will Edmondson
1899-1905

Joseph G. Edmondson
1919-1919

Amanda E. Edmondson
Jun 27, 1843
Sep 12, 1905

J. M. Edmondson
Feb 18, 1836
Jan 6, 1918

* *

BRYANT CEMETERY

Located one-half mile south of Mars Hill, and one-hald mile
west of Interstate - 65. Copied June 22, 1980 by Mr. Joe
Mack Hight of Greenbrier, Tennessee.

Florence A., dau of
J. D. & L. M. Bryant
Oct 3, 1890
Jan 21, 1892

Mariah G. Bryant
Jul 30, 1820
Oct 28, 1888
Age 68 yrs, 2 mos, 28 days

Alexander Bryant
Dec 14, 1818
Feb 29, 1904

Velma Clint, dau of
W. M. & M. A. Bryant
Apr 24, 1883
Nov 28, 1886

E. H. Alford
Dec 29, 1820
Aug 10, 1895

Elizabeth Jane, wife of
E. H. Alford
Jun 3, 1824
Mar 10, 1888

Infant Son of
M. D. & E. B. Alford
B&D Mar 15, 1888

Mollie A., wife of
W. M. Bryant
Feb 14, 1858
Jul 12, 1893

Few unmarked graves.

* *
END OF BRICK CHURCH QUADRANGLE

CORNERSVILLE QUADRANGLE

ADAMS-STILWELL CEMETERY

Located one-half mile south of Collins-Holly Road. Copied Dec 1, 1973.

J. L., son of
J. C. & C. Stilwell
Aug 30, 1868
Mar 1, 1889

Lee M. Adams
1854-1944
&
Dezza T. Adams
1856-1901

I. R. Adams
Jan 24, 1885
Oct 10, 1887

Several unmarked graves.

Jimmie Lee Osborn
Oct 15, 1899
Oct 28, 1899

* *

BRINTLE CEMETERY

Located just to the east of the site of Old Ebenezer Methodist Episcopal Church, in Ebenezer Hollow.

Said to be the Family Graveyard of John M. and Sarah Brintle. Several unmarked graves.

* *

HOBBY-PRUITT CEMETERY

Located on a hill near an old road which ran from Yell to Cornersville, behind the home of Mr. & Mrs. Clyde Conwell on the Yell Road. Copied April 15, 1976 by Ralph D. Whitesell and Frank Boyd.

Green Hobby
Feb 26, 1810
Aug 9, 1895

Sarah Hobby
Oct 23, 1815
Oct 6, 1890

About 40 unmarked graves.

Mattie Lee, dau of
----- ----- Hobby
Born Jan 28, ----
Died --- --- ----

Edy Bruse, son of
W. A. & S. F. Pruitt
Jul 23, 1879
Nov 4, 1880(6)

Eddie B., son of
William & Fannie Pruitt
Jul 20, 1879
Nov 4, 1886
(same as above)

Luler Emmer, dau of
W. A. & S. F. Pruitt
Aug 16, 1877
Aug 18, 1878

Luler E., dau of
William & Fannie Pruitt
Aug 16, 1877
Aug 13, 1878
(same as above)

* *

HOBBY CEMETERY

Located on Yell Road, north of Ostella, on farm of Mr. & Mrs. Shirley House. Copied Mar 27, 1976.

J. P. Hobby
Mar 6, 1851
Feb 17, 1909

Nettie Hobby
1863-1937

Maxie, dau of
J. P. & Nettie Hobby
Jun 5, 1888
Sep 18, 1910

1 other grave, unmarked.

* *

OLIVER CEMETERY

Located on Yell Road, north west of Ostella. Copied by Haskell Roden

Annanias T. Oliver
Mar 2, 1810
Nov 3, 1890
(3rd son of Frederick &
Rosanna Oliver)

Other graves, unmarked.   Located on part of the Old Mathew McGaugh Estate.

* *

CORNERSVILLE

BACHMAN CEMETERY

Located one mile north of Delina-Ostella Road, east of Ebenezer Hollow and near the mouth of Edwards Hollow. The cemetery has been destroyed. Known to be buried here are:

Daniel Bachman
1787-1868

The markers have all been moved from area of Cemetery. The markers have no inscriptions. Several graves.

Dorcas Bachman
1800- ca 1855

Sarah, wife of
Capt. John Doak*
Died ca. 1840

* Capt. Doak died at New Orleans in 1815

NOTE: Daniel Bachman born in Virginia, settled here prior to 1814. Was a large landowner. He operated a large tanyard on this farm.

* *

NIX-TAYLOR CEMETERY

Located on Collins Hollow Yell Road, north of Ostella, on farm of Herman Bigham. Copied Mar 27, 1976 by Haskell Roden, Ralph D. Whitesell, Foster & Charlene Nicholas.

W. A. Taylor
Jan 22, 1850
Oct 17, 1905

Altie M., wife of
A. W. Taylor
Jan 7, 1865
Oct 20, 1907

Lester E., son of
M. H. & V. A. Lowrance
B&D Jul 11, 1894

Several unmarked graves.

J. A. Taylor
Jun 27, 1823
May 2, 1906

A. M., wife of
J. A. Taylor
Jul 29, 1822
Oct 2, 1891

Mary E. Taylor Green
Jul 27, 1826
Jun 1, 1911
"A Worthy Mother".

Guy K., son of
M. H. & V. A. Lowrance
Mar 10, 1888
Oct 4, 1897

Johny Worth Coleman
Jul 12, 1884
Dec 19, 1888

Oscar Leonidas, son of
G. W. & M. A. Nix
Jun 3, 1878
Jan 5, 1880

Infant Dau of
G. M. & R. E. Taylor
B&D Jan 25, 1884

R. E. Taylor
Aug 10, 1820
Apr 14, 1876

Newton Thomas
B&D Jun 27, 1889
&
Frances E. Green Thomas
Aug 29, 1858
Mar 17, 1894

* *

DOWNING CEMETERY

Located on the hill about 200 yards north of the Old Downing ancestral log home, on land now owned by Charley and Grady Davis. About 2 miles west of Delina, on Delina-Ostella Road. Copied March 1973 by C. H. Roden.

R. C. Downing
Nov 22, 1836
Jul 12, 1860
Age 24 years

J. G. Downing
Jan 6, 1795
Sep 11, 1856
Age 61 years

Many unmarked graves.

Eliza, wife of
J. G. Downing
Born 1806
Died Aug 6, 1887
Age 81 years

Bettie Downing
Died Sep 11, 1856
Age 11 years

Mary P. Downing(Caldwell)
Jan 18, 1841
Feb 28, 1903
Age 62 years

Bird L. Downing
Died Sep 14, 1856
Age 12 years

Jane M. Downing
Jul 20, 1808
Jan 18, 1893
Age 85 years

Margaret A. Downing
Feb 4, 1843
Mar 12, 1863
Age 20 years

Elijah Downing
Jan 17, 1811
Nov 15, 1884, Age 73 yrs.

Jas. F. Downing
Jul 25, 1835
Dec 25, 1860, Age 25 yrs.

Martha M. Downing
Nov 1, 1838
Jun 15, 1862, Age 24 yrs.

* *

PARK CEMETERY

Located one-fourth mile south east of Ostella on Coffey Branch. This cemetery has been completely destroyed.

Moses Park
Born 1780 , Mar 12
Died (after 1850)

Mary Wier, wife of
Moses Park
Born Jan 26, 1779
Died Jan 19, 1859
Age 80 yrs, lacking 7 days.

CORNERSVILLE

BISHOP CEMETERY
Located on Petersburg-Cornersville Road on Pee Dee Branch near Archer, at site of the Old Bishop School.

Members of the Bishop Family is buried here. No signs of graves remain. 1979.

* *

BARNES CEMETERY
Located two miles south east of Ostella, on Coffey Branch.

G. E. Barnes
1830-1902   This the only grave.

* *

HARRIS CEMETERY
Located one mile south of Archer, Harris Fork of Pee Dee Branch. Copied April 5, 1980 by Ralph D. Whitesell, Helen and Tim Marsh.

James Harris Nov 7, 1772 Sep 27, 1845	Sarah Harris Born --- 7, 1788 Died Aug 3, 1858 (broken in many pieces)	Thomas Harris 1815-1850 (no marker)	Aletha Adaline (McCree) Harris wife of Thomas Harris Died in early 1900's (no marker)
Probably Elizabeth, dau of Jas. & Sarah Harris & wife of Samuel Davis.	A Daughter of James & Sarah Harris who married Isaac Park.		Perhaps members of the William Rosson Family &
	15 or more unmarked graves. * Native of Pittsylvania co.Va.		The McCree Family.

* *

BRADEN CEMETERY
Located on Coffey Branch, two miles south east of Ostella, in Coffey Hollow. Copied by Tim and Helen Marsh.

John W. Braden Dec 5, 1804 Aug 29, 1871	Harvey L. Braden Jul 7, 1863 Apr 27, 1914	Sintha Alis Braden Jan 1, 1861 Jan 5, 1865 (fieldstone, no inscription)	Several unmarked graves.
Sarah A. Braden (dau of Edmund & Sarah Taylor) Oct 28, 1821 Nov 17, 1898	Vera, dau of H. L. & J. E. Braden Mar 31, 1902 Jul 2, 1902	Perry Columbus Braden Apr 9, 1842 Feb 14, 1862 (CSA) (fieldstone, no inscription.)	

* *

HORTON-(HAUGHTON) CEMETERY
Located four-tenths mile on Delina Road off the Spring Place Road. Copied 1970 by Helen and Tim Marsh.

Albert C. Ealy 1864-1948 & Anna R. Ealy 1872-1961	Father (& Soldier) James Harvey Ralston Aug 23, 1819 Feb 13, 1883 & Mother Sallie Harris McGaugh Talley Aug 27, 1836 Feb 23, 1916	James H. Ralston Jan 23, 1877 Apr 4, 1927 & Icie B. Ralston Sep 22, 1890 ------------ Tom Haislip 1870-1919 & Cora Haislip 1875-1954	Henry V. Smith (Soldier) 1868-1956 & Bettie R. Smith 1868-1953 Felix R. Haislip Tennessee Sgt Central Inf Officers Training School Sep 7, 1895 Nov 26, 1919
Dana Harvey, son of A. C. & A. K. Ealy Jan 28, 1901 Sep 14, 1901			

CORNERSVILLE

Lawrence McGaugh
Aug 7, 1850
Jun 23, 1922

Mrs. Ammy McGaugh
Sep 4, 1851
Mar 26, 1920

Catherine J. Milton
Jan 30, 1924
Oct 19, 1925

D. H. Beasley
Jan 25, 1843
Jun 5, 1917 (CSA)

Mary A. Beasley
Jul 25, 1843
May 10, 1926

Mother
E. F. Thomas-Beasley
Feb 28, 1838
Jun 4, 1908

*
Susannah, wife of
F. R. McGaugh
May 27, 1813
Jun 14, 1897

Rev. F. R. McGaugh
May 30, 1813
Jul 25, 1896

Mattie Lou Wolaver
Jun 13, 1884
Jul 24, 1890

Robert G. Wolaver
Nov 30, 1844
Oct 14, 1896

Robert A., son of
S. M. & Laila Wolaver
Dec 1, 1903
Jul 11, 1904

Willie M., dau of
S. M. & Laila Wolaver
Apr 5, 1905
Sep 7, 1905

S. M. Wolaver
Dec 20, 1879
Jul 27, 1914

O. T. Baucom
1881-1962
(McDaniel FH)

Felix E. McGaugh
Apr 10, 1879
Sep 6, 1881

Annie Haislip
1899-1903

Jessie B. Harris
(no dates)

Ella Edwards
(no dates)(on big marker)

John L. Billingsley
(no dates, on big marker)

Mary M. Billingsley
(no dates, on big marker)

James S. Billingsley
(no dates, on big marker)

C. Billingsley
(no dates, on big marker)

Elmo O. O'Neal
1892-1947

J. Herman O'Neal
1909-1930

Arthur C. Edwards
1892-1954

Clara Mae Ealy McWaggoner
Sep 27, 1886
Apr 22, 1970

Nannie L., wife of
F. G. Crick
Mar 2, 1876
Aug 12, 1909

Lurindia E., wife of
F. G. Crick
Apr 17, 1878
Oct 29, 1905

Infant Dau of
F. G. & Lula Crick
Aug 5, 1905

E. J., wife of
J. W. Crick
Sep 30, 1835
Dec 31, 1896
(she is on also
 stone with her husband)

About 40 unmarked graves.

*NOTE:Dau.of James & Sarah(Yates)Harris

Mary M., wife of
P. M. Billingsley
May 5, 1838
Apr 12, 1877
&
James S. Billingsley
Apr 9, 1867
Aug 22, 1876
&
C. Billingsley
(no dates)
&
John L. Billingsley
Aug 18, 1874
Jan 28, 1904
&
Ella B. Edwards
Oct 13, 1869
Jan 11, 1904
&
Jessie B. Harris
(no dates)

Emma R., wife of
F. P. O'Neal & dau of
D. A. Ellison
Jun 15, 1868
Jan 12, 1910

F. P. O'Neal
Jan 21, 1862
Apr 16, 1924

Sam T. Ealy
1859-1937
&
Lou M. Ealy
1859-(no date)

Father
John W. Crick
Apr 5, 1830
Jul 13, 1912
&
Mother
Eliza J. Crick
Sep 30, 1835
Dec 31, 1896

William R., son of
J. W. & E. J. Crick
Mar 26, 1867
Feb 26, 1889

Jasper O., son of
J. W. & E. J. Crick
Dec 13, 1880
Aug 11, 1885

Mollie West O'Neal
1872-1933

Freemon N. Wakefield
Mar 14, 1885
Dec 18, 1956
&
Edna J. Wakefield
Nov 22, 1887
Nov 23, 1970

James T. Finley
1852-1921
&
Hortense Finley
1861-1951

Britton M. Finley
Tennessee
Mech Co F 6 Inf Repl Regt
WW I
Apr 28, 1896
May 11, 1964

J. R. Vaughn
Oct 30, 1872
Oct 11, 1895

Amanda Vaughn, 2nd wife of
William Barron
Died Oct 30, 1907
Age 67 years

J. H. Vaughn
Jul 3, 1850
Dec 30, 1892

James Thomas Campbell
1864-1941
&
Amanda Billingsley Campbell
1863-1956

John Baucom
Feb 26, 1820
Oct 31, 1904
&
Nancy D. Baucom
Oct 10, 1827
Aug 16, 1894

B. M. B.
(no dates)

William Baucom
1939-1958 (TM)

John J. Baucom
Apr 3, 1858
Apr 4, 1938
&
Cinthia Baucom
Feb 18, 1861
(no date)

* *

CORNERSVILLE

JOBE CEMETERY
Located near Yell on Yell Road, north of Ostells. Copied April 8, 1976 by Ralph D. Whitesell and Knox Bigham. This cemetery is at the home of William Earl Wells.

S. C. Jobe
Dec 27, 1827
Oct 8, 1906
&
Mary A. Jobe
Jul 29, 1836
Oct 10, 1904
(Mary may have been a Pyles)

Morgan J. P., son of
S. C. & Mary A. Jobe
Nov 24, 1861
Mar 8, 1879

Several unmarked graves.

Stephen F., son of
S. C. & M. A. Job
Aug 11, 1855
Aug 10, 1885

S. L. Job
Apr 18, 1857
May 18, 1894

Sarah Jane Jobe
Jan 10, 1862
Dec 10, 1913

* *

COBLE CEMETERY
Located on the Delina-Cornersville Road, one mile west of Old Ebenezer. Copied by Haskell Roden

William Coble, Sr.
Sep 15, 1794
Jul 10, 1860

Exie (Experience) Coble
Jul 17, 1804
Jul 15, 1886

Jimmy Jones
(no marker)

Several unmarked graves.

Henry Coble
Sep 22, 1840
Oct 18, 1861

Martha Huckaby
May 24, 1849
Aug 26, 1894

Nancy Ann Huckaby
Aug 17, 1874
Sep 4, 1876

* *

UNNAMED CEMETERY
Located on hill, east side of Ebenezer Hollow, one-half mile north east of sight of Ebenezer M. E. Church.

Several graves with fieldstones, two with pyramid type Rocks. This appears to be a very old graveyard. Some local historians think that members of the Franklin, Edwards and possibly Lawrence Families are buried here.

* *

ARTHUR CEMETERY
Located on the property of Harold Glenn near Yell. Copied by Knox Bigham, June 1, 1975.

M. L. "Boy" Taylor
1860-1933
&
Trenie Taylor
1861-1928

M. C. "Bud" Emerson
Mar 15, 1863
Oct 21, 1922

Ninna G. Emerson
Feb 11, 1899
Oct 24, 1917

Mother
Nora C. Emerson
Jun 6, 1879
Aug 3, 1956

J. L. Willis
Feb 16, 1874
Jul 25, 1897

Thomas H. Willis
Dec 30, 1820
Jun 11, 1879

"Vollie"
V. O. Willis
Feb 4, 1864
Jul 20, 1888

Fannie, wife of
J. E. Lee
Born Jul 8, 1866
Mrd Mar 11, 1888
Died Feb 10, 1911

J. E. Lee
Feb 6, 1847
Oct 16, 1911

B. C. Arthur
Sep 20, 1845
Jan 19, 1912

Addie Arthur
Jan 7, 1847
Mar 12, 1896

Bessie Norton Benedick
Oct 10, 1892
Jul 14, 1894

G. B. Arthur
Son of Bluford &
Mary Arthur
May 1, 1845
Aug 18, 1875

Mary O. Arthur
Aug 3, 1821
Oct 10, 1895

Bluford Arthur
Jul 14, 1809
May 14, 1872

J. B., Infant of
J. B. & M. J. Rainey
May 6, 1854
Mar 20, 1897
(dates may be wrong)

L. L. Oliver
Apr 4, 1845
Sep 28, 1896

J. A., wife of
L. L. Oliver
Dec 22, 1846
May 14, 1877

Tippie, wife of
E. B. Arthur
Sep 23, 1871
Sep 15, 1898

E. B. Arthur
Jun 4, 1867-Oct 11, 1909

CORNERSVILLE

Willie T. Fox
Jun 15, 1892
Feb 1, 1911

Ota D. Fox
Jun 24, 1871
Dec 6, 1895

Father
Thomas H. Pyles
Jul 15, 1850
Aug 26, 1910

Mother
Nan P., wife of
T. H. Pyles
Jun 27, 1852
Aug 25, 1914

Eddie Welch
Dec 13, 1892
Jan 2, 1914

Son of
Mr. & Mrs. W. M. Pettes
(no dates)

Daughter of
Mr. & Mrs. W. M. Pettes
(no dates)

J. A. Emerson
Mar 27, 1815
Apr 22, 1892

Mother
S. L. Hillard, wife of
John A. Emerson
May 16, 1826
Apr 7, 1906

Several unmarked graves.

William C. Hobby
Jun 18, 1841
Jun 22, 1903

Bettie Hobby
Oct 10, 1849
Apr 21, 1888

J. B. Hobby
Dec 12, 1877
Oct 12, 1957

Sirdelia Love, wife of
J. B. Hobby
Nov 17, 1879
Dec 20, 1905

F. M. Hobby
Aug 26, 1839
Oct 14, 1918

J. A. Haislip, wife of
F. M. Hobby
Sep 25, 1847
Apr 17, 1899

W. M. Pettes
Oct 21, 1857
Jun 26, 1905

Sarah J. Pettes Glenn
1858-1926

Tursie Caneer Arthur
Age 85 years
(no dates)

Father
William Ace Gillum
Feb 25, 1861
Aug 23, 1921

Mother
Vinie West Emerson Gillum
Feb 10, 1858
May 29, 1923

J. A. Crowder
Jun 22, 1828
Aug 4, 1907

* *

DAVIS CEMETERY
Located west of Ostella on the Cornersville-Ostella Road.
Copied Feb 17, 1974.

Lizzie A. Davis
Mar 12, 1876
Apr 8, 1906

Nannie M., dau of
Edd & Tellie Davis
Aug 20, 1910
Sep 2, 1910

Ethel, wife of
J. M. Clayton
Nov 20, 1881
Mar 9, 1906

Steel, son of
J. M. & Ethel Clayton
Feb 28, 1906
Sep 19, 1906

J. D., son of
S. E. & S. F. Moore
Aug 6, 1895
Jul 16, 1897

J. Garrett, son of
W. W. & Laura Crunk
Jun 19, 1900
Oct 8, 1900

Laura Garrett, wife of
W. W. Crunk
Sep 3, 1879
Jun 20, 1900

Mary E., wife of
N. C. Davis
Feb 1, 1818
Dec 22, 1856

Jesse J. Garrett
Oct 1, 1846
Feb 9, 1909
 & wife
Mary E. Garrett
Apr 1, 1848
Oct 30, 1881

U. B. Meadows
Sep 1, 1854
May 18, 1873

S. A. Meadows
Feb 17, 1826
Sep 26, 1896

A. F. Meadows
Dec 25, 1818
--- --, 187-
(broken)

In Loving Memory of
Daughters (Meadows)
Jamie Ruth
1892-1948
 &
Sarah Ellen
1898-1971

Annie A., wife of
A. N. Bligh
Oct 26, 1869
Jul 28, 1894

C. C. Meadows, wife of
_. J. Williamson
Born --- 25, 1850
Died (illegible)
(broken)

Louis A., son of
A. F. & H. B. Meadows
Jul 20, 1896
Apr 11, 1897

A. F. Meadows, Jr.
Nov 12, 1860
Dec 30, 1906

Mother Beulah Meadows
Jul 12, 1866
Feb 17, 1920

Leland & Leon, twin sons of
Turner & Vivian Garrett
Nov 29, 1918
Dec 19, 1918

W. T. Garrett
1841-1916
 &
S. A. Garrett
1842-1916

Andrew A. J., son of
J. A. & S. A. Davis
Apr 5, 1880
Aug 30, 1893

J. A. Davis
Jan 24, 1848
Jul 27, 1901

Levi Garrett
(illegible)
Feb 5, 1867
 &
Francis T. Garrett
May 24, 1818
--- 27, 1876
(stone broken & repaired)

Infant of P. L. &
L. A. Davis
(stone, no dates)

W. P. Childs
Jan 11, 1861
Oct 8, 1901

Roy N., son of
J. C. & A. E. Grimes
Mar 9, 1900
Jan 28, 1902

Talmage, son of
J. C. & A. E. Grimes
May 12, 1893
Jul 5, 1895

William Johnson, son of
A. F. & Sarah Ann Meadows
May 10, 1852
Sep 2, 1855

CORNERSVILLE

Nathan C. Davis
1814-1882
&
1st wife
Mary E. Davis
1818-1856
&
2nd wife
Sarah H. Davis
1827-1908
&
Amos C. Davis
1840-1917

S. E., dau of
A. F. & S. A. Meadows
Apr 15, 1856
Apr 29, 1856

and on same stone:
1st Set of Children:
Martha A., 1845-1855
James A., 1848-1901
Susan O., 1850-1850
&
1st Set of children:
John W., 1836-1853
Sarah E., 1838-1879
Susie F., 1842-1855
Mary J., 1844-1844
William M. 1851-1909
Nathan D., 1855-1855

E. D.
(fieldstone)

A. D.
(fieldstone)

and on same stone:
2nd Set of Children:
Richard E., 1859-1859
Steel C., 1862-1862
Albert E., 1863-1864
R. Lee 1865-
Addie E., 1867-
N. Harrison 1870-

Nathan C. Davis "Father"
Jan 12, 1814
Jun 23, 1882
(another stone)

J. D.
(fieldstone)

A. D.
(fieldstone)

Addison Davis
Jan 6, 1820
Sep 23, 186-
&
Jane Davis
Mar 25, 1824
May 21, 1877
&
J. H. Davis
Feb 26, 1812
Jul 5, 1897
&
Amos Davis
Jul 18, 1783
Oct 16, 1834
&
Elizabeth Davis
Apr 27, 1793
Oct   1867

Several unmarked graves.

* *

BEECHWOOD CEMETERY

Located at Cornersville. Seven miles south of Lewisburg. Copied April, 1967 by Deane Porch and partially re-ckecked 1979 by Helen and Tim Marsh.

John E. White
Apr 19, 1837
Died Dec 8, 1857
"Erected by his brother,
T. M. White"

Mary Eda, dau of
Thomas T. & Mary J. Burgess
Jul 7, 1853
Sep 5, 1854

John Edwards
Jun 9, 1797
Mar 14, 1860

Newton J. Vancleave
Mar 18, 1840
Apr 6, 1883
"Farewell, my wife and
Children, all"

Louisania J., wife of
T. J. Nance
Oct 24, 1828
Sep 15, 1854
"Dau of I. & L. Holden"

Fayette G. Poarch
1896-1960

Martha M. Woods
Feb 21, 1924

James C. Woods
Tennessee
Tec 5 579 AAA AW Bn CAC
WW II
Feb 27, 1925
Feb 14, 1956

L. Haskell Park
1868-1937
&
Sallie A. Park
1871-1964

John M. Alexander
1877-1944

T. E. Yarbrough
1913-1964   (TM)

Sim L. McConnell
Jan 24, 1875
Jan 12, 1947

Barry McConnell
Feb 20, 1953

Spart A. Crane
Sep 1, 1894
May 28, 1954
&
Ellis K. Crane
Oct 22, 1905
Feb 24, 1952

Carl Wayne Crane
Aug 26, 1946
Dec 25, 1946

George Robert Massie
1948-1960   (TM)

Aline Henson
1922-1953
(McDaniel FH)

Tim W. Crane
Sep 24, 1891
Mar 15, 1956
&
Nettie G. Crane
Aug 1, 1898
Jul 9, 1979

James W. Griggs
Oct 29, 1869
Oct 2, 1942
&
Sarah E. Griggs
Oct 23, 1882
Jan 19, 1975

W. Charlie Bates
1886-1959
&
Lucy L. Bates
1892-1964

Joe P. Rutledge
1880-1959
(London FH)

Mrs. Viola Rutledge
1883-1965
(London FH)

Mother
Laura E. Mitchell
1876-1961

Marie Phillips Gillum
1900-1953
(Emblem: Ladies Aux. VFW)

Mackey Burnett
Jan 18, 1890
Aug 23, 1963
&
Shirley Burnett
Sep 29, 1890
Feb 14, 1972

Marsh Haywood
1876-1952
&
Margaret Haywood
1896-

Horace C. Smith
1893-1953
&
Robbie G. Smith
1897-19

Samuel A. Smith
Tennessee
Cpl 306 Engineers 81 Div
WW I
Jun 12, 1891
Dec 9, 1950

Sam Cullen Smith, Jr.
May 28, 1958
May 29, 1958

Father
N. Harrison Davis
1870-1950
&
Mother
Lyzinka H. Davis
1874-1950

CORNERSVILLE

Loys Frances Clift
Mar 18, 1919
May 21, 1957

Father
Tom M. Clift
1882-1949
&
Mother
Lulie Clift
1895-1968

Samuel W. "Jack" McDaniel
Ohio
Pvt 920 ORD HAM Co WW II
Aug 6, 1906
Nov 2, 1954
&
Sadie Belle McDaniel
Jan 3, 1909

Warner J. McAteer
Dec 15, 1880
Oct 12, 1961
&
Annie Mai McAteer
Jun 10, 1887
Jun 17, 1976

Hobart A. Emerson
1897-1952
&
Doris D. Emerson
1911-

Thomas H. Martin
Oct 2, 1910
Jan 28, 1953

Nannie B. Martin
Apr 22, 1891
(no date)

Thomas L. Martin
Jan 17, 1885
May 20, 1961

Ladye R. Williams
Aug 26, 1929

James E. Williams
May 20, 1928
Mar 6, 1954

Asa D. Lunsford
1885-1960
&
Mary O. Lunsford
1885-1962

E. M. Lunsford
1881-1955
&
Rebecca J. Lunsford
1888-1961

J. Henry Bivins
Jun 29, 1886
May 27, 1962
&
Eva C. Bivins
Apr 15, 1891
Apr 30, 1966

Selma Lee Glenn
Jul 30, 1908
Feb 11, 1956
(Emblem: Ladies Aux. VFW)

James F. Key
1952-1952

James W. Gillum
Feb 12, 1869
Apr 16, 1952
&
Onnis Pruitt Gillum
Jan 27, 1875
Oct 23, 1959

Floree Edith Austin
May 19, 1892
Aug 15, 1936

Alva H. Austin
1895-1952
&
Mary Lois Austin
1900-
Alvia H. Austin
Tennessee
Cpl Co A 114 Machine Gun BN
WW I PH
Aug 25, 1895
Jul 28, 1952

Ellen Hope Jordan
1920-1947

Thelma Mae McAdams
1915-1936

Joseph W. McAdams
1936

Kenneth T. Stewart
1939

Father
Claud Stewart
Oct 9, 1886
Jan 24, 1950
&
Mother
Ollie Stewart
Sep 5, 1887
Feb 2, 1958

J. M. C.
(footstone)

Joseph E. McAdams
1872-1947
&
Nancy E. McAdams
1880-1950

William Oscar Johnson
Aug 14, 1870
Nov 7, 1934
&
Mollie Alexander Johnson
Feb 28, 1875
Sep 30, 1962

Virginia Johnson
Mar 30, 1840
Feb 16, 1927

T. Howard Fox
Oct 18, 1848
May 26, 1924
&
Cora B. Fox
Jun 10, 1876
Jun 30, 1959

MARTIN on Plot Marker:
James Marshall
Jan 6, 1857
Nov 19, 1935

MARTIN on Plot Marker:
Florida Buckloo
Feb 27, 1858
May 20, 1937

William B. Martin
Tennessee
Pvt 164 Inf 41 Div WW I
Feb 11, 1897
Nov 9, 1946

William Lee Johnson
Sep 26, 1904
Jan 14, 1939

Thomas Burgess
1913-1932

Cora C. Burgess
1884-1963

Dee Burgess
1874-1930

William Thomas Welch
Aug 2, 1871
Jun 26, 1925

Myrtle Gault Welch
Apr 23, 1874
Jul 16, 1943

Ross B. Welch
Jan 1, 1902
May 17, 1947

Son of
Mr. & Mrs. C. B. Welch
Sep 20, 1932
Sep 26, 1932

Thomas F. Welch
Oct 12, 1872
Dec 17, 1925
&
Della C. Welch
Feb 7, 1874
Apr 13, 1948

H. E. Bligh
1874-1929

T. E. Bligh
1866-1934

Florence E. Bligh
1860-1948

J. M. Bligh
1875-1953

Lou C. Arthur
1857-1951

Father
Joseph L. Fowler
1850-1895
&
Mother
Mattie A. Fowler
1860-1934

Vanmeter Watson
1876-1933
&
Fannie Watson
1881-1972

Joseph Lane Keller
1871-1944

James Porter Smith
1875-1947
&
Minnie Dail Smith
1879-1974

Emma Fox Wilson
1860-1945

James C. Taylor
1879-1952
&
Minnie M. Taylor
1884-1953

Free Taylor
1872-1954
&
Tommie Taylor
1877-1957

Gary L. Nix
1945-1947

William Lon Haislip
1898-19
&
Vivian B. Haislip
1903-1947

CORNERSVILLE

Ewell C. Sanders
Apr 14, 1881
Jun 3, 1956
&
Sarah E. Sanders
Jan 26, 1886
Oct 17, 1967

Lee K. Nix
Jul 14, 1911
Dec 2, 1957
&
Catherine F. Nix
Feb 27, 1919

Iceloe S. Doggett
1907-

Homer H. Doggett
1905-1965

Mother
Alma Doggett
1878-1965

Father
W. J. Doggett
1867-1943

Pvt William F. Wheeler
Co E 105 QM Regt
Nov 16, 1910
Killed in Service at
Fort Jackson, S.C.
Jul 29, 1941

Amack B. Wheeler
1882-1949
&
Mary E. Wheeler
1883-1964

John W. McCollum
1852-1936
&
Mehallie McCollum
1854-1933

James R. Tarpley
Jun 2, 1892
Apr 11, 1963
&
Lula W. Tarpley
Aug 27, 1902
Sep 17, 1963
James Robert Tarpley
Tennessee
Pvt STU Army TNG Corps
WW I

Addie Hickerson
Mar 29, 1893
Nov 29, 1969
&
Nannie A. Hickerson
Aug 21, 1855
Sep 5, 1933
&
Lillie Hickerson
Jan 5, 1880-Mar 6, 1965

Willie (H.) Hodge
Feb 7, 1887
Nov 26, 1964

Mary E. Hodge
Mar 30, 1868
Mar 13, 1947

Robert W. Hodge
Mar 6, 1863
Aug 3, 1927

Earl Wysong Crunk
1902-1965
&
Alta Park Crunk
1905-

Robert Leo Taylor
1879-1955

R. L. Taylor
1850-1939
&
Martha E. Taylor
1850-1925

Earl E. Smith
1880-1965

William M. Bryant
1856-1936
&
Sadie M. Bryant
1855-1934

M. Harris Kennedy
Jul 2, 1889
Dec 3, 1949

Marion S. Kennedy
Born once, Born again
(no dates)

Frances Bates Kennedy
May 1, 1903
Feb 18, 1945

Carrie Harris Kennedy
Sep 4, 1854
Mar 7, 1945

Neil B. Glenn
1847-1919
&
Mary E. Glenn
1847-1925

Everett Clay, son of
N. B. & M. E. Glenn
Oct 28, 1877
Jun 17, 1899

Jodie S., son of
N. B. & M. E. Glenn
Mar 18, 1873
Jul 9, 1875

Johnnie, dau of
W. T. & M. C. Jones
Jul --, 1868-Apr 5, ----

Father
Allen Polk Doggett
Pvt Co E 11 Tenn Cav
Confederate States Army
Nov 22, 1844
Nov 22, 1939
&
Mother
Hannah C. Doggett
Feb 13, 1850
Sep 18, 1923

Quincy Doggett
1886-1950
&
Elizabeth Doggett
1886-19

J. Bell Clark
1860-1920

Maggie Doggett Clark
1865-1923

Kenneth L. Clark
Tennessee
Pvt 3 Co Receiving Camp
WW I
May 1, 1891
Dec 15, 1950

Vera Edwards Clark
1895-19

Albert S. Beatty, Sr.
Oct 22, 1876
Mar 17, 1962
&
Willie M. Beatty
Jan 25, 1887
Dec 25, 1970

Bentley Davis London
Oct 20, 1878
Jun 4, 1963

Effie Harwell London
Jan 5, 1887
Nov 6, 1957

B. A. London
Oct 4, 1855
Dec 29, 1936

Mattie, wife of
B. A. London
Sep 1, 1857
Aug 26, 1942

B. F. Coleman
Sep 13, 1850
Jan 11, 1928
& wife
Cordelia Taylor Coleman
Feb 5, 1859
May 23, 1925

W. E. Coleman
1887-1924

Estelle A. Coleman
1894-1959

Fannie Massey
1851-1932

Mother
Mary Vanhoozer
1848-1928

Clarence Doggett
1871-1949

Charlie W. Worsham
May 1, 1870
Aug 21, 1930
&
Annie R. Worsham
Feb 17, 1874
Jun 8, 1933

Robert Bruce Worsham
Jul 22, 1897
Jan 25, 1958
&
Elizabeth A. Worsham
Nov 16, 1900

Father
James Richard Stepp
Feb 28, 1879
Dec 19, 1961
&
Mother
Lena Eaton Stepp
Jul 16, 1877
Jun 4, 1947

Vestal E. Nix
Tennessee
Pvt 1Cl Infantry
Apr 28, 1918
Oct 29, 1944
"He gave his life for his
Country's cause."

Marcus Nix
1880-1959
&
Mattie Nix
1892-1951

Elisha D. Richardson
1889-1956
&
Ellie R. Richardson
1887-1963

Jasper Smith
1872-1946
&
Bettie Smith
1875-1967

Lawrence Bryant
1883-1963
&
Clara S. Bryant
1893-1969

CORNERSVILLE

Orris Gene Gower
1928-

Herman O. Gower
1898-1963
&
Janie Bell Gower
1901-

Thomas Sheffer James
1894-1956

Lyndal James
1913-1946

Viva R. McKibbon
1890-19

William J. McKibbon
1889-1942

Mrs. Anna Mae Culp
1890-1962 (TM)

Orvie A. Smith
1864-1945

Ada Smith
1873-1970

Trim C. McCollum
Tennessee
Cpl 19 Co 157 Depot Brigade
WW I
Dec 31, 1889
Dec 29, 1964
&
Sadie B. McCollum
1882-1965

Earnie McCollum
1879-1931
&
Lela McCollum
1890-1974

W. B. Fox
1884-1961
&
Bessie G. Fox
1887-1959

Sidney A. Moffitt, M.D.
1870-1930
&
Lula Mae Moffitt
1887-1956

Sara Coleman
1912-1942

T. L. Coleman
1882-1950
"Circuit Judge
1934-1945"
&
Lubbie T. Coleman
1880-1966

Lowell S. Moore
May 12, 1931
Nov 12, 1933

Everett S. Hedgcoth
Oct 11, 1890
Apr 16, 1925

Estelle Hedgcoth
Jan 10, 1893
Jul 24, 1935

Ruth Hedgcoth
Apr 3, 1921
Aug 28, 1923

Cecil Palmer Simmons
Jan 30, 1889
Jun 6, 1919

Zada May Simmons
Dec 29, 1895
Apr 17, 1929

James Monroe Simmons
Oct 10, 1861
Mar 29, 1948

Mrs. Jennie Simmons
Dec 19, 1864
Mar 29, 1941

S. E. Moore
Feb 18, 1872
Aug 15, 1942

Sarah Frances, wife of
S. E. Moore
Jan 1, 1871
Apr 16, 1921

Joseph E. Hyde
Dec 15, 1858
Jul 5, 1939
&
Anna C. Dabney Hyde
Oct 12, 1859
Oct 3, 1932

Minnie Olivia Hyde
Nov 27, 1887
Jul 8, 1960

Chesley Chunn
1901-1941
&
Mattie D. Chunn
1896-19

Chesley Chunn, Jr.
1934-1934

Nellie Will Davis
Jul 25, 1919
Jan 4, 1926

Robert Tillman Davis
1898-1957
&
Era Brintle Davis
1898-19

James Buckanan Edwards
1857-1939
&
Susan Braden Edwards
1859-1938

J. Tillman Edwards
1888-1955
&
Hattie Lou Edwards
1902-

Charles L. Welch
1867-1941

Lela P. Welch
1875-1964

Bert Welch
1871-1942

Chloe Welch
1872-1951

Charlie B. Welch
1899-1964
&
Mary London Welch
1904-1962

Peggy Gayle Hamlin
1935-1946

Ada R. Hamlin
1876-1947

Charles Burch Fox
1895-1949
&
Nettie Gosnell Fox
1897-1974

Father
John C. Fox
1922-1959
&
Mother
Mary B. Fox
1925-

Wiley Allen Bridges, Jr.
Tennessee
FC D2 USNR   WW II
May 11, 1924
Aug 26, 1963

James Allen Bridges
FLT O Army Air Forces
WW II
1921-1976

Selma Edwards Bridges
1890-1977

Wyley Allen Bridges
Tennessee
Cpl FA CEN OFF TNG SCH
WW I
Aug 5, 1888
Mar 22, 1958

Milton Lafe Bridges
Oct 22, 1880
Feb 3, 1968
&
Minnie Word Bridges
Jun 13, 1880
Dec 3, 1951

Alford H. Holland
1884-1947

W. Brown Lanier
1894-1966
&
Lula F. Lanier
1894-1951

"Sisters"
Johnnie Hobby
1878-1951
&
Della L. Hobby
1868-1951

Eura P. Welch
1884-1960

C. W. "Ladd" Welch
1884-1949

Robert Eldridge
1916-1939

Claude Eldridge
1882-1950

Maury C. Ketchum
1883-1961
&
A. Sidney Ketchum
1877-1936

Steven Gail Ketchum
Aug 8, 1944

Martha Mae Ketchum
1947

Infant
Evelyn Taylor
Jul 3, 1935

J. Frank Taylor
Oct 10, 1896
May 26, 1963

Lionel P. Taylor
1866-1947
&
Fannie J. Taylor
1875-1960

Howard B. Taylor
Mar 5, 1906
May 18, 1935

CORNERSVILLE

J. C. Grimes
1863-1935
&
Addie E. Grimes
1867-1946

James Ozro Smith
1895-1936
&
Lera Harwell Smith
1895-197_

Fannie May Lowrance
1879-1956

Joe Lowrance
1876-1935

Virgil M. Fowler
1890-1960
&
Louise H. Fowler
1903-1976

Thomas L. Hambrick
Sep 25, 1880
Jun 26, 1962
&
Mary T. Hambrick
Jun 25, 1886
Nov 16, 1970

Faris May Hambrick
May 20, 1905
Sep 30, 1932

Alpheus L. Head
May 2, 1877
Oct 17, 1956
&
Beatrice F. Head
Jul 31, 1884
Dec 20, 1956

Lucy Neallie Cook Rainey
Jun 23, 1881
Aug 23, 1958

Walter Lee Rainey
May 26, 1881
Oct 30, 1963

M. D. Rainey
Sep 29, 1854
Apr 1, 1925

Annie Lou Harmon
Nov 16, 1895
Jul 23, 1965

Ervin L. Harmon
1869-1940
&
Della Harmon
1872-1932

Edward A. Beatty
Nov 19, 1876
May 24, 1958

S. A. "Duck" Beatty
1864-1955

John Nelson Brintle
1869-1958
&
Alice Beatty
1860-1947

Fred Marshall, son of
F. M. & Jennie Bowers
July 9, 1928

Fred Marshall Bowers
1890-1953
&
Jennie May Bowers
1898-
Fred M. Bowers
Tennessee
Pfc Co L 326 Inf WW I
Aug 2, 1890
Mar 22, 1953

Melvin C. Kincaid
Nov 20, 1893
Oct 9, 1963

Robert J. McClintock
Oct 10, 1891
&
Madaline H. McClintock
Oct 23, 1895
Sep 6, 1963

Cora McClintock
1869-1906

Emma McClintock
1831-1909

Joseph McClintock
1831-1911

Octa McClintock
1889-1944

Joe McClintock
1859-1947
&
Mollie McClintock
1859-1940

Lovey McClintock
1902-1904

W. Clyde McClintock
1890-1956
&
Lois C. McClintock
1901-1964

"Bobby"
Pfc Robert J. McClintock, Jr.
50th Engineers Co D
Born Feb 15, 1919
Killed in Action on Attu
May 29, 1943

Alby McClintock
Nov 1, 1911
Nov 4, 1922

Luther P. McDaniel
1880-1947

Lillie M. McDaniel
1882-1965

Angie Lillian McDaniel
Aug 15, 1916

A. N. Bligh
Apr 5, 1862
Mar 31, 1923
&
Callie Bligh
Oct 18, 1885

Robert Woodward
1890-1959
&
Ozell Woodward
1894-1978

Mattie J. Creecy
Jul 22, 1879
Dec 4, 1957

Mrs. Martha R. Lanier
1927-1955 (TM)

Father
Marcellus M. Fowler
1848-1936
&
Mother
Mary E. Willis Fowler
1854-1928

Luther G. Fowler
1872-1949
&
Jerena S. Fowler
1877-1951

George W. Gower
1868-1932
&
Beulah A. Gower
1880-1957

Infant
Thomas Riggs Harwell
1931

Judge
William E. Harwell
Nov 20, 1869
Jan 21, 1955

Mattie Beasley Harwell
Jul 7, 1874
Oct 31, 1954

Annie Katherine Harwell
1904-1938

Horace Riggs Harwell, Sr.
1871-1960

Katherine Gordon Harwell
1875-1961

Hurshell Gaston Doggett
Tennessee
Pvt 1 Engr Fors Repl Bn
WW I
Jul 25, 1894
Oct 4, 1951
&
Sarah H. Doggett
Mar 13, 1910

Eulie G. Hobby
1883-1960
&
Maggie Shaw Hobby
1881-1955

Mary F. Stockman
Dec 7, 1892

William E. Stockman
Oct 11, 1889
Aug 24, 1956

Charles O. Stockman
Tennessee
S/Sgt US Air Force
WW II PH
Dec 16, 1920
Apr 4, 1962

Newton H. Stewart
Aug 19, 1912

Lois Inez Stewart
Sep 9, 1916
Jan 7, 1960

S. Spencer Adams
May 10, 1886
Mar 12, 1956
(color picture)

Mary Foster Clark
Oct 5, 1888
Dec 14, 1963

Mother
Mary I. McMillin
1875-1954

Oscar Elgin Word
Dec 29, 1873
Apr 26, 1931
&
Sadie McLaurine Word
Sep 2, 1879

Hollis T. Redden
1903-1948
&
Lura E. Redden
1911-

CORNERSVILLE

Solomon B. Wade
1873-1947
&
Minnie E. Wade
1877-1966

A. C. Adams
Nov 25, 1893

&
Elizabeth Adams
Jul 13, 1894
Feb 28, 1923

Mother
Elsie Bond
Dec 1, 1897
Nov 24, 1934

Dave Allen
1888-1965 (TM)

Margaret Jackson
1926
&
Mary Jackson
1924
"Daus of
Andrew & Wilma Jackson"

Lee Andrew Jackson
1890-1958

Marcus A. Caneer
Dec 25, 1882
Jun 18, 1923

Mary E. Caneer
1861-1948

Atlas L. Caneer
Oct 27, 1858
Jan 30, 1920

Father
George A. Bond
Jul 14, 1871
May 7, 1937
&
Mother
Nannie Beatty Bond
Jun 3, 1871
Mar 14, 1920

Columbus Webster
Jan 14, 1890
Nov 10, 1964
&
Selma Lee Webster
Feb 10, 1894

Ransom Powell
Aug 30, 1883
Nov 8, 1961
&
Annie Powell
Oct 6, 1896

Robert Mack Wheeler
Mar 29, 1917
Aug 21, 1964
&
Sarah Frances Wheeler
Dec 10, 1920

M. Brown Nix
Jan 5, 1888
Nov 7, 1964
&
Pernina J. Nix
Jan 26, 1893

James McAden Peebles
1890-1951

Shirley Patrick Jones
1869-1961

R. Herman Arnold
1906-1963
&
Pauline D. Arnold
1904-

Claude E. Dale
Jun 1, 1897
Apr 30, 1960

Robbie M. Dale
Apr 30, 1895

Ernie E. Shaw
Apr 24, 1886

&
Kate M. Shaw
Sep 23, 1895
Dec 4, 1961

John W. Throneberry
1887-
&
Flora M. Throneberry
1894-1961

Hubert R. Gillum
1886-1961
&
Alberta C. Gillum
1894-

Willie L. Shaw
Aug 23, 1888
Sep 17, 1959
&
Evelyn L. Shaw
Mar 5, 1891

Annie Laura Upton
1933-1959

Bailey Paton Upton
Apr 27, 1872
Dec 5, 1964
&
Clara Dona Upton
Nov 20, 1875
Aug 26, 1959

Brittain Taylor
Mar 3, 1905
Jun 26, 1962
&
Ina Lee Taylor
Dec 7, 1907

Mrd Oct 20, 1928

E. M. Bates
1888-1966 (TM)

John M. Goodman
1888-1959
&
Katherine K. Goodman
1893-

H. Clate Howell
1890-
&
Molly K. Howell
1891-1958

Columbus Marsh
Died Dec 22, 1912
Age 56 years

Sallie A. Meadows
April 1846
February 1931

Pearl, dau of
Dr. L. L. & Ella Palmer
Murrey
Dec 15, 1874
Aug 14, 1957

Lula J., dau of
William J. & Ellen E.
Palmer
Aug 21, 1857
Jul 30, 1863

William J. Palmer
Born in Culpepper County,
Virginia, Jul 4, 1811
Died Apr 26, 1882

Ellen E., wife of
William J. Palmer
Feb 6, 1813
Jul 21, 1889

Minnie M. McBride
Nov 23, 1875
Oct 18, 1878

------- McBride
Aug --, 1862
Aug 2, 1868

Elizabeth Corinne, dau of
N. H. & M. C. Murrey
Jan 26, 1851
Dec 16, 1873

Myrtle, dau of
L. L. & E. W. Murrey
Oct 30, 1877
Jul 26, 1904

Mary E. Scales, dau of
Jo & Mary A. McBride &
wife of J. S. Scales
Jan 23, 1856
--- --, 1886

Mertle F. McBride
Nov 23, 1879
Apr 20, 1883

A. L. Ewing
Apr 28, 1833
Nov 21, 1911
& wife
Victoria Ewing
Mar 23, 1838
Mar 2, 1918

Lewis Palmer
Born near Culpepper, Va.
1783- Died 1865

Jane Palmer, wife of
Mack Wilkinson
Born in Culpepper, VA.
Jul 31, 1819
Died Dec 15, 1905

Mack Wilkinson
Nov 30, 1816
Oct 27, 1880

Mack Horace, Baby Boy of
G. R. & M. A. Summerhill
Nov 20, 186-
Oct 5, 1868

Grandpa & Grandma Wilkinson
Darling Baby, Agnes Viola,
Dau of G. R. & M. A.
Summerhill
Died Sep 7, 1877
Age 5 yrs, 3 mos, 3 days

Mrs. Araminta Acuff
Sep 29, 1800
Jan 21, 1866

John Acuff
Apr 12, 1800
Jun 28, 18--
(broken)

L. M. Grigg
Feb 14, 1809
May 23, 1868

Mrs. Mary A. Grigg
Dec 16, 1821
Jun 25, 1871

CORNERSVILLE

W. G. Massey
Jan 1, 1841
Feb 2, 1914

Lee Taylor
1866-1953

John P. Calloway
1885-1960
&
Forest S. Calloway
1879-1963

Mary Edith Calloway
Jun 20, 1920
Apr 11, 1922

Addie E. Welch
Jun 19, 1875
Jul 28, 1963

John T. Brown
Aug 12, 1891
May 23, 1959
&
Lizzie Brown
Dec 30, 1887

Margaret Elia Perry
(no dates)

James Simpson Perry
1835-1918
&
Hortensia Haywood Perry
1838-1919

George W. McCoy
Mar 28, 1875
Aug 5, 1957

Carrie Jane McCoy
1886-1944

S. Willis
Nov 10, 1812
Jan 15, 1887

Mary Elizabeth Parham
May 13, 1830
Jun 22, 1861
&
William T. Parham
Aug 3, 1822
Jul 15, 1858
&
Mary Cordelia Parham
Aug 14, 1854
Jul 1, 1855
&
William James Parham
Jul 23, 1850
Nov 22, 1857
&
Martha Elizabeth Parham
Jul 13, 1852
Jul 11, 1854

W. C. Deven
(footstone, broken)

P. B.
(footstone)

John Park
Born Nov 14, 1774
Embraced religion 1801
Died Jun 11, 1862

M. L. P.
(fieldstone)

Ann E., wife of
E. B. Rosson & dau of
J. B. & J. Neely
May 11, 1833
May 28, 1853

John Burgess Neely
son of J. B. & Jane Neely
Apr 22, 1855
Jul 15, 1856

W. D. E., son of
J. B. & Jane Neely
Apr 12, 1850
May 14, 1857

John Neely
May 10, 1812
Apr 3, 1885

J. D.
(fieldstone)

William T., son of
Richard & Eliza Davis
Mar 20, 1854
Jul 11, 1855

T. J. Ketchum
Oct 2, 1830
(no date)
& wife
Esther E. Ketchum
Feb 25, 1836
Aug 4, 1897

C. T., wife of
T. J. Ketchum
Sep 21, 1834
Jun 8, 1871
(on another stone:
Caroline T., wife of
T. J. Ketchum, same
dates)

James W., Husband of
Mary J. Brown
Oct 25, 1828
Aug 17, 1911

Mary J., wife of
J. W. Brown
May 11, 1835
Jul 21, 1906

Nancy E., dau of
J. D. & I. D. Hackney
Oct 27, 1845
Jul 30, 1847

Ellanor P., dau of
C. & E. P. Hood
Aug 18, 1848
Sep 24, 1848

Andrew Johnson
Born 1802
Died May 1885
&
Susan F. Johnson
Jan 12, 1816
Apr 21, 1898

Sarah J., wife of
J. F. Cunningham & dau
of J. A. & N. Rhodes
Jan 24, 1840
Mar 25, 1871

Martha, wife of
L. S. Paxton & dau of
J. & N. Rhodes
Jul 12, 1842
Aug 15, 1868

Nancy, wife of
J. A. Rhodes & dau of
H. R. & S. Fowler
Oct 27, 1814
Dec 1, 1879

J. A. Rhodes, Sr.
Mar 1, 1813
Dec 12, 1890

M. A. G.
(footstone)

H. R. F.
(footstone)

N. P., dau of
John L. & Rhody H. Fowler
Sep 22, 1835
Sep 15, 1851

John Alexander
1794-1861

M. B. Fowler, wife of
John Alexander
May 6, 1810
May 1, 1890

Holman R. Fowler, Jr.
Born Oct 8, 1826
Was wounded Feb 13, in the
Battle of Fort Donaldson
and died close to the Babe of
Bethleham Feb 20, 1862

Here lies
Sallie Fowler
Who was born
May 6, 1787 & Died
Dec 31, 1855
Age 68 yrs, 7 mos, 24 days

Here lies Till
Resurrection
Holman R. Fowler, Sr.
Who was born
Jun 11, 1783 & Died
Nov 15, 1854
Age 71 yrs, 5 mos, 4 days

Parollee Addeline, dau of
J. A. & Nancy Rhodes
Aug 16, 1854
Oct 16, 1854

Mary Elizabeth, dau of
J. A. & Nancy Rhodes
Jul 27, 1837
Nov 13, 1843

Nancy Frances, dau of
J. A. & Nancy Rhodes
Sep 8, 1847
Aug 25, 1848

Infant Son & Daughter of
James & Lucy Rosson
Jan 1845 - Oct 1845
May 1845 - Aug 2, 1855
&
Robert Palmer
Born in Culpepper Co., VA
in 1757. Died in 1835
Age 78 years.
(All of the above graves
are covered with a con-
crete slab)

James H. Collins
Died Oct 11, 1833
Age 22 years

Thomas H. Stratton
Jul 28, 1812
Apr 26, 1843

May Richardson
Died Nov 19, 1822
(no age given)

Thaddius Constantine
Sobieski, son of
J. A. W. & N. D. Andrews
Died Jun 5, 1836
Age 13 days

Martha Jane, Consort of
James W. Nance & dau of
Dr. J. S. & Frances M. Hunt
Jan 10, 1827
Nov 8, 1858

J. W. Nance
Nov 4, 1817
Jul 23, 1892
& wife
Mary Frank Amis Nance
Died Nov 2, 1903
(no age given)

CORNERSVILLE

Mable Nance
Died Jul 14, 1892
Age 22 years

Eloise Nance
Died Mar 15, 1887
Age 23 years

Mary Francis Hunt
Feb --, 1852
Aug 4, 1852

Malinda S. Bills, wife of
M. H. Nance
May 23, 1818
Mar 6, 1900

Healen M., dau of
Walker & Mary Brown
Jan 4, 1831
Jan 14, 1847

Sallie Walton
Nov 18, 1860
Dec 13, 1947

Willis R. Walton
Jan 28, 1826
Jan 28, 1888
&
Mary P. Walton
Mar 29, 1836
Sep 23, 1877

Ellen W. Walton
Jan 16, 1807
Nov 22, 1866

Ellen J., wife of
W. D. Kelly
Mar 12, 1856
Jul 7, 1885

LaFar, son of
W. D. & E. J. Kelly
Nov 18, 1883
Jul 11, 1884

William Fowler
Sep 5, 1816
Feb 12, 1879

Frank Hawkins, son of
W. D. & E. J. Kelly
Apr 22, 1885
Aug 29, 1885

Jane J. Fowler
Oct 3, 1827
Oct 24, 1896

Tabitha E. Walton
Nov 9, 1854
May 28, 1855

Infant Son of
J. R. & V. T. Fowler
Nov 26, 1870

John R. Fowler
Mar 18, 1833
Dec 20, 1899
&
Tennie Fowler
Feb 3, 1839
Dec 19, 1878

Jimmie Pillow Acuff
Feb 27, 1865
Mar 16, 1893

Joseph William Taylor
Feb 13, 1837
Dec 7, 1911

Alex B. Taylor
1875-1948
&
Lula A. Taylor
1873-1962

Effie Annie Caneer
Dec 27, 1896
Sep 17, 1904

Johnie Melvin Taylor
Aug 10, 1901
Nov --, 1907

William Eagleton Henderson
1884-1952

Bettie Eagleton Henderson
1858-1943

Annie & Mary Henderson
1879

Samuel Eagleton
May 28, 1877
Jun 1, 1877

Our Brother
T. R. Smith
Died Feb 8, 1891
Age 68 years

Samuel Smith Henderson
1857-1897

Rhoda Ann Henderson
1832-1893

William I. Henderson
Apr 9, 1822
Dec 17, 1872

William, son of
W. I. & R. A. Henderson
Died Jul 30, 1864
Age 9 yrs, 11 mos, 26 days

Bell Erwin
1861-1920
&
Robert Erwin (no dates)
&
Elvira Erwin (no dates)

Jane N., wife of
M. S. Hurt
Oct 3, 1825
May 17, 1851
&
Floridine M., dau of
M. S. & J. N. Hurt
May 7, 18--
May 15, 1849

Milissa E., wife of
E. P. Massey
Died Dec 13, 1848
Age 28 years
"I would not live
always."

Elizabeth, wife of
J. Henderson
Mar 2, 1790
Feb 4, 1852

John Henderson
Died Mar 18, 1846
Age 73 yrs, 6 mos, 2 days

Margaret Haynes
Aug 9, 1763
Jul 3, 1851

James S. Haynes, Esq.
Jul 7, 1788
Sep 23, 1873

Rizpah, wife of
J. S. Haynes
Died Dec 6, 1870
Age 72 yrs, 11 mos, 13 days

Minnie, dau of
J. S. & R. Haynes
Died Apr 23, 1861
Age 18 yrs, 8 mos, 13 days

Rev. R. G. Kimbrough
Jul 24, 1806
Jul 22, 1879

Newton C. Nix
1838-1914
&
Sallie E. Nix
1845-1923

Infant Son
May 1, 1917
May 2, 1917
(all on stone)

Cullen George, Jr.
Jul 16, 1919
Jul 16, 1919

Mrs. Will Taylor
Oct 29, 1874
Oct 11, 1918

George W. Brown
Tennessee
Pvt 339 FA BN 88 Inf Div
WW II
(sunken)

Bobbie Dee Ann Pearson
1963-1964 (TM)

John Rutledge
1890-1957 (TM)

R. A. Pigg
1884-1961 (TM)

James A. Bridges
Jan 29, 1848
Dec 19, 1906
&
Tennie S. Bridges
Jun 28, 1859
Mar 18, 1917

Edna May Park
Sep 14, 1866
Dec 5, 1957

W. A. Pruitt
Mar 11, 1847
Oct 8, 1934
&
Fannie Pruitt
Sep 4, 1856
Sep 28, 1943

Mattie J. Burlin
1864-1949

Flora, wife of
S. M. Turner
May 17, 1879
Jul 23, 1912

S. M. Turner
Feb 3, 1861
Nov 26, 1940

Effie Lou Turner
1889-1957

Mark Fowler
1873-1955

J. R. Dockrey
1853-1929 (TM)

Mrs. Bettie Dockrey
1860-1946

Alvie E. Walker
1886-1959
&
Gertrude A. Walker
1888-

Robert E. Walker
Aug 21, 1910
May 21, 1912

CORNERSVILLE

Ross Carter Bagley, Jr.
1920-1922

John Elam Cochran
1860-1939
&
Margret Cochran
1861-19

Walter Dockery
1884-1921
&
Ida Dockery Purdom
1886-1937

Thomas L. Caneer
1857-1932 (TM)

Owen Scott Cochran
1899-1966 (TM)

Allen Rutledge
1901-1960 (TM)

Bud Cochran
1862-19
&
Ada Cochran
1866-1939

Mary L. Riley
1862-1935

John J. Riley
1863-1940

Malinda F. Riley
1841-1922

Thomas Beatty
1858-1940
&
Mattie Beatty
1871-1948

Mrs. Hannah Caneer
1861-1950 (TM)

Charles A. Bagley
Sep 12, 1879
Dec 22, 1962
&
Ada Pettes Bagley
Dec 3, 1881

Bessie Bagley Brady
May 31, 1890

Mary Eliza Bagley
1888-1929

A. W. Taylor
1854-1933

Knox Albina, son of
A. W. & C. P. Taylor
1913

R. D. Bagley
Dec 8, 1847
Dec 12, 1912
&
Nancy C. Davidson Bagley
Nov 21, 1848
Jan 2, 1929

R. N. Nix
Nov 18, 1837
Dec 25, 1919

Mary E. Nix
Jun 25, 1838
Jun 27, 1920

Ivon Irwin Nelms
Jan 7, 1902
Dec 2, 1959

Sarah Martha Nelms
Feb 19, 1905

John Claiborne Meadows
Jan 29, 1898
Nov 10, 1964

Clifford Meadows
1900-1966 (TM)

Mrs. Berdie Meadows
1899-1966 (TM)

W. E. Thompson
1871-1942

Ada Mai Richardson
Oct 1, 1923
May 17, 1940

Dillie C. Davis
May 3, 1903
May 8, 1939

Maggie Richardson
Mar 9, 1900
Mar 16, 1928

Meldon Richard Calloway
1910-1957

John Clifford Steele
1890-1931

William Thomas Steele
1920-1920

J. E. Hyde, Jr.
Apr 23, 1891

&
Gertrude B. Hyde
Jul 23, 1900
Nov 24, 1919

Olie Head, Jr.
Sep 1935

Judith Louise Meadows
Feb 22, 1907
Feb 23, 1907

Bruce C. Meadows
1875-1945
&
Martha R. Meadows
1877-1933

Martha J. Gambill
Aug 29, 1859
Jul 19, 1931

J. B. Gambill
Nov 24, 1856
Aug 28, 1919

Edgar, son of
J. B. & M. J. Gambill
Sep 23, 1879
Oct 23, 1892

Mildred E. Alexander
1920-1936

Jackson Alexander
1848-1928
&
Harrett M. Alexander
1854-1913

Miss Effie Dockery
1893-1912

W. F. Hambrick
1858-1937
&
M. A. Hambrick
1863-1940

Max P. Hambrick
Jan 15, 1891
Sep 28, 1911

Mrs. Annie May Rainey
1890-1965

Jermie T. Hambrick
Jun 19, 1886
Jul 23, 1911

Flora McMahon Dysart
1839-1928

Sarah McClintock
1916-1918

Capt. Andrew R. Gordon
1835-1923
&
Rebecca C. Gordon
1839-1923

Annie Jones Gordon
1873-1959

Hoyte Nix
May 9, 1901
Jul 31, 1901

Hazel O. Nix
Jun 18, 1917
Oct 20, 1918

J. T. Nix
Nov 27, 1864
Oct 16, 1938
&
Naoma Nix
Aug 5, 1869
Oct 24, 1949

James E. Nix
Sep 5, 1872
Jul 7, 1935
&
Daisy E. Nix
Jan 16, 1879
Oct 28, 1938

Daniel P. Underwood
May 3, 1854
Jan 6, 1932
&
Sarah D. Underwood
May 6, 1865
Feb 16, 1937

Blanche Underwood
Jul 23, 1885
Nov 20, 1906

Alonzo H. Hedgecoth
Oct 3, 1871
Aug 9, 1915
&
Orpha Madge Hedgecoth
Mar 11, 1887

William B. Millsap
1857-1911
&
Addie Lee Millsap
1869-1950

J. T. Luna
Apr 7, 1837
May 18, 1902

Amitus, wife of
J. T. Luna
Jan 5, 1842
Jan 9, 1907

Susie Jane Rhodes
1881-1954

J. P. Rhodes
1867-1918

Jimmie Hemphill
1857-1927
&
Jennie Hamphill
1857-1934

Carrie, wife of
A. R. Whitaker
1877-1944

CORNERSVILLE

William J. Hunter
Mar 29, 1852
(no date)
&
M. Birdie Hunter
Jan 1, 1864
(no date)
&
Mary Elizabeth Hunter
Jan 28, 1905
Dec 7, 1911

John B. Williams
1861-1933
&
Molly T. Williams
1867-1940

Mary Hatchett
1879-

Flora Hatchett
1870-1957

Joel Hatchett
33 Reg Tenn Vol
1839-1929
&
Bettie Hatchett
1840-1904

Horace, son of
Jas. & Mattie Ashley
Aug 24, 1871
Mar 27, 1897
&
Joe, son of
Jas. & Mattie Ashley
Sep 4, 1868
Nov 21, 1898

Carrie Ashley, wife of
John P. Buchanan
Nov 15, 1876
Dec 8, 1905

James Ashley
May 22, 1846
Apr 28, 1910

R. P. Thornton Walker
Jun 29, 1852
Dec 31, 1914
&
Minnie Olivia Walker
Jun 1, 1858
Aug 11, 1921

Jesse C. McMurrey
Oct 12, 1873
Mar 31, 1931
&
Annie E. McMurrey
Sep 19, 1878
Jan 20, 1942

Charlie B. Chunn
1888-1955
&
Sammie L. Chunn
(no dates)

Charlie Boyd Chunn, Jr.
Jan 30, 1922
Jan 31, 1922

Newton Doggett
1870-1915
&
Fannie Doggett
1872-1960

Father
J. W. Cox
Nov 19, 1849
Jul 27, 1912
&
Mother
Florence A. Cox
Mar 20, 1858
May 4, 1935

Walter W. Word
1876-1961
&
Bessie B. Word
1888-

Walter Bryant Word
Feb 23, 1919
Nov 17, 1927

Bettie, wife of
W. W. Word & dau of
J. W. & Florence Cox
Born Mar 13, 1885
Married Dec 17, 1903
Died Mar 21, 1906

William J. Roberson
Oct 1, 1887
Mar 7, 1947

J. H. Roberson
1852-1919
&
Hettie Roberson
1853-1921

Father
James Baker Roberson
Apr 10, 1854
Dec 7, 1906
&
Mother
Bettie Bullock Roberson
Jul 30, 1856
Nov 19, 1906

Jennie W. Connelly
1855-1930

O. M. Connelly
Jan 27, 1858
Jul 7, 1916

Julia P. Connelly
Sep 11, 1887
Dec 2, 1911

Ida M. Dabney
1861-1935

Josie Dabney
1856-1935

Samuel Day Dabney
Dec 8, 1841
Dec 20, 1919
"A good Soldier, kind
husband & father"

Charles J. Dabney
Feb 14, 1843
Jan 7, 1897

Samuel A. Ramsey
1850-1929

Charles M. Ramsey
1862-1947

Joseph Ramsey
1824-1912
&
Isabell Ramsey
1839-1925

Georgia C. Wilkinson
Mar 21, 1863
Aug 4, 1959

Walter G. Wilkinson
Jun 23, 1859
Mar 3, 1939

T. W. Wakefield
Jan 30, 1850
Jan 8, 1910
&
Addie C. Wakefield
1851-1934

Bell Zana, dau of
T. W. & M. A. Wakefield
Mar 16, 1890
Feb 1, 1892

J. Harvey Word
Feb 23, 1839
Apr 27, 1920
&
Rellie J. Word
Apr 6, 1843
Aug 24, 1910

David Chalmers Kennedy
Jan 6, 1861
May 11, 1944
&
Lillian Stamps Kennedy
Oct 31, 1861
Dec 4, 1943

Frank M. O'Neal
Dec 18, 1856
Jan 11, 1925
& wife
Alice J. Word O'Neal
Sep 6, 1865
May 19, 1926

Uncle Foss
F. E. Word
Dec 12, 1831
Oct 11, 1911

Tennie Alexander, wife of
J. F. Nix
Born Jul 2, 1841(1844)?
Married Feb 7, 1871
Died Dec 25, 1903

John F. Nix
Sep 21, 1845
Dec 17, 1935

Nannie E. Nix
1874-1948

Rev. W. A. Bridges
Jul 26, 1847
Jun 20, 1892
& wife
Sarah F. Bridges
Nov 16, 1853
Jul 29, 1934

Sister
Susan A. Bridges
Feb 1, 1860
Jun 22, 1939

J. T. Glenn
1834-1919
&
Martha V. Glenn
1842-1894

William Cowden Glenn
May 16, 1871
Apr 30, 1926

Infant of
W. B. & Margaret G. London
May 20, 1913

Berry London
Jan 18, 1867
Sep 7, 1946
&
Maggie London
Jul 7, 1873
May 23, 1931

Clarence A. Ewing
1873-1940

Mrs. Gussie Ewing
1873-1960 (TM)

Bulah O'Neal, wife of
Allen Gates
Sep 25, 1877
Dec 10, 1912

Ollie Davis
1889-1963

Bettie Davis
1865-1949

CORNERSVILLE

Hubert T. Burt
1895-1919

Nattie M., wife of
H. T. Burt
Jun 5, 1876
--- --, 1899

Lon D. Burgess
1897-1964

T. K. James
Sep 6, 1859
Sep 15, 1898

Mrs. Emma Perry
1873-1948 (TM)

J. A. Burrow
Mar 5, 1843
Sep 11, 1920

Katie Burrow, wife of
A. L. Head
Sep 16, 1881
Apr 22, 1911

George E. Burrow
Aug 12, 1888
Aug 13, 1888

Nannie D., wife of
J. A. Burrow
Jun 30, 1857
May 6, 1890

George A. Morgan
1866-1943
&
Vernor Kennedy Morgan
1870-1939

Sam Blake Webb
1899-1899

Bettie E. Blake
1861-1884

Amanda E., wife of
J. F.(R) James
Aug 11, 1853
Oct 14, 1883

Mary E. Kennedy
1868-1918

Mamie Gordon, wife of
R. M. Kennedy
Mar 25, 1866
Oct 23, 1915

Richard Marcus Kennedy
Aug 26, 1864
Mar 11, 1896

James Mark Kennedy
Feb 24, 1892
Sep 18, 1903

James F. Kennedy
Oct 4, 1830
Sep 13, 1904

Hannah C., wife of
James F. Kennedy
Apr 2, 1834
Jul 8, 1887

My Mother
Mollie J. Peebles
Left us Aug 18, 1893
Aged 50 yrs, 5 mos.

Dr. E. A. Norton
May 5, 1837
May 4, 1907
& wife
Elizabeth E. Norton
Nov 25, 1840
Dec 14, 1907

Thomas Moore Hall
Oct 23, 1843
Feb 2, 1923
&
Mintia Bell Hayes Hall
Nov 14, 1865
Feb 20, 1919

Lillie B. Caneer
1882-1952

In Memory of our Mother
Anna R. Plattenburg
Mar 3, 1824
Dec 6, 1910
&
In Memory of our Brother
William W. Plattenburg
Dec 24, 1848
Jul 26, 1915

William E. Wilkinson
Mar 14, 1856
Mar 7, 1907
&
Mollie Holden Wilkinson
Dec 10, 1860
Feb 11, 1934

Robie L., dau of
W. E. & M. Wilkinson
Apr 20, 1890
Nov 10, 1898

Claude E. Perry
May 2, 1871
May 16, 1949
&
Della M. Perry
Jan 1, 1888

Max M. Jones
1873-1931

Kenneth Lane Jones, M.D.
1866-1922
& wife
Sadie D. Haywood Jones
1877-1960

Alfred Jones, M.D.
1839-1920
& wife
Maxie Harris Jones
1843-1938

Willis H. McConnel
Nov 16, 1822
Mar 13, 1907
& First wife
Winnie E. McConnel
Jan 16, 1826
Oct 10, 1891
& Second wife
Mary J. McConnel
Nov   1828
Oct 27, 1902

Mother
Mary Elizabeth Tally
Dec 3, 1843
Nov 25, 1910

E. F. Alexander
Jul 25, 1835
Dec 26, 1908
&
Amanda Glenn Alexander
(no dates)

Farris Inez, dau of
J. T. & E. L. Gillum
May 27, 1893
Jan 10, 1907

J. T. Gillum
Sep 9, 1852
Feb 15, 1930

Nora Lou, wife of
L. O. Simpson & dau of
J. T. & E. L. Gillum
Feb 29, 1884
Aug 22, 1909

Eva Lee Gillum, wife of
J. T. Gillum
Oct 8, 1859
Jan 8, 1921

J. C(G). Davis
Apr 18, 1860
Apr 5, 1887

Ernest Davis
Jan 1, 1867
Sep 9, 1888

Elisha R. Davis
Mar 23, 1801
Sep 6, 1890

Susan E. Davis
Died Nov 15, 1891
Age 62 years

Robert E. Davis
Apr 6, 1863
Jan 24, 1891

Audie Lee Throneberry
Feb 22, 1884
Jun 29, 1902

Sallie E. Throneberry
Mar 1, 1861
Nov 17, 1910

R. N. Throneberry
Nov 2, 1855
Nov 13, 1902

Minnie A., wife of
E. D. Richardson
Oct 20, 1890
Mar 4, 1916

Annie Sarah Richardson
Nov 26, 1912
Jan 28, 1923

J. P. Clark, Sr.
1865-1902

Fannie Clark McCollum
1877-1952

Floyd Benjamin Clark
Tennessee
Pvt US Army
Oct 13, 1918

Gwendolyn Fay Clark
dau of J. P. & Lois Clark
Aug 8, 1930
Jun 6, 1931

Louise Pigg
1906-1919

Wilma May Burrow
May 24, 1915
Jun 11, 1916

James L. Burrow
Apr 11, 1917
Jul 30, 1942

-- N. G. Fisher
1883-1943 (TM)

Berry Lee Fisher
Dec 29, 1908
Nov 14, 1911

Thomas Fisher
Jun 23, 1906
Sep 30, 1911

John Virgil, son of
T. F. & N. L. McCollum
Apr 6, 1908
Nov 19, 1911

CORNERSVILLE

Dorcie A. Jenkins, wife of
R. L. Davis
1871-1938

Jno. B. Jenkins
1846-1927

Nannie Jenkins
1844-1933

Laura Jenkins
1877-1900

Thomas O'Brien
Age 84 years
(no dates)

Mary O'Brien
Age 86 years
(no dates)

Blake McCollum
1911-1944

Palmer McCollum
1857-1916

Mary McCollum
Nov 20, 1857
Oct 15, 1901

Velma McCollum
Mar 10, 1893
Jun 1, 1894

Iva May McCollum
Dec 28, 1894
Feb 2, 1895

Mossie Jane, dau of
J. S. & M. W. Daily
Born Jan 22, 1889
Married J. L. McCollum
Sep 8, 1903
Died Feb 2, 1905

Dr. A. C. Clayton
Feb 22, 1842
Sep 18, 1928
&
Mary E. Clayton
Sep 6, 1856
Dec 18, 1885
&
Sarah E. Clayton
Dec 18, 1849
Jan 19, 1929

Infant Son of
John B. & Lula T. Allman
Nov 12, 1888
Jan 10, 1889

Infant Son of
Dr. W. H. & M. A. Wilks
Aged 2 years
(no dates)

Lotaimogen (?) Wilks
Aged -- Years
(no dates)

Our Babe
------ --- of
W. H. & M. A. Wilks
(no dates)

Willie E., son of
S. S. & J. A. Hall
Jun 11, 1850
Aug 14, 1851

Mrs. Jennie A., wife of
S. S. Hall
May 17, 1823
May 29, 1882

William Bradbury, son of
Jno. W. & Lizzie Clayton
Oct 26, 1877
Sep 13, 1883

M. Nancy, wife of
Jeremiah Holt
Died Sep 7, ----
(broken)

Milton McClure
1811-1869
&
Margaret B. McClure
1818-1887
&
William E. McClure
1842-1867

John B. Rodgers
1842-1925
"A loving Son & Brother
A loyal friend
A brave Soldier, C.S.A."

Father
James M. Rodgers
Oct 6, 1814
Jun 12, 1883
&
Mother
Susan Walker Rodgers
Sep 2, 1817
Jan 22, 1901

Roy M. Fowler
1887-1965 (TM)

Mrs. Emma Hyde Fowler
1889-1965 (TM)

Ione Dabney Robbins
Dec 6, 1836
Dec 23, 1916

Robert Presley Robbins
Aug 5, 1836
Nov 27, 1904

William Dabney Robbins
Nov 24, 1864
Feb 9, 1882

N. A. Tally
Mar 24, 1820
Apr 19, 1893

William T. Stamps
1817-1900

Mary R. Stamps
1823-1920

Sarah E. Timberlake
1842-1865

John T. Stamps
1845-1864

Lucy C. Stamps
Jan 24, 1854
May 18, 1939

Thomas Hall McClure
Oct 5, 1858
Aug 8, 1921

John Bell McClure
1869-1921

Anna E. McClure
1861-1946

Bobby, son of
W. D. & Mary O. McClure
Jun 2, 1853
Feb 8, 1866

Mary O. Pillow, wife of
William D. McClure
Sep 20, 1836
Sep 23, 1905

William D. McClure
Sep 20, 1830
Nov 29, 1893

Conrad H., son of
Dr. A. & Maxie Jones
May 25, 1863
Jun 17, 1878

Alfred Hershell, son of
Max & Anna May Jones
Aug 24, 1906
Aug 29, 1906

Kennedy
"She smiled & Slept"
(all on stone)

Bell, dau of
William & Caroline Harris
Mar 24, 1852
Jan 19, 1861

John A. Harris
Age 30 years
(no dates)

Lonnie Harris, wife of
Thomas H. Peebles
Jun 26, 1876
Mar 14, 1901

Sallie E. Jones, wife of
John A. Harris
Jan 25, 1844-Sep 30, 1914

William Harris
Aug 23, 1806
Jul 15, 1876
&
J. C. Harris
Apr 3, 1816
Jun 5, 1900

David B. Phillips
Feb 11, 1842
1900
&
Virginia G. Phillips
Nov 13, 1843
Feb 13, 1900

Willie Eugene, son of
W. E. & M. E. Baird
Feb 24, 1859
Aug 6, 1863

Robert Gordon, son of
W. E. & M. E. Baird
May 7, 1861
Aug 2, 1863

Horace Ney, son of
W. E. & M. E. Baird
Mar 24, 1857
Jul 28, 1863

William E. Baird
Oct 15, 1830
Apr 7, 1897
&
M. E. Gordon Baird
Jan 6, 1838
May 24, 1908

Jane E. Baird
Feb 26, 1806
Aug 4, 1874

Zenus Baird
Sep 24, 1804
Mar 1, 1874

C. A. Dabney
Nov 8, 1819
Dec 25, 1893
&
Sarah Dabney
Jan 23, 1829
Jul 3, 1908

Walton Jett Dysart
May 12, 1873
Feb 5, 1951
&
Clara Cox Dysart
Aug 19, 1881
Nov 29, 1947

Eva May, dau of
J. W. & F. A. Cox
Jun 13, 1894
Apr 18, 1895

CORNERSVILLE

Kate and
    Plattenburg
(on one side)
&
Dr. Levan G. Pillow
Aug 2, 1818
Apr 2, 1898
    &   wife
Mariah M. Pillow
(no dates)

J. C(G). Murrell
Apr 1, 1860
Sep 24, 1875

R. W. Murrell
Oct 9, 1843
Mar 3, 1876

C. F. Murrell
Jan 31, 1825
Sep 21, 1879

S. J. Murrell
Mar 9, 1820
Sep 30, 1896

Bernice S., dau of
L. A. & M. R. Wilks
Mar 28, 1885
Sep 26, 1889

William G., son of
M. T. & M. V. Head
Oct 5, 1875
    1876

Middleton T. Head
Jan 27, 1853
Oct 13, 1932
&
Mary V. Head
Aug 16, 1855
Mar 8, 1936

Sadie Bell, dau of
Mr. & Mrs. M. T. Head
Feb 19, 1894
Aug 10, 1913

Harriett Matilda Head
Jun 30, 1834
Jan 29, 1911

Enoch Head
Jan 3, 1826
Jan 6, 1894

Anna P., wife of
R. L. Griffis
Jan 1, 1855
Mar 13, 1900

Wiley Boatwright
Mar 25, 1895

&
Myrtle Boatwright
Mar 12, 1890
Dec 13, 1939

J. Wilson
(fieldstone, no inscription)

Mary Kerr, Who
Departed this life
Jul 24, 1835
Aged 42 years

James C. Haynes
Mar 2, 1793
Jul 22, 1854

W. L. Haynes
May 24, 1841
Feb 2, 1849

B. F. Haynes
Aug 8, 1839
Jul 6, 1843

George T. Allman
Oct 6, 1820
Apr 4, 1878

Eugenia, wife of
George T. Allman &
Dau of
Dr. T. J. & Elmira Kennedy
Jan 11, 1833
Married Jul 17, 1855
Died Aug 9, 1856

V. A. Sublett
Oct 31, 1829
Aug 17, 1855

Dr. Lucian Valentine Sublett
Aug 18, 1855
Jun 4, 1912

Laura C. Kennedy
May 5, 1837
Aug 24, 1846

Newton L. Kennedy
Oct 3, 1845
Oct 9, 1846

William B. Kennedy
Aug 3, 1843
Apr 22, 1849

Lucian T. Kennedy
Sep 15, 1847
Apr 23, 1849

Martha E. Kennedy
Mar 22, 1839
Apr 23, 1849

Thomas Jefferson Kennedy
Jan 21, 1800
Apr 15, 1879

Elmina Kerrick Lindsey,
wife of Thomas Jefferson
Kennedy
Dec 1, 1812
Jan 16, 1892

Mary Kennedy
Oct 22, 1779
Jan 9, 1865
Age 85 yrs, 2 mos, 17 days

Mary R. Kennedy
May 22, 1824
Apr 26, 1849

Emma Jane Kennedy
1855-1938

Alpheus Orlando Kennedy
Mar 9, 1850
Jul 30, 1914

Bessie Topp, wife of
A. O. Kennedy
Nov 6, 1868
Oct 10, 1898

Nelly Ewing McClure
Nov 17, 1792
Jul 29, 1872

William McClure, Esq.
Died Sep 10, 1854
Age 69 years

Miss Susan E. McClure
Apr 9, 1828
Aug 16, 1854

Minerva McClure
Died Feb 29, 1896
Aged about 63 years

George Ewing McClure
May 25, 1822
Apr 20, 1870

Elizabeth Cox
Sep 28, 1816
Oct --, 1855

J. J. Walker
May 6, 1828
Sep 12, 1900
    & wife
J. A. T. Walker
Apr 5, 1833
Jul 1, 1894

Presley T. Cox
Died May 26, 1873
Age about 70 years
&
Edgar E. Cox
May 5, 1835
Jan 11, 1889

Sarah E., wife of
Robert Cox
Mar 6, 1797
Sep 25, 1865
Age 68 yrs, 6 mos, 19 days

Laura E. Cox
Aged 9 years
(no dates)

---- Elizabeth, dau of
A. J. & S. E. Wolridge
May 12, 1857
Jun 1, 1857

James Owen Evans
Nov 26, 1854
Sep 26, 1858

Rebecker Ann Taylor
Dec 4, 1838
Jul 3, 1893

William C. McClure
Died Nov 16, 1881
Age 58 years

Harriet Esselman, wife of
W. C. McClure
Died Oct 28, 1894
Age 58 years

Laurent McClure
Oct 8, 1875
May 6, 1900

Maggie McClure Dean
1865-1903

Thomas Bligh
1831-1912

Leslie G., son of
Thomas & S. E. Bligh
Sep 17, 1876
Jul 5, 1904

Sarah E. Bligh
1839-1926

Joanna, dau of
Thomas & S. E. Bligh
May 1, 1873
Jul 31, 1873

Fairrie, dau of
Thomas & S. E. Bligh
Apr 17, 1868
Jan 8, 1871

Curran, son of
Thomas & S. E. Bligh
May 22, 1882
Aug 29, 1903

Anna S., dau of
G. T. & M. V. Allman
Sep 15, 1865
Aug 15, 1882

Willie F., son of
George T. & Martha V. Allman
Aug 13, 1859
--- --, 1867

Sadie B. Gordon
1911-1912

Howard B. Gordon
1921-1926

CORNERSVILLE

Father
W. T. Gordon
Jan 1, 1880
Apr 19, 1936
&
Mother
Ruby McCollum Gordon
Mar 1, 1887

Walter J. McCollum
Sep 19, 1860
Dec 19, 1947

Walter Lee Jordan
1884-1920
&
Cora D. Hyde Jordan
1885-1932

Thomas D. Jordan
Oct 16, 1913
Oct 24, 1913

Nannie, wife of
W. R. James
Apr 19, 1854
Jan 17, 1890
&
Virginia A., wife of
W. R. James
Sep 14, 1851
Jun 12, 1884
&
Nannie, dau of
W. R. & V. A. James
Sep 19, 1882
Dec 1, 1883

Andrew E. Blackburn
Apr 12, 1817
--- --, 1888

Neppie J. Kilgore
Feb --, 1846
Apr 22, 1874

My Husband
George Gray Collier
Jan 19, 1822
Aug 5, 1855

George Calvin, son of
George G. & Susan J. Collier
Jul 6, 1851
Oct 10, 1870

Eliza F., wife of
Rev. W. J. Collier
May 13, 1853
May 28, 1891

Presley T. Walker
Sep 24, 1824
Sep 18, 1852

Mother
Elmira Cox
Jun 22, 1808
Feb 12, 1854

Sister
Alice C. Cox
Oct 1, 1845
Jun 11, 1855

Father
John Cox
Dec 14, 1790
May 14, 1863

--------, dau of
James _. & Mary O. Reid
Jul 9, 1850
Aug 28, 1855

Mother
Susan V. Bond, wife of
Dr. J. R. Crutcher
Mar 6, 1830
Nov 29, 1866

Mary T. Crutcher
Nov 17, 1856
Sep 29, 1862

Jane E. Crutcher
Feb 26, 1861
Oct 1, 1862

William Lee Andrew Orr
Jul 5, 1872
Nov 5, 1888

Alonzo W., son of
R. W. & M. V. Worley
May 10, 1877
May --, 1878

Infant Son of
C. R. & M. B. Orr
Oct 30, 1872

Fanny E., wife of
W. D. Orr
Oct 3, 1844
Dec 2, 1872

William D. Orr
May 26, 1844
Sep 8, 1899

W. T. Cheatham
1837-1919

Jennie E., wife of
W. T. Cheatham
Sep 20, 1834
Mar 23, 1889

William Jackson
Mar 6, 1836
Feb 6, 1874

Lucinda McCrary
Nov 4, 1832
Jan 8, 1866

T. N. A. Kennedy
Dec 27, 1823
Jul 30, 1876

Margaret Kennedy
Jun 19, 1801
Sep 21, 1876

Mittie L. Throneberry
1867-1938

I. J. Throneberry
Jul 23, 1861
Mar 27, 1905

Mother
Adlaide Brown Hunter
Mar 14, 1863
Apr 29, 1893

Otto Cannon
Age 42 years
(no dates)

James Rosson
Jan 10, 1810
Jun 18, 1866

Lucy J. Rosson
Mar 10, 1817
Aug 8, 1859

Infant Daughter of
James & Lucy J. Rosson
May 6, 1856
Aug 10, 1857

America V. Rosson
Aug 2, 1847
Feb 8, 1856

Mary J. Rosson
Sep 13, 1843
Feb 7, 1856

Cordelia A. Rosson
Apr 15, 1837
Feb 11, 1856

Ada Lee McClelland
Jul 29, 1854
Mar 29, 1902

William Lee McClelland
Oct 23, 1815
Feb 8, 1883

Mother
Sarah Chambliss McClelland
Died Apr 10, 1900
Age 67 years

Lizzie S., dau of
W. L. & Mary J. McClelland
Jul 10, 1849
Nov 26, 1851
Age 2 yrs, 4 mos, 14 days

Mary J., wife of
W. L. McClelland
Died --- --, 1851
Age 29 years

Mary Eva, dau of
W. L. & Mary J. McClelland
Aug 3, 1847
Feb 22, 1856

Mother
Elizabeth Reeves Burgess
nee Chambliss, who left
us October, 1886, having
passed 67 useful years on
earth.

Father
J. J. H. Burgess
Who left us July, 1866,
having passed 54 useful
years on earth.

Kathleen Read Coontz
Jan 24, 1887
Oct 16, 1944
"Fortifier, Fideliter,
Feliciter."

L. J. D., son of
J. J. H. & E. R. Burgess
Apr 8, 1851
Oct 13, 1853
&
L. S. D., son of
J. J. H. & E. R. Burgess
Apr 8, 1851
Jun 11, 1856

----- Henry, son of
J. J. H. & E. R. Burgess
--- 5, 1847
--- 21, ----
(illegible)

Cordelia Tennessee, child
of R. G. & M. E. McClure
Mar 14, 1848
Jul 1, 1848

William Lee, son of
R. G. & M. E. McClure
Jul 6, 185-
Aug 15, 185-

Nancy L. Andrews
Jul 18, 1847
Nov 26, 1848

James Andrews
Died Dec 14, 184-
Aged 70 yrs, 5 mos, 27 days

Rebecca, Consort of
William Hudson
Died Aug 31, 1828
Age 29 years

Sarah Catharine Andrews
May 28, 1825
Mar 10, 1836
Age 10 yrs, 3 mos, 11 days

Johnnie McClintock
1881 (All on stone)

CORNERSVILLE

W. M. H.
(fieldstone)

A. L.
(fieldstone)

Zillah R. Molloy, dau of
J. S. & A. Haynes
Nov 7, 1821
Nov 13, 1859

Asenath, Consort of
James S. Haynes
Died Sep 7, 1827
Aged 34 years

Infant Son of
P. C. & M. Haynes
Died Apr 20, 1851
Age 3 days

Infant Son of
J. S. & A. Haynes
Died Nov 28, 1823
(no age given)

------ Erwin
Died Jul 18, 1855
Aged 2 years

William Henderson
Feb 10, 1777
Jan 14, 1830

Eleanor Henderson
Oct 13, 1780
Aug 12, 1848

William Alexander
Pvt N.C. Militia
Rev. War
1760-1839

Elizabeth Sturgeon Alexander
(no dates)

Mary, Consort of
A. B. Alexander
May 1, 1801
Jun 20, 1846

Mathew McGaugh
1774-1858
(inscription broken
away)

Nancy, Consort of
M. McGaugh
Oct 8, 1800
Jun 7, 1845

Nancy C., dau of
M. & N. McGaugh
Feb 23, 1845
Oct 26, 1856

Infant Son of
I. W. & M. J. Compton
Sep 3, 1852
Apr 8, 1853

Samuel W. Thompson
Feb 25, 1805
Apr 27, 1845
Age 40 yrs, 2 mos, 2 days

I. W. C.
(fieldstone)

Martin Slaughter Jones
May 5, 1802
Apr 11, 1882
& wife
Susan Maury Alexander Jones
Oct 30, 1803
Oct 11, 1869
& Dau
Sarah Ann Elizabeth Jones
Oct 13, 1834
Jun 14, 1854

In Memory of
Andrew & Eliza Mitchell
The former was born
May 5, 1809 & Died
Sep 29, 1864
Age 55 yrs, 4 mos -- days
The latter was born
--- --, 1807 & Died
Jan 22, 1865
Age ---
Andrew and Eliza Mitchell
was married -----

R. W. Pillow
Dec 14, 1809
Jul 1, 1895
& wife
Ann Pillow
Apr 24, 1815
Feb 7, 1900

Ida Walker
Jul 26, 1859
--- --, 1860

Ada Walker
Jul 26, 1859
Feb 29, 1860

G. W. Walker
May 29, 1830
Mar 31, 1862

Virginia Pillow Fowler
Born Jan 13, 1835
Married G. W. Walker
Nov 20, 1856
Died Feb 25, 1904

Here lies our Sweet Little
Oscar P., Son of
George W. & Jennie Walker
Aged 2 years & 28 days
1859

NOTE: In this part, both White and Colored
are buried.

I. U(M). Marsh
(no legible dates)

--llek Hall
(no legible dates)

Ronald Clay Walker
Feb 1, 1964 (TM)

Lula Ann Allen
1962-1963

Willie Dee Allen
Tennessee
Pvt US Army
Jan 28, 1927
Jul 31, 1961

Will R. Lumpkins
Tennessee
Pvt Co E 1 Res TNG BN
WW II
Jul 11, 1892
Oct 10, 1960

Callie Lumpkins
1878-1959

Mrs. Annie Mai Pitts
1899-1957 (TM)

John H. Brown
1891-1957 (TM)

Mr. Tom Walker
Dec 7, 1957
(only one date) (TM)

Mother
Jennie Hardy
1890-1951

George Lumpkins
1892-
&
Edna Mae Lumpkins
1890-1957

Harrison Walker
Tennessee
Pfc 44 PW Escort Co ASC
WW I
Feb 23, 1894
Aug 3, 1942

John McLLand
1869-1935
&
Fannie McLLand
1879-1947

McKinley Taylor
1905-1957 (TM)

Dorothy Lee Smith
(McDaniel-McClintock FH)

Allen Cross
Aug 18, 1883
Apr 5, 1957
&
Susie Cross
May 15, 1892

William London
Tennessee
Pvt 365 Inf 92 Div
Jan 9, 1940

Mrs. Vera McClure
Oct 10, 1868
Feb 22, 1933
Age 65 years

Brown London
1871-1936
&
Georgie London
1876-1926

Florence Davis
Dec 25, 1874
Sep 25, 1940

H. M. Kennedy
Died Feb 21, 1909
Age 50 years

Jonathan, son of
Irvine & Katie Allen
Jun 30, 1909
Nov 18, 1909

Mary Jane Allen
1868-1948

George Bates
Co A 110 USC Inf
(illegible)

Sarah M., wife of
G. W. Bates
Sep 15, 1859
Dec 23, 1907

Wymonia McLean
Died Jan 11, 1948
(no age given)

Willie D. Thomas
Jan 24, 1916
Jan 11, 1943
&
Daisy Thomas
Dec 5, 1897
Apr 22, 1944

Ervine Allen
1880-1953

Mable Hendrix
1893-1952

CORNERSVILLE

Ella L. Taylor
Born Dec 20, 1906
Died (illegible)

Carrie Hall
Died Jun 1961
Age 83 years

Mattie McClure
1868-1943

Will Walton
"Phillipe"

Alburtus A. Hall
1897-
&
Jennie Hall
1900-

END OF BEECHWOOD

* *

COX CEMETERY
Located in the town of Cornersville, in the back yard of Mrs. Tom Martin, formerly the Hunter home. Copied 1964.

In Memory of
Presley Cox
Departed this life on
the 18th of January 1827
Age 78 years

In Memory of
William Samuel Day
Who departed this life in
August 1821
Age 35 years

Jane, dau of
Samuel & Priscilla Day
Who departed this life
in the year 1820
Age 6 years

Sarah, dau of
Samuel & Priscilla Day
Who departed this life
in the year 1821
Age 3 years

In Memory of
Sarah P. Cox
Departed this life on the
17th of August, 1841
Age 84 years

In Memory of
Mrs. Priscilla, Consort of
William Samuel Day, Who
departed this life Sept
22, in the year of 1840
Age 42 years

All stones are piled in a fence corner.

* *

HAYWOOD-MARSH CEMETERY
Located two miles south of Cornersville, on Pulaski Highway. Copied 1958.

Sarah B., wife of
Dr. G. W. Haywood
Oct 25, 1809
Apr 16, 1894
Age 84 yrs, 5 mos, 22 days

Octie Lou, dau of
Dr. E. P. C. & Belle Haywood
Nov 3, 1874
Jul 3, 1898

George Cullen, son of
Dr. E. P. C. & Belle Haywood
Feb 27, 1880
Aug 23, 1898

Rena, dau of
Dr. E. P. C. & Belle Haywood
Oct 31, 1885
Feb 9, 1905

Dr. E. P. C. Haywood
Sep 5, 1845
Feb 5, 1919

Belle Marsh Haywood
Sep 13, 1850
Feb 29, 1925

Son of
Justin & Nina Leonard
May 3, 1915

About 55 unmarked graves.

Shelby H. C., son of
S. E. & Dorinda Marsh
Mar 27, 1855
Nov 1, 1857

Henry A., son of
S. E. & Dorinda Marsh
Jun 27, 1858
Feb 4, 1860

Isabella Marsh
Died Jul 28, 1846
Age -- years (illegible)

* Simeon Marsh
Died April 29, 1850
Age 66 years

Shelby B. Marsh
Nov 12, 1807
Mar 4, 1889

John S. Marsh
Aug 15, 1846
Mar 22, 1865

Dorinda Marsh
Aug 4, 1814
Apr 12, 1880

J. G. Click
Died 1884
Age about 65 years

Mary F. Fergeson
Oct 23, 1798
Jul 30, 1859

Francis Fergeson
Died Jan 9, 1854
Age 64 years

Benjamine, son of
N. P. Fergeson
Aug 18, 1851
Aug 1, 1852

N. P. Ferguson
Aug 15, 1811
Dec 23, 1886

J. W. Fergerson
Mar 20, 1862
Aug 1, 1880

R. W. Collins
Oct 22, 1811
Aug 28, 1837

H. C., wife of
J. W. Stevens
May 12, 1877
Aug 11, 1919

Mattie, wife of
J. W. Glasgow
Jan 21, 1878
May 15, 1903

George W. Stevens
Feb 21, 1890
Apr 11, 1913

Frank Stevens
1855-1942

Eva Stevens
1856-1924

Amanda K., wife of
W. R. James
Nov 3, 1849
Mar 25, 1878

Sarah J., formerly Butler
wife of W. D. White
Feb 10, 1820
Dec 8, 1852
Age 37 years

George W. Tanner
Nov 24, 1824
Mar 16, 1845

Nancy London
Died Sep 20, 1855
(no age given)

J. R. Hopkins
Nov 7, 1853
Jul 3, 1909

* Died in Shelby Co. Tn.

* *

CORNERSVILLE

HAISLIP CEMETERY
Located three miles north of Spring Place, near Gills Chapel, in Duckworth Hollow.

Jonathan Haislip, Son of Labon Haislip
Born 1801 (Tenn.)
Died after 1850
(no marker with inscription)

Betty Ruth Page, wife of Jonathan Haislip
Born 1811 (Ala.)
Died between 1870-1880
(no marker with inscription)

Marmaduke Myers
Born ca 1790 in Rowan Co., N.C.
Died ?
(no marker with inscription)

Eleanor Young, wife of Marmaduke Myers
Born ----
Died after 1866/70
(no marker with inscription)

Stacy L. Myers, wife of Levi Garrison Pyles
Born ca 1822 (Tenn.)
Died ----
(no marker with inscription)

Many unmarked graves.

* *

SHORT CEMETERY
Located at Spring Place or Richmond Cumberland Presbyterian Church, on Spring Place-Lewisburg Pike. Copied May 6, 1978 by Helen & Tim Marsh.

James T. Pigg
May 31, 1903
May 24, 1974
(picture)

John Deaumont Jordan
Oct 6, 1911
Jan 14, 1976
&
Vendal Pack Jordan

Ruby Lee Endsley Pack
(no dates)

Flournoy Brent "Dock" Pigg
Feb 17, 1915
Aug 5, 1970
&
Mildred Louise Pigg
Jan 19, 1923

Mrd Dec 14, 1940
(picture of both)

Bernie M. Adams
Jun 6, 1909
Oct 27, 1967
&
Rosa Lee Adams
Mar 19, 1919

Jim W. Agent
Aug 6, 1883
Jan 25, 1972
&
Delia M. Agent
Dec 4, 1886
Nov 16, 1962

Clifford Hopwood
1882-1958

Floyd T. Rudd
1880-1952
&
Tillie A. Rudd
1887-1963

Ernest D. Wolaver
Mar 7, 1880
Oct 11, 1951
&
Nancy B. Wolaver
Apr 11, 1886
Jun 22, 1971

Sara P. Wolaver
1908-1968

J. "Bud" Bowers
May 17, 1905
Apr 2, 1963
&
Annie W. Bowers
Feb 20, 1910
Apr 25, 1961

Betty Jo Anderson
Sep 5, 1929
Dec 4, 1929

James M. Cowser
1884-1959
&
Wennie W. Cowser
1886-1955

Thomas L. Cowser
1904-1973
&
Alene M. Cowser
1904-
&
J. B. Cowser
1926-1935

J. B. Finley
Mar 28, 1937
Apr 8, 1937

Barbara Ann Finley
Oct 18, 1938

J. B. Glazier
1880-1945
&
Ida Glazier
1875-1944

John T. Doss
1880-1949

Margaret Worley Doss
1876-1932

Willie (Ezell) Rudd
Dec 22, 1918

&
Forace (Coucharan) Rudd
Sep 25, 1910
Sep 17, 1971

Infant Son of
Mr. & Mrs. Ezell Rudd
Jun 7, 1941

Ernie J. Hemphill
Tennessee
Pvt Co C 26 MG BN WW I
Aug 21, 1889
Jul 25, 1958
&
Lela Hemphill
Oct 3, 1896

Infant Dau of
J. H. Oliver
1936

Porter Oliver
Oct 9, 1867
Jun 4, 1929
&
Eliza Ann Oliver
Jul 19, 1871
Jul 29, 1948

Joseph Brent Pigg
Feb 24, 1871
Jun 5, 1947
(picture)

Eldia Pigg Thompson
Jan 10, 1901
Apr 7, 1942
(picture)

William Carter Pigg
US Med. Corps Med Det E
321st A.F. A.E.F.
Wounded in Action
Sep 25, 1895
Oct 30, 1935
(picture)

Marvin Pigg
Nov 27, 1912
May 29, 1948

Ida Holley Pigg
Mar 12, 1875
May 15, 1951
(picture)

Earl L. Taylor
Oct 21, 1892
Sep 8, 1972
&
Carrie V. Taylor
Sep 16, 1905

(picture of both)

CORNERSVILLE

Sam R. Cummings
May 5, 1925
Apr 6, 1967

Theron Reed
Oct 16, 1904
Mar 23, 1974
&
Sallie Sue Reed
Jul 18, 1904

Alex Reed
1894-1950
&
Lillie C. Reed
1891-(no date)

Robert C. Reed
S1 US Navy
May 24, 1924
Jun 19, 1975

Thomas L. Jobe, Sr.
Dec 20, 1921

&
Audalene H. Jobe
Mar 3, 1921

Willie L. Worsham
Pvt US Army WW II
Apr 24, 1924
May 29, 1976

William Coy Lovett
Pvt US Army WW II
1913-1977

Father
Ralph V. Adgent
1925-
&
Mother
Hilda A. Adgent
1929-

Father
Lane E. Allen
1923-
&
Mother
Amanda A. Allen
1919-

Ernest E. Allen
May 17, 1898
Sep 9, 1977
&
Alla Mai Lane Allen
Jun 29, 1896
Oct 29, 1975

Thomas Allen Meadows
1909-
&
Mary Clayte Meadows
1900-

John L. Sowell
Aug 29, 1920
Nov 7, 1971
&
Louise H. Sowell
Mar 17, 1920

Mrd Dec 24, 1942

E. Clifford Vaughn
Jul 31, 1910

Robert L. Harris
Nov 27, 1918

&
Valta L. Harris
Oct 20, 1917

William H. Cowser
1908-19(78)
(death date not on stone)
&
Docie E. Cowser
1907-

Clarence F. Price
Feb 4, 1899
Sep 9, 1976
&
Tishie Mai Luker Price
Sep 5, 1900
Sep 9, 1961

J. Monroe Price
1864-1931
&
T. Elizabeth Price
1873-1951

Albert S. Reed
1882-1949
&
Mattie E. Reed
1880-1949

G. W. Causby (Wash)
Aug 14, 1844
Mar 8, 1931
& wife
Mary J. Nichols Causby
Feb 3, 1845
Mar 21, 1933

Ollie Bradford
1880-1948
&
Martha Bradford
1878-1965

Virgil Endsley
1893-1961

Erma G. Pruitt Endsley
1890-1931

Nora Sims Endsley
1907-1962

Zedrick Jobe
1900-1962

Lacy Jobe
1902-1977

Zedrick Jobe, Jr.
1920-1945

J. K. Jobe
Dec 7, 1860
Oct 24, 1941
& wife
Mary Emma Jobe
Apr 17, 1861
May 27, 1930

Billy Joe, son of
Mr. & Mrs. Clifford Haislip
Oct 8, 1932

Ernie L. Twitty
Mar 15, 1887
Sep 8, 1959
&
Lela Luna Twitty
Nov 30, 1890

Willis L. Luna
May 5, 1856
Feb 12, 1933
&
Ada G. Luna
Aug 22, 1867
Apr 29, 1927

Miss Anna Carroll
1883-1956
(London FH)

Lennis B. Luna
Aug 24, 1892
Aug 11, 1972

George V. Crick
Jun 3, 1879
Dec 6, 1918

F. L. "Mitch" Williams
Jan 11, 1908
Jun 12, 1953

Father
John R. Ketchum
1881-1945
&
Mother
Modena B. Ketchum
1888-1967
&
Son
Cecil R. Ketchum
1921

Infant Baby of
Mr. & Mrs. E. O. Park
(no dates)

Infant Baby of
Mr. & Mrs. E. O. Park
(no dates)

Father
Elmer O. Park
1893-1974
&
Mother
Herman B. Park
1892-1977

R. L. Compton
1876-1956
& wife
Nannie E. Swiney Compton
1880-1927

Claude Endsley
May 17, 1884
Apr 21, 1960
&
Josie Endsley
Jul 28, 1872
Aug 12, 1967

Dewey Duckworth
Jul 4, 1898
May 11, 1945

Lola A. Duckworth
Feb 2, 1900
Feb 22, 1961

Tripletts of
Dewey & Lola Duckworth
Aug 16, 1924
Aug 17, 1924

M. Christine Duckworth
Sep 13, 1927
Feb 27, 1930

Monte P. Murrey
Aug 24, 1893
Dec 26, 1975
&
Mai R. Murrey
Aug 30, 1891
Mar 28, 1968

Infant Son of
Mai - Monte Murrey
1922-1922

James L. Reed
1861-1937
&
Sarah C. Reed
1859-1944

Tempa Lou Reed
Sep 29, 1889
Mar 21, 1967

Rufus E. Glazier
1876-1949
&
Elizabeth A. Glazier
1883-1940

CORNERSVILLE

Clarence Glazier
1903-1947

Father
W. L. Turner
Mar 18, 1844
Jan 12, 1923
&
Mother
Elizabeth E. Turner
Nov 10, 1848
Oct 30, 1917

James H. Welch
May 3, 1879
May 1, 1950
&
Lena B. Welch
Sep 19, 1879
Jun 12, 1959

W. J. Rambo
Sep 29, 1864
Apr 19, 1918
& wife
Genevia Rambo
Mar 15, 1868
Apr 26, 1917

William Thomas Rambo
1890-1929
&
Maude Rambo
1890-1961

Father
Albie L. Carroll
Dec 5, 1881
Jul 2, 1955
&
Mother
Ana Bernice Carroll
Oct 16, 1886
Mar 3, 1952

W. Frank Oliver
Feb 26, 1892
Dec 11, 1972
&
Lillie Bell Oliver
Sep 18, 1892
Mar 5, 1968

Frank J., son of
W. F. & L. B. Oliver
B&D Jun 28, 1918

J. A. McConnell
1906-1965
(McDaniel FH)

Annie Lou McConnell
Jan 26, 1890
Mar 6, 1960

Willis Kelley
Died --- --, 1929
(McDaniel FH)

W. O. Kelley
Apr 9, 1912
Dec 23, 1974
&
Lillie B. Kelley
Aug 15, 1915

John Bradford
1848-1928
&
Maggie Bradford
1849-1927
&
Mattie Bradford
1873-1921
&
Tennie Bradford
1878-1958
&
Lorena Bradford
1892-1930

Lewis E. Randolph
1909-1946
&
Lizzie Lee Randolph
1914-

Raymond E. Johns
Sep 18, 1931

&
Annie V. Johns
May 16, 1932
Feb 4, 1973

Bessie Lee Cathey
Apr 30, 1880
Aug 23, 1963

Myron L. Taylor
Feb 4, 1886
Feb 19, 1965
&
Sarah Margaret Taylor
Nov 16, 1885
Dec 19, 1961

Randolph F. Leonard
Dec 18, 1882
Jan 25, 1967
&
Mary F. Leonard
Mar 15, 1893

William H. Bowden
Sep 15, 1925
Nov 15, 1959

Lex McCrory
May 30, 1898
Jun 19, 1956
&
Fannie McCrory
Oct 7, 1898
Feb 17, 1962

Vernie McCrory
1892-1976
&
Mary McCrory
1885-1956

Joe L. McCrory
1877-1956
&
Anna E. McCrory
1880-1969

Carlee Haislip
Feb 7, 1917

&
Margaret E. Haislip
Feb 22, 1919
Oct 7, 1972

James L. Short
Oct 20, 1883
Jan 15, 1944
&
Nannie F. Short
May 16, 1886
Oct 23, 1963

Lucille Short
Jan 3, 1908
Feb 26, 1929

Father
Morgan Massey
Jun 30, 1853
Feb 8, 1926
& wife
Mother
Martha Price Massey
Sep 20, 1854
Oct 4, 1953

J. Tom Harris
1888-1977
&
Nannie Harris
1888-1958

Annie Sarah Harris
1920-1943

Infant Dau of
Mr. & Mrs. J. T. Harris
1919

J. F. Harris
Dec 22, 1847
Jan 6, 1920
& wife
Ellen Harris
Dec 18, 1864
(no date)

W. A. Harris
1892-1967

Claudie Malcolm Harris
Apr 27, 1895
Jul 8, 1923

Rollie Gilbert Harris
Feb 13, 1898
Sep 23, 1924

John K. Harris
1890-1967
&
Eula V. Harris
1888-1946

John Roy, son of
John & Eula Harris
Jun 5, 1926
Dec 2, 1926

William H. Braden
1858-1937
&
Minnie S. Braden
1870-1954

Clarence R. Braden
Jan 19, 1896
Mar 27, 1926

Tennessee M. Chapman
Aug 3, 1896
Dec 27, 1966

Jimmie Howard Chapman
Jan 31, 1912
Jul 12, 1917

Lynn M. Chapman
1884-1940
&
Carrie A. Chapman
1884-1948

Charles M. Chapman
Tennessee
Pvt 30 Inf WW II
Jun 25, 1921
Aug 8, 1943

G. Worth Hobby
Sep 6, 1860
Mar 10, 1917

Mattie A. Hobby
Mar 30, 1865
Aug 1, 1923

H. M. Hobby
Jun 21, 1889
May 23, 1932

Frances Finley
1927-1927

James W. "Jim" Compton
Nov 5, 1893
Jul 27, 1973

Maggie C. Compton
1888-1922

CORNERSVILLE

Grady G. Ralston
1895-1964
&
Betty Lee Ralston
1891-

George G. Ralston
1870-1953
&
Mollie P. Ralston
1874-1963

Alma K., dau og
G. G. & M. P. Ralston
Aug 4, 1900
Aug 17, 1915

Father
B. F. Lane
May 2, 1865
Nov 21, 1917
&
Mother
M. L. Lane
Jun 10, 1873
(no date)

William B. Eldridge
1877-1917
&
Carrie E. Eldridge
1878-1949

Marshall Metz Eldridge
Apr 23, 1906
Mar 6, 1966

William A. Whitsett
Sep 23, 1903
Oct 11, 1965
&
Dallas E. Whitsett
Feb 23, 1905

Charlie C. Massey
Jun 17, 1874
Oct 16, 1967
&
Kate L. Massey
May 20, 1878
Feb 26, 1967

John, son of
C. C. & Kate Massey
Nov 6, 1900
Jan 30, 1919

Walter C. Massey
1887-1963
&
Carrie L. Massey
1889-1966

Willna, dau of
W. C. & A. C. Massey
B&D Jun 27, 1923

Jolene M. Garrett
1916-1943

Sue Farrar Garrett
Mar 22, 1937
Jul 27, 1962

Ace W. Rhodes
1909-1945

Ronnie Rhodes
US Army
May 30, 1943
Jun 25, 1976

Bryan Keith Rhodes
Oct 29, 1973
Oct 30, 1973

Earl Davis McCrory
BMC US Navy
Apr 4, 1918
May 17, 1966

J. Grady Davis
Jan 18, 1898

&
Lola B. Davis
Jun 16, 1902

Mrd Jul 29, 1923

Charlie H. Davis
Aug 21, 1906

&
Nona Irene Davis
Jul 22, 1909

Mrd Nov 18, 1928

Kenneth Loyd Haislip
Apr 20, 1927
Dec 9, 1968

James T. Williams
Jun 15, 1892
May 14, 1973
&
Mable G. Williams
Oct 5, 1905

James S. Massey
Nov 14, 1880
Mar 16, 1975
&
Ethel R. Massey
Apr 10, 1883
Feb 13, 1939

Cecil M., son of
J. S. & L. E. Massey
Apr 30, 1918
Jun 2, 1918

Mother
Eva M. Thompson
May 10, 1890
Feb 15, 1923

James V. Gullie
Oct 8, 1898

&
Selma M. Gullie
Apr 24, 1908
Nov 22, 1966

Alfred B. Gullie
Oct 20, 1891
Dec 23, 1917

H. J. Gullie
1858-1933
& wife
Sarah P. Gullie
1866-1922

A. O. Gullie
Jul 5, 1887
Mar 6, 1943

R. C. McCrory
Feb 4, 1879
Apr 20, 1956

Nettie I. McCrory
Feb 3, 1876
Jul 28, 1943

Minnie Lee McCrory
Jan 13, 1884
Dec 2, 1923

Roy V. McCrory
1902-1937

Volley D. McCollum
Dec 9, 1880
May 23, 1918
& wife
Anna May McCollum
Dec 26, 1881
(no date)

Lee Burdeene Holly
Dec 27, 1912
Nov 14, 1914
&
J. T. Holly
B&D Sep 29, 1915

R. Wheel Davis
1887-1938
&
Laura M. Davis
1894-

Tommie Jean Davis
1935

Emanuel Clark Ealy
1862-1946
&
Maggie Lee Ealy
1872-1946

Father
John F. Ledford
Feb 13, 1866
Oct 16, 1922
&
Mother
Altie O. Ledford
Aug 27, 1870
Mar 12, 1930

Nettie B. Murray
1869-1937

Tonnie Murray
May 4, 1896
Oct 17, 1918
"Served 5 months, 6 days in France. Killed in Battle of Molain Somme Front."
&
Lilburn L. Short
Oct 28, 1894
Oct 30, 1918
Co H 117th Inf A.E.F.

May Lois, dau of
Charlie & Ella King
Mar 28, 1913
Sep 7, 1914

Otis Charles, son of
Grady & Era King
1925-1928

Ava Lucile, dau of
Kelly & Hattie Lane
Jun 9, 1914
Jun 15, 1915

John T. Beard
1870-1931

Ida M. Beard
1880-1952

Myrtice Beard
Mar 6, 1916
Apr 30, 1975

Lottie, wife of
J. T. Williams
Feb 29, 1896
Jun 6, 1917

Jewel Chunn
1915-1933

Amy, wife of
J. W. Glymp
1899-1927
&
Martha E., wife of
J. G. Glymp
1859-1928

Infant Son (Massey)
Jul 17, 1918
Oct 27, 1918

CORNERSVILLE

John T. Massey, Sr.
Sep 23, 1889
Jul 27, 1964
& wife
J. Annie Pack Massey
Jan 8, 1890
Feb 14, 1919

William A. Massey
Aug 15, 1856
Jun 6, 1928
&
Tina Gant Massey
Jul 2, 1864
Jun 16, 1932

Father
J. L. McCrory
Sep 5, 1845
Apr 16, 1921
&
Mother
Margaret McCrory
Aug 23, 1852
Oct 20, 1929

J. W. McCrory
Sep 26, 1881
Sep 19, 1921

Olga L. Beard
1883-1961
&
Lela M. Beard
1887-1949

W. R. Stallings
Feb 13, 1851
Aug 14, 1927
& wife
Frances Stallings
Jul 14, 1856
May 19, 1936

Mark A. Stallings
Jul 17, 1890
Nov 20, 1958

Mother
Nelle Stallings, wife of
Dr. J. P. Scales
Feb 14, 1893
Jan 2, 1962

William E. Stevens
Apr 24, 1904
Apr 1, 1971
&
Cora Mag Stevens
Feb 20, 1904
Dec 11, 1958

James Howard Stevens
May 20, 1930
Nov 10, 1941

Joseph W. Powers
1916-1977
(Bills-McGaugh FH)

Charlie G. Powers
Dec 31, 1898
Jul 22, 1956

Father
James Ollie Haislip
Tennessee
Pvt Co G 309 Inf WW I
Dec 11, 1897
Oct 20, 1959
&
Mother
Rollen L. Haislip
1898-1974

Dolly Burgett Haislip Allen
Nov 20, 1880
Oct 23, 1959

Joe Paul Luna
Jul 28, 1910

&
Catherine M. Luna
Jul 5, 1917

Della Cole
Feb 5, 1887
Sep 23, 1965

Father
Edgar L. Pickle
Apr 14, 1907

&
Mother
Lillie O. Pickle
Mar 25, 1907

Mrd Jul 4, 1934

J. Carson Collins
1906-1933

J. N. Collins
Aug 28, 1858
Nov 23, 1932

Mattie (Massey) Collins
May 5, 1865
Oct 15, 1925

Johney May, dau of
J. N. & M. A. Collins
Dec 28, 1898
May 12, 1904

John B. Compton
1874-1945
&
Blanche Compton
1874-1930

Bertha E., dau of
J. B. & S. B. Compton
Jan 19, 1893
Aug 9, 1912

Earlene, dau of
J. B. & S. B. Compton
Dec 17, 1903
Dec 9, 1913

Kieffer Compton
1895-1943
&
Mary Compton
1902-19

Edward, son of
Mr. & Mrs. Kieffer Compton
May 25, 1921
Aug 28, 1928

C. O. Welch
Nov 6, 1876
Aug 11, 1937
&
Belle Welch
Aug 27, 1874
Sep 10, 1949

Horace E. Glazier
Tennessee
Cpl US Army
Jan 31, 1897
Oct 21, 1966
&
Dessa P. Glazier
Jul 15, 1897
Jul 22, 1978

Hobart Duckworth
Tennessee
Pfc Sup Co 70 Arty CAC
WW I
Jul 22, 1896
Aug 4, 1961

Frank B. Street
Aug 20, 1894
May 24, 1967
&
Ida Mai Street
May 1, 1898

Morgan Murdock
Aug 28, 1915

&
Elizabeth S. Murdock
Oct 16, 1914
Jul 13, 1960

Charles T. Bishop
Dec 10, 1859
Nov 4, 1927
&
Bettie G. Bishop
Feb 16, 1888
Dec 9, 1968

James C. Gant
1907-1973
&
Evelyn E. Gant
1909-19

William E. Gant
1874-1963
&
Lillie M. Gant
1874-1936

Cecil Howard, son of
W. E. & L. M. Gant
Nov 17, 1901
Sep 6, 1907

W. Z. Gant
(William Zachariah)
Aug 1, 1836
Jan 6, 1902

Adeline B. Gant
1843-1916

J. T. Hemphill
Jul 12, 1847
Feb 15, 1921

Ophelia, wife of
J. T. Hemphill
Jan 13, 1853
Mar 28, 1901

J. Bennie Hemphill
1881-1956
&
Bertha E. Hemphill
1885-1958
&
W. Hubert Hemphill
1903-1937

Emma B. Freeman
1864-1934

Virginia Talley, mother of
R. B. & J. L. & J. B.
Compton
Feb 26, 1837
Oct 12, 1915

Mattie H., dau of
R. B. & S. F. Compton
Jan 24, 1884
Dec 18, 1902

R. B. Compton
1857-1931
&
Sarah E. Compton
1858-1941

Sidney Compton
1898-1944

S. G. Bayless
Dec 15, 1843
Mar 10, 1909

Sarah J. Bayless
Sep 23, 1840
Dec 1, 1916

CORNERSVILLE

Father
Vollie Willis
Oct 27, 1890
Jun 26, 1960
&
Mother
Nena Pigg Willis
Sep 21, 1895
Mar 28, 1929

Bruce Pigg
Jul 11, 1876
Feb 4, 1936
&
Dora Bigham Pigg
Feb 10, 1879
Apr 1, 1958

Alice Wilkerson
Dec 5, 1875
Dec 20, 1940

Olgia Eugene Wilkerson
Feb 6, 1892
May 27, 1946

Geneva Wilkerson
May 7, 1919
Jul 15, 1922

F. P. Welch
Mar 16, 1853
Feb 15, 1922
&
Frances E. Welch
Jul 24, 1855
Mar 23, 1926

Jere P. Thompson
Nov 2, 1856
Oct 22, 1940

Fannie Thompson
Nov 14, 1867
Aug 14, 1930

George L. Thompson
Jul 7, 1901
Jul 8, 1934

G. W. Thompson
Mar 14, 1851
Jun 11, 1936

Nora, dau of
A. E. & M. E. Cathey
Oct 10, 1885
Aug 14, 1919

Mother
Frances Emeline Thompson
Dec 25, 1829
Feb 18, 1911

J. Clint Thompson
Mar 9, 1853
Jun 19, 1922

Mary E. Bishop
Feb 10, 1855
Apr 12, 1911

Josephine Harmon
Jan 15, 1854
Nov 25, 1933

M. C. Beasley
(Morgan Clayton)
1845-1900

M. W. Fowler
Sep 15, 1855
Aug 19, 1945
Son of J. E. &
Bettie Fowler
&
Emma Fowler
Sep 23, 1870
Dec 16, 1902
Dau of A. & Bettie
Beasley

A.(Archer) Beasley
Aug 5, 1836
Apr 24, 1914
& wife of
J. E. Fowler &
A. Beasley,
Bettie Beasley
May 16, 1837
Aug 12, 1898

Father
G. W. Rainey
Feb 4, 1830
Feb 12, 1902
&
Mother
M. L. Rainey
Nov 16, 1827
Apr 22, 1918

R. F. Rainey
Feb 14, 1834
Jan 11, 1905

Henry E. Richardson
Jan 4, 1887
Feb 15, 1887

Nancy Lou, wife of
J. W. Richardson
Jan 22, 1861
Jan 3, 1914

John W. Richardson
1857-1938
&
Cora Richardson
1874-1923

Z. T. Short
Aug 25, 1846
Apr 20, 1918

Addie Short
Apr 15, 1869
Jan 4, 1930

Z. T. "Bud" Short
Jun 26, 1896
Jun 17, 1957

** NOTE: Widow of Wm. McGaugh and dau.
of James and Sarah Harris

Howard Short
May 11, 1910
Oct 29, 1911

Nancy E. Short
Apr 7, 1901
Dec 11, 1902

NOTE: The following
Short Family are inside
Iron fence.

Parthenia G. Short
Died Nov 20, 1880
Aged about 70 years

John H. Short
Died Dec 27, 1879
Aged about 66 years

R. R. Short
(Richard H. Rudder Short)
Mar 22, 1817
Jun 15, 1863

Lizetta C., dau of
Thomas & Sarah D. Short
Nov 20, 1812
Sep 19, 1847

Mary H., dau of
Thomas & Sarah D. Short
Feb 14, 1819
May 10, 1844

* Thomas Short
Born 1773 in the State
of Virginia, Died in
Lincoln Co.
Nov 20, 1864

Sarah D., wife of
Thomas Short
Died May 9, 1821
Aged 32 years

Infant Dau of
T. & S. D. Short
(no dates)*
* Died before 1821
info from Lincoln Co.,
TN Court Records.

Infant Son of
T. & S. D. Short
(no dates)*
* Same as above.

End of Short Family
inside Iron fence.

Mary M. McGaugh
Feb 17, 1879
Mar 17, 1887

Will J. McGaugh
1858-1936
&
M. Lizzie McGaugh
1858-1929

E. P. McGaugh
Apr 27, 1904
Jul 14, 1968
&
Mary E. McGaugh
May 21, 1900
Nov 4, 1967

T. J. McGaugh
Jan 1, 1838
Apr 3, 1907

N. A., wife of
T. J. McGaugh
Jan 15, 1840
Aug 27, 1900

Eugene H. McGaugh
1865-1930
&
Josie McGaugh
1874-1965

** Lydia McGaugh
Aug 24, 1809
Feb 27, 1901

Margaret A. Crunk
1891-1950

Delina E. Crunk
May 3, 1865
Jan 4, 1941

Alvarion Wysong
Dec 2, 1848
Nov 20, 1898
"A Brother, dear,
lies buried here"

Alfred E. Cathey
1853-1936
&
Mary E. Cathey
1861-1942

Donald E. Haislip
1934-1978
(Cornersville FH)

Olen R. Locker
1892-1950
&
Myrtle E. Locker
1895-1973

Father
J. R. Endsley
Jun 14, 1867
Aug 24, 1926
&
Mother
Sallie Endsley
Jul 4, 1864
Mar 27, 1948

J. K. Endsley
May 18, 1824
Dec 28, 1907

* NOTE: Marriage Records of Davidson Co. Tn.
Thomas Short to Sally Reeder Nov. 29, 1808

CORNERSVILLE

Elizabeth Endsley
Apr 4, 1841
Jul 4, 1904

S. M. Endsley
1869-1938
&
Mattie R. Endsley
1864-1940

Will T. Helton
1881-1944
&
Myrtle A. Helton
1889-1954

Floyd Lee Eldridge
Tennessee
Cook 2 Billeting &
Sup Det   WW I
Oct 27, 1892
Apr 29, 1959
&
Emma B. Eldridge
Sep 27, 1892
Jun 7, 1968

R. M. S. Eldridge
Feb 20, 1852
Jan 2, 1914

Simmie D. Eldridge
Mar 31, 1884
Nov 22, 1943

Mrs. M. E. Eldridge
Jul 20, 1852
Dec 29, 1923

Roy Eldridge
Sep 7, 1890
Jun 8, 1917

Maggie Lou Adams Causby
Dec 18, 1893

Waman Clark Crigger
1911-
&
Louise Causby Crigger
1921-
&
Yvonne Crigger
1939-1943

Smith Dee Winnett
Pfc US Army WW II
Aug 27, 1916
Aug 16, 1976
&
Cora D. Winnett
Dec 14, 1915

Lewis A. Defoe
1886-1960
&
Mammie L. Defoe
1896-

Dorris P. Woodward
May 28, 1896

&
Ola G. Woodward
Apr 23, 1898

James H. Looney
Jul 29, 1906
Apr 11, 1975
&
Madelle Looney
Nov 25, 1905

Odis R. Word
Mar 6, 1906

&
Nancy L. Word
Mar 23, 1911

C. Hatten Archer
Jul 4, 1904

&
Thelma S. Archer
Sep 11, 1905
------------mrd Jul 29,1925

James Russell Pigg
1920-1977
&
Anita G. Pigg
1925-

Thomas D. Bone
Tennessee
Pvt US Marine Corps Res.
WW II
Jun 8, 1921
Jul 2, 1964

Fred Wilson Curtis
Tennessee
S Sgt US Army WW II
Mar 10, 1916
Apt 5, 1973
&
Elizabeth S. Curtis
1914-1977

Ollie Savage
1895-1973
&
Dallas Savage
1908-1973

W. A. Owens, Sr.
Oct 8, 1903

&
Pearl Owens
Apr 17, 1908
Jul 15, 1972

Calvin L. Burgett
Nov 30, 1908
Mar 2, 1969
&
Verdie L. Burgett
Aug 3, 1914

Oscar Lush Holly
Jan 21, 1886
Mar 26, 1957
&
Eula Burgess Holly
Mar 18, 1888
May 3, 1965

Father & Mother have gone
to meet their Infants
David W. Davis
Oct 16, 1855
Nov 6, 1855
&
John B. Davis
Aug 30, 1861
Oct 18, 1861
&
Father
James P. Davis
Jun 9, 1830
Dec 5, 1863
&
Mother
E. Jane Davis
Dec 29, 1828
Jul 28, 1896

Thomas O., son of
F. M. & S. E. Davis
May 4, 1873
Sep 15, 1877

Garner A., son of
F. M. & S. E. Davis
May 22, 1866
Jul 24, 1867

Martin B. Wood
Feb 20, 1900

&
Nola V. Wood
Apr 28, 1908
Dec 15, 1972
Mrd Dec 12, 1925

Mary Elizabeth Wood Burgett
Sep 22, 1926
Feb 16, 1954

Terry Sloan Burgett
1947-1948
(picture)

John D. Cecil Burgett
1901-1941
&
Elma Dee Burgett
1901-

Walter L. Fitzgerald
Nov 5, 1900
Sep 15, 1965
&
Bessie L. Fitzgerald
Jan 20, 1900

Robert H. Collins
Nov 7, 1899
Jan 23, 1973
&
Lounora W. Collins
Aug 23, 1900

Robert D. Pigg
Mar 30, 1921

&
Lynda T. Pigg
Jul 19, 1924
Nov 12, 1977
&
Roger D. Pigg
Sep 27, 1954
Nov 11, 1972

Father
Joe H. Duckworth, son of
Lawson & Etta Duckworth
Apr 29, 1907
Nov 7, 1976
&
Mamie, Irene dau of
Louie M. & Eva Daniel
Jan 19, 19--

Mrd Jun 10, 1930

Otha S. Short
1873-1941
&
Emma L. Short
1878-1958

Winfield Short
1847-1928
&
Margaret Short
1847-1921

Miss Dora Short
Apr 13, 1879
Jul 5, 1951
(1873-1951,R.H.Beasley FH)

Mary Ealmerd Allen
Sep 23, 1904
Sep 14, 1910

Levi Short
Feb 14, 1866
Apr 14, 1929
& wife
Icie D. Luna Short
Aug 6, 1868
Aug 2, 1927

CORNERSVILLE

Bessie Mai, dau of
L. V. & Icy Short
Oct 22, 1892
Jun 22, 1894

Hershal B. Flye
Jun 3, 1917

&
Mattie Lou Flye
May 9, 1918
Feb 21, 1978
&
Donald W. Flye
May 2, 1940

Hershal Flye, Jr.
Dec 10, 1944
Feb 28, 1972
&
Dianne V. Flye
Jul 4, 1944

Jam-- (Polly)
1911-(date gone)
(Bills-McGaugh FH)

Effie Lucille Polly
1942-1943
(Bills-McGaugh FH)

William E. Short
Pvt US Army
Feb 2, 1894
Jan 24, 1975

Bernice Short Welch
Oct 18, 1897
Jul 25, 1971

W. Thomas Short
1869-1901
&
Bettie B. Short
1872-1955

Joel Thomas Short
Feb 12, 1900
Nov 28, 1923

Cincinnati Cummings
Died Jul 17, 1895
Aged 54 yrs, 3 mos, 7 days

John Alvey Adams
Oct 1, 1859
Aug 7, 1909
&
Rachel Adams
Nov 12, 1820
Nov 24, 1890
&
Susan Bramlet
(no dates)

Sarah Lucille Adams
Aug 21, 1905
Jan 23, 1962

B. L. Adams
1867-1950
&
Nora Adams
1883-1938

Thomas Endsley
Jun 9, 1862
May 8, 1925

Alice Endsley
Sep 10, 1875
Dec 23, 1946

Clay, son of
T. M. & A. J. Endsley
Feb 24, 1895
Mar 30, 1896
&
Ulaler, dau of
T. M. & A. J. Endsley
Apr 5, 1897
May 25, 1898

Baby
Vernia May Bell Bland
May 20, 1910
Feb 28, 1912

J. G. Holland
1871-1958
&
Alice Holland
1865-1945

Bertha Haislip Holland
1897-1978
(Davis-Ralston FH)

Edd L. Haislip
1900-1955
&
Ada E. Haislip
1897-

Michael (Lavon) Haislip
May 9, 1952
Nov 26, 1971
(picture)

James L. Bradford
1870-1946
&
Leona E. Bradford
1871-1960

John Calvin Bradford
Mar 28, 1890
Jan 19, 1966
&
Lura May Bradford
May 19, 1880
May 21, 1971

Infant Son of
Calvin & Lura Bradford
B&D Jun 25, 1914

Joe M. Crunk
Jul 23, 1860
Mar 17, 1941
&
Lizzie E. Crunk
Apr 3, 1860
Jun 27, 1914

Next to above:
"Mother"
(no name or dates)

Breta, dau of
Josie & Horace Duckworth
Jan 22, 1894
Jul 10, 1904

Grace Duckworth
Mar 31, 1866
Jul 13, 1899

W. J. Duckworth
Mar 10, 1827
Nov 10, 1893
&
Sallie McGahey Duckworth
Apr 25, 1836
Apr 2, 1917

Leora Duckworth
1858-1943

Father
Erskin Luna
1888-1943
& wife
Fannie Luna
1884-1969
& dau.
Sara Luna
1914-1935

Willie Ford, son of
E. M. & F. M. Luna
Sep 9, 1910
Feb 1, 1911

O. M. Luna
Dec 25, 1876
Dec 30, 1901

T. Sidney Luna
Feb 11, 1880
Aug 6, 1893

Father
J. S. Luna
Oct 11, 1843
Apr 5, 1925
&
Mother
M. A. Luna
Oct 19, 1849
Jul 30, 1919

J. W. Wall
Jul 1, 1851
Mar 24, 1910

W. E. Young
Aug 21, 1883
Apr 11, 1931
&
F. E. Wall Young
Jul 27, 1875
Nov 12, 1949

J. S. Taylor
Nov 10, 1856
Feb 9, 1922
& wife
Viola Taylor
Jan 24, 1874
Jun 21, 1953

James O. Luna
1874-1958
&
Nannie E. Luna
1875-1970

Otho H., son of
J. O. & N. A. Luna
Jul 23, 1910
Mar 22, 1912

Joshua Young, Sr.
Sep 13, 1903
May 13, 1972
&
Ruby J. Young
Feb 9, 1911
Nov 8, 1976

Harold L. Young
1932-

Hellen Ruth Young
1928

N. F. Short
May 1, 1853
Jun 22, 1889

Martha C., wife of
H. M. Walls
Mar 31, 1828
Jun 29, 1889

Orlena Ellison
Oct 5, 1855
Mar 26, 1940

Mrs. Fannie Humbles
Dec 7, 1870
Nov 25, 1959

Effie Bell, dau of
J. L. & L. T. West
Feb 29, 1882
Aug 10, 1886

John Robert, son of
J. L. & L. T. West
Nov 28, 1884
Aug 15, 1886

James Clarence, son of
J. L. & L. T. West
Died Sep 4, 1893, age

CORNERSVILLE

Charlie J. Porter
Jan 21, 1886
Jun 6, 1954
&
Clemmie M. Porter
Feb 15, 1887
Jun 3, 1958

Martha S. Wilson
1863-1947

Ed T. McGaugh
Jun 22, 1884
Jun 19, 1954
&
Etna Wilson McGaugh
Nov 17, 1885
Sep 23, 1966

Lyndel M. Baucom
Jan 14, 1913
Jan 17, 1913

Marlin F. Baucom
Aug 6, 1915
Jan 20, 1918

Father
A. L. Baucom
1888-1922
&
Mother
C. P. Baucom
1891-1972

J. Lefley West
1856-1932
&
Tishey West
1862-1936

William Albert West
Dec 27, 1888
Feb 3, 1938

Ilia Irine West
Sep 8, 1894
Mar 15, 1963

E. Herman Baucom
Jun 12, 1915

&
Clari Mai F. Baucom
Aug 8, 1914
Apr 12, 1974

Braxton Fly
1876-1946
&
Alice W. Fly
1880-1972

Homer L. Fly
Aug 9, 1904
May 16, 1963
&
Clara Mai Fly
Jul 4, 1905

K. Doyle Adams
1930-1959
&
Nellie H. Adams
1930-
(picture, gone)

J. C. Wright
Dec 6, 1922

Michelle Chantai Adams
Jan 14, 1971
Jun 7, 1972
(color picture)

Tracie Lynn Adams
1969-1969
(London FH)

Father
Eugene Darnell
Jan 25, 1941
Jul 29, 1977
&
Mother
Elizabeth Darnell
Jan 9, 1942

Mrd Sep 23, 1959

J. R. "Pete" Causby
Jun 28, 1885
Jun 6, 1968

John T. Stovall
Dec 4, 1879
Apr 29, 1951

Molly Stovall
Oct 6, 1878
Jun 21, 1972

James M. Wright
Jun 25, 1921
Feb 1, 1972
&
Brownie E. Wright
Mar 6, 1919

Willie Jones
1907-1975
(Cornersville FH)

Jesse Joe Rogers
Mar 2, 1889
Aug 30, 1964
&
Ida Elizabeth Rogers
Sep 24, 1880
Oct 2, 1946

J. D. Rogers
Oct 26, 1911
Aug 30, 1941

Herschel Lee Fowler
Jun 13, 1907

&
Hannah Bell Fowler
Feb 6, 1914

Tull L. Franklin
May 1, 1886
Aug 3, 1954
&
Maudie Franklin
Apr 4, 1893
Feb 9, 1931

Willie Myrtle Franklin
Apr 23, 1929
Nov 22, 1929

Thurston Beard
1928-1931

W. O. "Bill" Beard
1907-1963

William Sim Foster
Apr 19, 1893
Mar 21, 1896

I. C., wife of
R. A. Wilson
Apr 4, 1826
Nov 14, 1891

Nancy, wife of
John Fue
Jan 10, 1833
Mar 4, 1893 "Mother"
& Daughter
Emily, wife of
Neal Dodd
Jan 12, 1870
Jul 5, 1888

Monroe, son of
J. F. & L. A. Wakefield
1884-1904

Lee Otis Wakefield
Oct 13, 1889
Jan 29, 1967
&
Annie Mae Thompson Wakefield
Mar 30, 1891

In Loving Memory of
John Kenneth Wakefield
Sep 21, 1919
May 4, 1963
"A Cancer victim who gave
his body for research that
others might live."

T. E. Wall
1897-1958
&
Mary Fannie Wall
1901-1935

Theo Wall
1894-1918

Bettie Lou Wall
1885-1904

Aggie Wall
1883-1903

Minnie Wall
1880-1903

Wall
(no dates)

Wall
(no dates)

Tommie Wall
1863-1899
&
Addie Wall
1865-1904

Roy, son of
R. M. & Ella Luna
Dec 2, 1890
Jun 15, 1891

Ella, wife of
R. M. Luna
Jun 3, 1861
Nov 1, 1893

R. M. L.
(footmarker)

Brownie Luna, dau of
R. M. & Ella Luna
Nov 8, 1882
Apr 30, 1901
Age 18 yrs, 5 mos, 22 days

J. E. Harmond
1859-1926

R. E., wife of
J. E. Harmond
Jul 26, 1859
Jun 20, 1903

Infant Son of
J. E. & R. E. Harmond
Jun 13, 1903
Jun 25, 1903

Mattie E. Harmond
Jul 18, 1869
Mar 18, 1933

Laura Bell Harmond
July 6, 1901

Will Edd Harmond
1929-1946
(picture)

Infant of Lush & Annie
McCrory   1917

CORNERSVILLE

Lush McCrory
1886-1956
&
Annie McCrory
1892-1969

Willie Lee Harmond
1894-1952
&
Mamie Kate Harmond
1901-19

George C. Sharp
1898-1959
&
Nannie B. Sharp
1912-

Arnold Townsend
Aug 21, 1917
Aug 31, 1955

George W. Townsend
Aug 11, 1878
Jul 25, 1947

Wilma W. Townsend
Jul 10, 1902
May 17, 1941

Luther Whitsett
Jun 30, 1871
Nov 26, 1952
&
Viola E. Whitsett
Oct 10, 1874
Mar 11, 1934

Minnie Whitsett Harmond
1875-1940
&
Roy E. Harmond
Tennessee
Pvt 49 Inf
1897-1931
&
Mazie H. Crabtree Harmond
1899-1968

T. O. Wall
1866-1943
&
Frances P. Wall
1866-1936

B. E., dau of
T. O. & F. P. Wall
Jul 10, 1905
Apr 24, 1906

Father
Willie G. Wall
1900-19
&
Mother
Bessie Mae Wall
1900-1933

Loyd O. Gault
1910-1973

Ora, dau of
J. F. & E. A. Freeman
Oct 27, 1867
Sep 20, 1889
Age 21 yrs, 10 mos, 23 days

John T. Smith
Nov 30, 1898
Apr 20, 1975
&
Dallas Smith
May 1, 1905

Father
J. Frank Freeman
Mar 16, 1841
Oct 1, 1903
&
Mother
M. A. E. Freeman
Oct 23, 1845
Sep 6, 1909

Lillie L. Freeman
Mar 27, 1882
Mar 1, 1906

Maggie Freeman
Aug 5, 1875
Feb 2, 1922

Tommie Florine, dau of
J. T. & W. H. Turner
Dec 21, 1901
Jun 25, 1903

Una Cloe, wife of
R. R. Collins
Feb 11, 1887
Jan 22, 1908

Edgar D., son of
E. A. & R. B. Rainey
Feb 12, 1881
Feb 11, 1896

R. B. Rainey
Oct 1, 1848
Jan 20, 1920

E. A., wife of
R. B. Rainey
May 23, 1858
Feb 26, 1908

W. P. Rainey
Oct 1, 1874
Dec 28, 1915

Sandy G. Rainey
Nov 3, 1845
Oct 13, 1932
&
Tiney M. Rainey
Oct 11, 1872
Dec 7, 1956

To Father
J. J. Dodd
Died Mar 17, 1909, age 95 yrs.

Thomas H. Dodd
Sep 18, 1869
Feb 7, 1918
&
Susie F. Dodd
Apr 18, 1872
Nov 25, 1911

George Wright
Feb 3, 1887
Apr 10, 1965
&
Emma D. Wright
Sep 13, 1889
Oct 23, 1970

Bessie Dean Wright
Jun 19, 1907
Mar 30, 1912

Timothy Vinal Endsley
1954-1955
(picture)

Melba Jeannette Adams
May 30, 1934
Jul 6, 1935

Solon B. Adams
Mar 2, 1905
Mar 24, 1972
&
Tishie Mae Adams
May 7, 1903
Jun 15, 1970

David M. Adams
B&D Sep 12, 1955

Salene Duckworth
1930-1960

Father
Fred T. Haislip
Jul 31, 1890
Oct 10, 1963
&
Mother
Otalene M. Haislip
Aug 24, 1894
Aug 6, 1975

Darlene Hudson
Jul 24, 1946

Father
John Thomas Allen
Mar 28, 1903

&
Mother
Elsie Lillian Pigg Allen
Dec 11, 1902

Mrd Dec 15, 1923

Ira L. Allen
1896-1963
&
Mary F. Allen
1907-1959

Felix Welcome Gentry
Jan 28, 1911

&
Mollie D. Pigg Gentry
Dec 2, 1910
------------Mrd Dec 2, 1928

Oscar Shield Pigg
Jul 15, 1876
Jun 30, 1951
&
Maud Elizabeth Pigg
Feb 18, 1879
May 15, 1956

------ B. Haislip
1905-1958
(London FH)

Clabe Haislip
Apr 23, 1893
Jan 16, 1946
&
Ada B. Haislip
Jan 4, 1897
Sep 12, 1928

Myrtle R., wife of
D. I. Nelms
Sep 13, 1876
Jul 6, 1919
"Mother"

Elizabeth Rayburn, dau of
D. I. & Myrtle Nelms
1907-1933

J. Melvin Burch
Jun 4, 1909
Mar 30, 1977
&
Virginia R. Burch
Jan 30, 1915

Mrd Jul 28, 1934

Infant Daughter of
J. T. & S. W. Robinson
Jul 11, 1922
Jul 12, 1922

Clarence L. Robinson
Mar 27, 1886
Dec 10, 1965

R. W. Robinson
Nov 6, 1883
May 21, 1925

J. T. Robinson
Jan 29, 1857
Jan 29, 1903

Callie V., wife of
J. T. Robinson
Mar 5, 1857
Nov 9, 1914

Hattie Robinson Clark
1879-1958

CORNERSVILLE

Alace L. Jones
Jan 1, 1860
Apr 14, 1904

Modena, dau of
Mr. & Mrs. O. C. Pigg
1908-1910

O. C. Pigg
Jul 16, 1847
Aug 22, 1908

Tina, wife of
O. C. Pigg
1870-1952

Penelopy, wife of
Joel Pigg
Apr 23, 1813
Mar 7, 1900
"Erected by
O. C. Pigg"

John Loyd Ledford
Dec 13, 1898
Sep 29, 1899

Lucile, dau of
G. G. & M. P. Ralston
Nov 29, 1897
Jul 19, 1899

Joel Oates Pigg
Jun 10, 1881
Oct 18, 1896

Willie Ezell Ledford
Jul 5, 1894
Oct 2, 1896

Sarah S., wife of
O. C. Pigg
Jan 13, 1847
Jan 13, 1890
"Mother"

W. H. Ellis
May 6, 1832
Mar 3, 1913

Jennette, wife of
W. H. Ellis
Jun 28, 1836
Dec 24, 1893

Catherine, wife of
W. H. Ellis
Jul 30, 1852
Mar 21, 1906

Eliza J. Daniel
May 9, 1843
Oct 10, 1903
"Erected by her son
J. T. Daniel"

J. T. Daniel
1871-1957

Emely Cochran
1936

Anna L. Cochran
1941

Roy E. Cochran
1906-1941
&
Verna Cochran
1909-1963

James H. Cochran
1873-1933
&
Annie W. Cochran
1880-1941

Frank Cochran
Nov 26, 1899
Apr 10, 1962

Zula F., wife of
W. H. Massey
May 14, 1884
Mar 27, 1907

Odie E. Massey
Jun 26, 1904
Oct 8, 1905

Bernice Irene, dau of
L. S. & A. C. Leonard
Mar 17, 1899
Jan 12, 1907

Lee D. Cox
Aug 23, 1844
Oct 31, 1923

Ronald R. Kinsley
Apr 4, 1912

&
Gladys C. Kinsley
Oct 10, 1910

Robert M. Chapman
Mar 26, 1886
Jun 16, 1962
&
Sallie R. Chapman
Feb 11, 1892
Feb 5, 1968

Capt. Clifford Chapman
1918-1978
(Bills-McGaugh)

Elmer Cochran
1883-1964

Pearl Cochran
1893-1956

Mary Frances Welch, wife of
Elmer Cochran
Nov 9, 1882
Jul 29, 1916
"Mother"

Infant Son of
T. E. & M. F. Cochran
B&D Jul 8, 1910

Mother
Josephine Welch
Feb 11, 1849
Sep 9, 1935

Walter Finley
1879-1954
&
Mary E. Finley
1879-1947

"Aunt Delia"
Cordelia Reynolds
Sep 8, 1874
Dec 17, 1934

Will T. Gault
1849-1925

Lela C. Gault
1872-1957

Willie F., dau of
W. T. & I. L. Gault
Feb 18, 1908
Jul 1, 1911

W. L. Caneer
Apr 25, 1832
Oct 27, 1913
& wife
Nancy E. Caneer
Mar 20, 1846
Dec 14, 1915

Nat L. Caneer
Apr 7, 1880
May 15, 1948

George T. Rainey
1863-1941
&
Caledonia F. Rainey
1874-1950

Infant Dau of
J. O. & G. R. Robinson
Jul 19, 1912

Lillie May, dau of
J. O. & G. L. Robinson
May 12, 1906
Oct 25, 1907

Infant Son of
J. O. & G. R. Robinson
Apr 7, 1911
Jan 18, 1914

Annie Mildred Robinson
1924-1926
"Daughter"

Nannie Wright
1864-1941
"Mammy is at rest"

J. Otis Robinson
1881-1942
&
Gleaner Robinson
1884-1948

Infant Son of
Mr. & Mrs. R. W. McCoy
1920-1920

Dorris Marie, dau of
Mr. & Mrs. Carl Robinson
Feb 9, 1926
Sep 17, 1931

Father
Tom B. Wakefield
1895-
&
Mother
Lucile P. Wakefield
1898-1957

Louise Wakefield
1916-1934

George Earl Wakefield
1918

Thelma June, dau of
Melvin & Virginia Burch
Sep 1, 1938

Rossie B. Pigg
Tennessee
Pvt Co A 26 MG Bn WW I
Apr 23, 1896
Jun 30, 1967
&
Lilyan A. Pigg
Marshall County
Feb 17, 1901
Dec 16, 1967

Infant Son of
Mr. & Mrs. R. B. Pigg
Jan 28, 1938

Joseph F. Bradford
Pvt US Army
Apr 10, 1890
Jul 1, 1975
&
Pearl Bradford
Aug 10, 1898
Aug 24, 1976
Mrd Sep 6, 1926

Dean Bradford
May 21, 1935
Oct 26, 1939

John O. Bradford
Aug 8, 1871
Mar 5, 1952
&
Mattie W. Bradford
Sep 29, 1895
Jan 27, 1961

CORNERSVILLE

Jimmie C. Pigg
Feb 12, 1891
Sep 17, 1944
&
Mazie E. Pigg
Aug 16, 1895
Apr 6, 1967

Laymon B. Edmondson
Jul 7, 1898
Mar 29, 1967
&
Mary C. Edmondson
Sep 4, 1904
Feb 10, 1953
Mrd Jul 4, 1920

William Monroe Hickerson
Tennessee
Pvt 7 Co 159 Depot Brig
WW I
Feb 2, 1894
Aug 24, 1966
&
Ornel W. Hickerson
1889-1955

J. Oliver Wright
Sep 3, 1898
Mar 24, 1963
&
Georgia Mai Wright
Jun 23, 1901
Dec 19, 1975

John R. Wright
Feb 3, 1929

Joe L. Wright, Jr.
1957-1957

Rev. G. A. Hester
1886-1972
&
Esther Hester
1894-1971

B. Leaman Bowers
Jan 16, 1900
Nov 16, 1968
&
Gladys E. Bowers
Mar 24, 1908

Sidney G. Caneer
Sep 23, 1869
Aug 17, 1958
&
Abbie D. Caneer
Jan 23, 1877
Dec 7, 1944

Davy Tell Wall
1899-1964
&
Beatrice C. Wall
1899-

J. W. Lane
Dec 26, 1884
Jan 16, 1973
&
Lillie H. Lane
Jan 29, 1890
Feb 23, 1970

T. Hill Lane
Dec 28, 1886

&
Jossie H. Lane
Dec 27, 1894

Infant Son of
Mr. & Mrs. Hill Lane
Aug 18, 1922

J. Lee Glenn
Mar 23, 1854
Dec 11, 1944

Elizabeth L. Glenn
Feb 28, 1818
Mar 3, 1915

Martha I. Fuller
Oct 3, 1861
Jan 1, 1897

J. G. Fuller
Jul 27, 1823
May 29, 1907

Mary L. Fuller
Sep 26, 1828
Jan 13, 1904

Father
O. C. Short
Nov 3, 1852
Feb 22, 1916
&
Mother
J. F. Short
Mar 29, 1856
Jun 16, 1890
& dau
Bettie Short
Nov 3, 1874
Oct 2, 1891

W. Silas Bradford
1855-1928
&
Realie Bradford
1858-1900

J. W. Haney
1860-1926
&
Lucy Ann Haney
1861-1933

Rev. J. C. Mials
Jul 3, 1833
Nov 16, 1890

H. M. Walls
Jul 23, 1829
Sep 3, 1912

J. H. T. Ketchum
Oct 11, 1849
Oct 22, 1901

Fannie Ketchum
1851-1928

Thomas J. Ketchum
Apr 8, 1886
Dec 11, 1908

Henry B. Ketchum
Dec 9, 1890
Oct 2, 1976
&
S. Howard Ketchum
Jul 6, 1896
Jan 11, 1968

Roy Bradford
1895-1947
&
Maggie Lou Bradford
1907-19

Infant Dau of
R. C. & E. E. Pigg
Feb 1, 1911

Doris Dean
1930

Lee Pigg
Oct 28, 1892
Aug 6, 1917
&
Narcie A. Pigg
Feb 13, 1890
Aug 5, 1967

Dulene Pigg
Sep 26, 1917
Jan 29, 1929

J. F. Larwood
Dec 5, 1849
Nov 1, 1920

Sallie C., wife of
J. F. Larwood
Oct 8, 1852
Apr 11, 1914

Robert C. Pigg
1870-1940
&
Elizabeth E. Pigg
1872-1958

George M. Tate
1878-1930
&
Dora E. Tate
1882-1952

Paterson Tate
1912-1928

Father
Jessie C. Tate
May 1, 1899

&
Mother
Eunice H. Tate
May 6, 1901
Mar 13, 1968

Fate Wolaver
Sep 26, 1870
Apr 16, 1956
&
Willie Wolaver
Jan 30, 1881
Aug 22, 1965

J. C. Brown
Tennessee
Pvt HQ Co 475 Inf WW II
May 3, 1924
Jan 29, 1972

Burtie Mae Brown
Sep 7, 1921

Walter Brown
1890-1963
&
Ida M. Brown
1896-

Mary Magdalene Salisbury
1910-1941

John Thomas Pigg
Jan 18, 1866
Feb 17, 1937
&
Emmadee Pigg
Jan 18, 1866
(no date)

Father
O. C. Pigg
1898-1956
&
Mother
Louise D. Pigg
1901-1956

May Lois Short, wife of
W. L. Ketchum
1897-1923

Earl Short
1889-1955
&
Vallie Short
1887-1974

W. Marvin Short
1891-1957
&
Iris D. Short
1895-1974

CORNERSVILLE

J. W. Davis
May 12, 1869
Apr 24, 1910

Dona Davis
Jun 14, 1868
May 16, 1935

Beulah M., dau of
J. W. & C. D. Davis
Sep 25, 1901
Mar 3, 1916

Raymond R. Short
May 16, 1897
Mar 18, 1962

Charles O. Short
Tennessee
Pvt 307 Inf 77 Div
May 8, 1923

James Thomas Short
Nov 16, 1882
Nov 11, 1902

Freddy M., son of
M. H. & E. L. Short
Mar 6, 1888
Oct 26, 1890

Eddie M., son of
E. W. & A: L. Short
Mar 30, 1887
Sep 30, 1892

Walter Short
1863-1930
&
Laura Short
1865-1945

John R. Lane
1859-1934
&
Jossie S. Lane
1857-1902
&
Alice H. Lane
1866-1938

Mary Lane
1882-1957

Lizzie W.(Lane ?)
1896-1896

Fannie W.(Lane ?)
1870-1898

Nora (Lane ?)
1889-1899

Father
Sambo Bowers
Jan 25, 1885
Feb 15, 1961
&
Mother
Bettie Lou Bowers
Oct 2, 1898-Nov 7, 1962

Monroe Bowers
Jan 18, 1880
Jan 20, 1914

Mary Bowers
1878-1942

Ewen W. Bowers
1918-1978
(Bills-McGaugh FH)

William H. Bowers
1840-1923
&
Livona Bowers
1848-1926

Infant Son of
J. F. & Eva Crick
B&D Sep 8, 1909

Infant Rudd
Jul 1, 1892
Sep 5, 1892

D. F. Rudd
Jan 27, 1854
(no date)
& wife
S. E. Price Rudd
Nov 30, 1858
Jul 1, 1892

James E. Pigg
Nov 1, 1871
Sep 1, 1934
&
Lula M. Pigg
Sep 30, 1875
Jul 22, 1950

Maggie Wilma, dau of
J. E. & L. M. Pigg
Mar 6, 1901
Sep 9, 1901

Desa L. Pigg
Mar 2, 1886
Sep 12, 1892

Father
T. M. Pigg
Jan 8, 1845
Apr 28, 1922
&
Mother
Elizabeth Pigg
May 12, 1850
Apr 5, 1915

J. M. Welch
Nov 28, 1874
Sep 19, 1901

Beulah L., wife of
W. S. Alexander
Died Apr 7, 1912
Age 32 yrs, 8 mos, 15 days

Paralee Coonradt
1859-19(no date)

Annie Lee Coonradt
1891-1946

Laura B. Stokes
1922-1922

Willie Stokes
Oct 6, 1904
Jan 6, 1921

Will M. Stokes
1871-1913
&
Emma Stokes
1866-1957

Montie G. Poarch
Sep 18, 1877
Jan 25, 1918

James L. Shaw
1879-1958
&
Lula B. Shaw
1881-1953

Thomas H. Fuller
1867-1930
&
Maggie B. Fuller
1879-1967

J. Albert Haislip
Nov 30, 1900
Feb 6, 1975
&
Clarice Haislip
Jun 20, 1909

Mrd May 27, 1929

Father
A. B. Haislip
Jan 17, 1868
Dec 24, 1959
&
Mother
Maggie B. Haislip
Apr 2, 1873
Jan 20, 1961

Billy L. Haislip
Dec 17, 1932
Jan 14, 1943

Father
A. Lee Haislip
Apr 25, 1904
Aug 31, 1962
&
Mother
Willia Mae Haislip
Nov 10, 1912

James P. Thompson
Tennessee
GM3 US Navy WW I
May 26, 1896
Apr 26, 1957
&
Cora L. Thompson
Oct 9, 1899
Oct 3, 1974

Wallace D. McConnell
1882-1963

Maggie Pearl McConnell
Sep 4, 1907
Jul 7, 1959

Mr. Jeriel Brown
1927-1977
(London FH)

J. Tom Turner
1875-1966
&
Waxie F. Turner
1878-1952

Malcolm Ezell, son of
J. T. & W. H. Turner
Mar 8, 1909
Oct 24, 1910

Frank A. Bigham
Dec 25, 1914

&
Sue B. Bigham
Apr 20, 1916

Eddie Lee Barnes
Jul 25, 1880
Oct 26, 1950
&
Bettie Pearl Barnes
Jan 11, 1883
May 16, 1931

Annie B., wife of
A. D. Crunk
Sep 5, 1886
Jun 10, 1915

J. Calloway Crunk
Aug 31, 1881
Nov 1, 1904

Dr. J. C. Crunk
1852-1933
&
Mary C. Crunk
1856-1948

Father
Grover C. McCrory
1884-1949

CORNERSVILLE

F. M. Ealy
Apr 20, 1846
Dec 7, 1925
&
Bettie Ealy
Jul 10, 1852
Mar 15, 1912

Jim Davis
1886-1949

Jane Davis
Oct 12, 1853
Dec 14, 1929

Ella May Johnson
Feb 14, 1878
Mar 20, 1948

Infant Son of
W. R. & L. C. Bowers
Aug 20, 1897
Aug 22, 1897

Sidney M. Bowers
Feb 20, 1915
Sep 17, 1933

W. R. Bowers
May 20, 1871
Jul 5, 1950
&
Clemma Bowers
Dec 10, 1878
Jul 22, 1942

Lillard F. Bowers
1902-1964
&
Pearl R. Bowers
1910-

Fred V. Bowers
Dec 22, 1910

&
Robbie C. Bowers
Oct 30, 1914

Mrd Apr 9, 1932

William E. Bowers, Sr.
Apr 12, 1913

&
Helen B. Bowers
Aug 24, 1917

Mrd Mar 16, 1940

John T. Bowers
Jan 18, 1874
Mar 22, 1948
&
Pearl E. Bowers
Oct 8, 1881
Jan 6, 1960

Robbie L. Bowers
May 27, 1917
May 2, 1973

John T. Bowers
Apr 4, 1909
Nov 23, 1911

Father
A. E. Bivins
May 28, 1850
Apr 3, 1911
&
Mother
Martha A. Bivins
Dec 6, 1855
Sep 1, 1936

M. M. Bivins
Apr 22, 1853
May 13, 1917

Sarah J. E. Bivins
Jul 15, 1846
Nov 3, 1906

S. L. Bivins
Jan 1, 1884
Aug 5, 1912

Zaner B. Bivins
Jul 23, 1889
Sep 12, 1912

M. E. J. Wilkerson
Oct 28, 1865
Mar 5, 1895
"Member of Christian
Church"

Elizabeth W. Golden
Aug 3, 1914

Fount W. Bowers
1873-1939
&
Mattie M. Bowers
1875-1963

Thomas Bowers
1908-1928

Robert Bowers
Feb 24, 1906
Nov 14, 1906

R. J. McCrory
Jun 9, 1841
Apr 30, 1902
&
M. F. McCrory
Aug 8, 1845
Aug 18, 1906

Thomas H. Hardin
May 12, 1820
Jan 22, 1893

S. S., wife of
T. H. Hardin
Mar 27, 1814
Jun 11, 1898

James Thomas Bryant
Jun 5, 1874
Aug 18, 1903

James L. Bryant
1848-1910
&
Nancy C. Bryant
1849-1924

Terrell B. Bryant
1892-1922

Father
T. A. J. Turner
Nov 13, 1846
Sep 8, 1908
& wife
Mother
M. L. Turner
Mar 12, 1843
Apr 12, 1918

Julius P. Turner
1875-1949
&
Florence S. Turner
1882-1954

W. U. Collins
Sep 8, 1872
Nov 6, 1928
&
Lenis O. Collins
Nov 17, 1871
Oct 2, 1946

Infant Son of
J. E. & Burnie Swiney
Dec 11, 1911

Infant Son of
J. E. & Burnie Swiney
Jun 2, 1916

J. Edgar Swiney
Jul 3, 1882
Sep 17, 1962
&
Bernie Freeman Swiney
Mar 13, 1885
Jan 17, 1920

Willie Riley Short
Jan 31, 1889
Apr 10, 1920

Marshall Swanner
Sep 19, 1849
May 28, 1934
&
Rebecca Swanner
Nov 19, 1856
Mar 12, 1933

Father
J. Lee Freeman
1869-1920

William L. Brown
Mar 19, 1910
May 22, 1977
&
Mattie H. Brown
Mar 26, 1910

Mrd Jan 19, 1928

J. Henry Wakefield
1881-1967
&
Gertrude E. Wakefield
1885-1938

John F. Wakefield
Oct 2, 1863
Nov 4, 1952
&
Lydia Wall Wakefield
Dec 8, 1862
Mar 10, 1941

James C. Bradford
Oct 27, 1884
Aug 5, 1966
&
Nettie S. Bradford
Aug 17, 1880

Mrd Jan 19, 1913

T. Morgan Tate
May 17, 1918
Apr 13, 1976
&
J. Kathryn Tate
May 17, 1923

J. Denver McCollum
1909-1974
&
Lillian H. McCollum
1917-

Audie L. McCollum
1882-1974
&
Hattie C. McCollum
1882-

Bee Baucom
Aug 8, 1894
(new grave, no date)
&
Elma T. Baucom
Nov 6, 1893

James Owen Harrison
Nov 30, 1898
Sep 21, 1962
&
Katy Vera Harrison
Apr 19, 1902
Feb 18, 1957

CORNERSVILLE

James Crunk McDaniel
Tennessee
S1 USNR WW II
Aug 16, 1925
Jan 6, 1945
&
Tyler V. McDaniel
Jan 4, 1906
Apr 14, 1971
&
Edna C. McDaniel
Feb 9, 1907

Andrew C. Crunk
1900-1959

W. Charlie Crunk
1863-1941

A. A. Malloy
Jul 20, 1872
Nov 25, 1928
&
Irene M. Malloy
Jul 27, 1893
Aug 19, 1937

Wade Shepard
North Carolina
Wagoner HQ 27 MG BN WW I
Apr 28, 1895
Feb 18, 1973
&
Porter C. Shepard
Dec 2, 1897

Asie F. Rhodes
Nov 17, 1889
Jan 15, 1926
&
Nana Tucker Rhodes
Dec 5, 1896
Dec 11, 1974

Thomas A. Rhodes
Jul 6, 1896
Sep 1, 1913
&
Sallie Rhodes
Jul 1859
Dec 1937

Ollie M. Coonradt
1887-1935

Fannie Brown
1868-1929

Elmer E. Coonrad
Feb 3, 1900
Oct 2, 1918

Vera Conradt
Apr 1, 1896
Dec 11, 1924

Herman Conrad
Mar 19, 1912
May 28, 1912

Velma D. Conrad
Mar 30, 1910
Dec 26, 1922

Rosalee, wife of
O. M. Conrad
Jun 12, 1889
Mar 19, 1912

Laura B. Brown
Jun 2, 1893
Aug 2, 1911

Andrew Alexander Thompson
Mar 9, 1841
Apr 5, 1907
&
Martha Jane Thompson
Dec 10, 1860
Jan 5, 1910

Martha, dau of
W. G. & Fannie Brown
Apr 21, 1902
Oct 1, 1903

Dewey Brown
Jan 28, 1902
Mar 10, 1930

Dock Brown
1857-1937

Betty Lyon Meadows Pierce
1862-1946

J. F. Haislip
Jan 15, 1827
Sep 3, 1904

L. F., wife of
J. F. Haislip
Jun 5, 1842
Feb 13, 1912

Father
J. T. McCrory
Aug 20, 1866
Jul 30, 1932

Mother
Ella V. McCrory
Dec 4, 1872
Sep 18, 1939

Father
Elmer Lee McCrory
1893-1937
&
Mother
Josephine H. McCrory
1892-1972

Bruce Cochran
1868-1963
&
Florence Cochran
1871-1962

W. C. Bivins
1880-1970
&
Sallie Bivins
1888-1934

W. C. Bivins, Jr.
Jun 4, 1918
Sep 23, 1923

Deborah McAdams
Sep 14, 1893

Frank Dixon
1897-1935

Elsie B. Dixon
Jan 29, 1901

&
Annie Pearl Dixon
Jul 24, 1922

Bodie Lee Calahan
Feb 9, 1921

&
Mary Jane Calahan
Aug 28, 1923

R. H. Hobbs
Sep 10, 1885
May 3, 1921
& wife
Cora Bivins Hobbs Davis
Jul 3, 1891
Aug 1, 1973

Vollie, son of
R. H. & Cara Hobbs
Dec 31, 1912
Sep 19, 1917

Selvage E. Hobbs
Sep 1, 1905

&
Willie D. Hobbs
Jun 25, 1909

Mrd Apr 19, 1927

William O. Bivins
1928-1928

Johnnie M. Bivins
Sep 18, 1907

Father
T. J. Bradford
Jan 3, 1860
Sep 14, 1928
& wife
Mother
Sidnie Bradford
Aug 24, 1865
Feb 26, 1934

Robert C. Bradford
Feb 13, 1887
Mar 28, 1904

William T. Bradford
Tennessee
Pfc US Army WW I
Jan 6, 1893
Mar 16, 1971
&
Bonnie S. Bradford
Dec 23, 1896
Feb 25, 1963
Mrd Feb 17, 1923

Thomas Shealey Pigg
Oct 8, 1882
Jun 25, 1971
&
Susie Massey Pigg
Dec 26, 1882
Aug 3, 1969
&
T. M. Pigg
Oct 27, 1911
Aug 1, 1912

Frederick Roscoe Foster
Mar 10, 1903
Feb 23, 1970
&
Irene Pigg Foster
Jun 20, 1904

William N. Wakefield
1860-1935
&
Sallie A. Wakefield
1866-19(no date)

Tullie R. Wakefield
1892-1956
&
Bertha E. Wakefield
1895-1974

M. N., son of
T. R. & B. E. Wakefield
Nov 29, 1917
Dec 3, 1917

Robert A. Tucker
Jan 6, 1854
Dec 5, 1927
&
Irene McKenzie Tucker
May 22, 1867
Oct 8, 1947

Edwin Newton Tucker
Tennessee
Pvt Co H 149 Inf WW I
Dec 16, 1893
Apr 7, 1963

"Daddy"
William Roy Luna
May 22, 1898
Oct 27, 1973

CORNERSVILLE

____e Luna
1869-1934
(McDaniel FH)

Clyde Luna
1911-1936
(McDaniel FH)

Marion L. Higgs
Tennessee
Pvt 2 Inf Repl Regt WW I
Sep 15, 1896
Dec 14, 1950

Elsie L. Higgs
Jun 29, 1901
Oct 9, 1937

William E. Barrom
1901-1976
&
Aline H. Barrom
1911-

Will Brown
Apr 20, 1896
Jul 19, 1968
&
Lillie S. Brown
Oct 6, 1904

Charles H. Wolaver
Tennessee
Pfc US Army WW I
Feb 11, 1889
Jan 2, 1962
&
Clara C. Wolaver
Sep 12, 1895

Tom U. Watson
1881-1963
&
Rosa B. Watson
1887-1948

James A. Finley
1866-1954
&
Minnie L. Finley
1878-1942

Father
Charlie Pack
1885-1941
&
Mother
Bessie Pack
1892-(no date, new grave)

Herman B. Fowler
1904-1953

A. D. Endsley
1917-1938

Arthur Endsley
Nov 4, 1889
Nov 5, 1936

Mollie D. Endsley
1892-1923

Louise Endsley
Mar 19, 1911
Jun 10, 1913

Ernest Lebert Massey
Apr 1, 1906
Dec 9, 1971

Windel, son of
E. L. & A. C. Massey
B&D Jul 11, 1913

Ernest L. Massey
Feb 2, 1894
Dec 15, 1918

Etter Lee Ketchum
Tennessee
Pvt 157 Depot Brigade
WW I
Jul 23, 1888
Jan 26, 1951

Dealma Massey
1882-1959
&
Loretta Massey
1893-1964

Breta, dau of
D. A. & M. L. Massey
Mar 22, 1914
Sep 3, 1914

Thomas H. Haislip
1842-1922
&
Lucy Dell Haislip
1867-1938

George W. Wakefield
Apr 29, 1890
Oct 26, 1957
&
Willie Mai F. Wakefield
Feb 28, 1894

Mrs. Mary D. Dunivant
1912-1978
(London FH)

E. Leonard Adams
Apr 11, 1918
Apr 13, 1977
&
M. Catherine Adams
Jul 15, 1938

Mrs. Brenda A. Dye
1943-1977
(London FH)

Maxie Shaw Cochran
1884-

Hattie Shaw Bagley
1882-1965

Father
R. F. Shaw
Sep 8, 1843
May 11, 1921
&
Mother
Martha Shaw
Feb 20, 1862
Apr 13, 1923

W. C. Jobe
1870-1932

Ada L. Jobe
1869-1934

Henry Morgan Jobe
Jul 30, 1890
Nov 14, 1963

J. R. Welch
Oct 15, 1841
Nov 24, 1920
&
Emily J. Welch
Aug 25, 1849
Jul 10, 1941

James Thomas Short
Aug 25, 1881
Dec 9, 1924
&
Mary Welch Short
Apr 27, 1881
Dec 9, 1968

Melba Dean Short
Mar 4, 1922
Jun 4, 1922

John Reavis Coggins
Jan 22, 1886
Dec 21, 1956
&
Neoma Short Coggins
Nov 13, 1908
Jul 27, 1975

Winfield Ezell Haislip
Tennessee
Pfc Field Arty WW II
Mar 26, 1919
Dec 7, 1957
&
Gladys P. Haislip
1919-1952

Infant Dau of
Mr. & Mrs. C. N. Park
1932-1932

Harold Wayne Park
1931-1934

END OF SHORT
* *

Clarence N. Park
Nov 21, 1893
Jul 1, 1976
&
Bertha W. Park
May 11, 1894
Apr 18, 1975

Carey T. Lowrance
Mar 12, 1872
Feb 3, 1956
&
Leona E. Lowrance
Oct 6, 1883
Nov 29, 1963

Vera Park Fann
Mar 4, 1903
Nov 7, 1974

Patrick Jason Allen
1972-1972
(Bills-McGaugh)

Traci Leigh Allen
Apr 27, 1966
May 1, 1966

Robert Carl Tallman, III
Nov 18, 1968
Jul 29, 1969

Roy Norwood
1925-1941
(R. H. Beasley FH)

Odell "Coot" Lowrance
Oct 27, 1907
Jul 17, 1972
&
Lena Mae Bivins Lowrance
Jan 14, 1912

J. R. Whitaker
Feb 22, 1877
Jan 6, 1955

W. E. Whitaker
Apr 18, 1869
Jan 30, 1937
&
V. V. Whitaker
Sep 3, 1882
Nov 6, 1959

Several unmarked graves.

CORNERSVILLE

NEW HOPE CEMETERY

Located two miles southeast of Cornersville Corporate limits, at Cherry Corner, on Cornersville-Ostella Road. The New Hope Methodist Church once stood near this cemetery. Copied April 15, 1978 by Helen and Tim Marsh.

Old Section:

Daniel McCray
Who was born
----- & departed this life
Feb 7, 1844

Silas McClelland
Who departed this life
Sept the 6th 1843
Aged 52 yrs, 10 mos, 25 days
"Weep not nor shead a tear for me, my tender wife & children dear"

Peggy C. McClelland, dau of
Silas & Jane McClelland
Born May 4, 1818
Died Aug 20, 1825   (Vault)
            W.M.D.

Jane McClelland, wife of
Silas McClelland
Born Dec 1798
Died Aug 1864

John F. McClelland
Dec 29, 1812
Jan 16, 1859

Lucinda R., Consort of
John F. McClelland
Jan 8, 1812
Oct 13, 1835 (Vault)

Sandy G., son of
William & Fanny Cook
Jul 19, 1816
Oct 27, 1840 (Vault)

Wife
Polly Cowden
(concrete marker, no dates)

Pioneer
John Cowden & wife
Elizabeth Norris
(Concrete marker, no dates)

John B. Cowden
(no dates)

William Cowden
1800-1840 (Vault)

William Frederick Edwards
Who was born Dec 7, 1823
& Died Jan 29, 1834
D.C. & N. C. Gillespie.
(Vault)

T. C. R.
(Vault, no dates)

W. W. R.
(Vault, no dates)

Payne Davis
 & wife
Sarah Cowden
(concrete marker, no dates)

John O. Davis
son of Wilson P. &
Sally Davis
Dec 27, 1831
Feb --, 1834
(chipped)

Solomon C., son of
Solomon & Lucinda Meadows
Jun 18, 1837
Oct 16, 1839 (Vault)

Mrs. Mary Hunter
Who was born
Apr 1, 1774
Died Dec 6, 1839

John D. Beasley
Feb 10, 1827
Apr 8, 1856
Age 29 yrs, 1 mo, 28 days

Mary E., wife of
John D. Beasley
Oct 5, 1834
Dec 15, 1883

Brandon Cowden
(concrete marker, no dates)

End of Old Section.

H. N. Cowden
Jul 1, 1816
Sep 23, 1886

Emiline, wife of
Humphry N. Cowden
Oct 20, 1821
Aug 10, 1857
Age 35 yrs, 9 mos, 20 days

E. A., son of
H. N. & Emiline Cowden
Died Jan 1856
Aged about 4 years

Susan J., dau of
H. N. & Emiline Cowden
Died Jan 1856
Aged about 2 years

Infant Son of
H. N. & Emeline Cowden
Died 1847
Aged about 2 days

Lula E. Cowden
Jun 19, 1869
Apr 4, 1872

B. Hay
(fieldstone)

Ano wife
Susan Cowden
(concrete marker, no dates)

George M. Cooper
Jun 24, 1831
Oct 6, 1862

Ada L., dau of
George & Maria Cooper
Nov 16, 1858
May 7, 1861

S. Ida, dau of
George & Maria Cooper
Dec 21, 1860
Feb 11, 1862

Margret J., dau of
W. G. & J. S. Clayton
Aug 9, 1858
Apr 30, 1865

Collin Claton
Died Jul 10, 1893
Age 46 yrs.
(fieldstone)

New Section:

A. C. McClelland
Jan 10, 1826
Mar 6, 1864

N. J. M., wife of
J. G. Burt
Jan 29, 1829
Jun 3, 1866
Age 35 yrs, 4 mos, 5 days
(Vault)

Mary J., wife of
J. G. Burt
Sep 29, 1839
Jan 28, 1869
(Vault)

M. L. Burt
(fieldstone)

B. N. P.
(fieldstone)

Mrs. R. B(?). Haislip
(fieldstone)

Minnie Jane, dau of
G. W. & L. F. McBride
Died Jan 14, 1886
Age 1 yr, 6 mos, 5 days

Mattie L. Leonard
Oct 27, 1882
Oct 17, 1885

Lucinda E. Scales
Apr 22, 1820
Mar 18, 1845
"Was a member of
Baptist Church"

William A., son of
S. & Loucinda Meadows
Apr 28, 1835
Aug 16, 1855

C.(Carey) T. Kelley
Died May 1, 1854
(no age)
(broken into 3 pieces)

Rosalie A., dau of
J. W. & L. J. Kelley
Jul 22, 1857
Jul 12, 1859

Jeremiah Gant
Born May 1780
Died Aug 7, 1855

CORNERSVILLE

Nancy, wife of
Jeremiah Gant
Born 1776
Died Jul 15, 1855

Susan A. P. Gand(Gant)
Mar 19, 1823
Jun 30, 1855
Age 32 yrs.

Roxannah V., wife of
E. A. McCollumn
May 17, 1835
Dec 27, 1857

W. M. P.
(fieldstone)

W. D. Powell
Jan 30, 1795
Sep 14, 1873
& wife
Celia Powell
Feb 27, 1802
Aug 20, 1859

Paul R. Garrett
1919-1931

Dyer Short
1915-
&
Merle E. Short
1917-1962

Avon E. Nelms
Jul 29, 1893
Apr 13, 1970
&
Ocie C. Nelms
Aug 7, 1895
(1978)

A. Frank Nelms
1857-1950
&
Nannie E. Nelms
1858-1926

Sam F. Allen
Jul 15, 1882
Aug 21, 1914
&
Leota Poarch Allen
May 11, 1882
(no date)

Mother
Ruth Allen Anderson
Jul 1, 1909
Jan 28, 1958

Malcom B. Allen
1907-1957
&
Maxie G. Allen
1918-

Mary Margie Poole
1905-1939

Newton C. Poarch
1865-1946
&
Etta Poarch
1872-1960

Ellen Jane Poarch
1916-1918

Lester Gilbert Pratt
Jul 25, 1928
Oct 20, 1928

William Floyd Franklin
Aug 8, 1897
Feb 27, 1977
&
Gladys N. Franklin
Aug 1, 1897

Clarence Lynch
1883-1920
"Father"

Maggie Lynch
1877-1922
"Mother"

A. Arthur Porter
Jan 5, 1876
Apr 14, 1961
&
E. Celia Porter
Jul 11, 1866
Jul 16, 1941

William Anderson Porter
Jun 30, 1840
Jun 4, 1922
&
Argustie Ann Porter
Mar 25, 1855
(no date)

James Henry Porter
Oct 2, 1888
Jan 2, 1953

N. M. Smith
Aug 8, 1847
(no date)
&
Sallie Todd Smith
Feb 16, 1849
Oct 31, 1918

Mother
Aunt Jennie Smith Hardin
1849-1921

Annie B., dau of
N. M. & S. E. Smith
Nov 4, 1882
Sep 18, 1908

M. Katie Porter
Mar 2, 1894
May 10, 1919

Veatrice N. Hamlin
Apr 16, 1880
Dec 22, 1918
"Farewell husband &
children dear"

A. D. Moore
Dec 13, 1828
Aug 9, 1897

Thomas S. Moore
Sep 17, 1882
Jun 16, 1975

Cleaveland A., Son of
A. D. & M. C. Moore
Apr 23, 1887
Nov 16, 1888

J. D. Moores
Mar 28, 1830
Mar 17, 1912
& wife
Lucy A. Moores
Apr 1, 1837
Jun 7, 1912
& dau
Mary Pearl Moores
Jul 22, 1878
Nov 4, 1899
&
William H. Moores
1868-1930

Ruie, dau of
T. N. & B. I. Burgess
Dec 9, 1894
Mar 7, 1896

T. N. Burgess
Jul 17, 1861
May 3, 1904

Father
Marshall L. Burgess
Oct 25, 1853
Apr 19, 1911

Eliza P. Burgess
Aug 18, 1862
Feb 26, 1945

Otis J. Burgess
1890-19(no date)
&
Irene Clark Burgess
1892-1928

J. B. Burgess
Died Oct 3, 1890
Age 30 yrs, 3 mos, 12 days
& wife
Ida G. Burgess
Died Feb 27, 1891
Age 27 yrs, 9 mos, 25 days
&
Infant Sons
(no dates)

Infant Dau of
J. H. & Ora Burgess
Jun 2, 1892
Jun 18, 1892

Adam Coble
1835-1893
&
Lucinda E. Coble
1843-1916

William Tucker
1874-1898

Otis Kent Tucker
Apr 15, 1896
Jul 31, 1915

John M. Poarch
1853-1933
&
Mollie R. Poarch
1859-1949

Robert Earl Harwell
Oct 17, 1919

&
Mary Frances Harwell
Jan 23, 1921

Clyde Cooper
Jul 1, 1869
Jan 1, 1961
&
Nannie J. Cooper
Dec 22, 1861
Feb 19, 1937

Reba Lou Cooper
Sep 16, 1896
Sep 1, 1897

W. F. Glazier
Jan 15, 1823
Apr 16, 1895

Jane, wife of
Young Burgess
Oct   1843
Dec 9, 1905

Mother
Nancy C. Griffis
1856-1943

C. Bugg Clift
1871-1949
&
Ana A. Clift
1877-1964

A. Gowan Clift
Apr 28, 1907
Jan 9, 1936

Herman Elmo Woodward
Apr 4, 1906
Jan 23, 1954

CORNERSVILLE

Thomas F. Garrett
Nov 27, 1910

&
Ruby C. Garrett
Feb 23, 1911
Jun 29, 1973

Robert Thomas Darnell
Dec 10, 1879
Sep 24, 1957

Eunice Woodward Darnell
Feb 28, 1881
Oct 30, 1952

E. L. Woodward
Jul 11, 1874
Jun 22, 1919

A. D. Woodward, Jr.
Jan 11, 1933

Thomas Riley Henry
May 22, 1888
May 26, 1977

Henry Clay Cook
1860-1943
&
Jennie Smith
1869-1953

W. Morgan Burt
1870-1942
&
Mary A. Burt
1877-1905

Joseph G. Burt
Mar 2, 1833
Feb 17, 1917
&
Millie E. Burt
Aug 20, 1840
Feb 9, 1924

Jesse W. Cox
Apr 1, 1908
Oct 8, 1974
&
Mary L. Cox
Apr 11, 1906
Mar 4, 1972

Floyd Cox
1871-1954
&
Ada A. Cox
1878-1941

Nancy Allen
Jan 16, 1831
Jun 7, 1906

Father
William E. Allen
1852-1931
    & Mother
Mary J. Allen
1857-1896

Dan Allen
1851-1935
    &
Nellie M. Allen
1854-1892
    &
Alice L. Allen
1878-1903

Russell A. Allen
May 9, 1912

    &
Lona Mae Allen
Aug 4, 1910

Mrd Dec 17, 1932

J. ?.
(fieldstone)

Infant of A. R.
& Mattie Garrett
Apr 7, 1917

Mary E., wife of
C. B. Clift
Jul 15, 1870
Mar 23, 1902

James H. Park
Jan 15, 1812
May 9, 1889

John M. Park
Jan 14, 1904
Nov 5, 1973

Joseph H. Park
May 11, 1874
Apr 8, 1891

Charlie D., son of
G. M. & M. J. Park
Oct 17, 1877
Aug 20, 1892

G. M. Park
Feb 9, 1844
Sep 12, 1902

Mary J., wife of
G. M. Park
Jun 13, 1851
Dec 10, 1896

J. C. Cowden
Dec 24, 1845
May 16, 1903
    &
Belle Park Cowden
Sep 8, 1848
Nov 17, 1910

A. Franklin Swiney
Co D 4 Tenn Cav C.S.A.
1823-1907

Hattie Cowden Fowler
Mar 23, 1873
Jul 1, 1908
    &
Edwin Cowden Fowler
Jun 26, 1908
Jul 15, 1908
    &
Joe O. Fowler
Sep 29, 1858
Oct 3, 1922

Father
J. B. Lowrance
May 14, 1852
Jan 13, 1933
    &
Mother
Mary P. Lowrance
Feb 5, 1858
Mar 11, 1924

Rudie Norton, Dau of
J. B. & M. P. Lawrance
Jun 1, 1888
Sep 17, 1888

Father
Joseph E. Lowrance
Jul 31, 1879
May 26, 1954

Mother
Bettie Burgess Lowrance
Jul 24, 1880
Dec 5, 1966

J. E. Woodward
1849-1931

Josy D. Woodward
1855-1890

Bettie J. Woodward
1849-1904

Delia Woodward
Oct 27, 1868
Mar 22, 1948

Nancy Swiney
Jan 29, 1823
Jul 20, 1893

W. F. Swiney
1846-1926
    & wife
Dicie C. Swiney
1850-1916

Robert W. McGaugh
Sep 27, 1811
Apr 16, 1899

Lillar, dau of
W. F. & D. C. Swiney
Dec 18, 1874
Aug 1, 1898

Bright Meadows
1880-1951

Ivor Swiney Meadows
1879-1956

William M. Glazier
1851-1896
    &
Elizabeth Glazier
1856-1901

Grace Clift
Jul 3, 1888
Oct 8, 1894

Ben Clift
1865-1936
    &
Ella Clift
1869-1947

E. D. Clift
Dec 17, 1877
Sep 8, 1961
    &
Fannie B. Clift
Jul 21, 1889

Father
A. G. Clift
Mar 10, 1834
Nov 25, 1915
    &
Mother
Mary E. Clift
Jan 31, 1841
(no date)

Jackson Park
Nov 18, 1852
Sep 5, 1906
    &
L. F. Park
Mar 26, 1864
(no date)

Andrew Park
Sep 3, 1883
Dec 29, 1906

Moses Park
Nov 26, 1881
Aug 12, 1912

Ethel Park
Aug 24, 1888
Jan 19, 1912

Tellie A. Park
Mar 19, 1885
Aug 25, 1957

Infant Son of
W. H. & J. E. Park
Mar 11, 1914

CORNERSVILLE

R. H. Clark
1865-1939
&
Mary E. Clark
1869-1936

R. S. "Sam" Clark
Apr 29, 1903
May 22, 1976
&
Berdie M. Clark
May 8, 1903

Valton Laverne, son of
Mr. & Mrs. R. S. Clark
1931-1935

Robert Norris Clark
Aug 13, 1922
Apr 27, 1952

Betty J. Clark
Jan 10, 1928
Aug 30, 1948

J. Harold Wise
1904-1974
&
Bess W. Wise
1904-

John Allen Wise
May 17, 1876
Mar 20, 1944
&
Ella Garrett Wise
Sep 2, 1877
Jun 25, 1959

Sarah Oxolene, dau of
Alfred & Flora Doggett
Wise
Apr 19, 1919
Jul 16, 1919

Harding House
1889-19(no date)
&
Clara House
1886-1938

D. C. Swiney
Oct 14, 1853
Feb 5, 1929
&
Mary Lou Swiney
Jan 14, 1857
Jul 21, 1925

John Thomas Woodward
1863-1950
&
Mary Addie Woodward
1878-1942

A. M. March
Nov 1, 1858
Sep 21, 1926

Nannie McCrory, wife of
A. M. March
Jun 13, 1871
Jun 15, 1906

R. W. McRory
Aug 29, 1841
Sep 16, 1908

N. M., wife of
R. W. McRory
Mar 7, 1838
Feb 27, 1901

Robert C. McRory
Mar 24, 1869
Jul 22, 1933

James M., son of
R. W. & N. M. McRory
Mar 20, 1867
Jul 10, 1894

John A. Oliver
1856-1904
&
Sallie B. Oliver
1866-1954

George Oliver
1893-1909

Marie Oliver
1927-1929

Alonzo L. Brewer
1891-1957
Tennessee
Pfc Btry D 318 Field Arty
WW I
Mar 8, 1891
Jan 19, 1957
&
Annie O. Brewer
1890-(died Dec 31, 1977
        Higgins FH)

Murratt Alvie Reed
Oct 2, 1887
Feb 27, 1919
&
Pearl Reed
Dec 23, 1890
Jan 31, 1964

J. W. Tucker
Oct 14, 1836
Apr 26, 1911

M. A. Tucker
Oct 26, 1837
Sep 28, 1916

Lurline, dau of
O. L. & D. L. McCollum
Aug 27, 1907
Jan 27, 1908

Dixie Lou, wife of
J. L. Sanders
Sep 21, 1886-Dec 10, 1917

Ollie McCollum
Aug 15, 1876
Mar 20, 1910

J. G. McCollum
Sep 2, 1881
(no date)
& wife
Mai Belle McCollum
Aug 29, 1888
Mar 6, 1910

Floyd A. Allen
1905-
&
Velma T. Allen
1907-

T. William Wise
1871-1953
&
Minnie Davis Wise
1877-1960

James Edward Wise
1908-1937

Louella Bayless Wise
Mar 16, 1870
Oct 11, 1943

James Marion Wise
Jun 3, 1870
Oct 12, 1937

G. T., son of
J. M. & L. E. Wise
Aug 29, 1902
Aug 3, 1903

Infant Son of
Will & Minnie Wise
B&D Mar 12, 1901

Parthenia Casteel
Apr 7, 1817
Feb 3, 1901

Father
Thomas M. Wise
Dec 18, 1842
Dec 16, 1922
&
Mother
Bettie G. Wise
Mar 8, 1849
Mar 19, 1916

Buford Hughey
Apr 2, 1906
Mar 31, 1971
&
Nellie A. Hughey
Jan 18, 1907
Jan 13, 1968

M. F. H.
_. L. H.
(fieldstone)

J. H. Jacobs
Aug 10, 1881
Nov 24, 1938

Walter L. McGaugh
Jun 13, 1893
Jul 8, 1976
&
Julia M. McGaugh
Feb 15, 1894

Mrd Dec 24, 1911

J. K. P. Lawrence
Nov 14, 1844
Jun 18, 1901
& wife
Martha A. Haynes Lawrence
Oct 22, 1843
Apr 30, 1886

W. T. "Tom" Wolaver
Jan 7, 1885
Feb 22, 1955

Euell Duckworth
1902-1955
&
Selma Duckworth
1903-

William Turner Garrett
Apr 16, 1885
Nov 29, 1965
&
Vivian Nelms Garrett
Feb 11, 1885

Dr. F. H. Gault
Nov 12, 1871
Apr 4, 1937

Sallie Tom, wife of
F. H. Gault
Feb 9, 1876
Oct 15, 1910

Ruby H. Wall
1918-1959

B. F. H.
(fieldstone)

A. Mack Beard
Oct 4, 1877
Dec 16, 1959
&
Mary May Beard
Dec 8, 1870
Mar 11, 1958

Rufe C. Park
1854-1926
&
Anna U. Park
1865-1959

CORNERSVILLE

George Oliver
Jan 13, 1924
Jan 7, 1961

Howell Worthe Oliver
Jul 8, 1904
Aug 25, 1972

Georg Rhiner
1865-1937

Elizabeth Rhiner
1867-1944

Father
George K. Love
Oct 30, 1876
Jul 25, 1961
&
Mother
Vance S. Love
Jun 12, 1880
Apr 13, 1974

Kathryn C. Love
Aug 26, 1904
Apr 20, 1921

Jessie F. Love
1838-1913
&
Eliza Jane Love
1838-1917

Ralph Myers
Apr 14, 1889
Oct 26, 1974
&
Mildred Love Myers
Mar 29, 1909
Dec 18, 1961

Ott F. Cook
Oct 17, 1889
Aug 13, 1963
&
Annie H. Cook
Jul 26, 1888
Feb 3, 1968

Ozro Cook
Dec 5, 1931
2 days

Melissa May Collins
1902-1938
(McDaniel FH)

W. R. Edwards
Aug 7, 1828
Apr 28, 1904
"He was a Private in Co C.
Third Tenn Vols in War with
Mexico in 1846".
& wife
Mary Louise Edwards
Jun 5, 1829
Feb 18, 1891

Jeannette M. London
1874-1902

Joe Clayton
Jul 25, 1883
Feb 13, 1922

J. Morgan Clayton
1871-1920

W. G. Clayton
Nov 6, 1817
Feb 4, 1887
&
Jane S. Clayton
Mar 25, 1816
Oct 17, 1909

H.(Henry) D. McCrory
1844-1928

Mary A. McCrory
Aug 29, 1844
Mar 25, 1905

Howard Clark
1899-1953
&
Lorena S. Clark
1898-19

Elaine Clark
Aug 16, 1922
Mar 31, 1936

John C. Clark
1872-1943
&
Hallie C. Clark
1872-1972

Mary Margaret Woodward
Jan 18, 1852
Dec 18, 1898

William Berbert Park
Jan 13, 1890
Jun 3, 1977

J. Herbert Park
Tennessee
Pfc 129 Inf WW II BSM
Feb 14, 1917
Sep 12, 1952

April Rhena Park
May 21, 1956

Shirley E. Larson
1910-1957

George W. London
1840-1896

Sarah J. London
1835-1899

John C. London
1878-1912

Hattie London
1871-1965

J. C. Hughey
Jul 15, 1866
Apr 29, 1930
&
Rhoda Hughey
Nov 5, 1875
Nov 29, 1950

Dean Allene, dau of
Robert & Allene Hughey
Dec 16, 1950

Father
A. B. Oliver
Sep 23, 1847
(no date)
&
Mother
M. C. Oliver
Aug 29, 1848
Jan 25, 1923

Otomar A. Oliver
Born May 13, 1871
Died in Manila
Jul 31, 1904

B. N. Swiney
Sep 19, 1861
Jan 18, 1912

W. H. Davis
Feb 21, 1871
May 28, 1950
& wife
Maxie L. Davis
Feb 16, 1870
Jan 18, 1918

Infant Son of
W. H. & M. L. Davis
(no dates)

Elizabeth C. Davis
Dec 15, 1850
Jul 11, 1907

Lucinda J. Harris
Feb 19, 1817
Jul 17, 1905

Baby
Ernie Hughey
Sep 21, 1895
Jan 9, 1897

B. F. Conrad
Died Feb 12, 1902
Age 59 yrs.

Curtis, son of
Mary & Ralph McFarland
Nov 16, 1913
Nov 30, 1913

Mary Purdom, wife of
Bascum Harness
Apr 20, 1909
Aug 1, 1928

Infant of
Mr. & Mrs. B. W. Clift
1906

Florene A., wife of
John P. Glenn
Oct 9, 1859
Dec 1, 1896
"Mother"

Forrest Scales, wife of
G. W. McBride
Mar 18, 1865
May 23, 1891

B. F. McGaugh
Dec 22, 1834
May 16, 1904

Newt McGaugh
1866-1942
&
Maggie McGaugh
1871-1956

G. W. McGaugh
Dec 22, 1834
May 12, 1886
&
Fannie A. McGaugh
Oct 25, 1841
Feb 29, 1912

James Hill Park
Mar 6, 1861
Nov 25, 1943

Mintie May, wife of
J. H. Park
Aug 12, 1869
Feb 23, 1917
Age 47 yrs, 6 mos, 11 days

F. M. Park
Sep 14, 1836
Apr 20, 1908
&
Elizabeth A. Park
Jul 1, 1841
(no date)

Dita, dau of
F. M. & E. A. Park
Aug 26, 1873
Jan 26, 1905

Jim H. Purdom
Mar 22, 1885
Mar 23, 1937

Anna Eliza Purdom
Nov 16, 1890
Feb 8, 1917

Roy W. Poarch
1901-1953

Fate Poarch
1874-1957

CORNERSVILLE

Alice Poarch
1874-1941

Golie J. Poarch
Nov 18, 1899
Dec 10, 1976
&
Lillie B. Poarch
Jul 12, 1903
Jun 6, 1968

"Our Baby"
Rosolyn Elain Poarch
Jul 18, 1941
Apr 23, 1943

Casey D. Poarch
Dec 12, 1915
Apr 5, 1959
&
Annie B. Poarch
May 23, 1914

Bunyan Clift
1886-1941
&
Maggie Clift
1885-

John T. Berlin
May 21, 1913
Nov 13, 1944

Mrs. Skida Kelley
1868-1958
(Oaks-Nichols FH)

Kenneth A. Murray
Jan 30, 1927
Aug 18, 1973
&
Annie R. Murray
Nov 7, 1932

J. Howard Clark
1877-1956
&
Mary W. Clark
1877-1967

Lillie T. Oliver
1879-1961

Willie C. Adams
Dec 15, 1897
Nov 10, 1955
&
Madlene Adams
Apr 19, 1904
Mar 8, 1951

Will P. Wright
Apr 19, 1870
(no date)
&
Davis Crabtree Wright
Sep 2, 1868
Jan 5, 1948

Senie Doggett
Mar 27, 1876
Dec 19, 1946

Buford L. Doggett
Nov 18, 1897
Mar 25, 1975
&
Sally L. Doggett
Mar 29, 1900

A. Everette Beard
Nov 18, 1897
Jan 11, 1969
&
Delia M. Beard
Jan 24, 1897

James L. Haislip
1867-1941
&
Ida D. Haislip
1871-19(no date)

Virginia Cook
1922-1945
(picture)

Lola Florence, dau of
W. S. & M. E. Chiles
(no dates)

B. F. Rambo
Oct 27, 1836
Aug 3, 1905
&
Sarah T. Rambo
Apr 18, 1840
Jul 18, 1917

Jesse J. "Boss" Clark
1895-1958
&
Esther Lee B. Clark
1885-1967

Orpha N. Rhodes
May 23, 1886
May 20, 1951

Bose Griffis
Feb 11, 1883

&
Vernie Griffis
Jul 28, 1886
Jul 10, 1953

Many unmarked graves

F. M. Wolaver
1856-1942
&
Leona D. Wolaver
1866-1942
(picture of both)

L. Garland Jacobs
Nov 24, 1899

&
Hattie Lou Jacobs
Oct 21, 1905
May 8, 1943

Larry Ward Nelms
Oct 13, 1942
Dec 18, 1942

Bessie H. Alexander
May 1, 1886
Aug 24, 1969

Richard Franklin Henry, Sr.
Apr 15, 1882
Apr 4, 1954
&
Lena Dee Henry
Sep 14, 1889
May 22, 1959

W. T. Harrison
1870-1948
&
Georgia Harrison
1872-(no date)

Laban Haislip
1754 - Dec 14, 1816
"A Revolutionary Soldier"
(buried here in unmarked grave)

END OF NEW HOPE

* *

END OF CORNERSVILLE QUADRANGLE

PETERSBURG
QUADRANGLE

MT. ZION CEMETERY

Located eight and one half miles from Lewisburg on Highway 431, turn right and go .3 mile. Three miles south of Belfast. Copied April 28, 1968 by Foster and Charlene Nicholas.

William D. Petty, son of
N. & L. Petty
Dec 12, 1849
Jan 9, 1853
(pyramid)

Nathan Petty
Dec 1, 1827
Oct 30, 1862
(Pyramid)

Louisa, wife of
Nathan Petty
Dec 14, 1823
Jun 3, 1857
(pyramid)

Nathan G., son of
J. B. Bagley
May 23, 1800
Sep 12, 1833
(pyramid)

Robert W., son of
N. & A. G. Bagley
Nov 15, 1825
Jun 5, 1842
(pyramid)

J. F. W., an infant of
W. & C. _. Petty
(no dates)

Isaiah F. Bagley
Aug 17, 1819
May 7, 1833
Age 13 yrs, 6 mos, 20 days
(pyramid)

Uriah Bagley
Jul __, 1805
Sep 10, 1829
(pyramid)

Bethaney Petty, dau of
Joab Bagley
Nov 10, 1803
Aug 27, 1829
(pyramid)

Father
Col. John Orr, Jr.
Feb 13, 1809
Mar 18, 1848

"Our Mother"
Emily J., wife of
Col. John Orr
Dec 24, 1813
Jan 22, 1886

John Armstrong
Aug 31, 1830
Apr 19, 1855
Age 24 yrs, 9 mos, 12 days

Sarah Ann Margaret, wife of
John Armstrong
Feb 13, 1834
Jul 27, 1854
Age 20 yrs, 5 mos, 14 days

Alice Elmina, dau of
John & Sarah Armstrong
May 17, 1854
Oct 25, 1854
Age 5 mos, 8 days

M. B. Gabbert
Nov 30, 1868
Dec 9, 1947
&
Corrie E. Gabbert
Jul 25, 1870
Jul 10, 1912

Joseph L. Orr
Nov 9, 1836
Oct 6, 1888

John C.(G) McAdams
Apr 20, 1867
Oct 13, 1901

H. D. McAdams
Sep 27, 1835
Dec 20, 1891

B. G. Orr, wife of
H. D. McAdams
Sep 1, 1839
Feb 20, 1903

Taz Newman McAdams
Dec 17, 1861
Jun 16, 1869

William R. Hastings
1862-1941
&
Josie W. Hastings
1861-1948

Marvin Bishop Hastings
1887-1962

Mrs. Brucile Martin
1862-1967

David W. Watson
May 28, 1835
Aug 27, 1920
&
Mary V. Waters
Apr 26, 1871
May 9, 1935
&
Raymond Waters
Sep 23, 1901
Dec 26, 1935

Archibald C. Nollen
Dec 15, 1825
Jan 23, 1892

Parthenia L. Nolen
May 12, 1825
Mar 31, 1902

Jno. F., son of
D. W. & S. B. Watson
Apr 10, 1882

Mother
Sarah B. Watson
Jun 29, 1838
Jun 22, 1922

James H. Watson
1867-1954

William H. Watson
1877-1955

Seraphna Adeliza, dau of
Sim & Georgiana Foster
Feb 8, 1875
Feb 28, 1876

Agness W., dau of
Frederick & Sally Foster
& sister of A. S. Foster
Jun 24, 1834
Aug 1, 1897

F. L. J., dau of
Jno. & Sallie Foster &
second wife of
A. S. Foster, Sr.
Mar 25, 1840
Jan 1, 1899

"Our Father"
A. S. Foster
May 9, 1816
Jun 16, 1902

Martha M., dau of
George & Nancy Cunningham
& wife of A. S. Foster
Feb 5, 1810
Mar 13, 1883
Age 73 yrs, 1 mo, 28 days

Fannie J. Crabtree
Jun 16, 1862
Nov 12, 1862

William Crabtree
Born 1828
Died Mar 13, 1893

Nannie Crabtree
Jun 9, 1837
Aug 2, 1913

Anthony S. Crabtree
1856-1919
&
John W. Crabtree
1858-1938

W. P. Ledford
Nov 22, 1837
Nov 24, 1916

Mary E. Ledford
May 2, 1841
Apr 27, 1916

William S. Ledford
Nov 25, 1863
Aug 2, 1879

Several unmarked graves.

* *

PETERSBURG

BRENTS CEMETERY

Located three-fourth mile north east of Tally Station and one half mile east of Highway 431.

Mary Emmeline Norman
Sep 12, 1854
May 2, 1885

Thomas Brents
was born Sept 3, A.D. 1773
and departed this life
July 12, 1841

Jane Brents
was born Jan 6, A.D. 1786
and departed this life
--- 12 A.D. 1842

10-12 graves marked with fieldstones.

* *

WELLS CEMETERY

Located two miles N.E. of Delina-copied in 1969 by Tim & Helen Marsh

J. Charles Harvey Ray*
1850-1934
(no marker)

James H. Ray*
son of Harvey &
Lizzie C. Ray
Died ca. 1876
(fieldstone, no inscription)

L. C. Ray (Lizzie)
Dec 16, 1853
Jul 7, 1902

T. B. Wells
Dec 14, 1811
May 30, 1900

Genie E., wife of
T. B. Wells
Apr 7, 1815
Apr 27, 1884

Ola Wells
Mar 26, 1881
Apr 14, 1926

Wesley Wells
Nov 15, 1845
Oct 2, 1925

Isibel Wells
Jan 5, 1840
Jun 23, 1900

J. T. Williams
1833-1906

Eliza J. Williams
1840-1908

Emmeline Williams
May 10, 1859
Mar 23, 1925

M. E., wife of
J. C. Haislip & dau of
E. E. Wakefield
Nov 13, 1861
Jan 29, 1884

W. S. T., son of
J. T. & E. E. Wakefield
Feb 16, 1866
Jul 28, 1899

Mrs. Will Wells (Lula)
1877-1937

Jimmie Wells
Apr 19, 1851
Aug 10, 1928

Mrs. Frances Wells
1856-1933

Note:
Adam Wells a native of Dinwiddie Co.Va.
and the progenitor of this Wells family
may be buried here in an unmarked grave
ED.

* info from T.R. Marsh

J. G. Wells
Jan 3, 1813
Jun 22, 1894

Susan, wife of
J. G. Wells
Sep 18, 1803
Jun 5, 1890

W. H. Wells
Mar 23, 1843
Sep 17, 1928

Francis A., wife of
W. H. Wells
Dec 19, 1844
Sep 30, 1910

Jim Watson
1856-1933

Watson
(all on stone)

Infant Son of
T. J. & M. C. Sullivan
May 10, 1884
Jul 21, 1884

John T. Wakefield
Jan 13, 1841
Dec 2, 1910
&
Elizabeth E. Wakefield
Feb 27, 1839
May 6, 1921

M. E. Franklin
Feb 14, 1845
Dec 1, 1901 (old marker)
Milton Franklin
Feb 29, 1846
Dec 1, 1901 (new marker)
&
Hannah Franklin
Dec 15, 1845
Feb 14, 1918

Will Frank Haislip
Aug 26, 1861
Nov 16, 1935
&
Lou Kate C. Haislip
Feb 15, 1867
Apr 9, 1932

Jimmie Lee Haislip*
(fieldstone, no inscription)

S. W. Wakefield
Apr 15, 1816
Mar 20, 1905

Mary Luna,* 1st wife of
S. W. Wakefield
1815-1851
(fieldstone, no inscription)

Malinda James,* 2nd wife of
S. W. Wakefield
(fieldstone, no inscription)

Several unmarked graves.

* *

NEW HOPE CEMETERY

Located on Fishing Ford Road near Talley Station. Copied
April 1969 by Nancye and Charlene Nicholas, recheckcked 1978
by Helen and Tim Marsh.

Joe Sidney Troupe
1891-1960 (TM)

Mrs. Hobert Ray
1896-1964 (TM)

Nellie Marris
Died Aug 16, 1897
Age 80 years

Father
Harris Troupe
Oct 29, 1852
Feb 6, 1899
&
Mother
Ada Troupe
May 10, 1859
Aug 8, 1924

Wash'n Cannon
Co. C 111th USCT
(no dates)

Sam Price
&
Eliza Price
&
Myrtle Price
(no dates)

Ralph B. Conrad
1883-1955
&
Vernie M. Conrad
1897-

Willis Hilda Nicholas
Jun 18, 1923
Aug 4, 1948

PETERSBURG

Martha V. Nicholas Pruitt
Oct 13, 1913
Mar 30, 1973

Willis Menefee Nicholas
Apr 8, 1892
Aug 10, 1933
&
Seraphna Foster Nicholas
Oct 20, 1891
May 19, 1947

Father
Lee Foster
Sep 9, 1866
Jul 9, 1930
&
Mother
Ida Foster
Dec 21, 1868
Feb 5, 1940

William Joseph Murphy
Born in County Meo,
Ireland, died
Dec 27, 1875
(no age given)

Imogene Hastings
May 22, 1890
Oct 17, 1933

Robbie, dau of
J. J. & M. E. Hastings
Dec 30, 1905
Aug 26, 1906

Lee, son of
J. J. & M. E. Hastings
Sep 25, 1888
May 17, 1899

Mother
Serephna, 1st wife of
Fred Foster
Jun 22, 1845
Aug 5, 1872
&
Father
Fred Foster
Sep 13, 1839
Jan 11, 1918
&
Mother
Mary Frances, 2nd wife of
Fred Foster
Apr 16, 1853
Oct 4, 1934

William Rufus, son of
Thomas H. & N. J. Holland
Dec 16, 1847
Oct 12, 1858
Age 10 yrs, 9 mos, 26 days

Mattie E. Hastings
Dec 18, 1864
Jul 26, 1893

Margaret & Elige Hammonds
(Sandstone, no dates)

Patsy Stephens
Apr 22, 1814
Apr 29, 1898

James Stephens
Born 1812
Died May 12, 1883

Stacy Lynn Brown
Jun 14, 1967

M. A., wife of
B. R. Stephens
Jun 2, 1861
Nov 21, 1904

Felix, son of
B. R. & M. A. Stephens
Jan 3, 1897
Dec 13, 1897

Albert Nathan, son of
B. R. & M. A. Stephens
Apr 8, 1882
Aug 26, 1892
Age 10 yrs, 4 mos, 18 days

John B. Holland
Feb 5, 1819
Nov 5, 1852

Infant Dau of
J. B. & M. Holland
B&D Sep 11, 1848

Thomas H. Holland
Jan 25, 1817
Jun 10, 1905

Narcissa J., wife of
Thomas H. Holland
Apr 11, 1827
Nov 22, 1912

Asa Holland
Mar 30, 1793
Aug 4, 1867

Sarah, wife of
Asa Holland
Died Mar 11, 1853
(no age given, in
1850 was 57 years old)

Andrew, son of
J. B. & M. L. Looney
Mar 11, 1909
Jul 9, 1910

J. Bascom Looney
1874-1951
&
Maggie Looney
1884-1952

Mrs. Elizabeth Luna
1908-1960 (TM)

Allen Loyd Luna
1903-1964 (TM)

Michel Wayne Dean
1967

Bobby Humbles
Dec 16, 1932
Dec 18, 1932

D. A., wife of
J. H. Humbles
Sep 12, 1869
Dec 14, 1908

Mary, wife of
W. D. Gillum
Sep 25, 1824
Jul 28, 1885

"My Husband"
William Gillum
Feb 14, 1827
Jul 12, 1912

T. Smith Foster
Oct 1, 1893
Sep 26, 1964
&
Elma Foster
Oct 17, 1888

George W. Foster
Feb 21, 1901
Oct 21, 1951
&
Retta R. Foster
Dec 7, 1903

R. Guy Foster
Apr 24, 1895
May 26, 1948
&
Mary T. Foster
Mar 11, 1898

William Morton Nix
1891-1960 (TM)

Ollie W. Nix
Jul 10, 1874
Jan 3, 1881

J. F. V. Nix
Jul 16, 1879
Aug 12, 1914

Father
W. M. Nix
(no dates)
&
Mother
Josephine Nix
(no dates)

Hugh J. Luna
Jan 1, 1841
Dec 8, 1882

Nancy Luna
Apr 11, 1850-Dec 21, 1922

Children of
P. W. & Julia Watt
Infant Son
Dec 12, 1892
Jan 21, 1893
&
James Floyd Watt
Feb 24, 1899
Jun 12, 1903

Infant Dau of
P. W. & J. A. Watt
May 9, 1906
Nov 9, 1906

P. W. Watt
Aug 14, 1852
Apr 3, 1924
&
Julia A. Watt
Dec 3, 1867
Jul 17, 1953

Infant Dau of
Rufus & Louise (Watt)
Oct 24, 1927

Louise, wife of
Rufus Watt
Jul 8, 1903
Dec 19, 1946

William Rufus Watt
Tennessee
Pvt Co K 113 Inf WW I
Feb 25, 1894
Sep 3, 1972

Quin_ilian Adams
Aug 12, 1854
Jun 10, 1891
(broken)

Lydia Dunivan
Apr 25, 1962
Apr 25, 1962

Andrew J. Umbles
Aug 10, 1840
Jul 12, 1932
"Nobly he fought for his
country"
&
Eliza A. Umbles
Oct 9, 1842
Dec 19, 1920

Nora, dau of
J. R. & I. E. Reynolds
May 6, 1904
Aug 13, 1905

Clifford Ernest, son of
J. R. & Ida E. Reynolds
Mar 25, 1894
Dec 8, 1895

John R. Reynolds
1867-1948
&
Ida E. Reynolds, 1877-1958

PETERSBURG

Dorothy Luna
1915-1924

W. H. "Billie" Hardin
1854-1938
&
C. C. "Dollie" Hardin
1861-1943

Laila Maxie Hardin
Jan 11, 1886
Aug 14, 1903

Ollie Thomas, son of
W. H. & C. C. Hardin
Apr 8, 1884
Sep 11, 1884

John Calvin Luna
Aug 18, 1859
Jan 1, 1933

T. J. Willis
Sep 11, 1867
Dec 6, 1897
&
M. D. Willis
Dec 22, 1866
Jan 25, 1903

J. D., son of
T. J. & M. D. Willis
Sep 12, 1893
Jun 7, 1894

Otie Willis
1869-1960

Jim L. Adams
Oct 2, 1872
Jan 25, 1946
&
Ozella C. Adams
Mar 26, 1884
Jun 15, 1956

Jimmie Lee, son of
J. L. & H. O. Adams
Dec 17, 1900
Apr 22, 1909

W. Clarence Adams
Mar 30, 1913
Feb 10, 1929

Mary Virginia Luna
Dec 27, 1851
Mar 18, 1916

Elizabeth Talley
1845-1923

Robert P. Adams
May 13, 1905
Oct 5, 1958

Macy, dau of
Pete & A. L. Adams
Dec 7, 1907
Dec 19, 1912

Pete Adams
Feb 2, 1876
Feb 17, 1935
&
Anlizzie Adams
Mar 10, 1876
Sep 26, 1935

Elmer Jane Oliver
Apr 18, 1891
May 1, 1958

Bob Adams
1882-1954 (TM)

Mary S. Luna
Jul 25, 1828
Nov 20, 1902

John B. Luna
Aug 29, 1844
Aug 19, 1904
&
Maggie Luna
Oct 24, 1851
Mar 28, 1940

Cecil B. West
1908-1977
&
Tisha M. West
1912-1963

Henry V. Adams
Apr 11, 1898
Mar 23, 1956

Roy Milton Adams
Apr 6, 1933
Jul 5, 1933

John A. Adams, Sr.
1903-1964
&
Irene J. Adams
1913-

J. G. "Polk" Adams
Dec 11, 1909
May 22, 1967

Tom L. Greggs
May 22, 1904
Oct 4, 1966
&
Gladys E. Greggs
Aug 31, 1916

George W. Norman
Sep 4, 1880

&
Georgia E. Norman
Jul 23, 1882
Mar 1, 1949

Elner B., dau of
G. W. & G. E. Norman
Feb 2, 1908
Jan 1, 1909

Father
William Henry Wells
1858-1937
&
Mother
Nannie O. Wells
1865-1936
& Daughter
Anna Liza Wells
1886-1976

Infant Dau of
W. H. & N. O. Wells
Feb 22, 1906

J. S. Troop
Dec 7, 1868
Aug 20, 1933

Mattie Troop
Feb 28, 1877
Dec 5, 1914

J. T. Holland
Jun 25, 1848
Oct 22, 1905

J. P. Holland
Sep 17, 1821
Nov 17, 1906

Emmaline, wife of
J. P. Holland
Mar 5, 1830
Mar 21, 1901

Sue Emma Holland
Mar 15, 1893
Jun 13, 1894

Infant Sons of
G. W. & Lola Fowler
B&D May 5, 1893
B&D May 10, 1894

Clifford, son of
W. A. & C. E. Craig
May 30, 1894
Jan 21, 1897

Noralee, wife of
G. H. Wells
Nov 29, 1882
Jun 21, 1912

Infant Son of
G. H. & N. L. Wells
Mar 26, 1909
Mar 29, 1909

Emmaline, wife of
R. A. Holland
Apr 17, 1862
Apr 16, 1900

Willie H., son of
J. T. & L. I. McCoy
Jun 13, 1916
Sep 9, 1918

Mrs. Lucy Irene McCoy
1893-1937 (TM)

Charlie Archer
1879-1932
&
Viola Archer
1876-1961

Infant Son & Daughter of
C. B. & Viola Archer
May 18, 1914
Jul 20, 1919

W. R. Archer
Apr 1, 1839
Apr 1, 1929

Mary Archer
Mar 17, 1839
Jan 11, 1911

William M. Twitty
1873-1913
&
Daisy Long Twitty
1879-1959

Mattie Maud Gambill
May 28, 1892
Dec 1, 1915

C. C. Troop
Aug 29, 1854
Jan 17, 1929
& wife
Sarah E. Troop
Jun 5, 1855
Apr 14, 1919
& Dau
Ida Belle Troop
Oct 29, 1876
Oct 4, 1878
& Son
Ollie Otus Troop
Nov 24, 1879
Aug 7, 1880

Hugh Virgil Luna
Tennessee
Tec 5 Co A 718 RY Opr BN T
WW II
Jun 12, 1922
Sep 27, 1967
&
Peggy Luna
Sep 10, 1930

Charlie H. Wells
Aug 12, 1890

&
Mattie H. Wells
Nov 11, 1898

Mother
Eula J. Jacobs Wells
Nov 19, 1891-Dec 24, 1926

PETERSBURG

Nannie Mai Wells
Apr 4, 1921

Alex D. Marsh
Tennessee
Pvt Co G 306 Armd Tank
WW I
Aug 28, 1889
Nov 7, 1967
&
Mary T. Marsh
May 12, 1900

Father
William Allen Wells
Mar 30, 1893
Nov 15, 1924

Mother
Elsie T. Wells
Apr 26, 1900

Mrs. Cora Couch
1874-1966 (TM)

Bill McCoy
1862-1935

Bedie E., wife of
J. B. Pearson
Apr 25, 1839
Mar 3, 1917

James B. Pearson
Mar 16, 1847
Jan 13, 1927
"A Confederate Soldier"

Freda Hastings
1912-1927

Edna H. Whitsette
1893-1921

Hugh Epps
1877-1942

Evie Epps
1870-1924

Milton Reed Whitsett
Oct 12, 1923
Dec 13, 1931

A. Mims Whitsett
Jul 23, 1894
Sep 24, 1960
&
Cara M. Whitsett
Nov 25, 1895

Benjamin F. Marsh
Dec 23, 1865
Apr 1, 1924
&
Mary Myrtle Marsh
Mar 7, 1874
Feb 28, 1953

Erskine D. Marsh
1901-1940
&
Julia M. Marsh
1903-19

Homer Harrison Henson
Aug 5, 1908
Dec 1, 1963

Thomas J. Blackwell
Jun 26, 1845
Apr 26, 1932
&
Irene T. Blackwell
Oct 7, 1851
Jan 29, 1950

James Robert Davidson
Dec 5, 1929
Dec 14, 1929

Raymond Whitsett
1918-1918

Martha Jane Whitsett
1870-1940

Thomas F. Whitsett
1866-1936

Sarah D., wife of
J. R. Wherley
Jan 12, 1852
Nov 10, 1923

J. R. Wherley
Nov 6, 1843
May 11, 1932

Robert A. Whorley
1889-1934
&
Ola May Whorley
1889-19

James E., son of
T. M. & L. M. Whorley
May 24, 1916
Apr 7, 1919

J. A. Causby
1853-1935

Roy A. Whorley
Mar 22, 1902
Sep 13, 1959
&
Clara P. Whorley
Feb 9, 1895
Oct 27, 1968

Roy Whorley, Jr.
Sep 25, 1926
Sep 28, 1954

Infant Dau of
Roy & Clara Whorley
Oct 27, 1925

Infant Son of
Roy & Clara Whorley
Sep 19, 1923

William C. Wherley
1873-1933
&
Elizabeth Wherley
1877-1930

Joe L. Wilkes
B&D Jun 16, 1964

Milton Whitsett
(no dates)

Sie Beard
Jul 24, 1886

&
Lelia H. Beard
Dec 19, 1890
Jun 29, 1968

Little Edith, dau of
S. E. & Leila Beard
1925-1926

Ida Shaddy Beard
1868-1948

Lacie Beard
1903-1935

Sammie D. Beard
1895-1959

"A True Boy"
Pvt Tommie L. Beard
Nov 28, 1892
Killed in action
Oct 25, 1918

James Edward McCoy
1953-1953 (TM)

Margaret Ann McCoy
1950-1950 (TM)

William Earl McCoy
1947-1947 (TM)

Robert Horton Brown
Jun 15, 1930
Oct 24, 1965

Bettie R. Williams
Jun 30, 1868
Feb 24, 1924

H. G. Wherley
May 7, 1857
Jun 7, 1930
(picture)

Infant Son of
Mr. & Mrs. T. C. Collins
Aug 6, 1917

Thomas C. Collins
1888-1950
& wife
Lessie Whorley Collins
1882-1934

D. F. Brown
Nov 24, 1827
Dec 6, 1915

Baby Lillian, dau of
L. A. & W. A. Lemond
Feb 5, 1897
Aug 1, 1897

Leland Whorley
Aug 8, 1888
Sep 4, 1921
(picture)

J. D., son of
J. N. & Mattie Wherley
Jan 3, 1892
Oct 8, 1913

J. N. Wherley
1855-1941
& wife
Mattie Wherley
Oct 17, 1870
Sep 5, 1894

Catherine Collins
Oct 22, 1841
Oct 3, 1899

Marguret M., wife of
Joel Wherley
Jan 28, 1819
Jun 29, 1903

Alice C. Hicks
Jun 5, 1861
Jun 8, 1914

Lola Crabtree, wife of
W. B. Long
Jan 3, 1872
Aug 11, 1909

J. P. Long
May 6, 1845
Jul 10, 1928

Mother
Paralee Murphey, wife of
J. P. Long
Oct 20, 1846
Mar 7, 1904

Minnie Lee, dau of
M. L. & C. C. Pyland
Jan 11, 1890
Mar 4, 1893

C. Cate, wife of
M. Lee Pyland
1872-1948

M. Lee Pyland
1869-1929

PETERSBURG

Mattie T., wife of
R. H. Hastings &
Dau of
W. N. & E. J. Pyland
Feb 17, 1874
Jul 27, 1893

Claud, son of
W. N. & E. J. Pyland
Jul 10, 1871
Jun 15, 1895
Age 23 yrs, 11 mos, 5 days

Willie, son of
W. N. & E. J. Pyland
Feb 10, 1879
Feb 17, 1899
Age 20 yrs, 7 days

Father
W. H(N). Pyland
Mar 15, 1842
Jul 4, 1926

Mother
Mrs. E. J., wife of
W. N. Pyland
Aug 29, 1848
Feb 28, 1905

Caroline Gold
Mar 13, 1904
Apr 19, 1922
(picture)

Willie Howard, son of
R. H. & A. E. Hastings
Sep 1, 1900
Jul 23, 1901

Jess Hastings
1872-1951
&
Annie Hastings
1877-1951

W. F. Yowell
Jul 1, 1866
Jan 3, 1921

Mother
M. J., wife of
W. F. Yowell
Feb 25, 1867
Apr 16, 1905
"She was a kind and affect-
ionate wife, a fond mother &
friend to all."

Hermon A., son of
W. F. & M. J. Yowell
Jan 22, 1896
Nov 8, 1896

J. N. B. Ketchum
Jun 9, 1859
Sep 11, 1860
Age 1 yr, 3 mos, 2 days

M. V. Luna
May 18, 1832
Feb 8, 1879

M. M., wife of
M. V. Luna
Dec 6, 1826
Jun 2, 1898

Joel A. Morris
Nov 23, 1834
Sep 25, 1896

R. Anna E. Morris
dau of Joel A. &
Sue M. Morris
Aug 1, 1856
Mar 22, 1883
Age 26 yrs, 7 mos, 21 days

Sarah E., dau of
M. V. & M. M. Luna
Apr 26, 1854
Mar 16, 1863
Age 8 yrs, 10 mos, 20 days

An Infant of
M. V. & M. M. Luna
B&D Dec 3, 1852

An Infant of
M. V. & M. M. Luna
B&D Sep 20, 1866

Sarah M., dau of
Joseph & Eliza W. Morriss
Oct 12, 1839
Sep 30, 1851
Age 11 yrs, 11 mos, 18 days

Elizabeth, dau of
Joseph & Eliza W. Morriss
Apr 4, 1837
Sep 17, 1846
Age 9 yrs, 5 mos, 15 days

(Marker, down & overturned
see pg 239, Eliza W. Morriss)

Joseph Morriss
Oct 6, 1801
Mar 4, 1861
Age 59 yrs, 4 mos, 29 days

Millie Letitia Morris
Feb 9, 1825
Nov 19, 1914

Willie M., son of
M. & L. R. Yowell
Jun 10, 1893
Oct 19, 1893

Maggie Murdock Warren
Jul 31, 1893
Mar 30, 1913

Infant of
J. N. & C. E. Murdock
B&D Aug 27, 1911

J. W. Hastings
Nov 18, 1839
Sep 12, 1916

Caroline M., wife of
J. W. Hastings
May 24, 1839
Jul 9, 1899

William W. Luna
Dec 21, 1856
Jul 27, 1939
&
Ella G. Luna
Nov 7, 1877
Nov 10, 1963

Deward G. Luna
Jul 31, 1896
Apr 8, 1928

Ramon Wright, son of
W. W. & E. G. Luna
Jul 21, 1903
Aug 22, 1904

Elizabeth C. Russell
May 22, 1839
Jul 3, 1871

George W. Russell
Nov 25, 1844
Sep 30, 1863

Mary A. Sweeney
Jul 9, 1850
Dec 20, 1916

Donia Mae Davis
Jul 12, 1867
Jan 30, 1936

Mattie Lee Davis
Oct 26, 1892
Dec 24, 1919

Julius Davis
Jan 29, 1897
Jun 4, 1944

J. Frank Cummings
Mar 4, 1895
(no date)

Joe S. Blackwell
1845-1933

Mother
Susie Bain Blackwell
Dec 6, 1859
Dec 19, 1900

Sister
Annie Pearl Blackwell
Sep 16, 1885
Dec 11, 1899

1812
Here lies the daughter of
Jesse & Rachel Riggs
was born & died the
25th Decr. 1812

1816
Here lies the Sun of
Jessie & R. A. Riggs
was born & Dec'd September
the 22, 1816

Mother Davis
Mar 14, 1827
Nov 30, 1900
&
Margaret Davis
Oct 5, 1859
Jan 14, 1880
&
John Davis
Feb 6, 1869
Sep 1, 1913

William Carroll Bryant
1858-1925
&
Anna L. Bryant
1870-1939

F. H. "Bud" Davis
Nov 15, 1890
Nov 8, 1964

W. A. "Bill" Davis
Mar 14, 1857
Feb 21, 1926

Maggie Davis
Sep 30, 1888
Apr 17, 1908

Here lies Rachel Riggs,
wife of Jessie Riggs, was
born April the 6th day,
1771 and was married Feb.
the 10th, 1791, Dec'd
September the 25th day,
1816, war the mother of
6 suns & 8 daughters.

Robert L. Cole
1898-

Joe Cole
1857-1914
&
Dora Cole
1862-1950

Mrs. Caldonia Cole Cummings
(no dates) (TM)

W. M. Whitestt
Mar 9, 1871
Jan 19, 1940

Archie Whitsett
Jul 16, 1891
Nov 19, 1950

Perlina B. Collins,
wife of G. M. Whitsett
Aug 27, 1873
Aug 7, 1914
&
Infant Daughter
Aug 7, 1914

Elisabeth Tucker, the wife
of Laban E. Tucker. She
was born April 15, 1803
married June 8, 1828, and
deceased March 31, 1829.
Age 25 yrs, 11 mos, 16 days
and with her
sleeps an Infant Daughter.
Their only child.

Mary Luna, wife of
Peter Luna
Departed this life
Sep 13, 1854
(no age given)

Eliza W., Consort of
Joseph Morriss
Jan 13, 1813
Aug 28, 1843
In her 31st year.

J. Claude Burns
Jun 26, 1873
Oct 26, 1958
&
Lessie L. Burns
Jul 9, 1880
Mar 16, 1939

Mary E., wife of
W. I. Luna
Apr 11, 1856
Feb 8, 1873

Thomas B. Bryant
1849-1932
&
Martha Frances Bryant
1858-1942

Husband
Edwin Bryant
Mar 30, 1866
Dec 13, 1928
&
Wife
Vertie Bryant
Aug 19, 1884
(no date)

James L. Bryant
Mar 25, 1827
Oct 20, 1881

Permelia, wife of
Jas. L. Bryant
Aug 20, 1828
Oct 17, 1900

Mary Jane, dau of
J. L. & P. Bryant
Sep 28, 1856-Nov 21, 1857

Welch Graves
(no dates)
&
Alice Graves
(no dates)
&
Mary Graves
(no dates)
&
Ann Graves
(no dates)

John Graves
May 20, 1844
Nov 8, 1894

Margret C., wife of
Jno. T. Graves
Nov 7, 1840
May 6, 1888

Tell F. Wells
Aug 17, 1895
Aug 24, 1970
&
Mary Wells
Jun 29, 1895
Feb 5, 1962

Billie Sue Wells
1930-1977
(Davis-Ralston FH)

Raymond L. Adams
Sgt with 1st Army in
Germany, WW II
1920-1947
(picture)

Patricia Gail, dau of
W. H. & Sue Wells
Jun 3, 1952
Jan 19, 1953

Albert L. Bryant
Feb 13, 1859
Oct 15, 1863

Myram O., dau of
J. L. & Mealy Bryant
Mar 30, 1866
Aug 5, 1866

Raney, dau of
J. L. & Mealy Bryant
Sep 28, 1862
Sep 27, 1869

Mary E., wife of
S. L. Littleton
Oct 25, 1846
Apr 29, 1903

Amy Hogan
1874-1952

R. E. Hogan
1866-1936

Lebert McCoy
Jun 5, 1892
Dec 22, 1965
&
Icie W. McCoy
Jan 30, 1892

James P. Luna
1845-1930
&
Eliza O. Luna
1854-1939

Grady Worth, son of
Thomas & Ada Cummings
Mar 8, 1893
May 11, 1894

W. T. Waters
Jul 18, 1827
Jan 24, 1866
"Erected by M. G. Waters"

Amos Crabtree
1910-1964
&
Elma Crabtree
1910-1939

Lillie, dau of
S. P. & M. A. Bryant
Aug 10, 1896
Sep 18, 1898

S. Purvis Bryant
Feb 27, 1868
Nov 24, 1949
&
Mattie A. Bryant
May 31, 1878
Jun 13, 1939

H. T. Benedict
Born in the State of
Connecticut
Oct 4, 1811
Died Mar 11, 1892
Age 80 yrs, 6 mos, 7 days

Martha Luna Benedict
First wife of A. H. Luna
Then the wife of
H. T. Benedict
Apr 3, 1822
Feb 28, 1891
Age 68 yrs, 10 mos, 25 days

Mattie, wife of
John C. McCrory
Nov 18, 1852
Nov 1, 1875
Age 22 yrs, 11 mos, 13 days

A. H. Luna
Nov 28, 1821
Dec 6, 1859

Evan J. Luna
Jul 10, 1849
Nov 1, 1931
&
Sarah E. Luna
Sep 28, 1850
Oct 25, 1924

James Luna
Born Jan 22, 1785
Died Dec 28, 1872
Age 87 yrs, 11 mos, 6 days
No. of children   12
Grandchildren   122
Gr-grandchildren   259
gr-gr-grandchildren   16
Total   409
&
There lies the mother &
Grandmother of all
Mary Luna, wife of
James Luna
Born Feb 24, 1788
Died Jul 16, 1856

J. A. Hogan
Nov 18, 1836
Jan 2, 1906

M. A., wife of
J. A. Hogan
Mar 20, 1843
Nov 4, 1899

W. D. Bonds
(stone gone)

Veturia E., wife of
W. D. Bonds
Oct 12, 1821
Feb 28, 1876

Cassa, Infant dau of
V. E. & W. D. Bonds
Dec 5, 1861
Jan 31, 1863

Thomas Logan Davis
Aug 2, 1913
Dec 3, 1959

A. L. Davis
Apr 14, 1872
Apr 14, 1918
&
O. M. Davis
Oct 4, 1875
Apr 14, 1946

Nellie Davis
Sep 18, 1898
Jul 11, 1899

Margaret West Troop
Mar 31, 1878
Oct 6, 1938

PETERSBURG

Jesse Edward Gambill*
Feb 21, 1872
Dec 28, 1940
(buried by Julia Gambill)
(no marker)

William Doyle Hastings*
Jul 29, 1899
May 22, 1900
(no marker)

Annie Grace Hastings*
Sep 24, 1907
Oct 27, 1908
(no marker)

Fred Foster Hastings*
Sep 13, 1905
Nov 11, 1906
(no marker)

Vera Beulah Hastings*
May 25, 1916
Jun 4, 1917
(no marker)

Morgan Bryant Smith*
Nov 2, 1925
Dec 5, 1925
(no marker)

Several unmarked graves.

* Info from Ralph Whitesell.

END OF NEW HOPE

* *

LUNA CEMETERY
Located one and one-half miles east of Delina, north of Petersburg and east of Wakefield Chapel Road. Copied April 6, 1973 by Haskell Roden.

Mrs. Bird McCree
Born Sep 15, 1854
Killed by Cyclone
May 4, 1914

J. K. Luna
Nov 29, 1847
Feb 20, 1921

S. T. "Toker" Edmiston
Aug 7, 1872
Sep 19, 1918

Mrs. Emma (McCree), wife
of S. T. Edmiston
1875-1952

W. J. Larwood
(no dates)

E. Larwood
(no dates)

Ollie Rhodes*
born ---
died Nov 20, 1928
& wife
Gaudie (Haislip) Rhodes*
born ----
died Nov 10, 1913
(no marker)

Jas. A. "Jimmy" Larwood
Apr 7, 1845
Dec 16, 1931

Mary A. ____ Larwood
Sep 2, 1849
Dec 26, 1924

* Info from Haskell Roden.

Several unmarked graves.

* *

HALL CEMETERY
Located north of Delina on Spring Place Road, west of Highway. Copied April 6, 1973 by Haskell Roden.

In Memory of
Mrs. Jane M. Hall
Who departed this life
Oct 19, 1857
&
Infant Son, who was
Born dead
Oct 16, 1857
"Mrs. Hall was born in
Green Cty., near Greenville,
Tenn. Feb 6, 1822. She was
married to D. C. Hall
Jan 25, 1848. Her age 35 yrs,
8 mos, 13 days. Her father
E. Y. Russell, died and was
buried in Paris _____(blank)
Her mother E. K. R. _____
in Fayetteville _____ 1848
(all on same stone)

Caroline M. Whittaker
Jun 27, 1826
Dec 19, 1862

Several unmarked graves.

* *

PETERSBURG

SANDERS CEMETERY

Located on Bert Watt Road, east of Talley Station.
Copied Dec 29, 1978 by Mrs. Thomas A. McAdams and
Ralph D. Whitesell.

Mary Ann Adams
Dec 29, 1823
Jun 22, 1900

N. S. C. Sanders
Sep 30, 1847
Jan 7, 1929

Julia E., wife of
N. S. C. Sanders
Nov 3, 1851
Oct 24, 1882

Mahulda, wife of
W. R. Sanders
Jul 3, 1843
Jun 26, 1897

Mary E., dau of
W. R. Sanders
Sep 21, 1871
Jan 17, 1898

Thomas West Sanders
Jan 29, 1875
Jan 10, 1907

* *

LEONARD CEMETERY

Located two and one-half miles north west of Petersburg,
at Leonard Bluff, on Liberty Valley Road. Copied 28 Jan
1968 by Lucie Leonard Baxter.

John Cowden
1854-1912

Mary H., wife of
Dr. John Cowden
Jan 23, 1887
Nov 29, 1907

Ida M. Cowden
Jul 17, 1868
Apr 1, 1891

William Griffith Cowden
Apr 14, 186_
Feb 3, 1863

Gracie Cowden
Feb 12, 1878
Oct 10, 1878

Sara E. Cowden, wife of
C. A. Sowell
Apr 7, 1882
Dec 17, 1910

Amos Clement Davis
Aug 25, 1840
Jan 15, 1917

Sarah Leonard Davis
Oct 12, 1845
Nov 24, 1919

Thomas Leonard
Oct 15, 1752
Apr 8, 1832

Hannah Leonard
Nov 2, 1752
Nov 3, 1842

Alpha W., wife of
N. W. Cowden
Sep 14, 1842
Jul 2, 1879

Father
Griffith J. Leonard
Sep 25, 1787
Sep 1, 1864
& wife
Mother
Nancy Porter Leonard
Jan 10, 1818
Apr 18, 1910

William B., son of
William M. & E. R. Lenard
Jun 15, 1842
Aug 27, 1842

S. C., dau of
William M. & E. R. Lenard
Jul 3, 1840
Aug 11, 1841

Elizabeth R., wife of
W. M. Lenard
Jun 3, 1814
Jul 20, 1842

Mary Jane Hill
1832-1902

William W. Porter
Sep 10, 1815
Feb 21, 1893

W. H., son of
Griffith Linord
Jan 18, 1831
Apr 29, 1831

Sarah Jane Lenard
Mar 4, 1829
Feb 28, 1831

Hannah Addeline Lenard
Born June 1831
(broken, even with ground)

Infant Son of
T. B. & M. P. Leonard
(no dates)

Samuel H. Hart
Mar 16, 1893
Oct 7, 1918

Edna E. Hart
Mar 16, 1876
Oct 12, 1892
and 2 nd marker:
Edna Earl, dau of
B. F. & Hettie Hart
Mar 16, 1876
Oct 12, 1892

Mattie Cella Leonard
Jan 18, 1881
Oct 9, 1947

John William Leonard
Jan 30, 1875
Jul 26, 1911

Mary Clementine, wife of
S. J. Leonard
Oct 7, 1843
Jun 9, 1915

Samuel J. Leonard
Jul 31, 1839
May 17, 1923

Nancy Leonard
Oct 24, 1854
Sep 12, 1926
&
Martha L. Woods
Apr 17, 1852
Mar 4, 1877

S. L.
(fieldstone)

Hezekiah Leonard
Jun 24, 1784
Mar 27, 1817

W. S. Leonard
Aug 21, 1857
Jul 22, 1943

Mary Leonard Campbell
May 5, 1754
Sep 8, 1844

Abigail Nichols
Jun 27, 1802
Aug 6, 1888

Charley Cowden, son of
Z. D. & Myrtle E. Jones
Jul 10, 1898
Oct 24, 1898

John Cowden Bills
Jan 23, 1887
Apr 1, 1888

Father
Joshua S. Conrad
Jul 9, 1835
Jun 16, 1918
&
Mother
Kittie C. Conrad
Sep 27, 1844
May 15, 1932

William C. Conrad
Oct 6, 1877
Feb 22, 1911

Alpha L., dau of
William D. & Hannah Moore
May 27, 1820
Aug 19, 1835
Age 16 years

PETERSBURG

Robert L., son of
J. J. S. & J. A. Gill
Mar 29, 1839
Dec 15, 1842

Several unmarked graves.

Little Jo, son of
J. J. S. & Angeline Gill
Nov 5, 1852
Jul 6, 1853

Thomas B., son of
G. J. & N. E. Leonard
Jul 27, 1848
Mar 15, 1901

Mary Burke Leonard
Sep 16, 1855
Jan 12, 1913

Tommye B. Leonard
Sep 18, 1889
Jul 21, 1915

Maria N. Leonard
Aug 16, 1860
Jan 6, 1936

* *

MEADOWS CEMETERY

Located near Wakefield Chapel. Copied by Helen and Tim Marsh, 1973.

Vance S. Edwards
Aug 19, 1904
Mar 20, 1961
&
Zora Lee Edwards
Jul 12, 1910
Feb 26, 1955

Vance S. Edwards, Jr.
Nov 4, 1930
Oct 20, 1932

H. M. Luker
Dec 26, 1862
Aug 2, 1938
&
Ada M. Luker
Jun 30, 1869
Mar 10, 1939

Several unmarked graves.

Willie Hoit, son of
H. M. & Ada Luker
Aug 18, 1899
Jul 23, 1900

Lela T., dau of
E. A. & S. L. Meadows
Aug 4, 1879
Aug 8, 1896

S. L., wife of
E. A. Meadows
Oct 1, 1849
Jun 16, 1910

E. A. Meadows
Mar 19, 1851
Dec 12, 1921

W. T. Beasley
Nov 29, 1867
Oct 10, 1932

Oda Beasley
Mar 26, 1876
Dec 22, 1948

Nola A., dau of
H. M. & Ada Luker
May 31, 1903
Mar 15, 1916

Wilma, dau of
H. M. & A. M. Luker
Apr 7, 1907
Nov 3, 1911

Dortha, dau of
H. M. & A. M. Luker
Apr 21, 1905
Dec 21, 1906

W. E., son of
H. M. & Ada Luker
Dec 26, 1892
Jan 13, 1904

Cora, wife of
V. A. Meadows
Nov 10, 1889
Jan 18, 1915

Vance Arthur Meadows
1889-1973 (TM)

Grand Ma Rhodes
(fieldstone, no insc.)

Minnie Koonce Meadows
(no marker)

* *

LUKER CEMETERY

According to a report made by Brevet Major General R. W. Johnson, stationed at Pulaski, Tennessee, June 22, 1865, he dispatched, the previous week, a party of Federal Cavalry to hunt down and kill Hill Looker, formerly a scout for Brig. General Starkweather. This they did. Killing him on the hill side on his farm and burying him on the spot where he fell. This grave is located two and one half miles north west of Delina on Goshen Ridge.

* *

LARWOOD CEMETERY

Located about 200 yards west of Meadows Cemetery, two miles north of Delina, Haislip Hollow. Copied 1973 by C. H. Roden.

Polly Larwood (Sister)
Ambers Larwood (Brother)
(no markers)

Johnny Watson
   & wife
Bessie Larwood Watson
(no markers)

* *

PETERSBURG

LARWOOD CEMETERY
Located one mile north east of Spring Place, in Larwood Hollow. Copied Jan 4, 1978 by Harden L. Brown and Ralph D. Whitesell.

Edmond F. Larwood
Jan 14, 1827
Dec 2, 1908

Louisa, wife of
E. F. Larwood
Dec 25, 1829
Apr 16, 1903

Several unmarked graves.

* *

COOK CEMETERY
Located on Duckworth Hollow Road. Seven miles south of Lewisburg, four miles north of Spring Place. Copied 1974 by Thomas Ross Turner and Ralph D. Whitesell.

John J. Cook
Dec 30, 1820
Jul 16, 1854
Age 34 yrs, 6 mos, 17 days

In Memory of
William Cook
Born Dec 1769
He departed this life
July 30th 1847
Age 77 years & 5 months

* *

WILKERSON CEMETERY
Located two and one-half miles north of Delina on the Old Zerry Wilkerson farm, Poarch Hollow. Copied Mar 1973 by C. H. Roden.

J. Z.(Zerry) Wilkerson
Born 27 Sept 1833
Died (no date)

Mrs. Zerry Wilkerson
(Fannie Short)
May 2, 1855
Feb 13, 1901

Sam Haislip
(husband of
Nannie Wilkerson)
Mar 2, 1871
May 16, 1901

John Thomas Wilkerson
1872-1905
(son of J. Z. Wilkerson)

Corp Joe Stacy McCormick
Oct 15, 1890
Oct 7, 1918
"Noble he fell, while
fighting for his Country".

Mrs. Stacy McCormick
(Ada Wilkerson)
Nov 14, 1892
Sep 1, 1916

Mrs. Luther Milton
(M. E. Wilkerson)
May 2, 1871
Dec 11, 1910

J. B. Short
Oct 22, 1878
Dec 19, 1917

Maggie Short
Sep 15, 1885
May 28, 1915

W. T. Poarch
Feb 14, 1887
Nov 9, 1901

* *

MURDOCK-HAISLIP CEMETERY
Located north east of Delina, near Old Wakefield Chapel. Copied by C. H. Roden, March 1973.

John Murdock
Jul 28, 1838
May 14, 1908

Amanda Caldonia, wife of
John Murdock
Mar 10, 1838
Dec 14, 1920

Nancy A. Haislip
Aug 21, 1858
Feb 24, 1950

G.(Green) N. Haislip
Nov 25, 1861
Apr 23, 1917

Olga F(L)., wife of
J. W. Haislip
Sep 8, 1874
Dec 13, 1917

Zack Haislip
1866-1937 (Apr 27)

Samuel Nathan Larwood
Feb 15, 1856
Sep 3, 1944
& wife
Nancy E. Larwood
Apr 4, 1854
Nov 20, 1933

Zach L. Haislip and 1st wife Sarah Davis Haislip &
Z. L.'s 2nd wife Mary Jane Wade Richardson, widow of
Drury Wade. (no markers) *

John Wesley Haislip *
(died young, no marker)

Green Austin Haislip*
Oct 11, 1830
Jul 12, 1916
& wife
Sarah Elizabeth Wakefield
             Haislip *
May 26, 1840
Nov 9, 1906
(no marker)

Modena Haislip *
(teen age girl, no marker)

Ewell Carter Haislip *
(died young, no marker)

John Haislip *
Born 1824
Died ca 1855, age 31 yrs.
(no marker)

PETERSBURG

James Travis Haislip *
& 2nd wife
Nancy Jane Wakefield *
(no markers)

Sherman Haislip *
Nov 25, 1864
Apr 5, 1905
& 1st wife
Saphronia Crabtree Haislip *
(no dates)
& daughter
Clemmie *
died Aug 18, 1914
Age 17 years
(no markers)

Sarah Ida Sophronia Haislip
Whitehead,*wife of
Harvey Whitehead
Jul 24, 1883
died ____.
&
1 Son & 2 daughters are
buried here
(no markers)

* Info furnished by
C. H. Roden, Cornersville,
Tenn. Route.

* *

CATHEY CEMETERY

Located one and one-half mile north of Delina, on Old Cathey home place, on a small hill west of Highway on land now owned by Robert Bigham, and just north of the former site of second location of Goshen School House, that burned in Fall of 1924. Copied by C. H. Roden, March 1973.

Alexander Cathey
Jan 1, 1806
Nov 20, 1885

S. B., wife of
Alex. Cathey
Aug 20, 1815
Mar 12, 1895

Cyrus M. Cathey
Jan 12, 1847
Nov 3, 1912

Clemma, wife of
Cyrus Cathey
Aug 6, 1858
Jul 18, 1899

Lula M. Cathey
(dau of C. M. & Clemma Cathey)
Aug 25, 1875
Died   1876

Daniel A. Cathey
(son of Cyrus & Clemma Cathey)
Born & Died 1883

Marion Cathey (son of
Cyrus & Clemma Cathey)
B&D 1893

Kizzie T. Dodd
Jan 1, 1829
Mar 3, 1917

L. I. Poarch
May 22, 1830-Jan 19, 1912

* *

CARUTHERS-DUCKWORTH CEMETERY

Located at Brown's Shop. Copied by C. H. Roden and rechecked by Helen and Tim Marsh, 1979.

Ora Watson
1881-1966

Inez Lestelle, dau of
H. C. & Nettie Watson
Mar 17, 1886
Jul 16, 1887

S. A. E., wife of
H. C. Watson
Mar 22, 1848
Jan 12, 1894
Age 45 yrs, 10 mos, 10 days

Henry C. Watson
1846-1905

Aletha Watson
1884-1906

Joe Rhodes
1918-1918

Charlie Rhodes
1920-1920

Golie Watson
1898-1955

C. Hatten Rhodes
Feb 26, 1884
Feb 14, 1926
&
Valleria W. Rhodes
Mar 13, 1890
Oct 10, 1970

Travis Haislip
Mar 31, 1863
Oct 3, 1951
&
Lou C.(Couser) Haislip
Feb 5, 1868
Dec 10, 1910

John E. Crabtree
1862-1935
&
Sizney C.(Couser) Crabtree
1870-1909

Pfc James Duckworth
1914-1944

J. B. Watson
Nov 5, 1844
Apr 6, 1926

S. M. "Bud" Crabtree
Sep 1, 1861
Apr 4, 1930
&
Nannie Couser Crabtree
Jul 13, 1865
Jun 23, 1889

James K. P. Couser
Aug 22, 1839
Sep 9, 1897
&
Elizabeth A. Russell
Apr 1, 1840
May 15, 1898

Willie Dee Duckworth
1886-Sep 8, 1915

Leora Duckworth
1880-1942

F. L. "Fate" Duckworth
1844-1925

Martha E. Duckworth
1851-1902

Sons of J. L. & M. E.
Duckworth
Erskine D. Duckworth
Oct 12, 1890
Sep 27, 1892
&
Clarence Duckworth
Sep 12, 1892
Oct 7, 1892

Lawson Duckworth
Sep 4, 1867
Aug 23, 1944
&
Etta Duckworth
Jul 2, 1872
Oct 23, 1941

Bettie Crick
1888-1934

Samuel Riley
Mar 1, 1823
Apr 28, 1870

Elizabeth (Duckworth),
wife of Samuel Riley
Apr 29, 1825
Aug 6, 1899

PETERSBURG

Amy Jane Riley
May 1, 1831
Aug 31, 1881

10 Infants of
Elizabeth & Samuel Riley
are buried her in
graves marked only by
fieldstones.

J. T(Tom). Davis
Feb 22, 1862
Jul 13, 1937
&
Edna D.(Dodd) Davis
(2nd wife)
Sep 12, 1881
Mar 12, 1962
(Tom's 1st wife was
Mattie, no marker)

"Little Joe" Duckworth *
died young, son of
Joseph McMillen and
Ann J. Patterson Duckworth
(marked with fieldstone)

Vida E. Davis
1902-1919

Samuel W. Davis
Jan 24, 1876
Apr 29, 1935
&
Ella May (Hemphill) Davis
Aug 29, 1875
Mar 13, 1968

D. H(Herman) Davis
1910-1935

Samuel Davis & wife *
Rebecca Haislip Davis
(unmarked graves)

Wyly Bradford
1850-1880

Mrs. Wiley Bradford *
(no marker)
Died Sep 29, 1929

E. Malina Duckworth
Nov 28, 1837
Apr 16, 1930

M(Morgan). D. Duckworth
Mar 6, 1845
Jun 29, 1928

Samuel Duckworth
Jan 16, 1795
Mar 4, 1868
Age 73 yrs, 1 mo, 18 days

Eliza, wife of
Samuel Duckworth
Apr 16, 1812
Jun 8, 1893

Many unmarked graves.
William Caruthers is said
to be buried here in one
such grave.

* Info from C. H. Roden.

* *

FINLEY CEMETERY
Located one mile north of Catapla Road, on Old Finley Farm.
Copied April 12, 1977 by Ralph D. Whitesell, C. H. Roden &
T. D. Young.

N. M.(Newton Marshall) Finley
Apr 23, 1842
Jan 1, 1918

James Newton Watson
1906-1926

Modena (Finley), wife of
Tommy Watson
Apr 7, 1883
Feb 8, 1915

Ella Mable Finley
Jul 31, 1877
Dec 21, 1901

Thomas H. Finley
Jan 10, 1890
Jul 6, 1899

Nancy E(Emaline)(Davis),
wife of N. M. Finley
Oct 29, 1841
Oct 12, 1889

Cordelia C., dau of
N. M. & N. E. Finley
Apr 17, 1874
Oct 17, 1892

Lucinda Caroline Davis
Aug 16, 1844
Dec 8, 1899

R. H. Finley
Aug 10, 1864
Jan 10, 1894

Several unmarked graves.

Charles C. Finley
Died Jun 17, 1870
Age 21 years.

James L. D. Finley
Died Mar 5, 1862
Age 22 years.

R. W. Eddins
Nov 18, 1842
Aug 28, 1904

Elender J. (Finley) Eddins
Oct 29, 1846
Sep 7, 1890

Nancy L., wife of
Francis Carroll Finley
Died Aug 5, 1854
Age 38 yrs.

W. M.(Wm. Martin) Finley
Mar 12, 1809
Jul 16, 1875

Amanda Finley
Jul 15, 1821
Jan 17, 1907

Francis M. Whitaker
Sep 5, 1821
Jun 1, 1892

Mary Ann (Finley) Whitaker
Mar 4, 1844
Jul 5, 1926

Francis Finley and his
wife Jane Caruthers are
said to be buried here.

* *

FINLEY CEMETERY
Located across the fence from the above Finley Cemetery, in
another field, is completely lost due to neglect. It is
believed to be the burial place of William Finley, born
April 1o, 1777 in North Carolina and died in Marshall County
in 1849. Another brother, Samuel Finley, born Dec 27, 1799
in North Carolina, died in Marshall County July 19, 1840
is buried in the Sowell Cemetery.

* *

PETERSBURG

DRIVER CEMETERY
Located on Delina-Petersburg Road, on side of road.
Copied by Ralph D. Whitesell, April 1971

Sacred to the Memory of
Moses Driver
from Hartford Cty, N.C.
Who was born July the
8th 1782 and died
June 12th 1815
Age 33 yrs, 11 mos, 24 days

James B. R., son of
G. G. & N. F. Watson
Dec 17, 1858
Oct 21, 1882

Several unmarked graves.

* *

BEASLEY CEMETERY
Located near Archer, on Pee Dee Branch, on Old Wash Causby Farm. All markers in this cemetery are fieldstones with no inscriptions. Information furnished by Timothy R. Marsh.

Liberty Beasley
1802-1879

Mary W. (Doak),
1st wife of Liberty
Beasley
1807-1862

Lucinda M.(widow Smith),
2nd wife of Liberty Beasley
(no dates)

Mary Ann, dau of
Liberty & Mary W. Beasley
(no dates)

Dorinda A., dau of
Liberty & Mary W. Beasley
1829-1901

NOTE: Liberty Beasley, son
of Archer Beasley, was born
in Nottoway Co., VA.

Frank P. Beasley
(no dates)

Sallie Wilkerson, wife
of Frank P. Beasley
(no dates)

NOTE: On site grave count made by Richard A., Tim & Helen Marsh in 1976.

* *

BRADFORD CEMETERY
Located on Pee Dee Branch, near Horton-Haughton Cemetery.
Copied 1977.

John Bradford
Dec 29, 1827
Apr 21, 1914

and

Martha E. Bradford
May 30, 1829
Dec 6, 1911

Other graves with
fieldstone markers.

* *

DUCKWORTH CEMETERY
Located across the fence from Sowell Cemetery, near Catalpa and Brown's Shop. Copied by Helen and Tim Marsh, 1976.

John H. Duckworth
Mar 28, 1840
Jan 28, 1884

Louisa, wife of
John H. Duckworth
Aug 6, 1844
Jan 7, 1914

Ottis Duckworth
Dec 19, 1870
Nov 19, 1912

All graves marked.

* *

SOWELL CEMETERY
Located near Catalpa and Brown's Shop. Copied 1976 by Helen and Tim Marsh.

Joseph Christopher, son of
J. F. & E. A. Pack
Oct 11, 1852
Oct 19, 1855

Leota P., dau of
B. F. & M. F. Pack
Jul 19, 1887
Jan 6, 1888

B. C. McKinney
Dec 15, 1827
Feb 7, 1900

R. L., wife of
B. C. McKinney
Dec 26, 1842
Jul 13, 1914

Rosie Wakefield, wife of
John B. McKinney
Oct 23, 1868
Jul 18, 1918

J. G. Luna
Jun 6, 1807
Aug 10, 1846

Rhody C.(Stephens), wife
of James G. Luna
Jul 18, 1805
Aug 1, 1880

Will Wells
1875-1931

James J. Gaunt, son of
Robert & Elizabeth Gaunt
Nov 2, 1855-Oct 15, 1856

J. C. Wells
Jul 29, 1838
Dec 4, 1917
&
M. E. Wells
Dec 5, 1844
Jun 14, 1922

Robert J. Wells
Aug 4, 1848
Jul 26, 1904

Susan J., wife of
Robert J. Wells
Sep 10, 1854
Jun 19, 1916

R. J. B. Gaunt
Nov 21, 1831
Mar 27, 1878
& wife
Elizabeth Gaunt
Feb 12, 1836
Jan 23, 1880

Hugh Eddins, son of
R. J. B. & Elizabeth Gaunt
Nov 20, 1870
May 18, 1884

Jackson Luna
Nov   1812
Mar 19, 1875

Nancy, wife of
Jackson Luna
Sep 27, 1817
Feb 19, 1909

William, son of
M. R. & Fanny Luna
Apr 17, 1843
Nov 23, 1863

M. R. Luna
Feb 14, 1810
Dec 8, 1880

Fannie, wife of
M. R. Luna
Jun 8, 1812
Mar 26, 1887

Martha L., wife of
J. B. Luna & dau of
W. R. & Martha Yowell
Sep 25, 1849
Oct 26, 1865

Margaret, wife of
Claborn A. Finley
May 7, 1848
Sep 8, 1882
Age 34 yrs, 4 mos, 1 day

Mary E., dau of
C. A. & M. L. Findley
Feb 3, 1871
May 28, 1887

Albert L., son of
R. J. & S. J. Wells
Aug 2, 1871
Dec 4, 1872

Infant Son of
R. J. & S. J. Wells
B&D Oct 18, 1873

Robert H., son of
Jackson & Nancy Luna
Sep 3, 1842
Feb 1, 1863

Ethel, dau of
S. S. & M. E. Hemphill
1877-1878

M. A. Robinson
Sep 5, 1821
Feb 8, 1889
Age 67 yrs, 5 mos, 3 days

Mary, wife of
M. A. Robinson
Feb 22, 1833
Aug 14, 1891

Dottie E., wife of
R. M. Welch
Dec 27, 1841
Sep 4, 1907

Mary E., dau of
R. M. & D. E. Welch
Aug 7, 1868
Apr 2, 1887

J. S. Malone
Died May 17, 1864
Age 25 yrs, 2 mos, 10 days

Mary E., dau of
Jackson & Nancy Luna
Jan 14, 1838
Feb 6, 1853

N. F., dau of
W. C. A. & S. J. Luna
Died Jun 20, 1858
Age 15 mos & 3 days

Sarah L., dau of
W. C. A. & S. J. Luna
Aug 22, 1866
Jul 16, 1867
Age 10 mos & 24 days

Lefrey Leo, son of
W. C(Charles). &
M. E. Findley
Jul 2, 1879
Apr 2, 1880

Walter, son of
W. C. & M. E. Finley
Oct 11, 1872
Nov 23, 1875
Age 3 yrs, & 18 days

M. L. D., dau of
J. C. & M. E. Wells
Feb 5, 1867
Jul 18, 1868

Susan Adaline, wife of
W. B. Ray
Feb 17, 1840
Mar 23, 1888

Martha T., dau of
W. S. & Mary Findley
Jun 15, 1856
Sep 10, 1894

W. S. Findley
Jul 5, 1819
Sep 8, 1893

Mary (Andrews), wife of
W. S. Finley
Jan 12, 1822
Nov 3, 1906

James J., son of
W. S. & Mary Findley
Dec 9, 1850
Oct 9, 1888
Age 30 yrs & 9 mos.

Samuel Finley, husband of
Harriet Finley
Dec 27, 1799
Jul 19, 1840

Harriet, wife of
Samuel Finley
Jan 22, 1800
Oct 29, 1850

Mary Emaline, dau of
S. & H. Finley
Jan 25, 1833
Oct 2, 1835

Richard Tanner
Jan 15, 1783
Jul 28, 1858

Elizabeth Tanner
May 3, 1795
Dec 28, 1874

William A., son of
Samuel & Harriet Finley
Nov 5, 1829
Apr 26, 1874
Age 44 yrs, 5 mos, 21 days
2nd marker:
W. A. Finley
Nov 5, 1829
Apr 26, 1874

Isabella (Murdock), wife
of W. A. Finley
Sep 29, 1837
Oct 18, 1909

David A. Ellison
Jan 25, 1845
Feb 5, 1921
& wife
Sarah O. Ellison
Oct 17, 1843
Aug 15, 1886

William T., son of
D. A. & S. O. Ellison
Jan 22, 1871
May 23, 1877

Mary Stephens
Mar 4, 1770
May 3, 1846

Wily B. Stephens
Jun 17, 1807
Sep 17, 1867

Nancy E., wife of
Jas. Isom
Mar 16, 1854
Sep 22, 1876
Age 22 yrs, 6 mos, 16 days

W. C. A. Luna
Nov 20, 1833
Dec 2, 1898

Sarah J., wife of
W. C. A. Luna
Jun 5, 1833
Jun 2, 1909

James M. Luna
Dec 16, 1835
Oct 30, 1902

Clarissa Luna
Dec 4, 1815
Oct 26, 1863
Age 48 yrs, & 22 days

Icey, dau of
J. T. & A. A. Luna
Nov 13, 1868
Apr 19, 1870

Robert Ervin, son of
A. P. & S. J. Hill
Dec 9, 1865
Jul 21, 1867

Mrs. Sarah Ann, Consort of
A. F. Collins
Mar 8, 1828
May 14, 1850

Catharine, wife of
P. W. Brooks
1791-Nov 1857

Sarah, dau of
-------- Sanders
Nov 11, 1855
Apr 10, 1857
(name gone)

PETERSBURG

James T. Kennedy
Aug 14, 1858
Oct 29, 1893

Hattie A., Consort of
N. W. Finley
Oct 9, 1839
Feb 7, 1868

Walter Bruce, son of
N. W. & H. A. Finley
May 23, 1862
Jul 2, 1864

William D. S., son of
N. W. & H. A. Finley
Mar 18, 1865
Feb 11, 1868

John M. Luna
Mar 23, 1847
Nov 24, 1915
& wife
Lucy A. Luna
Mar 20, 1852
Nov 22, 1925

Many unmarked graves.

Willie Clyde Luna
Mar 20, 1905
Sep 3, 1905
&
Infant
(no dates)
Infants of
J. E. & S. P. Luna

Ezekiel Sanders
Dec 18, 1799
Dec 20, 1862
Age 63 yrs & 2 days
(broken in many pieces)

Mary, Consort of
E. Sanders
Died Jun 27, 1858
Age 56 years

L. A. Sanders
Jan 30, 1822
Dec 18, 1874

James C. Sanders
Jan 9, 1840
Apr 8, 1863
Age 23 yrs, 2 mos, 29 days

James M. Sowell
Oct 28, 1819
Feb 23, 1907
& wife
E. T. Sowell
Jun 19, 1835
Jun 14, 1911

Daniel L., son of
J. M. & E. T. Sowell
May 7, 1859
Aug 6, 1885

Joseph L., son of
J. M. & E. T. Sowell
Oct 21, 1870
Dec 9, 1886

Infant Dau of
W. L. & F. J. Sowell
Sep 19, 1912
Sep 29, 1912

Edker L. Jacobs
Apr 13, 1912
Aug 29, 1912

Hattie, wife of
J. H. Jacobs
May 13, 1886
Aug 14, 1908

W. H. Sowell
Aug 22, 1852
Sep 30, 1929
&
Rosey A. E. Sowell
Dec 29, 1855
Jan 5, 1918

Infant Dau of
Mr. & Mrs. W. H. Sowell
Jul 29, 1900
Sep 21, 1900
&
Infant Son of
Mr. & Mrs. W. H. Sowell
Apr 11, 1878
Apr 11, 1878

"Sister"
Sarah J. Sowell
Jan 10, 1851
Jun 22, 1924
"In Memory of
Aunt Sallie"

T. L. F. Sowell
Jul 1, 1863
Jun 19, 1890

Silas D. Sowell
May 25, 1861
Sep 2, 1890

* *

TROOP CEMETERY
Located one mile south west of Talley Station, near Bryant Hollow. Copied by Helen and Tim Marsh, Jun 20, 1968.

John G. Troop
Oct 14, 1823
Oct 20, 1910

Martha M., wife of
Jno. G. Troop
Jan 28, 1822
Jan 21, 1863

Christiana, wife of
Jno. G. Troop
Sep 12, 1825
Dec 31, 1858

Sarah A., wife of
Jno. G. Troop
Born 1835
Died 1901

Elizabeth, wife of
George Crawford
Died Jan 14, 1859
(no age given)

George Crawford *
1786-1870
(fieldstone, no inscription)

NOTE: This was the Old George Crawford Farm.
*George Crawford was son of William & Rachel Sawyers Crawford of Augusta Co., VA. Elizabeth Crawford was dau of Samuel & Rachel Gray. Info by T. R. Marsh.

* *

BELL-HEMPHILL CEMETERY
Located one mile north east of Delina. Copied April 12, 1977 by Ralph D. Whitesell, C. H. Roden and T. D. Young.

John N. Hemphill
Dec 12, 1859
Oct 28, 1862

Martha J. Hemphill
Aug 7, 1842
Mar 6, 1863

W. C. Luna, Sr.
Mar 20, 1822
Apr 28, 1898
& wife
Mary A. B. Luna
May 17, 1823
Apr 10, 1885

Infant dau of
W. C. & S. E. Luna
B&D Apr 14, 1877

Martha E. Bell
Jul 28, 1837
Mar 21, 1862

Daisy D., dau of
R. W. & H. B. McRee
Oct 12, 1882
Nov 17, 1883

Elisha J. Luna
Sep 25, 1860
Oct 30, 1862

James M. Luna
Jan 21, 1857
Sep 26, 1862

Pyrmids, no inscriptions.

Several unmarked graves.

* *

PETERSBURG

HASTINGS CEMETERY
Located on side of road from Petersburg to Richmond, a short distance past the Arbor Hill Road.

J. M. Hastings
Jan 18, 1841
Oct 4, 1878

George Hastings
Born 1845
Died Aug 12, 1906
(no marker)

Bobbie, son of
R. H. & F. A. Hastings
Jun 23, 1871
Oct 22, 1875

Robert Hatton Hastings
Oct 8, 1838
Jul 7, 1892
(no marker)

Fannie A. Hastings
Aug 17, 1829
Aug 7, 1895
(no marker)

* *

YOWELL CEMETERY
Located two miles north of Petersburg, at the junction of Highway 130 and Arbor Hill Road. Copied 1970 by Helen and Tim Marsh.

John Caldwell
May 9, 1813
Feb 5, 1892

Mary, wife of
John Caldwell
(no dates)

James T. Caldwell
(no dates)

Samuel A., son of
J. & M. Caldwell
Feb 10, 1850
Oct 15, 1870

Margaret A., dau of
John & Mary Caldwell
Dec 28, 1839
Oct 10, 1867

Eliza C., wife of
J. L. Wisdom
Feb 8, 1845
Oct 18, 1867

Margaret F., wife of
Joel F. Yowell
May 20, 1813
Jul 26, 1838

Gabriel E., son of
Joel & Lucy Yowell
Died Sep 28, 1837
Age 19 years.

Doct. Thomas Woodward
Aug 8, 1786
Jun 25, 1836
Age 49 years.

Nancy, wife of
Dr. Thomas Woodward
(no dates)

R. R. Hanaway
Nov 7, 1835
Dec 20, 1897

Fannie W., wife of
R. R. Hanaway
Feb 22, 1848
Feb 1, 1902

Walter S., son of
R. R. & F. W. Hanaway
Dec 28, 1871
Aug 2, 1873

Elizabeth, wife of
W. J. Lancaster
Jun 28, 1850
Apr 21, 1884

B. L. Lancaster
Jan 8, 1815
Jul 28, 1882
"Lived a member of the
Church 49 years."
Was married
Aug 29, 1838 to
Asenith Vandiver.

Joel Yowell
Born 1771
Died Sep 26, 1855

Mrs. J. Lucy, late Consort
of Joel Yowell, Esq.
Died Aug 21, 1824, in the
41st year of her life,
left 10 children to lament
their loss.

Mrs. Nancy, 2nd Consort of
Joel Yowell
Died May 1, 1841
Age 60 years.

Mollie E., wife of
Alex Lancaster
Aug 30, 1854
Mar 4, 1890

Mary E., dau of
J. H. & A. J. Lancaster
Died Nov 19, 1880
Age 4 yrs, 7 mos, 12 days

Tyre B., son of
D. B. & Elizabeth A. Stamps
Apr 2, 1859
Jan 29, 1863

Charles Lee Davis
May 12, 1836
Dec 13, 1885

Mary, wife of
D. Wells
Apr 23, 1794
Aug 3, 1848

Jane, 2nd wife of
Drury Wells
Oct 16, 1816
Sep 14, 1858

Infant Dau of
J. A. & S. Yowell
B&D Nov 1827

John S., son of
J. A. & S. Yowell
(dates in ground)

J. W. V. Allen
Aug 11, 1838
Jul 10, 1856
Age 17 yrs, 10 mos, 30 days

Jane, wife of
David Moore
May 5, 1770
Feb 10, 1843
Age 72 yrs, 10 mos, 5 days
EX by S. C. M.
Dec 15, 1850

Martha Washington, wife of
W. B. Fonville & dau of
G. & C. M. Blackwell
Mar 3, 1837
Dec 4, 1854
Age 17 yrs, 9 mos, 1 day

Joseph E., son of
Stephen & Mary Read
Died Oct 11, 1837
in the 19 years of his
age.

Green Madearis
Jan 22, 1811
Oct 25, 1873

M. E., dau of
B. & E. Harwell
Dec 25, 1832
Jul 28, 1834

George W. Stone, Jr.
Mar 29, 1843
Jul 25, 1844

Many unmarked graves.

* *

PETERSBURG

GIBSON CEMETERY

Located on Arbor Hill Road. Copied 1978 by Helen and Tim Marsh

1820
Ephraim Loyd
Aug 16, 1773
Nov 11, 1819

1816
George, son of
Thomas and Mary Gibson
Born Mar 1807
Died   1816

1816
Anna, dau of
Thomas & Mary Gibson
Oct 26, 1800
Dec 27, 1816

* *

PORTER CEMETERY

Located off Liberty Valley Road, one and one-half mile east on Arbor Hill Road. Submitted by Mrs. Thomas A. McAdams and rechecked 1979 by Helen and Tim Marsh.

John Porter, Sr.
Feb 8, 1820
Feb 8, 1906

Lou Doss Porter
May 5, 1828
Dec 2, 1900

* Neil C. &
Elizabeth Cummings Whorley.

Several unmarked graves.

Stephen A. Porter
Sep 15, 1830
Apr 30, 1906

John Porter, Jr.
Died May 5, 1866
(no age given)

William Longmire, a
Revolutionary Soldier,
died 1815, probably buried
here in unmarked grave. He
left wife Hannah and several
minor children.

Mother
Maude Whorley Moore
May 10, 1881
Mar 3, 1905

Jessie, dau of
N. C. & E. C. Whorley *
Aug 11, 1903
Feb 25, 1907

NOTE: Longmire moved from
Fairfield in Bedford Co.Tn.
to this area in 1810. ED.

1816
Here lies the body of
William Longmire, the son
of William and Hannah
Longmire. He was born
Dec 31, 1810 and deceased
the 14th Sept 1816.

Rachel, wife of
Riley Leonard, who was
born 22nd Feb 1800 and
deceased 15 Sept 1831.

* *

SANDIFER CEMETERY

Located off Liberty Valley Road, two miles east on Arbor Hill Road. Submitted by Mrs. Thomas A. McAdams. (This is the Old Joseph and Stephen Porter Farm).

Moses Neely
Mar 8, 1809
Mar 25, 1877
Age 67 yrs & 17 days

Nancy, wife of
Moses Neely
Jan 22, 1810
Jan 7, 1893

Cyentha Owen
Died Feb 11, 1884
Age 26 yrs.

J. T. Whorley (Jess T.)
Sep 10, 1834
Dec 15, 1864

Nancy I., dau of
Ephraim and Sarah Loyd
Mar 5, 1820
May 12, 1825

Several graves were
illegible.

Several unmarked graves.

Cyntha, wife of
Joel Whorley
Born Sep 1802
Died   1853

William Thomas, son of
J. & C. Whorley
Born 1848
Died 1868

Nancy M., dau of
John & Jane Wakefield
Dec 5, 1816
Oct 25, 1838

W. H. Moore
Jan 22, 1821
Nov 10, 1864

Sacred to the Memory of
Mary Porter, wife of
William Porter, who was
the mother of 9 Sons and
5 Daughters, who departed
this life..(illegible)

Joseph Hall
Mar 6, 1792
Feb 24, 1871

Mary, wife of
Joseph Hall
Oct 12, 1810
Apr 9, 1837

Sacred to the Memory of
Isbell Miles. She was
born Mar 19, 1765
died Dec 22, 1830
(A Leonard Miles, born
1759, pension list of
Lincoln Co., TN, 1834)

William, son of
Joseph & Catherine Porter
Oct 30, 1812
Sep 22, 1823

Here lies all that was
Mortal of
Catherine Porter who was
born Aug 12, 1785 and
departed this life
Sep 12, 1823.
"The mother of 8 children."

Mary E., wife of
Stephen Porter
May 3, 1790
Jul 20, 1834
(She was 1st wife of S.
Porter. Copied from an
Old Bible owned by Mrs.
C. C. James, R # 2, Humbolt, TN 38343: Mother,
Mary E. Porter, born May 3
1790, buried in Uncle Jo
Porter graveyard, later
called Sandifer Graveyard.)

David Porter
Feb 14, 1822
Nov 27, 1834

Stephen Porter
Jan 22, 1789
Dec 28, 1854
(From Bible owned by
W. E. Porter: Stephen
Porter married 1st Mary E.
Jul 21, 1814; married 2nd
Jemima S. Quarles, Nov 5,
1841)

PETERSBURG

RIVES-CRUNK CEMETERY

Located one-half mile north west of Petersburg on the Old Petersburg-Belfast Road, now known as Liberty Valley Road. Copied by Mrs. Thomas A. McAdams and Ralph D. Whitesell.

Capt. William Crunk
Oct 11, 1787
Mar 13, 1869

Mary, wife of
William Crunk
Feb 28, 1790
May 6, 1852

Infant Dau of
J. W. & R. J. Crunk
Sep 26, 1860
Sep 29, 1860

Nancy J., wife of
(illegible)
Sep 11, 1830
Aug 6, 1880
(broken &
footstone: M.J.C.)

Fanny Delitha (Crunk),
Consort of
Pryor Buchanan, mother
of Sarah Minerva and
Mary Lettecia Buchanan
Jun 17, 1827
Feb 27, 1852

Margaret P., wife of
Dr. J. J. Crunk
Nov 8, 1823
Aug 17, 1877

Joseph J. B. Crunk
Apr 5, 1808
Oct 3, 1880

Mrs. Martha, Consort of
J. J. B. Crunk
Oct 14, 1813
Feb 23, 1852
"Joined the C. P. Church
Sept 1850"

Father
William J. Blakemore
Sep 22, 1825
Mar 16, 1891

Mother
Nancy S. (Crunk) Blakemore
May 12, 1834
Mar 21, 1910

Joe J. Blakemore
1863-1935

George Wesley Crunk
Nov 5, 1822
Mar 18, 1907
&
Eliza Jane Crunk
Aug 11, 1827
Mar 17, 1903

Lucy C., dau of
W. R. & M. L. Archer
Aug 9, 1870
Nov 3, 1881

Infant Son of
W. R. & M. L. Archer
(dates under ground)

Mattie, dau of
W. R. & M. L. Archer
Feb 25, 1865
Aug 5, 1867

Sarah, dau of
W. R. & S. Williamson
Born Nov 25, 1869
Died (illegible)

Infant of
W. R. & S. Williamson
Born Jun 6, 1879
Died (illegible)

Mary, dau of
L. & M. Landers
Sep 10, 1861
Jan 9, 1875

Mrs. Dollie Rogers
Mar 5, 1798
Apr 5, 1871

* Green Rives
Sep 14, 1776
Jul 29, 1859

Susan, wife of
Green Rives
Jun 15, 1804
May 14, 1849

G. W. Beasley
May 10, 1814
Feb 18, 1895

Many Tombstones are broken, unable to read.

Many unmarked graves.

* Native of Dinwiddie Co., Va.

* *

HOWZE-CAMPBELL CEMETERY

Located near the site of the Old William Moore Mill in Petersburg. The stones are now in a lot adjoining the residence of Mr. & Mrs. Holland Whittaker, just to the rear of the Morgan School. 1968.

Camilla C. Campbell
Feb 19, 1809
Nov 28, 1839

James W. Campbell, son of
G. D. & M. L. Campbell
Feb 15, 1851
Feb 17, 1851

Mary F., wife of
B. J. Allison
Born --- 8, 1828
Died Oct 18, 1851

NOTE: An article written to the Fayetteville Observer, September 4, 1905 by John Y. Gill which is recorded in the scrapbook of J. J. S. Gill. It states that John Y. Gill's great-grandfather Howze and great-grandmother Howze are buried in this cemetery, together with his grandmother Gill. In this article, he also states that he put together the pieces of the marker which was broken when the old Willow tree blew down, and it read as follows: " In Memory of Mary J. Gill, Died June 19th A.D. 1844, Age about 57 years."

* *

WILLIAMSON CEMETERY

Located on Delina-Cornersville Road. Members of the Williamson Family are buried here in unmarked graves.

Info. from C.H. Roden

* *

PETERSBURG

GREER CEMETERY
Located on Liberty Valley Road, one-half mile south of Leonard Bluff.

No signs of the graveyard remain today. Marshall County Deed Book "D", page 273, 1840, lists James Greer of Madison County, Alabama. He mentions Greer Burying Ground reserved from sale, this land was purchased by James Greer in 1811, 66 foot square.

* *

BILLS CEMETERY
Located three miles north west of Petersburg, one-half mile west of Liberty Valley Road. Copied Jul 29, 1964 by Richard W. Sassman.

Father G. W. Bills Apr 10, 1823 Aug 26, 1913 & Mother A. E. A. Bills Nov 24, 1819 Oct 30, 1914	John M. Bills Jul 21, 1865 Aug 4, 1888 M. E. Bills Mar 30, 1886 Oct 7, 1901	C. R. Darnall Jun 15, 1822 Nov 8, 1870 M. G.* wife of J. T. Holland Sep 29, 1859 May 8, 1898	Charlie G. Holland Nov 11, 1892 Jun 1, 1895 Our Babies (all on stone)

* When this cemetery was rechecked in December 1979 by Helen and Tim Marsh and Ralph D. Whitesell, this marker was lying about 100 feet north of the graveyard.

* *

BROOKS CEMETERY
Located on Fishing Ford Road, between Belfast and Talley Station. Copied January 1961.

George W. Brooks May 15, 1851 Aug 22, 1892 Willie Brooks Apr 1885 Nov 14, 1898 Mary Ann Brooks, wife of W. D. Gillum Apr 9, 1841 Jan 1, 1919	James M. Brook Apr 4, 1844 Sep 6, 1896 Thomas F. Brooks May 18, 1818 Jun 21, 1904	Sally E., wife of George W. Brooks Jan 22, 1860 Jun 20, 1909 Helen, wife of Thomas F. Brooks Jul 17, 1820 Oct 27, 1903	Robert Brooks 1858-1909 Amanda Crunk Apr 12, 1842 Jun 23, 1922

NOTE: This grave and six unmarked graves, are on the Price W. Brooks Farm, now owned by Mr. Henry Mitchell (1961), one mile south east of Talley Station, and one-half mile from the above Cemetery.

Arthur Brooks
Jul 4, 1774
Dec 11, 1819

* *

GABBERT CEMETERY
Located one and one-half miles north of Cane Creek Church of Christ, and one mile east of Talley Station. Cpoied May 1, 1960

Samuel H. Gowan Mar 8, 1864 Nov 20, 1929 Mattie A. E. Gowan(Gabbert) Feb 26, 1867-Apr 30, 1947	H. V. "Pete" Gabbert 1883-1937 W. S. Gabbert, son of Benton & Fannie Gabbert Dec 30, 1865-Sep 15, 1891	Fannie(Blakemore), wife of Benton Gabbert Jul 15, 1844 May 19, 1893	Benton Gabbert Apr 10, 1840 Jun 18, 1906 S. Elmer Gabbert 1875-1920

PETERSBURG

Daniel L. Gabbert
Oct 28, 1870
Jun 1, 1924

Infant Children of
James & Mattie Broadway
(no dates)

J.(Jonathan) F. Prosser
1852-1928

Several unmarked graves.

* Info by Mrs. T. A. McAdams.

J. E. Prosser
Dec 6, 1820
Feb 17, 1907

Hepsie (Johnston), wife
of J. E. Prosser
Aug 26, 1826
Apr 23, 1881

Ann M., wife of
Daniel Blakemore
May 17, 1810
Apr 12, 1885

Infant Son of
Benton & Fannie Gabbert
Mar 18, 1885
May 19, 1886

Allie, dau of
J. E. & H. J. Prosser
Apr 16, 1866
Jul 14, 1867

Sacred to the Memory of
Daniel Blakemore, who was
born Mar 10, 1794 & died
Oct 23, 1860.

Harriett H., wife of *
William Crunk
Jan 17, 1802
Jun 5, 1864

Fanny, Consort of *
Joseph Blakemore, who was
born Oct 6, 1770 & died
Sep 10, 1841. "She was a
member of the M. E. Church
for forty years."

* *

SORRELLS CEMETERY

Located north of Petersburg-Richmond Road on Sorrells Raod.
This cemetery is found on the Bellville Map. Copied Oct 24,
1978 by Helen and Tim Marsh.

J. E. Sorrells
Nov 2, 1833
Sep 9, 1908

Mahala C. Sorrells
Aug 13, 1835
Jul 26, 1921

E. E. S. (footstone)

6 unmarked graves.

* *

MOORE CEMETERY

Located one-fourth mile north of Petersburg on Highway 130.
Copied Oct 24, 1979, by Helen and Tim Marsh.

H. Bascom, son of
J. S. S. & Angelina (Moore)
Gill
May 22, 1850
Sep 2, 1895

James O. Andrew, son of
Jo J. S. & Angelina Gill
(dates broken away)

Alpha Moore Gill
Sep 29, 1841
Jun 16, 1910

J. J. S. Gill
Jun 16, 1816
Mar 16, 1902
&
Angeline Gill
May 18, 1818
Jul 21, 1913

Fannie M., dau of
Rev. W. T. & M. F. Gill
Died Oct 5, 1869
Age 2 years

Thomas David, son of
W. B. & Addie L. Moore
May 13, 1888
Jun 7, 1888

Tommie D., son of
W. C. & R. F. Moore
Jul 16, 1867
Dec 5, 1870

J. B. Fishback
Jun 20, 1812
Jun 9, 1864

Thomas David Moore
Jan 25, 1823
Oct 25, 1883
Age 60 years & 9 months
&
Fannie Buchanan Moore
May 5, 1839
May 15, 1887
Age 48 yrs & 10 days

W. D. Moore
Feb 7, 1792
Nov 1, 1855
Age 63 yrs, 8 mos, 21 days
(next to above is this
grave):
(<u>Hannah</u>) H. Moore, wife of
W. D. Moore
(broken into pieces, cannot
be read)

Amanda M. Moore
Dec 11, 1828
Mar 31, 1898

* *

PIGG CEMETERY

Located near Spring Place, in Pigg Hollow. Copied by
Helen & Tim Marsh and Ralph D. Whitesell, Nov 5, 1979.

Margaret L., dau of
J. H. & D. L. Pigg
Dec 30, 1878
Jan 29, 1900

Phoebe L., dau of
J. H. & D. L. Pigg
Feb 6, 1873
Nov 26, 1898

Joseph H. Pigg
Mar 24, 1841
Jul 8, 1910
& wife
Delinda L. Pamplin Pigg
Apr 21, 1843
Jun 1, 1917

Elijah L. Pigg
Oct 25, 1867
Aug 5, 1889

Sarah L., dau of
E. L. & L. H. Pigg
Feb 6, 1890
Feb 25, 1891

Delinda C., dau of
W. F. & S. L. Pigg
Jul 12, 1901
Oct 10, 1901

Infant Son of
W. F. & S. L. Pigg
Died Apr 9, 1891
(no age given)

PETERSBURG

W(Will). F. Pigg
Sep 26, 1864
Sep 15, 1918
&
Sarah L. Pigg
Dec 1, 1864
May 2, 1902

Louise V., dau of
W. F. & S. L. Pigg
Jun 24, 1897
Aug 7, 1897

Henry K., son of
W. F. & S. L. Pigg
Nov 24, 1888
Dec 23, 1888

May have been other unmarked graves.

* *

LYONS CEMETERY
Located one and one-fourth mile north west of Brown's Shop on Pee Dee Branch. Copied Nov 21, 1979 by Helen and Tim Marsh.

Father
William Lyons
Mar 29, 1850
Jan 29, 1915
&
Mother
Sallie Lyons
Jun 1, 1853
Apr 16, 1889

Purlia Ann, wife of
B. E. Franklin
Jun 2, 1871
Sep 8, 1892

James N. Franklin
Sep 4, 1890
Mar 7, 1891
Age 6 mos & 3 days
&
Clarence B. Franklin
Mar 7, 1892
Sep 19, 1892
Age 6 mos & 10 days
"Infant Sons of
B. E. & P. A. Franklin"

6 unmarked graves.

* *

SHORT CEMETERY
Located one mile east of Harris Hollow, south of Pee Dee Branch.

William M. Short
(no dates)
   & wife
Elizabeth H. McGaugh Short
(no dates)
(no marker)

Other members of the family.
No markers with inscriptions

* *

LUNA CEMETERY
Located one mile south of Talley on Old Fishing Ford Raod, one-fourth mile west of Highway 431. Copied Dec 5, 1979 by Ralph D. Whitesell, Helen and Tim Marsh.

Sophia S., wife of
G. D. Petty & dau of
A. & J. Hogan
Born Oct   1808
Died Jul 25, 1831
Age 25 yrs, 8 mos, 26 days

S. E. Hogan
Feb 5, 1815
Aug   1816

P. H.
(fieldstone)

Sacred to the Memory of
Peter Luna, who was born
October the 1st 1760 &
departed this life Feb the
16th 1851, aged 90 years,
4 months & 11 days.
(DAR Marked)

Mary Luna
(no dates)

* *

McKNIGHT CEMETERY
Located at junction of Pigg and Larwood Hollow, near Spring Place, on Rhodes Farm. 1979.

John McKnight and members of his family are said to be buried here, but no markers with inscriptions.

* *

TALLEY CEMETERY
(north section)

Located two miles north west of Petersburg on the Petersburg-Delina Road. Copied April 29, 1979 by Helen and Tim Marsh.

Ernest R. Hobby
Jul 7, 1886
May 23, 1969
&
Addie L. Hobby
May 9, 1886
Feb 20, 1971

John N. Watson
Jul 20, 1872
May 1, 1966
&
M. Ella Watson
Dec 30, 1883

Tellie Loyd Robinson
son of J. D. &
S. F. Robinson
Mar 19, 1892
May 21, 1894
&
Rosie Lee Robinson
dau of J. D. &
S. F. Robinson
Jul 10, 1889
Jul 27, 1889

Samuel L. Chesser
1892-1951

S. B. Chesser
Oct 2, 1827
Nov 25, 1911
& wife
S. M. Chesser
Oct 1, 1853
Nov 2, 1925

Martha, wife of
S. B. Chesser
Jan 7, 1825
Mrd Jul 27, 1846
Died Jan 16, 1879

Elizabeth J., dau of
S. B. & S. M. Chesser
Sep 19, 1850
Apr 15, 1888
&
Infant Son of
S. B. & S. M. Chesser
Sep 10, 1882
Sep 16, 1882
&
John Clinton, son of
S. B. & S. M. Chesser
Aug 24, 1880
Dec 25, 1896

M.(Matthew) Dixon
Mar 1, 1817
Feb 1, 1878

Susan P. Dixon
(dau of Henry & Mary Talley)
Jun 5, 1821
Feb 26, 1891

Maggie Pearl, dau of
G. L. & E. C. Butler
Sep 12, 1886
Oct 28, 1888

Dwight Butler
1908-1943 (TM)

Hallie Mae Butler
Nov 22, 1905
Jun 10, 1960

Earnest L. Butler
1880-1942
&
Clara S. Butler
1882-1963

Howard E. Butler
Tennessee
Tec 5 Engineers, WW II

Jessie D. Finley
1883-1955
&
Lizzie V. Finley
1885-1940

Irene Talley, wife of
R. M. Hickman
1891-1942

Fannie T. Arnett
1884-1916

Father
W. N. Talley
Nov 28, 1852
Dec 31, 1904
&
Mother
Mrs. M. F. Talley
Dec 9, 1859
Jul 31, 1944

Sina F. Talley
Apr 1, 1857
Mar 23, 1943

J. David Talley
Sep 10, 1865
Apr 21, 1926

Barrett W., son of
Henry & Mary Talley
Oct 29, 1826
Jul 14, 1867
Age 40 yrs, 8 mos, 15 days

Mother
Nancy A., wife of
B. W. Talley
Jul 8, 1832
Mar 28, 1915

Mary Eliza, dau of
B. W. & N. A. Talley
Jul 18, 1855
Jan 19, 1866
Age 10 yrs, 6 mos, 1 day

Thomas H., son of
J. B. & E. P. Talley
Apr 13, 1862
Jun 1, 1862

(name gone) Talley
Jun 2, 1844
Jan 11, 1861

Martha D., wife of
J. B. Talley
Mar   1821
Jun 2, 1856

Henry Talley
Nov 28, 1778
Mar 9, 1862
Age 83 yrs, 3 mos, 12 days
&
Mary Talley
Jun 24, 1788
May 9, 1865
Age 76 yrs, 10 mos, 16 days

Robert P., son of
Henry & Mary Talley
May 29, 1818
Feb 9, 1842
Age 23 yrs, 8 mos, 11 days

Patrick H., son of
Henry & Mary Talley
Jan 22, 1810
Mar 24, 1831
Age 21 yrs, 4 mos, 2 days

Susan J. J., dau of
William & Elizabeth Talley
May 4, 1838
Dec 28, 1839

R. P. Dixon
Jun 25, 1848
Aug 7, 1850

J. O. Dixon
May 13, 1859
Jul 22, 1860

Susan E., dau of
Jas. B. & Bethany A. Talley
Sep 10, 1846
Dec 22, 1846
Age 3 mos, 12 days

Mary F., dau of
Jas. B. & Bethany A. Talley
Nov 21, 1836
Feb 13, 1853
Age 16 yrs, 2 mos, 22 days

Robert H., son of
Jas. B. & Bethany A. Talley
Aug 12, 1832
Aug 3, 1854
Age 21 yrs, 11 mos, 22 days

James B. Talley
Jan 20, 1808
Mar 8, 1875

Bethany A., wife of
James B. Talley
Mar 22, 1811
Apr 23, 1855
Age 44 yrs, 1 mo, 1 day

Sarah E., wife of
J. P. Doss & dau of
James B. & Bethany A. Talley
Aug 13, 1834
Aug 27, 1854
Age 20 yrs, 14 days

John J., son of
Jas. B. & Bethany A. Talley
Feb 24, 1843
Dec 31, 1862
Age 19 yrs, 10 mos, 7 days

David E., son of
Jas. B. & Bethany A. Talley
Jan 20, 1841
May 14, 1864
Age 23 yrs, 3 mos, 3 days

J. L. Gibson
May 17, 1831
Jan 31, 1873
"His last words,
I want nothing."

David C., son of
J. L. & Martha A. Gibson
Jan 25, 1865
May 18, 1865

Mary Talley, wife of
G. W. C. Neill
1844-1881

P. H. Lee, son of
G. W. C. & Mary Neill
Aug 6, 1864
Dec 2, 1865

Paul Overton Talley
Nov 27, 1898
Mar 18, 1970
&
Thelma Ownby Talley
Jan 27, 1906

Tom D. Talley
Jul 11, 1869
Mar 8, 1957
&
Josie F. Talley
Dec 18, 1871
Dec 18, 1955

Infant Son of
L. C. & B. L. Neill
B&D May 23, 1868

Infant Son of
L. C. & B. L. Neill
B&D Oct 4, 1870

Infant Son & Dau of
W. A. & B. M. Williams
B&D Jun 14, 1887

Eunice, wife of
J. B. Talley
Jul 24, 1836
Aug 9, 1914

Beulah J., wife of
C. A. Talley
Jun 10, 1886
Jun 25, 1912

Sina F. Talley
Apr 1, 1857
Mar 23, 1943

Father
James M. Broadway
1856-1928
&
Mother
Mattie E. Broadway
1858-1927

Erskine C. Broadway
1884-1928

E. Buford Luna
Dec 13, 1888
Nov 24, 1971
&
Dean T. Luna
Aug 18, 1894
Aug 11, 1975

Mary Louise, dau of
E. B. & B. D. Luna
Sep 15, 1916
Jul 11, 1917

Susie E. Talley
Nov 13, 1870
Aug 11, 1949

Gifford, son of
Geo. & Susie E. Talley
Dec 20, 1906
Mar 27, 1916

G. T. Talley
Feb 14, 1851
Feb 5, 1912

Mary, wife of
G. T. Talley
Oct 30, 1857
Sep 25, 1900

P. L. Talley
1870-1929

William N. Talley
Jun 13, 1879
May 26, 1901

Father
James T. Talley
Mar 9, 1841
Mar 21, 1916
& wife
Mother
Martha F. Talley
Aug 5, 1845
Aug 6, 1890

Infant Son of
J. T. & M. F. Talley
Mar 5, 1868
Mar 12, 1868

Father
William Talley
Aug 10, 1814
Mar 31, 1885
Age 70 yrs, 7 mos, 21 days

Mother
Elizabeth A. Talley
Oct 10, 1817
Nov 28, 1881
Age 64 yrs, 1 mo, 18 days

Patrick H., son of
William & Elizabeth Talley
Dec 23, 1839
Jul 13, 1861
Age 21 yrs, 6 mos, 20 days
"Here lies the remains of
the Soldier Boy."

Infant Son of
William & Elizabeth Talley
(no dates)

Susanna Randolph
1797-1883

Sallie E. Wakefield
Jul 20, 1864
May 2, 1890

Sarah E., dau of
J. P. & S. E. Wakefield
Apr 27, 1890
Jun 7, 1890

Grace E., wife of
Nat. Talley
Jan 22, 1824
Jan 10, 1889

Samuel G., son of
N. & G. E. Talley
Jul 20, 1864
Aug 18, 1864

John C., son of
Nathaniel & Grace E. Talley
Feb 27, 1845
Killed in the Battle
of Murfreesboro
Dec 31, 1862

James N., son of
N. & G. E. Talley
Mar 18, 1854
May 29, 1855

E. L., dau of
H. H. & S. J. Talley
Sep 24, 1868
Jan 25, 1869

Mrs. D. J. Driver
Mar 3, 1837
Oct 16, 1885

Nancy Lucinda Blacknall
Jun 15, 1841
Aug 6, 1895

A. J. Blacknall
Mar 15, 1872
Nov 16, 1902
"Wait dear Alonzo, wait".

John T. Finley
Dec 31, 1858
Jan 16, 1921

Mary E. G., wife of
John T. Finley
Jul 15, 1859
Jul 13, 1906
Age 46 yrs, 11 mos, 28 days
"Gone before us,
wife & Mother".

Howard W. Daniel
Illinois
Pfc Medical Dept
Jan 5, 1908
Nov 6, 1969
&
Laura K. Daniel
Nov 8, 1900

Adolphus W. Daniel
1880-1934
&
Sallie W. Daniel
1880-1950

Wade Daniel
Sep 22, 1904
Mar 17, 1974
&
Edith Daniel
Nov 7, 1910

Harriet F., wife of
N. W. Cowden
Aug 23, 1846
Nov 2, 1883

Dennis Lee, son of
Kenneth & Evelyn Brown
Aug 15, 1949

Ida, dau of
W. A. & M. J. Darnall
born (cemeted through date)
died Aug 24, 1878

Anthony S. Foster
Aug 6, 1851
Feb 29, 1944
&
Mattie E. Foster
Feb 21, 1852
Jun 6, 1937

Calvin Luther Darnall
Jun 4, 1856
Jun 28, 1875

Nathaniel W., son of
C. R. & S. W. Darnall
Sep 27, 1859
Oct 10, 1859
&
Mary C., dau of
C. R. & S. W. Darnall
Apr 13, 1843
Mar 11, 1849

Father
Calvin R. Darnall
Jun 15, 1822
Nov 8, 1870
&
Sallie W. Darnall "Mother"
Jan 31, 1823
Jun 9, 1906

Mary Eliza, dau of
W. T. & Martha Talley
Jun 24, 1867
Jul 11, 1869
Age 2 yrs, 17 days

Sammie, son of
W. T. & Martha Talley
Apr 21, 1865
Apr 17, 1866
Age 11 mos, 26 days

PETERSBURG

William T. Talley
Jun 20, 1836
Mar 30, 1889

Martha, wife of
W. T. Talley
May 8, 1842
Jul 17, 1870
Age 28 yrs, 2 mos, 9 days

Eliza Jane, wife of
W. T. Talley
Oct 19, 1848
Dec 8, 1915

T. Duncan Talley
Jan 8, 1888
May 13, 1965

Samuel Talley
Sep 20, 1812
Jun 8, 1897

Lillie Ann, wife of
Samuel Talley
Died Sep 24, 1876
She was born in
Williamson Co., Tenn.
1813. She was for more
than 30 years member of
Church of Christ.

Sarah, wife of
Samuel Talley
Aug 18, 1826
Feb 23, 1890
Age 63 yrs, 6 mos, 5 days

Annie E., wife of
T. K. Broadway
May 1, 1858
Jul 15, 1883

Reuben J. Logan
Mar 28, 1854
Aug 31, 1893
& wife
Mattie A. Logan
1867-1934

Addie Logan
Sep 20, 1878
Dec 31, 1959

Charlie D. McCrory
Oct 18, 1875
Nov 29, 1955
&
Irene L. McCrory
Feb 5, 1876
Aug 8, 1960

Infant Dau of
Mr. & Mrs. C. D. McCrory
1901-1901

Son
Reuben D. Logan
Jun 10, 1912
Jan 10, 1944

Juranda Logan
Aug 21, 1880
Sep 3, 1970
&
Bertha McCrory Logan
Mar 20, 1883
Aug 25, 1950

May, dau of
J. L. & N. C. Butler
Oct 30, 1901
Oct 20, 1902

Claude Harris
Jan 3, 1869
May 14, 1942

Ann Eliza Talley Harris
Apr 18, 1875
Oct 4, 1952

Father
James P. Terry
May 16, 1856
Feb 23, 1933
&
Mother
Mary S. Terry
Apr 21, 1859
(no date)

Infant Son of
J. P. & M. S. Terry
B&D Dec 8, 1879

Ella Talley
Aug 22, 1876
Jul 22, 1952

Bertha, dau of
J. A. & Margaret Ann Talley
Jul 6, 1883
Feb 9, 1940

Mother
Margaret Ann, wife of
J. A. Talley
Dec 6, 1844
Apr 30, 1924

J. A. Talley
Oct 6, 1834
Jul 9, 1916

Delina Ann, wife of
J. A. Talley
Sep 17, 1837
Nov 1, 1868
Age 31 yrs, 1 mo, 14 days

Albert Sidney, son of
J. A. & D. A. Talley
Feb 16, 1866
Oct 1, 1867
Age 1 yr, 1 mo, 15 days

Benjamin Adrin, son of
J. A. & D. A. Talley
Jul 24, 1868
Sep 30, 1868
Age 2 mos, 6 days

Infant Son of
H. W. & S. A. Hampton
(no dates)

A. S., son of
H. W. & S. A. Hampton
Feb 3, 1876
Jul 14, 1876

Willie H., son of
H. W. & S. A. Hampton
Feb 26, 1883
Mar 31, 1884

Rachel, dau of
H. W. & S. A. Hampton
May 28, 1894
Jul 7, 1897

Father
Henry W. Hampton
Jun 17, 1848
Apr 19, 1914
&
Mother
Susan A. Hampton
Aug 5, 1852
Jul 30, 1918

Roy T. Sanders
1900-1930

Annie Hampton, wife of
W. T. Sanders
Jul 24, 1877
Oct 27, 1906

Herschell Hastings
Aug 27, 1886
Mar 13, 1967
&
Pearl H. Hastings
Jul 20, 1889
(no date)

Harold H. Hastings
Nov 8, 1919
Oct 25, 1944
Tennessee
Staff Sgt 19 Inf Div WW II

Annie Lee, dau of
G. H. & Pearl Hastings
Feb 1, 1916
Jun 21, 1917

Allen B. Talley
1898-1912

Nancy Elma Talley
1868-1915

Lucile Talley
1901-1916

William J. Talley
1859-1933

Infant Son of
Cecil & Rebecca Talley
1933

Delma T. Swanner
1892-1972

Gladys E. Talley
1894-1977

John F. J. Erwin
Nov 4, 1886
Jan 16, 1905

J. Robert Watters
Jul 6, 1887
Feb 27, 1966

Fannie L. Fullerton Watters
Feb 5, 1889
Oct 10, 1946

Mariemma Watters
May 4, 1918
May 21, 1948

Joseph Shuler, son of
J. W. & M. H. Powell
Mar 26, 1880
Dec 6, 1896

June Franklin
1872-1949
&
Sannah Franklin
1879-1947

Thomas F. Dixon
1856-1905
&
Annie B. Dixon
1860-1940

Clarence W. Dixon
Jan 16, 1891
Sep 2, 1968
&
Rufus J. Dixon
Mar 17, 1888
Sep 15, 1968

W. M. Dozier
Dec 15, 1834
Nov 24, 1902
&
N. C. Dozier
Oct 8, 1847
Aug 11, 1934

Infant Son of
W. M. & N. C. Dozier
Jun 26, 1871
Jul 7, 1871
Age 11 days

Will Z. Dozier
May 18, 1877
Oct 30, 1955

Infant Son of
H. M. & S. F. Neill
B&D Jul 9, 1873

PETERSBURG

Emma, dau of
H. M. & S. F. Neill
Feb 16, 1870
Jan 3, 1874
Age 3 yrs, 10 mos, 12 days

Erskine Neill
Jun 9, 1884
Jan 20, 1889

Henry Marshall, son of
James R. & Matilda Neill
Aug 8, 1845
Jul 1, 1890
&
Susan Frances Darnall, dau
of Calvin R. & Sally White
Talley Darnall
May 12, 1848
Nov 3, 1940
Mrd Aug 28, 1867

Maggie A., dau of
W. D. & M. E. Welch
Mar 22, 1884
Apr 11, 1908

W. D. Welch
Aug 21, 1846
Mar 7, 1921

Martha E., wife of
David Welch
Oct 28, 1845
Oct 2, 1915

Dee Petty
1873-1967
&
Lena Petty
1875-1967
&
Eck Petty
1851-1920
&
Fannie Petty
1853-1941

J. Luther Adams
1856-1934
&
Amanda L. Adams
1853-1939

E. Cooper Adams
1865-1933

Ona, wife of
E. C. Adams
May 12, 1871
Nov 21, 1908

Infant Son of
E. C. & Ona Adams
Mar 12, 1903
Nov 15, 1903

Tommie Anna, dau of
E. C. & Ona Adams
Jun 1, 1908
Feb 28, 1909

Richmond Campbell
Dec 18, 1808
Oct 14, 1893

Sallie S., wife of
Richmond Campbell
Dec 13, 1814
Jul 19, 1887
Age 72 yrs, 7 mos, 6 days

William H. Sanders
Nov 21, 1835
Sep 5, 1897

Susan A. Sanders
1838-1921

Edgar Moore Dixon
Jan 16, 1877
Jan 21, 1955

W. H. Dixon
Dec 8, 1839
Nov 25, 1905

Sarah E., wife of
W. H. Dixon
Apr 22, 1850
Oct 10, 1895

Emma, dau of
W. H. & S. E. Dixon
Oct 4, 1872
Oct 4, 1874

Samuel R. Murdock
Jun 3, 1845
Apr 20, 1922

Susan F., wife of
S. R. Murdock
May 7, 1849
Mar 20, 1910

Walter Lee Murdock
Apr 28, 1871
Nov 2, 1875
Age 4 yrs, 6 mos, 14 days

Lebert N., son of
S. R. & S. F. Murdock
Mar 25, 1881
Jan 22, 1897

Ruffus Dudley Murdock
Dec 15, 1892
Apr 14, 1913

L. Marion Jobe
1876-1952
&
Lela Jobe
1878-1959

Sam E. Jobe
Apr 21, 1905
Apr 3, 1923

C. F. Watson
1869-1955
&
Daisy Welch Watson
1870-1941

Roy M. Welch
1903-1959
&
Ann H. Welch
1913-

C. R. "Bud" Welch
1874-1940
&
Bertie Welch
1878-1957

Father
Samuel S. Hemphill
Oct 14, 1849
Apr 28, 1926
&
Mother
Mary M. Hemphill
Oct 14, 1860
Jun 17, 1950

Walter W. Welch
1876-1961
&
Emma H. Welch
1879-1951

Father
Will J. Hemphill
Sep 19, 1880
Jun 4, 1923
&
Mother
Alice L. Hemphill
Apr 17, 1884
Jan 18, 1962

Leonard Watson, son of
W. J. & A. L. Hemphill
Dec 20, 1914
Dec 26, 1914

Charles H. Hill
Nov 15, 1893
May 27, 1948

Albert S. Hill
1877-1954
&
Georgie A. Hill
1880-1965

Adeline Finley
Sep 3, 1860
Apr 1, 1945

Tillman B. Finley
Jan 22, 1816
Mar 2, 1883
Age 67 yrs, 10 days

Elizabeth, wife of
T. B. Finley
Jul 24, 1823-Jan 20, 1907

Mary M., wife of
W. M. Reedy
Nov 17, 1856
Jan 30, 1902

Wright W. Watson
May 1, 1819
Jul 17, 1890

Mother
Roxana L., wife of
W. W. Watson
Oct 27, 1827
Apr 23, 1896

Pinkney Dixon
Sep 26, 1854
Dec 29, 1925

M. E. McKinney, wife of
P. Dixon
Jan 19, 1856
Jul 10, 1917

William M. Dixon
1875-1877
&
Edna C. Dixon
1878-1878
"Children of
P. & M. E. Dixon".

Paul D. Wells
Aug 24, 1928
Apr 25, 1929

A. P. Hill
Aug 16, 1834
May 28, 1903

Sarah J., wife of
A. P. Hill
Dec 21, 1844
Oct 30, 1914

Charlie W. Hill
Nov 28, 1870
Jul 20, 1905

Mary C. Hill
Apr 24, 1873
Nov 30, 1962

Nolan E. Wells
Dec 5, 1874
Oct 13, 1925

Ava H. Wells
1867-1956

Nath Murdock
1870-1952
&
Bettie Murdock
1878-1954
&
Maude Murdock
1903-1974

PETERSBURG

Irene Murdock, wife of
Sam P. Bryant
Jun 28, 1900
Nov 3, 1918

A. Elbert Murdock
Sep 10, 1907

&
Dora C. Murdock
Sep 9, 1908

Ulyss E. Crabtree
1903-1949
&
Mattie A. Crabtree
1905-

W. A. Crabtree
Jan 6, 1880
Mar 15, 1953
&
J. A. Crabtree
Nov 9, 1881
Dec 23, 1940

Paul Conwell
1911-1937
&
Elizabeth Conwell
1911-19

Jerrill Wilson, son of
Paul & Elizabeth Conwell
Feb 17, 1937

P. S. Lovett
Aug 6, 1848
Apr 14, 1914
&
Martha F. Lovett
Dec 18, 1853
Apr 12, 1928

Infant Son of
M. R. & L. E. Luna
Mar 23, 1913
Apr 2, 1913

Liza E. Wells
Jun 18, 1875
Jun 2, 1906

Infant Son of
Mr. & Mrs. N. E. Wells
B&D Apr 5, 1906

Clayburn Wakefield
1886-1954
&
Maggie Sowell Wakefield
1887-1960

Mother
Annie Wakefield
1887-1910

J. B. Luna
1845-1932
&
Callie D. Luna
1847-1905

J. M. Brents
Oct 20, 1809
Jul 21, 1883

Rhoda Davis, wife of
J. M. Brents
Sep 7, 1811
Jul 9, 1899

Victoria Brents
Aug 23, 1847
Sep 2, 1932

Wilson P. Brents
Co H 41 Tenn Inf
C.S.A.

Charlie D. Brown
1895-1939
&
Gaynell M. Brown
1898-19

Edward M. Brown
Apr 17, 1921
Feb 10, 1970

Infant Son of
Mr. & Mrs. Cooper Darnell
Oct 16, 1942

J. Roy Brown
Sep 25, 1901

&
Lillian M. Brown
May 22, 1905

Infant Dau of
Mr. & Mrs. James R. Pack
Jan 21, 1946

Cecil Brown
1933-1937

Henry Haislip
May 20, 1893
Dec 23, 1967
&
Gertie M. Haislip
Apr 12, 1893

&
Brownie R. Haislip
Jul 13, 1925
Jul 13, 1925

Lee A. Brown
1864-1909
&
Tennie Brown
1868-1954

E. J. Brown
1862-1935
&
Martha Brown
1855-1917

N. E. Brown
1860-1929

Clara Brown
1867-1939

Ida D. Brown
1866-1904

Brother
Thomas L. Brown
1867-1933
&
Sister
Louella Brown
1881-(no date)

Mary, wife of
D. A. Ellison
Nov 2, 1844
Aug 19, 1908

James L., son of
Henry & S. J. Brown
Oct 19, 1873
Oct 19, 1892
Age 19 years

(name gone) Brown
Sep 6, 1875
Jan 3, 1886
Age 10 yrs, 3 mos, 27

Sophronia P., dau of
Henry & S. J. Brown
Sep 22, 1878
Aug 17, 1901
Age 22 yrs, 10 mos, 25 days

Henry Brown
Jul 5, 1833
Nov 20, 1909

Sarah J., wife of
Henry Brown
Jan 21, 1842
Aug 13, 1916

Charlie L. Brown
Apr 16, 1871
Jun 28, 1946
&
Lutie N. Brown
Nov 18, 1877
Sep 15, 1958

W. Larmar Meadows
1864-1933
&
Fanie H. Meadows
1869-1939

In Meadow's plot:
marker:
"Brother"

W. I. M.
Born Apr 1895
Died Nov 1955

L. O. Bostick
Jun 5, 1891

&
Maie M. Bostick
Jan 1, 1891
Jun 4, 1962

Everet Bell Bostick
Feb 2, 1915
Jun 17, 1916

Rev. M. B. Creek
May 24, 1832
Jul 3, 1909
"One Old Sinner saved
by grace"

Mary E., wife of
Rev. M. B. Creek
Nov 13, 1837
May 9, 1889
"Was a member of the
Baptist Church for
32 years"

William H. Wells
Jul 31, 1878
Oct 13, 1968
&
Marshall T. Wells
Dec 8, 1881
Jun 10, 1922

George, son of
J. A. & N. A. Creek
Nov 8, 1891
Feb 21, 1892

John A. Crick
1865-1923
&
Nancy A. Crick
1871-1952

Reuben L. Crick
Sep 25, 1902
Oct 25, 1902

John Hobert Crick
Feb 29, 1900
Sep 16, 1976

Clarence L. Crabtree
May 28, 1915
Nov 29, 1974

Willie Wade Wells
May 2, 1925
Aug 28, 1927

PETERSBURG

Leonard Poarch
Aug 31, 1906
Jul 3, 1937
&
Elsie M. Poarch
Apr 5, 1897
Feb 25, 1974

David Wells
Dec 13, 1957
Dec 15, 1957

Cleaburne Haislip
1886-1958
&
Pearl E. Haislip
1894-1970

Mildred Haislip Bradford
Feb 18, 1922
Aug 27, 1950

(End of North Section)

(Middle Section or 2nd Section)

Emmett C. Woodard
1905-1950
&
Clara Woodard
1908-

Jerry W. Woodard
1944-1945

William Loyd Archer
1922-1946
"William Loyd Archer died in the service of his country".
&
Edna Sarah Archer
1925-

Boyd Archer
Aug 10, 1899

&
Ethel Archer
Aug 23, 1903
Mar 19, 1973
Mrd Nov 24, 1918

Wiseman Lyons
Jun 4, 1873
Jan 4, 1960
&
Mary Luna Lyons
Sep 8, 1872
Nov 7, 1954

Guy E. West
1896-1972
&
Gertrude West
1900-1956

Alton J. Owen
Jul 22, 1905
Apr 5, 1968
&
Elizabeth M. Owen
Aug 30, 1926

Father
Andrew J. Murdock
Dec 29, 1874
Jul 8, 1942
& wife
Mother
Ada L. Murdock
Jun 9, 1875
Feb 10, 1917

Lota Murdock
Mar 9, 1901
Oct 16, 1923

G. J. Woodard "Father"
1861-1929
& wife
Mary E. Dixon Woodard "Mother"
1867-1927

Sarah Josiephene, dau of
G. J. & M. E. Woodard
Sep 6, 1892
Aug 27, 1914

William E. Woodard
Aug 24, 1888
Sep 9, 1931
&
Ida Mai Woodard
Mar 29, 1893

William A. Reed
1894-1949
&
Emma Dean Reed
1890-1944

Urban Lee Woodard
Aug 1, 1894
Apr 13, 1954

Mother
Edna W. Hastings
1898-1960

In Memory of
Walter L. Sowell
1884-1949
Buried in Lancaster, PA.

S. Other Sowell
Oct 27, 1888
Nov 30, 1968
&
Bonnie E. Sowell
Jan 31, 1892
Dec 25, 1918

Mother
Amanda P., wife of
Silas Sowell
Nov 11, 1860
Sep 26, 1933

Father
J. Nealy Sowell
Sep 26, 1890
May 11, 1917
&
Mother
Velna Sowell
Oct 7, 1894
Apr 17, 1959

Father
J. Ernest Sowell
Dec 17, 1886
Feb 20, 1917
&
Mother
Lake G. Sowell
May 27, 1889
Aug 4, 1977

William Vinson
Oct 8, 1850
Jun 22, 1913
& wife
Martha Vinson
Aug 3, 1852
(no date)

Joel Dyer
Aug 9, 1863
Feb 18, 1911
&
Dora Dyer
May 16, 1870
Apr 15, 1956

Clyde Dyer
1892-1961
&
Olga D. Dyer
1893-

Hugh, son of
Clyde & Olga Dyer
Aug 18, 1912
Dec 19, 1926

Hobert Dyer
1897-1956
&
Sadie Dyer
1899-

Dorcas Elaine Dyer
1924

Carolyn Ernestine Sowell
Nov 19, 1940
Apr 30, 1941

Rhonda Ruth Hastings
Oct 15, 1952
Jul 3, 1955

Jewell L. Sowell
Oct 19, 1909
Oct 22, 1973

Earl C. Stephenson
Tennessee
Sfc HQ & HQ Co 16 Sig BN
Korea   SS-PH

Alva Watson
1892-1950
&
Vera Watson
1899-1973

John S. Daniel
Mar 28, 1885
Oct 21, 1967
&
Rona B. Daniel
Jan 7, 1888
May 18, 1966

Infant Son of
Mr. & Mrs. John S. Daniel
1925-1925

Austin H. Hampton
Feb 13, 1887
Dec 5, 1942

Edna Earl Hampton
Oct 10, 1906
Jul 19, 1918

Lemuel Loyd Wilkerson
Jun 15, 1868
Jan 29, 1929   "Father"
&
Eliza Daniel Wilkerson
May 29, 1874
May 8, 1908   "Mother"
&
Carrie Sue Wilkerson
Nov 17, 1902
Aug 21, 1921 "Daughter"

Hugh Lane
1896-1913
&
Floyd Lane
1902-1913

Daniel Lane
1860-1944
&
Fanny Lane
1860-1947

R. J. Sowell
Aug 15, 1868
Sep 16, 1946
&
M. E. Sowell
Jan 31, 1874
Jun 24, 1922

Arthur Sowell
1890-1957
&
Erma Watson Sowell
1883-1956

Charlie Arthur Sowell
Feb 10, 1949
Feb 11, 1949

Mother
Mrs. Clay Luna Butler
Aug 18, 1869
May 22, 1940

W. A. Rainey
1866-1950

Minnie Luna, wife of
W. A. Rainey
Aug 7, 1872
Jun 16, 1927

Mrs. Josie P. Sowell
1908-1964

Robert L. Sowell
1894-1954
&
Mary Lou Sowell
1891-1932

Grady Dorris, son of
G. H. & C. J. Hastings
B&D May 29, 1918

Jane Jobe
1852-1935

J. Edward Jobe
1882-1960
&
Daisy L. Jobe
1883-1921
&
Minnie S. Jobe
1891-

Eddie B., son of
J. E. & D. W. Jobe
Jan 2, 1915-Feb 12, 1915

Sgt Paul T. Jobe
1912-1949

Baby
D. W. Jobe
1921-1921

Raymond Duckworth
1899-1955
&
Dessel Duckworth
1896-1972

Eris, dau of
R. W. & D. A. Duckworth
B&D Jun 12, 1923

Lawson Luna
1873-1943
&
Viola Luna
1882-1972

Father
W. H. Tate
Mar 9, 1863
Aug 28, 1931
& wife
Mother
Dora Tate
Mar 30, 1869
Apr 2, 1930

Fred Tate
Feb 28, 1891
Dec 29, 1956
&
Annie Tate
Jul 7, 1891
Oct 23, 1963

J. Ford Franklin
1892-1958
&
Nannie P. Franklin
1894-

Will C. Franklin
1867-1936
&
Dora E. Franklin
1872-1937

Mathew R. Luna
Dec 4, 1875
Nov 14, 1949

Letsie Tucker Luna
Jun 5, 1894
Sep 16, 1967

Vasta, dau of
M. R. & L. E. Luna
Jan 1, 1910
May 1, 1915

Father
Reuben H. Wilkerson
Dec 5, 1886
Feb 9, 1969

Mother
Maxie A. Wilkerson
Jul 20, 1888
Mar 26, 1921

Daughter
Mildred Wilkerson
Jan 16, 1909
Sep 27, 1941

M. A. Watson
Apr 24, 1851
Feb 21, 1926

Donald R. Watson
1941-1941

Roy E. Franklin
1895-1959
&
Edna W. Franklin
1895-1977

James A., son of
R. E. & Edna Franklin
Mar 22, 1925
Apr 10, 1925

Tony C. Plada
Jul 4, 1902
Jun 14, 1968
&
Leta W. Plada
May 28, 1908

Albert "Buddy" Watson
Aug 10, 1882
Mar 9, 1966
&
Ella Lyons Watson
Oct 8, 1874
Jul 23, 1941
&
Lorene O. Watson
Mar 7, 1903

Pattie L. Owen
Died 1977
(Davis-Ralston FH)

Dave Owen
1850-1929
&
Linnie "Sissie" Owen
1868-1951

Billy, son of
Mr. & Mrs. M. E. Partain
Dec 5, 1937

George W. Dodd
Dec 18, 1860
Mar 13, 1948

Elizabeth D. Dodd
Sep 18, 1869
Mar 31, 1937

William Edward Dodd
Jan 7, 1904
Apr 23, 1925
&
Gladys Mae Dodd
Oct 6, 1907
Oct 2, 1976

Clifton B. Wells
Mar 20, 1938
"Baby Boy"

John Rudd
1874-1963

Bert Rudd
Oct 19, 1903
Dec 9, 1945
&
Novella Rudd
Oct 20, 1905

William Pamplin
May 15, 1898
Jun 27, 1943
&
Gracie E. Pamplin
Jun 5, 1896

Gaston C. Anderson
Sep 30, 1898
Apr 15, 1975
&
Martha L. Anderson
Jan 12, 1913

Jeff C. Anderson
1871-1936
&
Ida Clay Anderson
1875-1964

William James Crick
1875-1964
&
Fannie Lee Crick
1873-1943

Mary Ida Crick
1902-1965 (TM)

James Walter Crick
1924-1975
(Davis-Ralston FH)

Emmett Lee Crick
Sep 20, 1888
May 9, 1953
&
Neva Eastland Crick
Mar 19, 1904
Apr 2, 1957

James A. Welch
Feb 12, 1951
Feb 15, 1951

PETERSBURG

Odie E. Dyer
Jun 27, 1888
Mar 12, 1952

Joseph Carlee Dyer   and   Ida Watson Dyer
Dec 7, 1889   Jan 16, 1890
Jan 26, 1971   Dec 18, 1973

Joe E. Dyer
1913-1955

(end of Middle or 2nd Section)

3rd Section

Dorth Y. Brown
Jun 5, 1936

&
Dora Mai Brown
Jul 14, 1966

J. J. Jones
May 4, 1900

&
Clara Mai Brown
Jan 12, 1900

Clyde Holley
Jul 26, 1917

&
Naomi Holley
Sep 12, 1913
May 31, 1967

Mother
Nannie Laura Holley
Jun 1, 1912
May 26, 1978

Robert R. McCormick
1904-1974
&
Ruby J. McCormick
1913-

N. C. Gardner
1888-1966 (TM)

Lillian Ashby
1915-1977
(Davis-Ralston)

Crystal Diane Cole
Dec 11, 1961
Mar 4, 1962

"Daddy"
Ronold Dean "Ronnie" Hargrove
SP 5 U.S. Army Vietnam
Jun 10, 1947
Sep 15, 1977

Logan McCrory
1913-1977

Oliver Omigga Conwell
1890-1976
(Davis-Ralston)

Father
Bobby Sowell
Jan 10, 1941
Oct 30, 1976
&
Mother
Betty Sowell
Sep 16, 1943

Mrd Sep 14, 1962

Garland Asberry Ashby
May 15, 1920
Oct 24, 1973

Aldon Jackson Ashby
1913-1973
(Davis-Ralston)

Eddelene Lentz
1933-1972 (TM)

Charles Everett Holland
1885-1970 (TM)

George Leon McElroy
Apr 28, 1931
Jan 24, 1970

George P. Smith
Sep 20, 1896
Dec 12, 1969

Lillie Wells
1877-(no date)

Mrs. Etta Davis
1899-1961 (TM)

Father
T. Clark McElroy
1899-1963
&
Mother
Ola D. McElroy
1897-1961

James Monroe Brown
Jan 26, 1904
Jan 14, 1973
&
Mary Logan Brown
Oct 16, 1907
Dec 18, 1968

James Conard Spray
B&D Aug 8, 1970

Father
John T. Epps
May 1, 1899
May 7, 1965
&
Mother
Betty O. Epps
Jun 12, 1901

Corbitt R(Roscoe). Luna
Feb 8, 1899
Apr 6, 1976
&
Maudie S. Luna
Dec 4, 1900

Ben H. Massey
Oct 25, 1911

&
Louise W. Massey
May 14, 1911
Feb 22, 1969

Garland L. Crabtree
Oct 6, 1894

&
Robbie Lou Crabtree
Aug 2, 1899

Hubert W. Wells
1910-1978
(Davis-Ralston)

Irvin Humphrey
Sep 3, 1899
Jul 21, 1969
&
Lela F. Humphrey
Oct 5, 1908

William F(Floyd). McClenney
Feb 15, 1952
Dec 27, 1971
&
Edith D. McClenney
Feb 7, 1953

Mrd Jul 1, 1969

James W. Spray, Jr.
Sep 5, 1961
Sep 16, 1961

Will L. Tate
Jun 19, 1897
Oct 16, 1958
&
Jewell Tate
Aug 3, 1905

Father
William E. Bigham
Oct 31, 1906

&
Mother
Velma A. Bigham
Nov 11, 1906

William L. Bigham
1883-1961
&
Clemmie A. Bigham
1883-1953

Joel Thomas McKinney
Nov 15, 1873
Jul 13, 1953

Andrew J. Archer
Apr 7, 1877
Nov 6, 1954
&
Ozella McKinney Archer
Mar 28, 1877
Feb 8, 1960

George Earl Woodard
Mar 10, 1902
Mar 29, 1966
&
Lizzie Mae Woodard
Mar 23, 1903

George C. Woodard
Aug 27, 1933
Jun 8, 1970
&
Ruby H. Woodard
Feb 29, 1940

Mrd Apr 15, 1960

Douglas Wayne, son of
George W., Jr. &
Wilma Sanders
B&D Jun 5, 1960

PETERSBURG

Clarence U. Hastings
Mar 2, 1889
Nov 15, 1970
&
Bessie H. Hastings
Oct 22, 1891
Dec 18, 1971

Lester P. Crane
1906-1966
&
Mary Pearl Crane
1908-

Mary Fannie Pigg
Jan 26, 1890
Jun 20, 1973

Mattie Enola Pigg
Dec 17, 1884
Oct 13, 1968

Paul Joseph Sowell
Oct 20, 1973
(Infant)

Jamie Dawn Welch
Jan 11, 1972
Jan 14, 1972

James A. Johnston
1875-1960
&
Sarah F. Johnston
1875-1962

Mary Ellen Rudd
April 24, 1953
(Infant)

James A. Mosley
Mar 12, 1899
May 6, 1974
&
Fannie M. Mosley
Dec 25, 1903

William Eldred Dodd
Tennessee
TEC 4 U.S. Army WW II
Nov 1, 1925
Mar 30, 1973
&
S. Helen Dodd
Oct 24, 1930

Father
Howard E. Franklin
Sep 10, 1907
Apr 17, 1968
&
Mother
Matilene T. Franklin
Oct 26, 1911

Mrd Feb 7, 1931

Father
Leonard A. Collins
Mar 1, 1915
Apr 25, 1977
&
Mother
Maybelle F. Collins
Apr 14, 1915

Mrd Jul 16, 1938

Will T. Watson
1870-1953
&
Viola F. Watson
1872-1962

Martha Jo Jett
1963-1965

Lee Roy Foster
Dec 31, 1896
Jul 7, 1973
&
Grace W. Foster
Dec 5, 1901

Kenneth V. "Pud" Watson
Aug 27, 1913

&
Lillian Pauline Watson
Feb 23, 1912

Mrd May 21, 1932

Otis Duckworth
Jun 24, 1897
Dec 28, 1967
&
Jewel R. Duckworth
Jan 15, 1907

Mrd Aug 31, 1924

Father
Raymond Earle Verlin
SSgt Army Air Forces WW II
Sep 26, 1921
Nov 9, 1975
&
Mother
Hulene D. Verlin
Mar 20, 1927

(end of 3rd Section)

4th Section

Byron Wynn Adams
Mar 19, 1942
Apr 21, 1975

Alfred W. Adams
Jul 30, 1921

&
Margaret M. Admas
Apr 7, 1923

Mrd Feb 4, 1939

Harry Eugene Sharp
Pvt U.S. Army WW II
Dec 29, 1917
Mar 21, 1976

James Willie Haislip
Jul 30, 1887
(no date)
&
Nannie Bell Haislip
May 24, 1905

Father
Audie T. (Taylor) Hemphill
Aug 1, 1892
Jan 16, 1976
&
Mother
Annie A. Hemphill
Aug 13, 1891

Mrd Dec 25, 1917

Father
Charley M. McCowan
Dec 23, 1903
Nov 27, 1976
&
Mother
Lena M. McCowan
Feb 16, 1906

Mrd Nov 25, 1923

Tommie Mitchell
Sep 23, 1885
Apr 9, 1972
"Our beloved Auntie,
Mother to all."

Lela L. Kerr
1889-1962

James B. Moore
Alabama
Major 484 AAA AW Bn WW II
Nov 16, 1912
Feb 17, 1969
&
Flora S. Moore
Mar 5, 1911

Robert J. Murdock
Mar 5, 1904
Dec 25, 1976
&
Mabel E. Murdock
Mar 7, 1907

David Nelson Murdock
Jun 9, 1957
Jun 5, 1972

(End of 4th Section)

* *

END OF PETERSBURG QUADRANGLE

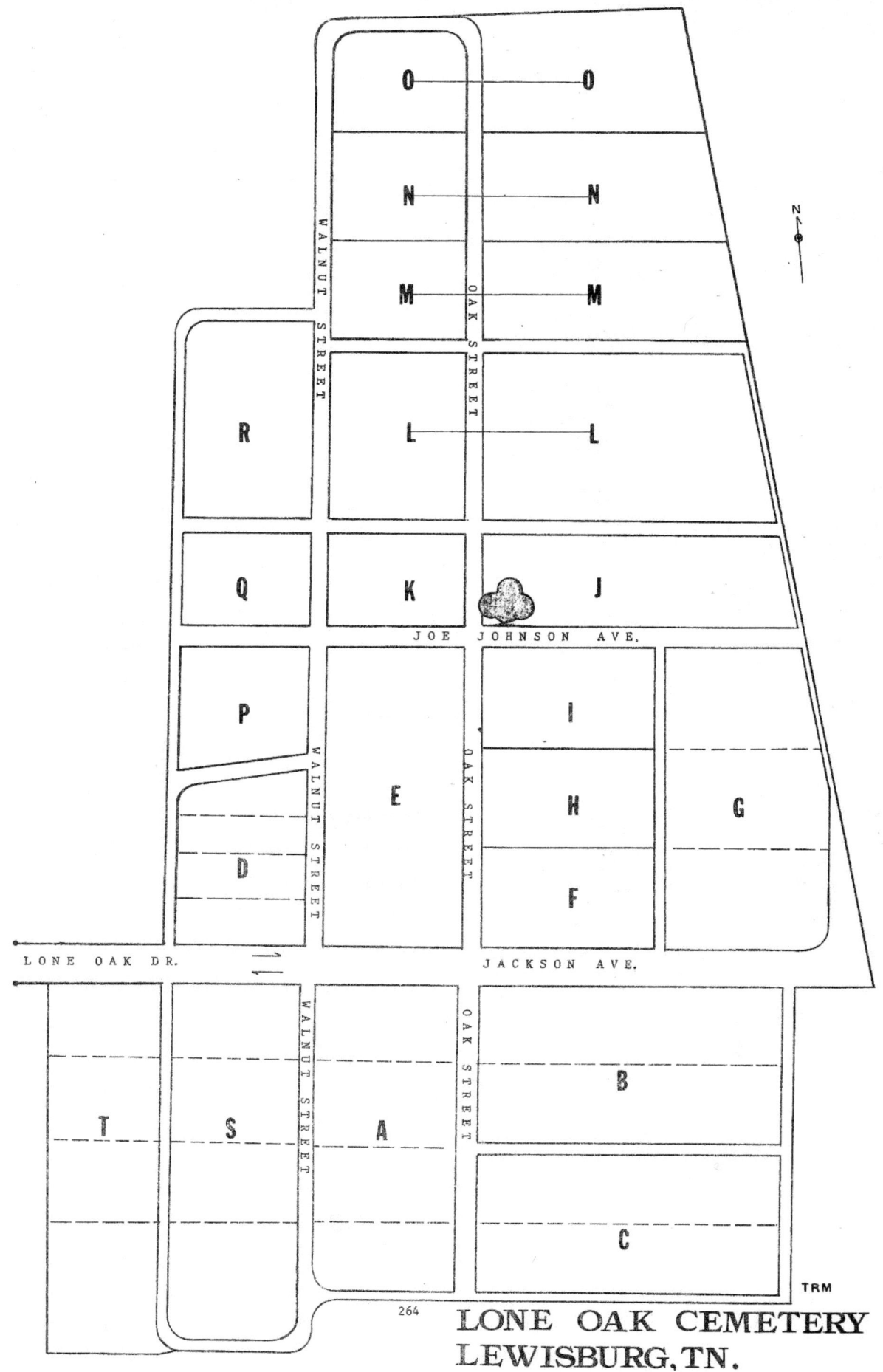

LONE OAK CEMETERY
LEWISBURG, TN.

LEWISBURG QUADRANGLE
LONE OAK CEMETERY

LONE OAK CEMETERY began with the sale of two (2) acres of land by Jesse Mercer Ledbetter and wife Sarah C. in January 1879 for the consideration of $132.00 to Trustees Alvin B. Ewing, Samuel T. Hardison, Jas. M. Hawkins, W. P. Bullock and Jo. A. Carter. In 1894, additional Trustees W. G. Loyd, W. K. Kercheval and A. N. Miller were named, when Mrs. Lucy E. D. Cowden, widow of William N. Cowden sold an additional one and one half (1½) acres, adjoining and to the west and south of the first tract purchased of Ledbetter. In the early 1900's, the cemetery was enlarged again by the purchase of more land from the Hendrix family, with additional purchases made later.

According to headstone inscription dates, there were a few burials here before 1879, on the private property of J. M. Ledbetter. Mt. Carmel Cemetery located about one half mile to the south west of Lone Oak Cemetery, across Rock Creek, was the main Lewisburg Burying Ground until the establishment of Lone Oak Cemetery in 1879.

Lone Oak Cemetery is located one half mile south of Lewisburg Public Square. Interments prior to January 1, 1981. Copied by Helen C. and Timothy R. Marsh.

SECTION "A"

T. W. "Toby" Caruthers
1902-1937
& wife
Mattie Lee Caruthers
1903-

John T. Carothers
1875-1956
&
Mary M. Carothers
1874-1947

I. D. Carothers
1900-1964

Nancy Jennie Osborne
1869-1945

James N. Cathey
1855-1938
&
Lula O. Cathey
1866-1939

Lester J. Miller
1884-1963
&
Gertrude Fox Miller
1886-1974

Richard P. Sharer
1862-1944
&
Mollie B. Sharer
1869-1939

Lillian Jean Guthrie
B & D Nov 23, 1939

Rosa Lee Rogers
Sep 20, 1892
Jan 5, 1970
&
Virginia Glaze
Oct 1, 1872
Nov 17, 1938

William Thomas Sharpe, M.D.
1867-1939
&
Susie Sewell Sharpe
1867-1948

A. H. Beckwith
Jul 18, 1888
Feb 14, 1969
&
Estelle S. Beckwith
Aug 13, 1899

Charlie L. Beever
Apr 28, 1883
Aug 25, 1943
&
Pearl U. Beever
Jun 5, 1900
Apr 27, 1969
mrd Jun 7, 1922

Ave Lucille Upchurch
1899-1956

Vance Luna
1885-1960
&
Iva E. Luna
1906-1960

Lorene Upchurch Clay
1913-1945

Thomas H. Collins
Jan 19, 1873
Oct 28, 1945
&
Eulala A. Collins
Sep 4, 1877
Nov 1, 1948

Nellie Sue Neece
Mar 10, 1961
Jun 26, 1963
(color picture)

James Edward McCoy
Aug 22, 1882
Jan 19, 1969
&
Rachel Hawkins McCoy
Apr 19, 1886
Jun 12, 1954

Charles Harry Beevers, Jr.
Tennessee
S/Sgt Cannon Co
WW II, BSM
Jun 6, 1923
Nov 2, 1960
&
Vernell Beevers
Mar 10, 1930
----
mrd Aug 24, 1946

Joseph E. Harris
1893-1957
&
Mary E. Harris
1892-1952

Edward Vernon Harris
Tennessee
Seaman 1cl USNR
Dec 11, 1925
Feb 3, 1945
"Glory to them that
die in this great
cause."

Baker Powell Harris
Jun 1, 1872
Mar 7, 1956

Irby E. Finley
Tennessee
Pvt Co K 126 Inf
WW I
Apr 18, 1896
Jul 19, 1951

Bertha Mae, wife of
Irby E. Finley
1906-1950

C. B. Brewer
1876-(no date)
&
Mary E. Brewer
1876-1941

Charlie R. Miller
1888-1942
&
Inez Hill Miller
1894-1964

Esker Richardson
Apr 19, 1878
Aug 12, 1943
&
Lizzie C. Richardson
Dec 23, 1878
Jun 30, 1963

Roy J. Bills
1886-1940
&
Carrie C. Bills
1891-1962

Roy J. Bills, Jr.
1917-1944

James Franklin Bryant
Jul 7, 1869
May 27, 1942

Claude C. Lowe
May 13, 1889
Jun 14, 1971
&
Sallie H. Lowe
Jul 9, 1896
May 30, 1942

Lovelace Lowe
Jul 12, 1900
Aug 25, 1979

Gertha Lowe
Nov 21, 1896
Aug 28, 1948

Father
William A. Lowe
1866-1953
&
Mother
Inez Smith Lowe
1870-1960

Robert Ross Lowe
Sep 11, 1898
Jan 30, 1977
&
Mary Charlotte Lowe
Oct 24, 1898
Nov 17, 1971

LEWISBURG

M. Edwina Fowler Cothern
Oct 10, 1919
Jul 30, 1945

Tye C. Dooley
May 10, 1911

&
Grace L. Dooley
Oct 20, 1913
Oct 21, 1968

Brother
Wade H. Dooley
1928-
&
Sister
Hattie B. "Belle" Dooley
1922-1978
(Bills-McGaugh)

Paul W. "Sofie" Johnson
1902-1949

Father
William W. McCrory
1873-1952
&
Mother
Martha C. McCrory
1872-1966

Otey M. Reed
1884-1943
&
Dulcie Reed
1890-1977

James Reed
Jan 6, 1918
Sep 20, 1955

George E. Musgrave
1898-1978
&
Ruby Ann Musgrave

Orville N. Baxter
1904-1979
&
Ruth Leonard Baxter
1909-1941

William Bernie Darnell
1925-1950

Jamie Darnell
1927-1950

Maudie May Darnell
1933-1943

Eugene Darnell
Mar 15, 1903
Feb 7, 1972
&
Nellie Darnell
Sep 15, 1908

Father
Earl H. Wilson, Jr.
Feb 10, 1918

&
Mother
Mildred G. Wilson
Apr 2, 1924
Jun 19, 1976

Hensley Wilson
Cpl US Army
WW I
Feb 26, 1894
Feb 15, 1977
&
Sarah L. Wilson
1898-1977

Infant son of
Cecil & Ophelia Scott
Jun 14, 1928

William C. Scott
Pvt US Army
WW I
Aug 5, 1895
Sep 20, 1976

Lacy O. Seagroves
Mar 11, 1903

Thomas Edward Gambill
1893-1956

Father
W. Thomas Wood
1903-1957
&
Mother
Joanna M. Wood
1903-

Elmer C. Rollins
1901-1980
&
Vera B. Rollins
1907-1960

Sam C. Rollins
1862-1947

Cyril A. Leonard
1880-1944
&
Lillie Leonard
1895-19

Frank Chapman
1872-1950
&
Sally Carpenter Chapman
1881-1945

Fletcher Chapman
1881-1951
&
Ella Chapman
1886-1960

Thomas Pickle
1870-1944
&
Fannie Pickle
1879-1951

Bedford Endsley
1884-1953
&
Frances Endsley
1890-1978

Joe Whitsett
Aug 5, 1878
Nov 24, 1949
&
Effie Lake Whitsett
Jul 20, 1882
Feb 16, 1944

Carl Edward Hinds, Jr.
Jul 7, 1939
Jul 16, 1944

William M. Connelly
Sep 12, 1891
Feb 27, 1979
&
Mattie Felts Connelly
May 20, 1888
Aug 2, 1970

"Aunt Belle"
Mary Belva Connelly
Sep 19, 1889
Feb 12, 1979

Mary K. Minor
1925-1943

Jim F. Ray
Sep 11, 1890
Jul 7, 1974
&
Lucile M. Ray
Jun 10, 1894
Aug 29, 1970

George M. Ray
1926-1943

Thomas V. Brown
1881-1957
&
Maude Brown
1887-1943

Robert Lee Stinson
1868-1944
&
Vertna Hobby Stinson
1886-1958

Father
Thomas Hunter Allen
Feb 12, 1912
Jun 6, 1972
& Mother
Catherine McCullough Allen
Oct 13, 1919

William Harris Allen
Jul 12, 1876
Dec 22, 1942
&
Ruth Hunter Allen
Aug 12, 1884
Oct 8, 1943

Jessie F. Brown
1884-1973

Fanny Brown
1927-1950

Herbert Brown
1873-1942

Mother
Mary Allen
Sep 10, 1870
Feb 15, 1958

John Thompson
1883-1943

J. Ben Green
1898-1941

Mrs. Claudia Green
1898-1969
(London)

Betty June Ray
Oct 23, 1920
Apr 10, 1943

Helen Montez Ray
Tennessee
2 Lieut Army Nurse Corps
Nov 29, 1917
May 12, 1942

Vance D. Whitsett
1942

Fletcher Hill Cathey
May 10, 1899
Jul 10, 1949
&
Margaret Neil Cathey
Nov 12, 1899
May 30, 1972
&
Fletcher Neil Cathey
Nov 17, 1923
Feb 12, 1941

Edgar W. Sims
1909-1948

Ruby Willis Cunningham
1908-1940

James W. Limbaugh
Oct 26, 1899
Oct 13, 1940
&
Thelma S. Limbaugh

LEWISBURG

James Monroe Carter
Apr 2, 1901
Dec 29, 1978
&
Ouida Sanders Carter
Nov 1, 1904

Will F. Richardson
Feb 18, 1868
Apr 18, 1945
&
Mattie West Richardson
Jun 28, 1864
Feb 3, 1941

Leland Clifford McCord
1886-1972
&
Louise Miller McCord

Ed M. Miller
1859-1940
&
Alice Miller
1860-1945

Ervin Miller
Mar 24, 1902

Hugh W. Miller
1885-1953

Maude Miller
Mar 5, 1937

Charles S. Miller
Apr 30, 1936

&
Catherine E. Miller

R. L. Richardson
Jul 12, 1873
Feb 19, 1936
&
Annie Collins Richardson
Nov 26, 1871
Feb 24, 1957

Thomas A. Thompson
Aug 18, 1885
Oct 18, 1967
&
Estelle C. Thompson
Sep 27, 1883
Oct 5, 1941

Dorris M. Little
Tennessee
Pfc Inf Korea
Dec 30, 1929
May 18, 1968

Carl Little
1895-1938
&
Josie Little
1895-

R. M. Glasscock
Oct 15, 1866
Oct 29, 1939
&
Ada D. Glasscock
Apr 4, 1870
Apr 21, 1951

Elizabeth Mallonee
(no dates)
&
Ella Sherman
(no dates)

John William Royster
1909-1946

Ruth L. Royster
1912-

Fay S. Ludington
1887-1970

Irene M. Ludington
1889-1977

John Thomas McCoy
1861-1938

Dona Andrews McCoy
1857-1939

Wilda Nix
Aug 24, 1934
Jun 19, 1935

James O. Nix
Jun 15, 1890
Mar 8, 1938
&
Odeylene Nix
Dec 31, 1892
Sep 19, 1973

John E. Evans
Aug 5, 1854
Oct 14, 1938

Lena M. Evans
Apr 10, 1861
Jun 22, 1937

Florence E. Evans
Feb 13, 1891
Aug 15, 1956

Joseph E. Evans, M.D.
Oct 27, 1898
Jan 25, 1939
Lt. US Navy
"Buried in Arlington
Cemetery, Washington,
D.C."

Will H. Evans
May 22, 1897
Dec 20, 1966

Mary Tate Evans
Apr 25, 1904

John Liggett Evans
Aug 19, 1932
Oct 16, 1953

William L. Barnett
1874-1948
&
Erma Halbert Barnett
1889-1959

Eugenia F. Johnson
1905-1927
&
Mrs. Charles F. Rich
1927-1950
&
Mrs. J. Floyd Murrey
1950-1967

Charles Franklin Rich
North Carolina
Sgt 2 French Mortar BN
Aug 21, 1897
Jul 21, 1938

George E. Hopper
1864-1939

Algie Long Hopper
1876-1938

George W. Yates
Apr 4, 1873
Jul 6, 1951
&
Modena L. Yates
Oct 12, 1879
Oct 15, 1966

Father
William David Farmer
1872-1961

Mother
Annie Mai Farmer
1879-1947

Barney Pickens Orr
Tennessee
Pvt 307 AM TN, 82 Div
Sep 5, 1887
Jul 17, 1937

Mary Farmer Orr Crawford

J. O. Wood
Dec 7, 1876
Aug 22, 1930
&
Nannie Wood
Jul 15, 1882
(no date)

W. Knox Bigham
1876-1949
&
Lena Bigham
1877-1938

Russell Bigham
Mar 11, 1911
Jun 11, 1932

William Virgil Welch
1888-1958
&
Sadie Hardison Welch
1899-1934

Marshall B. Kerr
1884-1947

Louemma H. Kerr
1888-1980

John A. Hargrove
1857-1932
&
L. Belle Hargrove
1860-1948

Chloe Nicholas
Feb 17, 1887
Oct 11, 1936
&
Bessie E. Nicholas
Sep 23, 1894
Dec 4, 1968

J. Wes Nicholas
1864-1948
&
Martha Nicholas
1862-1932

Walter Drake
Jul 16, 1860
Sep 21, 1938

Ida Crutcher Drake
Jun 21, 1867
Apr 2, 1933

Alta Drake
Dec 7, 1887
Aug 28, 1946

Walter Drake, Jr.
Nov 1, 1901
Jun 9, 1948

Joe R. Haynes, Sr.
May 14, 1883
Dec 3, 1962

Margaret Drake Haynes
Mar 12, 1891
Jul 22, 1955

Gideon Rufus Beckham
Mar 1, 1882
Jul 14, 1931
&
Olivia Duncan Beckham
Oct 7, 1888

Alden Lee Poplin
Sep 1, 1907
Apr 16, 1970

LEWISBURG

Tolley I. Cooper
Oct 13, 1886
Apr 9, 1954

Nell A. Cooper
Dec 13, 1886
May 5, 1978

Hunter Barnett
1910-1935
&
Elizabeth Barnett
1912-

William Edwin Poplin, Jr.
Sep 4, 1919
Oct 9, 1976

William Edwin Poplin, Sr.
Nov 16, 1881
Apr 21, 1951

Mabel M. Poplin
Jul 18, 1884
Jun 28, 1965

Mary Ruth Poplin
Jan 23, 1910
Mar 31, 1942

Sallie Cundiff Morton
Apr 5, 1855
Aug 6, 1935

Robert C. Armstrong
1872-1933

Steve D. Tally
Tennessee
Mus. 3 Cl, 114 Fd Arty
30 Div
Dec 12, 1894
Mar 18, 1933

Maxie T. Weaver
Aug 15, 1896

Carl L. Tally
Dec 4, 1916
Jan 3, 1940

Malcolm P. Edwards
1908-1976
&
Mary F. Edwards
1921-

Edd Lee Harris
Jul 11, 1897
Dec 11, 1934
&
Lois Edwards Harris
Jun 9, 1903
Dec 11, 1934

Adam Houk
Feb 24, 1866
Jun 28, 1936

Maggie L. Houk
1872-1940

Dan S., son of
Clayton & Ruth Baxter
1946-1946

Jane Clayton, daughter of
Clayton & Ruth Baxter
1941-1941

Dorothy Joan, daughter of
Clayton & Ruth Baxter
1936-1936

Charlie Stokes
1912-1940

Ruth Stokes
1916-1937

William O. Stokes
Dec 15, 1892
Jun 3, 1968
&
Beulah B. Stokes
May 28, 1891

Audie F. Green
Dec 28, 1880
May 15, 1958
&
Mary Thomas Green
Jan 12, 1885
Apr 1, 1942

Albert L. Sharp
1904-
&
Ethel C. Sharp
1906-1939
&
Georgiana R. Sharp
1915-1974

Albert George Weber, IV
1965-1965

James C. Dooley
1917-1941

John W. Dooley
1881-1957
&
Nannie May Dooley
1877-1955

Barbara E. Thomason
Jun 12, 1939
Aug 1, 1939
&
Bordie B. Thomason
Jun 12, 1939
Jul 30, 1939

Stanley Andrew Watson
1885-1967

Fain Haggard Watson
1889-1955

Stanley Winford Watson
1917-1949

Edna Beryl Watson
1915-1941

Louella Averitt
Jul 10, 1934
Jan 28, 1942

Father
Elmer Odell
Dec 26, 1888
Jan 8, 1964
(picture)
&
Mother
Lou B. Odell
Mar 10, 1899
Dec 27, 1967

James M. Wood
1867-1949
&
Elizabeth G. Wood
1868-1943

Kennie A. Allen
1880-1945
&
Pearl Harwell Allen
1887-1972

Alva C. Houk
Tennessee
Staff Sgt 372 Serv.
Park Unit, QMC
Apr 26, 1942

Margaret May Houk
1898-1948

W. Lawson Lowrance
1883-1943
&
Leota Orr Lowrance
1882-1950

Marvin Earonhart
1901-1943
&
Kate A. Earonhart
1896-

Cathryn Earonhart Simpson
and two infant sons
Feb 28, 1926
Dec 10, 1954

Harvey G. Earonhart
1879-1952
&
Minnie C. Earonhart
1881-1964

Willie M. Barrett
Alabama
Pvt 69 Engineers
WW I
Nov 5, 1892
Mar 13, 1952

Hellen H. Barrett
Jan 4, 1873
May 16, 1953

James M. Thornton
1886-1956
&
Virgie B. Thornton
1891-

Inez Snell White
Apr 5, 1881
Jan 4, 1944

Annie Nowlin
1875-1955

Harry C. Alderdice
1898-1953

Mark W. Cathey
1901-1954

Claudia S. Cathey
1907-1977

William C. Stewart
1883-1957

Mable T. Stewart
1888-1970

Camilla R. Stewart
1920-

Jesse F. Jones
Mar 29, 1886
Sep 12, 1957

Lessie H. Jones
Feb 20, 1897
Mar 10, 1977

W. A. "Babe" Hopper
1869-1952

Arzo Reavis Hopper
1872-1946

Charles Frederick Minturn
1876-1945
&
Leila Houston Minturn
1877-1950

Ellen P. Adams
1897-1943

Sam C. Cochran
1870-1967
&
Oma Alice Cochran
1863-1953

Sister
Delia Cochran
Dec 25, 1858
Dec 30, 1938

Josie Richardson Lankford
1861-1940

Edney Richardson
1871-1949

LEWISBURG

Father
George W. Martin
Sep 17, 1889
Jun 7, 1946
&
Mother
Lillie May Martin
Apr 23, 1894
Sep 1, 1953

Mary Frances Martin
1915-1938

Wilson Collins Beech
Tennessee
Pvt 109 Machine Gun Co
WW I
Oct 26, 1893
Jan 14, 1970
&
Dessa Barron Beech
1898-1937

Thomas J. Reavis
1869-1937

Mary T. Reavis
1877-1973

Raymond Leroy Allen
TEC 3, US Army
WW II
Jul 1, 1908
Apr 18, 1978

Loxie L. Doud
Tennessee
Pvt US Army
Apr 27, 1937

John O. Williams, Jr.
Jun 21, 1929
Apr 29, 1978

Robert N. Turner
1885-1976
&
Sallie E. Turner
1885-1941

Edward M. Woodward
1866-1938
&
Nannie T. Woodward
1864-1946

Martha Jane Derryberry
1936-1936

Mae E. Baxter
May 31, 1887
Oct 24, 1936

Edna L. Baxter
Nov 25, 1911
Apr 15, 1971

Earl Snell
1883-1965
&
Lois Snell
1891-1965

William Gaston London
Feb 4, 1894
Jun 2, 1970

Ercell Rambo London
Sep 11, 1894

Aubrey Williamson
1904-1935

Maud Nix Bacharach
Sep 15, 1886
Oct 22, 1944

Bennie F. Derryberry
1884-1967
&
Mamie Nix Derryberry
1886-

Eddie Derryberry
Nov 16, 1911
Jan 27, 1912

William R. Marshall
1874-1933
&
Kate Haggard Marshall
1873-1951

Sam W. Liggett
1870-1932
&
Olga D. Liggett
1872-1950

William Clay Davis
1884-1931

Verna Davis
1891-1969

John Houston Fitzpatrick
1914-1929

Mary Jane Fitzpatrick
1922-1933

John Paul Fitzpatrick
1884-1961
&
Mary Houston Fitzpatrick
1893-1967

William Akin Houston
Tennessee
Sea US Navy, WW I
Apr 7, 1896
Aug 29, 1955

Cyrus Clay Houston
1860-1936
&
Sallie Robinson Houston
1869-1938

David Ira Shires
1895-1957

William Pillow McClure
1866-1933
&
Alice Cartwright McClure
1869-1941

B. M. Woods
1885-1933
&
Vera Woods
1885-1973

Sherman Cheek
1882-1934

Willie Cheek
1880-1954

End of Section "A"

LEWISBURG

SECTION "B"

James Earnest White
1878-1946
&
Susie Lee White
1893-1972

Melvin A. Walker
1894-1948

Joe Walker, Sr.
Apr 11, 1868
Jan 25, 1951

Joe H. Walker
1889-1960
&
Edna J. Walker
1884-(no date)

Arthur V. Hough
1905-

John D. Weaver
Dec 19, 1878
Oct 2, 1955

Mary Ida Weaver
Oct 3, 1879
Nov 6, 1953

W. O. Weaver
1908-1960

John William Edwards
Apr 17, 1903
Feb 26, 1969
&
Lucille S. Edwards
Nov 9, 1898

Cameron E. Wood
Dec 23, 1922

&
Hilda H. Wood
Sep 27, 1920
Apr 17, 1972

Dorothy Jean Wood
Jun 16, 1946
Jun 19, 1946

A. P. "Aut" Malone
1872-1950
&
Della P. Malone
1882-1974

Mrs. Bessie Cozart
1889-1954
(London)

Mother
Berta Finley Crigger
1874-1948

Dyer Vaughn
1892-1947

Hattie S. Vaughn
1893-1976

Raymond L. Jones
1895-1975
&
Valta C. Jones
1895-1975

F. Edd Jones
1871-1961
&
Margaret F. Jones
1874-1947

Harris McCormick
Jan 1, 1901

&
Loyd McCormick
Dec 26, 1900

Charles W. McCormick
Tennessee
S 1, USNR, WW II
Apr 23, 1923
Mar 17, 1951

Joe Howard McCormick
Tennessee
AS US Navy
Mar 6, 1920
Mar 17, 1951

Addie F. Shaw
May 7, 1879
Feb 13, 1944
&
Willie M. Shaw
Feb 25, 1886
Apr 26, 1962

Thomas W. Cozart
Tennessee
Pfc US Army
May 11, 1943
Apr 3, 1967

William Clifford Cozart
born Jul 11, 1910
Age 38
died May 16, 1948

J. Albert Davis
Dec 3, 1867
Sep 11, 1943

J. Aubrey Collins
1889-1954

Maggie Collins
1883-1942

Rickey Joel Callahan
Dec 3, 1956-Jan 9, 1959
(picture)

Maxie Dockery
1891-1944

J. Marcus Hazelett
1904-1963

Ruby Hazelett
1907-1941

Tom Neal Twitty
1878-1943
&
Lela Mae Twitty
1877-1958

Boyd C. Redd
Jan 11, 1901
Dec 15, 1971
&
Mary T. Redd
Nov 1, 1907

Leslie Reynolds Woodward
1892-1961

Pauline Woodward
1891-1941

Charles David McNutt
1960

Lloyd T. Horner
1887-1941
&
Allie M. Horner
1893-1972

Calvin C. Harwell
1914-1942

Amos Graves
Apr 24, 1889
(no date)
&
Margaret Ann Graves
Jul 17, 1894
Dec 12, 1964

L. Joe Edwards
1870-1940

Sallie Jane Edwards
1867-1943

Odous W. Beatty
1879-1941
&
Addie C. Beatty
1880-1961

Sister
Simmie A. Crabtree
Mar 27, 1883
Sep 30, 1956

Mildred Elora Bennett
1922-1933

Father
H. R. Bennett
1880-1951
&
Mother
Roxie Ann Bennett
1882-1936

Jim L. Bennett
Tennessee
Cpl 16 Air Ship Co
Air SVC, WW I
Feb 9, 1900
Nov 9, 1962

John Lewis Collins
1892-1971

David Fuller Collins
Apr 28, 1887
Nov 29, 1931

Ila Whitehead Sharp
1916-1940

Jerry Duncan Blackburn
1936-1940
&
Jimmie Lee Blackburn
1938-1940

Leo B. Tillman
1872-1939
&
Lula M. Tillman
1879-1958

Zana Lee Osborn
Dec 30, 1890
Nov 20, 1952

Mrs. Annie Margaret Barron
1915-1940

William H. Powell
1857-1948
&
Hattie L. Powell
1865-1943

J. L. Branum
1870-1930
&
Kate Branum
1868-1960

Walter W. Bryant
Sep 6, 1886
Sep 13, 1943

Gladys R. Bryant
Oct 21, 1893
Jul 9, 1971

LEWISBURG

Arthur E. Gipson
Mar 22, 1883
Oct 13, 1939
&
Virgie B. Gipson
Jan 10, 1897

B. F. Tatum
Nov 23, 1850
Aug 20, 1936

Mary Sue Tatum
May 4, 1874
Jun 14, 1954

Father
Melvin T. McCrory
Dec 21, 1907
Sep 4, 1931
&
Mother
Etta M. McCrory
Jul 4, 1906

Loretta Sue McCrory
1961-1961
(Bills-McGaugh)

Robert Lee Davis
1867-1965
&
Clemmie May Davis
1873-1903

Robert Davis
1907-1975
&
Sallie Agnes Davis
1865-1953

John M. Tyree
Sep 17, 1867
Dec 15, 1929

Mary Reynolds Tyree
May 27, 1874
Nov 16, 1950

Columbus Lee Tyree
Sgt US Army, WW I
Jul 26, 1897
Jul 14, 1978

Salene Tyree
Dec 23, 1931
Dec 25, 1931

Jack W. Neese
1909-1930

James Wendle Tatum
Jun 29, 1926
Jul 19, 1930

James C. Gipson
Nov 1, 1903
Aug 14, 1935
&
Vesta G. Gipson
Jan 13, 1902
Jul 21, 1978

Ollie O. Pettes
Jul 7, 1879
Oct 27, 1934

Lillian Pettes Cranford
Nov 19, 1886
(no date)

Eugene Tillman
1911-1942
&
Mildred Tillman
1917-1968

Wallace Richard Tillman
1941

W. E. Purdom
1854-1931
& wife
Bittie Ewing Purdom
1864-1931

Robert Lee Graham
Tennessee
Carpenter's Mate 3 cl
US Navy
Mar 4, 1896
May 23, 1943

Bobby C. Graham
1930-1930

Lilburn R. Crick
May 9, 1890
Nov 1, 1959
&
Alliene P. Crick
Aug 9, 1890

Chesley C. Crick
Feb 2, 1859
May 25, 1930
&
Martha L. Crick
Feb 6, 1865
Sep 14, 1953

Sandy A. Moon
May 24, 1887
Oct 5, 1964
&
Lila C. Moon
Apr 18, 1892
Oct 30, 1976

W. Thomas Cathey
1870-1934
&
Cora P. Cathey
1873-1960

Lucille Duncan
1913-1933

Fred (Thomas) McGaugh
Dec 10, 1893
Jan 8, 1941

"Ike" Ray McGaugh
Aug 9, 1952
Mar 19, 1967

John S. Finley
Died Aug 9, 1930
Age 51 yrs, 1 mo, 29 days

Our Mother
Mrs. Talitha Williams
(no dates)

William Riley Sharpe
1876-1929
&
Delina M. Sharpe
1889-1975

William Sidney Thompson
1845-1935

Harold L. Bills
1899-
&
Emalene W. Bills
1898-

B. J. Adair
1851-1930
&
Georgie Adair
1854-1943

Cladie Simpson
1902-1935

Irene Simpson
1930-1935

Garland Simpson
1927-1935

Clemmie K. Morphis
Sep 11, 1859
Mar 28, 1933

Henry C. Morphis
Co F
1 Alabama Cav
Dec 13, 1842
Nov 8, 1931

Davis W. Hightower
Jun 4, 1899

&
Kate Marks Hightower
May 26, 1903
Jun 5, 1974
Mrd Aug 23, 1925

Ninnah B. Hightower
Sep 6, 1859
May 28, 1931

W. M. Endsley
1860-1931
&
Beatrice Endsley
1875-1945

William A. Bills
1863-1943
&
Annie L. Bills
1871-1959

W. Eric Bills
1895-1965
&
Virginia M. Bills
1911-1965

George Freddie Derryberry
1911-1970
&
Elizabeth A. Derryberry
1912-

John R. Andrews
1886-1967
&
Josie May W. Andrews
1890-1979

Louis B. Cannon
Sep 6, 1893
Sep 4, 1975
& wife
Margaret Andrews Cannon
1890-1930

Frederick H. Orr
1906-1980
&
Grace Adair Orr
1916-1978

Everett F. Adair
1887-1965
&
Allie Louis Adair
1894-1969

Preston
1918-1931
(in Adair plot)

J. Clyde Chunn
Mar 22, 1873
Apr 14, 1951
&
Susie L. Chunn
Jan 9, 1878
Nov 15, 1933

William C. Bowden
1885-1934

Clara M. Bowden
1885-1973

LEWISBURG

G. T. Simmons
1852-1929

Mary Simmons
1873-1964

Dave Stafford
1871-1954
&
Mary Lou Stafford
1877-1961

Cecil Stafford
1907-1930

Gillum Green Stacy
1869-1944

Sallie Wilson Stacy
1869-1930

Clara Mae Stacy
1899-1929

Robert Benton West
Oct 16, 1862
Sep 16, 1929
&
Carrie Cathey West
Feb 22, 1870
Oct 31, 1954

Father
Walter K. Hewitt
Jun 23, 1895
Mar 24, 1968

Mother
Julia H. Hewitt
Aug 31, 1897

Daughter
Mary Neil Hewitt
Feb 11, 1918
Sep 25, 1934

Roy Sharp
1880-1929
&
Venie M. Sharp
1883-1967

John Otis Minturn
1915-1974

Edna Moss Minturn
1919-1967

Joe Chase Adams
1863-1932
&
Margaret Bullock Adams
1865-1956

Ernest Henegar
1893-1965

Joe E. Wheeler
1880-1953

Willie Mai Wheeler
1885-1946

W. Loyd Thompson
1884-1963
&
Leah W. Thompson
1887-1975

Hallie Thompson
1881-1972

Mary Zana Thompson
1879-1933

Mary Jemima London Thompson
1859-1930

Father
William M. Davis
Aug 26, 1873
May 12, 1963
&
Mother
Pearl E. Davis
Dec 17, 1882
Nov 27, 1970

William Claude Cheek
Oct 4, 1884
Jan 3, 1958
&
Lelia B. Cheek
Aug 19, 1891
Aug 27, 1979

Dr. L. E. Wheat
1882-1933

Mattie P. Wheat
1890-1969

Lucile Wheat
Mar 16, 1912
Aug 24, 1936

Dr. Thomas A. Wheat
1915-1951

Bessie Wheat Hardison
1909-1959

Robert Paschall Wooten
B & D Jun 13, 1934

W. W. Mayes
1852-1933

Mary V. Mayes
1863-1950

Willie Mayes Carlton
1886-1971

Martha Mae Brown
1937-1937

Bobby Brown
1929-1934

Mary Catherine Cheatham
Apr 26, 1850
Nov 17, 1933

Cleo Dell Davis
1907-1935

Bob Bennett
Jul 4, 1898
Aug 1, 1965
&
Reilley Ann Bennett
Nov 16, 1900
Nov 5, 1974
Mrd Mar 15, 1915

James B. Savage
1923-1938

Charles Ray Waldrep
Nov 18, 1936
Dec 24, 1936

Maurice Bradford
Sep 18, 1935
Feb 25, 1936

Sister
Lena B. Herring
Nov 26, 1901
Mar 7, 1976

Elmer Paul Moffitt
Tennessee
Fireman 3cl US Navy
Oct 16, 1900
May 15, 1935
&
Jessie Lee Moffitt
Jul 15, 1904

Albert Nafus
1880-1969
&
Cynthia Nafus
1882-1970

Laurence B. Jean
Apr 3, 1897
Mar 20, 1933

William D. Savage
1897-1935
&
Hattie S. McCory Savage
1899-1973

Charlie L. Hickerson
1876-1949
&
Minnie Webb Hickerson
1876-1947 Mrd: Sep 3, 1902

Della Marie Hickerson
1937-1937

William L. Toseland
Jul 14, 1867
Jun 22, 1938
&
Ludie Toseland
Oct 15, 1877
Aug 1, 1963

Luther Milton Nichols
1877-1962
&
Ada Manetho Nichols
1879-1947

Joe M. Holly
1880-1960
&
Lizzie Holly
1884-1935

Peggy Sue Nichols
1937

Rufus George Nichols
Dec 4, 1898
Jan 17, 1972

Onis Holley Nichols
Jul 19, 1906
Oct 19, 1933

Charles H. Allen
Apr 2, 1934
Nov 2, 1947

Barbara Ann Allen
Oct 31, 1937
Apr 18, 1941

Betty Alice Allen
Feb 20, 1940
Apr 18, 1941

John Frank Allen
May 24, 1935
Apr 18, 1941

Edwin B. Moffitt
1874-1937
&
Melva R. Moffitt
1878-1950

Luther E. Wheat, Jr.
1926-1977

Bobby Wheat
1940-1946

H. E. Cox
1874-1951
&
Beulah Cox
1873-1945

Agnes V. Battershell
1873-1961

LEWISBURG

F. W. Mansell
Jan 3, 1887
Jun 6, 1946
&
Lola (Sexton) Mansell
Jun 2, 1902
Nov 10, 1976

Linda Fay Lasater
Feb 24, 1940
Sep 7, 1941

Carl William Lasater
May 9, 1944
Jun 16, 1945

Samuel Henry Rogers, II
Aug 16, 1929
Dec 26, 1929

Samuel Henry Rogers
Mar 15, 1896
Jan 13, 1941

Sarah Ogilvie Rogers
Nov 1, 1898
Mar 12, 1970

Joseph F. Hopkins
1924-1962

Marianne H. Hawkins
1927-1971

Herman A. Hopkins
1900-1979

Marilee W. Hopkins
1900-

Marcus F. Hopkins
1886-1937

Elsie B. Hopkins
1891-1970

Lena Hopkins
1890-1907

Frank M. Hopkins
1861-1908

Sarah F. Hopkins
1859-1929

Annie Lou Hopkins
1882-1968

Thomas M. Fisher
1884-1961

Clatie H. Fisher
1884-1961

Bruce K. Hill
1886-1974

G. Douglas Powell
1886-1940

Winifred Allen
1882-1974

Henry E. Foster, Jr.
1910-1939

Frances Hopkins
1921

Marie H. Warner
1927-1969

Robert P. Hopkins
1888-1950

Lucile Powell Hopkins
1889-1960

Robert Preston Hopkins, Jr.
1911-1966

Ann Wagonon Hopkins
1911-1977

Baby Hopkins
1951

Elmer Brady Bowden
1873-1947
&
Cora Maude Bowden
1874-1941

Walter Augustus Sterne
Tennessee
S1 USNR, WW II
May 16, 1906
Oct 6, 1958
&
Elizabeth Bowden Sterne
1907-1979

Ollie Turner
1878-1945
&
Aetna Turner
1887-1973

William L. Wheatley
Tennessee
Pfc 133 Inf 34 Inf Div
WW II
Apr 22, 1918
Apr 8, 1943

John A. Wheatley
Jun 25, 1916
Apr 7, 1973

Samuel H. Wheatley
1888-1959
&
Edith Lowe Wheatley
1886-1968

Virgil B. Cathey
Apr 8, 1878
Jun 30, 1952

Mother
Maggie Cathey
1877-1949

Newt Ledbetter
1888-1950

Robert W. McKnight
Tennessee
Pfc 818 Tank Destroyer BN
WW II
Jan 6, 1920
Nov 22, 1948

J. Edgar Davis
1872-1948
&
Tellie M. Davis
1880-1978

Howard C. "Dick" Davis
1909-
&
Grace B. "Tiny" Davis
1910-1978

John B. Bowden
Dec 29, 1901
Dec 25, 1974
&
Hazel T. Bowden
Jul 14, 1906

George William Blackburn, Jr.
Jan 1, 1941
Jul 10, 1941

George W. Blackburn
Tennessee
S3 US Navy
Feb 3, 1915
Nov 25, 1973

James Otis Sharp
1884-1948
&
Lena Bell Sharp
1893-19

James D. "Jimmy" Davis
1947-1960
&
James W. Davis
1924-
&
Thelma "Polly" Davis
1927-

Peggie Marie Isley
1934-1950

Lewis T. Trigg
1892-1953

Father
Ward Davis
Tennessee
Pfc Btry A 80 field Arty
WW I
Apr 9, 1891
Mar 27, 1957
&
Mother
Virgie Davis
1905-

Elizabeth "Pinkie" Galbreat
1892-1973

Paul C. Woodward
1915-1975

Jo Carol Woodward
1948-1952

Mary Frances McConnell
1919-1943

Claude F. Miller
Nov 25, 1897
Sep 23, 1953
&
Lena S. Miller
Jun 14, 1906

J. Nolan Battershell
1898-1957

Irene Battershell Bryant
1905-

Ernest W. Hopper
Tennessee
Pvt Co B 26 Machine Gun BN
WW I
Mar 31, 1895
Jun 14, 1961
&
Sara C. Hopper
Jul 23, 1897
Feb 27, 1969

Guy E. Smith
Dec 15, 1907

&
Annie Mae Smith
Feb 12, 1908

Charlie H. Davis
1869-1914
&
Cora Malone Davis
1875-1955

Arnold C. Carroll
Tennessee
Pvt Co E 165 Inf, WW I
Aug 16, 1893
Jul 18, 1961
&
Pallen H. Carroll
Feb 6, 1908

Elizabeth McDaniel
1870-1953

Gratton McCollum
1881-1962
&
Ella May McCollum
1892-1980

LEWISBURG

E. Chesteen Welch	Owen W. Staggs	Rev. B. Jack Staggs	Robert Barry Deason
1910-1950	1906-1969	1876-1948	Oct 19, 1950
			Aug 17, 1968
Leta Welch	Margaret W. Staggs	Rosa Lee Staggs	
1878-1954	1907-	1887-1967	

End of section "B"

SECTION "C"

Julian H. Green
Apr 27, 1909
Jan 10, 1980
&
Dean W. Green
Dec 10, 1914

R. "Hughes" Green
Oct 21, 1881
Apr 6, 1930

Julia "Moss" Green
Aug 3, 1880
Sep 20, 1967

Moss Green
Jul 12, 1903
Dec 7, 1967

Julia J. Green
Oct 11, 1902

Junior Derryberry
Oct 25, 1925
Feb 21, 1977

Ernest Estes
May 1, 1885
Apr 21, 1947

Nettie Estes
Dec 21, 1859
Dec 7, 1933

J. Thomas Dugger
1900-1934

Mildred Anderson Dugger

Thomas Porter Anderson
1874-1949

Golie Fisher Anderson
1876-1959

Jeff Purdom
1860-1937
&
Viola Purdom
1862-1953

Robert Earl Hayes

Sam H. Hayes
1881-1938
&
Josephine Hayes
1878-1951

William T. Wilsford

&
Pearl H. Wilsford

William Ervin Purdom
1865-1936
&
Effie Daisy Purdom
1888-1974

James T. Chapman
1882-1944
&
Manerva Jane Chapman
1882-1958

Kate B. Hayes

Bobbie Hayes, son of
Mr & Mrs H. G. Bryant
1938

H. Grady Bryant
1901-1966
&
Doris H. Bryant

Annie Moore Wilson
1904-1944

James H. Dark
Apr 28, 1879
Jan 26, 1961
&
Cora C. Dark
Jun 15, 1884
Mar 31, 1960

Charlie H. Dark
1910-1949

Mary Eva Dark
1910-1944

Sallie D. Hoskins
Aug 3, 1873
Nov 30, 1959

John Wesley Maddox
Dec 9, 1857
Mar 24, 1939

Albert C. Maddox
119 Inf 30 Div
Apr 30, 1894
Jan 10, 1938
&
Mary Lou Maddox
Feb 6, 1904
Jan 15, 1978

Herman Hooten
May 9, 1910

&
Hattie S. Hooten
Sep 16, 1914

&
Donald Hooten
Sep 29, 1932
Dec 10, 1939

William E. Greer
1891-1945

Father
J. Richard Brown
1893-1947
&
Mother
Johnie M. Brown
1895-

Melvin R. Crunk
Tennessee
Pvt 1458 SVC Comd Unit
WW II, PH
Jan 23, 1914
May 30, 1970

Larston R. Harwell
1890-1946

Father
Gus Harwell
1903-1955

Wyndall B. Kincaid
Tennessee
GM 3C US Navy, WW II
Dec 21, 1924
Feb 9, 1947

Hoyle M. Kincaid
Tennessee
Pfc 504 Mil Police BN
Aug 14, 1928
Aug 3, 1951

James Logan Kincaid
S/Sgt US Army
WW II
1922-1979

Jim Allen
born Dec 30, 1864
died (date in ground)

James R. Green
1883-1965
&
Mary Etta Green
1880-1953

Amos Davis
1878-1946
&
Fannie E. Davis
1882-1975

Haskell Whitsett
1904-1979
&
Sarah Whitsett
1907-
&
Paul Whitsett
1933-1946

John I. Sanders
1874-1947
&
May Etta Sanders
1876-1969

Jim Willie Coggin
1882-1961
&
Florence Williams Coggin
1888-1948

James Grady Coble
1900-1946

Martha Virginia Thomas
Oct 30, 1916
Mar 19, 1960

LEWISBURG

Father
Charlie R. Thomas
1873-1965
&
Mother
Katie Lee Thomas
1882-1971

Robert McCord Fowler
Sep 3, 1952

Uncle
Ben L. Thompson
1884-1949
&
Auntie
Janie L. Thompson
1891-19
Mrd Feb 5, 1911

Frank Cathey
Jan 27, 1878
Oct 1, 1952
&
Lonnie Cathey
Nov 22, 1888

Elbert McCord Fowler
Sgt US Army, WW I
Jan 12, 1895
Jun 15, 1979
&
Bonnie Neil Fowler
Dec 14, 1894
May 21, 1973

John Nelson Alford
1908-1961

Frances Alford Whitaker
1911-1948

Dodson B. Hardison
1895-1954

James Garlan Hardison, Jr.
1947-1947

William Howard Alford
1883-1959

Brownie Jones Alford
1883-1949

James Floyd Murrey
1884-1976
&
Pattie Battle Murrey
1884-1949

Vera Olivia Coffey
Nov 13, 1899
Jan 27, 1978

George O. Thomas
1879-1949
&
Sarah F. Thomas
1881-1967

Father
Alfred Isaac McCullough
Oct 15, 1892
Jul 27, 1975
&
Mother
Lela Coffey McCullough
Sep 4, 1890

Oliver R. Dawson
1880-1949
&
Roxie C. Dawson
1884-1978

Judy Louise Mayse
Aug 28, 1949
Aug 31, 1949

Henry C. McKay
1905-1951
&
Nina L. McKay
1915-

J. Buford Hastings
1885-1956
&
Emma P. Hastings
1888-1969

Thomas Porter Anderson
1899-1949
&
Lois M. Anderson
1900-1971

Rev. Calvin P. Cox
1882-1948
&
Katherine Rambo Cox
1902-1956

Edward E. Kincaid
Apr 3, 1888
Nov 12, 1970
&
Rachel H. Kincaid
May 27, 1892
Jan 21, 1969

Father
W. O. "Bill" Hazlett
Mar 6, 1899
Feb 22, 1955
&
Mother
Edna P. Hazlett
Apr 21, 1904

Scott A. McCurdy
1884-1957
&
Fannie May McCurdy
1889-1955

Paul S. Sharp
Tennessee
Pvt Mil Police Corps
WW II
Feb 25, 1910
Jan 4, 1971

Walter Knox Calahan
1881-1955
(Bills-McGaugh)

Cecil W. Talley
1906-1950
&
Rebecca H. Talley
1911-19

Cheryl L. Gallegly
Nov 28, 1958
Jul 3, 1960

Rodger W. Gallegly
Apr 3, 1957
Sep 16, 1957

Walter W. Tyree
1904-1975
&
Mable B. Tyree
1909-

Arthur Dean Buzan
Jan 24, 1901
Aug 16, 1971

Dorothy Bryant Buzan
Nov 9, 1918
Aug 25, 1974

Homer Allen Bryant
1893-1949

Albert L. Darnell
1911-1949
&
Ruby I. Darnell
1914-

Father
Orville Barron
Apr 9, 1887
Dec 5, 1957
&
Mother
Elnora G. Barron
Aug 7, 1887
Nov 9, 1974

Charles T. Higdon
1905-1961
&
Glendon W. Higdon
1921-1978

James Ross Woodruff
1952-1952

William Floyd Nix
Tennessee
CBM US Navy, WW II
Sep 12, 1921
Sep 16, 1970

Willie Jeanne Nix
1945-1954

John R. Smith
Jul 6, 1876
Aug 28, 1967
&
Jennie M. Smith
Dec 2, 1898
Mar 27, 1974

John W. Davis
Mar 26, 1910
Apr 2, 1966
&
Imogene W. Davis
Jan 11, 1917

Our Son
Gary Keith Davis
Sep 23, 1940
Oct 1, 1961

John A. Evans
1892-1952
&
Lucylle L. Evans
1891-19

Garland D. Cunningham
Nov 29, 1900
Oct 6, 1970
&
Willie A. Cunningham
Dec 31, 1902

Thomas Leigh Thompson
1863-1954
&
De Waller Thompson
(no dates)

Robert S. Escue
May 19, 1890
Jan 23, 1970
&
Edna E. Escue
Jul 22, 1891

Robin Lyle Smith
born in Wurzburg, Germany
Oct 27, 1968
Oct 28, 1968

Jimmie Sharp
1906-1954

LEWISBURG

Father
Willie B. Carroll
Jun 11, 1916
Mar 25, 1971
&
Mother
Melba W. Carroll
Jan 29, 1921

Mrd Jun 29, 1941

Father
Timothy P. Thompson
Oct 25, 1881
Feb 5, 1950
&
Mother
Angie Z. Thompson
Feb 2, 1880
Nov 4, 1962

Father
Jesse B. Baxter
1923-1961
&
Mother
Ruth E. Baxter
1921-1952

Buford Lee Baxter
1953-1953
(London)

Bozzie Brisby
1877-1949
&
Gertie Brisby
1879-1959

Sidney C. Wilson
Mar 25, 1900
Apr 9, 1955
&
Mildred B. Wilson

Kimberly Allison, dau of
Hilrey & Mary Frances Carr
Jul 11, 1961
Jul 17, 1961

Roy A. Petty
1884-1948

Laura Estes Petty
1887-1964

Frances B. Whaley
Jul 19, 1915
Sep 1, 1954

W. B. McAdams
Sep 27, 1879
Feb 10, 1958
&
Laila McAdams
Apr 18, 1883
May 18, 1952

Alex F. Nix
Dec 25, 1886
Jul 12, 1975

Sadie H. Nix
Aug 26, 1895
Jan 2, 1973

Travis Gipson
Jun 5, 1943
Sep 21, 1968
&
Peggy Gipson
Apr 7, 1950

Guy H. Bryant
1905-1952

Lucille Bryant
Apr 18, 1909
Jan 16, 1973

James F. Stafford
1874-1954
&
C. Caroline Stafford
1877-1963

James A. Stafford
1910-1980
(London)

Howard M. Wilson
1893-1959

Don W. Luna
1878-1950
&
Nannie L. Luna
1885-1956

Clyde Hoyt Cozart
Sep 5, 1912
Mar 13, 1969
&
Mamie L. Gifford Cozart
Oct 20, 1907
Dec 4, 1948

Wash H. Higdon (Father)
Nov 15, 1884
Feb 15, 1956
&
Josie S. Higdon (Mother)
Nov 6, 1885
May 21, 1973

Father
Shirley Hobby
Tennessee
Pfc Btry A, 80 field Arty
WW I
Jun 22, 1895
Dec 10, 1956
 & Mother
Pauline Hobby
1888-1959

Rufus E. Henry
husband of Jane T. Henry
Feb 6, 1909-Apr 23, 1971

J. Clifford Hardison
1905-1949
&
Jane T. Hardison
1910-

Charles H. Hosea
1902-1948
&
Sallie M. Hosea
1903-

E. C. Bud Brown
Cpl Btry A, 103 AAA
BN CAC, WW II
Jun 6, 1920
Nov 30, 1968
&
Martha B. Brown
Jan 10, 1920

Judy Carol Brown
1949

Earl K. Minor
Mar 24, 1890
Jun 3, 1970
&
Martha E. Minor
Sep 26, 1903

Earl W. Minor
1921-1948

Phillip Larry Murrell
Dec 6, 1948
Jun 22, 1968

Anthony S. Watson
1875-1947
&
Mary E. Watson
1885-1966

Charles Clarence Brown
Oct 27, 1898
Sep 2, 1973
&
Annie Ruth Brisby Brown
Jan 23, 1903
Sep 17, 1970

Walter L. Brown
1923-1947

Infant of
Mr & Mrs Charles Thomas
(no dates)

Cornelia A. Watson
Mar 19, 1881
Dec 7, 1962

Dora A. Cheek
May 10, 1868
Feb 7, 1953

Father
Robert Lee Roddy
Nov 5, 1888
Oct 24, 1956

Mother
Dora Mai Roddy
Apr 22, 1892
Nov 30, 1968

Father
Thomas E. Roddy
Jun 22, 1911
Jun 23, 1948
&
Mother
Ester Roddy
Apr 13, 1914

William L. McGaha
1887-(no date)
&
Alice E. McGaha
1885-1949

A. N. "Nick" Balthrop
Jul 11, 1899
Mar 21, 1949

Azzie A. Higdon
1890-1948
&
Dovie M. Higdon
1898-1972

Claudie Neal Cozart
Tennessee
Pvt US Army, WW II
Aug 19, 1906
Mar 4, 1963

John William Cozart
Jul 8, 1876
Nov 3, 1953
&
Jennie P. Cozart
Jul 5, 1877
Aug 13, 1953

William B. Cozart
Tennessee
Pfc 320 Inf 27 Inf Div
WW II
Dec 22, 1920
Nov 8, 1944

Bobby Gene Manly
S2 US Navy, WW II
Jul 19, 1930
Sep 3, 1947

Shula B. Davis
1898-1947
&
Bessie J. Davis
1907-

Dan Patrick Wiser
1947-1947

LEWISBURG

John Robert Boyett
Tennessee
Pfc US Marine Corps
WW II
Apr 20, 1909
Jan 13, 1973
&
Lois Ownby Boyett
May 17, 1913

C. Orin Barron
1894-1947
&
Eula M. Barron
1895-1959

William W. Barron
Capt. US Navy
Korea, Vietnam
Nov 25, 1923
Mar 29, 1979

Samuel Gratton Thompson
Dec 11, 1883
Mar 25, 1965
&
Alice Irene Thompson
Aug 26, 1901
Mar 8, 1972
Mrd Aug 8, 1918

John W. Cunningham
1873-1948
&
Mary F. Cunningham
1879-1967

A. Journal Trammel
1881-1957
&
Flora L. Trammel
1881-1963

Lenna Kyle, dau of
G. W. & L. A. Yarbrough
Aug 2, 1899
Nov 12, 1900

Father
George W. Yarbrough
Jan 16, 1844
Sep 1, 1918
&
Mother
Lucy A. Yarbrough
Dec 22, 1863
Apr 28, 1949

Cheryl Denise Keller
Jul 5, 1962

Nannie W. Ridner
Jun 10, 1863
Mar 7, 1948

Sarah Elizabeth Gopson Tyree
wife of Carl Tyree
Feb 23, 1907
Feb 20, 1971

Sessions L. Gipson
1902-1968
&
Gladys B. Gipson
1907-1970

Sister
Annie "Mary" Burlason
Aug 4, 1908
Jan 14, 1972

Father
Joe Sy Burlason
1882-1947
&
Mother
Annie T. Burlason
1885-1963

Wayne Middleton
May 22, 1913
Feb 5, 1980
&
Kathleen Middleton
Aug 18, 1913
May 8, 1977

Edna Middleton Sweet
1944-1976

Mrs. Lou Annie Dean
1923-1949
(London)

Elmer Collins Middleton
1916-1975

Inez G. Middleton
1916-1972

Flora Middleton
1879-1946

Clay Crane
1877-1931
&
Naomi Crane
1887-1946

Joe Loyd Wheatley
1895-1948

Etta Orr Wheatley
1869-1953

Seagal V. Wheatley
Feb 3, 1907
Jan 2, 1969

Daniel Ezekiel Powell
1870-1959
&
Nancy Margaret Powell
1873-1956

Charles Edward Neese
"Buddy"
1930-1950

Letha K. Neese
1948-1948

Theodore Joseph Miller
Jun 6, 1889
Mar 10, 1962

Myrtle Lee Wheatley Miller
Sep 21, 1898
Mar 28, 1957

John Cullen Beard, M.D.
Dec 16, 1895
May 7, 1946

Robbie May Beard
May 1, 1901

Frank F. Thomas
Mar 7, 1902
Sep 29, 1979
&
Mai Belle A. Thomas
Sep 3, 1904

Mrd Dec 22, 1922

Maggie Neeld Hill
1862-1948

Gladys Hill
1902-1963

Harold Manley
Jul 19, 1907
Jul 19, 1969
&
Will Eva Manley
May 23, 1910

Eugene A. Beasley
1887-1968
&
Myrtle C. Beasley
1888-1953

Father
Archie Glenn Vanhorn
Nov 10, 1890
Oct 9, 1972
&
Mother
Clelia Lowe Vanhorn
Sep 18, 1894

C. L. Harris
Jul 4, 1884
May 12, 1965

Rosa Lee Harris
Sep 15, 1883
Apr 21, 1952

Ruth Harris Weaver
Jul 6, 1913
Jan 28, 1961

Mrs. Susie B. Harwell
1918-1976
(Bills-McGaugh)

Cecil "Shorty" Harwell
1906-1968
"Pa Pa"

Paschell L. Bennett
Oct 13, 1903
Aug 5, 1968

R. L. "Bob" Brown
1866-1946
&
Mattie J. Brown
1866-1946

Earnest Guy Bigger, Sr.
Jan 10, 1895
Jan 12, 1952

Ozella Bigger
Apr 14, 1894
Mar 25, 1972

Earnest Guy Bigger, Jr.
Feb 9, 1926
Mar 6, 1946

Earnestine Bigger Watson
Feb 9, 1926
Sep 16, 1949

Robert C. McMillion
1874-1964

Mamie F. McMillion
1893-1970

Roy C. Luna
Tennessee
Mech Btry B 12 field Arty
WW I
Mar 25, 1892
Jun 22, 1966

Evelyn F. Luna
Apr 22, 1915

James H. Davis
Jan 29, 1884
Jun 24, 1970
&
Annie Bet Davis
Dec 21, 1890
Jun 10, 1952

John N. Lowrance
1878-1955
&
Leota G. Lowrance
1879-1965

John G. Bradley
1902-
&
Lena May Bradley
1903-

LEWISBURG

William H. Helmick
Nov 19, 1885
Feb 17, 1964
&
Corinne L. Helmick
Jan 24, 1890
Nov 15, 1972

William Lewis Doster
Jul 23, 1907
Feb 20, 1979
&
Edith P. Doster
Aug 9, 1910

Ollie F. Orr
1867-1960
&
Sallie E. Orr
1871-1944

Jesse B. Jones
1885-1957
&
Ruby B. Jones
1888-19

In Memory of
James E. Clark
who gave his life in
the defense of his
Country July 25, 1944
Age 29 years.

Mary Dorcas, infant dau
of J. A. & Alice F. Clark
Nov 26, 1913

James A. Clark
1874-1941

Alice F. Clark
died Jun 21, 1955
(no age given)

Morgan Cunningham
1903-1979

Steel B. Gibson
1869-1942
&
Carrie H. Gibson
1870-1949

George C. Gibson
1903-1939

Mercer D. Ledbetter
1883-1942
&
Effie N. Ledbetter
1884-1955

Clarence M. Petty
1875-1937
&
Ellen M. Petty
1880-1938

Ela E. Hayes
1883-1964
&
Zadie L. Hayes
1863-1946

Howard N. Liggett
Tennessee
Pfc 50th AMB Co, WW I
1890-1937
&
Mary S. Liggett
1898-1960

End of Section "C"

SECTION "D"

Odell Hobby
Nov 14, 1904
Mar 8, 1952
&
Sarah Hobby
Jun 11, 1914
Mar 28, 1976
Mrd Jan 3, 1928

H. Wilkie Emmerson
Dec 11, 1878
Jan 12, 1959

Jack A. Ownby
May 28, 1885
Jan 17, 1953
&
Fannie Mai Ownby
Jun 24, 1892

W. E. Thomason
Apr 7, 1888
Aug 16, 1953

Rainie B. Hargrove
Jun 20, 1897
Jun 27, 1967
&
Bessie E. Hargrove
May 10, 1898
Sep 29, 1955

Robert O. Montgomery
Oct 31, 1903
Jan 4, 1970
&
Louise T. Montgomery
Aug 19, 1907
Jul 28, 1964

Effie Harris
Mar 29, 1881

Ada Harris
Feb 28, 1878
Aug 28, 1952

James W. Chunn, Sr.
Tennessee
Pvt US Army, WW II
Nov 11, 1914
May 15, 1969

Velna Jones Chunn
1896-1961

Solone Collins
Nov 30, 1899
Oct 9, 1950

Tom L. Thompson
1870-1950
&
Sallie B. Thompson
1876-1953

Euel F. Thompson
1897-1955

Luther Allen Glasscock
Dec 30, 1886
Feb 15, 1962
&
Myrtle May Glasscock
Jan 15, 1889
Oct 24, 1952

Ernestine Davis Killingsworth
Jun 13, 1873
Sep 14, 1950

James R. Haskins
Jun 6, 1894
Mar 6, 1938

M. Georgia Haskins
Mar 5, 1898
Feb 16, 1969

Charles W. "Deete" Haskins
Sep 17, 1928
May 5, 1951

Nancy E. Haskins
Nov 18, 1915
Mar 28, 1917

James Douglas Burrow
1953-1953

Walter W. Whitehead
Jul 13, 1870
Jul 26, 1952
&
Lillie J. Whitehead
May 10, 1890
Dec 9, 1959

Mart Taylor Chilton
Tennessee
Mech Sup Co 115 Fd Arty
WW I
Dec 25, 1889
Mar 17, 1953
&
Minnie A. Chilton
1895-1974

R. Stanley Baxter
Sep 12, 1903
Sep 13, 1971
&
Ellis R. Baxter
Dec 2, 1906

Jesse C. Ingram, Sr.
1878-1952
&
Lela G. Ingram
1883-1966

Douglas Eugene Adkins
Feb 6, 1952
Feb 6, 1952

William Michel Steele
Sep 25, 1950
Sep 26, 1950

LEWISBURG

William H. Helmick
Nov 19, 1885
Feb 17, 1964
&
Corinne L. Helmick
Jan 24, 1890
Nov 15, 1972

William Lewis Doster
Jul 23, 1907
Feb 20, 1979
&
Edith P. Doster
Aug 9, 1910

Ollie F. Orr
1867-1960
&
Sallie E. Orr
1871-1944

Jesse B. Jones
1885-1957
&
Ruby B. Jones
1888-19

In Memory of
James E. Clark
who gave his life in
the defense of his
Country July 25, 1944
Age 29 years.

Mary Dorcas, infant dau
of J. A. & Alice F. Clark
Nov 26, 1913

James A. Clark
1874-1941

Alice F. Clark
died Jun 21, 1955
(no age given)

Morgan Cunningham
1903-1979

Steel B. Gibson
1869-1942
&
Carrie H. Gibson
1870-1949

George C. Gibson
1903-1939

Mercer D. Ledbetter
1883-1942
&
Effie N. Ledbetter
1884-1955

Clarence M. Petty
1875-1937
&
Ellen M. Petty
1880-1938

Ela E. Hayes
1883-1964
&
Zadie L. Hayes
1863-1946

Howard N. Liggett
Tennessee
Pfc 50th AMB Co, WW I
1890-1937
&
Mary S. Liggett
1898-1960

End of Section "C"

SECTION "D"

Odell Hobby
Nov 14, 1904
Mar 8, 1952
&
Sarah Hobby
Jun 11, 1914
Mar 28, 1976
Mrd Jan 3, 1928

H. Wilkie Emmerson
Dec 11, 1878
Jan 12, 1959

Jack A. Ownby
May 28, 1885
Jan 17, 1953
&
Fannie Mai Ownby
Jun 24, 1892

W. E. Thomason
Apr 7, 1888
Aug 16, 1953

Rainie B. Hargrove
Jun 20, 1897
Jun 27, 1967
&
Bessie E. Hargrove
May 10, 1898
Sep 29, 1955

Robert O. Montgomery
Oct 31, 1903
Jan 4, 1970
&
Louise T. Montgomery
Aug 19, 1907
Jul 28, 1964

Effie Harris
Mar 29, 1881

Ada Harris
Feb 28, 1878
Aug 28, 1952

James W. Chunn, Sr.
Tennessee
Pvt US Army, WW II
Nov 11, 1914
May 15, 1969

Velna Jones Chunn
1896-1961

Solone Collins
Nov 30, 1899
Oct 9, 1950

Tom L. Thompson
1870-1950
&
Sallie B. Thompson
1876-1953

Euel F. Thompson
1897-1955

Luther Allen Glasscock
Dec 30, 1886
Feb 15, 1962
&
Myrtle May Glasscock
Jan 15, 1889
Oct 24, 1952

Ernestine Davis Killingsworth
Jun 13, 1873
Sep 14, 1950

James R. Haskins
Jun 6, 1894
Mar 6, 1938

M. Georgia Haskins
Mar 5, 1898
Feb 16, 1969

Charles W. "Deete" Haskins
Sep 17, 1928
May 5, 1951

Nancy E. Haskins
Nov 18, 1915
Mar 28, 1917

James Douglas Burrow
1953-1953

Walter W. Whitehead
Jul 13, 1870
Jul 26, 1952
&
Lillie J. Whitehead
May 10, 1890
Dec 9, 1959

Mart Taylor Chilton
Tennessee
Mech Sup Co 115 Fd Arty
WW I
Dec 25, 1889
Mar 17, 1953
&
Minnie A. Chilton
1895-1974

R. Stanley Baxter
Sep 12, 1903
Sep 13, 1971
&
Ellis R. Baxter
Dec 2, 1906

Jesse C. Ingram, Sr.
1878-1952
&
Lela G. Ingram
1883-1966

Douglas Eugene Adkins
Feb 6, 1952
Feb 6, 1952

William Michel Steele
Sep 25, 1950
Sep 26, 1950

Father
Charles A. West
Oct 19, 1924

&
Mother
Lois Y. West
May 24, 1926

Mrd Oct 20, 1945

Tommie Dale West
    Oct 5, 1950

Edna Mai Bailey Parker
1922-1951

Coy L. Bailey
Tennessee
Pvt Sup Co 102 Inf
WW I
Sep 2, 1889
Jun 17, 1958
&
Ruth C. Bailey
1900-

Henry R. Ragsdale
Cpl Army Air Forces
May 11, 1923
May 21, 1974

Margaret Bailey Ragsdale
1925-

Thomas M. Ervin
Sep 30, 1903
Jul 17, 1954

Kennie M. Baxter
Aug 31, 1882
Oct 20, 1962
&
Sallie Baxter
Dec 6, 1885
Oct 1, 1962

Minnie Bell Burns
Aug 11, 1906
Aug 24, 1953

Jesse R. Darnell
1890-1962
&
Zana L. Darnell
1881-1965

Lindsey Dockery
1897-1978
(Bills-McGaugh)

Kineth Dockery
1895-1961

Father
James Thadeus Ownby
Mar 29, 1887
Jan 10, 1971
&
Mother
Winnie Lunn Ownby
Dec 21, 1891

Juanita Cooper
Jan 6, 1949
Jul 24, 1970

Mary C. Cooper
Oct 21, 1947
Jun 20, 1952

C. L. "Pete" Cooper
Jan 8, 1928

Wanda D. Cooper
Mar 15, 1928

George M. Rutledge
1899-1951
&
Lucile Rutledge
1900-1975

Joe Lee Steele
Apr 17, 1887
Feb 19, 1969
&
Nannie E. Steele
Jan 7, 1903

Nancy Sue Steele
1936-1952

J. E. McCord
Oct 9, 1885
Oct 27, 1954

Kate Davidson, wife of
J. Everit McCord
1893-1952

Adrain J. Calahan
1878-1953
&
Pearl R. Calahan
1886-1955

W. T. "Tom" Golden
Feb 6, 1879
Feb 26, 1969
&
Martha K. Golden
Jun 7, 1902
Mar 9, 1969

William John, son of
Mr & Mrs W. T. Golden
Jun 1, 1925
Oct 23, 1953

Luther C. Holly
Sep 2, 1882
Feb 5, 1963
&
Ozella Jobe Holly
Aug 15, 1886
May 19, 1954

Loyd Richardson
Mar 6, 1910

&
Tommie Richardson
Dec 7, 1909
Aug 11, 1955

J. D. Whitehead
1920-1953
&
Mary Whitehead
1913-

Tommy Dale Farler
Apr 25, 1974
Apr 25, 1974

Trudy Lee Roberts
Dec 27, 1964
Dec 29, 1964

Kenneth D. Hobby
1964-1964
(Bills-McGaugh)

Bernie M. Sharp
1912-1958
&
Mary L. Sharp
1912-

Ray Luker
May 9, 1937
Feb 4, 1972

Edgar L. Broadway
Tennessee
Wagoner Sup Co 318 Fd Arty
WW I
Feb 20, 1892
Aug 22, 1954

William E. Wilburn
Feb 16, 1929
Sep 28, 1967

Garland C. Carothers
1914-1954

Clint Carothers
Mar 8, 1891
Feb 26, 1965

Sallie B. Carothers
Sep 7, 1892
Jul 5, 1969

Thomas D. Carothers
Jun 14, 1916
Mar 9, 1976

J. P. Orr
Tennessee
Pvt Co D 26 MG BN, WW I
Feb 15, 1896
Mar 29, 1971
&
Lacie S. Orr
Jan 1, 1898
Apr 10, 1956

John T. Foster
Sep 3, 1908
Aug 1, 1972

Ethel Johnson Foster
1916-1953

Arthur N. Sawyers
Jun 12, 1909
May 17, 1979
&
Sarah B. Sawyers
Oct 7, 1916

Mrd Dec 8, 1938

Fowler Alex Cathey
Tennessee
Pfc Co A 26 Machine Gun BN
WW I
Nov 3, 1893
Mar 8, 1954
&
Annie Mae Cathey
1892-1971

Buford Richardson
Tennessee
S1 US Navy, WW II
Mar 3, 1921
Dec 12, 1971
&
Elizabeth Richardson
Jul 30, 1927

John T. Haynes
Apr 12, 1908
Dec 14, 1968
&
Annie R. Haynes
Nov 26, 1913

Mrd Oct 18, 1930

James L. Hargrove
Tennessee
TEC 4 US Army, WW II
Dec 20, 1925
Feb 13, 1968

Samuel James Chessor
Tennessee
M Sgt US Air Force
AM & 3 OLC, WW II
Sep 8, 1922
Mar 17, 1954
&
Imogene Chessor
Feb 23, 1922
Sep 4, 1980
Mrd Dec 1, 1943

John Capps
1899-1972
&
Hautie Mai Capps
1899-1955

LEWISBURG

Leslie B. Johnson
1884-1954

Media M. Johnson
1897-1960

Margie B. Fowler
May 17, 1880
Nov 15, 1954

Celina Antonia Foster
June 5, 1962

Ernest H. Millen
1901-1958
&
Morraine W. Millen
1911-

Joyce Hargrove
Aug 24, 1955

Lottie Edmondson
1898-1955

David "Dave" Thompson
Tennessee
Pfc 160 Co Trans Corps
WW I
Feb 22, 1890
Jun 13, 1954
&
Ida B. Thompson
Feb 7, 1904
Oct 6, 1976

James Martin Middleton
1868-1953
&
Lillie Frances Middleton
1878-1969

James Middleton
Jun 9, 1919
Feb 19, 1968
&
Dorlene Middleton
May 28, 1922

Homer Fullerton
Dec 5, 1884
Jul 22, 1978
&
Velna L. Fullerton
May 10, 1886
Jun 11, 1968

Father
Claud Jones
1885-1955
&
Mother
Minnie Jones
1890-1957

John L. Johnson
May 19, 1906
May 20, 1977

Annie B. Johnson
Aug 28, 1910
Mar 24, 1952

James Massey Rainey
ACAD USNR, WW II
Apr 14, 1923
Sep 28, 1955

James Rauden Rainey
Aug 3, 1893
Feb 5, 1954

A. Woodson Gates
1910-1959

Regina Gayle Gates
1947-1951

Ollie K. Wilkes
Jun 15, 1881
Feb 2, 1961

Regina R. Wilkes
Nov 21, 1884
Jan 30, 1964

Thomas F. Cheek
Apr 25, 1894
Jul 1, 1950

Elizabeth Hendrix Cheek
Dec 27, 1899
Oct 25, 1969

Father
Eddie Thomas Curtis
Sep 1, 1874
Apr 6, 1950
&
Mother
Bettie Curtis
Sep 21, 1878
Apr 4, 1963

Jake Crigger
1872-1950

Blanche Crigger
1886-1963

Mother
Minnie Fowler Meyer
Dec 14, 1876
Sep 24, 1950

Otis Wilson Cathey
Sep 5, 1898
Jun 23, 1956

Jim Willie Crigger
Aug 24, 1904
Mar 1, 1950

Jimmy Maxon Crigger
Jan 16, 1951
Mar 9, 1980

Earl Buford Ellington
1907-1972

Catherine Cheek Ellington
1908-

William Bernie Hendrix
1891-1960
&
Era H. Hendrix
1893-

Loyd C. Bates
1892-1950
&
Lucy T. Bates
1897-19

Herman M. Hayes
1901-1957
&
Lillie V. Hayes
1906-

Herman Mark Hayes
Tennessee
Pfc 351 Inf 36 Div
WW II
Mar 29, 1925
Sep 27, 1944

Paul W. Foster, M.D.
Jul 12, 1894
Feb 19, 1950

Saydie Powell Foster
Apr 4, 1906
Dec 28, 1979

Charles Cecil Hopper
Jun 16, 1898
Jan 4, 1969
&
Minnilee T. Hopper
Nov 17, 1901

Tom W. George
Jan 7, 1872
Jan 13, 1947

Mattie E. George
1876-1957

Maggie E. West
1897-1958

Fred E. Wegold
1889-1957
&
Henrie J. Wegold
1899-1978

Edgar Folk Lambert
1892-1949

Pauline Dance Lambert
1899-1971

J. M. Lambert
1866-1946

Martha Ann Lambert
1866-1948

Gertrude L. Childers
1888-1966

E. Folk Lambert, Jr.
Apr 5, 1917
May 20, 1971

J. T. "Tom" Chiles
Nov 22, 1869
Apr 3, 1961
&
Geneva J. Chiles
Jan 7, 1870
Jun 15, 1949

Jerry Wayne Hargrove
Nov 22, 1949
Aug 28, 1965
(picture)

Father
Otis M. Coggin
1879-1954
&
Mother
Emma C. Coggin
1881-1970

James McCord
Tennessee
Pvt 115 Inf 29 Inf Div
WW II
Sep 30, 1914
Aug 7, 1944

William E. McCord
Oct 22, 1880
Sep 11, 1948
&
Tommie P. McCord
Jun 16, 1888
Oct 23, 1961

Petrica Hargrove
Apr 4, 1954

M. L. Akins
1862-1951

Grady E. Fowler
Tennessee
Pvt US Army, WW II
Jan 13, 1908
May 9, 1960

Cecil Fox Fowler
1889-1959

William Fox Fowler
1905-1956

LEWISBURG

Spain Beasley Gibson
1909-1970
&
Thelma Farmer Gibson

Father
James M. House
Aug 19, 1884
Jan 22, 1969
&
Mother
Phoebe J. House
Apr 10, 1885
Nov 15, 1970
Mrd Feb 12, 1908

Ernest T. Williams
1892-1980
&
Clemmie W. Williams
1899-1957

John Washington Zumbro
1887-1977

Grace Victoria Stephens
      Zumbro
1895-1972

Harold R. Hagen
1893-1979

F. M. "Bud" Harwell
1876-1966
&
Tennie E. Harwell
1875-1947

Father
Ernest J. Glasscock
1897-1948
&
Mother
Zelna C. Glasscock
1897-

S. A. "Aud" Green
1904-1976
&
Verna H. Green
1906-

John Mark Wheeler
Mar 24, 1961
Jan 20, 1977

Willie L. Higdon
1904-1950
&
Ella M. Higdon
1910-

Tom Keel
1896-1955

Birdie Keel
1892-1966

Forrest E. Finley
May 15, 1901
Apr 7, 1971
&
Leah C. Finley
Mar 15, 1896
Jan 8, 1971

Alice Craig
1865-1950

Joe E. Collins
Aug 17, 1902
May 28, 1949
&
Annie M. Collins
May 21, 1904

Joe Fry London
Feb 17, 1902
Oct 2, 1963
&
Mattie Mae London
Oct 11, 1904

William Cobia Barron
1917-
Son of Ezra & Annie C. Barron
G/S of Thomas Jefferson
      Barron, 1852-1929
G/G/S of John Alexander
      Barron, 1825-1863
G/G/G/S of William Barron,
      1801-1868
&
Willie E. Farrior Barron
1913-
Dau of Julian Eugene &
      Gussie Green Farrior,
      Sand Mountain, Alabama

Edmund J. Vaughter
Tennessee
SM2 US Navy, WW II
Dec 13, 1923
Sep 26, 1950

Amos Crunk
1889-1972
&
Annie Crunk
1897-

Sidney A. Weaver
1895-1976

Atherton C. Holman
1876-1952
&
Susie A. Holman
1882-1961

Roy H. Roberts
1899-1954

End of Section "D"

Ezra Barron
1891-1963
&
Annie May Barron
1898-

Herman Purdom
Dec 6, 1910
Dec 27, 1975
&
Eula Lee "Sis" Purdom
Feb 13, 1909
Aug 21, 1948

Luther G. Hill
Apr 27, 1898
Jun 10, 1974
&
Elizabeth T. Hill
Jul 31, 1900

C. Alton Harrison
Sep 17, 1904
Mar 28, 1979
&
Margaret C. Harrison
May 7, 1903
Nov 7, 1969

James T. Wood
Jan 23, 1913
(Dec 12), 1980
&
Verna G. Wood
Oct 8, 1913

Thomas Cordell, son of
Mr & Mrs J. T. Wood
Mar 14, 1950
Apr 2, 1950

E. Birdwell Glasscock
Apr 10, 1894
Apr 16, 1966
&
Mamie B. Glasscock
Nov 11, 1895
Mar 19, 1964

Father
Jessie Louis Corbin
Feb 13, 1887
Mar 14, 1951

Will N. Garrett
Oct 16, 1881
Jun 7, 1933

Ozella M. Garrett
Jun 19, 1882
Jun 9, 1960

Richard Sampson
Tennessee
Cpl Co C 32 Inf 7 Inf Div
Korea, PH
Jul 29, 1930
Oct 16, 1952

Edward L. Garrett
Mar 22, 1904
Jun 9, 1950

E. Randalle Garrett
Mar 26, 1929
Feb 20, 1951

James H. Cheek
1890-1975
&
Ethel H. Cheek
1896-

Clyde Harold Vann
May 2, 1916
Jan 30, 1956

Rollie Ewell Lasater
1898-1963
&
Eddye Elizabeth Lasater
1901-1952

Mary Jobe Taylor
Aug 25, 1901
Feb 26, 1952

Father
John W. Hargrove
Tennessee
Pfc Co E 55 Inf, WW I
Jun 15, 1892
Apr 2, 1954
&
Mother
Sadie P. Hargrove
1903-

Lemuel S. Leonard
1877-1951
&
Alice C. Leonard
1878-1965

Ezelle D. Thompson
Tennessee
SC2 US Navy, WW II
Oct 18, 1911
Jan 3, 1953

Talmage Young
May 22, 1888
Nov 23, 1953
&
Bessie Young
Nov 3, 1896

Father
Arthur G. "Doc" Sampson
May 15, 1890
Feb 18, 1971
&
Mother
Elsie T. Sampson
Apr 26, 1900
Sep 1, 1974
Mrd Apr 25, 1929

LEWISBURG

SECTION "E"

William Otha Turner
1875-1936
&
Sallie Davis Turner
1877-1974
Infant
(All on stone, in Turner plot)

Robert H. Hayes
1858-1933
&
May Hilliard Hayes
1862-1954

Mary Jean Cowden
1922-

John Walter Cowden
1879-1937

Saleen Hayes Cowden
1888-1972

Oliver M. Lyles
Jul 18, 1893

Corinne H. Lyles
Jul 17, 1895
Oct 18, 1975

Gertrude "Trudie"
  Granville Poindexter
1880-1972

James Luther Collins
1884-1953
&
Nancy Lee Green Collins
1889-19

Thomas Newton Green
1880-1954
&
Willie M. Green
1881-1959

Father
J. W. Green
Jun 29, 1851
Dec 30, 1926
& wife
Nancy Swofford Green
Sep 23, 1847
Jul 26, 1909

Christine, dau of
Robert L. & Cleo Pierce
Jan 12, 1909
Jan 18, 1909

John M. Pierce
Oct 26, 1863
(no date)
& wife
Mollie Pierce
May 18, 1861
Nov 8, 1913
& wife
Ella Pierce
Sep 26, 1871
(no date)

Mother
Grace Gibson Cantrell
May 27, 1908
Jul 29, 1955

Max Erwin
1890-1969
&
Ladell Erwin
1896-1974

Zela Gantner
1894-1971

Robert L. Tally
Jun 30, 1866
Aug 14, 1929

Ora D. Tally
Sep 19, 1872
Mar 29, 1949

W. T. Duncan
1849-1934
&
Elizabeth Duncan
1851-1913

W. T. Luna
Apr 22, 1873
Aug 21, 1912
(3 unmarked graves
beside this grave)

Thomas Wallace
1900-1943

James Zack Wallace
Tennessee
1st Sgt 8 Co 55 Depot
Brig, WW I
Mar 6, 1890
Nov 23, 1957

Thomas A. Wallace
1861-1934

Lu Bine Billington Wallace
1871-1962

Myrtle Wallace
1893-1916

Lucille Wallace
1905-1955

Margaret Wallace
1897-1970

Jas. C. Redd
Aug 21, 1876
Oct 28, 1911

Beulah Ann Redd
Dec 16, 1877
Jan 27, 1947

Mabel Redd
Apr 25, 1911
Sep 13, 1945

Robert H. Harwell
1888-1960
&
Ida P. Harwell
1890-1975

Clara L. Harwell
Nov 1, 1907
Sep 8, 1908

Thomas C. Cunningham
Apr 4, 1903

Elizabeth Orr Cunningham
Apr 18, 1908

G. M. Taylor
Oct 29, 1844
Feb 13, 1917
"I have tried"
&
Roe E. Taylor
Sep 11, 1855
Jan 17, 1935

Ruth Hightower
Apr 30, 1912
May 5, 1912
&
Nell Hightower
Apr 30, 1912
May 6, 1912

Fred B. Hightower, Jr.
Dec 21, 1909
Mar 12, 1915

Nora Burrel Hightower
Dec 3, 1905
Jan 16, 1924

Fred B. Hightower, Sr.
Apr 4, 1870
Jul 28, 1953

Victory F. Woodward
1859-1917
&
Alice M. Woodward
1862-1946

Claud Marion Pigg
Aug 1, 1888
Oct 28, 1970
&
Anes Bond Pigg
Mar 12, 1893

Paul Preston Haggard
1893-1965
&
Ruth Hastings Haggard
1896-1970

William P. Hastings
May 18, 1867
Aug 16, 1948
&
Mary Friel Hastings
died Apr 4, 1939
(no age given)

Boyd W. Hastings
1899-1916

Mattie S. Hastings
1854-1925

Father
J. D. Turner
Dec 13, 1832
Apr 26, 1918
&
Mother
M. A. Turner
Apr 28, 1838
(no date)

Robert Clyde Turner
Jul 20, 1886
Oct 9, 1916

Father
William Howard Gates
Sep 8, 1909
Aug 27, 1976
&
Mother
Sadie Grace Gates
Jan 8, 1914

Marvin Woodard Gates
Feb 16, 1934
Apr 12, 1947

Father
John Franklin Woodward
Nov 16, 1877
Aug 31, 1954
&
Mother
Mary Hays Woodward
Jul 6, 1884
Dec 8, 1865

LEWISBURG

Palestine L. Martin
1861-1916
&
Huldah Jane Martin
1863-1936

George B. Baxter
Jan 20, 1899
Dec 22, 1968
&
Buena T. Baxter
Aug 27, 1902
Jul 28, 1980

John A. Taylor
Oct 16, 1843
Nov 20, 1917
&
M. Malvina Taylor
Mar 14, 1851
Apr 1, 1927

Father
Walter M. Collins
Oct 9, 1885
Jan 24, 1959
&
Maxie M. Collins
Apr 4, 1886
Nov 22, 1963

Berry B. Head
1882-1964
&
Pearl Duncan Head
1884-

Joe Tom Duncan
Apr 22, 1897

&
Nannie Mae Duncan
Oct 22, 1897
Dec 14, 1977

Mary L., wife of
J. T. Stafford
Oct 5, 1850
May 9, 1914

Sanford J. King
1874-1942

Carrie M. King
1875-1969

Otis B. Craig
Jun 11, 1899
Jan 8, 1924

J. L. Finley
Jan 5, 1852
Nov 4, 1918

Arthur Glenn Jean
1881-1979

Bertha Ewing Jean
1879-1924

Howard Payne Jean
1905-1941

Sallie Shires Jean
1891-1965

Ercy Noel Welch
1899-1966
&
Ruth Jean Welch
1903-

F. P. Harmond
1866-(no date)

Lavinie Harmond
1872-1940

Mable Harmond
1902-1912

James Alexander Bond
Feb 28, 1864
Feb 10, 1940
&
Mattie Hightower Bond
Aug 22, 1863
Jan 25, 1939

Argyle Bond
Mar 22, 1888
Jul 14, 1970

Lounora Bond Pickens
Nov 6, 1895
Oct 5, 1976

Elmo Bond
Jan 10, 1886
Feb 8, 1963
&
Ora Cheatham Bond
Feb 10, 1886
Dec 20, 1956

Francis L. Woods
Aug 6, 1840
Jun 4, 1909

Wilma Baxter Mitchell
May 22, 1892
Nov 20, 1965

Billy B. Mitchell
Tennessee
Pvt 8 Med BN
Aug 27, 1922
May 15, 1943
"He gave his all"

Will Nat Baxter
1900-1927

William H. Baxter
Tennessee
Pvt 248 Fd Arty BN, WW II
Apr 5, 1924
Apr 6, 1948

William P. Webster
Tennessee
Pvt 39 Inf 4 Div
died Apr 16, 1932
(no age given)

Milton Gross Nowlin
Feb 4, 1854
Dec 30, 1907
&
Mary Thomas Wilson Nowlin
Sep 13, 1865
Feb 11, 1930

Frank Wilson Nowlin
Nov 5, 1904
Apr 5, 1922

James E. Collins
1916-1916
&
Mary Ann Collins
1931-1931

Grover Collins
1888-1943

Mrs. Jennie Phifer Collins
Jennie Collins
1889-1938

Allen Newton Coffey
Dec 14, 1833
Nov 24, 1909
&
Mary C. Coffey
Sep 19, 1834
Jan 4, 1915

Infant of
Mr & Mrs V. C. Harwell
Mar 31, 1926

R. A. Fergus
1857-1918
&
Fannie C. Fergus
1861-1945

Margaret Fergus
1890-1961

Daughter
Fannie Vera Haney
1925-1926

Hattie V. Little
1917-1918

Edwin G. Fitzpatrick
1887-1925

James B. Marsh
Tennessee
Pvt 26 M.G.BN 9 Div
Mar 10, 1942

David Cannon Sanders
Nov 28, 1847
Feb 26, 1919
& wife
Laura Brooks Sanders
Jun 16, 1849
Aug 16, 1926

Annie Lui Sanders
died Nov 13, 1898
Age 22 yrs, 3 mo, 2 days

Robert Sanders
Co G
4 Tenn Inf
Sp. Am. War

Charles S. Sanders
1885-1949
&
Maxine B. Sanders
1888-

Jasper Lee Bailey
1864-1933
&
Alice M. Bailey
1867-1947

Father
Montie E. Chunn
Sep 24, 1889
May 7, 1958
&
Mother
Daisy E. Chunn
Dec 5, 1895
Jun 18, 1967

George Morrison
1849-1927

Eliza Morrison
1855-1938

A. B. Winford
1866-1929

Maggie Winford
1872-1932

Julius Winford
1895-1918
"Son"

Thomas Roy Turner
Sep 8, 1883
Mar 2, 1947
&
Willie Roberts Turner
Mar 5, 1886
May 14, 1968

J. Ben Turner
1859-1940
&
Mary Ann Turner
1864-1928

Wardell Harwell
Oct 9, 1900
Oct 19, 1914

Douglas McLean
1902-1970
&
Mary McLean
1902-
& Daughter
Nancy McLean
1935-1957

LEWISBURG

Thomas Leonard Cathey
1888-1964

Clifford B. Whitehead
Tennessee
Pvt Co E 1 Casual Regt
WW 1
Dec 8, 1897
Jul 23, 1962

J. M. Corbin
1860-1925
& wife
M. C. Corbin
1866-1923

Pvt Samuel Flones Corbin
Co 14, A. E. F.
Jul 12, 1893
Oct 7, 1918

Bruce A. Bryant
Oct 5, 1891
Jun 22, 1968
&
Callie B. Bryant
Aug 22, 1896
May 8, 1972

James E. Sanders
Jul 11, 1851
Jul 13, 1923

Father
William B. Trammel
Sep 16, 1848
Nov 25, 1922
&
Mother
Mary Jane Trammel
May 20, 1848
Jun 22, 1927

"Aunt"
Nan Trammel
Jul 3, 1845
May 3, 1934

Maxie Mae Trammel
Mar 27, 1907
Oct 23, 1923

Mittie T. McCurdy
1873-1957
"Sister"

Kelvia A. Wilson
Apr 13, 1883
Nov 11, 1971
&
Minerva Ewen Wilson
Dec 2, 1887
Apr 3, 1959

Father
J. Claud Garrett
Sep 30, 1887
Apr 10, 1967
&
Mother
Nora T. Garrett
Feb 27, 1892
Nov 14, 1974

William S. Ketchum
1865-1924
&
Melissa Ketchum
1868-1935

J. Lillard Ketchum
Dec 6, 1910
Nov 2, 1949

Thomas H. Wilson
May 25, 1854
Aug 6, 1935

May L. Wilson
Jan 16, 1872
Jul 19, 1946

Madge Wilson
May 28, 1904
Jan 9, 1926

John William Wilson
Dec 31, 1911
May 29, 1956

Mary C. Wilson
Jan 11, 1902
Feb 4, 1979

Mother Hopwood
1868-1927
&
Brother Hopwood
1893-1917
&
Sister Hopwood
1897-1927

Ray Gowens
Feb 22, 1894
Apr 2, 1943
&
Mabel Rebecca Nowlin Gowens
Nov 24, 1894
Jun 8, 1961

Peter Walton
May 16, 1845
Aug 7, 1908

John C., son of
H. F. & S. W. Barnett
1929

Robert L., son of
H. F. & S. W. Barnett
1933

John William Nichols
1870-1924
&
Ida Kercheval Nichols
1871-1930

Maynie Nichols
1901-1954

Claude E. Tillman
Apr 28, 1888
Apr 11, 1968
&
Nannie M. Tillman
Feb 23, 1892
Jul 6, 1971

Mother
Alice Jones Hurt
1868-1948

John R. Tillman
Aug 30, 1883
Dec 14, 1925
&
Ada F. Tillman
Aug 19, 1888
Feb 5, 1967

Thad N. Beasley
1881-1924
&
Levada Beasley
1883-1947

Jackson Beasley
Aug 22, 1921
Apr 15, 1937

Dorothy Sue Lee
Dec 2, 1909-
Jun 6, 1923

Claude J. Lee
Aug 29, 1876
Nov 3, 1927
&
Clara Ada Lee
Dec 6, 1877
Mar 2, 1965

John Clay Lee
1846-1926
&
Mary Jane Reavis Lee
1842-1926

Samuel M. Haskins
Sep 29, 1881
May 8, 1960
&
Mary C. Haskins
Apr 1, 1885
Jun 3, 1962

Tom Allen Little
1914-1980
(London)

William Tommie Little
Jan 26, 1893
May 4, 1924
&
Kitty A. Little
Jun 26, 1894
Jun 21, 1968

James E. Ramsey
Tennessee
TEC 5 541 Ord HV Maint
WW II
Dec 16, 1910
Sep 12, 1971

John Perry Ramsey
1883-1963
&
Seletha Gray Ramsey
1884-1954

Geraldine Ramsey
1904-1920
Age 16

Clarence C. Adams
May 1, 1896
Oct 7, 1937

Father
Robert A. Adams
Oct 7, 1852
Mar 28, 1924
&
Mother
Mollie E. Adams
Sep 14, 1852
Jul 4, 1928

Mother
Mary Emma Fowler
Apr 18, 1878
Feb 26, 1937

Burnie L. Collins
1889-1924

B. L. Collins, Jr.
May 25, 1920
Dec 4, 1920

F. Emory Burt
Nov 30, 1896
Mar 24, 1966
&
Lois A. Burt
Oct 20, 1896
Jul 24, 1977

Billie Burt
May 7, 1902
Feb 19, 1920

J. Floyd Burt
Apr 13, 1866
Dec 25, 1941
&
Tina M. Burt
May 13, 1874
Dec 1, 1957

LEWISBURG

Thomas H. Wakefield
1880-1918

Mother
Anna Wakefield
1879-1938
(another stone:
Anna Landis
Jun 5, 1879
Sep 12, 1938
Mrd to Thomas H Wakefield,
1906-1918 & to W. R.
Hightower, 1923-1938)

Michelle Gay, dau of
David & Marion Tyree
Aug 20, 1963
Nov 15, 1963

James T. Cheatham
1922-1959

Will T. Cheatham
1874-1935

Mary W. Cheatham
1894-1976

Infant Son of
Mr & Mrs Will T. Cheatham
B & D Dec 3, 1919

James S. Ledford
Dec 11, 1871
Dec 5, 1920

Eliza Ledford
Jun 2, 1872
Mar 14, 1950

Lewis A. Woodward
Aug 25, 1873
Oct 2, 1950

William Frank Ledford
Jan 8, 1899
Sep 10, 1976

Lenis B. Ledford
Aug 13, 1902

John R. Albright
Jan 14, 1902
Nov 16, 1957

Paul Stanley Batey
May 29, 1902
Aug 4, 1971

Joe L. Batey
Mar 10, 1856
Mar 5, 1941

Ellen Ledbetter Batey
May 13, 1869
Feb 22, 1947

James M. Batey
Aug 26, 1897
Sep 8, 1964

Robert L. Devin
Aug 1, 1869
Dec 26, 1909
   & wife
Clara B. Devin
Aug 31, 1873
Aug 11, 1965

Lee Allen
1868-1960
&
Lizzie Allen
1869-1956

Father
William R. Little
TEC 5 US Army, WW II
Jan 27, 1924
Jun 25, 1975
&
Mother
Donna M. Little
Jan 24, 1936

Mrd May 16, 1959

Lizzie Miller, dau of
Thomas M. & Bittie
McClary Little
Sep 22, 1890
Aug 14, 1975

Mac O. Little
1902-1951

McClary Foster, Infant
son of McClary Odell &
Nell Foster Little
Jun 6, 1937
Jun 8, 1937

Bobby Ray Averitt
1952-1952
(Bills-McGaugh)

Nannie M. Averitt
(no dates)
(Bills-McGaugh)

Mother
Rosa Bell Avrit
1902-1937

Walter Howard Averitt
(no dates)
(Bills-McGaugh)

Edd Ray
1877-1965
&
Emma S. Ray
1887-1956

Robert Ray
1908-1926

Seth E. Thomason
Jun 6, 1929
May 20, 1932

Julius H. Edwards
1866-1930

Florence Edwards
1874-1926

Dewey E. Long
1898-
&
Thomas Solon Long
1888-1960

Earl L. Neese
Tennessee
Pvt 27 AA Repl Tng BN
CAC WW II
May 16, 1897
Sep 3, 1948

William Martin Carter
1868-1936

Louise Carter
1910-1951

Lena Hawkins Carter
Jun 27, 1878
Jul 3, 1974

William Marion Carter
Oct 3, 1914
Nov 20, 1973

Robert Taylor Davis
Sep 30, 1902
Jun 25, 1975
&
Barbara Ray Davis
Nov 9, 1910

Wallace Green
1885-1906

Andrew J. Green
1851-1932
&
Margaret West Green
1859-1934

B. Neil Green
1890-

Hiram A. Murdock
1885-1945
&
Belle Green Murdock
1883-1978

Wallace, son of
Hiram & Belle Murdock
Dec 13, 1913
Jul 9, 1929

H. Sheffer Sharp
1896-1960

James H. Ealy
Jun 24, 1882
Sep 12, 1964

Stacie C. Ealy
Sep 11, 1880
May 31, 1969

Herbert, son of
J. H. & S. E. Ealey
Apr 23, 1903
May 14, 1927

J. Loyd Ealy
Aug 12, 1912
Aug 9, 1965

Eugene M. Swaim
Apr 7, 1883
Feb 17, 1935

Wiley J. Morris
1857-1929

Betty Swaim Morris
1860-1940

Aubrey M. Smith
Mar 4, 1903
Jan 16, 1929

Clara M. McCullough
Jan 14, 1908
Sep 23, 1971

Willie Byrd Caughran
1881-1971
&
Effie T. Caughran
1891-1971

Fulton R. E. Thompson
Tennessee
Pvt 307 Inf 77 Div
Oct 4, 1887
Sep 27, 1944

Maurice L. Woods
Mar 16, 1926
Jun 24, 1927

Herman F. Woods
Aug 11, 1892
Sep 5, 1968
&
Catherine C. Woods
Nov 20, 1892
May 6, 1977

Susan Ann Sharp
1959

Mary Joe Sharp
1926

Joseph E. Sharp
1869-1941

Sally B. Sharp
1872-1960

LEWISBURG

Jackson Jewell
1862-1927

Sadie Walker Jewell
1883-1933

Father
James M. Collins
1854-1935

Father
Scott Collins
1892-1938

Walter E. Collins
Jun 11, 1922

&
Shelia A. Collins
Aug 13, 1950
Jan 20, 1978

Elsie L. Collins
Feb 14, 1899
Jun 11, 1949

Scott Collins, Jr.
Jan 8, 1926
Jan 16, 1926

Jack M. Collins
Mar 23, 1917
Aug 20, 1950

Alice Z. Collins
Nov 13, 1918
Jul 29, 1943

Earle M. Armstrong
Jun 14, 1889
May 8, 1968
&
Kate Alford Armstrong
Nov 24, 1890
Mar 9, 1975

Mayme Alford
1880-1969

John Nelson Alford
1850-1936
&
Mattie Jones Alford
1858-1925

Joseph William Alford
1859-1951

Alpha Turnley Alford
1869-1923

Dr. Joseph William Alford, Jr.
1896-1976

M. P. Boyd
May 19, 1877
Oct 16, 1948

Bessie S. Boyd
Feb 14, 1886
Dec 27, 1963

Sarah F. Houston
1841-1929

John T. Boyd
1914-1960
&
Caroline C. Boyd

Sarah Belle L. Grissom
1904-1929

Lewis Edward Jordan
S1 US Navy, WW II
May 16, 1920
Feb 5, 1945

A. Fletcher Jordan
Sep 20, 1886
Feb 23, 1965
&
Vera W. Jordan
Oct 21, 1886
Jul 25, 1974
&
Bonnie L. Jordan
Jan 22, 1917

J. Sam Powell
1896-
&
Clara Rambo Powell
1896-1977

Jesse C. Carroll
Nov 28, 1899
Dec 19, 1979
&
Elizabeth T. Carroll
Oct 11, 1902

James Oliver Ewing
Jul 21, 1868
Aug 29, 1958

Alma Westbrooks Ewing
Jul 26, 1881
Jul 12, 1973

Helen E. Ewing
Nov 17, 1895
Jan 5, 1980

Anabel E. Ewing
Jan 24, 1897
Nov 22, 1978

J. Davis Chapman
1890-1958
&
Mary R. Chapman
1894-

Tom K. Luna
Dec 1, 1885
Sep 5, 1974
&
Maggie B. Luna
Sep 29, 1894
Feb 25, 1972
Mrd Jan 17, 1915

Rev. Jacob W. Madewell
Jan 6, 1872
Aug 23, 1934
&
Ella S. Madewell
Nov 27, 1887
Jul 1, 1957

Roy Elmo Madewell
1911-1928

George Raymond Ketchum
Nov 6, 1902
Jun 29, 1970
&
Louise Collins Ketchum
Dec 20, 1906

Infant Daughter of
Mr & Mrs George Ketchum
Jul 15, 1926

John A. Dillehay
Oct 8, 1889
Jun 8, 1953
&
Bertha T. Dillehay
Jun 27, 1891
Sep 2, 1977

Infant Son of
Mr & Mrs John Dillehay
1918-1918

Juanita Savage
Jun 1, 1928
Jul 8, 1929

Claud Davis
1878-1928
&
Lela Davis
1884-1958

Earl W. Davis
Sep 15, 1921
May 22, 1976
&
Tennie Lee Davis
Apr 19, 1922

Mrd Oct 27, 1940

Aaron B. Davis
Co L
4 Tenn Inf
Sp AM War

Otis Secrest
Apr 14, 1899
Mar 28, 1952
&
Lucile Secrest
Oct 20, 1902

Grover Eugene, son of
Mr & Mrs Ottis Secrest
Sep 6, 1925
May 8, 1928

Otis Neece
1917-1979
(London)

J. Sam Capley
Sep 10, 1871
Feb 17, 1962

Tennie W. Capley
Jan 24, 1878
Apr 18, 1955

Katie L. Capley
Sep 9, 1899
Mar 20, 1928

John Davis
May 8, 1883
May 29, 1946
&
Lena Davis
Mar 2, 1887
Nov 28, 1952

James T. Davis
Tennessee
Pfc 323 Inf 81 Inf Div
WW II
May 6, 1922
Nov 13, 1944

John L. Davis, Jr.
Sep 3, 1942
Aug 2, 1943

Thomas J. Sanders
Aug 21, 1852
Jan 25, 1928
&
Elizabeth Riner Sanders
Dec 27, 1856
Aug 31, 1949

Irene Coggin Blackwell
Oct 12, 1910
Jun 14, 1934

Mattie Sanders Fluty
Dec 12, 1887
Oct 31, 1974

LEWISBURG

John W. Weaver
(no dates)
&
Susie T. Weaver
(no dates)
&
Ana L. Weaver
(no dates)

Jimmie M. Tillman
Nov 21, 1897
Sep 27, 1970
&
Emma N. Tillman
Mar 7, 1890
Feb 3, 1967

End of Section "E"

SECTION "F"

Roy H. Fagan
1899-1970
&
Macel Fagan
1906-

Roy E. Bills
Mar 18, 1893
Oct 9, 1962
&
Alice W. Bills
May 24, 1894
Dec 2, 1971
&
Reverse side of
 marker:
In Memoriam
Lt. Edward Bills
Aug 18, 1914
Mar 11, 1945
"Interred in US
Cemetery in Belgium"

Leach Estes Petty
Oct 22, 1912
May 20, 1977

Father
James O. Hightower
Apr 24, 1906
Jan 6, 1980
&
Mother
Vera S. Hightower
Jan 8, 1908
May 10, 1962

W. D. O'Neal
Jun 2, 1895

&
Arbie B. O'Neal
Oct 24, 1898
May 23, 1969

George L. Butler
Jan 11, 1904
Feb 20, 1977
&
Martha E. Butler
Jan 19, 1909

Ewell B. Butler
Apr 28, 1901
Jan 24, 1974
&
Mary B. Butler
Mar 17, 1905

Uliver C. Butler
Aug 20, 1897
Sep 19, 1969
&
Birdie M. Butler
Oct 29, 1894

Thomas L. Wilson
Tennessee
Sgt Army Air Forces
WW II
Dec 12, 1906
Feb 14, 1972

Joseph R. Wilson
Tennessee
T Sgt US Army, WW II
Mar 24, 1909
Sep 30, 1971

Milton Elvin Hardison
1908-1956
&
Edna Andrews Hardison
1911-

Milton Ray Hardison
1934-1937

Elvin McVeigh Barras
Tennessee
PTR3 USNR, WW II
Jul 29, 1905
Dec 7, 1954

John R. Wise
Sep 6, 1896

&
Mary K. Wise
Oct 25, 1899

Ed Lawrence Baxter
Tennessee
Pvt 4 Service Comd
WW II
Sep 4, 1901
Feb 17, 1969
&
Vera W. Baxter
May 11, 1914

Ike Rhea Bigham
1895-1946

John W. Bigham
Oct 22, 1862
Jan 11, 1929
&
Hannah E. Bigham
Jan 29, 1865
Jan 14, 1929

Thomas Davis Bigham
Tennessee
Pvt Co B 117 Ammo Train
WW I
Mar 7, 1894
Sep 15, 1967
&
Clara Bell Bigham
Aug 5, 1896
Oct 26, 1974

Homer Cook
1896-1980
&
Macie H. Cook
1900-1968

Howard Sanders
Sep 26, 1896
Jun 17, 1971
&
Mattie Belle Anderson
         Sanders
Mar 26, 1907

Linda Gail Poarch
Aug 6, 1955
Dec 4, 1977

William B. Wheatley
Tennessee
Cpl HQ Co 114 Fd Arty
WW I
Nov 27, 1889
Apr 11, 1957
&
Edmonia W. Wheatley
Feb 21, 1897

Mrd Dec 22, 1919

Ruth Wheatley Foster
Jul 26, 1929
Jun 18, 1980

Porter Jones (Father)
Aug 25, 1911

&
Pearl C. Jones (Mother)
Sep 5, 1910-Jul 18, 1957

Ed Baxter Bryant
Oct 25, 1893
Jan 5, 1959
&
Jennie Maude Walker Bryant
Mar 23, 1896
Jan 3, 1959

James C. McRee
Tennessee
Pvt Co C 147 MG BN, WW I
Dec 29, 1889(8 on headstone
Oct 12, 1972
&
Virginia P. McRee
1893-1966

Dan Palmer McCrory
Tennessee
RDM3 USNR, WW II
Aug 3, 1903
Apr 8, 1961
&
Dorris P. Atchley McCrory
Jul 24, 1904
Nov 19, 1976

Father
Billie H. Chunn
Oct 20, 1879
Oct 16, 1960
&
Mother
Nellie J. Chunn
Nov 13, 1889
Mar 16, 1972

Edker Richardson
1878-1958

Willie Richardson
1880-1966

Father
Clifford S. Haislip
1912-1958
&
Mother
Louise C. Haislip
1917-

George Carl Pettes
Tennessee
S/Sgt Co B 50 Engr C BN
WW II, PH
Apr 18, 1912-Jul 22, 1956
&
Ozella A. Pettes
1909-

LEWISBURG

Robert Jeremiah Hardison
Tennessee
Pvt US Army, WW I
Dec 8, 1888
Nov 7, 1960

Dona Mai Hardison
1927-1928

T. Ownby Hardison
Feb 27, 1901
Mar 12, 1979
&
Estelle M. Hardison
Oct 9, 1906
Aug 22, 1976

Clarence C. McCrory
1867-1928

William C. McCrory
1866-1936

Vivian S. McCrory
1887-1940

Dan V. McCrory, Jr.
1914-1979
(Bills-McGaugh)

Dan Voorheese McCrory
Jul 4, 1878
Oct 31, 1961
&
Eunice McCord McCrory
Nov 13, 1888
Jul 27, 1958

Thomas J. Hickerson
Nov 21, 1882
Nov 19, 1967
&
Fronnie C. Hickerson
Oct 23, 1882
Feb 14, 1963

Ervin Lee Hickerson
1905-1928

Fronie Mae Deeryberry
1927-1933

Thomas W. Hickerson
1912-1973

Zuella H. Rockwell
1907-1979

Jackson J. Liggett
Jan 13, 1908
Oct 9, 1975
&
Josephine H. Liggett
May 2, 1915
Feb 11, 1973

George W. Cook
1865-1940
&
Ada Cook
1868-1928

Jack W. Cook
1902-1964
&
Violet M. Cook
1909-

Dan Allison Pruett
1909-1977
(Clark-Erwin)

Ellen Pruett
Mar 6, 1884
May 16, 1928

N. Cecil Wiley
Nov 26, 1893
Dec 13, 1966
&
Ocia A. Wiley
Oct 30, 1898
Aug 30, 1969

Father
Allen H. May
Nov 27, 1915
Mar 30, 1957
&
Mother
Nina F. May
Jul 23, 1916

Walter L. Binkley
1875-1957

Joseph W. Mills
Tennessee
F1 USNR, WW II
Jan 12, 1913
Feb 17, 1959
&
Christine Mills
Jan 2, 1920

Henry Elmer Harris
Pvt US Army, WW I
Jan 11, 1896
May 1, 1975
&
Elsie Harris
Oct 30, 1900

Sidney L. Leonard
1897-1977
&
Sadye D. Leonard
1898-1960

Frank Howard Helton
Aug 6, 1946
Apr 9, 1956

Sarah Leah Helton
Jul 7, 1912
Mar 19, 1959

William W. Marsh
1883-1951

Father
Charlie "Brown" Allen
1868-1955

Mother
Evalena Wiley Allen
1873-1944

Johnny Owen Hay
Tennessee
Pvt US Army
Mar 16, 1924
Jul 28, 1960

Mary F. Nicholas
1927-1954

Brownie Allen Hay
Mar 26, 1900

Evelyn Allen
1940

Blanche Allen
1909-1927

Father
Walter C. Garrett
Feb 16, 1889
May 19, 1970

Mother
Edna Bartlett Garrett
Oct 20, 1888
Jan 5, 1971

Daughter
Martha Josephine Garrett
Feb 15, 1910
Jul 24, 1927

Father
James M. Garrett
Dec 15, 1855
Oct 12, 1940

Mother
Hannah Haze Garrett
Sep 7, 1856
Oct 30, 1946

John W. McConnell
1885-1951

Eliza Glasscock
1876-1968

Loreen G. Bond
1899-1925

J. C. McKnight
1854-1928
& wife
Emaline McKnight
1856-1949

Virgie Lee Dyer
Mar 2, 1885
May 24, 1952

William Thomas McKnight
Apr 13, 1885
Jul 14, 1965

Mary Ethel Endsley
           McKnight
Jan 3, 1886
Sep 7, 1951

Addie Claude Hopwood
Nov 1, 1891
Jun 1, 1966
&
Bessie Hall Hopwood
Feb 22, 1902
Feb 12, 1951

Claude L. Hopwood
1924-1926

Alf H. Richardson
Jan 1, 1867
Mar 17, 1948
&
Ruth J. Richardson
Feb 27, 1869
Dec 20, 1944

Edd R. Collins
Aug 9, 1890
Apr 22, 1964
&
Maicel S. Collins
Mar 24, 1895

John M. Davis
Feb 8, 1866
Mar 29, 1954
&
Beulah J. Davis
Feb 5, 1867
Apr 18, 1926

Will Ray
Feb 15, 1876
Oct 9, 1924

Lou Doud Ray
Jun 26, 1881
Jul 29, 1943

J. K. Doud
Apr 6, 1852
Mar 18, 1930
&
E. V. Doud
Dec 8, 1860
Apr 10, 1928

Easter Susanna Scoggins
May 5, 1869
Sep 5, 1951

Louis Sylvester Bailey
Jan 7, 1921
Feb 19, 1931

Elmer Jack Bailey
Feb 10, 1925
Sep 17, 1926

LEWISBURG

Roy K. Bailey
1892-1967
&
Maudie M. Bailey
1904-1957

Floyd K. Bailey
Feb 8, 1927

&
Rhoda Blackwell Bailey
Jan 22, 1926
Sep 7, 1970

Mother
Mary R. Moore
Mar 26, 1927
Nov 25, 1957

"Pappy"
James Claude Lee, Sr.
Pvt US Army, WW II
Aug 16, 1911
Aug 5, 1977
&
Louise H. Lee

Sarah Elaine Guthrie
Sep 23, 1945
Oct 9, 1955
(picture)

Herman B. Craig
1891-1967

Mary Clair Craig
1891-1971

Ewell Braly Craig
1913-1960

James L. Jordan
1916-1947

Hartford Blount Jordan
Mar 23, 1889
Jan 18, 1941
&
Adell Harris Jordan
Jun 7, 1892
Sep 24, 1973

Clement L. Jordan
Apr 30, 1841
Aug 19, 1928
&
Annie H. Jordan
Jan 1, 1857
Jun 6, 1940

J. K. P. Thompson
Nov 24, 1844
Oct 4, 1936
&
Mahala F. Thompson
Feb 6, 1851
Mar 16, 1929

William Horace Jordan
Dec 15, 1890
Nov 14, 1921

Hazel Jordan Cochran
Sep 19, 1893
Jan 7, 1962

George H. Marshall
Tennessee
Pvt Co B
2 Development BN
WW I
Nov 13, 1887
Aug 14, 1956

Edmonds Marshall Murphree
1899-1959

Thomas Scott Marshall
1881-1946
(London)

James B. Marshall
May 8, 1845
Jul 12, 1926

Sarah A., wife of
J. B. Marshall
Feb 22, 1842
Jun 4, 1909

Carrie M. Haggard
1869-1958

Nina Marshall
1882-1965

Robert M. Haggard
Texas
Pvt 109 Mil Police
WW I
Jan 12, 1895
May 7, 1950

Jane Clayton, Daughter
of R. E. & Della C. Lee
Nov 2, 1920
Nov 5, 1920

George T. Stephenson
1878-1964

Lucile Clayton Stephenson
1883-1959

Dan B. Clayton
May 11, 1855
Aug 14, 1935

Cora McCord Clayton
Dec 5, 1861
Nov 13, 1953

William Marvin Clayton
1886-1963

Rachel W. Clayton
1892-1942

William Marvin Clayton, Jr.
1924-1961

Joseph M. Glenn
Aug 30, 1829
Jan 21, 1877
&
Martha E. Glenn
Mar 5, 1836
Jan 28, 1880

E. Bodie Glenn
Aug 4, 1861
May 22, 1923

Alf. J. Glenn
1874-1954

Elizabeth Fisher Glenn
Dec 5, 1870
Jan 1, 1910

Mother
Carrie Taylor Glenn
1877-1927

William J. McConnell
(no dates)

Pamela Jane, wife of
William J. McConnell
Jun 27, 1851
Dec 7, 1945

R. Grady Ketchum
1894-1956
&
Anna Lacy Ketchum
1900-1940

S. G. K. (Ketchum plot)
(no dates)

S. M. K. (Ketchum plot)
(no dates)

N. Hunter Bills
Aug 3, 1901
May 26, 1966

Ruby C. Bills
Dec 12, 1903

Samuel Elam Crutcher
Jul 7, 1870
Oct 5, 1943

Mary Louise Crutcher
Mar 2, 1866
Feb 22, 1941

Dr. R. D. Crutcher
1867-1937

Annie Kercheval Crutcher
Dec 29, 1859
Jan 3, 1945

Dr. Robert D. Crutcher, Jr.
Tennessee
Pvt Ordnance Corps, WW I
Sep 15, 1895
Apr 16, 1968

Floyd H. Collins
Oct 18, 1897
Jan 22, 1970
&
Ruth B. Collins
Apr 21, 1900
Jun 12, 1970

Alex Holmes Collins
1867-1934
&
Ada Twitty Collins
1870-1936

Flav Collins
May 23, 1901
Apr 16, 1923

David L. Collins
Aug 8, 1906
Aug 9, 1967

J. J. Collins
1855-1917
&
D. M. Collins
1863-1939

W. Vance Collins
Sep 9, 1903
Aug 3, 1968

Zeb Vance Turner
Tennessee
Pfc Air Service, WW I
May 7, 1891
(May 7, 1889 on headstone)
May 14, 1965

Alonzo C. Turner
1903-1927

Oscar K. Turner
Sep 5, 1860
Oct 12, 1932
&
Melissa E. Turner
Jan 6, 1862
Jul 9, 1941

Nancy L. Turner
Aug 10, 1854
Mar 12, 1925
Age 70 yrs, 7 mo, 2 days

Marcus W. Turner
1880-1953
&
Lena J. Turner
1886-1975

Ozro T. Bryant
Jul 30, 1875
Dec 11, 1917

Laura Fuller Bryant
1875-1944

LEWISBURG

Lewis A. Bryant
1871-1948
&
Inez E. Bryant
1873-1962

Tolbert F. Hooten
Jan 29, 1868
Feb 14, 1943
&
Lillie R. Hooten
Oct 28, 1868
Jan 21, 1929

Bessie P., wife of
Harry Logue
Jun 5, 1896
Jan 13, 1916

Robert L. Turner
1880-1963
&
Cleolia C. Turner
1881-1966

Robert Paul Turner
Nov 23, 1915

&
Betty Lee Turner
Oct 23, 1934
Jul 9, 1978
Mrd Jun 2, 1962

Frances Chunn
1918-1918

John C. Turner
1885-1951
&
Ethel C. Turner
1883-1960

Mrs. L. J. Rainey
Jun 26, 1858
Mar 30, 1923

Colie L. Hamlin
1883-1937
&
Anna B. Hamlin
1893-1968

Rufe T. Collins
Apr 6, 1905
Apr 8, 1972
&
Lucille B. Collins
Oct 22, 1906

Saline C. Ratcliffe
Jun 5, 1909
Jul 26, 1977

Infant son of
E. N. Callins
Oct 16, 1918

Elisha Neil Collins
1881-1949
&
Mary Maxie Collins
1886-1949

Jewell Caldwell
Sp4 US Army, Vietnam
Jun 16, 1947
Nov 16, 1975

John G. Caldwell
1904-1951

Zula A. Collins
1879-1963
"Marshall Co. Teacher"

Father
L. B. Collins
1841-1923

Mother
Josie Collins
1853-1941

Thomas Cleophas Holly
Tennessee
Pfc US Army, WW I
Jan 30, 1895
Jun 30, 1961
&
Flossye Luna Holly
Jun 23, 1894
Dec 17, 1974

Blanche Galloway Wyatt,
wife of Rev. William E.
Phifer, Sr.
Jul 25, 1886
Jan 10, 1916

Therese Ray
Aug 3, 1913
Jun 18, 1915

Bernard Haynes Ewing
S/Sgt Army Air Forces
Feb 4, 1906
Aug 30, 1975

Allison Haynes
1891-(1980, new grave)

Myrtle Haynes
1887-1968

Columbus Reed Haynes
1845-1931
&
Mary Elizabeth Haynes
1851-1937

C. D. Calvert
1854-1924

Pearl H. Calvert
1879-1953

M. A. Darnell
1859-1922
&
M. J. Darnell Glasscock
1859-1945

John A. Darnell
1881-1947
&
Jennie Mae Darnell
1880-1976

Monroe S., son of
J. A. & Jennie Mai Darnell
1916-1919

Father
James Monroe Darnell
1880-1915
&
Mother
Della Jane Darnell
1879-1928

Father
Thomas M. Darnell
Tennessee
TEC5 HQ 1, QM SALV Dep
WW I
Feb 11, 1902
Jun 30, 1965

William Thomas Jones
1836-1915
&
Mary C. Glenn Jones
1849-1930

Stacey Lynn Griffin
Aug 10, 1964
Nov 24, 1964

Effie Carothers
1881-1962

E. D. Carothers
Jan 11, 1844
Mar 29, 1915
&
Mary M. Carothers
May 11, 1850
Jul 21, 1938

William L. Ledbetter
1926-1977
&
Pansy M. Ledbetter
1927-

Luther Morton
Aug 17, 1912
Jul 22, 1974
&
Ruby L. Morton
Mar 2, 1913

Jesse Thomas Ledbetter
Apr 10, 1911
Mar 12, 1927

Levi R. Ledbetter
Jan 25, 1887
Nov 30, 1954
&
Nina Lee Ledbetter
Nov 22, 1888
Jul 30, 1969

John R. Kimmins
1857-1913
&
Flora S. Kimmins
1865-1937

Father
William J. Watson
Jan 26, 1839
Dec 5, 1926
&
Mother
Lena Kerr Watson
1856-1934

Berdie Watson
Nov 29, 1883
Nov 16, 1959

Infant of
James & Sallie Woods
Jul 10, 1914

J. Tom Garrett
1850-1932
&
Maggie L. Garrett
1857-1914

Kathrine Braden
1890-1931

Carl Cecil Braden
Tennessee
Sgt HQ TRP 82 Div, WW I
Jul 18, 1893
May 11, 1947

Doctor Franklin, son of
W. W. & Augusta Braden
Jun 8, 1891
Jun 22, 1914

W. W. Braden
Sep 28, 1862
Jan 9, 1950

Augusta Evelyn Braden
Oct 22, 1866
Jun 8, 1947

Ocie Braden Hardison
1887-1955

Lyman V. Braden
Sep 2, 1889
Nov 16, 1971
&
Helen W. Braden
Apr 27, 1907

Mrd Jul 9, 1939

LEWISBURG

Sallie P. Duggan
Oct 15, 1886
Feb 11, 1971

Myra Elizabeth Welch
B & D Jun 2, 1915

William R. Welch
May 17, 1909

Roberta D. Welch
Dec 5, 1913
Feb 2, 1935

Oliver C. Welch
Jul 29, 1877
Jan 6, 1968
&
Lamyra M. Welch
Aug 31, 1881
Feb 7, 1964

George A. Welch
Sep 22, 1910
Mar 24, 1935

Nannie Johnson
Nov 1861
Oct 1934

W. H. "Bill" Loyd
1896-1967
&
Rhoda Hastings Loyd
1895-1965

Mary Jane Loyd
1949-1963

John Alexander Patterson
Sep 22, 1873
Jan 11, 1913

Beritta Mc. Patterson
1845-1920

Mother
Betty P. Clifford
1871-1931

Miss Moody Patterson
1876-1941

John H. Rutledge, Sr.
Jan 18, 1902
Mar 29, 1968
&
Hazel P. Rutledge
Dec 10, 1899

Father
William Park
1877-1928

Wilma Park
Jul 18, 1889
Nov 15, 1962

Hilda Park
Jul 5, 1913

Lillie Almeda, wife of
William Park
Jul 7, 1879
Apr 25, 1915

Lillie Almeda Park
Apr 15, 1915
Aug 31, 1915

J. A. Rhodes
Mar 4, 1845
Nov 21, 1934
& wife
Mary E. Rhodes
Dec 11, 1844
May 1, 1913
& Daughter
Mary Bessie Rhodes
Apr 26, 1878
Apr 29, 1913

William Edward Rhodes
Tennessee
Pvt Co B 1 Regt ALA Inf
Spanish American War
Jan 25, 1870
Dec 30, 1957

William A. Morris
Mar 10, 1867
Feb 3, 1960

Dorothy Morris
1911-1913

Father
H. C. Murrell
Jun 2, 1853
Nov 29, 1927

Mother
Ida S. Murrell
Mar 8, 1857
Jun 3, 1912

Richard S. "Dick" Murrell
Feb 26, 1886
Jan 16, 1967

Lillian M. Murrell
Jan 20, 1890
Jun 13, 1964

Julius L. Brents
Aug 29, 1903
Feb 3, 1912

Cora J. Brents
Nov 14, 1869
Feb 15, 1955

A. C. Brents
Oct 15, 1851
Jan 10, 1926

George M. Brandon
1824-1872

Sue A. Brandon
1841-1912

Jennie L. Brandon
1867-1880

James M. Brandon
1865-1954

Daisy M. Brandon
1875-1962

Mary T. Brandon
1869-1939

Howard B. Wilson
Jun 23, 1904
May 7, 1977
&
Sara D. Wilson
Dec 13, 1906

S. L. Davis
Nov 3, 1838
Sep 23, 1922
&
Mollie J. Davis
Jun 29, 1859
Jan 31, 1921

John M. Davis
Oct 19, 1836
Feb 18, 1921
&
Lucy A. Davis
Mar 31, 1849
Jun 30, 1914

J. Edwin McKnight
1869-1947
&
Lillie G. McKnight
1878-1956

Joseph McKnight
Nov 10, 1842
Feb 27, 1920
& wife
Mattie J. McKnight
Aug 12, 1847
Apr 22, 1912

John R. Wilkes
1903-1977

Lawton D. Downing
1889-1912

Virgie E. Downing
1890-1946

Robert Gabrel Loyd
Pvt US Army, WW I
Jun 29, 1891
Jan 23, 1979

Maisy Loyd
1893-19

Father
James A. Loyd
1868-1914

Cricket Loyd
1868-1962

End of Section "F"

LEWISBURG

SECTION "G"

Claud Cawthon
Jun 22, 1908
Jun 22, 1970
&
Hudie Cawthon
Dec 25, 1900
May 22, 1971

Robert T. Ervin
Feb 23, 1909
Aug 2, 1967
&
Clemie L. Ervin
Oct 3, 1900

Shannon Doyle Reese
1968-1968
(London)

Willie G. Reese
Feb 28, 1888
Mar 30, 1968
&
Elizabeth Reese
Nov 16, 1890
Oct 20, 1976

Patricia G. Agent
Mar 3, 1942
Apr 5, 1967
"Patsy"

Charles A. Collins
Jan 25, 1907
May 13, 1967
&
Eloise C. Collins
Feb 28, 1908

Mrs May 17, 1930

Father
Joel Raymond Jobe
Feb 3, 1908
Jul 30, 1966
&
Mother
Mildred Irene Jobe
Dec 18, 1914

Mrd Jun 18, 1932

Clyde J. Liggett
Mar 3, 1897
Mar 12, 1967
&
Josephine P. Liggett
Mar 23, 1902

Bobby J. Liggett
Nov 4, 1930
Mar 17, 1979
&
Jolantha Liggett
Feb 18, 1930

Mrd Dec 18, 1952

Oscar D. Reese
Oct 4, 1914
Sep 26, 1967
&
Janie H. Reese
Jul 18, 1919

Mrd Jul 15, 1939

Douglas W. Reese
May 18, 1940
Nov 23, 1965
&
Juanita D. Reese
Nov 10, 1945

Fred B. Reese
1916-1965
&
Lola Vern Reese
1921-

Clarence S. Long
Oct 11, 1883
Mar 28, 1966
&
Lena Darnell Long
Feb 5, 1885
Apr 16, 1965

John M. Lumpkins
1934-
&
Shirley J. Lumpkins
1937-1964

Father
Malvin Redd
Oct 7, 1902
Oct 13, 1971
&
Mother
Susie K. Redd
Mar 17, 1911

Felix R. Redmond
Jun 4, 1906
Sep 10, 1963
&
Mary Elizabeth Redmond
Jul 31, 1908

Father
Homer W. Wilson
Apr 2, 1885
Jul 24, 1963
&
Mother
Cora M. Wilson
Mar 4, 1894

Robert Joe Sharp
B & D Nov 28, 1963

Presley Merritt
Apr 10, 1883
Feb 4, 1965
&
Jennie M. Merritt
Jun 28, 1881
Jan 28, 1964

Johnnie M. Boatright
Aug 8, 1890
Mar 19, 1963

Thomas A. Hedgecoth
Tennessee
Ens US Navy
Apr 6, 1936
Aug 22, 1969

Wilson Shaw
1918-1962
&
Bettye C. Shaw
1918-1980

Robert Collins Holly
1924-1926

Margaret Holly, wife of
Thomas P. Brew
1918-1974

Judge Robert Cecil Holly
1891-1961

Erline Collins Holly
1893-1979

Jamie Crunk
Mar 28, 1912

John T. Nicholas Crunk
Apr 2, 1889
Mar 7, 1962

Sarah May Crunk
May 19, 1916
Jan 3, 1977

Ed Ray, Jr.
Feb 21, 1914
Mar 28, 1971
&
Kathryn G. Ray
Mar 13, 1924

&
Patricia Ann Ray
Jun 8, 1945
Dec 27, 1963

Edward M. Criger
Apr 17, 1914
May 21, 1962

Jessie F. Crigger
Feb 23, 1914

Dockery
Twin Boys
1963-1963
(London)

Willie A. Finley
Sep 1, 1884
Jul 4, 1964

Janet Lynn Barnes
Feb 25, 1963
Feb 26, 1963

Luther Allen
Tennessee
Pfc Med Det 255 Inf, WW II
Feb 12, 1911
May 19, 1963

Charles A. Houston
Sep 10, 1912
Sep 5, 1965

John W. Thompson
1904-1960
&
Ethel B. Thompson
1908-

William I. "Buddy"
                Lawrence
May 14, 1905
Dec 11, 1966
&
I. Pearl Lawrence
Aug 6, 1901
Jul 11, 1973

Nat B. Cheatham
Aug 24, 1912

&
Clarissa H. Cheatham
Aug 27, 1915
Sep 9, 1959

Jessie Willoughby
1881-1955
&
Mary Willoughby
188_-(no date)

Father
Allen Nix
Apr 21, 1915
Oct 8, 1957
&
Mother
Jessie Lee Nix
Mar 23, 1925

R. Dysart Phillips
Jan 31, 1886
Mar 19, 1974
&
Bessie P. Phillips
Jan 3, 1887
Nov 1, 1976

LEWISBURG

Guy L. Bragg
Sep 29, 1900

&
Virginia D. Bragg
Nov 29, 1912
Jun 19, 1966

Valton M. Edwards
1922-1955
&
Peggy E. Edwards
1911-

Byrd Harden
1897-1955
&
Ella M. Harden
1895-1973

Melvin Collis Rucker
1910-1955
(London)

W. D. McNeese
Mar 11, 1889
Oct 10, 1964
&
Lizzie M. McNeese
Oct 30, 1890
Aug 12, 1961

Father
Vance H. Wallace
1910-1964
&
Mother
Byrdie M. Wallace
1922-

Raymond E. Thomason
Jun 30, 1903
May 8, 1960
&
Allie R. Thomason
Dec 2, 1905

Carl Sidney Luther
Jan 24, 1919
Feb 4, 1966

Edgar C. George
Sep 4, 1911
Oct 29, 1977
&
Wilma R. George
Apr 4, 1912

Everett Garrett
1889-1965
&
Willena Garrett
1892-

Stacey George
1930-
&
Virginia George
1927-1964

Paul N. Tyree, Sr.
Aug 8, 1901
Aug 8, 1979
&
Georgie D. Tyree
Dec 2, 1903

Baxter Hilliard
1900-1975
&
Mamie Hilliard
1900-1965

Frank L. Howard
Oct 5, 1905
Jun 17, 1968
&
Gladys W. Howard
Mar 17, 1914

C. J. Pickle
Mar 22, 1880
Apr 17, 1970
&
Vinnie L. Pickle
Oct 16, 1882
Jan 24, 1967

Leonard C. McDowell
Aug 13, 1903
Jul 26, 1966
&
Nancy Jane McDowell
Aug 7, 1909
Aug 29, 1966

Howard A. Woodward
1910-1966

Father
Houston A. Williams
Jan 26, 1917
Jan 11, 1964
&
Mother
Mable D. Williams
Aug 10, 1917

(picture)

Minnie S. Millen
Sep 28, 1872
Oct 26, 1965

Ethel M. Green
Nov 21, 1895
Mar 28, 1965

R. J. "Bob" Jett
Jun 15, 1885
Mar 4, 1963
&
Mattie S. Jett
Sep 2, 1898
May 17, 1972
(picture)

George Foster Nicholas
Mar 6, 1962-Mar 8, 1962

Father
J. Tom Davis
Jan 16, 1895

&
Mother
Maggie O. Davis
Feb 16, 1893
Jul 30, 1962

J. Edd Cothren
Jul 31, 1879
Feb 9, 1963
&
Etta T. Cothren
May 2, 1883
Mar 26, 1968

Willie M. Adams
Jan 6, 1885
Jun 11, 1963
&
Bessie I. Adams
Nov 9, 1895
Apr 18, 1963

A. C. Simmons
Mar 21, 1912

Pauline R. Simmons
Mar 24, 1922

Floyd Haislip
Nov 24, 1900
Aug 27, 1967

Jessie S. Haislip
Oct 14, 1904

Homer M. Rhiner
Dec 14, 1908

Eva S. Rhiner
Apr 2, 1910
Oct 20, 1975

N. B. Wingo
Nov 17, 1903
Sep 11, 1980

Ethel S. Wingo
Oct 29, 1906

Joe Cowden Hunter
1946-1963

Allen Claiborne Hunter
1912-1965

Charles B. Bailey
Tennessee
Pvt Army Air Forces
WW II
Aug 3, 1915
May 5, 1964

William H. Little
1893-1964
&
Dora C. Little
1895-1969

Father
Ralph Hulshof
1900-1963
(picture)
&
Mother
Ruby Hulshof
1914-
(picture)

Billy W. Hulshof
Nov 25, 1939

&
Bobbie J. Lasater Hulshof
Apr 22, 1938
May 22, 1978

Leola Mai Hulshof
Jan 8, 1965
Apr 6, 1965
(picture)

Zenious Max McCord
Tennessee
Pvt US Army, WW I
Mar 4, 1896
Feb 17, 1966
&
Brownie B. McCord
Jul 29, 1901
Dec 26, 1970

Huey K. Polly
1932-
&
Christine S. Polly
1919-
Mrd Jul 11, 1957

Mother
Lena Cooke Shaw
Oct 31, 1895
Mar 22, 1966

Father
Joe A. Agent
1918-
&
Mother
Edith A. Agent
1920-1966

Houston E. Marsh
TEC5 Quartermaster Corps
WW II
Oct 23, 1926
Apr 7, 1967
&
Helen V. Marsh
Feb 24, 1926

LEWISBURG

Father
George Allen Harber
1924-1966
&
Son
George Allen Harber, Jr.
1953-1966
&
Mother
Flossie J. Harber
1929-

Ronald Edward Hargrove
Aug 30, 1950
Jan 6, 1968

Nancy Joyce Wright
Oct 14, 1947
May 12, 1967
(picture)

Joseph Tyree Gordon, M.D.
Aug 7, 1912
Mar 19, 1966

Willis S. Earonhart
Oct 17, 1885
Jun 14, 1964
&
Lessie D. Earonhart
Oct 15, 1896
Aug 23, 1972

Leonard H. Turner
Alabama
Pfc 230 AAA SLT BN
CAC, WW II
Jan 9, 1911
May 17, 1964

Blanche Nix Turner
Dec 15, 1910
Feb 9, 1972

Raymond J. Hunter
May 8, 1910
Sep 5, 1965

Allen Woods Hunter
Apr 27, 1884
Jan 10, 1954

Kitty Smithson Hunter
Jan 7, 1888
Nov 29, 1966

Hubert L. Nix
1917-1978
(London)

Reva M. Wise Nix
Sep 2, 1927
Jul 3, 1966

R. E. Hunter
Aug 25, 1892
Apr 13, 1972
&
Leila Y. Hunter
Sep 7, 1898
Feb 29, 1972

Paul S. Ealy
Tennessee
S/Sgt 28 Mecz. Cav
Recon SQ, WW II
Aug 29, 1910
Jun 29, 1965

Alice Frances Ealy
Oct 11, 1920

Eldon V. Crunk
Sep 17, 1889
Dec 22, 1979
&
Gladys F. Crunk
Dec 15, 1921

Father
Marvin Estes
1888-1966
&
Mother
Josephine Estes
1894-1967

William A. Ledbetter
Dec 26, 1904
Dec 12, 1964
&
Mary Lou Ledbetter
Dec 8, 1929

Carrie V. Taylor
Jan 21, 1890
Dec 19, 1974

Edna P. Davis
Nov 22, 1928

&
Father
Herman C. Davis
Dec 9, 1904
Oct 22, 1975
&
Mother
Lavetor B. Davis
Feb 28, 1908
Jul 12, 1978

Kimberly C. Sharp
Dec 31, 1964
Apr 19, 1965
(picture)

Father
John Fredrick Scarbrough
1890-1964
&
Mother
Maggie Tucker Scarbrough
1891-1975

Lillie M. Crigger
Feb 4, 1933
May 27, 1968

J. Milton Adams
Jul 21, 1893

&
Brownie F. Adams
Sep 25, 1914
May 31, 1968

Father
William A. Middleton
1919-1964
&
Mother
Mabeline C. Middleton
1920-

Father
James Cecil Hobbs
Jun 15, 1927
Jan 29, 1965
&
Mother
Edna Earl Hobbs
May 5, 1926

Roy B. Hobbs (Father)
Oct 12, 1892
Nov 26, 1970
&
Malor G. Hobbs (Mother)
Aug 12, 1898
Apr 25, 1979

Father
Willard Carroll
Mar 20, 1926

&
Mother
Billye M. Carroll
Jul 7, 1936
Mar 31, 1971

Mack Allen Carroll
Sep 25, 1958
Oct 24, 1965

"Son"
Willard Lucius Carroll
Mar 18, 1955
Nov 26, 1971

Dennis Jay Culbertson
Apr 27, 1965
Apr 28, 1965

Robert Troy Culbertson
Oct 29, 1965
Oct 31, 1965

William A. Lowe, Jr.
Jul 24, 1904
Dec 8, 1972
&
Beatrice T. Lowe

Mrd Oct 26, 1932

John M. Raymond Towry
Tennessee
T/Sgt Quartermaster Corps
WW II
Feb 14, 1914
Mar 23, 1966

Claude F. McCord
Aug 6, 1890
Apr 3, 1961
&
Verle L. McCord
May 21, 1896
Nov 18, 1967

Jimmy J. Miller
Jan 22, 1950
Jun 17, 1965

Lonnie G. Miller
1956-1956

Father
O. Perry Garrett
Jul 21, 1882
Jul 28, 1959
&
Mother
Susie W. Garrett
Mar 6, 1885
Mar 29, 1969

John Thomas Cochran
Jun 12, 1872
Nov 13, 1955
&
Millie Bell Cochran
Jan 30, 1881
Mar 19, 1967

Roy L. Gupton
Jul 26, 1885
Jun 14, 1969
&
Maxie E. Gupton
Jan 8, 1896

W. Riley Killingsworth
May 29, 1874
May 11, 1952
&
Mattie L. Killingsworth
Jul 27, 1895

Sheri Michelle Bryan
B & D Aug 10, 1967

Sidney Robert Agent
Sep 26, 1908
Jan 26, 1962

J. L. Blackwell
Jan 22, 1895
Oct 2, 1979
&
Bertha E. Blackwell
Mar 7, 1897

Mrd Jun 6, 1914

LEWISBURG

Thomas L. Carlton
Nov 18, 1908
May 19, 1967
&
Ethel T. Carlton
Jul 20, 1914

Ernest G. Tyree
Sep 4, 1897
Sep 6, 1975
&
Nell L. Tyree
Oct 15, 1892

Father
George E. Curtis
Mar 1, 1918

&
Mother
Edith L. Curtis
Nov 19, 1924
Jul 6, 1967

William C. Miller
Sep 10, 1906
Jul 6, 1965
&
Grace J. Miller
Mar 14, 1907

Mrd Jan 1, 1925

William Clifford Twitty
May 22, 1905
Jun 18, 1966
&
Elizabeth Twitty
Sep 7, 1912

End of Section "G"

SECTION "H"

Herman A. Clayton
Oct 18, 1894
Mar 3, 1973

Joseph Ramsey Clayton
Feb 21, 1897
May 25, 1959

Edward Steele Clayton
Dec 24, 1862
Feb 14, 1955

Caroline Ramsey Clayton
Jul 31, 1868
Nov 30, 1956

(name gone) Talley
(date gone)-1959
(Bills-McGaugh)

Cecil Cundiff Wallace
1879-1948
&
Angie May Gill Wallace
1888-1969

Cecil Gill Wallace
1916-1944

Mrs. Joanne S. Wallace
1928-1980
(Bills-McGaugh)

John William Corlett
1873-1940

Blanche Wallace Corlett
1875-1935

Herman Wallace
1881-

Kinney Wilson Wallace
1882-1901

John Laws Wallace
1846-1919

Georgia Cundiff Wallace
1850-1921

James Kelly Wallace
1888-1930

John Ralph Wallace
1891-1947

Mary Nance Wallace
1892-1921

Lewis Jackson Wallace
1921-

Brother
Sam Jones Nix
1894-1969
&
Sister
Susie Nix Helmick
1880-1928

Mattie E. Nix
May 31, 1859
Nov 5, 1923

Father
J. L. Marshall
Jan 30, 1850
Sep 8, 1920
&
Mother
Martha Steel Marshall
Jan 5, 1864
Feb 11, 1918
&
Leslie Marshall
Dec 12, 1888
Jul 9, 1972

Frank Phillips White, Sr.
Aug 20, 1908
Aug 28, 1957
&
Janie Thomas White
Jan 3, 1910

Raymond H. Eaves, Sr.
1915-1978
&
Carolyn M. Eaves
1920-

Joe Cephas Mayes
1888-1956
&
Ruth Clayton Mayes
1892-1954
&
William C. Mayes
1917-19

John J. Richardson
Sep 30, 1867
May 30, 1914
&
Josie J. Richardson
Nov 6, 1877
Jul 17, 1956

Erskine D. Houk
Tennessee
MUS3 CL 114 Fd Arty
WW I
Aug 14, 1895
May 17, 1970
&
Lula R. Houk
Oct 30, 1896

Mrd Sep 10, 1919

L. C. Hawkins
Apr 23, 1850
Aug 6, 1917

R. E. Blackwell
Aug 19, 1881
May 17, 1931

Sulie Blackwell Bennett
Aug 12, 1883
Mar 11, 1967

W. C. Wooten
Feb 2, 1889
Mar 1, 1918

Mollie A. Wooten
Nov 11, 1856
Oct 21, 1943

John W. Chiles
1873-1925

Cornelia A. Chiles
1875-1963

William Ernest Pickens
1883-1949

Margaret Pickens Follis
1880-1932

William David Pickens
1845-1918

Mary Ann Pickens
1853-1945

Erwin Vance, son of
Mr & Mrs James Wilson
Mar 26, 1917
Nov 23, 1917

Fannie Edna, wife of
James Wilson
Aug 17, 1891
Jul 12, 1917

Mary Elizabeth Reed
Jun 21, 1898
Oct 27, 1972

J. Woods Hunter
1887-1919

Alice McCord Hunter
Nov 15, 1886
Jan 6, 1931

Will McCord Hunter
Sep 9, 1918
Jul 12, 1919

Father
Robert Williams Orr
Apr 30, 1884
May 7, 1935

Mother
Birdie C. Orr
Mar 29, 1884
Mar 18, 1970

Robert W. Orr, Jr.
B & D Mar 4, 1924

LEWISBURG

Mother
Mattie E. Cunningham
Apr 18, 1857
Oct 5, 1916

Mother
Georgia C. Williams
Nov 3, 1886
Nov 13, 1969

Thomas Kelly Davidson
1876-1947
&
Maude Wallace Davidson
1877-1941

John Thomas Davidson
1907-1974
&
Ann Watson Davidson
1914-

Maj. Joe Wallace Davidson
1939-1979

Kathy Patterson
Oct 10, 1947

Mary Patterson
Aug 20, 1952

Frank Wallace Patterson
Tennessee
S/Sgt 33 MECZ CAV
Recon SQ, WW II, SM
Oct 16, 1913
Jan 18, 1965

Ann Patterson Twitty
Jan 10, 1921
Oct 6, 1946

Alden Patterson
Apr 7, 1890
Apr 11, 1932

Octa Wallace Patterson
Oct 23, 1885
Aug 17, 1975

Kathryn Patterson Twitty
Mar 11, 1925
Jun 8, 1972

Marshall Gray Patterson
Nov 20, 1901
Sep 6, 1968

Franklin Robert Patterson
Feb 7, 1864
Aug 27, 1943

Mattie Gray Patterson
May 3, 1870
May 25, 1937

Thomas Allen Patterson
Nov 8, 1882
Oct 5, 1958

Roy Thomas Patterson
Feb 22, 1879
Jun 14, 1963
&
Della Wilson Patterson
Jul 18, 1880
Sep 30, 1973

Dorothy May Patterson
Apr 26, 1919
Mar 12, 1920

Tilmon E. Bivins
1911-1969
&
Mary E. Bivins
1911-

Birdell W. Adams
Sep 20, 1894

&
Clella May Adams
Mar 11, 1898
Jan 26, 1966

Whit W. McDaniel
Jul 4, 1872
Sep 7, 1956
&
Nettie D. McDaniel
Feb 23, 1888
Feb 6, 1970

Braden Wilson
Mar 3, 1906

&
Annie Lee Wilson
Jan 2, 1911

Johnny W. Wilson
Sep 20, 1946
Sep 21, 1946

Billie Gordon Wilson
Feb 10, 1943

W. A. Davis
Dec 2, 1842
May 24, 1919

Lena Mae Pickens
Feb 7, 1909

Clint A. Pickens
1891-1977
&
Effie S. Pickens
1896-1949

William Homer Sharpe
Jan 4, 1894
May 18, 1929

Cecil E. Sharp
1904-1925

Rev. W. E. Sharpe
1865-1938
&
Martha A. Sharpe
1865-1938

Charley R. Holden
Sep 29, 1856
Sep 14, 1949

Thomas W. McCrory
1849-1919
& wife
Fannie Holden McCrory
1849-1934

A. H. Simmons
1897-1964
& wife
Climmie Simmons
1905-1926

Will F. Darnell
Tennessee
S/Sgt 3298 Ord Base
Dep Co, WW II
Oct 2, 1914
Apr 23, 1956

Billy Lyndon Blalock
Sep 25, 1931
May 30, 1956

Calvin D. Adams
Oct 5, 1893
Dec 30, 1974
&
Bertha C. Adams
Dec 25, 1893
Mar 5, 1958

Virgil G. Miller, Sr.
Oct 12, 1895

&
Iva Pearl Miller
Jun 30, 1890
Jan 31, 1967

T. H. Hawkins
Dec 22, 1888
Dec 22, 1960

Rozelle H. Hawkins
Feb 16, 1891
Feb 29, 1968

James Trimble, son of
Evelyn & T. O. Harris
Jan 15, 1945
Jun 3, 1956

Infant
Luther Fagan
1928-1929

Robert J. Fagan
1861-1946
&
Mattie E. Fagan
1863-1936

James Samuel Turner
Tennessee
Pvt HQ Co 10 ARMD Inf BN
WW II, BSM PH
Jan 29, 1917
Mar 19, 1956
&
Louise Turner
1919-

W. Lee Turner
Apr 7, 1906

&
Lois Hughes Turner
Mar 24, 1908
Dec 18, 1961

Bruce H. Pickens
1873-1956
&
Mary M. Pickens
1888-19

William H. Hill
Tennessee
Pvt CAS Det Sta Com, WW II
Sep 25, 1900
Jul 16, 1969

Carrie Mansfield Hill
Dec 18, 1894

Logan E. Bellamy
1884-1938

Nat B. Tankersley
Aug 19, 1889
Dec 2, 1974
&
Ada E. Tankersley
Dec 28, 1899
Dec 29, 1977

Vance T. Tankersley
Tennessee
Pfc 2 Casual Co USMCR
WW II
Apr 1, 1916
Jan 23, 1959
(color picture)

James B. McCabe
Tennessee
Cpl 2 Engineer TNG Regt
WW I
Feb 20, 1894
Jul 16, 1958
&
Mattie B. McCabe
Mar 23, 1889
Jul 7, 1962

Father
E. Leach Estes
1898-1958

LEWISBURG

C. D. "Dolly" Jordan
1888-1959
&
Lela K. Jordan
1892-1959

Cecil T. Jordan
1885-1958

Father
Chesley E. Hardison
Feb 18, 1878
Aug 13, 1958
&
Mother
Margaret M. Hardison
Feb 18, 1879
Sep 6, 1973

W. Everett Hardison
1907-1957
&
Martha O. Hardison
1914-

Coleman W. Davidson
1904-1958

W. Howard Cochran
May 16, 1906
Apr 28, 1963
&
Louise H. Cochran
Jan 16, 1909

James Clifford Bethshares
Jan 12, 1905
Dec 13, 1957

Ralph Penton Andrews
Alabama
SK3 US Navy, WW II
Jun 1, 1927
Jun 26, 1958

Claude "Brad" Bradford
Aug 13, 1899
Apr 14, 1961
&
Anne B. Bradford
Dec 11, 1905
Sep 21, 1975

Marvin Hugh Crigger
Tennessee
SO3 US Navy
May 31, 1935
Nov 17, 1957

Melba M. Crigger
Jun 26, 1916

Paul C. Crigger
Sep 29, 1915
May 2, 1973

Mother
Mary B. Hartley Hinson
Oct 15, 1893
Jun 19, 1972

John V. Walton
Tennessee
TEC5 991 Fd Arty BN
WW II
Mar 20, 1918
Dec 24, 1961
&
Lorene H. Walton
Oct 24, 1927

Father
Allen R. Holder
Jun 10, 1910
Sep 6, 1960
&
Mother
Alice P. Holder
Mar 22, 1912

Father
Dee Loyd Gipson
Tennessee
SUP Sgt Coast Arty Corps
WW I
Dec 13, 1894
Mar 15, 1966
&
Mother
Carrie M. Gipson
Nov 18, 1900
Jul 27, 1973
Mrd Jan 21, 1918

Father
Roy Gipson
May 26, 1912
Dec 8, 1965
&
Mother
Mildred Gipson
Sep 24, 1920
Dec 15, 1977
Mrd Mar 9, 1955

Ulie G. Fox
Oct 5, 1884
Apr 7, 1965
&
Kitty E. Fox
Mar 1, 1891
Dec 10, 1959

M. Trinkle Shelton
1903-1965
&
Rachel "Ted" Shelton
1912-19

Father
Mark Tate
Apr 25, 1892
Jun 4, 1969
&
Mother
Era F. Tate
Sep 5, 1898

Father
Mayfield S. Ledbetter
May 16, 1890
Nov 11, 1965
&
Mother
Ives L. Ledbetter
Dec 6, 1893

Zetta H. Marshall
1900-1961

George Hobby
Tennessee
Pvt Co G 309 Inf
WW I
May 8, 1897
Mar 11, 1960
&
Myrtle A. Hobby
Aug 19, 1904

Hooper Holder
Dec 7, 1912
Aug 8, 1959
&
Irine T. Holder
Mar 14, 1919

Harvey F. Word
Mar 20, 1888
Oct 7, 1960
&
Bessie W. Word
Mar 13, 1889
Oct 17, 1979

Oakley Alexander Burk
Feb 19, 1957
May 29, 1960

Father
Bruce Damon Pickens
Aug 13, 1910
Jan 19, 1962
&
Mother
Eccle Mae Pickens
Aug 29, 1914

James Howard Curry
Michigan
SF2 USNR, WW II
Mar 16, 1907-Nov 20, 1965
&
Vera L. Curry
Aug 13, 1920 -

Thomas Norris Curry
Aug 31, 1949
Nov 20, 1970

Clifford Allen Hill
1884-1978

Mary Yarbrough Hill
1897-1966

S. D. Musgrave
Dec 17, 1887
Jul 16, 1966
&
Beulah F. Musgrave
Oct 1, 1896
Oct 1, 1960

Donald J. Buska, Jr.
Dec 15, 1962
&
Kim A. Buska
Dec 15, 1962
"Infants"

Will H. Fitzpatrick
Tennessee
Pvt Co B 787 Mil Police BN
WW II
Dec 24, 1905
Sep 5, 1964

"Son"
Lou S. White
Aug 25, 1945
Apr 23, 1966

Hugh R. Smith
Kansas
Pfc 37 Inf, WW I
Aug 21, 1900
Aug 28, 1987

Father
Leonard Hobby
Tennessee
TEC3 485 Ord MAM Co, WW II
Sep 30, 1920
Nov 14, 1966
&
Mother
Ruby T. Hobby
Oct 7, 1921

Ennis G. Hayes
Jan 31, 1907
Nov 6, 1974
&
Addie C. Hayes
May 13, 1911

Mrd Sep 12, 1931

LEWISBURG

Bonnie Ethel Walker
Nov 10, 1888
Sep 9, 1967
&
Mattie Jane Carson
Jun 6, 1898

"Sisters"

George T. Edwards
Oct 28, 1879
Feb 11, 1967
&
Lucile Edwards
Oct 28, 1903
Jun 13, 1966

Perry Frank Polly
Feb 25, 1951
Jan 31, 1967
(picture)
"Son"

E. Marvin Pruitt
Jun 22, 1886
May 22, 1973
&
Maggie S. Pruitt
May 16, 1891
Aug 19, 1969

Mother
Roberta Darnell
Nov 24, 1903
Oct 19, 1967

J. Calvin Edwards
1899-1978
&
M. Elsie Edwards
1901-1967

End of Section "H"

SECTION "I"

Father
A. W. Wysong
Feb 15, 1859
Sep 5, 1910

Mother
Lula Clementine Wysong
Sep 30, 1871
Dec 10, 1948

Father
J. Fletcher Finley
May 30, 1886
Mar 1, 1964
&
Mother
Virgie H. Finley
Oct 27, 1891
May 15, 1964

Rev. W. T. Gill
Jan 12, 1836
Sep 9, 1909

Father
Calvin J. Orr
Aug 10, 1836
Jan 28, 1928

Mother
Jane R. Orr
Mar 14, 1846
Dec 6, 1909

Narcissa R. Cooper
May 1, 1828
Dec 17, 1917

"Sister"
Anna M. Orr
Aug 7, 1947
(only date)

Harvey H. McClanahan
1888-1918

"Sister Ida"
Ida E. McClanahan
1868-1952

William Earnest Harrison
Jun 28, 1881
Jul 7, 1963

Elmer D. Lowe
Jul 11, 1888
Jan 20, 1925
&
Lillie Lowe
Dec 17, 1895
Jun 1, 1942

Charlotte Ann Adams
Mar 2, 1941
Jun 29, 1965

Henderson Adams
May 10, 1851
Sep 6, 1934

Donna Florence Adams
Jan 27, 1870
Jun 1, 1957

Sallie L. Davis
Jun 29, 1867
Oct 6, 1930

B. R. Irvine
1868-1924
&
Bell Irvine
1872-(no date)

Alvie Turner
1880-1963
&
Fannie N. Turner
1877-1976

Newton C. Duncan
died Aug 10, 1913
Age 76 years

Lucile Lowe
1899-1937

Father
J. R. Lowe
Mar 17, 1859
(no date)
&
Mother
Sarah C. Lowe
Jun 21, 1866
Aug 25, 1917

Carl Woodward
1886-1962
&
Ella B. Woodward
1890-

Covie Barrom
1894-1930
"K.O.T.M."

Will Howard Darnell
1910-1915

Mary Eugenia Darnell
1915-1918

Jim T. Wilson
1882-1930

Green Wilson
Mar 1, 1854
Jun 15, 1925
&
Mary K. Wilson
Apr 21, 1856
Apr 12, 1929
&
Daughter
Mary Kade Wilson
Apr 13, 1888
Mar 13, 1913

William Thomas Darnell
1872-1960
&
Eugenia Armstrong Darnell
1879-1965

Mable West Crooks
Jun 29, 1902
Feb 20, 1979

James Wat West
Jun 18, 1880
Sep 23, 1938
&
Katie Wilson West
Mar 2, 1880
Jul 11, 1947

Mary Katherine West
Dec 16, 1916
Jun 6, 1918

Adolphus Wilson
Feb 12, 1878
Apr 1, 1968
&
Sallie M. Wilson
Dec 31, 1882
Jun 24, 1969
Mrd Aug 10, 1902

John R. Andrews, Jr.
Dec 28, 1916
May 7, 1976
&
Kathryn P. Andrews
Mar 31, 1917

A. S. Coffey
1855-1924

Rena Coffey
1857-1930

Thomas D. Coffey
Oct 28, 1856
Dec 7, 1939
&
Mollie E. Coffey
Jan 4, 1862
(no date)

J. Trim Kercheval
Apr 23, 1850
Apr 22, 1919
&
Mary Kercheval Roberts
May 29, 1867
Jul 27, 1954

LEWISBURG

Dr. Charles W. Womack
1839-1925

James McCutcheon Murrey
1854-1920
&
Bettie Woodall Murrey
1857-1938

G. O. McRady
1860-1919

Katie B. McRady
1870-1935

Joe Fletcher McRady
Tennessee
Pvt Ste Army TNG Corps
WW I
Aug 19, 1897
Aug 14, 1950

George Craig McRady
Jul 18, 1900
Jun 23, 1978

Vance Duncan
Feb 22, 1886
Mar 31, 1954

Atlas Gratton Duncan
1830-1920
&
Wynefred Elizabeth Duncan
1846-1908

Pearl Duncan
Nov 16, 1896
May 15, 1968

Rev. Colet Pliny Thogmorton
1883-1940

Bettie L. Murrey Thogmorton
1888-1966

William Henry Hardison
Nov 14, 1874
Apr 20, 1953
&
Maykate Duncan Hardison
Aug 1, 1880
Mar 26, 1957

Annie Vera Hardison
1904-1928

Thomas E. Ralston
Tennessee
Cpl 603 Coast Arty (AA)
WW II
Oct 16, 1908
Apr 16, 1951

O. Z. Barron
1870-1955

Lonzo Barron
Jul 11, 1871
Jul 6, 1932

S. R. Fox
May 20, 1864
Sep 14, 1940
&
Alice Fox
Feb 28, 1867
Dec 12, 1924

Mattie E. Fox
1895-1942

William James Hamer
Oct 30, 1915
Mar 31, 1918

John Thomas Thrasher
1876-1943
&
Lula Bell Thrasher
1882-1959

Hamilton H. Baxter
Jun 24, 1897
Aug 26, 1950
&
Bessie D. Baxter
Aug 4, 1898

W. H. Thrasher
1900-1923

Father
Will O. Whitehead
Aug 6, 1858
Feb 10, 1930
&
Mother
Lela R. Whitehead
Sep 24, 1873
Jul 18, 1957

Loyd Bailey
Aug 3, 1915
Jan 12, 1939

Mrs. Maude Bailey
1891-1979
(London)

Charles H. Richardson
Sep 19, 1879
Apr 23, 1919
"K.O.T.M."

W. C. Whitesell
Feb 7, 1858
Aug 9, 1919
&
Dempie E. Whitesell
Dec 12, 1857
Apr 26, 1919

Father
Persie A. Sharpe
1888-1948
&
Mother
Annie W. Sharpe
1890-19

William Thomas Sharp
Jul 2, 1913
Nov 14, 1968

John W. Turner
1865-1932

Jennie B., wife of
John W. Turner
1869-1926

James Oliver Pickens
Feb 19, 1886
Sep 17, 1961
&
Mettie Turner Pickens
Nov 27, 1896

Thomas N. Stewart
1891-1950

Frank M. Wheatley
Jul 17, 1864
Nov 5, 1925
&
Victoria Calahan Wheatley
Jun 24, 1867
Mar 4, 1952

William Leroy Wheatley
Aug 8, 1888
Jul 5, 1943

J. B. Thompson
1854-1929
& wife
Annie Lou Thompson
1864-1936

William Guy Lawrence
1900-1957

Maude T. Lawrence
1897-1968

Jones Flanagan Rutledge, Sr.
1897-1955
"Druggist"
&
Minnie Taylor Rutledge
1900-

Charles D. Boatright
1902-1955

M. T. "Pete" Lowe
1890-1964
&
Corrinne Lowe
1896-1930

Sema M. Lowe
1886-1969
&
Bernice E. Lowe
1895-1940

Ollie Gail Smith
Nov 4, 1964
Nov 5, 1964

Paul Dewey Smith
Nov 16, 1898
Jul 22, 1975

A. T. Smith
1874-1939
&
Ada B. Smith
1884-1937

Douglass Smith
1922-1923

L. C. Bigger
1848-1922

Ott Wood
1890-1933
&
Janie Sharp Wood
1894-1977

Nadine Wood Wilson
1923-1944

William A. Ramsey
1877-1960
&
Inez Ramsey
1880-1942

Father
Oley Eugene Wood
1921-1978
&
Mother
Ellen Rebecca Wood
1923-1960
(color picture)

Father
Leroy Wood
Sep 6, 1907
Dec 15, 1977
&
Mother
Kate H. Wood
Oct 23, 1911

Mrd Oct 29, 1927

Robert H. Shaw
Aug 31, 1931

&
Kareen H. Shaw
Oct 18, 1937
Jul 6, 1957

J. "Howard" Williams
Jul 13, 1906
Sep 23, 1970
&
Flora J. Williams
May 11, 1908

Jesse S. Bills
1890-1958

LEWISBURG

Kate Culley Turner
1859-1959
"Auntie"

Virginia Sue Hooten
Oct 16, 1917
Jan 31, 1979

Father
Walter Scott Hooten
Jun 21, 1880
Nov 8, 1961
&
Mother
Mae Tarkington Hooten
Sep 10, 1893
Nov 13, 1972

Mary Kathryn Hooten
Jan 10, 1913

J. Will Turner
Nov 23, 1903
Feb 21, 1960

Lucille Wiles Turner
Feb 10, 1910

Father
George A. Ray
Tennessee
Pvt Co I 122 Inf, WW I
Dec 12, 1895
Jul 11, 1968
&
Mother
Bertha K. Ray
Nov 4, 1896
Aug 13, 1980
Mrd Nov 2, 1919

Miss Barbara A. Medley
1939-1960
(London)

Margaret J. Griffin
Aug 4, 1920
Nov 20, 1977

Laura Mai Blackwell
Sep 4, 1957
Dec 15, 1957

Father
Leonard Blackwell
Apr 24, 1916

&
Mother
Robbie Mai Blackwell
Sep 14, 1924
Oct 9, 1962
(color picture)

Mazie Blackwell
Sep 17, 1887
Dec 5, 1956

Leslie H. Blackwell
B & D Nov 27, 1973

Tessie Diane Blackwell
B & D Nov 4, 1975

Leo E. Weaver
1894-1959

Samuel Melvin Coak
1912-1958

Jefferson Lawrence Davis
Jun 26, 1960
Jul 13, 1960

James Hobert Lamb
Nov 11, 1898
Aug 23, 1960
&
Pearl Eley Lamb
Nov 21, 1905

Wesley G. Manns
Jun 12, 1920
Oct 21, 1969
&
Nannie M. Manns
Apr 25, 1925

Roy N. Manns
Tennessee
SP4 Co B, 39 Inf
9 Inf Div
Vietnam, PH
Dec 17, 1945
May 3, 1967
&
Edna L. Manns
Dec 30, 1947

James Harvey Hooten
Jul 1, 1882
Jul 13, 1964
&
Mary Ethel Hooten
Oct 21, 1887

Aubrey Gene Cooper
B & D Dec 20, 1964

Mrs. Ruby Mae Dalton
1923-1980
(London)

Kenneth Ray Dalton
Sep 15, 1960
Feb 9, 1961

Cheryl Darlene Beever
Oct 11, 1960
Feb 25, 1961

Dr. James M. Jones
Aug 14, 1881
Jul 5, 1970
&
Estha McLain Jones
Jul 13, 1886
Jun 7, 1965

Frank P. Clendening
1889-1960
&
Gladys E. Clendening
1909-1969

Leland Forrest Gates
Mar 29, 1909
Oct 24, 1964

Father
Connie C. Garrett
Mar 23, 1891
Jun 15, 1964
&
Mother
Ola Bryant Garrett
May 27, 1899

Edward H. Watson
Dec 2, 1926

&
Christine G. Watson
May 25, 1925
Dec 20, 1975

Father
John W. Guthrie
Dec 25, 1886
(no date)
&
Mother
Mollie M. Guthrie
Jun 21, 1895
Feb 13, 1966

Delia Price Scribner
Jul 15, 1889
Sep 11, 1971

Father
Earl W. Wilson
Apr 12, 1892
Feb 20, 1967
&
Mother
Clara B. Wilson
Jul 13, 1902

Clarence W. Wiggins
Nov 28, 1884
Mar 23, 1966
&
Maple F. Wiggins
Sep 15, 1906

Jame C. Kennedy, Jr.
Tennessee
SP4 Co A 3 BN
64 Armor
Oct 18, 1948
Aug 19, 1967

End of Section "I"

LEWISBURG

SECTION "J"

Mother
Ruby P. Raymer
Apr 14, 1908

&
Daughter
Nancy P. Curtis
Jan 14, 1928

Steve L. Hudlow
Dec 24, 1860
May 21, 1921

Mary Lou Sturm
Jun 14, 1960
Jan 26, 1961

Ruby Harwell, wife of
A. C. Hopwood
1893-1919
&
Addie, son of
A. C. & Ruby Hopwood
1913-1913

Orville C. Miller
Aug 15, 1882
Aug 2, 1960

Amelia Dianne Looney
Sept 1, 1962

Mother
Reba Little
1904-1972

Jana Shanell Barron
Aug 25, 1979
Oct 5, 1979

Marcus A. Barron
Pfc 168 Inf, 34 Red Bull
Inf Div, WW II, 5 Army
Feb 13, 1920
Apr 18, 1945
&
Ollie Mae L. Barron
Mar 17, 1922

James O. Barron
Feb 27, 1876
Feb 13, 1913

Alvie Turner
1880-19
&
Lelia Turner
1877-1933

Rev. Robert Hardin, D.D.
Jan 3, 1789
Licensed to preach the
gospel Oct 10, 1814,
served Christ in the
Ministry 51 years,
Slept in Jesus
Sep 4, 1867
Aged 78 yrs, 8 mo, 1 day
(NOTE: Autobiography states
actual burial was in the
Bethel Cemetery at Old
Belfast. He was a Minister
of the Presbyterian Church.)

Mary J. Davidson, wife of
Rev. Robert Hardin, D.D.
1827-1903

Mary Lake Hunter
1877-1956

W. A. Hunter
1845-1907

Nannie Hunter
1852-1925

Louis C. Garrett
Jun 21, 1880
Oct 27, 1946

Samuel Logan
Nov 18, 1834
Apr 20, 1918

Emily Holden
Feb 15, 1843
Feb 13, 1908

Ellen Boyette
Jan 9, 1888
Jan 13, 1919

Harry H. Garrett
Jan 12, 1875
Sep 3, 1957

Maggie Sue Garrett
Jan 31, 1872
Jun 25, 1956

Will A. Hopwood
Apr 24, 1888
Jan 17, 1974
&
Nettie E. Hopwood
Sep 2, 1889
Apr 7, 1968

Andy J. Hopwood
1853-1904
&
Bell Turner Hopwood
1852-1941

Hybride Barron
Sep 27, 1898
Feb 21, 1963
&
Annie H. Barron
Nov 8, 1894
May 12, 1969

Infants
Effie Lee &
George Hybride, Jr.
1930-1936
(in Barron plot)

Earl Sanders
Tennessee
MUS1 Cl HQ Co 114 FA
WW I
Jan 25, 1898
Oct 10, 1969
&
Mary F. Sanders
Mar 10, 1899
Mar 1, 1973

Infants of
Mr & Mrs Earl Sanders
(no dates)

David Monroe, son of
Monroe & Ouida Carter
Nov 28, 1936

J. H. Glasscock
1847-1928

Nannie E., wife of
N. Glasscock
1830-Feb 24, 1898

Glenn G. Braly
Mar 6, 1902
Jan 17, 1908

Sallie J. Braly
Feb 21, 1871
May 11, 1940

Gaston F. Braly
Sep 9, 1871
Mar 23, 1947

Wista B. Ogle
Sep 13, 1894
Apr 28, 1942

Salome Braly
Jul 20, 1900
Nov 6, 1947

Herman Kelly Morton
US Army
Aug 29, 1895
May 27, 1978

Nathan T. Jones
1865-1954
&
Lula W. Jones
1869-1964

Walter B., son of
W. A. & M. E. London
Mar 1, 1881
Dec 31, 1881

Father
W. A. London
Nov 23, 1857
Jan 18, 1914

Mary E., wife of
W. A. London
Apr 8, 1860
Feb 11, 1894

Mary, infant dau of
W. A. & M. E. London
Feb 4, 1894
May 28, 1894

Laura London Wheatley
Nov 21, 1885
Aug 16, 1908

Melvin F. Wheatley
Jun 20, 1886
Mar 26, 1936

Emma Davis London
Jul 22, 1870
Jan 17, 1958

L. Josie, wife of
N. S. Hopwood
Feb 28, 1856
Mar 16, 1894
Age 38 years

Neal S. Hopwood
1847-1932
&
Zetta Hopwood
1871-1934

Brother
Willis S. Hopwood
1903-1953

J. Ralph Beard
1913-1977
&
S. Christine Beard
1918-

H. Clay Gates
Apr 1, 1876
Apr 15, 1958

Iris Welch Gates
1881-1949

LEWISBURG

Father
J. Anderson Forrest
Aug 14, 1850
Jun 29, 1922
&
Mother
Amanda Forrest
Nov 15, 1847
Jul 20, 1928

Lillie Pearl Gates
1886-1918

Father
Woodson C. Gates
Jul 18, 1820
Sep 5, 1905
&
Mother
Rhoda M. Gates
Dec 25, 1847
Aug 15, 1927

Walter R. Johnson
1871-1923

Wife
Ollie Edwards
1878-1965

C. Presley Richardson
1875-1952

Jesse M. Craig
1871-1935

Ora D. Craig
1873-1965

C. Jeff Davis
1862-1956

Sallie, wife of
C. L. Davis
Jun 27, 1839
Jul 9, 1896

J. M. Ledbetter
Jun 15, 1849
Apr 12, 1918
&
Hattie M. Ledbetter
Dec 11, 1850
Dec 17, 1920

Jessie M. Ledbetter
Mar 25, 1814
May 5, 1881
&
Sarah C. Ledbetter
Jul 13, 1828
Nov 28, 1901

Dollie, Infant dau of
J. H. & M. D. Ledbetter
Mar 30, 1888
Jun 23, 1888

Maples S. Nance
May 30, 1865
Sep 27, 1896

Louis J. Nance
Jul 15, 1862
Feb 25, 1930

Carrie G. Nance
Jun 25, 1880
Jun 9, 1946

Ruth, youngest dau of
J. W. & M. F. Nance
Jul 31, 1872
Aug 23, 1905

A. Hobson
Confederate Veteran
Co C. 17 Tenn
Oct 5, 1836
May 12, 1892

Lucy Spillman Hobson
Oct 8, 1839
May 11, 1900

M. A. Edwards
Jul 7, 1841
Jun 17, 1913
&
W. V. Edwards
Mar 15, 1837
Aug 22, 1907
& Dau
Iva A. Edwards
Jun 28, 1884
Aug 22, 1903

Dr. J. B. Edwards
Aug 19, 1860
Dec 20, 1943

Medora Johnson Davis,
wife of Dr. J. B. Edwards
May 31, 1863
Aug 10, 1928

Edwin D. Erwin
1850-1913
&
Lucy S. Erwin
1863-1893

F. E. Smith
Sep 11, 1823
Dec 2, 1884

J. T. Edwards
Aug 11, 1850
Jun 20, 1922
& wife
Siddie Edwards
Aug 13, 1849
Aug 21, 1891

Lena T., dau of
J. T. & Siddie Edwards
Nov 29, 1883
May 16, 1915

Ewell O. Edwards
Jan 5, 1885
Mar 23, 1967
&
Lillie M. Edwards
Apr 15, 1888
Nov 8, 1968

James F. Cunningham
1836-1915

Marsena M. Cunningham
1858-1914

Mary Ann Nash Hopwood
1824-1899

Sophia W. Rodgers, wife
of R. L. Phillips
1848-1882

Robert Lee Phillips
1841-1918

Frances Jane Phillips
1848-1940

W. M. Duncan
Dec 8, 1832
Sep 16, 1879

William Riley Phillips
1830-1922

Dr. James Buford White
Jun 21, 1883
Jan 5, 1964
&
Kate Phillips White
Jul 17, 1882
Mar 2, 1966

John Wells
1875-1922

Emma Wells Davidson
1869-1913

John H. Wells
1831-1888

Rebecca M. Wells
1839-1912

Sallie Wells
1871-1885

John P. Atkisson
Oct 29, 1853
Jan 10, 1916

Lillian, daughter of
W. G. & L. M. Patterson
Mar 3, 1905

Thomas Braly, son of
W. G. & K. B. Patterson
Dec 31, 1894
Aug 23, 1897
&
W. G. Patterson
Nov 19, 1866
Jun 11, 1907
& wife
Kittie Braly Patterson
May 11, 1869
Jun 8, 1902

Brother
Samuel D. Graham
Jan 1, 1895
Jun 28, 1969

Father
Joseph F. Graham
Jun 2, 1861
Apr 10, 1947
&
Mother
Emma E. Graham
Jun 27, 1873
May 16, 1930

Charles F. Waddington
Georgia
1 Lieut Inf, WW I
Jun 22, 1883
Jan 3, 1948

Llewellyn Ewing Waddington
Feb 10, 1897
Apr 3, 1960

Mittie Pauline Ewing
Jun 20, 1885
Sep 21, 1965

George W. Ewing
&
Alice H. Ewing
(large marker down,
G.W.E. & A.H.E. on
footmarkers)

Pattie, dau of
George & Alice Ewing
Sep 23, 1889
Jul 7, 1894

Geneva McCord
1888-1951

Infant Son of
L. C. & Louise McCord
(no dates)

Cowden W., son of
R. A. & Bettie McCord
Apr 17, 1883
Aug 6, 1887

Infant Daughter of
R. A. & Bettie McCord
Jul 15, 1893
Jul 22, 1893

LEWISBURG

R. A. McCord
1859-1924

Bettie McCord
1859-1943

Robbie McCord
1881-1966

James A. Woods
1848-1891
&
Nannie McCord Woods
1856-1945

Annie Margaret Woods
Aug 30, 1889
Jan 2, 1912

James Woods
1882-1955
&
Sallie Woods
1882-1971

Charles Royster
Jan 5, 1826
Aug 18, 1910

Mary J. Gibson Royster
Mar 10, 1833
Apr 15, 1903

Peyton Carter Smithson
Jul 15, 1851
Apr 8, 1943
&
Ellen McClure Smithson
Aug 31, 1855
Oct 6, 1919
  their children
Nona Carrie, Ellen Nellie,
Mariannie & Noble Doak
  Smithson.

Ellen Nellie Smithson
Dec 6, 1883
Nov 30, 1894

Mariannie Smithson
died Sunday A.M.
Oct 18, 1925
(no age given)

Dr. R. G. McClure
Born Greenville, Tenn.
Apr 12, 1824
Died Lewisburg, Tenn.
Jun 18, 1881
  & wife
Mary E. Ewing McClure
born Marshall Co., Tenn.
Oct 2, 1828
Died Oct 24, 1906
  their children:
Cordelia T., Alexander D.,
William L., Anna E.,
Carrie E., Robert G.,
Mary L., & Leila S.

J. G. Stinson
1861-1926
  & wife
Mittie E. Stinson
1869-1946

Clara S. Cathey
Nov 8, 1886
Nov 18, 1962

M. Lou, wife of
J. L. Marshall
1847-1881

Annie Swanson, dau of
T. A. & Emma Orr Swanson
Apr 3, 1871
Feb 2, 1960

Susan Ordway
R. L. & Lakestelle
Ordway
(dates in ground)

William C. Roberts
1858-1945
&
Bird A. Roberts
1869-1925

R. L. Atkisson
Oct 26, 1864
Feb 28, 1886

Ella Atkisson Crawford
Jul 14, 1862
Jan 26, 1945

P. L. Atkisson
1825-1892
  & wife
Mary O. Atkisson
1832-1902

(name gone)
Born (date gone)
Died Sep 3, 1898

J. C., son of
J. V. & Clarrissa Richardson
Nov 19, 1862
Jan 7, 1899

W. M. Emerson
Jul 8, 1835
Jun   1920
  &
Martha C. Emerson
Oct 14, 1833
Sep 29, 1914

H. Bruce Liggett
Dec 17, 1868
Apr 25, 1947
  &
Lola D. Liggett
Jun 29, 1870
Apr 15, 1962

Wynefred E. Liggett
Nov 3, 1903-Mar 27, 1975

Gladys L. Galloway

Ellen Wood
1890-1898

Harley B. Duncan
1876-1899

Life of Eula Hardison
wife of W. D. Hardison
Sep 12, 1873
Mrd Dec 29, 1898
Died Nov 26, 1899

Annie, dau of
Dr. S. T. & Georgie
Hardison
Mar 13, 1886
Apr 16, 1903

C. O. Hardison
Mar 10, 1871
Oct 15, 1896

George Lee, son of
George & Martha McGucken
Aug 31, 1874
Apr 20, 1886

Joe B. Hardison
1883-1940

Katherine Hardison
1880-1961

Dr. C. C. Hardison
Jul 28, 1869
Feb 27, 1945

Dr. Samuel T. Hardison
Feb 13, 1841
Dec 31, 1927
  &
Georgia Ann Hardison
Feb 12, 1849
Dec 2, 1920

Johnnie B. Steele
Sep 4, 1875
Oct 7, 1877
  &
Julia A. Steele
Nov 29, 1843
Sep 22, 1895

Thomas F., son of
J. A. & M. Snell
Jan 28, 1850
Jun 14, 1913
  &
Mahala, wife of
J. A. Snell
Jun 14, 1814
Feb 18, 1905

Idella, dau of
A. N. & A. I. Miller
Feb 5, 1883
Apr 11, 1883

Brother
Edward Pearsall
Sep 30, 1875
Apr 18, 1883

Joseph "Dickie" R. Hart
Apr 5, 1953
Mar 16, 1962

Irline, dau of
Ben & Bettie Calahan
Mar 24, 1893
May 2, 1894

M. C. West
Dec 11, 1820
Dec 9, 1891

M. Jane, wife of
M. C. West
Oct 18, 1825
Sep 24, 1902

Ben Brecheen, father of
Maggin Edwards
(no dates)

Henry H. Edwards
1860-1929

Maggie E. Edwards
1861-1937

John Edwards,
brother of Henry Edwards
(no dates)

Magness Thornton Jones
Oct 9, 1902
Jul 28, 1959

Nell Edwards Jones
Feb 10, 1902

Carrie, dau of
H. H. & M. E. Edwards
Oct 5, 1888
Sep 20, 1898

Athey David Helmick
Apr 1, 1879
Jan 3, 1904
  & wife
Mary Newton Davis Helmick
born Apr 1, 1878 in
Lewisburg
died Aug 18, 1932

James W. Helmick
Jul 7, 1856
Apr 11, 1931
  &
Sarah J. Helmick
May 9, 1859
Mar 4, 1936

Margrett, wife of
Marlin Young
Mar 12, 1836
May 23, 1899

LEWISBURG

Mary E., wife of
John M. McCrory
Nov 8, 1858
Feb 11, 1910

W. M. Hopwood
Feb 1, 1813
Oct 24, 1893
Age 80 yrs, 8 mo, 23 days

Julia W., wife of
W. M. Hopwood
Mar 23, 1821
Apr 8, 1894
Age 73 yrs & 15 days

Josie Cosby
Oct 13, 1861
Jul 1, 1878
"Placque: 1st buried
  in Loan Oak
  July 1, 1878"

W. W. McLean
Nov 15, 1861
Jul 30, 1909
&
Nannie May McLean
Mar 26, 1867
Nov 5, 1941

George W. Davis
Oct 19, 1855
Jan 2, 1897
&
Marie E. Davis
Apr 10, 1861
Sep 8, 1934

Nat L. Burton
1871-1939

Mabel D. Burton
1880-1964

Josephine Virginia, dau of
P. D. & Margaret Houston
Jun 22, 1899
Jul 2, 1901

Edward Ennis Murrey
Mar 2, 1883
May 17, 1967

Daisy Houston Murrey
Nov 29, 1881
Apr 3, 1979

Charles Raymond Sisco
Mar 29, 1898
Sep 17, 1973
&
Lena Mae McGehee Sisco
May 20, 1905

Mrd Jun 30, 1928

Jim Nance McCord
1879-1968
Mayor, Magistrate,
Congressman
1945 Governor of
Tennessee 1949
&
In Memory of
Sula Sheeley McCord
1891-1966, beloved
wife of Jim Nance McCord
buried at Paris, Tenn.
&
Vera Kercheval McCord
1879-1953
"Hers was a radiant life.
1945 First Lady of
Tennessee 1949

In Loving Memory of my
late husband,
Jim Nance McCord
"I give thee thanks for
all our sacred memories,
for his devotion, patience
in suffering and for all
that endeared him to the
multitudes of mankind"
Nell Spence McCord.

Wilson Y. Jones
Jul 29, 1898
Jul 29, 1903

Harriett M. Jones
Oct 8, 1900
Aug 8, 1902

Mary Houston, dau of
Thomas Max & Josephine H
Crockett
Apr 14, 1903
Apr 16, 1903

Thomas Max, Jr., son of
Thomas Max & Josephine
Houston Crockett
Born in Lewisburg, Tenn.
Jan 15, 1907
Died in Nashville, Tenn.
May 2, 1908

Thomas Maxey Crockett
May 15, 1872
Jun 27, 1943

Josephine Houston Crocke
Jan 2, 1877
Jul 5, 1922

End of Section "J"

SECTION "K"

Hugh Wallace Willey
Col., US Army, Ret.
Legion of Merit
1906-1975
&
Sarah Adams Willey

William A. Adams
1878-1970
&
Mary Orr Adams
1893-1977

R. L. Adams
Jun 15, 1833
Jun 16, 1902
&
Jane E. Adams
Sep 22, 1839
Jan 13, 1915

Richard W. Davis
1913-1964
&
Mildred C. Davis
1913-

Emma L. Adams
1866-1954
&
Effie L. Adams
1873-1959

Irene H., wife of
W. A. Adams
Jul 27, 1881
Nov 25, 1906

Will A., son of
W. A. & Irene H. Adams
Aug 17, 1903
Oct 17, 1904

W. L. Welch
Jan 2, 1871
Sep 12, 1903
&
Janie E. Welch
May 19, 1870
Jul 30, 1951

William Welch, Jr.
1900-1980
(London)

Effie May, dau of
W. L. & Janie Welch
Apr 18, 1899
Oct 1, 1900

Infant Son of
W. L. & Janie Welch
Jul 15, 1895

Father
John L. Robbins
Dec 18, 1826
Sep 14, 1898
&
Mother
Louisa M. Robbins
Jan 14, 1836
Feb 8, 1914

William Allen, Jr., son of
Dr. W. A. & Fannie McCord
Jan 8, 1893
Mar 19, 1899

W. A. McCord, M.D.
Nov 6, 1858
Nov 13, 1905
& wife
Fannie McCord
Jan 23, 1863
Aug 9, 1902

Zana Phifer, wife of
A. L. Turner
1884-1902

Algie L. Phifer
1853-1929

Mary Phifer
1852-1920

Fannie Phifer
1854-1901

L. B. Davis
Mar 8, 1835
Aug 2, 1893

LEWISBURG

Ernest Fergus
1891-1918

Donald, son of
R. A. & F. C. Fergus
1895-1896

Bessie Dale, dau of
R. A. & F. C. Fergus
1893-1894

Maisy, dau of
R. A. & F. C. Fergus
1884-1889

Joe H. Murray
1887-1909

Dean P. Murray
1889-1909

Thomas A. Murray
1825-1897
&
Martha L. Murray
1838-1912

Infant
Maude Cooper
1920

Thomas E. Murray
1885-1894

A. D. Murray
1874-1892

Robert L. Murray
1867-1889

Willis Crunk
Nov 4, 1877
Aug 10, 1962
&
Nora W. Crunk
Oct 27, 1881
Jul 10, 1965

Infant Thompson
Dec 15, 1890

Father
L. A. Thompson
Oct 16, 1848
Nov 16, 1896
&
Mother
Mary Ellen Thompson
Jan 7, 1854
Jan 12, 1933

William P. Thompson
1884-1953

Parnell O. Causey
1908-1953

T. L. Cunningham
Jan 27, 1849
Aug 11, 1903
& wife
Louisa A. Cunningham
Feb 14, 1839
Nov 23, 1896
&
Augusta C. Cunningham
1866-1935

_. E. McCary
1895-1964
(Bills-McGaugh)

William Coleman Harris
Feb 14, 1879
Aug 26, 1897

Charles Austin Harris
1856-1934

Docia Cunningham Harris
1855-1935

William Edward Ownby
Nov 14, 1889
Dec 20, 1965
"Vet of WW I
&
Lee Anna W. Ownby
Aug 26, 1899

Hattie Moss
Jul 23, 1876
Jan 3, 1925

H. K. Moss
Feb 11, 1844
May 5, 1908
& wife
Jennie Moss
Jan 3, 1852
Apr 7, 1934

Maggie Mai, wife of
Granville E. Lipscomb
Sep 9, 1874
Mar 11, 1902

Helen Moss, dau of
G. E. & M. M. Lipscomb
Jan 3, 1902
Sep 6, 1902

Hattie, wife of
Alex McCurdy
1842-1912

James J. Murray
Jun 20, 1830
Feb 12, 1902
&
Mary Ann Murray
Mar 3, 1846
Dec 1, 1932

Mary Ida Murray
Aug 8, 1871
Sep 14, 1957

Lillie M. Murray
1873-1966

Jimmie Joe Murray
1877-1947

Martha J. Murray
1866-1963

Richardine Ogilvie
1895-1904

W. W. Ogilvie
1856-1916

Zana McClelland Ogilvie
1861-1935

William P(Preston) Murrey
Pfc US Army
Feb 24, 1890
Jun 24, 1974

Natilee Ogilvie Murrey
1892-1961

Frank Bush, Jr.
1900-1950

F. L. Bush
Jul 11, 1865
May 7, 1918

Emma I. Bush
Dec 11, 1868
Jun 19, 1959

Jas. C. Snell
Jul 22, 1833
Feb 25, 1905
& wife
Melissa J. Snell
May 6, 1850
(no date)

Lula Lee Arthur, wife of
W. E. Tally
Oct 10, 1875
Mar 31, 1903

J. W. Arthur
May 1, 1853
Jul 19, 1918
&
C. F. Arthur
Mar 15, 1855
Sep 17, 1915

Ernest H. Arthur
1890-1927

Henry C. Huggins
1875-1932
&
Ora C. Huggins
1882-1978

Charles Earl Crutcher
1888-1980
(Bills-McGaugh)

Pallen McCurdy Morris
1903-1926

George Birch Bryant
Oct 13, 1870
Oct 20, 1940
&
Nannie Lowry Bryant
Mar 27, 1871
Jun 27, 1926

S. R. Thompson
May 7, 1878
Apr 23, 1928

Georgia Thompson
Apr 26, 1881
Sep 11, 1960

William A. Davis, Jr.
Tennessee
Pfc 164 Ordnance Maint Co
WW II
Apr 27, 1916
Dec 1, 1963

Lucille Thompson Davis
Sep 29, 1919

J. Allen McClary
Oct 25, 1900
Aug 21, 1974
&
Bessie A. McClary
Aug 16, 1906

Malonie Ann, dau of
Mr & Mrs J. A. McClary, Jr.
June 16, 1975

Mary McKnight Sharpe
1899-1928

John F. Crutcher
1858-1942
&
Hattie C. Crutcher
1859-1947

Dr. Robert Bruce Berry
1884-1969
&
Lena Crutcher Berry
1890-1979

End of Section "K"

LEWISBURG

SECTION "L"

James L. Reed
Died Jan 21, 1891
Age 70 yrs.
& wife
Mary Reed
Died Feb 21, 1894
Age 66 yrs.

M. J. Gill
Sep 22, 1845
Jan 2, 1918

T. D. Williamson
Mar 24, 1833
Dec 11, 1895

Mabel Troy, dau of
J. E. & S. A. McRady
Nov 12, 1879
Oct 7, 1895
&
J. E. McRady
May 5, 1853
Nov 25, 1902
& wife
Susan Alice McRady
Dec 22, 1858
Mar 2, 1937

Ella Peach, wife of
W. H. Merritt
Sep 4, 1851
Sep 17, 1892

John Lloyd Rainey
Mar 12, 1889
May 25, 1975
"My beloved Husband"

Fannie M. Rainey
Apr 8, 1865
Oct 27, 1933

Mother
Josie E. Rainey
Oct 12, 1854
May 23, 1886

Stephen J. Rainey
Jan 19, 1850
Jan 17, 1926

Blythe Preston, son of
P. F. & Ella Lewis
Died Sep 3, 1877
Age 1 year & 16 days

S. J. Turner
Oct 25, 1869
Oct 10, 1941
& wife
Essie A. Turner
Jul 19, 1874
Mar 22, 1903

Bettie Collins London
Jan 6, 1878
Feb 19, 1956

J. W. Collins
Feb 15, 1832
Mar 8, 1917
& wife
Mary E. Collins
Feb 28, 1827
Jan 16, 1907

T. E. Reed, M.D.
1857-1926

Virginia Mc. Reed
1862-1945

Virginia Reed
1882-1903

Kathleen R. King
1887-1972

George F. Chadwell
Sep 25, 1854
Nov 8, 1924

Bulla Chadwell
Nov 28, 1858
Apr 5, 1921

A. J. Edwards
Feb 14, 1826
Feb 15, 1891

Mary A., wife of
A. J. Edwards
Jul 11, 1828
May 20, 1891

Josie V. Duncan
1857-1943

Abb M. Duncan
1853-1891

Girthie Duncan
1890-1911

S. R. Collins
Jan 3, 1848
Oct 1, 1902
& wife
Sallie Collins
May 5, 1856
Feb 14, 1931

Lucile, dau of
S. T. & Sallie Collins
Apr 9, 1883
Apr 18, 1883

Claude D. Seagroves
Tennessee
Pfc Engineers, WW II
Mar 11, 1918
Sep 29, 1964
&
Nancy L. Seagroves
1926-

John T. Collins
Aug 26, 1839
May 25, 1918
&
America A. Collins
Aug 21, 1836
Mar 20, 1909

Robert Lee, son of
J. T. & A. A. Collins
Sep 17, 1871
Sep 16, 1879

Alice Fay, dau of
C. L. & Addie McKnight
Born Feb 3, 1874
Age 4 yrs, 8 mo, 12 days

William Hopwood
Charlottie T. Hopwood
  their children
Michael J., Susan, Emma,
Will, Alice, Annie E.,
and Addie McKnight
(no dates)

W. E. McAteer
Aug 8, 1832
May 29, 1893

Sarah J., wife of
W. E. McAteer
Oct 10, 1830
Jun 26, 1894

Mary A., wife of
E. A. Loyd
Died Jul 30, 1884
Age 31 yrs, 5 mo, 2 days

Robert, son of
E. A. & M. A. Loyd
Aug 17, 1882
Aug 8, 1884

W. G. Loyd
Apr 26, 1838
Dec 18, 1909
&
V. C. Loyd
Mar 2, 1847
Feb 14, 1934

Bess C. Loyd
1885-1960

Charles R. Arthur
1906-1964

Samuel R. Woods
1903-1967
&
Mildred A. Woods
1903-

Thomas E. Arthur
1873-1929

Effie L. Arthur
1878-1941

Samuel P. Boren
1860-1911

Elizabeth L. Boren
1870-1960

Harriett E. Lee
Aug 7, 1815
Apr 3, 1891

Virginia E. M. Meadows
Jun 20, 1847
Dec 10, 1902
&
Irma Meadows
Feb 24, 1886
Jun 10, 1903

G. W. Collins
Nov 23, 1850
Jun 9, 1910
&
Manetho E. Collins
Sep 10, 1860
Jul 19, 1905

Rev. George D. Logan
Nov 6, 1858
Mrd Fannie Neren
Jun 29, 1887
Died at Grenada, Miss.
Oct 1, 1891

"Aunt"
Sallie Jones
Jan 13, 1824
Sep 14, 1906

Mary M., wife of
J. O. Pickens
Jun 13, 1820
Aug 17, 1890

Father
P. D. Houston
Jan 8, 1843
Aug 2, 1921
&
Mother
Dora Houston
Oct 8, 1847
Oct 26, 1911

Infant dau of
P. D. & M. A. Houston
B & D Aug 24, 1879

Alfred M., son of
P. D. & M. A. Houston
B & D Apr 24, 1890

LEWISBURG

Manie Hawkins
Died Oct 10, 1878
Age 4 years
&
Walter Hawkins
Died Oct 15, 1878
Age 2 years
Children of
J. M. & Lou A. Hawkins

J. M. Hawkins
1837-1916
&
Louise A. Hawkins
1848-1919

Herman H. Hawkins
1881-1942

James Trimble Hawkins
1883-1946

George Ewell Hawkins
1870-1944
&
May Cowden Hawkins
1877-1957

Robert J. Kercheval
Jan 7, 1862
Jul 1, 1908

T. E. Garrett
1836-1922

Bettie Garrett
1854-1940

Thomas W., son of
T. E. & E. M. Garrett
May 24, 1884
Feb 4, 1899

Thomas Garrett
1911-1921

Novella Garrett
1881-1934

George E. Garrett
1886-1954

Roy, son of
S. R. & S. B. Lee
Jun 11, 1891
Oct 22, 1892

Samuel R. Lee
1854-1944

Dr. Roy Erskine Galloway
1892-1962
&
Elaine Kercheval Galloway
1886-1969

N. E. Scales
Jan 22, 1857
Nov 10, 1930
&
H. E. Scales
Jan 22, 1859
Feb 27, 1925
&
G. M. Scales
May 6, 1883
Feb 26, 1928
&
N. R. Scales
Jan 28, 1899
Jul 14, 1925

Bessie A. Scales
Sep 2, 1902
Dec 6, 1902

Fred Kercheval
1884-1942

Mary W. Kercheval
1894-1972

Howard Kercheval
1877-1943

William K. Kercheval
Jun 3, 1852
Jul 22, 1915
&
Mary W. Kercheval
May 24, 1858
Feb 26, 1940

Lou Willie, dau of
W. K. & Mollie Kercheval
Dec 10, 1880
Oct 6, 1882

W. P. Irvine
Aug 1, 1845
Jan 10, 1905
&
Eliza P. Irvine
Aug 18, 1845
May 21, 1921

Mamie, dau of
W. P. & E. P. Irvine
Apr 10, 1878
Feb 10, 1888

C. A. Armstrong
1846-1928
&
Maggie Armstrong
1846-1886
&
Earl Armstrong
1876-1878

Infant son of
C. A. & Carrie Armstrong
Died Feb 18, 1888
Age 18 days

Carrie Mattison Armstrong
1860-1943

Sallie M., dau of
R. C. & H. A. Williams
Jun 2, 1858
Dec 28, 1878

Bert H. McKinney
Tennessee
Pfc Co B 321 Machine Gun BN
WW I
Oct 3, 1892
Aug 13, 1969

John B. McKinney
1860-1937
&
Maggie McKinney
1870-1961

Willie C., son of
R. A. & F. A. Neeld
Sep 12, 1875
Jul 3, 1881

C. C. McKinney
Dec 10, 1825
Oct 29, 1902
&
Mary McKinney
Feb 22, 1829
Jan 13, 1904

William P. Bullock
Jan 13, 1832
May 6, 1906
&
Mary C. Bullock
Jun 7, 1837
Oct 26, 1882

Ed C. Bullock
1st Lieut Co D
324 Inf 81st Div A.E.F.
1876-1931

John Holden Bullock
1862-1915

J. D. Wiley
Dec 18, 1818
Mar 1, 1901
&
N. A. Wiley
Jan 18, 1822
Sep 28, 1900

Mother
Mary E. Wiley
1856-1893

Mattie W. Estes
Oct 19, 1856
Sep 12, 1912

W. J. Davis
(no dates)

Thomas Ritchie
Sep 1, 1863
Sep 21, 1935
&
Nannie Ritchie
Sep 1, 1871
Jun 1, 1907
&
Eva Ritchie
Nov 5, 1882
Jan 6, 1965
(TM: Mrs. Eva B.)

Emma Ritchie
1880-1945

Florence Ritchie Hendrix
1872-1957

Jimmie L., son of
J. D. & M. C. Johnson
Nov 30, 1864
Oct 8, 1885

Burney M., son of
J. D. & M. C. Johnson
Feb 9, 1866
Mar 23, 1888

Johnnie T., son of
W. A. & _. _. Braly
Mar 12, 1881
May 19, 1881

Sammie L. Roper
Jan 30, 1876
May 24, 1880
&
John H., son of
G. W. & S. A. Roper
Apr 7, 1874
Sep 5, 1875

Dr. J. D. Johnson
Mar 20, 1818
Aug 28, 1884

Mary C., wife of
Dr. J. D. Johnson
Dec 16, 1825
Jul 26, 1888
&
Mark, son of
Louis & S. C. Esterhasy
Born June 28, 1881

Father
John G. Stinson
Nov 16, 1822
Jun 2, 1886
&
Mother
Martha J. Stinson
Nov 9, 1825
Nov 3, 1915

LEWISBURG

John Braly
1881-1881
(Johnnie R.
Mar 17, 1881
May 19, 1881)
&
Carrie Braly
1886-1915
&
Lome Braly
Oct 10, 1875
Jan 25, 1899
&
Evelyn P. Braly
Oct 22, 1893
Aug 30, 1898
&
Albert Braly
1848-1913
&
Mary Braly
1851-1931

Rachel Ellen Braly
Apr 15, 1831
Jul 17, 1893

Mary Elizabeth Long
Jan 30, 1864
Jul 19, 1925

Newton B. Walker
Jul 4, 1856
Dec 13, 1910

Lulamay Ewing, wife of
Newton B. Walker
Feb 20, 1869
Nov 6, 1903
Age 33 yrs, 9 mo, 16 days

Father
Lockard O. London
Aug 9, 1907
Oct 7, 1960
&
Mother
Edrie F. London
May 7, 1908
Jul 24, 1962

Daniel C. Sanders
1889-1914

William Newton Ewing
1867-1954
&
Annie Mai H. Ewing
1877-1947

Edward Stanley Ewing
1903-1950

Narcissa, wife of
S. S. Arnold
Mar 18, 1859
Jul 2, 1890

Maggie Lou, dau of
W. H. & Amanda Maxwell
Dec 7, 1876
Dec 28, 1878

James J. Long
Oct 22, 1848
Feb 14, 1929

G.H.A.
(footstone)

John T. Finley
Sep 7, 1850
Jul 1, 1917
&
Mary E. Finley
Apr 10, 1848
Feb 15, 1925

Elizabeth, wife of
T. L. Sowell
Aug 15, 1872
Aug 26, 1903
&
Emma (Finley)
Feb 15, 1883
Oct 9, 1899
"Daus of J. T. &
M. E. Finley"

Tommie Sowell, wife of
J. T. Nowlen
Sep 20, 1890
Feb 19, 1918

Trim K. Chunn
Dec 3, 1908

&
Annie S. Chunn
Dec 6, 1906
May 16, 1979
Mrd May 16, 1926

I. N. Ledbetter
Mar 17, 1859
Mrd Sallie Brecheen
Dec 18, 1882
Died Sep 15, 1890

Sallie Lancaster
1867-1929

William Brecheen
Feb 19, 1830
Jun 3, 1915
&
Nannie J. Brecheen
Jul 2, 1844
Feb 24, 1920

Beulah, wife of
Lawson Eady
Mar 19, 1873
Apr 18, 1915

H. L. Eady
1878-1968
&
Ida B. Eady
1880-1971

Mike P. Eady
1854-1934
&
Mary E. Eady
1852-1940

Ernest, son of
Mike & Mary Eady
Jan 11, 1883
Oct 8, 1907

Calvin, son of
Mike & Mary Eady
Jul 16, 1880
Mar 27, 1898

Jordan, son of
Mike & Mary Eady
Aug 30, 1889
Aug 6, 1907

John Thompson
Co B, 41st Tenn Inf
C.S.A.
1840-1908

Martha E. Thompson
1845-1919

Aunt Fannie
Frances L. Thompson
Mar 6, 1876
Oct 26, 1952

Newton W. Wiley
1859-1938

Kate S., wife of
N. E. Wiley
1860-1935

Thomas E. Thompson
1920-1934

Frances M. Thompson
1914-1925

Wilma C. Thompson
1910-1915

Loyd E. Thompson
1912-1913

John W. Thompson
1868-1934
&
Lillie May Thompson
1882-1953

Charles L. Tillman
1885-1966
&
Julia W. Tillman
1889-

Ben P. Weiler, Sr.
1880-1966

John W. Weiler
1848-1911
&
Henrietta W. Weiler
1852-1931

Wilhelmina W. Ingle
1870-1903

Bernie F. Webb
Oct 15, 1901
Dec 29, 1975
&
Mary B. Webb
Aug 8, 1904

George F. Weiler, Jr.
Jun 24, 1902
Sep 20, 1980
&
Sarah L. Weiler
Jun 24, 1914

George F. Weiler, Sr.
1874-1951

Mary H. Weiler
1875-1943
"Buried at Clayton, Ala."

William A. Buchanan
1837-1906

Martha S. Buchanan
1845-1928

Roy B. Buchanan
1871-1931

Robert C. Enloe
1873-1941

Lena B. Enloe
1878-1974

Paula Caderas
1967-1967
(Bills-McGaugh)

James McKinney McLean
May 1, 1848
Jan 4, 1924
&
Alice McLean
Nov 28, 1850
Dec 27, 1928

James Scott McAfee
Indiana
Cpl 42 Rainbow Div
WW I
Jan 8, 1891
Sep 3, 1950

Sallie Jones McAfee
1858-1936

Ella Eshman, wife of
Rev. W. J. Willis
Sep 13, 1869
Sep 2, 1904

Cynthia Ann Eshman
Sep 1, 1862
May 23, 1948

J. G. Marshall
1851-1919

Mary A. Marshall
1857-1938

Rev. J. M. Brown
Jan 29, 1836
Jan 11, 1923
& wife
Amanda Brown
Sep 17, 1842
Apr 4, 1899
&
Annie Brown Dunn
Mar 13, 1867
Jan 4, 1924

W. M. Marshall
1881-1937

Mabel Marshall
1882-1936

Billy Marshall
1914-1928 (W.M.M. on footstone)

Will Norris Cowden
Dec 6, 1888
Nov 18, 1940

William W. Cowden
May 3, 1860
Feb 28, 1935

Effie Cowden Wilkes
Dec 24, 1865
Dec 2, 1943

William N. Cowden
Dec 6, 1836
Jun 11, 1892
& wife
L. E. Cowden
1840-1923

John A. Cowden
Sep 18, 1855
Died Dec 3, 1887
Kansas City, Mo.
(stone broken at dates)

Aimee (Cowden)
Feb 24, 1889
Jul 31, 1918

Sandra Hendricks
Jun 16, 1942
Jun 17, 1942

R. G. Hendrick
Jan 8, 1848
Jul 21, 1921

Mattie Hendrick
Feb 9, 1862
Jul 11, 1938

Will T. Hendrick
1882-1932

Pearl P. Hendrick
1893-1960

James A. Yowell
1856-1940

Julia A. Yowell
1866-1931

Alice, dau of
James A. & Julia Yowell
Apr 26, 1890
Mar 16, 1895

Father
W. R. Yowell
May 8, 1820
Jan 29, 1912
& wife
Mother
Mary S. Yowell
May 22, 1818
May 12, 1896

Mary Yowell Gill
1853-1922

Minor Cowden Wilks
Tennessee
Yeoman 1C1 US Navy
Jan 6, 1941

Joe C. Dougherty
Aug 16, 1856
Nov 9, 1897
&
Lula A. Dougherty
Dec 26, 1864
Sep 22, 1936
& our children
Infant
Dec 1, 1889
&
Paul C. Dougherty
Nov 3, 1890
Jun 6, 1979
&
L. Wallace Dougherty
Mar 7, 1893
Aug 23, 1975
&
Joe C. Dougherty
Oct 8, 1894
Oct 9, 1914
&
Gordon B. Dougherty
May 6, 1897
Nov 30, 1975

Robert Dougherty
Was born 1766 and
departed this life
1823.
Aged 57 years
(Memorial Plaque)

Richard P. Bayly
1883-1928
&
Bessie P. Bayly
1890-1957

Richard P. Bayly, Jr.
1917-1924

E. O. Parr
Oct 11, 1923

&
Elizabeth B. Parr
Dec 28, 1920
Dec 27, 1979

Frank O. Roberts
Sgt 1 Tenn Inf
Nov 24, 1879
Sep 17, 1944

Elizabeth Hendrick Roberts
Jan 29, 1881
Jul 18, 1921

Charles C. Dabney
1859-1927

Ella Brents Dabney
1865-1940

James W. Brents
1859-1920

Dr. Thomas W. Brents
Feb 10, 1823
Jun 27, 1905
& wife
Elizabeth Jane Brents
May 1, 1825
Apr 26, 1895

J. Brents McBride
1893-1979

Sue Bryant McBride
1895-

R. L. McBride, Sr.
1864-1945

Ida Brents McBride
1869-1950

Louise Crutcher McBride
1902-1968

R. L. McBride, Jr.
1903-

Nona H. McBride
1929-

Joe Fussell Moss
Dec 2, 1882
Dec 9, 1966
&
Effie May Hendrick Moss
Mar 14, 1886
Sep 16, 1966

Joseph Hendrick Moss
Aug 2, 1907
Feb 25, 1970

Charles A. Burns
Oct 14, 1928
Jan 7, 1969
&
Helen M. Burns
Nov 3, 1937

George R. Gillespie
Feb 19, 1876
Jul 25, 1927

Mattie Gill Gillespie
Dec 16, 1875
Oct 23, 1963

Harold Young Gillespie
May 25, 1907
Mar 1, 1910

Wilma Clark
Feb 26, 1909
Feb 23, 1930

LEWISBURG

John A. Hardison
Tennessee
Captain Medical Corps
WW I
May 15, 1877
Apr 6, 1952

Elizabeth C. Hardison
Oct 2, 1878
Dec 1, 1940

John Armstrong Marshall
1867-1940

Margaret Marshall
1901-1905

Susie Brandon Marshall
1871-1932

Annie White Marshall
1896-1976

End of Section "L"

Rowland R. Lunn
Sep 7, 1881
Apr 2, 1958

Jamie W. Lunn
Jul 12, 1901
Jun 2, 1968
Mrd Apr 13, 1921

Sarah F. Lunn
Feb 20, 1924
Mar 29, 1927

Jim Wesley Lindsey
May 4, 1937
Sep 7, 1968

Peggy Lunn Lindsey
Mar 12, 1938

Mrd Dec 22, 1958

Robert Finley
1881-1956

Jean Clark McLelland
Aug 26, 1896
Apr 11, 1947

Joe W. Cowden
1871-1950
&
Leo Pettit Cowden
1890-1968

L. Erskine Cowden
1867-1962
&
Lula M. Cowden
1870-1945

John T. Murray
1863-1935
&
Maude B. Murray
1865-1928

James V. Wilson
Jan 21, 1887
Dec 26, 1968
&
Hettie M. Wilson
Feb 16, 1902

James Elijah Trotter
Aug 5, 1889
May 24, 1976
&
Ollie Weakes Trotter
Apr 3, 1889
Mar 11, 1976

James C. Gregory
Tennessee
MMC US Navy, WW II, Korea
Mar 26, 1913
Feb 6, 1969
&
Ouida T. Gregory
Sep 26, 1914

Phyllis C. Porterfield
Oct 30, 1930
Sep 1933

Jessie L. Porterfield
Nov 24, 1900
Nov 11, 1968

Emma L. Porterfield
Jan 6, 1906
Apr 30, 1945

SECTION "M"

Tom Henry Dennis
Feb 29, 1890
Aug 29, 1928

James W. Dennis
Jun 14, 1853
Jul 30, 1927
&
Caldonia Dennis
Jul 17, 1855
Sep 10, 1914

William J. Cozart
1853-1939
(London)

Mrs. Sarah P. Cozart
1849-1923
(London)

Ben A. Cozart
1886-1922
(London)

Eugenia Cozart
1895-1976
(London)

Father
David Jean
Sep 19, 1845
Sep 19, 1919
Age 74 years.

Father
H. B. Jean
Mar 30, 1867
Sep 17, 1922

Willie, wife of
H. B. Jean
Sep 26, 1874
Mar 26, 1905
&
Herman, son of
H. B. & Willie Jean
Oct 7, 1903
Mar 24, 1904

Ann Neeld, wife of
David Jean
Jan 19, 1842
Mar 29, 1896
&
Ada Jean Berry
Mar 10, 1870
Dec 15, 1903

Mollie Park
1857-1937

Thomas P. Shires
1901-1961
&
Mary V. Shires

Caroline B. Smith, wife of
Ira Shires "C.S.A."
1837-1922

Emmett Roscoe Shires
Tennessee
Cpl 133 Ord Depot Co, WW I
Feb 15, 1893
Jul 18, 1952

D. I. B. Shires
Nov 27, 1861
Oct 15, 1900
&
Mattie Hardison Shires
Sep 23, 1871
Sep 28, 1959

Martha V. Orr
1877-1929

Charles H. Biggs
1885-1972
&
Elia O. Biggs
1883-1978

Harold, son of
W. J. & Verdie Wade
Apr 1900
Sep 1900

Mary King, wife of
Rev. R. J. Orr
1849-1939

Vulake Duncan, wife of
W. E. Tally
Nov 26, 1898
Feb 23, 1915

Robert Christopher
Jul 12, 1880
Jul 6, 1896

O. S. Christopher
Apr 15, 1834
Mar 15, 1893
(broken)

T. D. N.
(fieldstone)

Father
G. S. Conwell
Apr 14, 1854
Jan 23, 1914
& wife
Mother
Mollie A. Conwell
Mar 4, 1859
Apr 29, 1921

Mattie Cleo Conwell
Mar 20, 1885
Nov 20, 1917

Minnie Duggan
Feb 9, 1899
(Adult, no other date)

Craig Coggins
(no dates)
&
Carrie Coggins
(no dates)

LEWISBURG

Father
E. M. McAdams
Jan 3, 1833
Feb 7, 1907
&
Mother
Phronia McAdams
Feb 5, 1832
Jul 26, 1916

Joseph Henry McAdams
Sep 7, 1856
Jan 3, 1913

W. B. McAdams
Dec 3, 1868
Feb 6, 1909

Walter F. Cortner
May 6, 1904
Jul 8, 1966

End of Section "M"

Clarence W. Corbin
Dec 29, 1911
Jan 23, 1966

Thomas W. Harwell
Aug 5, 1897
Nov 27, 1967

John W. Polly
Tennessee
Pfc 546 Engr Lt. Ponton Co
WW II
Dec 25, 1909
Jan 18, 1961

Mack Harwell
Jul 20, 1890
Sep 15, 1923

George Brewer
1823-1889
&
Nancy Ann Brewer
1851-1923

Steven Lynn Cozart
1974-1974
(London)

Vickie Carrell Cozart
Sep 30, 1966
Oct 1, 1966

Mrs. Addie Roddy
1902-1949
(London)

Maggie Sue Corbin
(dates gone)
(TM)

Beulah Corbin
(dates gone)
(TM)

Joe Sidney Corbin
(dates gone)
(TM)

Will Corbin
(dates gone)
(TM)

Phillip Mealer
May 21, 1960
Apr 1, 1961

Father
Richard "Dick" Harwell
1830-1902
&
Mother
Tempie Lou "Sis" Harwell
1852-1932

Daughter
Jennie Harwell
1875-1951

Connie Faye Crane
Feb 13, 1974
Aug 31, 1974

Mr. Grover Duncan
1912-1978
(London)

Mrs. Mary Toomey
1914-1980
(Bills-McGaugh)

SECTION "N"

James A. Avrit
1875-1937

Mrs. Reba May King
1911-1938
(Bills-McGaugh)

Earnest Mason Wilson
Aug 23, 1884
Jun 20, 1938
&
Eliza Harwell Wilson
Apr 14, 1881
Jan 11, 1941

Christie Ann, Infant dau
of Dianne & Johnny Williams
Sep 2, 1972
Oct 10, 1972

Tommy L. Keel
Dec 4, 1960
Aug 6, 1970

Willie Joe Keel
Tennessee
AS USNR, WW II
Apr 30, 1913
Jun 16, 1970

Mother
Mrs. Ida E. Thomas Laster
May 17, 1892

Lillie E. Laster
1919-

Albert Laster
Tennessee
Pfc Btry A, 178 FA BN
WW II
Mar 11, 1917
Nov 27, 1966

Thomas P. Laster
Tennessee
Pvt 42 General Hospital
WW II
Apr 22, 1908
Apr 23, 1969

Everett Jones
Mar 28, 1884
Oct 18, 1969

End of Section "N"

John David Watson
Jan 6, 1880
Apr 29, 1967
&
Martha T. Watson
Aug 12, 1903

Rainey Buford Hargrove
Jun 7, 1936
May 25, 1969

Lorene W. Hargrove
May 18, 1921
Oct 19, 1978

Elizabeth Louise Jett
1968-1968
(Bills-McGaugh)

John W. Cook
Sep 5, 1924
May 18, 1971

William "Bud" Toseland
May 28, 1911

&
Sarah S. Toseland
Dec 15, 1919
Jan 31, 1971

John H. Williams
Tennessee
Pfc US Army, WW I
Jan 5, 1897
Jun 4, 1973

Lois S. Stockstill
1938-19(date gone)
(Bills-McGaugh)

Paul E. Mathis
1905-1977

Hope Renea Henson
1977-1977
(London)

Kelvin Johnson
1980-1980
(London)

LEWISBURG

SECTION "O"

Patricia Ann Jones
1966-1966
(London)

Pamela M. Kelly
(no dates)

Judy Blackwell
B & D Aug 12, 1939

James R. Shepherd
Aug 17, 1912
Nov 7, 1942

Mother
Annie Leva Ette
1892-1946

Buck Holder
Dec 25, 1910
Jan 24, 1946

Lillie Holder
Jan 19, 1884
May 30, 1949

Mrs. Della Conwell
1888-1980
(Bills-McGaugh)

Next to above is:
name gone
1877-(date gone)
(Bills-McGaugh)

Gene Patrick Goolsby
1969-1969
(Bills-McGaugh)

Loney Melson
1902-1964
(Bills-McGaugh)

Fergus Leroy Ardis
1902-1964
(Bills-McGaugh)

Father
Melvin Lee
Tennessee
Pfc 29 Inf Div, WW II, PH
Aug 6, 1924
Jun 9, 1972
&
Sarah Lee
Jul 12, 1926

Patricia Diane Lee
Mar 1, 1959
Mar 1, 1959

Father
Henry J. Lee
1893-1949
&
Mother
Elsie V. Lee
1894-1950

James A. Lee, Sr.
Tennessee
TEC5 736 Engr HV Shop Co
WW II
Aug 20, 1918
Aug 7, 1969

Milton Prichett
Apr 22, 1903
Mar 21, 1932
 "Nephew"

Flora Ernestine Prichett
Feb 6, 1928
Jan 26, 1934

End of Section "O"

SECTION "P"

Thomas Lane Thompson
Aug 31, 1952
Jan 6, 1970

Jackson H. Thompson
Jul 11, 1916

&
Emma Lois Thompson
May 25, 1919
Oct 10, 1975

Father
Eugene Hickman
Jun 26, 1919
May 20, 1977
&
Mother
Cordie B. Hickman
Jun 19, 1922

Mrd Nov 29, 1939

Leroy Crigger
Feb 7, 1906
Aug 31, 1979
&
Frances Crigger
Feb 8, 1915

Edward C. Capley
Dec 11, 1910
Dec 24, 1972
&
Lillis M. Capley
May 9, 1916

Sevastion Stacey Stinnett
Tennessee
Sgt US Army, Vietnam
Apr 18, 1946
Oct 27, 1971

Father
John Miller
Sep 6, 1928

&
Mother
Martha Miller
Aug 9, 1932

&
Son
Ray Miller
Dec 1, 1951

Mother
Mary L. London
Sep 1, 1912
Apr 13, 1972

Nick Allen
Dec 29, 1899

&
Macie E. Allen
Mar 21, 1909

Martha Sue Wilson
Jun 1, 1934

Wilburn Collins
Jun 14, 1903
May 13, 1975
&
Gladys Collins
Apr 23, 1904
Oct 22, 1973

Isaac N. Ledbetter
Tennessee
Pvt US Army, WW I
Oct 31, 1895
Jan 29, 1972

Arthur Douglas Hendrickson
Mar 22, 1903
Nov 2, 1971
&
Iona Agnes Hendrickson
Apr 14, 1909

Robert Melvin Lewis
Feb 26, 1929

William Edward Jones
US Army, Korea
Oct 5, 1931
Nov 19, 1976
&
Mary F. Jones
Sep 17, 1931

Mrd Feb 27, 1954

Carmon Michael
Aug 20, 1905
Apr 6, 1976

Thomas E. Cozart
Tennessee
Pfc US Army, WW II
Sep 25, 1923
Feb 14, 1972

W. B. Robison
Pfc US Army, WW II
Aug 18, 1925 (stone: 1924)
Mar 25, 1978
&
Patsy Robison
1953-

Mom
Mamie Bee C. Robison
Jan 30, 1894
Jan 31, 1971

Rodney A. Sanders
B & D Sep 14, 1969

Claude Dean, Sr.
1884-1973
(London)

Adrain Duel Vega
"Andy"
Jul 12, 1937
Dec 23, 1977

Audie G. Hargrove
1961-1980
(London)

Wesley Norman Vincent
Jan 8, 1969
Jan 19, 1969

End of Section "P"

LEWISBURG

SECTION "Q"

Ernest Gattis
May 9, 1909
Jul 16, 1971
&
Helen Gattis
Apr 20, 1916

John L. Murphy
Dec 29, 1923

&
Nehoma H. Murphy
Feb 4, 1936

Deloris "Lori" Fay Jones
Mar 6, 1958
Jul 12, 1972

Lee Clark
Sep 30, 1911
Oct 18, 1972
&
Alta M. Clark
May 15, 1912

William L. Cole
Oct 20, 1907
Feb 22, 1974
&
Aline Cole
Jul 20, 1907

Otis C. Isley
Mar 23, 1907
Mar 20, 1974
&
Delsie R. Isley
Nov 27, 1904

James "Red" Uselton
Jun 24, 1912
Oct 2, 1973
Tennessee
Pfc US Army, WW II
&
Mattie Sue Uselton
Jul 25, 1916

Wallace M. Thompson
Jan 24, 1913
Oct 22, 1972
&
Maggie C. Thompson
Mar 5, 1907

Odell Farler
Jan 13, 1925
Aug 22, 1977
&
Mary Farler
Jul 30, 1921

Edward Moyers
Feb 13, 1916
Aug 10, 1972
&
Mable Moyers
May 14, 1918

Father
Willis O. Bailey
Sep 5, 1900
Dec 2, 1975
&
Mother
Lutie W. Bailey
Apr 9, 1900

Father
Aubrey L. Horner
Aug 11, 1924

&
Mother
Helen B. Horner
Aug 29, 1927
Sep 6, 1974
Mrd Nov 26, 1943

Cecil Everett Horner
Oct 9, 1911
Mar 6, 1972
&
Thelma Rhea Horner
Sep 12, 1914

John A. Simms
Aug 19, 1892
Jun 14, 1971
Alabama
Pfc US Army, WW I
&
Aline B. Simms
1897-

John W. Porter
Tennessee
TEC5 Co C 774 Tank BN
WW II, PH
Jun 8, 1922
Jul 27, 1971

James M. Holly
Dec 11, 1894
Sep 6, 1972

Tomye O. Holly
Feb 9, 1901

Turner R. Bailey
Tennessee
Pvt US Army, WW II
Feb 26, 1910
Feb 24, 1972

Luna C. Logue
Jul 7, 1909
Sep 9, 1977

Mattie H. Logue
Jun 17, 1913

M. Thomas Clendening
Apr 17, 1914
Oct 1, 1972
&
Grace S. Clendening
Jun 17, 1914
Sep 3, 1972

James Ray Bailey
Dec 3, 1938
Dec 5, 1977
&
Mary Ann Bailey
Sep 17, 1942

Mrd Jun 15, 1963

Charles E. Humbles
Aug 1, 1897
Jan 9, 1975
&
Arneta P. Humbles
Oct 4, 1908

William H. Lentz
1904-1975
(London)

Merrill F. McCord
May 29, 1893
Dec 16, 1975

Merrill F. McCord, Jr.
Feb 17, 1918
Jun 4, 1976
TEC4 US Army, WW II
&
Louise D. McCord
May 5, 1930

"L.P.N. Nurse"
Mrd. Jul 9, 1948

Glenn H. Vise
Oct 9, 1896
Feb 6, 1973
&
Bertha A. Vise
Feb 18, 1896
Mar 13, 1977

Willie B. King
Feb 14, 1908
Jan 30, 1971
&
Etta Mae King
Jan 8, 1907

A. J. Spencer
Jan 20, 1923
Oct 6, 1974
&
S. Elizabeth Spencer
Aug 8, 1916

Mrd Jul 5, 1947

John Christopher, son of
Mr & Mrs Charles W. Irwin
Feb 12, 1970
Oct 23, 1975
(color picture)

Claude R. Harwell, Sr.
Oct 7, 1914
Sep 30, 1970

End of Section "Q"

LEWISBURG

SECTION "R"

Earl P. Powell
Jul 23, 1890
Sep 22, 1979

Kate B. Powell
Aug 18, 1897

Father
Joseph L. McKnight
Apr 4, 1895
Aug 29, 1969
&
Mother
Iris M. McKnight
Apr 4, 1909

Grover C. Stinnett
Tennessee
US Army, WW I
May 9, 1895
Nov 18, 1973
&
Minnie S. Stinnett
Mar 18, 1906

Jones Alford
Feb 5, 1918
Dec 25, 1968
&
Brownie Alford
Jul 29, 1924
Jan 23, 1975

George C. Houston
1895-1970
&
Annie H. Houston
1896-

Father
Earnest W. Kelley
Apr 15, 1933

&
Mother
Betty J. Kelley
Jul 22, 1934
May 27, 1976
Mrd Jun 26, 1952

Thomas H. Chapman
Mar 17, 1906

&
Katie Lee Chapman
Jan 5, 1911
May 16, 1969

Jackie "Wade" Rosey
May 24, 1950   Perryman
May 31, 1971
(color picture)

Roger Joe Doggett
Sep 6, 1946
Mar 11, 1972

Marie Wentzel
Nov 24, 1896

David E. Stocstill
Pvt US Army
Aug 6, 1927
Aug 9, 1974

Father
Charles "Chas. S." Sharp
Jul 12, 1921

&
Christine "Chris. H." Sharp
Mar 25, 1923
Jan 12, 1973

James Thomas Bivins
Sep 3, 1914
Nov 18, 1974
&
Annie Pearl Bivins
Jun 22, 1915

Nolen H. Cope
Aug 18, 1929
Dec 16, 1975
&
Bradean W. Cope
Jun 29, 1934

Mrd Jul 10, 1965

Vigle R. Roberts
Aug 24, 1907
Jul 30, 1977
&
Nona E. Roberts
Jun 19, 1912

Mrd Aug 15, 1933

Dessa Ledbetter
Nov 13, 1888
Nov 6, 1972
&
Ivis Adcock Ledbetter
Feb 28, 1912

W. M. "Bud" Bowden
Nov 7, 1902
Jul 29, 1973
&
Sara T. Bowden
Jul 26, 1908

Thomas Ray Liggett, Jr.
1966-1969

Father
Howard P. Garrett
Aug 1, 1917

& Son
Don P. Garrett
Nov 10, 1953
May 27, 1973
&
Mother
Zela S. Garrett
Jul 6, 1920

George Clebert Sharpe, Jr.
SSG US Army, Korea, Vietnam
Apr 6, 1928
Nov 6/7, 1977
&
Marie F. Sharpe
Dec 4, 1925

Mrd Mar 28, 1962

Billy Wayne Blackwell
SP4 US Army
"Lewisburg Police"
&
Nancy Jeanne Blackwell
May 11, 1951

Walter C. Jones
Nov 23, 1911

&
Virginia A. Jones
Dec 20, 1921

Father
Joe Walter Jones
Tennessee
A2C US Air Force, Vietnam
Dec 20, 1943
Oct 30, 1969
&
Mother
Vadis C. Jones
Nov 3, 1943
Oct 30, 1969
&
Daughter: Vonda K. Jones
Nov 4, 1967
Oct 30, 1969

Clifford T. Collins
Tennessee
Sgt Co D 52 Inf 6 Div, WW I
Jan 25, 1889
May 7, 1972
&
Sadye B. Collins
Dec 16, 1902
Nov 2, 1978

Gordon B. Casteel
Sep 30, 1910
Mar 7, 1974
&
Virginia W. Casteel
Jul 28, 1914

Mrd Dec 12, 1931

Grandaddy
J. Reavis Thompson
Jun 30, 1903
Oct 9, 1975
&
Granny
Mattie Lee Thompson
Feb 1, 1910

Mrd Feb 28, 1951

Father
Earl B. McDonald
Apr 12, 1919
Mar 15, 1975
&
Mother
Maibelle H. McDonald
Feb 27, 1915

Hoyle R. Sharp
Jul 15, 1907

&
Faye M. Sharp
Mar 28, 1907
Apr 4, 1972

W. Frank Turner
1911-1969
&
Wilma J. Turner
1915-

Cecil Garner
Mar 17, 1897
Apr 29, 1972
&
Myrtle W. Garner
Sep 26, 1925

Morgan D. Sharp
Dec 13, 1912

&
Opal K. Sharp
Aug 4, 1921

Lynn B. McCaffrey
Jul 11, 1912
Nov 8, 1970

Dr. Christine Brask
1882-1979

LEWISBURG

B. C. Thompson
Oct 4, 1897
Jan 3, 1975
&
Delia Mai Thompson
Oct 28, 1896
Mar 26, 1969

Glen M. Clift
Aug 7, 1925

&
Mildred M. Clift
Aug 29, 1921
Nov 1, 1969

James W. Garrett
Jan 31, 1930

&
Inez H. Garrett
Dec 7, 1927
Apr 15, 1973
Mrd Apr 13, 1957

Marshall Q. Chambers
Jun 6, 1918

&
Lois J. Chambers
Feb 8, 1918
Feb 1, 1970

James F. Moffitt
Feb 24, 1904
Jun 3, 1971

Garland H. Phillips
Tennessee
S1 US Navy, WW II
Jun 1, 1908
Apr 25, 1972

Father
Burr McCoy
Nov 30, 1898

&
Mother
Adell McCoy
Dec 31, 1897
Jun 21, 1972

Edwin M. Barron
Jul 31, 1923

Joseph Emmett Barron
Tennessee
Pvt US Army, WW I
Sep 26, 1889
Nov 9, 1970

Flossie K. Barron
Apr 1, 1892
May 26, 1974

Little Selma K., dau of
E. & F. Barron
Apr 25, 1918
Jul 1, 1920

Father
James A. Lawrence
Aug 11, 1911
May 24, 1973
&
Mother
Eva Lee Lawrence
Feb 16, 1921

Charles E. Thompson
Tennessee
Pfc US Army, WW II
May 14, 1922
Dec 7, 1973
&
Ruth R. Thompson
Feb 19, 1924

William Howard Alford
1904-1972

Jane Wallace Alford
1913-

Elisha Hays Burnett
1912-1974
(Bills-McGaugh)

Steven Ray Darnell
Feb 16, 1969
Aug 8, 1974

Rickey "Rick" L. Lee
Apr 20, 1953
Jun 29, 1974
"Have a nice one"

David Scott Meredith
Jun 21, 1958
Apr 6, 1975
"Burt"

George T. Hazlett
Dec 25, 1927

Charles Wade McPeak
Nov 30, 1904
Nov 14, 1970
&
Lemma Erlon McPeak
Oct 12, 1910

Edwin Hampton Wintermute, III
Jul 31, 1897
Nov 25, 1970

Jerry Thomas Moore
1950-1975

J. C. Cole
Jan 9, 1923

&
Virginia Cole
Aug 14, 1928
Mar 21, 1978

Mattie L. Thomason
Sep 16, 1932

"I do my thing, and you do
your thing. I am not in
this world to live up to
your expectations and you
are not in this world to
live up to mine. You are
you and I am I, if by
chance we find each other,
its beautiful"

Holmon T. Boshers
Oct 1, 1900
Jan 31, 1975
&
Maggie L. Boshers
Jan 5, 1902

Oslin C. Butler
Jun 27, 1903
Oct 10, 1974
&
Maude B. Butler
May 27, 1900

Mrd May 20, 1923

Elmo E. James
Jul 13, 1917
Mar 9, 1973
&
Louise James
Oct 7, 1920

Ezra O. Phillips
Aug 18, 1888
Apr 18, 1961
&
Ellen B. Phillips
May 11, 1896
Dec 21, 1970

Robert W. Talley
May 17, 1912
Feb 27, 1972
&
Mary Ann L. Talley
Sep 12, 1922

Milton O. Crews
1905-1975
(Bills-McGaugh)

Mrs. Alice Crews
1912-1976
(Bills-McGaugh)

Jerald Claude Talley
Jul 11, 1942
Jul 27, 1974

Charles Albert Deason
Oct. 5, 1930
Apr 3, 1974

Father
Lambert P. Davis
Dec 10, 1906
Jul 10, 1973
&
Mother
Bernice A. Davis
Mar 1, 1911

Mrd Jul 12, 1926

Father
Oscar Rodgers (Rogers)
Pvt US Army, WW II
1914-1978
&
Mother
Margaret Rodgers (Rogers)
1918-

Albert C. Lewis
Pfc US Army, WW II
Jul 12, 1914
Nov 10, 1976
&
Carrie M. Lewis
1916-

William C. Sanders
Aug 29, 1912

&
Velma R. Sanders
Apr 20, 1923

Tatum W. Fuller
1911-1975
&
Mozelle J. Fuller
1917-1978

Hershel Blackwell
Jan 5, 1908
Nov 2, 1974
&
Maggie Blackwell
Jul 17, 1910

Orvis Wise
Oct 18, 1902

&
Rose Lee Wise
Aug 3, 1909
May 1, 1975

W. Earl Harper
Dec 8, 1911
Sep 7, 1977
&
Martha C. Harper
Apr 5, 1909
Dec 25, 1975

Charles E. Moser
Jul 5, 1898
Nov 13, 1973

LEWISBURG

Henry Luther Cole
Mar 4, 1903
Oct 20, 1974
&
Zula Mae Cole
Oct 17, 1904
Jul 2, 1975
Mrd Jan 29, 1922

James H. Blackwell, Jr.
May 6, 1945
Sep 7, 1974
"A Pilot, friend of
Jesus, father &
husband"

Father
James H. Blackwell
Pvt US Army
Jul 11, 1922
Sep 3, 1975
&
Mother
Marie M. Blackwell
Aug 18, 1926

Mrd Dec 9, 1946

End of Section "R"

William Thomas Cheek
1916-1975
(London)

Emily J. Cheek
1938-1976
&
Helen L. Cheek
1920-
"Tenn. Licensed
Practical Nurse"

Father
Edd Roberts
Jun 24, 1913
Jan 2, 1976
&
Mother
Mary E. Roberts
Jun 22, 1915

Mrd Aug 12, 1933

SECTION "S"

Mrs. Rozzella Calahan
1946-1977
(London)

James Lester Blade
Jul 28, 1945
Feb 17, 1977

Charlie D. Stegall
1899-1977

Mary Brisby Stegall
1905-

Clinton D. Bradford
Sep 8, 1937
Sep 5, 1976

John C. Howard
1921-
&
Gladys S. Howard
1922-1978

C. Edgar Stegall
1906-
&
Sammie H. Stegall
1910-

Charlie A. Barton
US Army, WW II
Sep 26, 1917
Mar 28, 1977

Robert H. Allen
1913-
&
Nannie B. Allen
1915-

Ruth H. Ewing
Died Jan 26, 1977
(no age given)

Mr. Dorris S. Brashears
1922-1980
(London)

End of Section "S"

E. Forrest "Bob" Darnell, Jr.
Mar 1, 1957
Apr 4, 1976
"Son & Brother"
(color picture)

Hugh L. LeFever
Apr 20, 1935
May 31, 1976
&
Jo Ann LeFever
Dec 6, 1941

Mrd Sep 11, 1966

Wallace Cathey
Aug 16, 1925

&
Beverly Fox Cathey
Oct 31, 1925
Jul 25, 1976

James E. Lovett
Oct 6, 1896
Jan 6, 1937
&
Maude E. Lovett
Sep 24, 1896

Carl M. Orr
Nov 17, 1897

&
Margaret Z. Orr
Mar 24, 1904
Aug 16, 1977

Wayne M. Lasater
Jul 20, 1931
Apr 29, 1977

Clarence Wayne Hastings
Oct 3, 1926
Jun 19, 1978
&
Rachel Ann Hastings
May 13, 1936

Father
Porter Roberts
Sep 26, 1906
Jan 4, 1976
&
Mother
Mai Bell Roberts
Mar 25, 1911

Tillman Dockery
Apr 16, 1920
Apr 14, 1980
&
Sue T. Dockery
Dec 10, 1921

Mrd Nov 10, 1939

Mrs. Laberta Mallory
1935-1980
(Bills-McGaugh)

Lara Vaughan Wilson
Jan 12, 1978
Mar 21, 1978

Horace Cochran
1910-
&
Mildred H. Cochran
1908-1980

Harry Rasmussen
born in Bellingham, WA
Aug 27, 1894
Oct 23, 1979
&
Sadie Rasmussen
born in Lake Lillian, MN
Jun 1, 1895
Oct 23, 1978

Mrs. Verline R. Davis
1925-1980
(Bills-McGaugh)

Berry McBill Rhea, Jr.
Oct 31, 1949
Nov 12, 1977

James LaFayette Bryant
1899-1976
&
Jessie Mae Cheatham Bryant
1904-

Leroy Cozart
Dec 30, 1904

&
Louise S. Cozart
Nov 30, 1912

Mrd Jan 28, 1933

J. C. Petty
1912-
&
Edith Barlow Petty
1914-1978

Marie Bryant Williams
1928-1978

Grey C. Harwell
1917-1980
&
Reba C. Harwell
1922-

Mrs. Beulah Ayers
1905-1977
(Bills-McGaugh)

Amos Logan Smith
1939-1980
(London)

Winford "Fuzzy" Rodgers
Mar 23, 1933
Aug 19, 1979

J. Hershel Glascock
Dec 13, 1916
Mar 5, 1980
&
M. Adell Glascock
Nov 25, 1922

Mrd Jun 11, 1944

LEWISBURG

SECTION "T"

Clyde T. Roberts
Jan 4, 1899
Jul 18, 1979
&
Ethel A. Roberts
Sep 26, 1903

Mrd Mar 7, 1920

George Townsend, Jr.
Dec 3, 1924

&
Lula Kate Townsend
Feb 22, 1930
Oct 9, 1979
Mrd Oct 12, 1946

Mike Miodragovic
1914-1980
(Bills-McGaugh)

Jackie Curtis Reese
1945-1980
(Bills-McGaugh)

John T. Nix
1897-1979
& wife
Lucy F. Nix
1907-
Mrd Aug 6, 1927

Charles E. Hay
Apr 22, 1921

&
Julene H. Hay
May 25, 1929

Ben T. Wheeler
1900-1980
&
Cleathol S. Wheeler
1908-
Mrd Feb 23, 1929

J. C. "Jack" Cook
Dec 24, 1918
Jul 28, 1980
&
Annie J. Cook
Aug 12, 1917

Mrd Sep 25, 1938

Father
Lucis Otis Philpot
Nov 24, 1907
May 3, 1979
&
Mother
Bertha Mae Philpot
Jan 14, 1908

Mother
Clatie H. Davis
1900-
& Daughter
Jean D. Prince
1924-

Luther L. Prentice
Nov 18, 1902

&
Minnie Lee Prentice
Aug 22, 1902
Jun 7, 1978
Mrd Jun 16, 1926

Mary A. Shires
1897-1979

William L. Thompson
1890-1980
(London)

Hubert J. Helton
Nov 8, 1909

&
Rose G. Helton
Jan 8, 1911

Leonard A. Bradford, Sr.
Jun 10, 1906

&
Catherine B. Bradford
Mar 19, 1912
Feb 29, 1980

Father
J. Claude Webb
Feb 14, 1939
Jan 14, 1979
&
Mother
Fay C. Webb
Aug 31, 1943

Mrd Aug 7, 1964

Donald "Don" Ray Holder
Sep 20, 1960
Nov 27, 1977

Enloe D. Walker
1904-

Lucille A. Walker
1902-

Mother
Dorothy P. Squires
Oct 14, 1923
Dec 15, 1979
"You and me against
 the world"

William Vet Patterson
Feb 10, 1913
Oct 16, 1978
&
Richie Dean Patterson
Jul 7, 1914

Rev. Charles A. Littleton
Nov 13, 1919
Nov 4, 1979
&
Mary E. Littleton
Dec 25, 1921

Father
Ricky D. Jett
Nov 10, 1950
Dec 19, 1978
&
Mother
Beverly S. Jett
Oct 16, 1957

Mrd Nov 29, 1974

Jesse H. Jackson
Aug 31, 1912
Aug 22, 1978
&
Sylvia S. Jackson
Jan 28, 1916

Barbara R. Thompson
1926-1979

Horace Lusby
Oct 28, 1893
Jun 27, 1977

Joseph R. Thompson
1898-1978

Father
Albert S. Reeves
Apr 16, 1916

&
Mother
Nona C. Reeves
Feb 10, 1919

Mrd Sep 5, 1939

Bland B. Houston
Dec 23, 1895
Oct 6, 1979
&
Sara H. Houston
Oct 17, 1903

Mary E. Colburn
Sep 4, 1929
Sep 29, 1977

J. Paul Stallings
1893-
&
Mary L. Stallings
1900-1978

Gaston Henson
Jan 13, 1905

&
Maggie Henson
Aug 10, 1907

Ewell R. Jordan
1912-
&
Elaine H. Jordan
1914-

Father
Cecil E. Hargrove
1923-
&
Mother
Sally E. Hargrove
1924-

John W. Hargrove
May 12, 1921

&
Mable V. Hargrove
May 21, 1928
May 10, 1978

Joseph Timothy "Tim" Gillum
Mar 24, 1958
Jun 2, 1977

Ralph Wallace Patterson
Jul 21, 1952
May 7, 1967

Virginia Hitt Patterson
Jul 31, 1916

James Ralph Patterson
Cpl US Marine Corps
WW II
Jul 18, 1911
Aug 22, 1976

Richard D. Burgess
Feb 24, 1923

&
Brownie Y. Burgess
Mar 23, 1922

&
Lanny Burgess
May 27, 1947

LEWISBURG

Mr. Loyd Eldridge, Sr.
1911-1980
(London)

Floyd C. Hazlett
Apr 13, 1916

&
Frances B. Hazlett
Mar 18, 1917

James M. Watson
Dec 25, 1912
Jul 4, 1980

Evelyn E. Watson
Oct 22, 1916

End of Section "T"

End of Lone Oak Cemetery

* *

EVANS CEMETERY

Located on the Evans farm about four miles west of Lewisburg and on Highway 50-A. Supplied by Don Jeter, Lewisburg, TN. Family Records indicates that the following are buried there:

John Evans   wife:
Oct 3, 1787
Mar 18, 1832

Elizabeth Boatright West Evans
Born 1805
Died Jun 30, 1879

Children:

Edward Hampton Evans
Oct 31, 1822
May 1, 1825

Joseph Wesley Evans
May 8, 1824
May 5, 1825

Salina Jane Evans
Nov 19, 1825
Mar 22, 1829

Eliza Ann Evans
Sep 29, 1827
Jun 18, 1829

William Henderson Evans
Jan 27, 1829
Oct 6, 1849

* *

NAME INDEX

A

Abernathy: 35
Acuff: 200, 202
Adair: 1, 8, 42, 52, 53, 271
Adams(Adms): 2, 12, 15, 29, 37, 88, 139, 151, 152, 154, 157, 158, 159, 160, 161, 162, 165, 166, 167, 169, 173, 175, 176, 177, 178, 179, 182, 183, 185, 187, 189, 199, 200, 211, 218, 219, 220, 226, 232, 235, 236, 239, 241, 258, 263, 268, 272, 285, 294, 295, 297, 299, 305
Adcock: 61, 167
Adgent: 19, 37, 94, 212
Adkins (Atkins): 70, 279
Adrin: 90
Agee: 77
Agent: 211, 278, 293, 294, 295
Akins: 281
Albright: 286
Alderdice: 268
Aldred: 13
Aldridge: 2, 8, 13, 53, 55, 56, 69
Alexander: 30, 195, 210, 203, 205, 209, 223, 232
Alford: 12, 65, 184, 185, 275, 287, 315, 316
Allen: 7, 29, 32, 34, 35, 36, 37, 80, 100, 123, 176, 183, 184, 187, 200, 209, 212, 215, 217, 220, 226, 228, 229, 230, 249, 266, 268, 269, 272, 273, 274, 286, 289, 293, 313, 317
Allison: 38, 39, 60, 174, 175, 251
Allman: 206, 207
Anderson: 13, 64, 79, 85, 87, 97, 111, 151, 152, 156, 173, 175, 177, 178, 179, 211, 228, 261, 274, 275
Andrews: 32, 33, 40, 52, 55, 95, 137, 175, 201, 208, 271, 298, 299
Angus: 99
Anthony: 108
Appleby: 85, 86, 87, 89
Archer: 169, 217, 236, 251, 260, 262
Ardis: 313
Armstrong: 104, 163, 164, 169, 175, 233, 268, 287, 308
Arnett: 255
Arney: 96
Arnold: 58, 91, 148, 173, 174, 200, 309
Arthur: 193, 194, 196, 306, 307
Ashby: 262
Ashley: 204
Atkinson: 28
Atkisson: 303, 304
Austin: 47, 196
Averitt (Avrit): 268, 286, 312
Ayers: 102, 103, 317

B

Baber: 154
Bacharach: 269
Bachman: 190
Bagley: 203, 226, 233
Bailey: 64, 65, 66, 128, 280, 284, 289, 290, 294, 300, 314
Bain: 100
Baird: 54, 206
Baker: 35
Ball: 60, 61, 64, 66, 95
Balthrop: 276
Barham: 32
Barnes: 43, 69, 191, 223, 278, 293
Barnett: 118, 155, 160, 267, 268, 285
Barras: 288
Barrett: 119, 268
Barrom: 226, 299
Barron (Barro): 86, 101, 128, 133, 134, 135, 138, 140, 143, 144, 145, 170, 192, 270, 275, 277, 282, 300, 302, 316
Bartlett: 126, 151, 152, 153, 161
Barton: 317
Bass: 170
Bates: 195, 200, 209, 281
Batey: 103, 286
Batten: 79, 80, 81, 82
Battershell: 272, 273
Baucom: 192, 219, 224
Baxter: 32, 33, 37, 79, 80, 86, 90, 113, 120, 125, 148, 266, 268, 269, 276, 279, 280, 284, 288, 300
Bayless: 215
Bayly: 310
Beard: 56, 163, 168, 214, 215, 219, 230, 232, 237, 277, 302
Bearden: 23, 136, 146, 181
Beasley: 18, 55, 107, 130, 139, 146, 188, 192, 216, 227, 242, 246, 251, 277, 285
Beatty: 32, 33, 87, 114, 164, 169, 187, 197, 199, 203, 270
Beckett (Becket): 131, 135
Beckham: 36, 103, 120, 146, 267
Beckwith: 265
Beech: 67, 69, 70, 142, 177, 269
Beever: 265, 301
Beisinger: 67
Belcher: 24
Bell: 13, 46, 62, 65, 80, 93, 152, 163, 248
Bellamy: 297
Benedict (Benedict): 193, 239
Bennett: 125, 270, 272, 277, 296
Bensinger: 278
Berlin (Burlin): 187, 202, 232
Berry: 104, 306, 311
Bethume (Bethune): 161, 166
Bethshares: 298
Biega: 187
Bigger: 27, 51, 52, 66, 75, 155, 172, 277, 300
Biggs: 311
Bigham: 118, 119, 122, 223, 262, 267, 278, 288
Billingsley: 192
Billington: 31, 45, 46
Bills: 78, 82, 84, 87, 88, 92, 105, 115, 126, 129, 137, 139, 140, 141, 144, 145, 151, 152, 153, 159, 161, 169, 202, 241, 252, 265, 271, 288, 290, 300
Bingham: 41
Bingaman: 172
Binkley: 289
Birmingham: 132
Bishop: 171, 173, 176, 191, 215, 216
Bivins (Bevins): 48, 186, 196, 224, 225, 297, 315
Black: 64, 95
Blackburn: 208, 270, 273
Blackmore: 59
Blacknall: 256
Blackwell: 7, 17, 26, 63, 79, 84, 147, 157, 162, 166, 237, 238, 249, 287, 295, 296, 301, 313, 315, 316, 317
Blade: 317
Blake: 205
Blakemore: 127, 251, 253
Blalock: 53, 63, 297
Bland: 218
Blanton: 178
Bledsoe: 82, 185
Bligh: 194, 196, 199, 207
Block: 86
Boatright (Boatwright): 105, 182, 207, 293, 300
Bobo: 139
Bodie: 155
Bolin: 80
Bond (Bonds): 60, 87, 89, 200, 239, 284, 289
Bone: 142, 217
Boren: 91, 92, 152, 307
Boring: 103
Boshers: 316
Bostick: 5, 259
Bowden: 101, 103, 114, 141, 178, 213, 271, 273, 315
Bowers: 199, 211, 222, 223, 224
Bowling: 64
Boyd: 12, 22, 24, 103, 104, 106, 107, 108, 287
Boyett (Boyet): 44, 48, 112, 115, 134, 137, 277, 302
Braden: 14, 43, 50, 51, 191, 213, 291
Bradford: 212, 213, 218, 221, 222, 224, 225, 245, 246, 260, 272, 298, 317, 318
Bradley: 33, 47, 90, 92, 151, 174, 177, 277
Bradshaw: 167
Brady: 203
Bragg: 154, 294
Braly (Braley): 131, 139, 302, 308, 309
Bramblett (Bramlet): 93, 218
Brandon: 292
Brannon: 81
Brantley: 171
Branum: 270
Brashears: 317
Brask: 315
Braswell: 151
Brecheen (Bercheen, Brechen, Breecheen): 120, 125, 134, 152, 309
Brents: 234, 259, 292, 310
Brew: 293
Brewer: 147, 230, 265, 312
Bridges: 198, 202, 204
Briggs: 186
Brintle: 189, 199
Brisby: 67, 103, 276
Brittain: 11, 12, 82
Broadway (Broadaway): 9, 70, 253, 256, 257, 280
Brock: 79
Brooks: 69, 247, 252
Broomley: 82
Brown: 13, 16, 33, 34, 36, 39, 53, 58, 66, 68, 70, 72, 73, 75, 95, 97, 107, 116, 143, 151, 152, 159, 161, 165, 172, 176, 187, 201, 202, 209, 222, 223, 224, 225, 226, 235, 237, 256, 259, 262, 266, 272, 274, 276, 277, 310
Bruce: 62
Bruin: 12
Bryan: 11, 295
Bryant: 34, 41, 100, 101, 102, 103, 105, 123, 128, 131, 137, 144, 184, 197, 224, 238, 239, 259, 265, 270, 273, 274, 275, 276, 278, 285, 288, 290, 291, 306, 317
Bryles: 14
Buchanan: 204, 251, 310
Buckingham: 82

Bullock: 308
Burch: 220, 221
Burgess: 87, 172, 195, 196, 205, 208, 228, 318
Burgett: 117, 217
Burks (Burk): 65, 298
Burlason: 277
Burlen: 151
Burnett: 195, 316
Burns: 17, 79, 239, 280, 310
Burris: 96
Burrow: 67, 73, 80, 81, 135, 205, 279
Burt: 164, 205, 227, 229, 285
Burton: 18, 305
Bush: 36, 306
Buska: 298
Bussart: 175
Butler: 31, 39, 210, 255, 257, 261, 288, 316
Buzan: 275

C

Caderas: 310
Calahan (Callahan): 33, 34, 74, 112, 130, 132, 165, 166, 167, 168, 170, 225, 270, 275, 280, 304, 317
Caldwell: 82, 249, 291
Calhoun: 60
Calloway: 201, 203
Calton: 115, 148
Calvert (Colvert): 67, 85, 97, 98, 106, 107, 291
Campbell: 62, 106, 192, 241, 251, 258
Caneer: 97, 133, 134, 146, 200, 202, 203, 205, 221, 222
Cannon: 85, 157, 208, 234, 271
Cantrell: 283
Caperton: 175
Capley: 81, 28, 287, 313
Capps: 81, 280
Carlton: 76, 87, 272, 296
Carothers: 95, 156, 265, 278, 280, 291
Carpenter: 87, 172, 187
Carr: 30, 276
Carroll: 124, 142, 212, 213, 273, 276, 287, 295
Carson: 299
Carter: 62, 157, 267, 286, 302
Caruthers: 245, 265
Cary: 66
Caskey: 107
Cason: 185
Casteel: 98, 176, 184, 230, 315
Cates: 82

Cathey: 2, 8, 9, 21, 42, 53, 68, 90, 92, 114, 139, 150, 155, 171, 213, 216, 244, 265, 266, 268, 271, 273, 275, 278, 280, 281, 285, 304, 317
Caudle: 137
Caughran: 50, 135, 161, 164, 169, 286
Causby: 212, 217, 219, 237
Causey: 306
Cavnar (Cavanar, Cavender): 98, 104, 167
Cawthon: 293
Cawthron: 55
Chadwell: 2, 36, 37, 307
Chambers: 316
Chambliss: 208
Chapman: 65, 83, 122, 126, 150, 153, 158, 170, 178, 179, 183, 213, 221, 266, 274, 278, 287, 315
Charlton: 184
Chatman: 70
Cheatham: 39, 41, 48, 111, 208, 272, 286, 293
Cheek: 33, 40, 41, 46, 55, 57, 102, 110, 116, 132, 269, 272, 276, 281, 282, 317
Cheeves: 80, 174
Cherry: 1, 26, 27, 35, 74
Chesser (Chessor): 255, 280
Chestnut: 2
Childers: 281
Childress: 116, 124
Childs: 42, 194
Chiles: 232, 281, 296
Chilton: 93, 147, 155, 180, 278
Chisam: 37
Chopin: 36
Christmon: 29
Christopher: 89, 131, 132, 311
Chunn: 31, 37, 38, 50, 115, 198, 204, 214, 271, 179, 284, 288, 291, 309
Church: 33, 89, 116, 132
Claiborne: 79
Clark: 19, 63, 64, 66, 70, 71, 84, 98, 101, 185, 197, 199, 205, 220, 230, 231, 232, 279, 310, 314
Claxton: 58, 75, 78, 79, 160
Clay: 64, 265
Clayton (Claton): 194, 206, 227, 231, 290, 196
Cleek: 80
Clendening: 132, 301, 314
Cleveland: 153
Click: 210
Clifford: 292
Clifft (Clift): 34, 136, 183, 196, 228, 229, 231, 232, 316

Clinard: 18
Clinton: 55
Clyde: 17
Clymore: 34, 125
Coak: 301
Coble: 92, 183, 193, 228, 274
Cochran: 42, 64, 88, 112, 116, 117, 119, 121, 124, 131, 133, 161, 203, 221, 225, 226, 268, 290, 298, 317
Cocrill (Cockrill): 120
Coffey (Coffee): 102, 155, 158, 159, 172, 173, 174, 176, 178, 275, 284, 299
Coggins (Coggin): 120, 142, 226, 274, 278, 281, 311
Colburn: 318
Coldwell: 172
Cole: 13, 19, 20, 33, 57, 136, 215, 238, 262, 314, 316, 317
Coleman: 131, 190, 197, 198
Collier: 101, 208
Collins: 1, 3, 5, 6, 7, 8, 16, 34, 36, 48, 50, 67, 71, 78, 86, 87, 94, 105, 115, 120, 121, 122, 124, 127, 131, 132, 139, 141, 142, 146, 154, 186, 201, 210, 215, 217, 220, 224, 231, 237, 239, 247, 263, 264, 270, 278, 279, 282, 283, 284, 285, 287, 289, 290, 291, 293, 307, 313, 315
Colvett: 96, 102, 106, 123, 184, 185
Compton: 209, 212, 213, 215
Conley: 60
Connelly: 204, 266
Conrad: 231, 234, 241
Conwell: 259, 262, 311, 313
Cook (Cooke): 68, 69, 72, 93, 94, 116, 173, 227, 229, 231, 232, 243, 288, 289, 312, 318
Coonradt (Conradt, Conrad): 223, 225
Coontz: 208
Cooper: 24, 49, 58, 67, 70, 71, 72, 76, 82, 140, 227, 228, 268, 280, 299, 301, 306
Cope: 315
Copeland: 60
Corbin: 282, 285, 312
Corlett: 296
Cortner: 170, 183, 312
Cosby: 305
Cothern: 266, 294
Cothran: 295
Couch: 237
Couser: 244
Covington: 4, 58
Cowan: 185

Cowden: 149, 227, 229, 241, 256, 283, 310, 311
Cowser: 211, 212
Cox: 5, 204, 206, 207, 208, 210, 221, 229, 272, 275
Coyle: 99, 100, 101
Cozart: 147, 270, 276, 311, 312, 313, 317
Crabtree: 162, 166, 176, 233, 239, 262, 270
Crafton: 65, 71, 72
Craig: 11, 32, 164, 172, 176, 177, 178, 236, 282, 284, 290, 303
Crane: 138, 195, 263, 277, 312
Cranford: 271
Crawford: 55, 65, 168, 248, 259, 267
Crawley: 100
Creecy: 199
Creek: 259
Cress: 278
Creswell: 8, 90
Crews: 316
Crichlow: 42
Crick: 49, 192, 212, 223, 244, 259, 261, 271
Crigger: 52, 53, 54, 55, 118, 217, 270, 281, 293, 295, 298, 313
Cristwell: 13
Crockett: 21, 64, 305
Cromartic: 100
Cromer: 17
Crooks: 299
Cross: 97, 182, 209
Crowder: 41, 44, 72, 194
Crowell: 48, 76, 77
Crunk: 119, 162, 194, 197, 216, 218, 223, 225, 251, 252, 253, 274, 282, 293, 295, 306
Crutcher: 19, 40, 63, 68, 69, 70, 84, 140, 143, 165, 208, 290, 306
Culbertson: 70, 75, 150, 152, 154, 295
Culp: 198
Cummings: 129, 161, 162, 164, 165, 167, 169, 173, 174, 175, 212, 218, 238, 239
Cundiff: 2, 32, 34
Cunningham: 40, 152, 164, 201, 233, 266, 275, 277, 279, 283, 297, 303, 306
Curl: 32
Curry: 298
Curtis: 5, 172, 175, 179, 217, 281, 296, 302

D

Dabney: 181, 204, 206, 310
Daily: 206
Dale: 200
Dalton (Dolton): 13, 60, 61, 155, 301
Daniel: 11, 36, 56, 74, 80, 175, 217, 221, 256, 260
Dark: 2, 31, 37, 38, 39, 43, 55, 56, 57, 274
Darnell (Darnall, Darnal, Darnel): 79, 120, 155, 172, 173, 219, 229, 252, 256, 258, 259, 266, 275, 280, 291, 297, 299, 316, 317
Daugherty (Daughrity, Daugarety, Dougherty): 62, 64, 69, 124, 127, 310
Davidson: 44, 158, 173, 179, 237, 297, 298, 303
Davis: 4, 16, 34, 43, 44, 49, 52, 54, 70, 71, 78, 81, 87, 95, 101, 110, 111, 117, 120, 121, 124, 127, 130, 131, 134, 137, 140, 141, 143, 145, 147, 150, 163, 164, 165, 166, 168, 170, 171, 178, 185, 194, 195, 198, 201, 203, 204, 205, 206, 209, 214, 217, 223, 224, 225, 227, 231, 238, 239, 241, 245, 249, 259, 262, 269, 270, 271, 272, 273, 274, 275, 276, 277, 286, 287, 289, 292, 294, 295, 297, 299, 301, 303, 305, 306, 308, 316, 317, 318
Daws: 169
Dawson: 275
Day: 133, 181, 210
Dazey (Dazy): 15, 35, 39, 59
Dean: 1, 5, 9, 34, 39, 67, 81, 147, 207, 222, 235, 277, 313
Deason: 274, 316
Deeryberry: 289
Defoe: 217
Dennis: 311
Denton: 146
Derryberry: 1, 8, 9, 36, 49, 51, 53, 269, 271, 274
Dettman: 74
Devin (Deven): 135, 201, 286
Dickens: 78, 82
Dickson: 71, 98
Dies (Die): 11, 17, 67, 161

Dillard: 35, 77, 150, 152, 177
Dillehay: 287
Divin: 118
Dixon: 95, 225, 255, 257, 258
Doak: 190
Dobyns: 145
Dockery (Dockrey): 168, 202, 203, 270, 280, 293, 317
Dodd: 219, 220, 244, 261, 263
Dodson: 7, 26, 99
Doggett: 95, 106, 107, 122, 145, 183, 184, 185, 186, 187, 188, 197, 199, 204, 232, 315
Donaldson: 185
Dooley: 266, 268
Doss: 211, 255
Doster: 279
Doud: 52, 269, 289
Dowdy: 26
Dowell: 48
Downing: 190, 292
Doyles: 31, 46
Dozier: 63, 65, 69, 257
Drake: 32, 41, 90, 178, 267
Drapchaty: 182
Driver: 246, 256
Dryden: 94, 171
Duckworth: 212, 215, 217, 218, 220, 230, 244, 245, 246, 261, 263
Duddy: 156
Dudley: 27
Duggan: 30, 56, 292, 311
Dugger: 105, 181, 274
Duling: 85, 86
Duncan: 2, 121, 122, 123, 136, 138, 142, 145, 271, 278, 283, 284, 299, 300, 303, 304, 307, 312
Dunivant (Dunivan): 226, 235
Dunn: 310
Dye: 55, 226
Dyer: 71, 134, 161, 260, 262, 289
Dysart: 85, 86, 150, 154, 155, 159, 160, 172, 173, 174, 180, 203, 206

E

Eady: 11, 309
Eagle: 75
Eagleton: 202
Eakes: 170
Eakin: 64
Ealy: 187, 191, 192, 214, 224, 286, 295
Earonhart: 268, 295
Easley: 155
Estherhasy: 308

Eatherly: 66
Eaves: 296
Eddins: 245
Edmiston: 240
Edmondson: 6, 95, 185, 186, 188, 222, 281
Edwards: 30, 43, 65, 100, 103, 122, 132, 134, 135, 145, 192, 193, 195, 198, 227, 231, 242, 268, 270, 286, 294, 299, 303, 304, 307
Elder: 64
Eldridge: 198, 214, 217, 319
Eley: 7
Ellington: 43, 281
Elliott: 6, 61, 77, 115, 127, 130, 139
Ellis: 163, 221
Ellison: 150, 163, 192, 218, 247, 259
Elrod: 49
Emerson (Emmerson): 116, 123, 136, 137, 145, 193, 194, 196, 279, 304
Endsley: 51, 57, 88, 116, 127, 165, 172, 174, 175, 176, 177, 178, 179, 212, 216, 217, 218, 220, 226, 266, 271
Enloe: 310
Ephlin: 185
Epperson: 81, 278
Epps: 237, 262
Ervin (Erven): 57, 102, 143, 280, 293
Erwin: 111, 155, 156, 202, 209, 257, 283, 303
Escue: 275
Eshman: 310
Esselman: 95, 207
Estes: 6, 64, 65, 186, 274, 295, 297, 308
Ethridge: 80, 108
Ette: 313
Eubank: 102
Evans: 18, 37, 38, 71, 105, 155, 207, 267, 275, 319
Ewell: 159
Ewing: 84, 85, 86, 87, 88, 89, 90, 99, 114, 123, 130, 131, 143, 159, 160, 172, 200, 204, 287, 291, 303, 309, 317
Ezell: 12, 22, 23, 27, 28, 59, 65, 66, 82

F

Fagan: 6, 19, 68, 88, 288, 297
Fain: 44
Falcon: 178
Falkenberry: 113
Falwell (Fallwell): 15, 16, 24
Fann: 226

Farler: 74, 170, 280, 314
Farlow: 66, 94
Farmer: 140, 184, 267
Farrior: 282
Farris: 45, 46
Faucett: 30
Fergus: 284, 306
Ferguson (Furgeson, Fergeson): 12, 13, 17, 65, 66, 67, 68, 75, 104, 210
Ferrell: 11
Finley (Findley): 33, 34, 61, 69, 89, 118, 143, 147, 192, 211, 213, 221, 226, 245, 247, 248, 255, 256, 258, 265, 271, 282, 284, 293, 299, 309
Fishback: 253
Fisher: 5, 33, 42, 47, 60, 66, 86, 87, 89, 90, 91, 119, 143, 176, 205, 273
Fitzgerald: 18, 217
Fitzpatrick: 129, 269, 284, 298
Flanakin: 135
Fleming (Flemming): 23, 60, 100, 106, 154
Flippin: 19
Flodeen: 7
Floyd: 34, 35, 36
Fluty: 287
Fly (Flye): 218, 219
Fogleman: 5
Follis: 183, 278, 296
Fonville: 249
Forbes: 65
Forehand: 145
Forrest: 23, 63, 303
Foster: 132, 157, 165, 169, 170, 187, 219, 225, 233, 235, 256, 263, 273, 280, 281, 288
Fowler: 42, 84, 92, 103, 116, 123, 124, 125, 137, 146, 152, 185, 196, 199, 201, 202, 206, 209, 216, 219, 226, 229, 236, 275, 281, 285
Fowlkes: 35
Fox: 73, 102, 105, 110, 125, 126, 136, 140, 141, 165, 194, 196, 198, 298, 300
Fraley: 114
Fralix: 182
Frank: 60
Franklin: 116, 193, 219, 228, 234, 254, 257, 261, 263
Fraser: 106, 140
Freeland: 101, 109
Freeman: 35, 63, 82, 116, 118, 161, 185, 215, 220, 224
Fry (Frye): 97, 100, 101
Fue: 219
Fuller: 85, 222, 223, 316

Fullerton: 281
Fulton: 12, 27
Funderburke: 102
Funk: 153

G

Gaalaas: 50
Gabard: 68, 70, 72
Gabbert: 157, 167, 233, 252, 253
Gabriel: 186
Gaines: 154
Galbraith: 75
Galbreath: 69, 273
Gallegly: 275
Galloway: 54, 55, 304, 308
Gambill (Gamel): 63, 89, 117, 203, 236, 240, 266
Gant: 107, 215, 227, 228
Gantner: 283
Gantley: 81
Gardner: 124, 184, 262
Garner: 315
Garrett: 14, 38, 52, 61, 64, 67, 70, 84, 96, 109, 125, 151, 194, 214, 228, 229, 230, 282, 285, 289, 291, 294, 295, 301, 302, 308, 315, 316
Garrison: 158
Garron: 109
Gates: 31, 43, 74, 126, 204, 281, 283, 301, 302, 303
Gattis: 314
Gault: 62, 70, 220, 221, 230
Gaunt: 246, 247
Gentry: 21, 40, 61, 68, 72, 220
George: 87, 89, 141, 202, 281, 294
Ghee: 11, 16
Gibson: 108, 120, 250, 255, 279, 282
Gilbert: 115, 135
Giles: 6, 23, 25, 59, 65, 66, 68, 69, 151
Gill: 242, 251, 253, 299, 307, 310
Gilleott: 155
Gillespie: 54, 55, 57, 81, 310
Gilliam: 49, 54
Gillum: 116, 117, 118, 194, 195, 196, 200, 205, 235, 252, 318
Gilmore: 112
Gipson: 126, 132, 138, 140, 142, 145, 271, 276, 277, 298
Glasgow: 210
Glasscock (Glascock): 47, 74, 81, 82, 83, 161, 162, 267, 279, 282, 289, 291, 302, 317
Glaze: 265

Glazier: 211, 212, 213, 215, 228, 229
Glenn (Glen): 27, 28, 88, 89, 126, 127, 131, 136, 158, 162, 164, 172, 176, 177, 194, 196, 197, 204, 222, 231, 290
Glymp: 214
Gold: 150, 151, 152, 180, 238
Golden: 224, 280
Goldman: 98
Goodman: 200
Goodrich: 130
Goodrum: 95
Goolsby: 313
Gordon: 128, 203, 207, 208, 295
Gossage: 180
Gowan: 252
Gowens: 285
Gower: 186, 187, 198, 199
Gracey: 100
Gragg: 167, 168, 170, 173
Graham: 91, 170, 271, 303
Grammer: 48, 186, 187, 188
Graves: 59, 239, 270
Gray: 3, 20, 32, 33, 63
Green: 5, 26, 32, 35, 38, 43, 44, 45, 50, 54, 55, 66, 77, 78, 90, 91, 92, 119, 144, 156, 169, 190, 266, 268, 274, 282, 283, 286, 294
Greer: 61, 156, 252, 274
Gregg (Greggs): 57, 106, 236
Gregory: 178, 311
Griffin: 61, 70, 71, 81, 143, 278, 291, 301
Griffis: 105, 106, 187, 188, 207, 228, 232
Griffy: 65
Griggs (Grigg): 66, 70, 195, 200
Grigsby: 63
Grimes: 194, 199
Grinstead: 155
Grissom: 103, 287
Grove: 100, 105
Grubbs: 103
Gulley (Gully, Gullie): 36, 39, 214
Gupton: 98, 99, 102, 103, 132, 139, 145, 146, 295
Gurney: 23
Guthrie: 166, 265, 290, 301
Gwedon: 68

H

Hackney: 201
Hagen: 282
Haggard: 90, 91, 283, 290
Haislip: 145, 191, 192, 196, 211, 212, 213, 214, 215, 216, 218, 220, 223, 225, 226, 227, 232, 234, 243, 244, 259, 260, 263, 288, 294
Hale: 140
Haley: 26, 187
Hall: 18, 24, 85, 113, 123, 125, 157, 205, 206, 209, 210, 240, 250

Hallock: 147
Hambrick: 199, 203
Hamer: 300
Hamilton: 68, 72, 135
Hamlin: 132, 198, 228, 291
Hampton: 150, 257, 260
Hanaway: 169, 249
Handly: 184
Haney: 36, 222, 284
Harber: 42, 80, 295
Harbor: 76, 78, 81
Hardin (Harden): 126, 127, 171, 224, 228, 236, 294, 302
Hardison: 2, 30, 33, 40, 42, 44, 45, 49, 50, 51, 52, 53, 55, 56, 57, 68, 79, 87, 97, 99, 106, 272, 275, 276, 288, 289, 291, 298, 300, 304, 311
Hardy: 129, 165, 209
Hargrove: 1, 5, 8, 9, 67, 71, 74, 81, 147, 262, 267, 279, 280, 281, 282, 295, 312, 313, 318
Harmon (Harmond): 1, 138, 199, 216, 219, 220, 284
Harness: 231
Harper: 1, 3, 36, 70, 316
Harris (Hariss): 1, 11, 13, 31, 33, 34, 37, 42, 55, 57, 60, 67, 68, 75, 76, 97, 106, 108, 128, 143, 144, 145, 148, 149, 152, 153, 162, 166, 167, 183, 191, 192, 206, 212, 213, 231, 257, 265, 268, 277, 279, 289, 297, 306
Harrison (Harison): 65, 142, 224, 232, 282, 299
Harshaw: 70
Hart: 41, 73, 241, 304
Harwell: 186, 199, 228, 249, 270, 274, 277, 282, 283, 284, 312, 314, 317
Hashaw: 140
Haskins: 77, 80, 163, 279, 285
Hastings (Haistings): 93, 94, 157, 233, 235, 237, 238, 240, 249, 257, 260, 261, 263, 275, 283, 317
Haston: 80
Hatchett: 131, 204
Hatfield: 188
Hatley: 125
Hawkins: 116, 123, 166, 273, 296, 297, 308
Hay: 82, 227, 289, 318
Hayes: 1, 32, 69, 87, 91, 152, 153, 154, 274, 279, 281, 283, 298
Haynes: 12, 21, 22, 34, (cont'd)

Haynes: (Cont'd): 61, 65, 78, 79, 80, 94, 202, 207, 209, 267, 280, 291
Hays: 52, 89, 125
Haywood: 127, 195, 210
Hazel: 48, 63
Hazelett (Hazlett, Hazelette): 21, 116, 173, 175, 176, 270, 275, 316, 319
Hazelwood: 8, 167
Head: 144, 186, 187, 199, 203, 205, 207, 284
Hedgcoth (Hedgecoth): 118, 119, 198, 203, 293
Helmick: 142, 182, 278, 279, 296, 304
Helton: 63, 79, 113, 168, 217, 289, 318
Hemphill: 203, 211, 215, 247, 248, 258, 263
Henderson: 107, 202, 209
Hendricks (Hendrix, Hendrick): 57, 110, 144, 209, 281, 308, 310
Hendrickson: 313
Henegar: 272
Henly: 22
Henry: 107, 108, 117, 125, 142, 229, 232, 276
Henson: 51, 195, 237, 312, 318
Herndon: 132
Herring: 272
Herron: 25, 90, 154
Hester: 71, 222
Hewitt: 183, 187, 272
Hickerson: 185, 188, 197, 222, 272, 289
Hickman: 71, 106, 186, 188, 255, 313
Hicks: 50, 89, 91, 237
Higdon: 124, 145, 275, 276, 282
Higgs: 41, 145, 226
Hightower: 89, 111, 136, 271, 283, 288
Hill: 39, 41, 49, 50, 51, 52, 53, 66, 73, 76, 79, 87, 88, 91, 92, 94, 101, 102, 104, 115, 128, 129, 136, 137, 143, 154, 178, 241, 247, 258, 273, 277, 282, 297, 298
Hillard (Hilliard): 33, 124, 144, 294
Hinds: 266
Hinkle: 55
Hinson: 298
Hinton: 174
Hobbs: 185, 225, 295
Hobby: 113, 117, 185, 189, 194, 198, 199, 213, 255, 276, 279, 280, 298
Hobson: 303
Hodge: 98, 182, 197
Hoffman: 155
Hogan: 239, 254
Holden: 131, 297, 302
Holder: 61, 68, 70, 71, 100, 298, 313, 318

323

Holdman: 64
Holland: 16, 198, 218, 235, 236, 252, 262
Holly (Holley): 106, 122, 129, 214, 217, 262, 272, 280, 291, 293, 314
Holman: 282
Holt: 12, 48, 108, 142, 165, 206
Holton: 57, 67, 68, 71
Hood: 201
Hooten: 53, 139, 140, 274, 291, 301
Hoover: 28
Hopkins: 76, 175, 183, 210, 273
Hopper: 73, 78, 79, 80, 81, 93, 94, 267, 268, 273, 281
Hopwood (Hoopwood): 117, 129, 156, 211, 285, 289, 302, 303, 305
Horner: 270, 314
Horton: 1, 93, 94
Hosea: 276
Hoskins: 274
Hough: 270
Houk: 268, 296
House: 230, 282
Houser: 82
Houston: 84, 89, 129, 130, 139, 152, 269, 278, 287, 293, 305, 307, 315, 318
Howard: 6, 7, 294, 317
Howell: 61, 200
Howze: 251
Hoyle: 153, 161
Huckaby: 193
Hudlow: 302
Hudson: 14, 104, 106, 208, 220
Hudspeth: 36
Huey (Hughey): 63, 230, 231
Huggins: 39, 128, 306
Hughes: 14, 137, 141
Hulshof: 294
Humbles (Umbles): 218, 235, 314
Humphrey: 262
Hunt: 201, 202
Hunter: 35, 41, 42, 75, 85, 86, 90, 92, 132, 152, 155, 162, 173, 204, 208, 227, 294, 295, 296, 302
Hurt: 46, 66, 67, 105, 107, 123, 151, 202, 285
Hussey: 48
Hutton: 75
Hyde: 3, 11, 25, 181, 198, 203

I

Ingle: 309
Ingram: 279
Ingrum: 103
Irvin: 7
Irvine: 299, 308
Irwin: 314
Isley: 85, 113, 147, 273, 314
Isom: 11, 247

J

Jackson: 44, 55, 107, 108, 129, 130, 143, 150, 200, 208, 318
Jacobs: 230, 232, 248
James: 13, 86, 188, 198, 205, 208, 210, 316
Jarrett: 8
Jean: 272, 284, 311
Jeanette: 174
Jenkins: 33, 206
Jennette: 13
Jernigan: 170
Jeter: 98, 182, 187
Jett: 57, 85, 87, 89, 182, 183, 263, 294, 312, 318
Jewel (Jewell): 113, 287
Jobe: 116, 121, 193, 212, 226, 258, 261, 293
Johns: 213
Johnsey: 77
Johnson: 12, 14, 15, 30, 33, 46, 64, 77, 83, 95, 102, 132, 140, 152, 154, 157, 165, 196, 201, 224, 266, 267, 281, 292, 303, 308, 312
Johnston: 263
Jones: 10, 31, 36, 38, 39, 41, 49, 62, 63, 64, 66, 71, 76, 79, 80, 91, 100, 101, 126, 129, 133, 134, 144, 148, 158, 167, 173, 175, 176, 181, 193, 197, 200, 205, 206, 209, 219, 221, 241, 262, 268, 270, 279, 281, 288, 291, 301, 302, 304, 305, 307, 312, 313, 314, 315
Jordan (Jourdan, Jordon): 5, 37, 49, 56, 67, 76, 116, 124, 140, 166, 196, 208, 211, 287, 290, 298, 318
Joyce: 3, 17, 18, 27, 28, 68
Junge: 150

K

Kaiser: 185
Karnes: 48
Keel (Keele): 80, 81, 147, 156, 184, 282, 312
Keller: 196, 277
Kelly (Kelley): 116, 202, 213, 227, 232, 313, 315
Keltner: 36, 55
Kennedy: 102, 108, 128, 150, 197, 204, 205, 206, 207, 208, 209, 248, 301
Kephart: 92
Kercheval: 123, 299, 308
Kerr: 47, 95, 171, 172, 207, 263, 267
Kesterson: 155
Ketchum: 50, 63, 88, 145, 169, 198, 201, 212, 222, 226, 238, 285, 287, 290
Key: 196
Kidd: 161
Kilgore: 208
Killingsworth: 137, 138, 141, 279, 295
Kimbro: 25
Kimbrough: 202
Kimmons (Kimmins): 26, 291
Kincaid: 6, 67, 95, 199, 274, 275
King: 1, 67, 72, 85, 96, 98, 101, 102, 136, 139, 161, 162, 214, 284, 307, 312, 314
Kinnard: 174
Kinsley: 221
Kirkland: 97, 99, 102
Kiser (Keiser): 106
Knight: 34
Knowis: 31, 32, 43
Knudson: 125

L

Laird: 10
Lamb: 8, 9, 11, 18, 42, 49, 51, 301
Lambert: 281
Lancaster: 156, 157, 164, 249, 278
Landers: 75, 251
Landis: 168
Landy: 88
Lane: 22, 42, 67, 88, 93, 155, 157, 178, 214, 222, 261
Langley: 102
Lankford: 268
Lanier: 4, 10, 35, 198, 199
LaRue (Larue): 85, 136, 173
Larson: 231
Larwood: 222, 240, 242, 243
Lasater: 151, 162, 165, 166, 169, 170, 273, 282, 317
Laster: 312
Latham: 181, 182
Laurence: 78
Lavender: 43, 44, 62, 69
Lawrence: 56, 69, 88, 133, 193, 230, 293, 300, 316
Laws: 39, 63, 67, 85
Ledbetter: 3, 126, 127, 273, 279, 291, 295, 298, 303, 309, 313, 315
Ledford: 101, 103, 163, 174, 214, 221, 233, 286
Lee: 18, 48, 68, 71, 72, 107, 115, 117, 118, 119, 176, 184, 193, 285, 290, 307, 308, 313, 316
Leeper: 89, 90, 172
LeFever: 317
Lemond: 237
Lentz: 262, 314
Leonard (Lenard, Linord): 61, 84, 123, 162, 163, 165, 167, 169, 176, 179, 210, 213, 221, 227, 241, 242, 250, 266, 282, 289
Lester: 7
Leverette: 7, 65
Lewis: 307, 313, 316
Liggett: 31, 32, 33, 42, 47, 52, 56, 57, 66, 136, 151, 269, 279, 289, 293, 304, 315
Lillard: 52, 54
Limbaugh: 266
Lindell: 123
Lindsey: 207, 311
Lines: 145
Lipscomb: 306
Little: 16, 21, 24, 71, 87, 116, 139, 155, 267, 284, 285, 286, 294, 302
Littleton: 239, 318
Locke: 183
Locker: 216
Lofton (Loftin): 20, 21, 64, 92, 93, 146
Logan: 5, 153, 156, 257, 302, 307
Logue: 64, 66, 68, 70, 71, 291, 314
London: 96, 114, 115, 124, 126, 128, 132, 133, 134, 136, 137, 144, 145, 146, 154, 177, 188, 197, 204, 209, 210, 231, 269, 282, 302, 307, 309, 313
Long: 19, 42, 83, 139, 151, 152, 173, 237, 286, 293, 309
Longmire: 21, 250
Looney: 217, 235, 302
Louge: 72
Love: 13, 36, 37, 155, 231
Lovett: 212, 259, 317
Lovings: 13
Lowe (Low): 59, 158, 265, 295, 299, 300

Lowrance: 98, 99, 146, 183, 190, 199, 226, 229, 268, 277
Lowry (Lowrey): 98, 172, 173
Loyd: 250, 292, 307
Ludington: 267
Luker (Looker): 242, 280
Lumpkins: 209, 293
Luna: 48, 74, 116, 157, 162, 203, 212, 215, 218, 219, 225, 226, 235, 236, 238, 239, 240, 246, 247, 248, 254, 256, 259, 261, 262, 265, 276, 277, 283, 287
Lunn: 9, 10, 55, 56, 57, 311
Lunsford: 196
Lusby: 103, 318
Luther: 294
Lyles: 283
Lynch: 228
Lynn: 59
Lyons: 166, 254, 260

M

Maddox: 274
Madewell: 287
Madison: 52, 102, 135, 150, 170, 185, 187
Majors: 178
Mallard: 38, 39, 54
Mallonee: 267
Mallory: 317
Malloy: 225
Malone: 116, 128, 137, 183, 270
Mangrum: 8, 78
Manier: 23, 69, 70
Manly: 276, 277
Mannan: 91
Manns: 301
Mansell: 273
March: 230
Marchand: 278
Marchbanks: 107
Marlin: 20, 24, 25, 59, 66
Marris: 234
Marrow: 83
Marsh: 134, 163, 168, 169, 200, 209, 210, 237, 284, 289, 294
Marshall (Marshal): 18, 42, 52, 58, 68, 71, 144, 269, 278, 290, 296, 298, 304, 310, 311
Martin: 9, 27, 34, 35, 37, 41, 42, 52, 56, 57, 68, 72, 79, 94, 106, 156, 158, 166, 169, 179, 187, 196, 233, 269, 284
Massey (Massie): 95, 102, 195, 197, 201, 202, 213, 214, 215, 221, 226, 262

Mathis: 98, 134, 312
Matney: 33, 63, 135, 146
Mattox: 37
Maupin: 37, 56
Maxwell: 309
May: 91, 289
Mayberry: 54, 55
Mayes: 172, 272, 296
Mayhew: 93
Mays: 1
Mayse: 275
Meador: 68
Meadows: 130, 194, 195, 200, 203, 212, 227, 229, 242, 259, 307
Mealer: 63, 64, 68, 70, 71, 147, 312
Medearis (Madearis): 170, 249
Medley: 301
Melson: 313
Melton: 69
Menifee: 115
Meredith: 316
Merritt: 293, 307
Meyer: 281
Mials: 222
Michael: 313
Middleton: 277, 281, 295
Miles: 250
Millen: 281, 294
Miller: 20, 38, 43, 50, 59, 64, 80, 81, 86, 88, 103, 145, 150, 165, 174, 175, 176, 265, 267, 273, 277, 295, 296, 297, 302, 304, 313
Mills: 289
Millsap: 203
Milton: 192, 243
Mincy: 37
Minor: 266, 276
Minton: 29
Minturn: 268, 272
Miodragovic: 318
Mitchell: 96, 107, 195, 209, 263, 284
Moffitt: 116, 118, 198, 272, 316
Molder: 71, 79
Montgomery: 35, 37, 40, 56, 139, 153, 154, 163, 164, 165, 279
Moon: 271
Mooningham: 62
Moore (Moores): 5, 9, 36, 97, 98, 105, 121, 129, 131, 161, 186, 194, 198, 228, 241, 249, 250, 253, 263, 290, 316
Morehouse: 36
Morgan: 39, 71, 205
Morphis: 271
Morris (Morriss): 8, 75, 78, 103, 119, 155, 238, 239, 286, 292, 306

Morrison: 284
Morton: 29, 35, 44, 48, 49, 63, 66, 69, 97, 108, 268, 278, 291, 302
Moser: 55, 316
Moses: 4, 6, 20, 30, 37
Mosley: 150, 151, 157, 170, 174, 176, 263
Moss: 306, 310
Mount: 152, 153, 154, 155
Moyers: 314
Mullikin: 62
Mullins: 100
Murdock: 15, 20, 26, 215, 238, 243, 258, 259, 260, 283, 286
Murphey (Murphy): 144, 235, 237, 314
Murphree: 290
Murrell: 207, 276, 292
Murrey (Murray): 14, 139, 168, 200, 212, 214, 232, 267, 275, 300, 305, 306, 311
Muse: 175
Musgrave: 151, 153, 266, 298
Myers (Myres): 135, 211, 231

Mc

McAdams: 157, 158, 161, 162, 163, 164, 165, 166, 167, 168, 170, 174, 176, 178, 179, 196, 225, 233, 276, 312
McAfee: 310
McAteer: 132, 135, 136, 142, 196, 307
McBride: 69, 70, 171, 172, 200, 227, 231, 310
McCabe: 113, 297
McCaffrey: 315
McCall: 9
McCary: 306
McCay: 118
McClain: 2, 168
McClanahan: 81, 299
McClarey (McClary): 86, 87, 89, 136, 306
McClaren: 18
McClean: 43
McClelland: 208, 227
McClenney: 262
McClintock: 184, 199, 203, 208
McClure: 96, 108, 183, 186, 206, 207, 208, 210, 269, 304
McCollum: 20, 95, 117, 178, 179, 197, 198, 205, 206, 208, 214, 224, 228, 230, 273
McConnell (McConnel): 50, 97, 99, 102, 103, 104, 105, 125, 129, 130, 133, 136, 139, 146, 195, 205, 213, 223, 273, 289, 290

McCool: 167, 170
McCord: 15, 26, 50, 52, 59, 139, 145, 181, 182, 267, 278, 280, 281, 294, 295, 303, 304, 305, 314
McCorkle: 120, 131, 133
McCormick (McCormack): 93, 243, 262, 270
McCowan: 263
McCown: 93
McCoy: 122, 201, 221, 236, 237, 239, 265, 267, 316
McCray (McCrary): 95, 208, 227
McCree: 191, 240
McCrory: 66, 69, 131, 160, 213, 214, 215, 219, 220, 223, 224, 225, 231, 239, 257, 262, 266, 271, 288, 289, 297, 305
McCullough: 150, 151, 152, 275, 286
McCurdy: 41, 42, 275, 285, 306
McDaniel: 113, 133, 135, 142, 161, 162, 164, 165, 168, 169, 196, 199, 225, 273, 297
McDill: 152
McDonald: 155, 315
McDowell: 294
McDowra (McDoura): 118, 120
McElhaney: 6, 7, 9
McElroy: 262
McFarland: 231
McGaha: 276
McGahey: 172, 174
McGaugh: 192, 209, 216, 219, 229, 230, 231, 254, 271
McGee: 137
McGibbon: 100, 101
McGregor: 130, 138, 146
McGucken: 304
McGuffee: 25
McGuire: 151
McKay: 175, 275
McKee: 158, 159
McKelvy: 101
McKibbon: 102, 103, 198
McKinney: 167, 168, 169, 246, 258, 262, 308
McKnight: 48, 56, 103, 105, 108, 110, 131, 138, 254, 273, 289, 292, 307, 315
McLain: 161, 163, 164, 165, 166, 168, 169, 170
McLane: 164
McLean: 5, 39, 43, 54, 55, 152, 164, 209, 284, 305, 310
McLelland: 311
McLin: 187
McLLand: 209
McMahon: 184, 186

McMillon (McMillin, McMillion): 106, 199, 277
McMorris: 130
McMurry (McMurrey): 12, 70, 204
McNail: 86, 159
McNeese: 70, 294
McNutt: 270
McPeak: 316
McQuiddy: 53, 73, 87
McRady: 123, 300, 307
McRee: 86, 168, 248, 288
McRory: 230
McWaggoner: 192
McWhirter: 176

N

Nafus: 272
Nance: 96, 195, 201, 202, 303
Neathery: 1, 61, 68, 70, 72
Neece: 265, 287
Neeld: 308
Neely: 21, 24, 63, 84, 178, 201, 250
Neese (Niece): 59, 63, 71, 79, 81, 132, 142, 271, 277, 278, 286
Neil (Neill): 2, 4, 21, 36, 37, 38, 42, 44, 46, 90, 92, 120, 159, 161, 163, 176, 177, 178, 255, 256, 257, 258
Nelms: 203, 220, 228, 232
Nelson: 2, 3, 130
Newcomb: 19
Newland: 96
Newton: 156
Nicholas: 75, 77, 234, 267, 289, 294
Nichols: 131, 235, 241, 272, 285
Nickens: 43, 73, 77, 183
Nix: 106, 140, 182, 183, 185, 190, 196, 197, 200, 202, 203, 204, 236, 267, 275, 276, 293, 295, 296, 318
Noah: 72
Noblett: 94
Noblin: 152, 159
Norman: 234, 236
Nolen (Nollen): 233
Norris: 227
Norton: 205
Norwood: 226
Nowlin (Nowlen): 85, 86, 90, 97, 126, 127, 129, 268, 284, 309

O

Oakley: 72
O'Brien: 206
Odell: 268
Ogilvie: 14, 15, 26, 28, 38, 40, 69, 306
Ogle: 302
Old: 44
Oliver: 189, 193, 211, 213, 230, 231, 232, 236
O'Neal: 44, 75, 82, 83, 91, 159, 161, 180, 192, 204, 288
Ordway:
Orr: 17, 88, 90, 97, 98, 99, 100, 102, 103, 108, 109, 145, 151, 153, 159, 162, 163, 165, 166, 168, 172, 182, 208, 233, 267, 271, 278, 279, 280, 296, 299, 311, 317
Osborn (Osburn, Osborne, Orsborn): 51, 52, 79, 88, 111, 128, 133, 134, 135, 138, 189, 265, 270
Oslin: 35
Osteen: 5, 36, 39
Overholser: 175
Overton: 94
Owen (Owens): 25, 217, 250, 260, 261
Ownby: 30, 44, 117, 279, 280, 306

P

Pack: 211, 226, 246, 259
Page: 211
Palmer: 151, 200, 201
Palmore: 68
Pamplin: 261
Pardee: 82, 85
Parham: 201
Park (Parks, Parke): 66, 75, 97, 136, 152, 184, 187, 190, 191, 195, 201, 202, 212, 226, 229, 230, 231, 292, 311
Parker: 280
Parr: 310
Parsons: 94
Partain: 261
Patrick: 95, 173
Patterson: 1, 2, 16, 21, 32, 37, 57, 62, 63, 64, 65, 70, 71, 96, 130, 292, 297, 303, 318
Patton: 51, 55, 156
Paul: 68, 69, 70, 71
Paxton: 117, 201
Payne: 65
Peach: 25
Pearcy: 26
Pearson (Pierson): 31, 81, 167, 168, 202, 237, 304
Peartswheimer: 98
Peay: 36
Peebles: 200, 205, 206
Perkins: 123, 130
Perman: 183
Perry: 74, 77, 78, 79, 98, 101, 106, 184, 201, 205
Perryman: 6, 70, 71, 77, 81, 315
Peterson: 78
Pettes (Pettus): 124, 188, 194, 271, 288
Petty: 161, 164, 165, 166, 167, 233, 254, 258, 276, 279, 288, 317
Pewitt: 37
Phifer: 48, 49, 51, 78, 122, 130, 132, 179, 291, 305
Phillips: 101, 121, 126, 134, 138, 139, 145, 146, 153, 176, 206, 293, 303, 316
Philpot: 318
Pickens: 98, 99, 102, 103, 104, 105, 177, 186, 284, 296, 297, 298, 300, 307
Pickle: 30, 62, 83, 140, 152, 177, 178, 215, 266, 294
Pierce: 183, 225, 283
Pigg: 109, 121, 125, 126, 166, 202, 205, 211, 216, 217, 220, 221, 222, 223, 225, 253, 254, 263, 283
Pillow: 206, 207, 209
Pinkston: 20, 186
Pitts: 209
Plada: 261
Plattenburg: 205, 207
Plummer: 75, 78
Poarch: 182, 195, 223, 228, 231, 232, 243, 244, 260, 288
Poindexter: 59, 283
Polk: 114
Pollard: 37
Polly: 218, 294, 299, 312
Poole: 228
Poplin: 267, 268
Porch: 15
Porter: 54, 55, 67, 157, 219, 228, 241, 250, 314
Porterfield: 311
Poteet: 48
Potts: 1, 64
Powell: 3, 26, 35, 54, 55, 62, 67, 69, 70, 76, 77, 82, 84, 92, 139, 145, 200, 228, 257, 270, 273, 277, 287, 315
Powers: 215
Pratt: 10, 228
Prentice: 318
Price: 22, 81, 84, 140, 173, 175, 212, 234
Prichett: 313
Prosser: 168, 170, 253
Pruett: 289
Pruitt: 7, 49, 67, 117, 118, 119, 120, 189, 202, 235
Pugh: 66, 79, 80
Purdom: 68, 88, 89, 118, 143, 146, 203, 231, 271, 274, 282
Putmon: 62
Pyland: 83, 159, 171, 237, 238
Pyles: 116, 193, 194, 211

Q

Quarterman: 50

R

Raden: 102
Ragan: 20
Ragsdale: 4, 64, 280
Rainey (Raney): 4, 18, 26, 39, 58, 89, 102, 117, 193, 199, 203, 216, 220, 221, 261, 281, 291, 307
Rains: 33
Ralston: 69, 191, 214, 221, 300
Rambo: 112, 113, 118, 124, 127, 132, 137, 138, 143, 213, 232, 278
Ramsey: 20, 33, 62, 64, 65, 70, 85, 87, 113, 141, 148, 154, 158, 172, 182, 186, 204, 278, 285, 300
Randolph: 213, 256
Rankin: 176, 179
Ransom: 38, 154
Rasmussen: 317
Ratcliffe: 100, 291
Ray: 49, 50, 52, 163, 166, 167, 234, 266, 286, 289, 291, 293, 301
Raymer: 302
Read: 249
Reavis: 82, 83, 100, 269
Reaves: 145
Record: 141, 149
Redd: 270, 283, 293
Redden: 199
Redding: 101
Redman: 26, 63
Redmond: 12, 66, 68, 293
Reed: 44, 46, 52, 67, 114, 140, 152, 169, 171, 212, 230, 260, 266, 296, 307
Reedy: 140, 258
Reese: 293, 318
Reeves: 65, 318
Regen (Regin): 42, 177
Reid: 4, 208
Renfro: 110
Reynolds: 8, 9, 38, 42, 49, 50, 51, 52, 63, 107, 141, 221, 235, 278
Rhiner: 121, 231, 294

S

Rhodes: 129, 201, 203, 214, 225, 232, 240, 242, 244, 292
Rice: 43
Rich: 267
Richardson: 30, 36, 121, 133, 136, 144, 145, 197, 201, 203, 205, 216, 243, 265, 267, 268, 280, 288, 289, 296, 300, 303, 304
Rickman: 17, 24, 28, 64, 66
Ridner: 143, 277
Riggs: 14, 22, 238
Riley: 3, 203, 244, 245
Riner: 185
Ring: 1, 2, 12, 45, 67, 166
Ritchie: 128, 308
Rives: 85, 251
Roane: 14
Robbins: 206, 305
Roberson: 9, 16, 17, 26, 204
Roberts: 23, 41, 49, 60, 87, 107, 125, 144, 147, 167, 177, 178, 183, 185, 187, 280, 282, 299, 304, 310, 315, 317, 318
Robertson: 83
Robinson: 17, 22, 36, 64, 74, 75, 77, 88, 92, 93, 167, 220, 221, 247, 255
Robison: 313
Rockwell: 289
Roddy: 276, 312
Rodgers: 71, 148, 175, 185, 206, 316, 317
Rogers: 62, 67, 147, 219, 251, 265, 273, 316
Rohelier: 185
Roland: 183
Rollings: 121
Rollins: 266
Rone: 45, 46, 59, 84, 111, 143, 144
Roper: 308
Ross: 96
Rosson: 191, 201, 208
Rowland (Rowlin): 69, 71, 72, 163
Royall: 103
Royster: 14, 267, 304
Rozell: 71
Rucker: 62, 294
Rudd: 211, 223, 261, 263
Rushing: 98
Russell: 7, 26, 85, 89, 148, 238, 240, 244
Rutledge: 55, 57, 87, 141, 195, 202, 203, 280, 292, 300

Salisbury: 169, 222
Sampson: 282
Sanders: 113, 125, 162, 166, 169, 173, 197, 230, 241, 247, 248, 257, 258, 262, 274, 284, 285, 287, 288, 302, 309, 313, 316
Saunders: 93
Savage: 140, 217, 272, 278, 287
Sawyers: 280
Scales: 12, 200, 215, 227, 308
Scallorn: 101
Scarbrough: 295
Schuessler: 91
Scoggins: 289
Scott: 5, 30, 36, 37, 66, 68, 72, 266
Scribner: 301
Seagroves: 266, 278, 307
Seaton: 157
Seay: 47
Secrest: 31, 32, 103, 287
Sellars (Sellers): 3, 84
Sewell: 103, 167
Shanks: 96
Sharer: 265
Sharp (Sharpe): 50, 141, 182, 183, 220, 263, 265, 268, 270, 271, 272, 273, 275, 280, 286, 293, 295, 297, 300, 306, 315
Shaw: 64, 66, 69, 70, 71, 91, 110, 117, 118, 157, 172, 200, 223, 226, 270, 293, 294, 300
Shearin: 67, 73, 177
Sheffield (Shuffield): 23, 24, 25, 65
Shehane: 133, 136
Shelton: 298
Sheppard (Shepard, Shepherd): 8, 68, 70, 80, 115, 225, 313
Sherman: 267
Shires: 21, 31, 56, 57, 80, 269, 311, 318
Shirley: 87, 89, 147, 148, 161
Short: 213, 214, 216, 217, 218, 222, 223, 224, 226, 228, 243, 254
Shriver: 176
Siler: 23
Simmons: 36, 48, 64, 97, 107, 125, 198, 272, 294, 297
Simpson: 6, 117, 268, 271
Sims (Simms): 40, 266, 314
Singleton: 94
Sisco: 305
Sissom: 179
Skinner: 5, 64, 65
Slate: 92

Slaughter: 11, 23, 66, 78
Smiley: 12, 68, 70, 157, 173
Smith: 2, 5, 9, 13, 17, 18, 23, 37, 79, 90, 99, 117, 120, 124, 132, 140, 151, 155, 157, 158, 165, 174, 175, 178, 181, 185, 186, 191, 195, 196, 197, 198, 199, 202, 209, 220, 228, 229, 240, 262, 273, 275, 286, 298, 300, 303, 317
Smithson: 17, 61, 79, 184, 304
Snell: 87, 89, 115, 132, 179, 269, 304, 306
Sorrells: 253
South: 137
Sowell: 52, 124, 212, 241, 248, 260, 261, 262, 263
Spain: 51, 56
Spencer: 43, 45, 66, 314
Spray: 165, 166, 170, 262
Squires: 141, 318
Stacey (Stacy): 34, 68, 137, 145, 272
Stafford: 134, 272, 276, 284
Staggs: 274
Stallings: 152, 156, 165, 215, 318
Stammer (Stammers): 17, 23, 27, 66, 69
Stamps: 206, 249
Stanley: 16, 44
Steagal (Stegall): 15, 136, 159, 317
Steele (Steel): 39, 96, 203, 278, 279, 280, 304
Steete: 185
Stem: 36, 107, 278
Stenbeck: 110
Stephens: 235, 247, 282
Stephenson: 74, 80, 81, 82, 173, 260, 290
Stepp: 197
Sterne: 273
Stevens: 71, 210, 215
Stewart: 43, 44, 49, 50, 51, 52, 56, 87, 88, 89, 93, 179, 196, 199, 268, 300
Stewman: 48, 51
Stillwell (Stilwell): 131, 132, 139, 141, 189
Stinnett: 36, 313, 315
Stinson: 266, 304, 308
St. John: 18
Stockman: 199
Stockstill (Stocstill): 312, 315
Stockton: 175

Stokes: 183, 185, 223, 268
Stone: 97, 102, 107, 187, 249
Stovall: 219
Stratton: 90, 201
Street: 14, 215
Studivan: 19
Sturm: 302
Stutts: 42
Sublett: 207
Sullivan: 234
Summerford: 146
Summerhill: 200
Summers: 31
Sutton: 81
Swaim: 5, 12, 278, 286
Swain: 65, 71
Swanner: 224, 257
Swanson: 62, 87, 304
Sweeney (Sweney): 17, 153, 157, 160, 178, 238
Sweet: 277
Swiney: 177, 224, 229, 230, 231

T

Talley (Tally): 137, 178, 187, 191, 205, 206, 236, 255, 256, 257, 268, 275, 283, 296, 306, 311, 316
Tallman: 226
Tankersley: 45, 50, 51, 94, 117, 297
Tanner: 11, 17, 33, 68, 72, 210, 247
Tarpley: 197
Tarry: 141
Tate: 91, 101, 102, 141, 166, 184, 222, 224, 261, 262, 298
Tatum: 56, 271
Taylor: 3, 24, 42, 61, 63, 64, 65, 100, 125, 126, 151, 190, 193, 196, 197, 198, 200, 201, 202, 203, 207, 209, 210, 211, 213, 218, 282, 283, 284, 295
Teal: 67
Temple: 15, 151
Templeton: 55
Tennison (Tenison): 150, 171
Terry: 98, 107, 257
Thacker: 26
Thogmorton: 300
Thomas: 1, 6, 8, 9, 11, 18, 30, 42, 47, 61, 64, 84, 85, 86, 88, 92, 102, 139, 152, 155, 173, 190, 209, 274, 275, 276, 277
Thomason: 39, 119, 139, 144, 268, 279, 286, 294, 316

Thompson: 41, 48, 50, 54, 66, 70, 71, 73, 112, 113, 118, 124, 128, 132, 133, 137, 138, 147, 163, 166, 171, 175, 176, 186, 203, 209, 211, 214, 216, 223, 225, 266, 267, 271, 272, 275, 276, 277, 279, 281, 282, 286, 290, 293, 300, 306, 309, 313, 314, 315, 316, 318
Thomson: 84
Thorne: 68, 178
Thornhill: 33
Thornton: 268
Thrasher: 167, 300
Throneberry: 200, 205, 208
Tiller: 153, 168
Tillman (Tilman, Tillmon): 128, 142, 143, 144, 154, 270, 271, 285, 288, 309
Timberlake: 206
Timmons: 94
Tindell: 33, 44, 55, 56
Tomlin: 63
Tomlinson: 61
Toomey: 312
Topp: 207
Toppin: 9
Toseland (Tosland): 141, 161, 272, 312
Towner: 128
Townsend: 59, 185, 187, 220, 318
Towry: 295
Trammel: 113, 277, 285
Tribble: 56
Trigg: 125, 273
Trollinger (Trolinger): 81, 82
Troop: 49, 234, 236, 239, 248
Trotter: 311
Tucker: 12, 115, 167, 183, 185, 225, 228, 230, 239
Turner: 63, 88, 90, 105, 116, 117, 134, 136, 140, 165, 178, 183, 202, 213, 220, 223, 224, 269, 273, 283, 284, 290, 291, 295, 297, 299, 300, 301, 302, 305, 307, 315
Twitty: 120, 127, 161, 162, 163, 167, 169, 212, 236, 270, 296, 297
Tyree: 271, 275, 277, 286, 294, 296

U

Umbles (see Humbles): 235
Underwood: 203
Upchurch: 265
Upton: 200
Ursy: 107
Uselton: 75, 314
Ussery: 106

V

Vaden: 2, 64
Van Cleave: 67, 97, 185, 186, 195
Vandiver: 249
Vanhooser (Vanhoozer): 141, 197
Vanhorn: 277
Vann: 282
Vaughan: 54
Vaughn: 16, 18, 24, 25, 26, 192, 212, 270
Vaughter: 282
Vega: 313
Verlin: 263
Vernor: 90
Vest: 29, 62, 63
Vickery: 174
Victory: 13
Vincent: 68, 101, 108, 109, 313
Vincon (Vincion): 67, 68, 260
Vise: 314

W

Waddington: 21, 303
Waddy: 89, 155
Wade: 120, 167, 182, 200, 243, 311
Wadley: 96
Wakefield: 192, 204, 219, 221, 224, 225, 226, 234, 246, 250, 256, 259, 278, 286
Waldrep: 272
Walker: 6, 7, 16, 49, 51, 60, 85, 88, 94, 97, 106, 118, 137, 145, 151, 163, 164, 171, 183, 184, 202, 204, 207, 208, 209, 270, 299, 309, 318
Wall (Walls): 59, 67, 68, 218, 219, 220, 222, 230
Wallace: 9, 20, 36, 37, 45, 46, 143, 145, 188, 283, 294, 296
Wallis: 10
Walton: 202, 210, 285, 298
Warden: 96
Warner: 68, 74, 75, 140, 273
Warren: 92, 238
Waters (Watters): 40, 163, 167, 168, 233, 239, 257, 278
Watkins: 17, 66, 72, 183, 185

Watson: 31, 165, 168, 169, 196, 226, 233, 234, 242, 244, 245, 246, 255, 258, 260, 261, 263, 268, 276, 277, 291, 301, 312, 319
Watts (Watt): 65, 235
Weaver: 33, 44, 45, 52, 66, 137, 268, 270, 277, 282, 288, 301
Webb: 31, 137, 205, 309, 318
Weber: 268
Webster: 200, 284
Wegold: 281
Weiler: 309
Welch: 112, 120, 143, 144, 162, 168, 194, 196, 198, 201, 213, 215, 216, 218, 221, 223, 226, 247, 258, 261, 263, 267, 274, 284, 292, 305
Wells: 12, 58, 96, 107, 167, 234, 236, 237, 239, 246, 247, 258, 259, 260, 261, 262, 303
Wentzel: 315
West: 38, 106, 174, 218, 219, 236, 260, 272, 280, 281, 299, 304
Whaley: 37, 39, 276
Wheat: 272
Wheatley: 125, 273, 277, 288, 300, 302
Wheeler: 197, 200, 272, 282, 318
Wherley: 161, 164, 237
Whitaker (Whittaker): 73, 88, 177, 203, 226, 240, 245, 275
White: 7, 21, 58, 63, 69, 71, 80, 81, 82, 115, 195, 210, 268, 270, 296, 298, 303
Whitehead: 2, 5, 6, 7, 34, 38, 93, 147, 187, 244, 279, 280, 285, 300
Whitesell (Whitsell): 46, 47, 54, 134, 141, 142, 147, 169, 300
Whitman: 75, 93
Whitsett (Whitsette): 119, 161, 166, 168, 187, 214, 220, 237, 238, 266, 274
Whitt: 135
Whitworth: 25
Whorley (Worley): 76, 147, 208, 237, 250
Wiggins: 301
Wiggs: 46, 85, 89, 154
Wilburn: 280
Wiles: 39, 42, 53, 54
Wiley (Willey): 112, 289, 305, 308, 309
Wilhoite: 14, 93

Wilkerson: 216, 224, 243, 260, 261
Wilkes (Wilks): 85, 96, 101, 102, 103, 104, 105, 108, 129, 184, 185, 186, 187, 206, 207, 237, 281, 292, 310
Wilkinson: 200, 204, 205
Williams: 13, 15, 51, 81, 96, 116, 123, 129, 132, 140, 158, 159, 166, 179, 182, 187, 196, 204, 212, 214, 234, 237, 256, 269, 271, 282, 294, 297, 300, 308, 312, 317
Williamson: 54, 98, 194, 251, 269, 307
Willis: 125, 165, 193, 201, 216, 236, 310
Willoughby: 293
Wilsford: 274
Wilson (Willson): 2, 3, 6, 11, 19, 20, 21, 24, 38, 44, 59, 60, 63, 71, 73, 94, 97, 98, 103, 114, 124, 126, 134, 139, 142, 143, 146, 150, 159, 167, 174, 178, 196, 207, 219, 266, 274, 276, 285, 288, 292, 293, 296, 297, 299, 300, 301, 312, 313, 317
Winford: 284
Wingfield: 161
Wingo: 294
Winn: 35, 66
Winnett: 217
Winston: 96
Wintermute: 316
Wisdom: 182, 183, 249
Wise: 230, 288, 316
Wiser: 276
Wolaver: 192, 211, 222, 226, 230, 232
Wolridge: 207
Womack: 300
Wood: 49, 118, 173, 177, 178, 179, 217, 266, 267, 268, 270, 282, 300, 304
Woodall: 35, 37
Woodard: 260, 262
Woodruff: 275
Woods: 47, 52, 87, 88, 108, 134, 154, 155, 157, 173, 174, 175, 176, 183, 184, 195, 241, 269, 284, 286, 291, 304, 307
Woodward: 42, 46, 49, 52, 126, 150, 151, 153, 157, 158, 165, 169, 170, 178, 179, 199, 217, 228, 229, 230, 231, 249, 269, 270, 273, 283, 286, 294, 299
Woosley: 68, 142

Wooten: 48, 272, 296
Word: 151, 199, 204, 217, 298
Work: 14
Worsham: 197, 212
Wortham: 61, 64, 81
Wright: 19, 33, 91, 138, 147, 169, 170, 182, 184, 219, 220, 221, 222, 232, 295
Wynn: 74
Wysong: 216, 299

Y

Yarbrough: 33, 50, 57, 151, 195, 277
Yates: 104, 267
Yell: 79
Yoes: 52
Young: 62, 64, 79, 137, 141, 163, 181, 211, 218, 282, 304
Yowell: 36, 238, 247, 249, 310

Z

Zumbro: 282

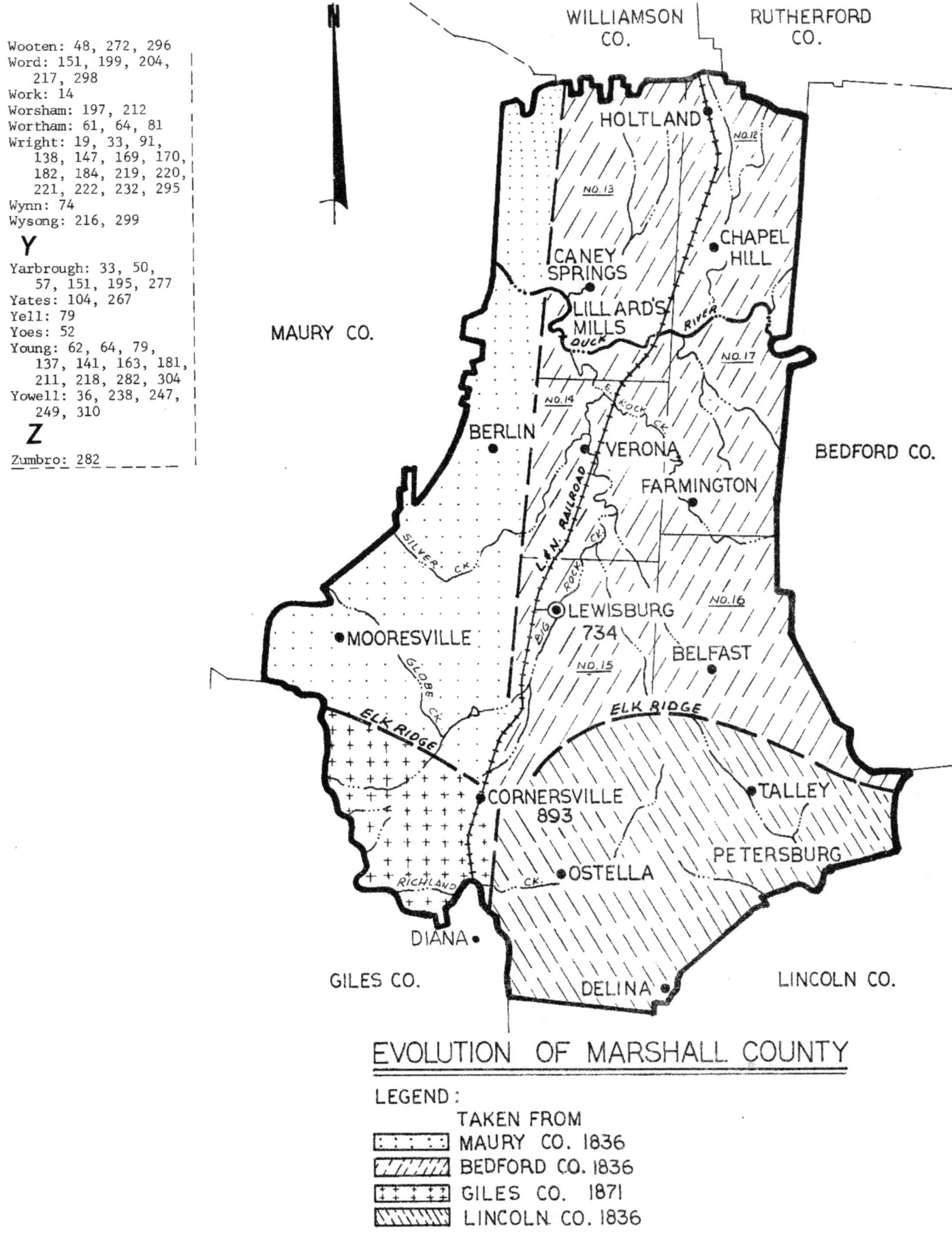

EVOLUTION OF MARSHALL COUNTY

LEGEND:
TAKEN FROM
- MAURY CO. 1836
- BEDFORD CO. 1836
- GILES CO. 1871
- LINCOLN CO. 1836

www.ingramcontent.com/pod-product-compliance
Lightning Source LLC
Chambersburg PA
CBHW060507300426
44112CB00017B/2578